THE GROWTH

OF

ENGLISH INDUSTRY

AND

COMMERCE

IN MODERN TIMES.

THE GROWTH

OF

ENGLISH INDUSTRY

AND

COMMERCE

IN MODERN TIMES.

BY

W. CUNNINGHAM, D.D.

FELLOW OF THE BRITISH ACADEMY; HON. FELLOW OF GONVILLE AND CAIUS COLLEGE,
FELLOW OF TRINITY COLLEGE, CAMBRIDGE, AND ARCHDEACON OF ELY;
FORMERLY LECTURER ON ECONOMIC HISTORY IN HARVARD UNIVERSITY.

THE MERCANTILE SYSTEM

CAMBRIDGE:

AT THE UNIVERSITY PRESS

1907

CAMBRIDGE UNIVERSITY PRESS
Cambridge, New York, Melbourne, Madrid, Cape Town,
Singapore, São Paulo, Delhi, Tokyo, Mexico City

Cambridge University Press
The Edinburgh Building, Cambridge CB2 8RU, UK

Published in the United States of America by Cambridge University Press, New York

www.cambridge.org
Information on this title: www.cambridge.org/9781107672673

© Cambridge University Press 1905

First published 1905
First paperback edition 2011

A catalogue record for this publication is available from the British Library

ISBN 978-1-107-67267-3 Paperback

IN MEMORIAM

E. L.

obiit a. d. xvii kal. Sept. MDCCCXCI.

PREFACE.

THIS book has been planned with a double object. On the one hand I have endeavoured to show how intimately the political and the economic history of the English nation have been interconnected, and on the other I have set myself to describe, and account for, the actual course of the material progress of the country.

Since the second edition of this work was issued, I have had, as a college lecturer, repeated opportunities of going over the ground it covers and I have come to see many of the matters dealt with, in truer proportion. I have given more attention to the economic affinities of different political personages and parties; I have noted more definitely the disastrous effects of the Civil War on the social and industrial organisation of the Realm; and I have been able to write more justly of the Restoration period, which so closely resembles our own. Earnest efforts were consciously made at that time to build up the world-wide commercial empire which Britain now holds. The medal represented on the title page, by the kind permission of the authorities of the British Museum, dates from the era when the factories of the great Joint-stock Companies were being planted in all parts of the world.

In modern times, when society is very complex, and the ramifications of different branches of industry and commerce are so far-reaching, it is particularly difficult to make the best use of the abundant materials which lie to hand, so as to bring the main outlines clearly into view. I have endeavoured to weave the threads of the story into a continuous narrative in the text; while in the notes I have inserted additional illustrations, and occasional allusions to analogous changes in other times and places. I have been careful to give detailed reference to my authorities, especially in those cases where they are not accessible in ordinary libraries, for the benefit of students who desire to follow up my work, so that they may be better able to correct, if they cannot confirm, my conclusions. There is ample room for numberless monographs on the history of particular localities, or of specific branches of industry and commerce. I can only hope that my effort to call attention to the broad features of the changes in economic life may be found useful by others who devote themselves to more specialised studies.

With the view of rendering this volume more suitable to the objects for which it is intended, I determined to recast it entirely; hardly a paragraph has been incorporated in this edition without alteration, and the greater part of it has been more than once re-written. In carrying out this task I have had unwearied assistance from Miss Lilian Tomn. Not only have my manuscript and the proof sheets had the advantage of her criticism, but I have been permitted to draw throughout on her unrivalled knowledge of the sources of English Economic History; while she is responsible for the chapter on Lord Burleigh, the transcripts of the documents printed in the Appendix, the Bibliography and the Index. It is impossible for me to appreciate accurately, far less to make clear to others, how immensely the book has gained from her constant and generous co-operation. I am also indebted to Professor Ashley of the University of Birmingham, for his kindness in reading my manuscript;

and for many suggestions and much valuable information to Mr Hubert Hall of the Public Record Office; as well as to Miss Maud Sellers, and to Dr Scott of the University of S. Andrews.

Twenty-five years have elapsed since I first began, almost accidentally, to devote myself to English Economic History. Since then I have given my best energies to it, and have found an ample reward, not only in the fresh light it has thrown on perennial problems, but also in the sympathetic interest of many friends, the sense of comradeship with fellow-workers, and the undying stimulus of one cherished memory. I had little idea at first of the wide range of the subject, or of the amount of time which must be spent in order to depict any incident in its proper colouring, and to draw their full significance from illuminating details. I now realise these difficulties so far, that it is with a very deep sense of its limitations and deficiencies that I put forth this contribution to the story of the Growth of English Industry and Commerce.

TRINITY COLLEGE,
16 *August*, 1903.

PREFACE TO THE FOURTH EDITION.

DURING the last four years, the study of the Modern Economic History of England has been carried on with remarkable vigour and success. Valuable monographs on special topics have been published in France and Germany as well as in England and America; while the investigations, which have been undertaken in connection with the Victoria County History, into the social and economic changes in particular districts, have been most fruitful. I have endeavoured to incorporate the results of these researches, so far as possible, in the present edition: it has been necessary to rewrite §§ 174 and 235, which deal with enclosure in the seventeenth and eighteenth centuries and the disappearance of small holdings; but the additional information which has come to hand serves, on the whole, to illustrate and amplify the views expressed in previous editions of this work. I am indebted for suggestions and assistance to Dr E. A. McArthur, Dr L. Knowles, Miss M. Sellers, and Miss M. F. Davies.

TRINITY COLLEGE,
CAMBRIDGE,
24 *Aug.* 1907.

CONTENTS.

INTRODUCTION.

ECONOMIC DIFFERENCES BETWEEN MEDIAEVAL AND MODERN SOCIETY.

VI. THE MERCANTILE SYSTEM.

I. Of the Mercantile System in General.

164. National Ambition for Maritime Power. The rising patriotic spirit of Englishmen in the Elizabethan age took the form of an ambition for maritime power; this might serve as the mainstay of national defence, as an effective instrument of attack on commercial rivals, and as a means of expansion. The growth and persistence of this sentiment, through all constitutional changes, show that it was deeply rooted in public opinion. Among the means to this end much attention was given to the increase of shipping, of seamen, and of naval stores; as well as to the development of maritime commerce, especially in corn. **13**

165. Public and Private Interest. When the State undertakes to foster economic life, its action must necessarily affect private interests, either favourably or unfavourably; and there is great difficulty in detecting where the public interest really lies. Even in retrospect it is not easy to estimate the effect of particular restrictions on the welfare of the nation as a whole, and to discard the standpoint of private interests. Increased respect for private interests is a noticeable feature in the seventeenth, and still more in the eighteenth century. **16**

166. The Crown and Parliament. Towards the close of Elizabeth's reign and in the seventeenth century, the constitutional question was raised as to whether the Crown, or the House of Commons, should be responsible for enforcing public good. In so far as *laissez faire* is impracticable, an autocratic government may be the best instrument of economic regulation, as democracies are even more liable to be inefficient and corrupt in dealing with trade affairs. The story of the Mercantile System may be naturally divided into three periods, (1) of full monarchical responsibility; (2) of the delegation of royal powers and attacks upon royal interference as unnecessary; and (3) of control by the Whig majority in the House of Commons. This division proves convenient, partly because of the different economic problems which came to light in successive periods, and partly because of the increasing areas which had to be habitually taken into account.   **18**

PART 1. THE REIGN OF ELIZABETH.

II. Nationalisation.

167. The Statute of Artificers. In Elizabeth's reign, the rules of municipal authorities were superseded by a national system of labour legislation; it aimed at reducing the existing chaos to order, and it survived with little modification for about 250 years. The chief things that demanded a remedy were the decay of corporate towns, the unsatisfactory training of village artisans, and the insufficient supply of agricultural labour. The main feature of the new measure was compulsion to service in husbandry, while the yearly hirings would tend to reduce vagrancy. In town and country alike, apprenticeship was to last seven years at least, as was the custom in London, and limitations were laid down as to the choice of employments, so as to favour rural districts and corporate towns, at the expense of market towns. These rules introduced greater uniformity throughout the country, and were a barrier to change of occupation ; but they did not prevent the growth of capitalism. The Act appears to have arrested the decay of corporate towns, and it incidentally determined the form which the settlement of the new immigrants assumed. There seems to have been less complaint of the harshness of the Act than of neglect to enforce it. The measure contained no adequate provision for the enrolment of apprentices, but the custom of a seven years' apprenticeship came into general vogue. The growth of local industrial companies was probably connected with the desire to enforce this national system, though it served other purposes as well. **25**

III. The Policy of Burleigh.

IV. The Landed Interest.

measures, supervise the quality of products and goods exposed for sale, and punish offences in connection with buying and selling. The local requirements of different districts were also considered by the Privy Council. In the time of Elizabeth, revenue was obtained on exported corn by taxation, and by occasional licences under Charles I. Considerable success had attended royal efforts to promote rural prosperity both in connection with tillage and with cattle breeding. **85**

V. The Moneyed Interest.

PART 2. THE STUARTS.

VI. The Necessities of State.

X. Economic Investigation and Maxims.

PART 3. PARLIAMENTARY COLBERTISM.

XI. The English Revolution.

XII. Public Finance.

XIII. Currency and Credit.

XV. Changes in the Organisation and Distribution of Industry.

XVI. SPIRITED PROPRIETORS AND SUBSTANTIAL TENANTS.

XVII. THE BEGINNING OF THE END.

VII. LAISSEZ FAIRE.

I. The Workshop of the World.

II. The Introduction of Machinery in the Textile Trades.

III. Aggravations of the Evils of Transition.

IV. Human Welfare.

Most of the evils, which were brought to light, had attached to cottage industry, and parents deserve a large share of blame as well as masters. The Commissioners of 1833 tried to isolate the question of child labour, and hoped that shifts would be organised. Limits were imposed on the employment of children; and inspectors, acting under a central authority, were charged with enforcing the Act. The over-working of children could not be checked effectively till the hours for women were restricted; and a normal working day of ten hours and a half was at length established, in spite of the forebodings of experts who ignored the results of Owen's experience. **774**

270. Distress of Hand-loom Weavers. The low standard of comfort of hand-loom weavers was not treated as a subject for State interference. The power-loom was superseding hand work; the concentration of weaving in factories gave facilities for supervision, and encouraged regularity and honesty, so that cottage weavers had no constancy of employment. The depression in the linen trade, during the transition to power weaving, was aggravated by the competition of Irish, and of cotton weavers; and in the silk trade, by the habitual spreading of work. The application of power to cotton-weaving was delayed through the cheapness of hand work, and led in the worsted trade to labour shifting. The woollen weavers had lost their abnormally high rates, and suffered a period of depression. State action seemed impracticable, but there has been improvement of wages from other influences, and the conditions for health of factory employment compare favourably with those that characterised cottage industries. . . **790**

271. Conditions of Work in Mines. The conditions of work in various industries were the subject of enquiry, and a strong case was established for interfering in regard to mines, when a Commission reported in 1840. The employment of young boys in mines had been increasing, but was now prohibited, as well as that of women under-ground, and a system of State inspection was organised. **802**

272. Conditions of Life in Towns. The conditions in which labourers lived attracted attention at the outbreak of cholera in 1831, in insanitary districts; and, after thorough enquiry, a Health Department was organised, but on an inadequate scale. The work of providing for the housing of the poor has been partly dealt with by building societies, though the problem is increasingly difficult either for individuals or municipalities. The new administrative machinery for social purposes is very different from that of the Stuarts, both in its aims and its methods. . . . **806**

V. FACILITIES FOR TRANSPORT.

273. Railways and Steamers. The demands of manufacturing districts for improved transport were met by the development of railway enterprise, which was a boon to the public generally; but it accelerated the decline of rural life in England, especially after the system was introduced in America. The application of steam power to ocean transport was more gradual, and it has greatly benefited the commercial, but not the landed interest. **811**

274. Joint-Stock Companies. Under the influence of new conditions, facilities were given for the formation of joint-stock companies with limited

POSTSCRIPT.

APPENDICES.

INTRODUCTION.

161. WITH the reign of Elizabeth we enter on the *The Eliza-bethan age is charac-teristically modern.* modern era of our history; the renewed breach with Rome, and the popular anxiety to escape from the shadow of Spanish domination, combined to rouse a patriotic enthusiasm that had been hitherto dormant. Englishmen had at last attained to a full consciousness of national unity, and showed a resolute determination in pursuing the new national mission. Hence we cannot but feel that the men of that era lived and moved on the same plane of thought as ourselves. While the partisans of the White Rose or the Red, and the heroes of the Hundred Years' War, seem strangely far away, the political designs of such men as Burleigh, or Gresham, or Raleigh, come home to us at once. We can sympathise with them completely in the objects they pursued, and have little difficulty in appreciating the means by which they strove to attain their ends.

This is particularly noticeable in the views then current *The im-portance of money for purposes of war* as to the acquisition of money for purposes of State. In Western Europe, as early as the fifteenth century, the command of wealth in a readily exchangeable form was of supreme importance, with a view to international conflicts. Landed proprietors, with their retainers, could not hold their own against professional soldiers; the prince, who commanded large feudal levies, was likely to be worsted by an enemy whose purse enabled him to put well-trained mercenaries into the field. A large territory, manned with dependents, was no longer such a source of strength; and money, which had been a useful adjunct, became the prime necessity[1] for supplying the "sinews of war[2]."

was generally recognised;

The political desire to accumulate wealth in the form of money or treasure had been strongly felt in the fifteenth century; and it was whetted by the opportunities for its gratification, which were opened up by the geographical discoveries of Vasco da Gama and Columbus. The Portuguese obtained possession of a lucrative line of commerce, and the Spaniards set themselves to monopolise the mineral resources of the new world. During the reign of Elizabeth,

and England, by engaging in the international struggle for wealth,

England entered the field as a competitor for a share in these newly-discovered sources of treasure. The Spanish monarchy under Charles V. and Philip II. seemed to have inexhaustible stores of bullion at its command, so as to threaten the very existence of independent European states; a successful attack on the plate fleet not only replenished the English supply of silver, but struck an effective blow at the dreaded foe. Very similar motives were at work in the sixteenth and seventeenth century schemes for developing commerce. A country which had no mines of the precious metals, could only hope to obtain a supply of them by means of trade; and under the new conditions of geographical knowledge, maritime enterprise was organised on a scale that had been hitherto unknown. Commercial jealousy took a new form; it was no longer concerned with maintaining exclusive

---

[1] Abundant illustrations may be found, in sixteenth century history, of the straits to which generals were occasionally reduced for want of ready money. Compare Marchand's remarks on the difficulty of keeping French armies in the field (*Charles 1ᵉʳ de Cossé*, 132, 159). M. de Brissac was frequently hard put to it for want of money (*Ib.* 273), and because of the frauds of officials (*Ib.* p. 586). Financial conditions were the determining causes of Charles V.'s successes against the Schmalkaldic League, and of his failure to hold his own at Innsbruck. (Ehrenberg, *Das Zeitalter der Fugger*, I. 139, 153). The action of Elizabeth, in detaining the treasure which was being transmitted to Alva, very seriously crippled his plans.

[2] Ehrenberg (*Das Zeitalter der Fugger*, I. 6) calls attention to the fact that Machiavelli criticised this position (*Discorsi sopra la prima deca di Tito Livio*, II. 10), and argued that, on the contrary, war was a source from which treasure could be obtained. This was undoubtedly the view of the English buccaneers in their attacks on Spain; and the mercenary troops and condottieri of the Middle Ages had engaged in fighting with the view of making it pay On Hawkwood, the captain of a celebrated English Company of this character, see Fortescue, *History of the British Army*, I. p. 51.

privileges at particular depots or securing a control over *was drawn into keen competition with other nations.* special routes; rival powers fought for a monopoly of access to some vast continent. Trading operations, and the conflicts to which they gave rise, assumed unexampled proportions. Throughout the Elizabethan and Stuart periods, the desire of obtaining ample supplies of money[1], either directly from the mines[2], or indirectly by means of trade, became the very powerful factor in international politics, which we find it to be to-day[3].

Though the exigencies of military operations pressed less *The English Crown, like other governments,* heavily on England than on several of the continental states, there were other reasons which forced the English Crown to

[1] There have been considerable changes of opinion among publicists and economists as to the precise importance of money: so long as natural economy held its own, there was no temptation to overrate it; in fact the schoolmen were inclined to stigmatise it as merely conventional, in contradistinction to natural riches. Since Adam Smith wrote, the political importance of money has been merged in the idea of wealth, but in this more general form it has been regarded as of supreme importance for the community. In quite recent times there has been a distinct reaction against the undue appreciation even of money's worth; and much attention is being given to elements of human welfare which the economic calculus." See below, p. 880.

[2] It is difficult to form any opinion as to the extent to which the precious metals were procured in England and Wales at different dates. There is evidence that a good deal of silver was obtained, in conjunction with lead, at Combe Martin in Devonshire in the time of Edward I., again under Edward III., and also in the reign of Elizabeth (Fuller, *Worthies of England* (1840), I. 395). The argentiferous lead in Cardiganshire had been worked by the Romans and Danes, and again in the reign of Elizabeth (Fuller, *op. cit.* III. 482); the most systematic working appears to have taken place in the time of Charles I., when Thomas Bushell minted Welsh silver for the use of the royal troops. (See his *Just and True Remonstrance of His Maiestie's Mines-Royall in the Principality of Wales*, 1642.) The Romans appear to have been accustomed to extract the silver from British lead, before making it up into pigs, both in the time of Claudius and of Nero (Way, *Relics of Roman Metallurgy* in *Archaeological Journal*, 1859, XVI. 26, 27), and there is no reason to suppose that the art died out altogether. Still, it is hardly likely that silver was obtained in any considerable quantities, as ancient writers speak of tin and lead as the metals which were found in abundance in Britain (*Archaeological Journal*, XVI. 14). The language of Bede seems to show that the supplies obtained in his time were unimportant (*Hist. Eccl.* I. i. § 5). That vast amounts of silver were taken away from England in the couple of centuries before the Norman Conquest is certain; the ravages of the Danes and the payment of Peter's Pence effected a considerable drain; but whether the supply was replenished by mining, or by means of trade, appears to be quite uncertain.

[3] The military resources of the Transvaal were largely due to the control which President Kruger exercised over the mining interests, and the demarcation of spheres for exclusive trade is a main part of the policy of Russia and France in China.

1—2

depend on a regular money revenue. The royal estates no longer yielded a sufficient income; and the centralisation of government had rendered it inexpedient for the king to move from one place to another, where stores had been collected for the subsistence of the court. Owing to the fall in the value of money, the traditional payments of tenths and fifteenths were quite inadequate; and the necessity of providing a permanent navy, instead of relying on the mercantile marine for ships in time of war, was an additional expense. The need of money affected internal affairs as well as foreign relations. Elizabeth was singularly successful in drawing upon the loyalty of her subjects for unrequited service, but the expenses of government could not be systematically and regularly provided, without regular supplies of money; and these could only be procured for the use of government in the requisite quantities by means of taxation. Under the pressure of new requirements, all questions as to ways and means of levying taxes assumed fresh importance[1]; and the desire of statesmen to increase the "funds" from which contributions could be drawn, led them to take account of the condition of every class of the subjects. Experience had shown that this form of revenue could not be permanently available unless the country was in a prosperous condition; "the King cannot have treasure when his subjects have none[2]." It thus came to be generally recognised that the economic interests of the government and the governed are identical in the long run. The oppression of the trading[3] or of the agricultural[4] classes had proved a short-sighted and disastrous policy, and rulers realised that it was prudent to develop the material welfare of their subjects. The existence of taxation, as the chief means of defraying the expenses of the State, is presupposed in all the political economy of modern times. The requirements of the new system of finance forced statesmen to interest themselves in the development of national resources, the extension of commerce, and the pros-

was forced to rely on taxation for revenue;

and this rendered it necessary to take more account of the resources of the country,

the extension of trade, and the welfare of the people.

[1] J. Bonar, *Philosophy and Political Economy*, p. 59.

[2] J. Hales, *A Discourse of the Commonweal*, p. 35.

[3] For the mischief resulting from the oppression of the rich in the later Roman Empire, compare Cunningham, *Western Civilisation* i. 186.

[4] Encouragement of tillage was a special feature of English policy; see below, pp. 87, 104.

perity of industry, far more seriously than was necessary in mediaeval times.

It is on these grounds that the Elizabethan period is *The economic features of society were of a modern type.* rightly included in the economic history of modern England. At first sight we might be inclined to demur; recent improvements in mechanical appliances, and in the means of communication, have occasioned such striking progress in every department of manufacture, and in the volume of trade, that the domestic industry and struggling commerce of the sixteenth and seventeenth centuries seem to have a closer affinity with mediaeval society than with that of our own day. But a more careful consideration of the economic features of society, as distinguished from mechanical processes, shows us where the turning-point may be found. In the time of Elizabeth, England had already entered on the race for wealth as a competitor with other nations; and the necessity of a new revenue system and of dependence on taxation, with all that it involved and implied, was becoming apparent. The crisis is so important that we must look a little more closely at it, to appreciate its political and its economic significance.

162. The age of geographical discovery had revealed the *The changes occasioned by the discoveries of the fifteenth century, were accelerated by the rise of nationalities, not only in a political but in an economic sense.* possibility of extending the range and increasing the scale of maritime enterprise; but besides this, the new forms of political organisation, which were coming into prominence, were important factors in progress, as they enabled the peoples of Western Europe to take advantage of the new commercial openings. The process of consolidating duchies and petty kingdoms into large territories, controlled by a single authority, had gone some way. The fifteenth and sixteenth centuries saw the rise of nationalities, not only in a political, but in an economic sense as well; since industry and commerce were beginning to be organised for national objects and on a national basis. The town no longer held its position as the chief organ of economic life. City states had come to the front as the centres of civilisation in the ancient world, and they had maintained their importance in regard to manufacture and trade all through the Middle Ages; but the time had at length arrived when they were to be superseded altogether.

Certain cities had been forced   In the thirteenth and fourteenth centuries, each of the leading towns of continental Europe had formed a separate economic centre, which not only regulated its own internal affairs, but pursued its own policy in its trading relations with other places[1]. Each of them had to solve the problem of its own food supply; each tried to apportion the opportunities for business fairly among the different citizens; each endeavoured to make the most of its facilities for commerce, and to prevent outsiders from taking undue advantage of *to take account of wide areas,* them. At first the interests of these civic entities were somewhat restricted; but as time passed, and they grew in importance, they were forced to look beyond their walls. Some were compelled to extend the sphere of their influence over the area from which the provisions necessary for their inhabitants were drawn, and others found it prudent to take account of the supply of wool, required for their manufactures, and of *and thus served as an object lesson in the government of a large territory, containing urban and rural districts,* other raw materials. As the expansion of town possessions went on apace, partly by purchase and partly by conquest, the mutual dependence of rural and urban life came into clear light, and served as an object lesson to rulers of large territories. Agriculture, manufacture and commerce have each a part to play in the 'natural progress of opulence,' and the prosperity of one element reacts upon the others as well. The separate factors are distinct, and they are occasionally in opposition[2], but they may be so controlled as to co-operate for the good of the community as a whole. It is in the superseding of the particularised interest of the separate cities, and the attempt to treat a large territory, containing many *as an organic whole.* towns and much intervening area, as one organic whole, and to foster its prosperity, that we find the nationalist economic policy which is characteristic of modern times.

Civic economic life had been little developed in England,   In some parts of Europe the life of the towns was imperfectly merged in that of a nation, and separatist civic interests continued to assert themselves, with considerable effect, all through the seventeenth century; this was especially the case in Holland[3], and it proved to be an element of

[1] Cunningham, *Western Civilisation*, II. 149; Schmoller, *Mercantile System*, 11.

[2] On the fact that all schemes for promoting national welfare must necessarily give special favour to some interest, see below, p. 16.

[3] Pringsheim (*Beiträge zur wirthschaftlichen Entwickelungsgeschichte der*

weakness. In England, on the other hand, the conscious sub- *and was* ordination of civic to national development seems to have *easily superseded,* begun as early as the time of Edward I.; it had been pursued *in one sphere* with success by subsequent monarchs, and by the time of the *after another,* Tudors the whole of the active economic institutions of the country had assumed a national character. The steps had been gradual; under Edward I. there had been a common system of weights and measures, a uniform coinage and a similar administration of justice throughout the country; after the Black Death, rules and institutions for the regulation of wages, and the treatment of the unemployed, were imposed upon the people generally by Statute; it was possible *by national* for Elizabeth not only to codify the whole of these arrange- *regulation.* ments, but also to impose the same conditions of technical training throughout the length and breadth of the land.

Such minute regulation of the economic life of the nation *The im-* as a whole would have been impossible, while each city was *portance of the change* practically independent, so far as its industry was concerned, *comes out* and commerce was intermunicipal[1]. The close interconnec- *in connec-* tion between the various parts of each realm becomes more *economic* noticeable, when we consider the steps that were taken, in *progress;* different European countries, to promote economic progress. Each had to strike out a path for itself. In the Middle Ages there had been much similarity between the institutions of one city community and another; the customs of one could be transferred by affiliation[2] to another without serious inconvenience. But in modern times, the economic life of each *these took a* nation presents special features of its own, since the native *different shape for* products and appropriate industries of each territory are *different* distinct. The physical conditions of England are so different *ties.* from those of France that the economic policy, which seems most favourable to the development of the one, would be unsuitable to the other. Even countries, like England and Holland, which have both aimed at maritime greatness, have been led to pursue the same object in different fashions.

Vereinigten Niederlande in Schmoller's *Forschungen*, **x.** p. 2) shows how this affected both the industrial development and the commercial undertakings of the Dutch.

[1] Vol. I. p. 186.

[2] Vol. I. p. 223.

Considerations as to the special advantages and natural connections of each country have necessarily modified the schemes of various rulers who were trying to develop national prosperity[1].

New facilities for the formation of capital rendered it possible to give effect to these schemes,

163. In modern times it has been possible to devise undertakings on an enormous scale, and there are also unexampled facilities for carrying these schemes into effect. In the Elizabethan and in all subsequent periods, there have been far better opportunities for the formation, and greater scope for the investment, of capital than was at all possible in the Middle Ages. The discoveries of the precious metals in Mexico and Peru opened up such large supplies[2], that the material means of hoarding[3], and of forming a capital fund, were very widely diffused. So long as natural economy continued to predominate in rural life, there was difficulty in amassing wealth; corn, and other raw produce, cannot be stored indefinitely without loss; the prudent man was prepared to be frugal in the use of his possessions, but he had no facilities for accumulating wealth. When gold and silver came more generally into circulation, it was possible for many people, who had never thought of it before, to lay up a hoard.

and there were increased opportunities for investment.

There was, besides, an even more important change, which was due to the improved facilities for investing money in business; the far-seeing man was no longer compelled, by the force of circumstances, to have his hoard lying idle; he could find the means of employing it at a profit. The restrictions, which mediaeval public opinion had imposed on the lending of money for interest, had broken down; wealthy men and wealthy communities had got into the way of making advances on remunerative terms to impecunious

Loans were negotiated by monarchs,

princes. The monarchs were forced to realise the importance of maintaining their credit, and of conforming to the expectations of business men in their management of their finances[4]. Goldsmiths, who were prepared to undertake the

---

[1] On the development of a cosmopolitan, as contrasted with a national economic policy, in recent times, see below, p. 867.

[2] See below, p. 165.

[3] Cunningham, *The Use and Abuse of Money*, 75.

[4] Cunningham, *Western Civilisation*, II. 168.

farming of taxes, or to supply loans in anticipation of revenue, *and goldsmiths developed a banking business.* were glad to receive deposits; and few men scrupled to take a moderate interest from merchants who had the means of making still larger profits themselves[1]. As current opinion altered, there came to be greater facilities for transferring accumulated wealth into the hands of men who would use it to advantage.

While the obstacles to the transference of capital were being removed, commercial business was being re-constituted *Commercial business expanded* on lines which made it possible for larger numbers of men to engage in it; as expenses were reduced, there was more inducement to embark in traffic. Foreign trade had for centuries been conducted by moneyed men, who adventured with their cargoes and hoped to replace their outlay at a profit; but the regulations of the ports which they visited, or the rules of the societies of which they were members, must have rendered it very difficult for them to push their trading connections. The discoveries of the fifteenth cen- *after the age of discovery,* tury rendered expansion inevitable; the greatly extended commerce, which resulted from direct communication with the East, did not readily adapt itself to the old institutions. Antwerp rapidly rose into importance as the chief mercantile *and was constituted on modern lines at Antwerp.* depot for northern Europe; and in this city, the restrictions on individual enterprise, which existed in many other places, were almost unknown. Strangers were as free to come and buy or sell, as they were at one of the great fairs; but while each of these only lasted for a limited period, Antwerp served as a mart all the year round. New commercial methods developed in these new circumstances, as merchants were not only able to trade on their own account, but were permitted to carry on business on commission[2]. At the older mercantile centres, the right of buying and selling had been carefully restricted to the citizens and gild members, or to specified bodies of traders; but Antwerp was the pioneer of modern commercial practice, and the opportunities it afforded were

---

[1] On the changes in public opinion and the transitional forms of bargain, especially the *contractus trinus*, see Ashley, *Economic Hist.* I. ii. p. 440; see also below, p. 153.

[2] Ehrenberg, *Das Zeitalter der Fugger*, II. 6.

The struggle between the old and the new business methods continued all through the seventeenth century; open to any man who had capital and could take advantage of them. This proved to be the commencement of the conflict between mediaeval and modern methods of business; it went on in all parts of Europe and we hear a great deal about it in England in the sixteenth and seventeenth centuries. The Merchant Adventurers and other bodies of merchants would have preferred that privileged and regulated trade should be maintained; while the independent capitalists, who were *with the result that merchants obtained freedom to employ their capital as they found profitable.* stigmatised as interlopers, claimed freedom to conduct their business at the places and in the manner which they found most profitable. The full significance of this change, in the character of trade, will become apparent when we come to discuss the Industrial Revolution[1]; at present, it may suffice to say that modern merchants have obtained new facilities for trade, while they are also in a position to command the use of additional capital on easy terms.

From time immemorial foreign trade had been capitalist in character, but the circumstances of the sixteenth and seventeenth centuries gave great opportunities for opening up new markets, and for enlarged transactions in some of the old lines of commerce. In regard to many industrial pursuits, however, it is true to say that, in the Middle Ages, they had been so organised that the possession of capital would have given a man no advantage in starting or carrying them on. The craftsman would possess the necessary tools; but he would often work on materials furnished by the 'consumer.' The gilds took measures to secure a high standard of workmanship, and the thorough training of apprentices; but the craftsmen catered for a known and limited market. Pains were taken to see that no man should engage in unfair competition, or push his wares either to the detriment of his neighbours, or *The extension of commerce re-acted on industry* to the disparagement of the trade. But gradually, as commerce increased, and men began to practise industries, which were dependent on a supply of imported materials, or set themselves to produce for distant markets, the moneyed man came to have an advantage in the prosecution of these callings. Capitalists resented restrictions, such as those on the number of apprentices, since they interfered with success in

[1] See below, p. 611.

the development of business. In some cases the wealthy *and the* members captured the gild organisation[1], in others, and *gilds no longer* more especially in the cloth trade, they evaded it, by going *availed to check its* outside the municipal bounds[2]; but, by one means or another, *expansion;* the institutions, which hindered the employment of capital in industry, had practically broken down, before the accession of Elizabeth. Manufacturing was not left unregulated; but the regulation was for the most part of a type that was perfectly consistent with the increasing introduction of capital into industrial pursuits. The crucial difference *so that industrial* between mediaeval and modern industry lies in the fact *pursuits were also* that, under the older system, the necessary oversight was *recon-* exercised by the officers of a gild over its members; while *stituted on a larger* in modern times, the employer is individually responsible for *scale and under* the organisation of business and supervision of the work *capitalist super-* carried on by his *employés*. *vision.*

The management of land was also coming, more and more, *Estate manage-* to be pursued with reference to the market for products, and *ment was* therefore as a trade. The scheme of self-sufficing economy, *also revo- lutionised,* which had been taken for granted by Walter of Henley or Robert Grosseteste, was felt to be out of date. Landowners were inclined to develop their estates on lines that gave opportunity for the investment of capital. This was especially noticeable in connection with pasture-farming; the price of wool was so high, at times, during the Tudor period[3], that there was a great temptation to convert large areas into sheep-runs; but in the seventeenth century cattle-breeding, in conjunction with cultivation, was proving more remunera- tive than sheep-farming. As increased facilities became *as tillage* available for the export of corn, there were new inducements *was pur- sued with a* to pursue tillage as a trade, and to cater for distant *view to the markets,* markets. Land management had been reconstituted on the basis of money economy in the fifteenth century; and as it came to be regarded more generally from a view to possible profit, the spirit of competition began to affect it,

---

[1] The tailors of London seem to have been originally a body of craftsmen (Clode, *Memorials of the Merchant Tailors' Company*, 513), but in the sixteenth century many of them were traders (Clode, *Early History*, I. 245). A similar change occurred at Bristol (Vol. I. p. 437, n. 5).

[2] On the migration of industry to suburbs see Vol. I. p. 518.

[3] This was especially the case in the decade beginning with 1540, when the price had nearly trebled.

and the possibility of enhancing rents rendered it profitable especially as regards the determination of rent. The enhancing of payments to the landowner took place in consequence of the increased demand for pasture, but rack rents for ordinary farms were common enough in the early part of the seventeenth century. These changes rendered some important economic movements pos- *to sink capital in improving the land.* sible. The landlord who sunk capital in the improvement of his estate could look for a return on his outlay from the increased rents on which he could count; there was a prospect of success in undertaking large operations, in the way of reclaiming land by banking and draining, and for this it was necessary to obtain capital[1]. The moneyed man was able to play a part, not only in commerce and industry, but in the working and development of landed property.

The energy of capitalists, which was controlled under the mercantile system, The predominance of capital is the leading feature which distinguishes modern economic conditions from those of the Middle Ages. There undoubtedly were energetic and vigorous men in all eras of history; but they had no opportunity of displaying their powers, in the industrial sphere, till facilities were available for forming capital, and there was freedom for employing it in many kinds of business. This state of affairs existed, to some extent, in the Elizabethan era, and it has become more and more common in subsequent times. The moneyed men, who organise labour on a large scale and bring it to bear in the directions which offer the best prospect of a profit, have given a feverish, restless character to modern life, that seems to us to have been lacking in mediaeval days. This feature, too, suggests a principle of division which may be conveniently applied to the modern, as distinguished from the recent, economic history of England. During many reigns persistent efforts were made to control the energy of capitalists, so as to force it into those lines which were of *gradually obtained free play.* political advantage to the realm as a whole; but, for a century or more, we have been content to let the business men manage their own affairs in their own way. The aims and working of the Mercantile System, and the subsequent triumph of Laissez Faire, are the subject of the present volume.

---

[1] See below, p. 111. On the need of capital for the development of mining, see p. 529 below.

VI. THE MERCANTILE SYSTEM.

I. OF THE MERCANTILE SYSTEM IN GENERAL.

164. A NATIONAL spirit was arising in many of the *The rising patriotic spirit of Englishmen* countries of Europe in the sixteenth century, and it was specially vigorous in England, where the physical conditions of the realm helped to determine the special form which the patriotic ambitions of Englishmen were destined to assume. Popular sentiment had run for many generations in national, rather than merely in civic, or provincial, channels; the memories of the glorious achievements of the Black Prince, or of Henry of Monmouth, inspired the descendants of their soldiers with a sturdy sense of independence. When the power of Spain, and later of France, threatened to extermi- nate their liberties altogether, Englishmen were roused to a determination to hold their own; they were especially anxious *took the form of an ambition* to make the most of the natural defences which were afforded *for mari- time* by the sea. The dreams of continental conquest faded away *power,* from the minds of the rulers, and ever-increasing attention was given to the development of maritime power.

This was to be the mainstay of national independence; *which might serve as the* and gradually, as the strategical importance of the sea was *mainstay of national* more fully recognised, the military organisation took a sub- *defences,* ordinate place in the eyes of those who were concerned with the national defences. As events proved at the time of the Armada, it was impossible for an enemy, however powerful, to transport and land his troops in the face of an effective fleet. At the beginning of the reign of Elizabeth, when the fortunes of England were at a very low ebb, and the govern- ment was destitute alike of ordnance and military stores and of any means of procuring them, all that could be attempted was to fix attention on the best means of repelling attacks.

and as an effective instrument of attack on commercial rivals In the later part of the reign, when this danger was less pressing, and during the seventeenth century, it was possible to take offensive measures against the Dutch and other powers ; and the navy proved a most effective weapon for this purpose. Maritime power had been cultivated at first, as the necessary condition for political freedom; in later days it was consciously developed, so that England might secure *and of expansion.* the command of the sea for commerce, and that her shipping might serve as the basis for building up a world-wide empire.

The growth and persistence of this sentiment, The strength of national sentiment in regard to sea power is very remarkable ; it grew in force as generation succeeded generation. In the sixteenth century, it took definite shape from the dread of Spanish invasion. In the seventeenth, it was stimulated by a conscious readiness to model our practice on that of the Dutch, for Englishmen were eager to imitate them in the hope of eventually outstripping them. In the eighteenth century, it inspired the effective attacks on the French power in India and in Canada. One steady purpose runs through the whole of the national life ; so that *through all constitutional changes,* despite the constitutional changes which England underwent, she still held the even tenour of her way towards maritime supremacy. Charles I. spent an immensity of pains on the organisation of a royal navy ; the exploits of Blake and Penn testify to the interest which was felt in the matter under the Council of State, and by Cromwell; and Charles II., and his brother of York, did not a little to increase our colonial importance. But maritime power was not merely the pet *shows that it was deeply rooted in public opinion.* ambition of a succession of rulers ; it had caught the popular imagination. There must always be a difficulty in gauging the force of public opinion, as apart from governmental action, but there is much to show that, in this matter, the authorities were content to follow a popular movement. Elizabeth's preparations lagged behind the desires of her subjects[1]; the inefficiency of the admiralty arrangements under Charles I. disgusted the trading classes and the seamen, and directly prepared the way for the fall of the monarchy The English nation has been willing to forgive much to those princes who

---

[1] Oppenheim, *The Administration of the Royal Navy*, Vol. I. p. 116.

have contributed to the greatness of England on the sea. The achievements of her reign have shed a halo of glory round the figure of Elizabeth, and the military despotism of Cromwell is half forgotten in the excellence of his naval administration. This determination to obtain maritime power, which rests on a long-standing and wide-spread national conviction, has been the principal factor in determining the economic policy of the country.

The statesmen, who were responsible for giving effect *As means* to the national aspiration after power on the sea, naturally *to this end, much* gave great attention to the improvement of English shipping, *attention was given* as the best means of attaining this end. In the first instance, *to the increase of* at all events, they were chiefly concerned in fostering the *shipping,* mercantile marine; as ships which were ordinarily engaged in commerce would serve, if need should arise, to repel any foe who might attempt to cross the channel. It was also *of seamen,* necessary that the ships should be properly manned; and much encouragement was consequently given to the fishing trades, as these were rightly regarded as an excellent school for seamanship. Pains were taken to preserve the timber, *and of* and procure the hemp, sailcloth and naval stores, which were *naval stores,* required for building and fitting ships; and special attention had to be given to the supply of ordnance.

It was clearly understood, moreover, that increased *as well as* facilities for remunerative employment would do more than *to the development* anything else to stimulate the energies of shipbuilders and *of maritime commerce,* shipowners. Efforts were accordingly made to enforce a *merce,* practicable navigation policy[1], and to keep the active trade of the country in the hands of native merchants; the men of the Hanse League were ousted from their privileged position, and negotiations were opened with the view of organising a trade in the Baltic. The authorities devoted much attention to fostering new forms of production, which might furnish additional commodities for export. The Hanse towns, and the men of the Low Countries, had developed a corn trade, which continued for many years to be the backbone of the commercial prosperity of Holland[2]; and

---

[1] The beginnings of this scheme can be traced back to the time of Richard II. (Vol. I. p. 394.)

[2] See below, p. 209.

especially in corn. successive governments, from the time of Burleigh till the passing of the Corn Bounty Act of 1689, sought to find employment of a similar character for our ships. It is unnecessary to multiply illustrations of the all-pervading character of the legislation which was drafted in the hope of encouraging shipping; the projects, which were devised with the view of directly, or indirectly, increasing maritime power, had ramifications which affected every department of industry and agriculture, as well as commerce, so as to control them and force them to co-operate for the attainment of this particular object of national ambition.

When the State undertakes to foster economic life, 165. Up till the time of Adam Smith, men of all parties in England were agreed that government was wise to pursue a definite economic policy and to aim at the acquisition of particular forms of wealth. And if it is desirable that there should be State intervention in these matters, one thing is clear,—Any scheme of controlling economic affairs for *its action must necessarily affect private interests, either favourably or unfavourably;* the public good must involve an interference with private interests. Some of them may be favoured, and some may be injured, but it is inevitable that very many should be affected in one way or another. In Tudor times, there was a consensus of opinion to the effect that the private interest of the graziers was detrimental to the community; the government had no scruple in opposing the development of sheep-farming, by imposing legislative restrictions. On the other hand, it was generally felt that the shipping and fishing trades were highly advantageous to the realm, and that the private interest of men engaged in such callings should be allowed free play, and might even be encouraged, as a *and there is great difficulty in detecting where the public interest really lies.* means of promoting the public good. The problem, which confronted the government, was that of detecting and pursuing the welfare of the community through the maze of private interests,—of discouraging some and fostering others, so as to obtain the best results for the nation as a whole.

Even in retrospect it is not easy It is necessary to bear this fact in mind in order to pronounce a fair judgment upon the Mercantile System, or any other national system of economic policy. English regulations were unfavourable to the progress of the colonies, but in so far as this interference was necessary in the general interest, not merely of the Mother Country but of the *to estimate the effect of particular restrictions on the* English realm as a whole, the sacrifice of particular settle- *welfare of* ments was quite defensible; the principle is thoroughly sound. Laws were adopted, which favoured the shipowners *the nation* as compared with manufacturers or landowners; but it would *as a whole,* be absurd to say that these enactments were simply passed in the interests of a class, and that the object of promoting the maritime power of the country was a mere pretext. In order to appreciate the action of the government aright, we must try to consider each measure in its wider bearings, and to take account of its probable effect on the welfare of the community, as far as we can. To attempt to judge of any *and to discard the* measure, from the point of view of private interests, is merely *standpoint* idle; some private persons were injured, and some were *of private interests.* benefited, in every case. This may be admitted at once; but the really important issue, as to the influence on the public weal, cannot be settled by weighing these personal or class considerations against each other. We shall not always find it easy to be wise after the event, and we need not be surprised that some of the measures adopted failed to produce the expected results. But we shall at least be better fitted to be intelligent critics, if we can enter into the reasons of public policy which weighed, at different times, with honest and sensible men and induced them to take a course, which was inimical to certain interests and unduly favoured others.

Elizabethan sentiment, in regard to the respect which *Increased* ought to be paid to private interests, differed very widely from *respect for private* the feeling which became current in the eighteenth century on *interests* the same subject. Tudor legislators, in their efforts after the public good, did not seem to take any account of private convenience. The sixteenth century statutes contain phrases which convey the impression that Parliament regarded as criminal the conduct of a man who ventured to urge his own gain[1], where any matter of public advantage was concerned.

---

[1] Vol. I. p. 480. See also the order of the Privy Council in 1622. "This being the rule, by which both the woolgrower, the cloathier and merchant must be governed, That whosoever had a part of the gaine in profitable times, since his Majesty's happie raigne, must now in the decay of Trade . . . . . beare a part of the publicke losses, as may best conduce to the good of the publicke and the maintenance of the generall trade." E. M. Leonard, *English Poor Relief*, 148.

is a notice-able feature in the seventeenth A modification of this view had become general, at the outbreak of the Civil War; and Parliament issued a pronouncement, which seems to imply that they were only justified by the existence of common danger in setting private interests *and still more in the eighteenth century.* aside[1]. The eighteenth century approximated more and more to the view that private interests, if allowed free play, would co-operate for the public good ; and, when this position was once explicitly adopted, the whole basis of the Mercantile System was sapped. But so long as the scheme lasted, it constituted a serious effort to pursue the good of the realm as a whole, with as little injury as might be to the separate and conflicting interests of distinct areas, or different trades.

The constitutional question was raised 166.   The constitutional struggles of the seventeenth century, which seem to have left the commercial policy of the country almost untouched, were nevertheless fraught with important consequences in regard to the economic side of national life.   The issue, which was fought out, turned on the question whether the King or the House of Commons *as to whether the Crown or the House of Commons should be responsible for enforcing public good.* should be responsible for detecting and enforcing the public good, amidst the claims of conflicting private interests.   The task must always be a difficult one ; we are inclined to think, at first sight, that full discussion, in a democratic assembly where all parties are represented, will afford the best facilities for exercising a wise control over industrial and commercial affairs.   It is true that democratic institutions have been consonant with the freedom for individual enterprise, which has been the vitalising principle of economic progress in all branches of the Anglo-Saxon race, and that the victory of the Parliamentary forces over Charles I. turned out to be an *Where laissez faire is impracticable* important step in the direction of *laissez faire*.   But the times were not ripe for repudiating State-interference in business affairs; all parties were agreed that governmental action was necessary, in order to foster industry and promote commerce.   When we ask the question whether, admitting

---

[1] "Whereas in times of common danger and necessity, the Interest of private persons ought to give way to the publike." *A declaration of the Lords and Commons assembled in Parliament, for the Incouragement of all such Apprentices as have or shall voluntarily list themselves to go in this present expedition for the defence of Religion the preservation of this City, the King and the Kingdome under the command of his Excellency the Earl of Warwick*, Nov. 7, 1642. [Trin. Coll. Camb., Y. 1. 9 (37).]

such control to be necessary, we should prefer to have it exercised autocratically, or through the machinery of popular government, we may see that difficulties, from which a personal ruler is free, arise in democratic states. Efficiency *an auto-cratic government may be the best instru-ment of economic regulation,* is one of the chief things to be aimed at in the control of business matters; and there can be little doubt that the Council under Elizabeth or Charles I., and the Committee of Trade under Charles II., were better able to administer industrial and commercial affairs with promptitude and despatch, than was possible under parliamentary rule in the period of Whig ascendancy. It is at all events clear that English public opinion did not set in the direction of *laissez faire*, until the country had had long experience of the evils of the Mercantile System as reconstructed by a constitutional government.

Corrupt as administration has often been under an autocrat, when important affairs have been left in the hands of court favourites, a democratic government has no immunity from similar evils. A personal ruler, who is a strong man, like Cromwell in England or Henri IV. in France, has an immense advantage over any popular government in his power and opportunities for choosing subordinates, and filling the various posts with men who will serve the country scrupulously and well. In a modern monarchy, in which the revenue is raised by taxation, the interest of the government will approximately represent that *as democra-cies are even more liable to be in-efficient and corrupt.* of the community; while there is a real danger that a democratic assembly may offer opportunities for particular persons, or classes, to obtain such influence, that they can utilise public resources for private advantage. Democratic institutions make very great demands on the public spirit of the citizens. When questions of fostering industry and directing commerce are under consideration, it must be singularly difficult for business men, who are engaged in framing or modifying the economic policy of the country, to lay aside all thought of their personal interests in the matter. There is in consequence, under parliamentary government, a possibility that the prosperity of the realm as a whole will be overlooked, in the effort to meet the requirements of powerful interests which demand legislative support. This particular evil is less likely to arise under an absolutism, though that system has other disadvantages of its own.

The story of the Mercantile System may be natural- ly divided into

During a period of more than two centuries, from the beginning of Elizabeth's reign till the accession of Pitt to power, the effort to promote economic progress by governmental action was steadily maintained. There was very little departure from the broad lines of the policy that had been laid down by the great Lord Burleigh; but despite this continuity, remarkable changes occurred in the administrative machinery for regulating industry and fostering commerce.

the three periods, of full monarchi- cal respon- sibility;

In the reign of Elizabeth, the royal power was paramount; the royal officials, including the justices of the peace and clerks of the market, were the chief agents by which control was exercised. General instructions were given to them in the form of royal proclamations, though specific directions on many *minutiae* were added in the letters of the Privy Council. This body was ready to call the local authorities to account for neglect; and to enforce the statutes of the realm or the royal mandates; royal patentees for special trades, as well as common informers[1], were the unpopular predecessors of the government inspectors of the present day. This phase of industrial and commercial regulation presents many interesting analogies with the thorough-going system of governmental control and royal initiative which flourished in France. The English Crown was never able to carry its supervision so far as was done by Colbert, but it is extraordinary to see how closely the central authority succeeded in keeping in touch with officials in all parts of the country.

of the delegation of royal powers and

With the change of dynasty and accession of the Stuarts, the system of royal administration entered on a period of great difficulty. The very progress that had been brought about during the Elizabethan age was a cause of trouble. Commerce was greatly enlarged; experiments in colonisation were beginning, and new industries were being planted; it

---

[1] Elizabeth had to issue orders for the protection of common informers from "light and evil disposed persons" (Proclamation 10 Nov. 1566); but legislation was also necessary to check the abuses of which they were guilty (18 El. c. 5 and 31 El. c. 5). See below, p. 99 n. 1.

was difficult for any government to keep pace with these developments or to continue to take stock of all matters of economic interest. A system of delegation became inevitable; the Crown found it convenient to establish companies for particular branches of foreign commerce, and to adapt the system of granting patents to the exigencies of internal economic life; while it also issued occasional commissions of enquiry into the condition of affairs. The mere existence of privileged bodies of traders and manufacturers was in itself a cause of jealousy, while their manner of exercising their rights stirred up an angry agitation against the authority from which they derived their powers. There were, moreover, other influences which interfered with the smooth working of the system. A sentiment, which was destined to deepen and grow, against any government control, began to make itself felt, especially on the part of some merchants engaged in foreign trade; while the feeling became *attacks upon them as unnecessary;* common that general legislation would suffice, and that the constant supervision which the Crown attempted to exercise was unnecessary. In this fashion, the economic grievances of manufacturers and traders came to be taken up by the agitators, who were endeavouring to safeguard the constitutional position of the House of Commons; they hoped for a solution of the difficulties, by establishing popular rather than royal control over economic affairs. The justices of the peace were in many cases anxious to be relieved of the burden of duty which the Elizabethan system had thrown upon them; but the strength of the opposition to the royal methods of economic administration, lay with the mercantile classes in London. They wielded immense political influence, and seem to have been deeply attached to the principle of representative government both in church and state; their presbyterian proclivities, and their dislike of occasional interference in trade, rendered them bitterly hostile to Charles I. and his advisers. A few years' experience of economic anarchy under the Commonwealth convinced them, however, that there was much to be said for re-establishing the exercise of economic authority by the Crown, subject to parliamentary criticism. This was the system which came into vogue at the Restoration, and it showed to great advantage under Charles II. His very inability to trouble himself about business was a guarantee against frequent meddling and left room for the employment of experts; a remarkable body of able men were induced, during his reign, to give their best attention to public affairs; and the control of industry and commerce appear to have got into admirable hands. There was hardly any element of economic grievance in the agitation which led to the English Revolution; this was forced on chiefly by anxiety in regard to ecclesiastical affairs. Still, the constitutional changes in 1689 necessarily involved considerable alterations in the *and of* economic administration. The Whig jealousy of arbitrary *control by the* power divested the executive of personal control over com-*Whig majority in* merce and industry; and the authority, which had been *the House of Com-* exercised by the Crown, passed almost entirely into the *mons.* hands of the House of Commons. This new *régime* had some advantages; the commercial expansion and agricultural improvement, which occurred during the first half of the century, may fairly be placed to its credit. But after all, the Lower House was quite unsuited for much of the work for which it became responsible. Popular assemblies have never been seen at their best in the government of dependencies; there was, in the American Colonies, a considerable body of loyal feeling towards the Crown, which was alienated by the pretensions of a Parliament in which they were not represented. Some of the darkest blots on the record of English dealings with Ireland, have been due to the unwisdom of elected legislators, rather than to the tyranny of a personal ruler. It is true that the political liberties, which were secured at the Revolution settlement, were well worth purchasing; but it is also true that the constitutional change involved the introduction of a less efficient and less public spirited system, so far as the administration of industry and commerce was concerned. For the present, however, it must suffice to draw attention to the turning points which give the most convenient lines of division; under Elizabeth, we have the direct and unquestioned power of the Crown exercised through its own officials; under the Stuart kings, we find the delegation of royal authority to privileged bodies and to

patentees, and may note the increasing success of the House
of Commons in criticising and, to some extent, in controlling
the systems adopted by the Crown; while the very definite
scheme of policy, which was in vogue during the period
of Whig ascendancy, was carried into effect through the
instrumentality of the legislature.

When we take the history of the Mercantile System in *This division proves convenient,*
these chronological periods, according to the nature of the
authority by which similar principles were carried into
effect, we shall find that the divisions which we thus
obtain prove convenient from other points of view.

In each of the three periods that have been marked out *partly because of the different economic problems, which came to light in each period;*
for separate treatment, a new economic problem came into
prominence; since in each of them the everlasting question
of ways and means assumed a new form. In the time of
Elizabeth, the government was concerned to control the
production of certain commodities and particular kinds of
goods. Under the Stuarts, it had become possible to procure
the needed supplies by purchase, and attention was chiefly
fixed on the possibilities of obtaining money. During the
eighteenth century, this particular aim became much less
prominent; for the facilities, which had been provided by the
development of credit, rendered the amassing of bullion a
matter of less importance.

Moreover, these periods differed from one another in the *and partly because of the increasing areas,*
extent of the areas, of which account was habitually taken
for purposes of economic regulation. In Elizabeth's time, the
purview of the legislator did not extend beyond England
itself; Scotland was an independent kingdom; and Ireland,
outside the pale, was a wild territory, dotted with some
imperfectly successful experiments in plantation. Government gave attention, not only to the development of physical
resources, but to the introduction of new industrial elements
as grafts into the original stock; it was intended, however,
that these should be assimilated to English national life, and
be the means of invigorating native skill. With the Stuart
accession, a wider range of responsibility was opened up;
statesmen did little for the benefit of the northern kingdom,
but there were several systematic attempts to reduce Ireland

to order, and to take measures for the improvement and enrichment of that island. As the century advanced, and our commercial interests and colonial possessions increased in importance, a new vista was opened up; the extraordinary *which had* development of enterprise, which occurred in the Restoration *to be* *habitually* period, was of lasting importance; and the statesmen, of the *taken into* *account.* era which succeeded the Revolution, were forced, in their efforts to foster English prosperity, to take account of commercial considerations in the most distant parts of the globe. In the eighteenth century, too, it was possible to exercise a more effective control from Westminster over both Scotland and Ireland; the parliamentary union in the one case, and the diminished authority of the Crown in the other, gave the British House of Commons a very real voice in determining the destinies of all the three kingdoms. Both in regard to the management of internal industry and to the fostering of foreign commerce, the sphere, which had to be taken into cognisance, was much larger in the eighteenth century than it had been in the time of Elizabeth.

I. THE REIGN OF ELIZABETH.

II. NATIONALISATION.

167. THE reign of Elizabeth marks an important era in *In Eliza-* the history of Economic regulation. As long before as the *beth's reign* *the rules of* time of Edward I., the central authority had made a be- *municipal* ginning in taking over the work of local bodies, and now *authorities* the whole industrial system of the country was brought under national rather than municipal control. In the fifteenth century the State had tried to establish such commercial relations with other countries, that artificers in England generally might enjoy favourable conditions for carrying on their work. The prohibition of the importation of foreign goods, such as cutlery and hardware, was continued in this reign[1]; and pains were taken to prevent any diminution of the advantage which English weavers enjoyed from the excellence of English wool[2], and to insist on the consumption of native manufactures[3]. The Parliament of Elizabeth was not content, however, to secure

---

[1] 5 El. c. 7. An Act for avoyding of dyvers forreyne Wares made by Handy-craftesmen beyond the Seas. Compare 3 Ed. IV. c. 4 and 1 Richard III. c. 12. See also the prohibition of the importation of wool-cards, 39 El. c. 14. On the other hand the Company of Pinmakers failed in 1598 to get an act passed prohibiting the importation of foreign made pins. *Hist. MSS. Com.* IV. Ap. p. 117.

[2] 8 El. c. 3.

[3] Elizabeth insisted that her subjects should wear English made caps. The trade had apparently been very extensive: London alone had maintained 8000 workers, and it had also been practised in Exeter, Bristol, Monmouth, Hereford, Bridgnorth, Bewdeley, Gloucester, Worcester, Chester, Nantwich, Alcester, Stafford, Lichfield, Coventry, York, Richmond, Beverley, Derby, Leicester, Northampton, Shrewsbury, Wellington, Southampton, Canterbury, and elsewhere; the division of employment had been carried very far in this science of capping, for carders, spinners, knitters, parters of wool, forcers, thickers, dressers, walkers, dyers, battelers, shearers, pressers, edgers, liners, and bandmakers are all

A.D. 1558
—1603.

were super-seded by a national system of labour legislation ;
favourable market conditions, but sought to regulate the *minutiae* of industrial life of all kinds, both in urban and rural districts, according to the best type. A great labour code was accordingly framed, which lasted till the early part of the nineteenth century. The rise of the New Monarchy had made it more possible for the central government to deal with such details in all parts of the country; and under the Tudors, the power of the legislative assembly had so far asserted itself over chartered towns, that there was no longer any practical hindrance to prevent statesmen from controlling and organising all separate activities, so as to work for a common end. Power had been conferred on the judges to abrogate any gild ordinances[1] that they regarded as prejudicial, and their approval was necessary to the validity of new regulations. When the craft gilds were thus brought under national, not merely municipal, control[2]; they could in some cases be trusted with extended powers so as to serve as agents for the regulation of an industry beyond the bounds of their own particular city[3]. It is probable, however, that the powers of the gilds had been so much affected by the legislation of Edward VI.[4] that they had but little influence either for good or evil. There were large numbers of workmen, who were carrying on their trades, in places where no municipal industrial authority had ever existed. The legislation, and the attempted legislation[5], of the decade from 1550 to 1560

it aimed at reducing the existing chaos to order,

mentioned; but it was alleged that people had left off wearing caps, that many who had been busily occupied were thrown into beggary, and that there were fewer personable men to serve the Queen in time of war. On every Sunday and Holy Day every person of six years and upwards, with some few exceptions, was to wear on his head one cap of wool fully wrought in England, and if he neglected to do so, was to pay a fine of three and four pence for each offence. 13 El. c. 19.

[1] 19 Henry VII. c. 7.

[2] Under Henry VI. Parliament had endeavoured to check gild abuses, not by independent action, but by strengthening the hands of the municipalities and re-enforcing the traditional practice of insisting that gild ordinances should be subject to municipal approval. 15 Henry VI. c. 6.

[3] Vol. I. p. 513.   [4] Vol. I. p. 522.

[5] The *Commons Journals* of the period show a constant activity in attempting to check the decay of corporate towns. In 1550 (Vol. I. p. 15) we have a *Bill for retaining of journeymen* and a *Bill for apprentices* (22 Jan.), and in 1552 (20 Feb. p. 18) *The bill for divers Handicraftsmen to dwell in Corporate Towns*, also a *Bill touching journeymen and prentices* (11 Apr. p. 22). In 1553 there were bills *For artificers to dwell in cities and towns corporate* (15 Mar. p. 25), and *For appren-*

reveals a curious state of chaos in regard to all questions A.D. 1558
—1603. connected with the training of workmen, the conditions of employment and the terms of payment. It was one of the first tasks of Elizabeth's second Parliament to pass a measure, *and it sur-* which not only dealt with the special difficulties of the time *vived with little modi-* in a statesmanlike fashion, but served to create a permanent *fication for about* system for the national regulation of industry. The Statute *250 years.* of Artificers purports to be little more than the codification of existing measures, and it certainly is based on the experience of the past; but those who framed the enactment were not slavish imitators of any model. They did not attempt to revive the institutions that had proved unworkable, nor did they fall into the mistake of creating a cast-iron system which should stereotype and perpetuate the rules devised to meet the special requirements of their own time. There was far less rigidity and far more room for independent growth than in the corresponding system which eventually grew up in France[1], and this is perhaps the reason why the labour legislation of Elizabeth continued to hold its own, without substantial modifications, for so many years.

But little information has survived to help us to follow *The chief* the preliminary enquiries[2], or the ineffectual drafts[3] which *things that demanded* preceded this remarkable enactment. So far as we can *a remedy were*

---

tices to be taken at *Bristol as London or Norwyche* (17 March, p. 25). In the first session of Mary's reign there were bills *For certain artificers to dwell in towns* (16 Oct. p. 28), and *For divers persons not to sell mercery, grocery or Haberdashe wares by retail in towns, not dwelling there* (20 Nov. p. 30), a measure which apparently became law as 1 and 2 P. and M. c. 7. We also have a special bill to compel craftsmen in Devon to dwell in towns (*Commons Journals*, I. 24 Nov. 1554, p. 38), and an attempt to revive the highly protective Statute of 3 Ed. IV. (21 Dec. p. 40). In 1558 there was a bill *For apprentices to be taken in divers towns notwithstanding the Statute* (11 Feb. p. 48), and there were several bills bearing on the difficulty in the first year of Elizabeth's reign.

[1] Cunningham, *Essay on Western Civilisation*, II. 210, 213.

[2] It appears from the interesting letter (3 Sep. 1561), printed by Prof. Hewins, that Cecil was making enquiries into some of the matters dealt with by this Statute. *Economic Journal*, VIII. 341. S. P. D. El. XIX. 43.

[3] Simon D. Ewes, *Journals*, p. 47, Tuesday, Feb. 14; p. 54, 18th April; and p. 55, 25 April, 1559. See also *Commons Journals*, I. under these dates (pp. 54, 60), also (16 March, p. 56), *A bill for Artificers in the County of Kent to dwell in Townes*; also (April 21, p. 60), *The Bill for a good order of Servants and Artificers and their wayes.*

A.D. 1558
—1603.

*the decay
of cor-
porate
towns,*

*the unsatis-
factory
character
of village
artisans
and the*

judge, however, one of the pressing difficulties, which occasioned the introduction of the measure, was the continued decay of corporate towns; to this the Statute Book bears testimony[1]. With it was closely associated an increase in the number of village artisans; these men were not all well trained[2], and no effective control could be exercised over them; some were inclined to engage in pasture-farming, and also to embark in the wholesale cloth trade, and there was a danger that tillage would fall into neglect. It was by no means easy to frame a measure that should be applicable to all employments alike; the cloth trade, which was by far the most important manufacture, was already organised, at any rate in certain districts, on capitalist lines[3]; while many other callings were carried on, without the intervention of a capitalist employer, and without any effective supervision by gilds. The Act, as passed, supplied a scheme which might help to meet the social difficulties, that had been actually felt in town and country; on the one hand, it endeavoured

[1] (1) Item, Whereas divers ancient cities, boroughs and towns corporate within this realm of England, have been in times past well and substantially inhabited, occupied, maintained and upholden, as well by reason of making of broad woollen clothes and kersies, as also by divers other artificers inhabiting then in the said towns, at which time also the villages and husband towns flourished, and husbandry and tillage was well maintained, to the great benefit of the realm and all the people therein: (2) Forasmuch as divers years past, such persons as do use the feat or mystery of cloth-making, not contented to live as artificers, and with the trade wherein they have been brought up, do daily plant themselves in villages and towns, being no cities, boroughs nor corporate towns, and there occupying the seat and place of a husbandman, do not only engross divers farms and pastures into their hands, displeasing the husbandmen, and decaying the ploughs and tillages, but also draw with them out of the cities, boroughs and towns corporate, all sorts of artificers, whereby not only divers ancient cities, boroughs and towns corporate are utterly decayed, destroyed, and depopulated, but also husbandry and tillages very much decayed, to the great hurt, damage and prejudice of this realm and the people therein, if speedy remedy be not foreseen: (3) And forasmuch also as the weavers and workmen of clothiers when they have been trained up in the trade of cloth-making and weaving three or four years, do forsake their masters, and do become clothiers and occupiers for themselves, without stock, skill or knowledge, to the great slander of the true cloth-making, besides a great number of inconveniences which do grow to the commonwealth of this realm thereby, as daily experience teacheth. 4 and 5 P. and M., c. 5 § 21.

[2] Lohmann, *Die Staatliche Regelung der Englischen Wollindustrie*, 25, in Schmoller's *Staats und Socialwissenschaftliche Forschungen*, xviii.

[3] Vol. I. p. 437. The crisis in the Suffolk trade in 1527 shows that the trade had assumed a capitalist form. Schanz, *Englische Handelspolitik*, I. 71 n. 7.

to provide for an adequate supply of agricultural labour; A.D. 1558
—1603.
while on the other, it gave special protection to corporate *insufficient*
towns as centres of the industrial arts. *supply of*
agricul-
All able-bodied men became liable to serve as agricultural *tural*
labourers, and could be compelled to do so under the Act[1], *labour.*
The main
unless they could prove that they were exempt from the *features of*
the new
obligation, on some one or other of the grounds which are *measure*
carefully specified. These reasons did not hold equally good at *were com-*
pulsion
all times of the year, as all artificers could be compelled to work *to service in*
husbandry,
in the fields during harvest[2]. Another clause insists that all *while the*
hirings of servants in husbandry[3], as well as of artificers in *yearly*
hirings
ordinary trades[4], should be for no shorter period than a year,
and there were severe penalties for leaving service or dis-
missing a servant before the time was out. Labourers and
artisans were to have testimonials from their last employers
whenever they left their parish; and they could not obtain
fresh employment without presenting such letters[5]. The
general purpose of the measure was to give stability to
society by insisting on long engagements for artisans, and
by checking as much as possible the migration of servants
in husbandry and of other artificers and labourers[6]. These *would tend*
to reduce
clauses, by prohibiting irregularity of employment in all *vagrancy.*
cases where it could be avoided, aimed at providing a
machinery by which the army of tramps and vagrants, with
which the country was infested, might be absorbed by the
demand for agricultural labour. From this point of view, the
connection between this enactment and the Elizabethan
legislation for the relief of the poor comes out; they may be
seen to be two parts of one great policy for regulating the
lives and promoting the welfare of the working classes[7].

A serious attempt was also made to insist that all artificers, *In town and*
country
either in rural or urban districts, should undergo a regular *alike,*
apprenticeship[8]; this was to last for seven years at least; *apprentice-*
ship was to
last

---

[1] § 7.   [2] § 22.   [3] § 7.
[4] § 3.   [5] §§ 10, 11.

[6] Those employed in the building trades worked by contract (§ 13), and under
some circumstances engagements were made for the day or week (§ 10).

[7] This comes out rather in the action of the Privy Council than in mere
legislation; see below, p. 51.

[8] § 31.

A.D. 1558
—1603.

seven years
at least,
and their service was to be continued till twenty-four, if they were learning a craft in a corporate town[1]. Contemporary opinion held that it was neither good for society nor trade, that the young man should enjoy any independence. "Untill a man growe unto the age of xxiiii yeares he for the moste parte, thoughe not allwayes, is wilde, withoute Judgment, and not of sufficyent experience to governe himselfe. Nor (many tymes) growen unto the full or perfect knowledge of the arte or occupation that he professed[2]." After the age of twenty-four, however, he was to be at liberty, if a householder, to set up in business for himself and to take apprentices of his own[3].

In fixing on seven years as the minimum period of apprenticeship, the legislature was greatly lengthening the period of training and service which had been in vogue in many places. Not a few craftsmen had been bound for five, four, three, two years or less; they were alleged neither to be efficient workmen themselves[4] nor able to train others properly. This was in itself an evil, and it was unfair to the industrial centres that were striving to preserve a better

as was the
custom in
London,
standard. London, and the towns which followed the custom of London, had always insisted on a seven years' apprenticeship; this was a period, not only of manual training[5] but of novitiate for life as a freeman of a town. This portion of municipal custom was adopted by Parliament and enforced throughout the nation generally; after the passing of the Act, the rural artificer was no longer able to offer to train boys in a briefer period than the townsman; and thus a positive disadvantage to which the urban craftsman had been exposed, in obtaining apprentices, was removed.

and limita-
tions were
laid down
as to the
choice of
employ-
ments
The Statute also contains some remarkable clauses on the choice of employment, which was open to boys, according to

[1] § 26. Agricultural apprentices might by agreement have completed their service at twenty-one years. § 25.

[2] S. P. D. El. xciii. 26. It occurs in an interesting discussion of the inconveniences of the statute, xciii. 26—36.

[3] § 26.

[4] This is alleged by a writer, in 1572, who complains that the statute had not succeeded in rectifying the abuse, S. P. D. El. lxxxviii. 11.

[5] Seven years was an unnecessarily long period for learning some arts; it was never adopted in Scotland. See also below, p. 658.

their parentage and circumstances; it thus attempts to
mediate between rural and urban interests at the point at
which they had been already found to conflict[1]. It was per- *so as to favour rural districts*
missible for any boy to be apprenticed to husbandry, or to
the employments which were necessary for country life, such
as those of smiths, wheelwrights[2], ploughwrights, millwrights,
carpenters and the weaving of household cloth. If, however,
any youths aspired to other callings and desired to become
clothiers, mercers, goldsmiths or grocers, then a distinct *and corporate towns*
preference was given to the corporate towns, over market
towns, as places of training. The rural districts and the
corporate towns were each placed at an advantage, relatively
to the market town; clothiers, and other capitalists residing in the latter, could not take the sons of 40s. free-
holders to be their apprentices, but only the sons of men *at the expense of market towns.*
who had a 60s. freehold[3]. Discriminating rules in regard to
the choice of apprentices must have had many curious results
on local industries; and the Act, by rendering apprentice-
ship more definite and precise, gave it a new importance. *These rules introduced greater uniformity throughout the country and were a barrier to change of occupation;*
The insistence that a boy should have served for seven
years, as a necessary preliminary to practising any craft in
any part of the country[4], not only introduced a greater uniformity than had previously existed, but also offered a new
barrier to change of occupation[5]. It laid down the framework of an industrial system for the whole country on very
precise and definite lines.

[1] Apprenticeship to the clothing trades proved so attractive in the time of Henry IV. and Henry VI. that it had been necessary to forbid men in towns and boroughs to take boys from the class of rural labourers as apprentices (7 Henry IV. c. 17). This statute proved such a grievance that it was set aside in favour of London and Norwich (8 Henry VI. c. 11 and 11 Henry VII. c. 11), but not for either Oxford (*Rot. Parl.* v. 205) or Bristol, *Commons Journals*, I. 25 (17 March 1553). The restriction on the taking of apprentices seems to have been a real grievance as far as the corporate towns were concerned, and this measure met the urban complaint by extending the disability in an aggravated form to village artificers. [2] § 30.

[3] §§ 27, 29, 32. This preference was also given to the corporate towns, over most of the rural districts, in regard to the taking of apprentices for the manufacture even of household cloth. This restriction was removed by 5 and 6 Will. and Mary, c. 9.

[4] Occasionally a boy who had completed one apprenticeship began to serve another. W. Hutton, *History of Derby* (1791), 192, 194.

[5] Vol. I. p. 345. The desire to remove these barriers was a strong motive for the abandonment of apprenticeship. *Reports*, 1806, III. 604.

A.D. 1558
—1603.

*but they
did not
prevent
the growth
of capi-
talism.*

*The Act
appears to
have
arrested
the decay
of cor-
porate
towns,*

At the same time the rules now brought into operation were not too rigid ; Elizabethan legislation did not present any additional barrier to the introduction of the capitalistic organisation of industry, where it was found desirable[1]. In this respect, the new code differed very much from previous legislative attempts to regulate the clothing trades[2]. No limitation was now placed on the number of apprentices which any clothier might take, so long as he preserved a due proportion between the number of boys he undertook to train and of journeymen he employed[3]. A restriction, in this form, would not hinder the development of factories ; but it would prevent the overstocking the trade with apprentices to the disadvantage of journeymen and small masters.

This measure marks an era in a very remarkable way: from this time onward the complaints, which had been so common for more than a century, of the decay of corporate towns seem to come to an end. The clothiers, who had established themselves in rural districts, were not forced back to the towns[4]; but there does not seem to have been a continued drain from urban centres. The raising of the standard of rural training, together with the change by which burgesses were permitted to draw on a lower social grade than heretofore for apprentices, seems to have checked the trend of the artisan class from corporate towns to market towns and rural districts.

[1] An exception to this may perhaps be found in the rule (27 El. c. 18 § 2) which limits the Queen's subjects in Devon and Cornwall, and forbids any of them to have more than three looms in his house. This tallies with the proof of the existence of the domestic system given by Westcote (*View of Devonshire in* 1630, p. 61); apparently the independent workmen held their own in Devonshire, Yorkshire and the north of England, while the capitalist system was in vogue in the Eastern Counties, and in the Wilts and Somerset districts.

[2] Compare 2 and 3 P. and M. c. 11.

[3] 5 El. c. 4 § 33.

[4] To extinguish the rural trade, after the existing generation had died out, was the policy of 4 and 5 P. and M. c. 5 § 32, which remained unrepealed till 21 Jas. I. c. 28 § 11; but the attempt to prevent the perpetuation of the trade would have been disastrous in many ways; and the existence of clothiers outside corporate towns was tolerated from the first, in Wales, the Northern Counties, Suffolk, Kent and Cornwall (4 and 5 P. and M. c. 5, § 36); this liberty was afterwards extended to Bocking, Coggeshall and Dedham by 1 Elizabeth, c. 14. The practice of weaving outside corporate towns was also legalised by 18 El. c. 16 for Somerset, Gloucester and Wilts, by 27 El. c. 23 for Boxstead and Langham in Essex. The existence of weavers "in market towns and elsewhere," as well as in corporate towns, is recognised as legal by 27 El. c. 18, which regulates the manufacture of cloth in Devon and Cornwall for exportation.

The Act not merely favoured the corporate towns rather than the country districts, in regard to industry, but it also operated to the advantage of the native, as against the alien. The Walloons and Huguenots were practically compelled to settle as industrial colonists, on special conditions[1]; this Act, with its insistence on a seven years' apprenticeship, was a serious hindrance to immigrants who wished to reside in a locality and compete with the native workmen[2]. In this matter the policy of the Act harmonised with popular feeling. A proof of the wisdom of the measure seems to lie in the fact that we hear of no complaints as to these restrictions in the Act or proposals for amending the clauses, but that, on the contrary, there was, on more than one occasion, a demand that it should be vigorously enforced, so that the industrial system of the country should be really reduced to order[3].

A.D. 1558 —1603.

and it incidentally determined the form in which the new immigrants settled.

There seems to have been less complaint of the harshness of the Act than of neglect to enforce it.

---

[1] See below, p. 82. Colchester, 12 C. II. c. 22; Norwich, S. P. D. Cromwell, cl. 6, *Calendar*, 3 Oct. 1655, p. 367.

[2] Cunningham, *Alien Immigrants*, 164—170. In towns, action was taken against aliens by the companies, as e.g. in the case of the Shrewsbury Mercers in 1481 (F. A. Hibbert, *Influence and Development of English Gilds*, p. 82). See also the Hull Cordwainers (J. M. Lambert, *Two Thousand Years of Gild Life*, p. 316). Compare the Mayor's Proclamation for the London Gilds in 1581 (Clode, *Early History of the Guild of Merchant Taylors*, i. 199 n.). In London the opposition to foreigners was particularly strong; the Londoners obtained the repeal (3 and 4 Ed. VI. c. 20) of the clause in Edward VI.'s Combination Law (2 and 3 Ed. VI. c. 15 § 4), which allowed native or naturalised workmen to practise certain crafts in corporate cities where they were not free and did not inhabit. The Common Council passed acts against them in 1606 and 1712 [Brit. Mus. 816. l. 3 (25, 26)], also in regard to their dealings in Cloth Halls in 1678, *An Act of Common Council for Regulation of Blackwell Hall, etc. and for prevention of foreign Buying and Selling* [Brit. Mus. 712, g. 16 (22)]. The City authorities also demanded in 1662 that all trades should be managed by regulated companies, so as to exclude aliens from commerce. *Petition for reducing all foreign trade under government* [Brit. Mus. 517. k. 16 (2)].

[3] There is a long and very interesting paper on the working of the statute in 1572, which deals especially with the evasions in rural districts, and advocates the binding of apprentices generally by indenture according to the custom of London (S. P. D. El. LXXXVIII. 11). The same remedy is suggested by Fleetwood, the City Recorder, when writing to the Privy Council in 1583 (British Museum, *Lansdowne MSS.* XXXVIII. 14). The evil appears to have continued, however, for we find similar complaints in 1606 (?) (S. P. D. J. I. XXIV. 72, 73), and in 1619 there were numerous cases of persons practising trades to which they had not been duly apprenticed (S. P. D. J. I. CV. 78, 79); a commission was appointed to deal with them, but it did not prove answerable to His Majesty's intention, and was revoked in 1621 (*Proclamations*, 10 July 1621). The difficulty continued under

C. 3

A.D. 1558
—1603.

It con-
tained no
adequate
provision
for the en-
rolment of
appren-
tices

The difficulty of enforcing the seven years' apprenticeship clause, especially immediately after the passing of the Act, must have been very great[1]: a similar effort had been made for the weaving trade by Edward VI., but it had been necessary to abandon it after a few months' trial[2]. The chief practical difficulty in the Elizabethan law appears to have arisen from the fact that there was no sufficient provision for the enrolment of apprentices, so as to keep a record of their service, except in the towns of London[3] and Norwich,

Charles I. (S. P. D. C. I. Vol. ccclxxvii. 1, 1637): and we hear of it in 1662, after the Restoration, S. P. D. C. II. liii. 93.

[1] Under the Elizabethan statute it was permissible for persons who had already exercised the trade for three years to continue in it, § 4.

[2] 5 and 6 Ed. VI. c. 8, and 1 Mary, st. iii. c. 7.

[3] *Notes of the braunches or articles of the Statute 5 El. c. 4 towchinge artificers, whereupon the erecting and making of this office and officer is chieflye grounded*, in *Lansdowne MSS.* cxiv. 3, S. P. D. El. xciii. 34. The Act assumed that the system in London was satisfactory and did not need to be altered; but there were citizens who would have been glad to have certain of the provisions of the Elizabethan act extended to London, and to remedy the existing laxity in some particulars. In London the Merchant Taylors had encroached on the sphere of the Clothworkers, and flooded them with apprentices; the Clothworkers failed to obtain redress or to enforce a limitation or secure supervision (Clode, *Early History*, p. 199). Similar irregularities were taking place in other lines of business, and persons who had been apprenticed in one trade were following others. As a remedy it was proposed on one side, that the supervision of the trade should be retained by the company with the right of search; but that those, who had served their time in one trade and were freemen, might have liberty to carry on any craft, so long as they submitted to the rules of that craft (see the petition in Clode, *op. cit.* p. 205). This policy was embodied in a Bill *That all the Freemen of the City of London may use the Mysteries and Trades within the same City lawfully*, which passed the Commons (Feb. 1575, *Journals*, i. 105, 106, 107), and was read a second time in the Lords on 9th March, 1576 (*Journals*, i. 734, 745), but which proceeded no farther. This measure would apparently have defined, and given greater scope for a practice as to apprenticeship, which rested on ancient custom in the City, and which was not touched by 5 El. c. 4 § 33; the citizens of London continued to exercise their ancient freedom despite the statute (*Index to Remembrancia*, by Overall, p. 91). There was also an effort on the other side to extend the provisions of 5 Eliz. c. 4 to the City, and to prevent anyone from working at a trade to which he had not been apprenticed; this was embodied in certain ordinances (Overall *op. cit.* p. 154), and apparently in *A Bill prohibiting the Exercise of any Art or Mystery, saving to such as have been Apprentice to the same*, mentioned in Stow's *Survey* (Bk. v. p. 252); according to this scheme each calling would be confined to those who had served their time in that trade; it maintained the trade monopoly of each company more stringently than ever. The advocates of greater liberty desired that the freemen should be permitted to exercise any trade, but that the monopoly of the freemen should be maintained against outsiders; though not sanctioned by any Act either of Parliament or of the Common Council, so far as I can learn, this was the policy

where indentures were requisite[1]. We hear of many com- A.D. 1558
—1603.
plaints, after the Act had been in operation for ten years or
so, and it was proposed to establish an official[2] who should
be responsible for the enrolment of apprentices, but no
amendment was introduced. The measure appears to have *but the*
been eventually successful in diffusing the custom of a seven *custom of a seven*
years' apprenticeship throughout the country[3], even when *years' apprentice-*
the forms of the statute were not carefully observed. *ship came*
into general
The desirability of obtaining some machinery for en- *vogue.*
forcing this enactment would appear to have been one of *The growth of local*
the reasons which led to the resuscitation of industrial *industrial*
companies in the latter years of Elizabeth's reign[4]. These *companies*
companies were different in many ways from the craft gilds,
even when they were erected upon their ruins[5]. They were,

which gradually triumphed. Even those companies which were able, by charter
or statute or prescription, to exercise an effective supervision over the men who
worked at a trade, would not necessarily bestir themselves to exclude a freeman,
who submitted to their regulations, from carrying on a business to which he
had not been regularly apprenticed. The custom of Chester in the seventeenth
century was of the stricter type; no one might exercise a craft unless he had
the freedom of the 'company whereof he desires to trade' as well as of the city.
Gross, I. 118, n. 2.

[1] Very full information about the apprentices, as well as about the Walloon
colony, appears to have been preserved by the Corporation of Norwich (*Hist.
MSS. Comm.* I. Ap. 108).

[2] Brief of the suit desired by Sir W. Russell and Sir Thomas Gorges, Knights,
for an office for keeping on record all such things as are appointed to be done by
5 El. c. 4 (British Museum, *Lansdowne MSS.* cxiv. 5). A similar proposal was
made in 1626 (?) (S. P. D. C. I. xliv. 29), but nothing resulted.

[3] The system of apprenticeship appears to have had a very firm hold in many
industries, at the time when the clauses rendering it compulsory were repealed.
See below, p. 660. Sir John Nickolls writes in 1754, severely condemning the
whole system (*Remarks on the Advantages and Disadvantages of France and
Great Britain*, p. 139), but the language he uses would be quite inappropriate if it
was not an established usage.

[4] This is, at all events, illustrated by the scheme under Charles I. for incorporating the artisans in the London suburbs (1636, S. P. D. C. I. cccxviii. 44),
and by such legislation as that of Charles II. for the York weavers (13 and 14
Charles II. c. 32).

[5] Vol. I. p. 524. The extent to which the old institutions retained their
property and influence would differ in different towns: some of the London
companies appear to have had recourse to doubtful practices in order to retain their property (Stow, *Survey*, Vol. II. Bk. v. 253; Nicholl, *Ironmongers*,
137); and they had difficulty in exercising any real control over the trades in
which they were formed. This is the substance of the complaint in a petition
sent in by fourteen of the London crafts in 1571. (Clode, *Early History of
Merchant Taylors*, p. 204). It is implied in the constant complaints of decay in
the trade in connection with the reorganisation of Companies at Hull in 1598; the

A.D. 1558
—1603.

*was pro-
bably con-
nected with
the desire
to enforce
this na-
tional
system*

for the most part, bodies of capitalists rather than of crafts-men[1]; and their powers emanated from Parliament, or the Crown, and not from mere municipal authority[2]. They thus served as the local agents for carrying out a national in-dustrial policy[3]; they appear to have been careful about keeping records of entered apprentices, they made some efforts for improving the quality of wares[4], and they cer-tainly busied themselves in the localities where they were allowed, in protecting the craftsmen from the competition of alien workmen. A curious instance of the companies' efforts to enforce a monopoly, and of the permission which the towns-men had to grant, in self-defence, for outsiders to work in the

very form of the grants, as compared with that to the tailors, seems to show that they had no regularly elected officers and that the company had practically to be called into being anew. (Lambert, pp. 236, 273); see especially the cordwainers who were empowered "to be a company of themselves" in 1564 (*Ib.* 316). In-direct evidence of the decay of gilds may be derived from the cessation of the mistery plays in Coventry; they were revived (Sharp, *Dissertation on Pageants*, 39) about the time when several of the companies were resuscitated in 1586. In Norwich the gilds had been very active under Henry VIII., but they took no part in the pageants when Queen Elizabeth visited the town in 1578 (Blomfield, II. 148). For the re-organisation at Shrewsbury see Hibbert, p. 77.

[1] Compare the London Upholsterers, Stow, *Survey*, Bk. v. 229. The functions of Capital, in the Elizabethan Company, as partly industrial and partly trading are noted by Unwin, *Industrial Organisation*, 103.

[2] In some cases, as in Queen Elizabeth's Charter to Winchester, the Mayor and Burgesses were empowered to create companies (Lambert, *Two Thousand Years*, p. 382). The proceedings of the Carlisle Burgesses in re-organising the crafts in 1561 were subsequently confirmed by the Crown (R. S. Ferguson and W. Nanson, *Municipal Records of Carlisle*, pp. 29, 30). The Mayor of Newcastle seems to have exceeded his powers in the privileges he conferred on the cooks of the town in 1575 (Mereweather and Stephens, *The History of Boroughs and Municipal Corporations*, 1323), and the Hull Mayor, who alleged rights in this matter (Lambert, *op. cit.* 271) appears to have failed to support the bricklayers in enforcing their privileges against an Englishman from Amsterdam who professed to be able to rectify smoking chimneys. The Mayor and Jurats of Hythe established a fellowship of Cordwainers in 1574 (*Hist. MSS. Comm.* IV. Ap. 430).

[3] Compare the regulations for weaving in Wiltshire in 1603, and the permis-sion for the creation of fellowships in boroughs and market towns, *Hist. MSS. Comm.* 1901, *Various Collections*, I. 75.

[4] In the clothing, and some other trades, this function was partly discharged by royal officials, see below, p. 296. So many trades were sometimes combined in one company, that no single set of wardens could be expected to carry out an effective search. The union of trades in one company had been noticeable earlier (Gross, I. 118), but it now became very striking. The Goldsmiths' Com-pany in Hull included, in 1598, the goldsmiths, smiths, pewterers, plumbers, glaziers, painters, cutlers, musicians, stationers, bookbinders and basketmakers (Lambert, 262). At St Albans, the various trades were combined in four com-panies, and eventually the Mercers and Innholders absorbed all the rest (A. E. Gibbs, *Records of St Albans*, 10). A composite body of this sort would be quite able to enforce the Elizabethan law in all the trades it embraced.

town, is related from Hartlepool[1]. Though some of these A.D. 1558 —1603.
companies were created with the view of introducing or
regulating particular manufactures, it seems not improbable *though it served*
that the protection of the natives of corporate towns from *other pur-*
competition was the main motive for their revival[2], as the *poses as well.*
time of the Revolution, when this jealousy of aliens was
dying out, synchronises with the period when these revived
companies fell into inactivity.

168. The industrial code of Elizabeth deals not only with *With the*
the training of workmen, but with the terms of employment; *view of providing*
there are interesting clauses laying down the method by *that wages should be*
which the rates of wages should be authoritatively settled[3]. *assessed according*
The legislators recognised the fact that account should be *to plenty or*
taken of the variation in local conditions, and the prime *scarcity*
responsibility lay with the justices of the peace, but they
were to act under the supervision of the central authority[4].

---

[1] On April 15, 1673, it was ordered at a general guild " that whosoever he be of any merchant trade or housecarpenter, joyner, shipcarpenter, drayper, taylors, plumers, glaisers, cordiners, butchers, glovers, and skinners, whitesmiths, black-smiths, wallers, wine coopers, tallow chandlers, et alias, that shall presume to come in, and within the liberty of this corporation to trade or occupye any such trade, without the liberty or consent off any such who are injoyned, to the pre-judice of the free trades and companyes within the corporation, as now is ordered for the good off the free burgesses and inhabitants thereoff, and for the better preservation off all the companijes and encouragement of them to them and their successors forever hereafter we doe hereby order and have fully agreed upon, that whatsoever he be that shall come within the corporation aforesaid, shall paye to the use of the mayor and burgesses of this towne, for every such time offending as he or they shall trade, complaint being made by one or two more of the companys aforesaid, to the major and burgesses, for every such offence xs." The companies of tradesmen " shall from time to time, and at all times here-after within their hall, or common hall and meetings, order, and with the consent of their warden and major partt of them at theire quarterly meetings, make such lawes and orders, for the better encouragement of their trades and callings here-after, for the better suppressing of all those that shall hereafter make any brash [assault] within the corporation to the damage of all or any of the said companyes aforesaid, shall upon every such offence pay to the warden of the said company, over and above the fine above mentioned, for every time offending the sum of xs." In 1675 the monopoly of the trades was broken in upon, and the mayor was empowered to grant license, to any of the tradesmen formerly mentioned, to come within the liberties of the town, when the freemen will not work at a reasonable rate (C. Sharp, *History of Hartlepool*, 84, 85).

[2] Compare the ordinances issued by Bishop Cotton for Salisbury in 1598 (*Salisbury* by Benson and Hatcher in R. C. Hoare's *Modern Wiltshire*, p. 304). On the re-organisation of the crafts by the mayor in 1612, see *ib.* 312.

[3] For an example of a typical assessment see Appendix A.

[4] Until 1598 (39 El. c. 12), the rates decided on by the Justices of the Peace were certified in Chancery, and issued in the form of a royal proclamation; but

A.D. 1558
—1603.

A very bitter attack has been recently made on the Elizabethan legislators for their alleged motives in passing this measure[1]; but it may at least be said that their own statement of their intentions is fully borne out by the precise modification they introduced into the existing

Parliament brought the justices into direct relations with the Council.

machinery for regulating wages. They removed the maximum limit, which had hitherto been imposed by statute, and thus left the justices free to propose as high a rate of wages as they might deem desirable; the rule they suggested only became authoritative, after it had been submitted to the Privy Council for approval, and proclaimed by the Sheriff[2].

The assessment of wages was not new,

The assessment of wages by the justices of the peace was no new thing; it had been introduced in the time of Richard II.[3], when the impracticability of the attempts to drive down wages by legislative enactment[4] had become apparent. There can be no doubt that the system was originally devised as a method of keeping the rates of wages down; in 1445[5], and in 1496[6], and again in 1514, the powers of the justices were limited by the enactment of a statutory maximum. Whether restricted by these rules, or not, the powers of the justices appear to have been habitually

after that date, the control exercised by the Crown was only occasional, not part of the regular machinery. The direct supervision of the Privy Council had apparently a great deal to do with the vigour of the English system of poor relief (E. M. Leonard, *The Early History of English Poor Relief*, 94, 164); and it seems possible that the increased independence, which was given to the local authorities in 1598, tended to irregularity in the assessing of wages.

[1] J. E. Thorold Rogers, *Six Centuries*, ii. 398. The evidence adduced by Miss E. M. Leonard, as to the manner in which the authorities had recourse, between 1629 and 1640, to the machinery of the statute to check the effects of competition in driving down weavers' wages, goes to show that the statute was not used as an engine of oppression. *The Relief of the Poor by the State Regulation of Wages*, in *English Historical Review*, xiii. 91. For additional cases in point see B. L. Hutchins, *Regulation of Wages by Gilds and Town Authorities*, in *Economic Journal*. x. 405.

[2] 5 El. c. 4 § 15.

[3] 13 Richard II., st. i. c. 8.

[4] The fixing of a rate had been tried under Edward III. and by 12 Richard II. c. 4.

[5] 23 Henry VI. c. 13.

[6] 11 Henry VII. c. 22. This measure appears to have been regarded as oppressive and was repealed, so far as artificers were concerned, in the following year (12 Henry VII. c. 3), though it was practically re-enacted in 1514 (6 Henry VIII. c. 3); but London was exempted from this later measure (7 H. VIII. c. 5).

exercised, through the fifteenth century and under the A.D. 1558
Tudor kings[1].   —1603.

In framing a great labour code, however, the Parliament *but the*
of Elizabeth finally abandoned the attempt to enact a *maximum limit was*
maximum limit; they recognised that wages were often *now done*
oppressively low[2], and that the justices should be free, subject to the approval of the Council, to assess them at higher
rates, so as to "yield unto the hired person, both in the time
of scarcity and in the time of plenty, a convenient proportion
of wages." It would be interesting if we had more information as to the practice of the justices in discharging this
duty[3]. In corporate towns they might be able to follow the
line adopted by the craft gilds[4], or they might have some
traditional method of settling what was fair by common estimation[5]. There may have been some rough and ready rule

---

[1] Miss E. A. McArthur (*A Fifteenth Century Assessment of Wages*, in *English Historical Review*, XIII. 299) has published a unique example of these early assessments. It offers an interesting illustration of the practice of the time, as it may be gathered from the charge contained in the *Boke longyng to a Justice of the Peace*, which went through several editions in the earlier part of the sixteenth century (E. A. McArthur, *The Boke longyng to a Justice of the Peace, and the Assessment of Wages*, in the *English Historical Review*, IX. 311).

[2] "Although there remain and stand in force presently a great number of acts and statutes concerning the retaining, departing, wages and orders of apprentices, servants and labourers, as well in husbandry as in divers other arts, mysteries and occupations; (2) yet partly for the imperfection and contrariety that is found, and doth appear in sundry of the said laws, and for the variety and number of them, (3) and chiefly for that the wages and allowances limited and rated in many of the said statutes, are in divers places too small and not answer-able to this time, respecting the advancement of prices of all things belonging to the said servants and labourers; (4) the said laws cannot conveniently, without the great grief and burden of the poor labourer and hired man, be put in good and due execution: (5) and as the said several acts and statutes were, at the time of the making of them, thought to be very good and beneficial for the commonwealth of this realm (as divers of them are): so if the substance of as many of the said laws as are meet to be continued, shall be digested and reduced into one sole law and statute, and in the same an uniform order prescribed and limited concerning the wages and other orders for apprentices, servants and labourers, there is good hope that it will come to pass, that the same law (being duly executed) should banish idleness, advance husbandry, and yield unto the hired person, both in the time of scarcity, and in the time of plenty, a convenient proportion of wages." 5 El. c. 4, preamble.

[3] An interesting account of the hiring system in Yorkshire in 1641 will be found in H. Best, *Rural Economy* (Surtees Soc.), 132.

[4] B. L. Hutchins, *op. cit.* 404.

[5] Compare the proclamation of wages for Kingston-upon-Hull dated June 8th, 1570, "We, the aforesaid Mayor and Justices have limited rated and assessed the wages in manner and form aforesaid, for that it seemeth to

A.D. 1558
—1603.

*It is diffi-
cult to see
on what
principles
the Justices
proceeded,*

of thumb for making an estimate; but it is difficult to see on what principles they could have acted in framing or revising these rates. The justices appeared to have aimed at laying down a rate which was reasonable, and could be insisted on by either party[1]; this is explicitly stated in the assessment for Hull in 1570[2]; but they sometimes specified that the sum quoted was a maximum, and that lower rates were permissible. It would hardly be possible to judge of the actual operation of the statute on the standard of comfort unless we could construct a Tudor labourer's "family budget" and see what proportion of his income[3] was expended in bread and other commodities which varied directly with the price of corn, and how much was devoted to house rent, or other payments, which would hardly be appreciably affected. There is another difficulty of a theoretical character[4]. If money wages were raised by the justices in time

divers discreet and sage men of the said town and county whose advice and opinions we have taken herein that the same is most convenient both to the giver and taker." The Rutland assessment of 1564 was made "upon consyderation of the great pryses of lynnen, wollen, lether, corne and other victuals."

[1] The London rule of 1573, quoted by Miss McArthur, provided for the punishing of men who refused to work for the rates assessed. *English Historical Review*, xv. 453. See also *The book of John Fisher*, p. 156, for an inquisition on this point at Warwick in 1586. In the corresponding enactment in Scotland, the justices of the peace were instructed to enforce the rate they assessed, neither more nor less. Acta 1617 c. 8, §§ 14, 17.

[2] Dyson, *Proclamation Book*, 77. All manner of persons were straightly charged to observe in all points the said rates for wages under pain of forfeitures. This occurs also in the Higham Ferrers, Rutland and Cardigan examples; it seems to be the regular form. The Nottingham (County) assessment of 1724 provides that lower wages may be given where they have been customary (Brit. Mus. 1882. d. 2 (192), and many of the assessments imply this by stating that e.g. the rate is to be "not above 40s." (Lincolnshire, 1621, *Hist. MSS. Commission*, xii. Ap. iv. p. 461.) This may have been necessary to provide for different grades of skill in the same calling; these are distinguished as of the first, second, and third sort, in the Middlesex Assessment of 166– (Brit. Mus. 190. g. 13 (202)). On the other hand the statute, which brought weavers' wages definitely under the authority of the justices, expressly regards the rate proclaimed as binding on the employer (1 Jas. I. c. 6 § 7); and this is confirmed by an act of Charles II. in regard to the Yorkshire clothing trade (13 and 14 Charles II. c. 32). A great deal of information in regard to the action of the justices in the North Riding (1680) has been preserved (J. C. Atkinson, *Quarter Session Records of Yorkshire*, Vol. vii. p. 34); several men were punished for paying too much (*Ib*. 45, 47, 48). Apparently the assessed rate for dairy maids had not altered since 1658 (Vol. vi. p. 3), but employers generally were giving more.

[3] Howlett, in *Annals of Agriculture*, xxv. 604, 612.

[4] Those who considered the possibility of re-enforcing the assessment of wages, at the close of the eighteenth century, when it had long fallen into desuetude,

of scarcity, the labourer would have more power of purchas- A.D. 1558 —1603. ing food; but as the 'effective demand' would be increased, without any increase in the available supply of food, we would expect a further rise of price to result from attempts to relieve the poor by this expedient[1]. In the sixteenth century, when prices, as well as wages, were still frequently settled by authority[2], the competition of the labourers for food would not have such immediate effects on prices as in modern times; the regulation would tend to hasten the entire exhaustion of the supply, rather than to bring about a further rise of price. At all events, it seems that the practical diffi- *though the* culties were not so grave as to prevent the system from *practice appears to* coming into operation, in the fifteenth century, and being *have been wide-* widely adopted before the close of the reign of Elizabeth[3]. *spread.*

No schedule was appended to the Act, but the assessments which survive are similar in form and have the same general character; and some of the common features throw a good deal of light on the general conditions of the times. Wages *Summer* are separately rated for summer and winter; as the wages *wages were always* are lower and the food allowance smaller for the shorter *assessed higher than* days during the winter months, though the expenses of main- *winter,* taining the standard of comfort would be greater, it does

regarded this difficulty as insuperable. See the speeches by Whitbread, Fox and Pitt, *Parl. Hist.* XXXII. 700; XXXIV. 1426. The repeal took place in 1813, by 53 Geo. III. c. 40; Hansard, XXV. 594. Compare the excellent discussion of the policy of the Act by D. Davies, *The Case of Labourers in Husbandry* (1795), 106; also T. Pownall, *Considerations on the scarcity and high price of bread and corn.*

[1] Sir T. Bernard in the *Reports of the Society for bettering the condition of the poor* (1805), v. 27.

[2] See below, p. 94. Compare the order of the Privy Council in 1542 for the fixing of prices at Hull so that workmen might live on their wages, E. M. Leonard, *op. cit.* p. 52; also E. A. McArthur on the regulation of prices at Woodstock in 1604, *English Historical Review*, XIII. 711.

[3] The statute (1 James I. c. 6 §§ 2, 4) gave me the impression that the assessment of wages had been greatly neglected during the reign of Elizabeth, and this view was taken in the second edition of this book; the preamble runs, "Whereas the said act hath not, according to the true meaning thereof been duly put in execution"; see also § 4. Still, the law had admittedly "been found beneficial for the commonwealth." Additional evidence moreover shows that assessment was regularly practised in London and Middlesex (E. A. McArthur in *English Historical Review.* XV. 451) and in Wiltshire from 1602 to 1685 (*Hist. MSS. Commission* 1901, *Various Collections*, I. pp. 161—176). Dyson, who collected the Elizabethan proclamations in 1618, puts this note in his index after the Proclamation rating wages in Cardigan for 1595: "Note. The like Proclamations and rates were published yeerely since 5 Elizabeth in euery Countie" (Brit. Mus. G. 6463, p. 5).

*and there-
fore could
not have
been starva-
tion rates.*

not seem that the summer payments, at all events, can be considered to be starvation rates. The more highly skilled and responsible workmen were regarded as entitled to more liberal allowances for diet than those which sufficed for labourers of a lower grade; the wages of apprentices in their third or fourth years are frequently stated.

*The details
given in
particular
localities
are re-
markable,*

The assessments exemplify the practice which was common to the whole country; even greater interest attaches to particulars which are specified in some cases and not in others. The list of trades, of which account is taken, is occasionally very long, and different grades of labour are carefully distinguished; this is particularly noticeable in Middlesex. At Hull, the authorities enter into considerable detail and discriminate between the payment due for digging a ditch according as it runs through sand, gravel, clay or stony ground; and at York the duties of different individuals are enumerated with some care. We read of the bailiff in husbandry, "that in these parts is called an overman, that is hired with a gentleman or rich yeoman, that doth not labour himself, but putteth his whole charge to his servants"; of a "miller that is skilful in mending of his mill," and a "woman servant that taketh charge of brewing, baking, kitching, milkhouse or malting, that is hired with a gentleman or rich yoemen whose wife doth not take the pains and charge upon her[1]." Some of the justices evidently endeavoured to fulfil their task very thoroughly; and the statute gave ample opportunity for modifying the assessed rates. Every year in each locality and each corporate town the justices were to assemble before June 10th, "and calling to them such discreet and grave persons...as they shall think meet and conferring together respecting the plenty or scarcity of the time, and other circumstances necessary to be considered" should limit and appoint the wages for every kind of manual labour, skilled or unskilled, by the year, week or day, and with or without allowances of food; six weeks after, they might revise their decision as to wages for the year, if they thought fit to do so.

*and the
Justices
had ample
oppor-
tunity of
revising
their de-
cisions.*

[1] Interesting rules for the management of the servants in a large household will be found in Sir J. Harington's *Nugae Antiquae*, I. 105. The fines appear to be heavy considering the value of money in 1592.

It is by no means easy to form any sound opinion on the interesting question as to the survival of this system. At the beginning of the nineteenth century, when the apprenticeship system was still a living reality, the assessment of wages was evidently regarded as a mere legal curiosity. Occasional examples have survived from the eighteenth century, but they appear to have been called forth by special exigencies[1], and hardly serve to show that the system was in anything like regular operation[2]. At the time of the Restoration, the existence of the practice[3] was taken for granted in legislating for the Yorkshire clothiers, and a wages assessment for Middlesex was apparently prepared with a view to repeated issue; though the special difficulties, caused by the fire, called forth a new enactment[4] to settle the wages of the London builders. Miss McArthur has conclusively shown[5] the danger of relying on the argument from silence in this matter; but in default of fuller evidence, it is difficult to resist the impression that the system had little vitality, outside Yorkshire, in the period after the Restoration[6]. Going further back, we

A.D. 1558 —1603.

The question as to the survival of the system presents many difficulties. Recourse was had to it, in special exigencies, in the eighteenth century;

[1] The grounds for this view, as regards the eighteenth century, will be found in my article on a *Shrewsbury Assessment* in the *Economic Journal*, iv. p. 516; I am glad to find that Prof. Hewins' impression on the point coincides so closely with my own. *Economic Journal*, Vol. viii. p. 345.

[2] In cases where it was maintained as a matter of form, it did not determine the actual rates paid. *Reflections on various subjects relating to Arts and Commerce* (1752), 63, 74 (Brit. Mus. 1144 (8)).

[3] It is referred to as a recognised duty by W. Sheppard, *Whole Office of the County Justice of the Peace* (1652), i. 124. Also *New Survey of the Justice of the Peace* (1659), 93.

[4] 19 C. II. c. 3.

[5] *Regulation of Wages in XVI century*, in *English Historical Review*, xv. 447.

[6] Sir Matthew Hale appears to be unaware of any legal provision against the starvation rates of pay of which he complains (*Provision for the Poor*, 1683, p. 18). In 1701 C. Povey writes as if he were quite ignorant of its existence in the *Unhappiness of England as to its Trade by Sea and Land truly stated*. He says (p. 32) "Let an Act of Parliament be made for the Redressing of all Wrongs and Abuses...." He proposes that in the act "a select Number of Wise and Good Men well skill'd in Trade" be appointed in every town. "They ought also to have power," he continues, "to set a value on Day Labour." Also on p. 46 he says "This Royal Community may undertake to settle a certain Price on most poor Peoples Labour, for 'tis the want of such good Orders that makes the Poor so numerous... This is the State of our meaner sort of poor People, but it might be soon otherwise if the price of every Man's Labour were fixed; as 'tis among the City Carr-men, Coal-meters, Hackney Coachmen, Fellowship

A.D. 1558
—1603.

*though
more often
mentioned
in the early
part of the
seventeenth
century,*

*it seems
to have
fallen into
neglect, as
a general
practice,
in the latter
part of that
century.*

*After the
Reforma-
tion*

find that one attempt was made to enforce it generally during the Interregnum[1]. As to its ordinary operation under James I. and Charles I., we have little evidence[2], but interesting testimony to the practice occurs in George Fox's *Journal* for 1648[3]; and there is, besides, an inherent improbability that a usage, which had prevailed so extensively under Elizabeth, should have suddenly fallen into desuetude There are, moreover, a considerable number of examples or allusions[4], from these reigns, and it is clear that the authoritative assessing was regularly carried out in London and Middlesex[5]. The reign of Charles II. may probably be assigned as the posterior limit, for England generally, of a practice which had been commenced as early as the time of Richard II.

169. Ecclesiastical authorities were so far shorn of power and wealth at the Reformation, that they were no longer able to take a substantial part in the work of providing for the poor. Their inability to discharge this duty properly had long been evident. Many of the towns had endeavoured to make arrangements of their own for the maintenance of the necessitous[6]; and in 1536, an act was passed, which gives

Porters and Watermen. All these have their several Labours equitably valued which makes them live much more happily than the rest of Labouring Men " (p. 47).

[1] Gardiner, *Commonwealth*, I. 44; *Commons Journals* VI. 180.

[2] Compare the action of the Council in insisting on Wages' assessments in 1630. Leonard, *op. cit.* 162. A similar system was introduced in Massachusetts in 1633. Weeden, *Economic and Social History of New England*, I. 83.

[3] This is the one contemporary complaint of the justices as oppressive in their action, "And at a certain time, when I was at Mansfield, there was a Sitting of the Justices, about hiring of Servants; and it was upon me from the Lord, to go and speak to the Justices, That they should not oppress the Servants in their Wages. So I walked towards the Inn, where they sate; but finding a Company of Fidlers there, I did not go in, but thought to come in the Morning, when I might have a more serious Opportunity to discourse with them, not thinking that a seasonable time. But when I came again in the Morning, they were gone, and I was struck even blind, that I could not see. And I inquired of the Inn-keeper, where the Justices were to sit that day? And he told me, At a Town eight miles off. And my Sight began to come to me again; and I went, and Ran thitherward, as fast as I could. And when I was come to the House, where they were, and many Servants with them, I exhorted the Justices, Not to oppress the Servants in their Wages; but to do that which was Right and Just to them: And I exhorted the Servants, To do their Duties, and serve honestly, etc. And they all received my Exhortation kindly; for I was moved of the Lord therein " (George Fox, *Journal* (1694), 17).

[4] See Appendix B. [5] E. A. McArthur, *op. cit.* 455.

[6] E. M. Leonard (*Early History of English Poor Relief*, 7) gives an exhaustive

expression to a sense of responsibility on the part of civil A.D. 1558
—1603. authorities for the condition of the poor throughout the country[1]. But little was done either under Edward VI. or Mary to meet the increasing difficulty; and it was left for Elizabeth and her advisers to build up a system for the relief of the poor, which was at once secular and national.

The need of some effective machinery for dealing with *the duties of relieving the poor* the poor was pressing, for pauperism of every kind seems to have obtruded itself more than it had ever done before, not only in England, but in Western Europe generally. The break-up of feudal society, as well as the disbanding of retainers and of mercenary troops, appear to have brought about an increase of vagrancy, and bitter complaints on this subject were wide-spread; but there were special causes which affected England in particular. The progress of enclosing, in the Tudor reigns, had been accompanied by depopulation[2] and the addition of fresh bands of recruits to the armies of beggars. The doles, which were dispersed from the monasteries, may not have done much to relieve poverty effectually[3]; but the sudden cessation of these gifts, at the dissolution, would set loose a crowd of idlers to prey upon society at large. According to contemporary literature, *and dealing with vagrants* the frightful prevalence of vagrancy called for stern restrictive measures; while there seems to have been no public demand for increased provision for the impotent poor. Awdeley, a London printer, published an extraordinary account of the *Fraternity of Vagabonds*[4] in 1561; a few years later, Thomas Harman, a Kentish magistrate, issued a similar but more elaborate work, which was specially designed to open the eyes of kindly disposed persons to the real character of the beggars who were maintained by indiscriminate almsgiving[5]. His enumeration of 'rufflers,' or disbanded soldiers,

account of the earlier experiments and expedients, from which much of the matter in the following paragraphs is drawn.

[1] 27 Hen. VIII. 25.　　　　[2] See below, p. 101; also Vol. i. 448, 531.

[3] Leonard, *op. cit.* 18, 63.

[4] This has been reprinted along with Harman's and other tracts by the Early English Text Society, Extra Series, Vol. ix.

[5] His *Caveat* (1566) is dedicated to Elizabeth the Countess of Shrewsbury, who was in the habit of not only caring for the poor of her own and neighbouring parishes, but of 'abundantly powringe out dayley' her 'ardent and bountifull

'upright men,' who were the beggar kings, rogues, and others, is very curious, and gives a vivid picture of the wide-spread evil with which the authorities were especially called on to deal; though improved provision for the impotent poor went on simultaneously with a vigorous war against tramps.

came to be discharged by civil rather than ecclesiastical authorities.

The chief legislative changes in the earlier part of Elizabeth's reign consisted in the complete substitution of civil for ecclesiastical authority—of overseers and justices for churchwardens and bishops—in the endeavour to provide for the relief of the poor. In 1563, the magistrates were empowered, if the bishop's exhortation failed, to insist on obtaining weekly contributions from persons who neglected the duty of charitable almsgiving[1]; while the Act of 1572 goes further; it does not merely provide for compelling the obstinate, but arranges for the assessment, by the justices in the country and the mayors in the towns, of a definite sum to be paid by each householder in a parish[2]. At the same

Parliament provided for the appointment of overseers to collect rates under compulsion, to distribute relief and to afford facilities for working.

time, provision was made for the appointment, by the justices, of persons who were responsible for collecting the poor rates, and of overseers, who became the agents for the distribution of parochial relief. A further duty was put upon local authorities by the Statute of 1576; the justices were instructed that a stock of wool, flax and other materials should be provided in all corporate and market towns[3], so that the poor might be set to work at remunerative occupations, under

charytie' upon all such as come for relief unto her 'luckey gates.' Early English Text Society, Extra Series, ix. p. 19.

[1] 5 El. c. 3 § 7.   [2] 14 El. c. 5 § 16.

[3] 18 El. c. 3 § 4. " To the intent youth may be brought up in labour......also that rogues may not have any just excuse in saying they cannot get any service or work......and that other poor needy persons being willing to work may be set on work." There is some evidence of action being taken in accordance with the terms of this statute. "This year (1581) a great deal of money was laid out about S. James's Church, in fitting it up and preparing it for a Workhouse, for the employment of the poor in making of Bays, &c., which not answering the charge was in a short time disused.... Divers poor people were this year (1586) set to work at the new building at S. James's in dressing of Hemp and making Strings and Tows for Fishermen." This whole attempt must have come finally to an end when the church was pulled down in 1623. Mackerell, *History of Kings Lynn*, 229.

A poor-house at Waltham Cross was undertaken, and John Stinton a chapman was empowered to collect benevolences for it. His wife got leave to pass

the penalty of being sent to a House of Correction. These A.D. 1558
were the main elements, which were tentatively introduced —1603.
and eventually codified in the poor law of the later part of
the reign. The whole conditions were carefully reviewed[1], *This*
and an elaborate scheme formulated in 1597[2]; this was *national scheme*
continued with little change in 1601[3], and remained as the
basis of all arrangements for the relief of the poor, till it
was substantially altered in 1834[4].

In framing a national system, Parliament was able to *was modelled*
draw on the experience which had been accumulated by *on the knowledge*
various municipalities in their efforts to deal with the *gained in*
problem, and especially to follow the experience of London. *municipal experience*
The establishments, for grappling with the difficulties of the
situation in the City, were completed before 1557 by the
institution of a house of correction at Bridewell[5]; the
vagrants, who were lodged there, were subjected to the dis-

through the country at the time the plague was raging in Leicester (1593). *Hist. MSS. Com.* VIII. Ap. i. 432.

At a later time we hear of similar efforts in Beverley. In 1599 it was stated that the town had become impoverished by the removal of the staple to Hull, that four hundred tenements were utterly decayed and uninhabited, and that the town expended the annual sum of £105 in support of the poor, besides the charge of maintaining and educating eighty orphans, in knitting, spinning and other works of industry, according to the provisions of an Act of Parliament passed 39 Eliz. (Oliver, *Beverley*, 192). Also at Leicester (*Leicester Corporation MSS.* in *Hist. MSS. Com. Report* VIII. Ap. i. pp. 430—432):—

(VII.) 2 June, 1584. Letter from Thomas Clarke, Mayor of Leicester, to the Earl of Huntingdon, respecting an arrangement for setting the poor of Leicester to work on spinning. Also two other letters touching a proposal to entrust Blase Villers, gent., a marchant of the Staple, and one of our company, with £100 of the common charge of our town, who therewith will set the poor to work on spinning.

(I.) 22 Feb. 1591. Letter from the Earl of Huntingdon to the Mayor, Recorder and Aldermen of Leicester. About "a note of receipt of coles" for the benefit of Leicester, and about the relief of the poor of the same town.

(V.) 2 June, 1592. Letter from the Earl of Huntingdon to the Mayor of Leicester. For the payment of £70 of "the cole money" to one Thomas Elkington of Langar, County Nottingham; the same to be used "to the benefit of the poor of Leicester, by setting them aworke about clothing."

(XIII.) 9 Feb. 1596. Mem., that, by the appointment of the Earl of Huntingdon, the Mayor and burgesses of Leicester have lent to Thomas Moseley, of Leicester, the sum of ten pounds, wherewith to "sett and keepe poor children in Leicester on worke in knitting of Jersey stockings."

(XVI.) 28 July. Letter from the Earl of Huntingdon to the Mayor and others. Recommending to them Thomas Clarke and Margaret his wife, as competent persons to receive a loan of money for setting the poor to work.

See also p. 433. (XVII.) 12 Sept. 1598, and (XXIII.) 7 Jan. 1599.

[1] Leonard, *op. cit.* 73.   [2] 39 El. c. 3.   [3] 43 El. c. 2.
[4] See below, p. 768.   [5] Leonard, *op. cit.* pp. 37, 39, 98.

A.D. 1558
—1603.

cipline of steady work under effective control; and arrangements were made for the practice of various employments, such as milking and baking, which were necessary for the establishment, as well as of nailmaking, weaving and other

especially in London, crafts. The municipal machinery for the relief of the poor, which was organised in London, became a model for other places[1]; and the 'custom' of London[2] in this matter was practically extended to the country generally, by the legislation of 1576 and 1597. It was unnecessary, however, to maintain a municipal system of administration, so soon as the parochial machinery was reconstructed. The municipalities had been excellent pioneers, but even the Lord Mayor of London had not been able, without parochial assistance, to obtain sufficient funds to maintain the system

but the civil parish eventually became an administrative unit for this purpose. which the city had started[3]. The civil parish was adopted in 1572 as the best administrative unit for the collection of funds: overseers acting under the supervision of the justices were primarily responsible[4] for the relief and employment of the poor; while the magistrates everywhere were provided with powers, which enabled them to coerce and punish the floating population of tramps. The mere creation of machinery, to deal with the problem in every part of the country, would in all probability have been of little avail[5],

The Privy Council were very active in bringing pressure to bear on local bodies, if it had not been for the action of the Privy Council, as a central authority, that was eager to bring pressure on the local officials and insist on their doing their duty[6]. The correspondence, which survives, shows that the Council were well informed as to the special requirements in different counties; the Devonshire justices are blamed for the insufficient provision they have made for old soldiers and sailors[7], while the Norfolk[8] magistrates are commended

---

[1] Leonard, *op. cit.* 36.

[2] Compare Vol. I. p. 224. London, Norwich and other towns were also forced to prevent new-comers from obtaining a settlement and establishing a claim to relief. This local custom was nationalised in 1662. Leonard, *op. cit.* 107.

[3] Leonard, *op. cit.* 96, 99.   [4] *Ib.* 78.

[5] The corresponding legislation in Scotland appears to have been quite ineffective, and was soon forgotten.

[6] See the *Orders and Directions* for the Commissioners of 1631. Rymer, xix. 231, and Brit. Mus. *Add. MSS.* 12,496, f. 262; also for the Commissioners' circuits, *ib.* f. 299.

[7] A. Hamilton, *Quarter Sessions from Queen Elizabeth to Queen Anne,* 19.

[8] S. P. D. El. c. xxxiii., No. 56.

for their vigilance in sending stubborn servants and rogues A.D. 1558 —1603. to the house of correction. The overcrowding of the poor, in tenement houses, had become a serious evil in Cambridge, and the Mayor and Vice-Chancellor were instructed to take action in the matter[1]. This business arose in the ordinary course of affairs; but there were occasional causes which brought about a sudden increase of pauperism, and at such times the Privy Council intervened by the issue of General *and in issuing* Orders. After the rebellion of the Northern Earls, a number *general* of disbanded retainers had been let loose on the country; *orders,* *in times of* they formed a disturbing element, and a careful search was *special* *difficulty,* instituted for them, not only in the northern shires but in other parts of the realm as well[2]. The Council inaugurated a regular whipping campaign, and shortly afterwards additional powers for punishing tramps were conferred on the magistrates; by the act of 1572, vagrants were to be whipped and branded for the first offence, to be adjudged felons on the second, and to be hanged if found guilty a third time[3]. It seems probable that the steady application of these measures resulted in the gradual suppression of vagrancy; and the principal causes, which had produced it, must have to some extent ceased to operate; the gain from sheep-farming had ceased to be the main incentive to enclosure[4] and there must have been fewer bodies of disbanded retainers. It is interesting, however, to find indications of the influence which contributes most noticeably to the sufferings of the poorer classes in modern times—the sudden changes to which they are forced to submit because of fluctuations in trade. In the sixteenth century, the clothing trade depended for its prosperity on access to foreign markets; and weavers and spinners might be suddenly cut off from all opportunity of

---

[1] Cooper, *Annals of Cambridge*, II. 398.

[2] Leonard, *op. cit.* 81.

[3] This very severe statute did not remain a dead letter. Some men who had been whipped and branded as vagrants in March, 1575, were accused in June " of being over eighteen years old and fit for labour, but masterless and without any lawful means of livelihood. They pleaded guilty and were sentenced to be hung....In the ten weeks between 6 Oct. 32 El. and 14 Dec. 33 El. seventy-one persons were sentenced at Middlesex Sessions to be whipped and branded for vagrancy." Leonard, *op. cit.* 70.

[4] See below, p. 101.

C.   4

A.D. 1558
—1603.

*such as
a depres-
sion of
trade*

employment, when intercourse with continental countries was interrupted through political complications. The Tudor government, backed by public opinion, took a very strong line as to the duty of capitalists, either as merchants or employers[1] under such circumstances; it was thought only right that they should bear the risk of loss, which arose from increasing their stocks while there was no sale abroad, rather than to condemn the workmen to enforced idleness. Wolsey had met the difficulties in this fashion in 1528; he had insisted that clothiers should continue to employ workmen[2]. In 1586 it was reported to the credit of the clothiers of Gloucestershire, that they had not diminished employment, although they were losing heavily on each cloth[3]; and the Ipswich employers[4] were compelled to set the poor at work in 1591. The most striking exemplifications of this principle occurred during the great depression in the clothing industry of 1622 and 1623[5] when the Privy Council issued Proclamations insisting that the clothiers should continue to employ the weavers as they had done when trade was good[6].

---

[1] See below, p. 206.

[2] *Letters &c. of Henry VIII.* Vol. IV. Pt. 2, Nos. 4058, 4276. See also 4239.

[3] S. P. D. El. CLXXXIX. 50. The loss was stated to be 6s. 8d. per cloth.

[4] E. M. Leonard, *op. cit.* 115.

[5] On the attitude of employers at this time compare R. F. Butler in *Victoria County History, Gloucestershire*, II. 159.

[6] E. M. Leonard, *op. cit.* p. 147. In Feb. 1622 the Council sent to the justices of ten of the clothmaking counties. They say letters have been written to them setting forth the "decay of cloathing and the great distresse thereby fallen upon the weavers, spinners and ffullers in divers counties for want of worke." They recognise that so great a trade cannot always proceed with equal profit, but upon it the "livelihood of so many poore workmen and their families dependeth" that they let the justices know that they "have taken a course with the merchants" for the purchase of cloths in the clothiers' hands; and "we hereby require you," they write, "to call before you such clothiers as you shall thinke fitting and to deale effectually with them for the imployment of such weavers, spinners and other persons as are now out of worke. Where wee maye not omitt to let you know that as wee have imployed our best endeavours in favour of the clothiers both for the vent of their cloth and for moderation in the price of wooll (of which wee hope they shall speedily find the effects). Soe may wee not indure that the clothiers in that or any other countie should att their pleasure and without giving knowledge hereof unto this Board, dismisse their workefoolkes, who being many in number and most of them of the poorer sort are in such cases likely by their clamours to disturbe the quiet and government of those parts wherein they live. And if there shalbe found greater numbers of poore people than the clothiers can reviue and imploy, Wee thinke it fitt and accordingly require you to take order for putting the statute in execution, whereby there is provisione made

The authorities were also concerned to mitigate the A.D. 1558 sufferings of the poorer classes in times of dearth; and —1603. attempts were made to obtain grain which might be sold *or a time of dearth.* to the poor at low rates. In connection with this point, we may again notice how municipal experience was embodied in the national system; for those, who were responsible for regulating the corn-supply of London and other towns, had constantly endeavoured to supply the labouring classes at special rates[1]. This was doubtless one of the conflicting motives which determined the complicated and shifting regulations of the corn trade[2]. The Privy Council intervened in 1572 to force farmers to bring corn to market, as the scarcity was attributed to the greed of speculative dealers who were holding their stocks. In 1587, a very elaborate system was devised for obtaining information as to the stock of corn available, and for insisting that it should be put on the markets for home consumption at reasonable rates. The scheme was held to have answered; for similar orders were issued by the Council in the more serious dearth of 1594–97, and under the earlier Stuarts, especially in 1630—31[3]. The existence of this method of regulating prices, must, as has been already pointed out, have had a considerable effect on the possibility of assessing wages in time of scarcity.

The manner in which the Privy Council took immediate *They took* cognisance of such matters as trade depression and the *a large view of* dearness of provisions, gives us some conception of the *their* broad view which they adopted of their responsibility with *duties,* regard to the assistance of the poor. They were concerned to see, so far as possible, that the industrious man should not fall into poverty ; they recognised a duty in regard to all those who were not economically independent. The

---

in that behalfe by raising of publicke stockes for the imployment of such in that trade as want worke. Wherein if any clothier shall after sufficient warning refuse or neglect to appeare before you or otherwise shall obstinately denie to yeeld to such overtures in this case as shalbe reasonable and iust, you shall take good bonds of them for refusing to appeare before us and immediately certifie their names unto this board."

[1] E. M. Leonard, *op. cit.* 23, 40; also p. 152. On town granaries see below, p. 318.

[2] See below, p. 92.

[3] Leonard, *op. cit.* 185.

A.D. 1558
—1603.

and in
their
attempts
to relieve
the impo-
tent
relief legislation was more restricted in its scope, and the parochial officers who administered it treated the 'poor' as including only the vagrants and the impotent. The final measure, which embodies all the experience of the reign, endeavoured to secure that overseers should provide, for those who could not work, assistance in their own parishes out of a compulsory rate; those, who were able to work and would not, were to be subjected by the justices to whipping..., and to be confined in houses of correction. The Act also encouraged

and to give the young a start in life the apprenticing of pauper children and the organising of opportunities for training them to earn their living. Many municipalities[1] were at pains to give effect to these suggestions, but this part of the state machinery, for dealing with poverty, could not be set agoing or kept in motion without great difficulty. It was at this point that public action was

their efforts were supplemented by private beneficence. most frequently supplemented by private beneficence, in the Elizabethan and Stuart periods. Mediaeval benevolence had founded many hospitals for the sick and aged; this form of benefaction did not cease in the sixteenth[2] and seventeenth centuries, but other forms of charity became more prominent. Especially noticeable were the endowments devoted to the purpose of teaching children to spin[3]; they served as a means of rescuing many persons from destitution, and they had an important bearing on the development and diffusion of the staple industry of the country. It is not easy to date the epoch when the practice of spinning wool was established, as the mainstay of rural householders in many parts of the country, but the fact that the art had acquired a firm hold, in the eighteenth century, appears to show that the efforts of the philanthropists, who founded spinning schools, were not without result.

---

[1] Leonard, *op. cit.* 95—118. See the enquiries of the Council in 1634. *Hist. MSS. Comm.* III. Ap. 71.

[2] Compare Burleigh's foundation at Stamford. Peck, *Desiderata Curiosa,* I. pp. 23, 26.

[3] A spinning-house was erected at Cambridge by Hobson the carrier. Cooper, *Annals of Cambridge,* III. 204.

III. The Policy of Burleigh[1].

170. The more we examine the working of the Eliza- A.D. 15¿ —1603. bethan scheme for the administration of economic affairs, the more do we see that the Council was the pivot of the *The poli pursued* whole system. The county justices were the agents who *the Adm istratioⁿ* saw to the enforcing of laws and the execution of orders *was directed* generally; and by their help the Council was kept in touch with the state of affairs in all parts of the country, and was therefore ready to take prompt and special action when occasion arose. In this inner circle there was one master mind. William Cecil, Secretary of State and later Lord *Lord Burleig* Treasurer, had clear ideas as to the economic policy which ought to be pursued; and during his long career, he was able to impress his views upon the life of the country. His great reputation in the field of politics has eclipsed the importance *who wa economⁱ* which attaches to him as an economist. He was constantly engaged, throughout the reign, in foiling the diplomatic schemes of France and Spain, and in taking precautions for safeguarding the life of the Queen. These great political cares did not, however, absorb his whole energies; there was no department of State which he could afford to neglect; and in particular he gave unremitting attention to every element of economic life.

Cecil's tenure of office was long; he had been Secretary *as well* of State under Edward VI.[2]; though not in office during the *a poli- tician* reign of Mary, he was constantly appealed to by the government[3]; he also acted as Elizabeth's factor[4], and helped to manage her private property. The day after Elizabeth came to the throne, Cecil returned into power as Secretary; he

---

[1] The whole of this chapter has been quoted with some trivial alterations, from an unpublished Essay by Miss Lilian Tomn, who undertook to investigate the matter at my suggestion.

[2] Sept. 1550.

[3] Lloyd, *State Worthies*, 2nd Edition, 1670, p. 474, "When he was out of place he was not out of service in Queen Mary's days, his Abilities being as necessary in these times as his Inclination, and that Queen's Council being as ready to advance him at last, as they were to use him all her Reign."

[4] M. A. S. Hume, *The Great Lord Burleigh*, p. 63.

became Lord Treasurer in 1572, and held the office till his death in 1598. During this long period he devoted his relentless activity not only to meeting immediate emergencies, but to carrying out a definite policy for the development of national resources. It is possible to form some idea of *with a genius for detail.* his energy from the many thousands of State Papers, endorsed, annotated or drafted by this indefatigable Secretary, which still exist; nothing was too trifling for him to take in hand, and he never seems to have been too busy to attend to the countless demands which were made on his time[1].

There is plenty of material, which affords an insight into his personal opinions The documents which survive often render it comparatively easy to distinguish Cecil's personal views and personal initiative in connection with many matters to which he had to attend on behalf of the Queen or the Council. The Secretary had a delightful habit of making, on all possible occasions, little memoranda which he headed, *Things to be performed*, or *immediately performed*[2]. Sometimes, too, he drew up a paper with the *pros* and *cons* of any plan he was meditating, and this gives an indication of the decision that

---

[1] Mr Secretary's name is rarely if ever missing from the list of those attending the Privy Council (*Acts of the Privy Council*), and he seems to have been a member of every commission of importance during the reign, e.g. on the recoinage (S. P. D. El. xiv. 33) and on the bill for the increase of tillage and the maintenance of the navy (S. P. D. El. lxxviii. 17, May 7, 1571).

[2] There are no less than twenty of these memoranda extant, between November 1558 and January 1561; they show the points on which he was engaged at the moment, and some of tho lists have as many as eighty things to be seen to. The two examples subjoined are typical.

1. *Thyngs necessary for the Conservation of this realme in savety and good order.* S. P. D. Eliz. xii. 6. April 12, 1560.

In primis, that your Counsell maye dilligently kepe the dayes of Counsell, and that the matters accorded uppon, may be distributed amongst them for more expedition. *Item*, that the realme may not be thus desolated for lack of Bishopps but that some may be specially appoynted to take chardg thereof. *Item*, that the realme may be distributed to lieutenants, and in any wise that one or twoo thousand pownd may be bestowed in arranging and instructing the realme to warr. *Item*, that the care be committed to iii or iiii to provide monny, and that therin your Majesty trust not to much to fayre words. *Item*, that men of service that have reasonable suytes may be well answered, and not discomforted as they be. *Item*, that the Navy be further prepared and all thyngs therto putt in redyness. *Item*, that the earle of Sussex may departe with spede into Irland and accord made with hym for the manner of governance thereof. *Item*, to appoynt certen of the Counsell to consider the state of the ordynance armory.

Thyngs necessary to be Considered upon the dout of K. Phillips breach with england. To send an express man to Tho: Gresham to confer with hym for

was forming itself in his mind[1]. In addition to his own A.D. 1558 —1603. letters, the letters addressed to him furnish another valuable source of information, as they contain references to correspondence of his own which has not always survived; they *as to the requirements and resources of the State,* prove the interest he was taking in such projects as the development of mines and the settlement of aliens, while they also testify to the importance in which he was held. His drafts of proclamations and statutes, and his corrections on drafts by other people, seem to show that he was allowed a very free hand by his royal mistress. He certainly deserved to be trusted, for his methods of work were extraordinarily painstaking and careful. His handwriting is very unusual and quite unmistakeable; it is remarkably clear and readable, even when it dates from the time when he was an old man and suffered from gout in the hands. His drafts are models of artistic conveyancing, and he is at pains to alter any slovenly expressions in papers drafted by other people; sometimes he inserts clauses[2] in proposed bills; he

the state of the Queen's Treasure, powder and such lyke. To give warning that the marchants do forese to there goods there. To practise with a nomber of merchants here how the vent of clothes might be issued unto Holst or other places.

2. *Notes of Thyngs to be performed,* S. P. D. El. ccliii. 103 (1595).

The book for provisions for the ordnance to be perused by the Earl of Essex, the Lord Admiral and Lord Chamberlain and such portions provided as present need requires. Bargains to be made for saltpetre and powder from Stade with the Merchant Adventurers, and underhand by Sir Francis Vere, with the merchants of Amsterdam. The Royal Co of miners to certify what copper they have, and how much they owe to the Queen. The number of unserviceable pieces provided by Sir Thomas Gresham to be made useful. Customer Smiths executors to answer for copper delivered. To deal with the gunmakers of London, as to what quantity of muskets they can serve monthly and to speak with Mr Grovenor of Shropshire about the same. Sir Robert Sydneys demands to be considered as to powder for Flushing wherein are some extraordinaries of great charge. Some bargains to be made for corn to be delivered about Christmas in Counties Hants, Wilts, Somerset & Devon. Letters to be sent to Cookham and Purbeck to cause the guns taken out of the Spanish burnt ships to be restored to the ordnance. Like letters to other forts on the sea side, to receive brass ordnance from London; also to Sir Ferd. Gorges, to take charge of the new fort at Plymouth; to consider what numbers are required to guard it. The armoury to be repaired, and its wants supplied. The fortifications of Milford to be carefully inspected. The ordnance to be shipped from Dieppe for the charge of which Otwell Smith requires £180 which he has laid out and cannot obtain anything from the governor. Letters to be written to choose gentlemen in maritime shires to survey the forts, and how the captains ward the same, with their companies allowed.

[1] As an illustration compare his reflections on the proposal by the French king for peace with Spain in S. P. D. El. cclxvi. 3.

[2] Clause 36, as to one dish of flesh being allowed to three of fish in 5 El. c. 5,

was most careful to maintain the Queen's prerogative, and especially to secure that the Queen's power to alter measures by proclamation should be safeguarded[1]; it was, as we have already seen, the most effective and reliable instrument of government at this time. The notes on petitions submitted to him show how carefully he read them, while he sometimes conducted a royal commission on his own account, and col-

and testi-
fies to his
activity
lected very many papers containing expert opinions from various quarters[2]. He was also constantly at work in revising the estimates and cutting down expenses[3], with the view of rendering the administration as efficient as possible. The collection of the revenue and the customs[4], the management of the navy[5], the ordnance[6], and the mint[7], were all overhauled by him in the hope of checking abuses and securing a reasonable amount of honesty; and he set a very remarkable example of impeccability. He was scrupulously

and incor-
ruptibility.
careful to avoid profiting in any way by his political influence[8], and refused the gifts from successful suitors which

and the clauses exempting fishermen from service as soldiers (41) and in regard to the spreading of false news (40) were drafted by Cecil (S. P. D. El. xxvii. 72).

[1] S. P. D. El. xxviii. 17, 18.

[2] Compare his enquiries before the recoinage, S. P. D. El. xiii. 27, 34.

[3] British Museum, *Lansdowne MSS.* xxi. 62—67. There is a very interesting paper extant in which he reviews the expenses of the Queen's Household; he makes a number of regulations which would do credit to a modern housekeeper; the ladies' maids are not to dine in their mistress' room, but at the common table (No. 67), the selling of meat out of the kitchen is to be "barred utterly," and a book is to be drawn up with the number of the servants and their rations. There are other curious *minutiae* also in his own handwriting such as "To defalk (deduct) for the drynk in bottells so much out of the allowance. No bottels to be allowed but to Counsellors, no private juggs to be allowed at tables, but if any be allowed, the less to be sent to the tables." Burleigh notes an increase of expenditure which was partly due to the larger quantities of victuals consumed and partly to the rise of prices.

[4] S. P. D. El. ccliii. 14, July 14, 1595; also S. P. D. El. ccxxxviii. 58, Feb. 1591.

[5] British Museum, *Cottonian MSS.* Otho E. viii. No. 147, p. 169. See also below, p. 64, n. 1. He was also the first man according to Peck (*Desiderata Curiosa*, p. 29) to see that the soldiers were apparelled, and that their money was paid into their own hands, and not to captains, who seem to have kept it back.

[6] Stow, *Survey* (1584), Bk. i. p. 106.

[7] S. P. D. El. cliv. 64. S. P. D. El. cxxii. 19, Jan. 1578.

[8] Two foreigners, Jean Carré, a merchant of Antwerp, and Pierre Briet, a Lorraine glass maker, petitioned to have exclusive licence to erect a glass furnace in London to make glass after the Venetian fashion. In their petition (S. P. D. El. xliii. 43) they offer Cecil a percentage on the glass as well as a present, "Supplions tres humblement a vostre seignourie quil luy plaise accepter ceste

were at that time the accepted method of making pay- A.D. 1558
—1603.
ments for work done[1].

The most pressing necessity, at the moment of Elizabeth's *The diffi-culty of* accession, was a means of supplying the realm with ordnance[2]. *supplying* The loss of Calais had deprived England of her principal *the country with* arsenal for munitions of war; the state of the defences was *ordnance* deplorable; and the country was in imminent danger of an *and gun-powder* attack by a combination of the Roman Catholic powers. Supplies of saltpetre and sulphur for gunpowder, and of iron and copper for ordnance, could only be procured through ports that were controlled by prospective enemies; there is no wonder that the Spaniards should have contemptuously calculated that it would be an easy matter to conquer England, because she lacked armour. Cecil immediately took the matter in hand, and with such success that in 1591 the Spaniards acknowledged the superiority of English cannon, and vainly endeavoured to procure them[3]. This *was over-come.*

charge (to be their protector) et prendre de bonne part le petit present ou offre que nous luy faissons pour ce commencement." This was refused although Cecil spoke on their behalf to Her Majesty, "Il nous a dict aussi que vostre seigniourie est bien contente de nous faire encorre a ladvenir toutz les plaisirs quelle porra mais quelle ne voeult accepter loffre que nous luy faisons par nostre premier et second escript que nous appellons les secondz fruictz Chosse quy nous a rendu aucunement perplex. Car puis que des le commencement Dieu nous la ainsy mys au Coeur nous y sasteferions vollontier " (S. P. D. El. XLIII. 44). This bears out his biographer Peck who says (*op. cit.* 19), "In cases of justice none could ever do him a greater dispight then to offer him anie thing, as myself can witness. For I have sene him refuse a bribe and many pieces of plate at new yeres tide. And to offer him money was to offend him so, as they fared the worse who did so." Peck adds "God send us more such, and that his example maie cause other to imytate his vertues."

[1] His mode of dealing with suitors is brought out in a letter to Mr White in Ireland, Sept. 1582 (Brit. Mus. *Lansdowne MSS.* CII. 108), "And as for my respondency to plesure particular sutors I thynk sometyme I am not so forward to plesure mens appetites as is required; my Conscience saveth me harmless in that I never forbeare to help any whom I thynk worthy for verteu or for actuall good service; and yet therin I mak to myself a rule that alweise I preferr the Queen's Maiesty and the Common Weale afore all sorts."

[2] S. P. D. El. VII. 5, Oct. 4, 1559.

[3] S. P. D. El. CCXLIV. 116. They offered 19*s*. to 22*s*. a cwt., and a pension of 40 ducats a month for life to the man who would smuggle them over. See also the Proclamation of Sept. 1591 (p. 89 below). The draft of this proclamation, in Lord Burleigh's own handwriting, is in Brit. Mus. *Lansdowne MSS.* CIV. 47. He refers to the attempts of the king of Spain to get these same munitions by "corruption of some of our undutiful subjects and of strangers inhabityng our countries."

rapid improvement is all the more remarkable because, at the time of Elizabeth's accession, this country was much behind the rest of Europe in all industrial arts, and could only hope to advance by importing skilled artisans[1], and encouraging enterprising men to undertake the risks of intro-

The grant-
ing of
monopolies
began
ducing new manufactures. They were frequently protected by royal letters patent; while the objects which Cecil had in view are often set out very fully in the grants themselves. The preamble of a patent granted to Sir Thomas Smith, Cecil, Leicester, and Sir Humphry Gilbert, for changing iron into copper[2] by heating it with blue vitriol, gives the reasons that this "notable invencion, if God graunte good successe to those that shall farther travayle therein, will be very profitable to us, our heirs and successors, for the making of our ordnance and other munitions for the warres uses. We therefore, greatly likyng of all good services and wyse and learned inventions tending to the benefit of the commonwealth of our sayde Realme and Domynions and serving for the defence thereof, and myndynge, as behoveth so good and excellent an Invention so hardly and so happelye come to, to farther and advaunce the skilfull first fynder thereof graciously to reward, as to us in honour in such cases doth appertayne, do therefore, to contynue the memory of the same Invention and of our gracious acceptynge thereof, as of a service done greatly to our honour and the benefit of our realme," confer the privileges asked for.

The Crown could not afford to engage in mining operations or establish factories for itself; but we find that many members of the Middle Classes were ready, during this reign, "to introduce, under the direction of the Crown but at their own charges, certain industries[3], the provision of which was considered indispensable for the safety and independence of

---

[1] The armourers at Woolwich were Germans. S. P. D. El. v. 2, 3, also VIII. 3.

[2] For an account of this affair see Strype's *Life of Sir T. Smith* (1820), p. 100. cap. XI.; also Pat. Roll, 17 El. Feb. 14.

[3] Spanish mining in the New World was carried on by a similar reliance on private capital, which was largely supplied by Germans; the French government on the other hand was able to provide the necessary funds for economic improvements (Fagniez, *L'Économie sociale de la France sous Henri IV.* 119, 181), and left less opportunity for private enterprise.

the realm[1]." The monopoly system was originally employed[2] A.D. 1558
with the object of reviving or re-introducing certain mining $\overline{}$ 1603.
and metallurgical industries; and it is in connection with *with*
the development of mines throughout the country that we *mining and metallurgi-*
see Cecil at his busiest. In 1561 a company was formed *cal projects,*
to work the mines in Northumberland, and also to search
for copper at Keswick[3]. Germans were brought over to
work these, and we find Gresham giving a bond to the
Fuggers for their expenses[4]. The mining adventurers were
in frequent communication with Cecil[5], who requested to be *in which Cecil was*
informed of the progress of the works. There is a letter *keenly*
extant from Daniel Hochstetter[6] to Alderman Duckett, in *interested,*
London. "Yt ys joyfull newes to us to understand that
Mayster Secretarye hath shewed hymesellfe so fryndly and
fforward in this our worke of our Minerall and that his
mony hathe beene so redye wythe the ffyrste, and allso so
willinge ffor the next paymente, prayinge you to call ernestly
uppon the Reste that paymente maye be made, and yf
they wyll not ffor you, then we pray you desyre the helpe of
Mayster Secretary in that behaulffe ffor in the wourkes
of the mynnes there must be no wante of monny." In 1568
the Company of Royal Mines was incorporated[7], but the
undertaking does not seem to have been very remunerative[8];
though the mines were eminently successful in the political
object[9] with which they were started, of providing iron and

---

[1] E. W. Hulme, *History of the Patent System*, in *Law Quarterly Review*, XII. 145.

[2] It was subsequently applied to new manufactures of every kind, but on these as well as on their constitutional character, see below, p. 76 also pp. 287, 293.

[3] S. P. D. El. XVIII. 18 (July, 1561).

[4] S. P. D. El. XL. 73 (Sept. 1566). On the part taken by German projectors in this matter compare R. Ehrenberg, *Hamburg und England*, 4 n.

[5] S. P. D. El. XVIII. 18 (July, 1561), XXXIV. 59, 60 (Sept. 1564), XXXVI. 25 (March, 1565), *ib*. 43 (April), *ib*. 59 (May), *ib*. 87 (July), *ib*. 91 (July), XXXIX. 80 (May, 1566), XL. 14 (June, 1566), *ib*. 64 (Sept.), 79, XLII. 27, 37 (March, 1567), etc.

[6] S. P. D. El. XXXIX. 57 (April 23, 1566).

[7] Stow, *Survey*, Bk. v. p. 246.

[8] S. P. D. El. CCLXXV. 145 (Dec. 1600).

[9] See a letter from the Council to Lord Scrope in June, 1559, "Great cost has been bestowed upon the copper works of the royal mines near Keswick, far above any commodity that has come to the Company by them; for their desire was that Her Majesty and the realm might be served with that commodity to make ordnance rather than stand to the courtesy of strangers who served the realm as they pleased." S. P. D. El. CCLXXI. 40.

copper for the ordnance[1]. At the end of the reign we get proclamations[2] forbidding the export of iron ordnance, and several of the smelting works were suppressed by government owing to the consumption of timber. Cecil was the Governor of the Mines Royal[3], and continued to take an active interest in the question of procuring a native supply of useful metals in Somersetshire as well as in the northern counties. He was financially interested in the mining and metallurgical enterprises which were floated by William Humphrey[4], and were incorporated under the name of the Mineral and Battery Company on the same date as the Company of Mines Royal[5]. They undertook to dig for Calamine stone, which was essential for the manufacture of brass, to dig for iron, tin, and lead, and to erect a mill for drawing wire, which was set up at Tintern[6]. Cecil corrected all the indentures for these patents, and paid the expenses of the foreign workmen whom Humphrey required in order to enable him to set up his plant[7].

and patents were also given for the manufacture of brimstone

Considerable pains were also taken to furnish native supplies of gunpowder; in 1565 an exclusive patent for the production of sulphur was given to Wade and Herlle for thirty years[8]; patents for saltpetre occur early in the reign[9], and were continued despite protests[10], since this substance

[1] S. P. D. El. xcv. 70, 79 (1574). A licence for founding or selling ordnance was required in 1574. S. P. D. El. xcv. 22—62.

[2] 1591 (Dyson, 296), 1592 (*ib.* 309), 1597 (*ib.* 351).

[3] S. P. D. El. colxiv. 30 (1597).

[4] S. P. D. El. xxvi. 83 (July), also xxxvii. 30, 43, 44 (Sept. 1565).

[5] Stow, *Survey*, Bk. v. p. 246. See also the charters granted by James I. in 1604. G. G. Francis, *Copper Smelting in Swansea District*, 30, 42.

[6] S. P. D. El. xlviii. 43. See also draft Act in 1593. *Hist. MSS. Comm.* iii. Ap. 8.

[7] S. P. D. El. xl. 30.

[8] Rymer, Vol. xiii. p. 650, Ad Sulphur et Oleum conficiendum de Concessione.

[9] S. P. D. El. xvi. 30 (Mar. 1561), "Articles of agreement between the Queen and Gerard Honrick, a German captain who undertakes the making of salt petre." England was dependent on importation from Naples, *ib.* 32. Imported saltpetre was cheaper than the native manufacture in 1575. S. P. D. El. cvi. 41.

[10] A grant made in January, 1587 gave rise to considerable trouble, and was recalled in 1589; the proclamation reciting the evils and the remedy was printed in 1595. Dyson, 278, *A Proclamation for the calling in and frustrating all Commissions for the making of salt peter granted forth before that to George Evelin and others, the* 28 Jan*ry* 1587 *whereby many of her Maiesties subjects were greatly abused.* etc.

had to be procured at the cost of any inconvenience. "There is another Patent," said the younger Cecil, "for Saltpeter, that hath been both accused and slandered: It digs in every man's House, it annoys the Inhabitant and generally troubleth the Subject; for this I beseech you to be contented . . . . Her Majesty means to take this Patent unto herSelf, and advise with her Council touching the same. For I must tell you the Kingdom is not so well furnished with Powder now as it should be[1]." The House appeared to be perfectly satisfied with this arrangement, and the exemption was retained in the Act of 1624; although the practical inconvenience caused by the operations of the saltpetre-men must have been very hard to tolerate[2]. The monopoly of the patentees was set aside in 1641[3], so that there might be free importation and unrestricted manufacture of gunpowder; but the practice of allowing patentees to dig for saltpetre was revived by Parliament during the Civil War[4]. Eventually the East India Company was able to furnish a proper supply for the manufacture of powder[5], and the minute regulations for native production, such as those about the paving of stables, were discarded.

There is a curious contrast between the economic policy which Cecil adopted in directing English energies, and that which was being pursued by the arch-enemy Spain. Our countrymen were giving attention to the mining and manufacture of useful metals[6], while Spanish prosperity was dependent on success in working the precious metals; England was developing her own native resources, while Spain was exploiting those of a distant dependency. Spaniards were eager to secure treasure, as it would give them the means of procuring mercenaries and munitions

A.D. 1558—1603.

and salt-petre.

Cecil aimed, not as the Spaniards did, at obtaining a treasure,

---

[1] S. D'Ewes, *Journals*, 653.

[2] See below, p. 291.

[3] 16 Charles I. c. 21, *An Act for the free bringing in of gunpowder and salt-petre from foreign parts and for the free making of gunpowder in this realm.*

[4] 1644, c. 35, Scobell, I. 68. The right was granted for two years. S. R. Gardiner, *History of England*, IV. 2—6.

[5] See below, p. 263.

[6] Some silver mining was attempted, but it was on a very small scale and attracted little attention. See above, p. 3.

and ships whenever they were wanted[1]: Cecil was not content
to possess purchasing power[2], he wished to have the country
supplied with the things themselves. It was in this way
that his policy worked out into so many ramifications, as he
but at procuring a supply of useful commodities. was compelled to look at the possibility of securing a permanent supply of all the necessaries of the national life. Thus,
while the economic system of Spain was concentrated on the
possession of treasure, the English scheme, at its first
inception, was devised with careful thought for useful commodities of every kind, and was free from any undue
hankering after bullion. Towards the close of Elizabeth's
reign, responsible statesmen[3] were perfectly aware of the
weakness of the Spanish economic system[4], and exposed its
defects with admirable clearness[5], and Cecil acted in a

[1] The Hanse ships supplied them with provisions for two years to victual and
fit out the Armada and a number of large Hanse ships formed part of the Spanish
fleet on that occasion. See *Lansdowne MSS.* civ. 30 (1591). In this paper, drawn
up in 1591 by Lord Burghley, he justifies Elizabeth's interference with the Hanse
corn ships. At the time of the Armada, he says, "the Easterlings had covertly
in ther Great Hulks, outwardly fraughted with peaceble merchandize, duryng
the space of ii yeres, conveyed into Spain the gretest part of all the Masts, Cables,
Cordage, Sayles, Copper, Saltpeter and powder, that served to furnishe the sayd
Navy, beside the furniture of the Spanish Shipps with such provisions; ther war
no greter nor stronger shipps in that army, than was a gret nomber of the Hanz
towns, whereof besyde the prooff that was had of the sight of them, the King of
Spayne had caused books to be published," in which were given their burden,
masters and number of mariners. The Hanse alleged that they were compelled
to serve; Burleigh replies "but he cold not have constrayned them if they had not
come thyther furnished as ships for the war." He goes on to say that "without
havyng of masts, boords, cabeles, cordag, pitch, tarr, copar out of the Estland, all
Spayn is not hable to mak a Navy redy to carry the meanest army that can be Ima-
gined, and if his money brought out of the Indies shold not tempt the Hanzes to bryng
hym these provisions, Spayn wold not offer to make war by sea with England."

[2] He was quite aware of the importance of treasure, but he did not put it in
the first place. See below, p. 176. See also Stow, *Survey*, v. 303.

[3] A proclamation of 1591 which deals with exactly the same points was drafted
by Lord Burleigh throughout. Brit. Mus. *Lansdowne MSS.* civ. 47.

[4] "Of late," Lord Burleigh says, "some number of Eastland shipps war stayed
on the Cost of Spayn, whan they war redy to have entred into the havens of Spayn
and Portyngale with ther full ladyng of victells and munitions....The shipps
that war arrested war shipps of the Est, laden with corn and other victells with
masts, cables and all kynd of cordage, and very many other thyngs proper to serve
the King of Spayn for his shipps and his army,...and without which he could not
renew his rent and spoyled navy." *Lansdowne*, civ. 30. This appears to be the
incident of the Lisbon ships in 1589, referred to in *Hist. MSS. Comm.* ii. Ap. 41.

[5] Dyson, 351, Sep. 1597, "*A proclamation publishing certaine just causes for
prohibition and stay of cariage of Victual and other provisions of Warre by Seas
into Spaine for continuance of the King of Spaines purposes to invade most*

fashion which showed he realised that it would not be wise A.D. 1558
—1603.
to try and outrival Spain by imitating her methods.

171. Though Burleigh was keenly alive to the necessity
of providing armaments, he yet seems to have been more *Burleigh*
ready, than any previous statesman, to place his main re- *began
the syste-*
liance, both for defensive and offensive purposes, on maritime *matic
develop-*
power. It occupied his thoughts at the very moment when *ment of
English*
he came into power[1]; and however pressing other needs *maritime
power ;*

uniustly her Maiesties Dominions: With authoritie for the stay thereof by Sea."
It recites the iniquities of the King of Spain who will not live at peace with his
neighbours. "And though these his violent hostilities to the trouble of a great
part of Christian dominions, are mightily mainteined by reason of the abundance
of his said treasure from the Indies, yet it is manifestly seene that to mainteine
his sayd Armies, and to renew his shipping, his Moneyes would not in their
proper nature suffise, if hee were not continually mainteined with victual, and
furnished from Forein countreys with munitions whereof neither his Indies, nor
Spain, nor any other parts of his own countreys, are able to serve him: but the
same is knowen to be brought into Spaine and Portugall from other forein parts,
not in his subiection, and that specially from the North East parts by Sea, where
the sayd King by abundance of his money with his Factors for that purpose in
the most part of the Port townes of Eastland, doeth buy and prouide the most
part of his victuals, wherewith he feedeth and maintaineth his Armies, and all
kinds of prouisions for the building and furnishing of his Navy, and without
which he could not continue his great hostilitie, but should be unable to offer so
great offence to his Neighbors, and thereby he and all other his Neighbors should
live in peace: For this cause, the Queenes Maiestie being amongst other Princes
most interested for defence of her selfe and her Countreys and Subiects, against
the sayd kings great preparations of his Navies and Armies by Sea: and manifestly perceiuing that if his sayd prouisions for hostilitie to be brought by Sea
from the sayd East parts might be staied untill he might be disposed to live in
peace, her Maiestie might thereby forbeare to continue her charge in mainteining
her forces both by Sea and Land, which she is constrained yeerly to renew and
continue only for her defence.

"And though some of the Kings in those East countries, that have interest in
certain Portes of the sayd East countries... have bene friendly required by her
Maiestie to prohibite their subiects to carry or send by sea into Spain such kindes
of victuall and munition as properly do mainteine his armies, and furnish his
ships of warre with all things requisite for to serve for his uniust warres:
... therefore her Maiesty doth by these presents notifie to all maner of persons of
all conditions, that shall send or carry into Spaine or Portugall any maner of
graine, or other victuals, or any maner of provisions to serve or build or arme any
shippes of warre, or any kinde of munitions for the warre... she will not onely
authorise her owne Admirals, ... but will allow and approve all other her subiects
to arme their ships at their will and with them to impeach and arrest all ships
that shall saile either out of the East parts or out of the Low countries with
intention to pass to Spaine or Portugall, having on board any such victuall
or other provisions of warre." Those who chose to fit up ships for this purpose
were to notify the High Admiral and to give bonds for their good behaviour.

[1] In the memorial dated November 18, 1558, S. P. D. El. I. 3 "to consider the
things of the Admiraltie" is one of the things to be "immediately performed."

might be, he never allowed himself to lose sight of this prime necessity.   There had been anticipations of his policy of fostering a mercantile marine, but he gave it a prominence which it had never had before, and which it has never since lost ; he was sufficiently far-seeing, too, to attend to all the sources of permanent maritime prosperity, and did not content himself with building ships of war and fitting out a well-appointed fleet[1].   There was no side of industrial or commercial life which was left unaffected, for good or for evil, by the policy which Cecil devised for increasing the shipping and employing the seamen of the country.

he went behind the work of naval adminis-tration,

The few ships which were added to the royal navy, at the beginning of the reign, were kept in good repair[2]; but in this, as in other things, Cecil's efforts were mainly directed to drawing out the energies of the subjects.   The bounties on building ships were more regularly paid[3], and great pains were expended on the preservation of the necessary materials.   A statute was passed in 1558[4] insisting that no timber was to be cut down for iron smelting within fourteen miles of the coast[5], a limitation which interfered with the development of

and took account of the preser-vation

---

[1] He gave very great attention, however, to the details of naval administration : he sat on almost every naval commission (see e.g. S. P. D. El. clxii. 50), and drafted nearly all the instructions for the navy (see *Armada Papers*, ed. Laughton, *Navy Record Society*, i. and ii. *passim*).   Sir John Hawkins attributes his own success in carrying out reforms and in checking official dishonesty to the aid he received from the minister's skill.   Oppenheim, *op. cit.* p. 147 quoting from S. P. D. El. clxx. 57.   Cecil would have wished to spend money much more freely on the navy than Elizabeth would allow, though he occasionally succeeded in having his way.   In 1597 he promises to send the *Lion* to Essex, and says that the vessel is to be victualled for three months by the Queen's command, "though she stuck at that at first" (S. P. D. El. cclxiv. 50).   Again Hawkins writes, "I do perseve hir Maiestie is not well sattysfied concernyng the imploymentes of the great somes of mony that have byne reseaved into th' office of the navye although your Honour dyd very honourably bothe take payne and care to see the strycte and orderly course that ys used in thoffice, and thereupon delyver your mynd playnely to her Maiesty as your Lordship fund yt, for which I shall ever acknowledge myself dewtyfully bownd to honour and serve your Lordship to the uttermost of my abillytie" (S. P. D. El. ccxxxi. 83).   The point in Cecil's policy is that while he attended to the royal navy thoroughly well, he was far-seeing enough to give constant consideration to the ultimate sources of maritime power.

[2] On the good condition of the fleet at the accession of James I. see Oppenheim, p. 184.

[3] S. P. D. El. ccl. 33.   Oppenheim, *op. cit.* 167.

[4] 1 El. c. 15.   See also 23 El. c. 5 and 27 El. c. 19.

[5] Cecil's personal interest in this matter may be gathered from the letter

the iron trade both in Kent, Sussex and the Forest of Dean[1]. An enquiry was instituted as to the condition of timber on episcopal and other lands[2], and the bishops were warned to be careful, while they almost unanimously protested that the fault lay with their predecessors. The Secretary also found occasion to remonstrate with the Countess of Rutland[3] on the destruction of the trees in her forests. His anxiety in regard to any waste of wood[4] is brought out by the order he drafted to the effect that no clapboards or barrels may be exported from London, as they are required for the navy[5]. Though timber, as the main requisite, is the chief object of solicitude, attention was also devoted to the production of the materials that were necessary for fitting ships, especially to the growth of hemp and flax[6] and the manufacture of canvas[7].

A.D. 1558 —1603.

of timber,

the supply of hemp and sail-cloth,

which he drafted to the Marquis of Winchester about preserving timber for ship-building especially at Lewisham in Kent. S. P. D. El. vii. 11, 21 (Oct. 1559). Compare also his notes S. P. D. El. xli. 76.

[1] In the early part of the reign exceptions were made in favour of existing iron-works in Kent and Sussex, but increasing limitations were imposed in the later statutes. Cecil was most anxious to promote the use of sea-coal for smelting, so that timber might be spared. See below, p. 523.

[2] There had been some reckless felling of woods by the Master and Fellows of Queens' College, Cambridge, who desired to erect a brewhouse (S. P. D. El. cxxxvi. (Jan. 1580) 6, 8, 9, 22), and destroyed the "ornament bewty and defence of that Colledge." See also the Bishops of Rochester (*ib.* 33), of Salisbury (*ib.* 45), of Worcester (*ib.* 65), the Archbishop of Canterbury (*ib.* 71), the Bishops of Lincoln (*ib.* 79), of London (cxxxvii. 9—12), Bath and Wells (*ib.* 33), and of Hereford (*ib.* 72).

[3] British Museum, *Lansdowne MSS.* ciii. 80 (1594).

[4] It was important that ships when built should be retained under English control, and not sold to foreigners. See *A Proclamation against selling of shippes*, Dyson, 12 (1559). "The Queenes Maiestie understanding out of sundrie partes of her Realme, and specially of such as be nigh to her Sea costes, what great scarcitie of Tymber there is, and in long time not to be recouered, meete for the building of Shippes, either for her owne Maiesties Nauie or for the Marchants of her Realme, hath by the aduice of her Counsell thought meete...to command... that no maner person borne within her obeysance shall sell or by any maner meanes, directly or indirectly alienate any maner Shippe or Vessell of what burthen soever the same shalbe, being meet to saile vpon the seas, to any maner of person either borne or resident out of her Highnesse dominions as the same will answere at their vttermost peril."

[5] Everyone who exports seven tons of beer is to bring in two hundred clap-boards. S. P. D. El. clxxxvi. 2 (Jan. 1586).

[6] Burleigh's calculations as to the yield of hemp per acre are extant (British Museum, *Lansdowne MSS.* cxviii. No. 39 f. 41 and xxvi. No. 47). He also corrected the draft of the proclamation by which the statute 24 Hen. VIII. c. 4 was re-enforced. Dyson, 185 (15 Jan. 1579). Brit. Mus. *Lansdowne MSS.* xxv. No. 99 f. 215. See also S. P. D. lxxviii. 34, 35.

[7] See below, p. 82, n. 4.

The Secretary was also at pains to re-enforce the measures, which had been taken in previous reigns[1], for the preservation of ships, both by the construction of harbours and the

suppression of piracy. The condition of the harbours is the second thing mentioned in Cecil's coronation memorial, and there are endless letters on the subject in the Privy Council Records and among the State Papers. The first proceeding was to enquire into the state of the havens; and in 1565, on the information thus received, a warrant was issued for commissions under the Great Seal for the superintendence and care of ports and havens, as well as for repressing pirates, against whom a vigorous crusade was being carried on. The instructions[2] are very elaborate; a return was to be made of all the inhabitants, ships, boats and vessels in any port or landing place, with the names of the owners and their trade; no ship is to be victualled or to put to sea without licence. Considerable ingenuity had sometimes to be shown in devising expedients to raise money for the repair of harbours: Cecil writes to the town concerned to know how much can be contributed, and frequently urges the inhabitants to make a special effort to give a little more[3]. Collections for this object were made by Lord Burleigh's permission all over the country, and those that brought in money were allowed a commission of fourpence in the pound. Letters were sent to all the sheriffs to advance the cause as much as possible. Forced labour was frequently employed, by royal warrant, on the harbours; and we get proposals for certain duties to be set aside for the purpose of repairs; licences were granted to Great Yarmouth and other places to export grain to pay for their expenses. A tax of half-a-crown was imposed on every new licence for an alehouse

---

[1] Vol. I. p. 497.

[2] These instructions were corrected by Cecil, and a list of persons was drawn up for the several counties of England and Wales; many of the names are added in Cecil's own hand. These men were to act as commissioners for the ports and havens, and to view them once every month at the least. S. P. D. El. xxxvii. 47, 49.

[3] The City Companies were specially urged to assist, and collections were authorised in all the churches; there was also a great lottery for the object in London. Clode, *Early History of Merchant Taylors Co.*, I. 228. R. R. Sharpe *London and the Kingdom*, I. 506—508.

throughout the kingdom, and the proceeds were devoted to A.D. 155 the repair of Dover harbour[1]; the government helped to pro- —1603. vide materials for such works by issuing warrants for the delivery of timber.

Ships would, however, be of little avail unless there were *as well as the* seamen to man them, and Cecil was keenly alive to the *increase* importance of training boys for a seafaring life. The sea- *mariners* *With the* fisheries formed an admirable school for this purpose, and *view he* *couraged* no expedient was overlooked which might encourage these *fisheries* trades[2]. There seemed to be little opportunity for increasing the sale of fish in foreign countries, as Norway, Scotland, Flanders not only satisfied their own demands, but had a surplus to export[3]. France employed 1500 men in New-foundland, and sent annually a fleet of five hundred sail to fish for herrings on the English coast[4]. But something could

---

[1] S. P. D. El. cxxxvi. 85, cxli. 46.

[2] The efforts of the government appear to have been successful, if we may judge from the following certificate from Trinity House, Jan. 26, 1580. "We the masters, wardours, and assistants of the Trinitie house at Deptford Strond made dilligent enquirie of all the costmen that be here at this instant at the cyttie of London, what fisher boates have been encreased sythence the last parliament as by particulers may appear. That is to say from Newcastle to Portsmouth 114 sayle betwene 15 & 40 tonne a piece. Which boates doe maintaine for every 20 tonne 8 men and a boy at the least which are betwene 1000 men ready to serve in her majesties shippes." S. P. D. El. cxlvii. 21. Some idea of the current opinions in 1580 on the development of fishing as an industry may be gathered from *The Politic Plat*, 1580, printed in Arber's *English Garner*, ii. 133. It contains an elaborate scheme for diminishing the number of idle vagabonds, and increasing the prosperity of decayed towns. Its author, Robert Hitchcock, had served in the Low Countries, and had, while there, seen how profitable an industry fishing could be. His scheme was not adopted, although it was laid before Parliament, but his tract gives an interesting account of the fishing trade during this period. He was anxious to develop whale fishing. "The killing of the whale is both pleasant and profitable, and without great charges." *Ib.* 158.

[3] "The Flemings and other nations...seeing our careless dealing have not only taken this beneficial Fishing from us, but very warily doth sell the same commodity unto us; and thereby carrieth out of this land both Gold and silver and a marvellous quantity of double beer, and other thinges, satisfying us with these fishes, which, through our owne slothe, we lose" (Hitchcock, *Politic Plat*, in Arber's *English Garner*, ii. 144).

[4] Despite numerous efforts there does not seem to have been much success in establishing an export trade in herrings or in securing their position in the Newfoundland fisheries. On the pretext that cod and ling were badly packed in barrels by aliens, the importation was wholly forbidden in 1563 (5 El. c. 5, § 10). Licences to import were obtainable however in 1564 (S. P. D. El. xxxv. 36), and permission to import them was afterwards accorded to English subjects "using uprightness and truth in the barrelling of such fish" (13 El. c. 11, § 3). The English

A.D. 1558
—1603.
be done to encourage the home consumption. Cecil was particularly zealous[1] about the desirability of increasing the English demand, by insisting on the observance of fish days each week and of the whole of Lent, not as a religious dis-

and in-
sisted on
the observ-
ance of
Fish Days.
cipline but from political motives. A Statute had been passed, in 1549, directing that people were to eat fish on Friday, Saturday, the Ember days, Vigils, and Lent; and ten years later, a proclamation in favour of the observation of this political Lent was issued[2]. A woman, who kept a tavern at the sign of the Rose at St Catherine's beyond the Tower, was set in the pillory for having flesh in her house in Lent, and four women who took thereof were set in the stocks all night[3]. The fish days were not allowed to be a

merchants took advantage of this permission and "for their private gain" engrossed salt fish in foreign countries, though it was inferior in quality, and "great masses of money" were sent abroad to pay for it (23 El. c. 7), by reason of which "unnatural dealings" of merchants and fishmongers, the shipping of the realm had suffered to the extent of 200 sail and more of ships, which had once found employment in the Iceland trade. No salt fish was now to be imported, unless from Iceland or Newfoundland, except on the payment of additional duties corresponding to those charged by the different foreign countries on the importation of English cured herrings; and it was expected that English fishermen and English skippers would be able to supply the whole of the home demand. But these hopes were doomed to disappointment; protection did not serve to call forth enterprise, and it was stated in 1597 (39 El. c. 10) as the result of experience, that "navigation of this land is no whit bettered by the means of that act, nor any mariners increased nor like to be increased by it; but contrariwise, the natural subjects of this realm, not being able to furnish the tenth part of the same with salted fish of their own taking," the trade had really fallen into the hands of strangers and aliens, who had much enriched themselves, greatly increased their navigation and had "extremely enhanced" the price of fish; while the shipping of England had rather suffered than otherwise. The trade was consequently allowed to revert to the same condition in which it had been when English merchants had practised their unnatural dealings, but had at least done active and remunerative business in the importation of foreign cured fish. Almost a century was to elapse before the continual struggle was to be crowned with success, and Englishmen were to oust their foreign rivals from this branch of maritime trade.

[1] Compare the paper numbered S. P. D. El. xxvii. 71, which consists of notes for a speech in Parliament, drawn up by his secretary and copiously corrected by Cecil himself.

[2] Feb. 1559, Dyson 4.

[3] Stow, *Survey*, I. 257. This was in 1563. See also the case of the Innkeeper of the Star at Wells in 1609, *Hist. MSS. Comm.* III. 350; also Kingston-on-Thames in 1576, *ib.* III. 332; Abingdon in 1578, *ib.* II. 150, and Coventry, *ib.* I. 101. In 1596 the Archbishop of Canterbury granted a licence to William Newport to eat flesh on forbidden days on a payment of 13s. 4d. to the poor of the parish, *ib.* I. 33. The respective rights of the Archbishop and the King to taxation in connection with such licences were discussed in 1623, *ib.* IV. 316. See below, p. 72.

mere empty form; and in 1563 Cecil advocated a bill, which A.D. 1558 —1603. passed into law[1], for the "increase of fish and navy days" by adding Wednesdays as well. The same measure contains a clause which exempted fishermen and mariners from serving as soldiers on land; it is a significant indication of the changed conditions of strategical policy, when the importance of sailors in the defence of the realm is fully recognised.

A paper which Cecil corrected[2] gives a most interesting *He studied the reme-* analysis of the causes of injury to English shipping, some *dies for* of which seemed remediable by legislation while others were *existing evils;* not[3]. He was particularly concerned at the decay of mariners[4], and notes that the expedients hitherto tried had proved insufficient. "Some other thing must be provided to increase the navy and to multyply mariners, ... and therby, by Goddes grace, be hable to defend the realme against all foreyn power ..... The very ground that naturally serveth to brede mariners is the trade or conversation upon the sea; which is divided into three sorts; the one is to cary or re-cary marchandizes, the other is to take fish; for the thyrd, which is the exercise of pyrecy, is detestable and cannot *he de-nounced* last[5]." The Elizabethan privateers gave this detestable *the piracy* practice a new lease of life in the Channel. On the quarrel with Alva, in 1568, they had a merry time in scouring the seas for trading ships, which they brought into Dover, where the cargoes were disposed of, and the Spanish grandees were auctioned off to anyone who liked to keep them in irons on the chance of a ransom[6]. The heroes of maritime warfare in

---

[1] See below, p. 72, n. 3. [2] S. P. D. El. xxvii. 71.

[3] The decline of the trade of Venice with the East, re-acting as it did on the English trade with the Mediterranean, was one of the mischiefs which could not be cured by legislative action; so, too, was a recent Navigation Act passed in Spain, which forbade the wares of the country to be exported in foreign bottoms when native shipping was available. The recovery of Iceland into the hands of the King of Denmark and the augmentation of his tolls at the Sound had affected English commerce on the north, and the fact that the towns of Riga, Revel and Nerva had fallen into the hands of the Muscovites also told against English shipping.

[4] In a memorial dated May 1, 1560 (S. P. D. El. xii. 14) we find Cecil noting that 3000 men are to be got to serve upon the seas. It may have been the difficulty of collecting these men that led Cecil to complain of the decay of mariners.

[5] On piracy compare Oppenheim, *op. cit.* 177.

[6] Froude, ix. 486.

the Elizabethan age carried on the African slave trade[1] with reckless boldness, in defiance of the laws which closed the Spanish colonies against them; the seamen may have sympathised with such doings[2], but ship owners had other views. The founders of our modern trade were the London merchants, who formed the Companies, and not the gentlemen privateers, who merely preyed on the commerce of other nations. The East India Company were prepared to defend their ships from attack, but they were able to distinguish between legitimate trading and mere piracy; they had probably no great sympathy with the exploits of the channel rovers. This seems to come out in their determination " Not to employ any gentleman in any place of charge or commandment in the said voyage, for that, beside their own mislike of the imploying of such, they know the generality will not endure to hear of such a motion, and if they should be earnestly pressed therin, they would withdraw their adventure." They wished " to sort their business with men of their owne qualety[3]."

which was commonly practised,

Attempts had been made in previous reigns to encourage the employment of English ships, especially in the wine trade, and a Statute imposing discriminating duties on the lading of foreign ships was passed in the first year of Elizabeth's reign[4]. Cecil was not an enthusiast for this policy; he seems to have felt that this mode of developing the shipping of the country was disadvantageous in other ways, and contrasts it with his favourite scheme of promoting the fishing trades. A paper in his hand headed " *The Inconveniences of enlargyng any power to bryng any more wyne into the realme*" is a masterly discussion of the whole subject,

and he condemned the Navigation Acts

[1] Compare S. P. D. El. XLIV. 7 for the African Slave Trade.

[2] A question which was discussed at one of the earlier meetings of the committee of East India governors shows the manner in which sailors regarded these opportunities for gain. " Whereas this assemblie were acquainted that ther hath bene some question made by some of the mariners what allowance they should have uppon such reprisalles as may happen in the voyage, it is uppon that question aunswered, that there is noe intention to make anie attempte for reprisalles, but only to pursue the voyage in a merchauntlike course" (Stevens, *Dawn*, p. 118). This is a marked difference from the time of Chaucer and a contrast with the contemporary practice of Hawkins

[3] Stevens, *Dawn*, p. 28.

[4] 1 El. c. 13.

and is particularly interesting as it contains a very clear A.D. 1558 —1603. statement of the doctrine of the balance of trade. "It is manifest," he says, "that nothyng robbeth the realm of England, but whan moore marchandisees is brought into the realme than is carryed furth," because the balance "must be payd with mony." "The remedy herof is by all pollycyes to *both on* abridg the use of such forrayn commoditiees as be not neces- *mercan- tilist* sary for us." "Of all these iii excessees" (wine, spices and silks), he holds "that none is more hurtfull to the realm than wyne," and this for four reasons. In the first place the trade "enrycheth France," in the second, the wines from Bourdeaux and Rouen must be paid for in money, "for in Burdeaux they have an ordonance forbyddyng barteryng with Englishmen for wynes," so that the gold brought home by merchants from "Spain or the Low Countries ... is con- veyed into France" instead of enriching England; thirdly, *and on moral* the multiplying of taverns is "an evident cause of disorder *grounds,* of the vulgar people, who by hauntyng thereto wast ther small substance which they welly gett by ther hand labour, and commit all evills that accompany drunkenes; fourthly, the excessyve drynkyng of wyne deminisheth the use of ale and beare, and consequently decayeth tillage for grayne which of all labors in the realme wold be favored, and cherished and preferred before such an unnecessary forrayn commoditee as wine is[1]." It would be difficult to find a more interesting example of the manner in which he traced out the remoter consequences of proposed interference with trade, and took account of them all. The encouragement of

[1] S. P. D. El. xli. 58. The matter was very arguable, and he discusses the pros and cons at considerable length; the allegation that the non-enforcement of the navigation policy was responsible for the decrease in the number of ships at some ports he answers by saying that this was partly due to the larger size of the ships, since one hoy could bring in as much in one year as ten merchant ships had formerly imported in two years. The usurpation of the fishing trades by foreigners seemed to him a much more important matter. He complains that Yarmouth fishing is yearly occupied by six hundred Flemings and Frenchmen, the North Coast fishing by four hundred Flemings and some Frenchmen, the fishing in the narrow seas by the French, the herring and salmon fishing (which is always spoken of as coast and sea fishing) is in the hands of the Scots, while the Southern coasts of Ireland are fished by the Spaniards. There was a prohibition against buying herrings from foreigners, unless they were shipwrecked, in the Statute of 1563, while Englishmen were allowed to export fish without paying any tax.

A.D. 1558
—1603.

*while he
held that
no similar
evils re-
sulted from
fisheries.*

the fishing trades, by a compulsory increase of the home consumption[1], appeared on the other hand to entail no disadvantages worth mentioning[2]; the policy was therefore enforced with greater stringency in 1563[3], and in 1576 there

[1] There is an interesting paper extant as to the diet at Cecil's own table on a fish day. The first course consisted of Ling, Salmon or Herrings, Pike, Plaice or Whiting, Haddock or Codfish or back meat. The second course of Conger, or Lamprey, or Roefish, Smelts. Tart. (British Museum, *Lansdowne MSS*. vi. 5.)

[2] This regulation for diet had the additional advantage of being more economical. Calculations which were officially circulated in 1595 reckoned 67,500 cattle as the saving which would arise if London kept all the fish days strictly. *A briefe note of the benefits that growe to this Realme by the observation of Fishe daies* (Brit. Mus. 21. h. 5 (1)). We see from a paper drawn up in February 1581, that a man's diet on a fish day only cost a penny half-penny, and on a flesh day three pence; it is added that in time of an army royall put to the seas, Wednesday now being a fish day doth save 80 oxen at least for that day (S. P. D. El. cxlvii. 82). Calculations as to the proportions of victuals required by seamen on fish and flesh days respectively were made in 1639. (*Hist. MSS. Comm.* iii. Ap. 79.)

[3] At the end of four years there was a complaint that the fish days were insufficiently observed, and the justices are instructed to be diligent in punishing offenders. We see from the account of the victuallers who supplied the troops at Newhaven and elsewhere, that the soldiers at least were made to keep fish days. Again in 1571 the Council were pursuing a very energetic policy with regard to fish days, and returns from Lincolnshire, Middlesex, Northampton and Bucks. in April 1572 show that the Justices of the Peace were actively promoting the observance of the law (S. P. D. El. lxxxvi. 21, 22, 27, 28).

It is clear, however, that continued pressure had to be maintained in order to keep the public up to their duty in this matter. In December 1576 the Council are writing to the Archbishop of Canterbury on the subject as well as to the Sheriffs of the Counties, though a special exemption from the general rule is granted to Colchester, which is allowed to see to its own fish days. There are similar instructions to the Sheriffs in 1578 (*Acts of Privy Council*, x. p. 156), and in the following year there are complaints of the laxity of the citizens of London: Burleigh, writing to the Lord Mayor in 1582, thought it quite unnecessary to license any butchers to kill meat in Lent, as invalids were allowed to have poultry; three butchers appear to have been licensed however, but a fourth could not be permitted in the City, even at the request of Lord Howard of Effingham. Every butcher licensed had to pay a sum of money towards the relief of maimed soldiers. Overall, *Remembrancia*, p. 395. Eventually it seems that Burleigh was content to give up the struggle to enforce the observance of Wednesday (S. P. D. El. clxxvii. 33 (Mar. 1585)), in districts five and twenty miles or more from the sea; and by the statute, as passed in 1585, the remission of this day is extended to all parts of the realm, though the insistence on the observation of the two remaining days became more marked in the Proclamations. The policy of prescribing a political Lent was frequently advocated, and seems to have been to some extent enforced till the time of the Civil War. On the enforcing of fish days in 1585 at Leicester, see Leicester Corporation Records, in *Hist. Manuscripts Commission*, Report viii. Ap. 432, February, 1585 (xxvi); also for privileged persons, *ib*. p. 433 (xx), 16 January, 1598. For other remarks on the subject see

seemed to be reason to believe that it had been successful in bringing about an increase of seafaring folk[1].

Cecil's policy was carried into effect, and while so much *The old method of developing a marine was discarded in his time,* attention was given to developing fisheries, there was little effort either to revive old legislation or to introduce new[2] for promoting the employment of mariners in carrying and re-carrying merchandise[3]. It may be said that the government was more careful to encourage English merchants than to limit them entirely to English ships; the merchants of the Staple and the Merchant Adventurers were exempted from the operation of the Navigation Act of 1559, at the time of their regular shippings; if the higher rates it imposed on goods sent in foreign ships had reduced the volume of trade

H. Robinson, *England's Safety in Trades Encrease* (1641), p. 16; also the numerous *Proclamations* in *Fœdera*, xvii. 181 (1619), 134 (1619), 661 (1625), xviii. 268, 822 (1626), 961 (1627), xix. 116 (1629) 329 (1631), 376 (1632). On the strictness with which it was enforced at Hull, Andrews, W., *Curiosities of the Church*, 71. For Warwick see *The Book of John Fisher*, ed. Kemp, pp. 150, 162: E. Jeninge, *Brief discovery of the damages that happen to this realme by disordered and unlawfull diet* (1593).

[1] Compare a paper dated 10 March, 1576, and headed *The increase of shippes and other vessels since the first makinge of the statute for the maintenance of the navie.* "Wee, whereof maniee be hereunto subscribed do testifie and wilbe redy to prove that the Townes and places whiche are here underneath written are encreased of Sea-fisher botts and Barks from Ten Tons of Burden to 30 tons to the nomber of cxl sayles from the tyme of the makinge of the statute from abstynence of fleshe on the Wenisday untill this presente. And if the said Lawe had not bin made wherby these botts and barks are increased, so many in number or rather more wolde have bin decayed within this realme.... And so whensoever the Quenes Maiestie shulde have any occasion to send her Highnes shipps to the seas, there wolde not be found sea-faringe men to man the same" (S. P. D. El. cvii. 67). There is a list of 51 new ships built since 1571 (*ib.* 68). Similar evidence is given by the authorities of Trinity House in 1581 (S. P. D. El. cxlvii. 21, 22). See also below, p. 176, n. 1.

[2] The traditional policy of encouraging English shipping, especially in the wine trade, had been discarded under Edward VI. (5 and 6 Ed. VI. c. 18), possibly because the navy of England was so far reduced in his reign that it did not suffice to serve the merchants properly; in the first year of Elizabeth, however, something was done to restore the old rule, and at the same time to increase the customs revenue. It was asserted that foreign powers had retaliated on England by enforcing a strict navigation policy of their own, and a remedy was provided by charging the customs due from aliens in the case of those subjects who shipped goods in foreign bottoms. Thus the differential rate was in favour of the employment of English ships; but since foreign ships could be used if the higher rate was paid, there was less danger of reducing the volume of trade and thus of affecting the customs revenue or of provoking retaliation (1 El. c. 13).

[3] Compare an interesting account of some places with which England traded in 1595 (?), and of the exports and imports in S. P. D. El. cclv. 56.

at these seasons, there might have been a serious reduction in the customs[1] and an inconvenient restriction of manufacturing. Cecil appears to have taken the far-seeing view that there was comparatively little to be gained by competing with foreigners for existing commerce, and that the wisest course was to open up new markets. With this object, he encouraged voyages of exploration[2] and favoured the formation of trading companies; and as a matter of fact Englishmen did succeed in pushing their active commerce in many directions during this reign[3].

but he interested himself in voyages of discovery,

The breach with Spain, and the interruption of the Netherlands trade, led to the transference of the Merchant Adventurers' factory from Antwerp to Hamburg, where the trade was carried on successfully for some ten years, till the Hansards drove them out. Elizabeth retaliated, in 1578, by abrogating all the special privileges which the men of the Hanse enjoyed in England, and placing them on the same footing as other aliens, as well as by granting a charter to the Prussian or Eastland Company[4], who were competitors in the Baltic trade: she gave the English merchants a more complete organisation than they had possessed under the patent from Henry IV.[5] After the old routes to the East were superseded, the active trade of the Venetians declined, and in 1587 it came to an end. The last of the argosies sent out by them to Southampton was totally wrecked off the Needles; Sir William Monson gives a graphic description of the disaster, of which he was an eye-witness[6]. On the suggestion of London merchants, Elizabeth had already sent an emissary to try to open up direct commercial communi-

and encouraged English merchants to seize every opportunity

---

[1] See above, Vol. I. p. 490.

[2] Cecil drew up instructions for Frobisher and paid £50 towards the expense of one of his voyages, S. P. Colonial E. I. (1576), 24, 33; S. P. D. El. cxix. 36, 46; cxxvii. 11. See also the copy of accounts of trading voyages made for Cecil and annotated by him, *Lansdowne MSS.* c. (2), (3).

[3] On the struggle with the Hanse League and the victory of the English Company see Ehrenberg, *Hamburg und England*, also the *Epistle to the most noble and illustrious Lords Edzart and John, Erles of Eastfriezland, Lords of Emden* (1564), (Brit. Mus. *Sloane MSS.* 818; also among *Yelverton MSS.* in Lord Calthorpe's possession, xxi. f. 296, and *Hist. MSS. Comm.* III. 115).

[4] 17 Aug. 1579, Stow, *Survey*, Bk. v. p. 262.

[5] Vol. I. p. 415.

[6] Sir W. Monson, *Naval Tracts*, IV. in Churchill's *Collection* (1732), III. 400.

cation with the subjects of Amurath III. the Sultan[1], and in   A.D. 1558 —1603.
1581 the Levant Company was regularly incorporated. In
1584 they pushed by the Persian Gulf to Goa[2]. The trans-   *of pushing their trade.*
ference of this trade, from Venetian to English merchants,
had another ultimate result; Southampton, which had been
the Italian depot, declined[3], and London was enriched, as
the Eastern trade was now drawn into the Thames. Besides
forming these new companies, Elizabeth showed some care
for the interests of the Muscovy Merchants, who had been
already incorporated, and who had pushed their trade by
means of the Russian river system eastward into Persia[4].
The Company had had many difficulties to contend with[5],
but they were able to maintain their position. An attempt
was also made, by some London merchants, to organise a
trade with Barbary, and a company was formed, but not
apparently with much result[6]. The fruits of all this new
activity became apparent in the seventeenth century, but
there is ample evidence that Burleigh saw the value of these
forms of enterprise and was eager to encourage them. The
great organisations of aliens, who had carried on the active
trade of the country, were ceasing to have any importance,
and Englishmen were beginning to take their own place in
the various branches of distant commerce.

172. Allusion has already been made to Cecil's eager-   *Burleigh made de-*
ness to utilise the mineral resources of England with the   *liberate*
assistance of aliens, so as to obtain a supply of ordnance;   *efforts to foster*
but this, though a most important instance, is only an illus-   *native industries,*
tration of a carefully thought out and deliberate policy. He
was exceedingly anxious to develop English industry of every
kind, so that the country might not only become economically independent, and be able to dispense with some of
its imports, but might also have valuable commodities to
export to foreign markets. The best hope of bringing about   *and*
a considerable improvement at small cost, lay in the granting   *granted patents*
of patents to men who had enterprise enough to plant a new   *for new enterprises,*
art, or introduce a new manufacture. They might be en-   *after full enquiry*
couraged to make the attempt if they were allowed special   *into their effects on existing trades,*

[1] Macpherson, *Annals*, II. 165.   [2] *Ib.* II. 198.   [3] S. P. D. CLVI. 43, 44.
[4] Camden, *Elizabeth*, anno 1569 (ed. 1688), p. 124.
[5] *Ib.* anno 1583, p. 285.   [6] *Ib.* anno 1585, p. 325.

A.D 1558
—1603. privileges of manufacture for a limited period[1]. One or two illustrations may be given of the careful enquiry which seems to have preceded the granting of such patents. In 1567, there is a petition from a body of workmen for exclusive rights in the window-glass manufacture for twenty-one years. It seems that, in a conversation with Cecil, it had been represented on behalf of the Crown that some of the Queen's subjects, who had long worked at such business, might be discontented, if this licence were granted; whereupon communications had been opened with the Chidding-

as e.g. in regard to glass, fold glassmakers; they were asked whether they had made or could make the above glasses or no? and they replied that they could not. Finally the patent was granted[2]; the patentees had to bind themselves to teach Englishmen the same science or art of glassmaking, so that at the end of their term it may be perfect and substantially used by Englishmen. Another instructive case, which illustrates the practice in the reign, is mentioned by Stow[3], in regard to

sugar refining, a patent for which Henry Newell and Sir Thomas Mildmay had been suing unsuccessfully, and which was finally refused in 1596[4]; the projectors had desired to have a patent for refining sugar for a term of years, and offered to pay a rent to the Queen. They argued that their undertaking would " cause no Hindrance to her Majesty's customs, no prejudice to any Merchant Adventurer, no Damage to the Grocers of London, no Inconvenience to the Commonwealth although

---

[1] For a list of these patents and a discussion of their legal character compare E. W. Hulme, *The History of the Patent System,* in the *Law Quarterly Review,* xii. 141 and xvi. 44 (April 1896, January 1900).

[2] Hulme, *English Glass Making in the Sixteenth and Seventeenth Centuries,* in *The Antiquary* (1894), xxx. 210.

[3] Stow, *Survey,* Bk. v. p. 244.

[4] In deference in all probability to the strong expression of opinion by the Commons several useful patents were refused at this time (E. W. Hulme, *History of the Patent System,* in *Law Quarterly Review,* xvi. 53). One of these was for the ingenious machine which had been invented by Mr William Lee, of St John's College, Cambridge, who in 1589 constructed a stocking frame, and thus gave rise to a new and important branch of industry. He is said to have been much put out, when paying his addresses to a young lady, by the sedulous interest she gave to her knitting (*Reports, etc.* 1845, xv. 15), and he determined to find a mechanical means for doing such work. The public, and the Queen in particular, regarded his ingenuity as so perverse that he found it impossible to work his machine in England. Under the patronage of Sully he successfully established a business at Rouen, but his Protestantism prevented him from carrying it on

it might be called a Monopoly: but the Lord Treasurer A.D. 1558
—1603. (who would never consent to such things without hearing what could be said by others against it) received Reasons why the Refining of Sugars should not be granted to one, two or three private persons only "; accordingly the patent was not granted. Whatever grievance may have been caused by these patents, to justify the complaints in the session of 1601, there can be no doubt that the government granted them in a discriminating manner, and with a statesmanlike intention to introduce new industries without displacing the old; they did in many cases affect articles of common consumption, because these were the very things of which it was best worth while to plant a native manufacture. The manu- *salt* facture of salt[1], a trade for which England was well adapted, was naturalised at this time. Some salt was obtained from Droitwich[2], a great deal had been imported, and treasure was conveyed to foreign parts to pay for it. We find Cecil writing in 1563 to Gaspar Seelar[3], a German, saying that he has obtained for him the Queen's licence to manufacture common salt in England, and advising him to come over directly. In 1565 a grant was made to Francis Berty[4], a stranger born, but this was subsequently surrendered to the Earl of Pembroke and others, who for twenty years had the sole right to use a new process in the manufacture of white salt and bay salt. This patent was perfectly satisfactory according to modern ideas, for it did not interfere with the existing arts, and the new process was not protected against foreign importers; it simply was assigned to the inventor and certain capitalists who might make the most of it[5]. On

---

without disturbance. Before his death more successful efforts were made to work his invention in Nottinghamshire, but he died, like most of his race, a disappointed man. The manual art was only introduced about 1564. Hasted, *History of Kent*, I. 420 n.

[1] We have several projects for undertaking the manufacture, S. P. D. El. xxviii. 5 (Mar. 1563); xxxvi. 93, 94 (1565); xliii. 1 (1567); lxxxiii. 12, 13 (1571); but in 1589 the Queen refuses to grant the privilege to the Germans for the making of salt as many of her subjects make salt of salt water (S. P. D. El. ccxxiv. 50).

[2] Harrison, in Holinshed (1807), I. 403.

[3] S. P. D. El. xxviii. 5; also for indenture see S. P. D. El. xxxiii. 5.

[4] This grant is corrected in Cecil's hand.

[5] 8 El. c. 22. On later patents for salt, see below, pp. 289, 309.

A.D. 1558
—1603.
and starch.
the other hand Sir John Pakington's patent for the manufacture of starch[1] brought him into serious conflict with the
Grocers in 1595; they had recently introduced this article
from abroad and had a large sale for it, and the patentee
and his assigns claimed a right to seize and destroy all
foreign starch.

The plant-
ing of new
industries
was under-
taken by
capitalists,
some of
whom were
English-
men,
The study of these patents has brought into prominence
the very interesting facts, that the planting of new industries
was a capitalist undertaking, organised by moneyed men[2], who
were prepared to wait some years for the full return on their
outlay, and also that many of those who took advantage of
the encouragement were not aliens, but Englishmen. This
is good evidence of progress in the formation of capital and
in skill to employ it; but at the same time there was something unsatisfactory in the manner in which protection
was afforded to native enterprise. The practice of granting
letters to protect aliens was unduly extended, when it was
used to confer exclusive privileges on certain selected Englishmen[3]. As long as the patent was given to a man, alien or
English, who brought in a new process or introduced a new
branch of industry, there is no reason to award anything
but praise for the ingenuity of the minister who could get
valuable trades started at practically no expense to the Crown.
Such was the patent to make white soap granted to Stephen
Groyett; this was to be void on proof of defective manufacture; the patent to Cockeram and Barnes to make saltpetre;
to George Cobham for a dredging machine, the licence to
Gylpin to make ovens; all of which were to be void if they
proved extortionate in their charges. Elizabeth aimed at
introducing the manufactures of alum, glass, soap, oils, salt,
saltpetre, and latten, which had hitherto been imported.
Novelty was the test for the patent. The patents became
oppressive when the trade in certain articles was given over
to a grantee, and all Cecil's care[4] did not suffice to prevent
the occurrence of serious abuses.

---

[1] Stow, *Survey*, Vol. II. Bk. v. p. 177. Hulme, *History of Patent System*, in
Law Quarterly Review, XVI. p. 49.

[2] Vol. I. p. 525.

[3] E. W. Hulme, *op. cit.*, *Law Quarterly Review*, XII. 144, and XVI. 54.

[4] In the case of Drake's patent for vinegar, Cecil intervened and insisted on

Though the political conditions of Europe were in many ways prejudicial to English commerce, they were extraordinarily favourable to Cecil's plans for the development of industry, since there was a steady flow of highly-skilled Protestant refugees to this country.   There had been an intermittent immigration of weavers, and others, since the time of the Norman Conquest; they were attracted, especially in the reign of Edward III., by the economic facilities which were offered in a well-governed and little-developed country; but, owing to the religious differences and persecutions in their native districts, a greatly-increased immigration occurred in the time of Edward VI.   A colony of Walloon weavers was settled by Somerset[1] at Glastonbury; and a German-speaking congregation was organised at Austin Friars in London.   In the reign of Queen Mary, many of these strangers were forced to return to the continent[2], but at the accession of Elizabeth they flocked to England in increased numbers.   They were exactly the class of men whom Cecil was trying to attract[3] through the agency of capitalist patentees, but their advent in such large bodies raised many difficult questions.   There was, of course, a certain amount of local jealousy, on the part of craftsmen who feared the competition of more skilled workmen.   This seems to have led to temporary difficulties at Norwich, and in some of the Essex towns.   But the real problem, so far as the refugees were concerned, lay deeper; Elizabeth and her advisers were trying to reduce the realm to order by the creation of an elaborate ecclesiastical industrial and eleemosynary system; in so far as the immigrants were

A.D. 1558 —1603.

and the political conditions of the time favoured the immigration of skilled artisans

of whom many were religious refugees.

These men could not be easily absorbed either

in the ecclesiastical, eleemosynary, or industrial system of England,

the insertion of a new clause after the grant was fully passed. Hulme, *op. cit.* in *Law Quarterly Review,* XVI. 50.

[1] Cecil was also their patron, especially after Somerset's fall. Strype, *Memorials of Cranmer,* Bk. II. Ch. XXIII. pp. 346 f.

[2] Apart altogether from the new danger of religious persecution to which they were exposed, there would be difficulty in the way of their remaining in England. Philip strongly objected to the loss of so many subjects; at a later time the strangers in London were deliberately planted out in different parts of the country, so that their numbers might be less likely to attract the attention of the Spanish Ambassador, and rouse his remonstrance. Cunningham, *Alien Immigrants,* 155.

[3] His intention was that they should instruct English apprentices in the practice of new arts (S. P. D. El. XLIII. 29).

A.D. 1558
1603.
willing and able to become denizens[1], they would of course have to adapt themselves to English institutions, but how were outsiders to be treated? They had suffered much for their own religious convictions, and they were not willing lightly to accept the Anglican system; many of them were in great poverty, but they had no claims to relief from the rates: they were highly skilled workmen, but they were unaffected by the restrictions imposed by the Statute of Artificers. It was not easy to arrange matters, so that they should be kindly welcomed, without at the same time giving them unfair advantages over native-born subjects and increasing the difficulty of executing wholesome laws.

so that there was considerable difficulty about their status
The eleemosynary difficulty was merely temporary, as the strangers were soon able to set an example by their generosity in providing for their own poor; the religious question only arose at certain centres, such as Canterbury, Norwich and London, where the aliens were gathered in considerable congregations; but the industrial question was raised in many places and in connection with many trades. The policy of the realm, since the time of Richard III., had been one of insisting that immigrant aliens should not keep their arts to themselves, but should instruct Englishmen. They had been forbidden to take alien apprentices, other than their own children, or to employ more than two alien journeymen, or to keep their trade secrets from Englishmen[2].

and supervision
The Cordwainers, Weavers, and other city companies, made vigorous efforts, in 1562, to exercise a supervision over the aliens, who were flocking to London and its suburbs. The disputes that arose were sometimes complicated by questions of jurisdiction, for many of the immigrants had settled in the region between London and Westminster, where they were not under any effective municipal control, either as to the conditions on which they did their work, or the quality

in the towns where they settled,
of the goods they exposed for sale. There is a long series of complaints, on this latter point, from different bodies in London; and various expedients were devised to meet the difficulty. In Norwich, the settlers were frankly treated as

---

[1] Somerset's settlers at Glastonbury became denizens.
[2] Cunningham, *Alien Immigrants*, 165.

aliens; they were only allowed to sell wholesale and not by A.D. 1558
—1603. retail; and some attempt seems to have been made to appoint hosts with whom they should dwell. Letters patent were granted in 1576 to Mr William Tipper for hosting strangers in London[1] and elsewhere; and some years later Mr Edward Dymock, and again Sir Thomas Mildmay, offered to supervise all the strangers in England. The tragedies of Evil May Day had been re-enacted in 1586, and there were very general complaints of the aliens, especially of their engaging in retail trade; a roll was to be kept of them, with full details of their names, families, time of residence and so forth. But the government were not inclined to impose any unnecessary restrictions[2]; the fresh trade, which the immigrants brought to such towns as Norwich, tended to remove much of the jealousy that had been felt of them; and they were doubtless gradually absorbed into the ordinary life of many towns. But this result was only gradually attained; in 1615, the London companies started a vigorous agitation[3] against strangers; and it seems possible that the reconstruction of industrial companies[4], in such towns as Hull, where it apparently occurred about 1598, was partly connected with the desire to exercise a more complete super vision over aliens, or even to exclude them altogether. The revived life of these companies lasted during the whole of the seventeenth century; they apparently sunk into unimportance, not so much through actual changes in trade—for they were already capitalist in character—as through the growth of public sentiment in favour of the general naturalisation of foreign Protestants.

---

[1] S.P.D. El. cviii. 19, cxiv. 47; also cxxx. 25. Compare Moens, *The Walloons and their Church at Norwich*, 39.

[2] An act for the maintenance of English craftsmen, which proposed to insist on foreigners undergoing a seven years' apprenticeship was drafted in 1592, but seems to have made no progress. *Hist. MSS. Comm.* iii. Ap. 6, 7. Also ix. Ap. 306 (e), 316 (k), (l), (o).

[3] On the activity of the City Companies in London see W. D. Cooper, *Lists of Foreign Protestants and Aliens*, Camden Society, p. viii. For other complaints see *Hist. MSS. Comm.* iii. Ap. 71; also the petition of artificers in 1641 as to the unfair competition and insanitary habits of the strangers. *Ib.* iv. Ap. 97.

[4] See above, p. 35.

C.   6

A.D. 1558
—1603.

*and in
some places
they
formed
separate
colonies.*

In several cases, a definite colony of aliens was planted within the limits of the town; and special agreements[1] were drawn up between the strangers and the townsmen as to police and trading regulation. This occurred both at Canterbury[2] and Norwich[3]. In the former town the strangers secured a number of privileges which must have rendered them unpopular with their neighbours. Not only did they obtain freedom to practise their worship, and rights for the supervision of their industry, but they were allowed to have bakers and carriers of their own.

*The immi-
gration of
labour
brought
about a
great
develop-
ment of
new
branches
of the
cloth
manufac-
ture,*

The industrial arts, which were introduced or improved by this incursion of aliens, are very numerous. They attempted to introduce the linen manufacture[4], but for some reason this has never been acclimatised in England. Their chief work was in connection with new branches of the staple industry of the country, and the manufacture of worsted, serges and bays developed very rapidly. An export trade soon sprang up, and the new drapery appears to have been to some extent preferred to the old in the home market[5]; the manufacture was widely diffused. Its beginning can be traced to the immigration of 406 persons, who were driven out of Flanders in 1561; some of them were settled at Sandwich and Canterbury, and thirty families were established at Norwich, a town which was still suffering from the consequences of Kett's rebellion. The most important centre of the manufacture however was at Colchester, where eleven households arrived in 1570. About fifty of those who had fled from Flanders to Sandwich, had come

---

[1] These were often submitted to Cecil, and the details of planting the aliens were supervised by him, S. P. D. El. XLIII. 28 (July 21, 1567); also XLII. 71.

[2] F. W. Cross, *History of the Walloon and Huguenot Church at Canterbury*, 28. See also Overend, *Strangers at Dover* in *Huguenot Society Proceedings*, III. 111.

[3] Moens, *The Walloons*, 18.

[4] The colony, which Cecil planted at Stamford, tried to establish linen weaving among other trades (S. P. D. El. XLIII. 11). They do not seem to have done anything for the manufacture of sailcloth, an industry in which Burleigh was most keenly interested, from its bearing on the maritime resources of the realm; he brought pressure to bear on the townsmen of Stamford to undertake it (S.P.D. El. XVII. 48, 49; XVIII. 22), but the experiment does not appear to have met with success, and it was left for a later generation of religious refugees to introduce it afresh.

[5] Stow, *Survey*, v. 298. The aliens are said to have introduced "foreign fashions and inventions to the ruin of honest English Handicrafts Tradesmen whose Manufactures thereby become a Drug."

on, hoping to obtain leave to reside and ply their trades at A.D. 1558
—1603. Colchester, and others were anxious to follow. They wished to make needles and parchment, and weave sackcloth and fine cloths, known as bays. None of these arts were commonly practised in the town at the time; and the bailiffs, who did not like to act on their own responsibility, wrote to the Lords of the Privy Council asking that the strangers should be allowed to remain and settle. The Council, who were engaged in allotting the immigrants to different towns, were much pleased at the manner in which the Colchester people had received the new-comers. The burgesses were to protect them, in the exercise of their crafts, as long as they conducted themselves well, and to give them facilities for buying and selling[1]. The Flemish colony appears to have flourished on the whole; though the English weavers were somewhat jealous of them, and complained that they assembled as a Company in their Hall, and made ordinances in an illegal fashion[2]. But James I. continued their privileges, and they were protected both in the exercise and regulation of their trade[3].

It is highly probable that another staple English trade *and the introduction or improvement* was introduced by these immigrants. The cotton manufacture[4] had been a flourishing industry at Antwerp—a port where the necessary materials[5] were easily procurable from Egypt; its first beginnings in England are very obscure[6], but it had begun to attract attention as an important trade in the rising town of Manchester in the earlier part of the seventeenth century. The beginnings of the manufacture in Lancashire appear to follow very closely on its decline at Antwerp, and there is at least a considerable probability in ascribing the development of this highly-skilled textile art to the immigration of refugees.

---

[1] Morant, *Essex*, I. 75.

[2] See above, Vol. I. p. 454.

[3] Morant, *Essex*, I. 77.

[4] The fustian manufacture had been carried on with great success in Ulm in the fifteenth century, but declined during the sixteenth. Nübling, *Ulms Baumwollweberei im Mittelalter*, 141, 158, in Schmoller's *Forschungen* IX.

[5] Cotton was probably only used as the woof on a linen warp.

[6] The Manchester cottons referred to in 1558 appear to have been woollen goods (4 and 5 P. and M. c. 5, §§ 11 and 13). There is another mention of the trade in a list of exports in 1595. S. P. D. El. CCLII. 56; Brit. Mus. *Lansdowne MSS.*, c. 25; see also S. P. D. El. CCLXIX. 45 and Strype's *Stow*, v. 297.

There are similar reasons for ascribing the rise of Birmingham, as an industrial centre, to these refugees; in
Leland's time, some iron-working appears to have been
carried on there; but the brass manufacture, for which it has
of glass-
manu-
facture,
since been especially celebrated, is not mentioned. It is
surely significant that this trade, along with glass-manu-
cutlery,
facture and engraving[1], the making of needles and of cutlery,
should be arts for which we are by common tradition indebted to the refugees. The development of such trades
at one centre, within a century of the great migration, is
highly suggestive of their probable origin.

Attempts had been made in previous reigns to introduce
paper-
making
paper-making[2], but from this time onwards the art seems to
have been completely established; thread-making was begun
at Maidstone[3], and silk-weaving at Canterbury. More widely
and other
trades.
diffused was the art of lace-making, which found a home in
the region round Honiton, in Bedfordshire and in Bucking-
hamshire; while potteries appear to have been started in
the neighbourhood of London, and in other districts as well.
We have no means of measuring the industrial progress that
was made between the beginning and the close of the sixteenth century, but there is every reason to believe that it
was incomparably greater than that of any previous period.
It is not a little remarkable that a reign, which was distinguished by the passing of a stringent measure of regulation, should also have been marked by rapid improvement
in the industrial arts. The new impulse was chiefly due to
that immigration of refugees which Cecil encouraged; he
warmly sympathised with them on religious and political
grounds. He was opposed even to the enforcement of laws,
which might render strangers less ready to frequent England
temporarily, and he was keenly alive to the economic advantages which would accrue from their settling in England[4].

---

[1] Cunningham, *Alien Immigrants*, 177.

[2] *Ib.* 127 (note).

[3] Hasted, *History of Kent*, II. 109. Pennant ascribes an improvement in
gardening to those who settled in Kent, *Journey*, I. 104.

[4] Stow, *Survey*, Bk. v. 303.

IV. THE LANDED INTEREST.

173. Three distinct objects have been prominently kept *A.D. 1558 —1603.* in view by the English government, at different times, in making regulations for the trade in corn. Until the latter *In regulating the* part of the fourteenth century, attention was given almost *corn trade* exclusively to the interest of the consumers[1]; and their *government have had* needs were not forgotten in the sixteenth century. Cheap *three distinct* food was advantageous to the artificers who were manu- *objects in* facturing for foreign markets; it might attract immigrants *view—the interest of* to settle in this country, and it certainly was beneficial to *the consumer,* the poor. There were times, however, when it became clear that the interest of the producer must not be disregarded, *of the producer,* or tillage would decline, and the food supply would be permanently reduced; this side of the matter was brought into light by the progress of sheep-farming, at the expense of tillage, in the century which succeeded the Black Death[2]. The legislature realised the danger; and in 1399, and 1426, and 1437[3], Statutes were passed, which gave a measure of freedom for the export of corn, and thus enabled the farmer to count on getting a better price, especially in years of plenty; while, in 1463, there was a restriction on import[4], which gave him advantages in the home market. The corn trade could also be considered as a source of revenue[5], with- *and of the revenue.* out any special thought for the interest either of the consumer or the producer. During part of the fifteenth century, and under Henry VII. and VIII., export was restricted; and after 1515 the issuing of licences to export corn, despite the prohibition, proved to be a considerable source of royal income and was not unpopular. According to changes of circumstance, of which no record may now remain, one or other of these three objects might become specially promi-

[1] W. Naudé, *Die Getreidehandelspolitik der europäischen Staaten*, 70.

[2] There is a very marked change of public opinion as expressed in Parliament between the years 1376 and 1393. Compare *Rotuli Parliamentorum*, II. p. 350, No. 156; III. p. 141, No. 54, with *Rot. Parl.* III. p. 320, No. 39.

[3] 17 R. II. c. 7, 4 H. VI. c. 5, 15 H. VI. c. 2.   [4] 3 Ed. IV. c. 2.

[5] R. Faber, *Die Entstehung des Agrarschutzes in England*, 57, in Knapp and Brentano, *Abhandlungen aus den Staatswissen. Seminar zu Strassburg*, v.

nent at any particular date; and there is in consequence very great difficulty in finding a clue, which renders the policy of any given reign completely intelligible.

No rules could be rigidly enforced,

There is another element of confusion; there were doubtless great dissimilarities between the agricultural conditions in one part of the country, and those which obtained in another neighbourhood. It is obvious that a rainy season, which did comparatively little harm in some districts, might cause disastrous floods along the course of the rivers[1]; or that a drought might be much more serious in one county

as there were great differences in local conditions and opportunities,

than in another. Apart from such variations, however, there was a marked difference between the districts which had easy access to outside markets, and those which were chiefly concerned in supplying the requirements of the resident population. The wants of the people of London[2] created a constant demand for corn from the southern and south-eastern counties; while the same districts were able, in times of plenty, to take advantage of their seaboard and export corn to Calais, to Flanders, and other less fertile districts[3]. The laws regulating the export of corn are general in form, and would have had, in all probability, but little effect, if it had not been for the frequent action of the

which received attention from the Commissioners of grain and victuals.

Commissioners for Restraint of Grain and Victuals; they were a most active body[4], who were at constant pains to inform themselves as to the stocks of corn, and avert the risk of famine, either generally or in particular localities[5]. As regards the Tudor Kings, it seems impossible to detect

---

[1] See below, p. 112.

[2] Much evidence in regard to this trade may be drawn from the records of the Privy Council intervention to regulate it. *Acts of the Privy Council*, VIII. pp. 135, 139, 140 (1573), also pp. 173, 299 (1574); Vol. x. pp. 288, 299 (1576).

[3] There seems to have been occasional export from the northern counties to Scotland. *Rot. Parl.* II. p. 287, No. 22 (A.D. 1364); also *Acts of Privy Council*, XIII. p. 34 (1581). The extraordinary wealth of the hundreds of Norfolk adjoining the Wash is difficult to account for as due either to fishing or to the cloth manufacture. It may possibly have been brought about by the fertility of the country and the facilities for the export of cereals, especially barley. Compare Vol. I. p. 507, n. 3. Corn was also exported from the Severn valley, but its destination is not specified. 34 and 35 Henry VIII. c. 9.

[4] *Acts of the Privy Council*, Vol. VIII., p. 210 (1576), and Vol. x., p. 220 (1578); also *passim* in preceding and succeeding years, see Index *s.v. Restraint*.

[5] In 1579 exportation was allowed in Devon (*Acts of Privy Council*, XI. 186, 192, 282), and restrained in Northampton (*ib.* 614).

any settled policy about the food supply of the realm; they A.D. 1558 —1603.
appear to have used their power of granting licences for
export, merely as a means of raising revenue and without
much consideration as to the effect on tillage.   Under
Queen Mary, permission was indeed given to export corn,
but only when the price of wheat was not more than 6s. 8d.
the quarter; as it rarely fell so low, there was little opportunity of taking advantage of the permission[1].   The policy
of legislating in the interest of the agricultural producer *Protection*
was not definitely adopted till the reign of Elizabeth; *for the producer is*
this had been the scheme recommended by John Hales[2], *the main object of*
and though it was not maintained with any persistence, the *Eliza-bethan*
policy was viewed with increasing favour; experience at last *policy;*
confirmed the wisdom of his suggestions[3].   We may also
notice that the Elizabethan legislation, on this subject, is
distinguished by one particular feature from that of previous
reigns; the fostering of agriculture is consciously associated *it was con-*
with the improvement of the mercantile marine.   At first *nected with a desire to*
sight, there seems to be little relation between the two; but *foster maritime*
if corn were grown in larger quantities for export, there *trade,*
would be another native commodity available for the employing of English ships, and it might be possible to compete
with the men of Zeeland and Amsterdam in the profitable
trade they carried on, by supplying the Mediterranean lands
and Iberian Peninsula with Baltic corn[4].   The clause, which
permits the export of grain at any port approved by the
Council, when the price of wheat does not exceed 10s., occurs

[1] 1 and 2 P. and M. c. 5. The specified price of wheat is the same as in the
statute of 15 Henry VI. c. 2, viz. that wheat may not be exported when it exceeds
6s. 8d. the quarter, but there had been a general rise of prices since that date,
and the average rates for some years after 1554 ranged over 17s. Rogers, *Agriculture and Prices*, IV. 290.

[2] *Discourse of Common Weal*, ed. Lamond, p. 53. The Doctor proposes "To
make the proffitt of the plow to be as good, rate for rate, as the proffit of the
grasiers and sheep-masters."

[3] Graswinckel writing in 1651 shows that the English policy of his day was not
very favourable to the producer in practice. *Die staatswissenschaftlichen An-
schauungen Dirck Graswinckels*, by G. Liesker, p. 66.

[4] The Baltic corn trade had been very important as the mainstay of the
prosperity of Dantzig and other Hanse towns; and it continued throughout the
seventeenth and eighteenth centuries to be the foundation of the maritime greatness of the United Provinces. Naudé, *op. cit.* 305, 333, 334.

in an "Act touching certain politic constitutions for the maintenance of the Navy[1]." In 1571 the restrictions were still further modified, with a view to the "better encrease of Tyllage and for the mainteinance and encrease of the Navye and Mariners of this Realme[2]." No definite figure at which export should cease was now specified; but the justices of

but export was frequently subject to restraint by the justices in the interest of consumers,
the peace, and higher authorities, were to be responsible for prohibiting shipments, when prices were not reasonable and moderate. Full power was reserved for the administration to deal with the matter, from time to time, and the Records of the Privy Council show how careful they were to supervise the action of the local authorities, and if necessary, to set them in motion. There must have been constant variations in the condition of the trade; as any prohibition, temporarily made, was allowed to cease if the justices of the peace found that it had become "hurtfull to the County by meanes of Dearth, or to be a greate Hyndraunce to Tyllage by meanes of to much cheapnes." Within a few months of the passing of the Act, it was necessary to take action; the prices of 1572 ranged high, and the crop seemed so short that the Queen issued a proclamation on the 16th of September; it alludes to the "sodayne increase of the pryces of grayne, for the more part universally in the Realme, as it is to be coniectured, partlye by the unseasonablenesse of the late harvest tyme, and partlye by reason of excessive transportation of grayne out of the Realme, into the partics beyonde the seas, whereby, yf stay be not speedily made for anye further transportation, there may follow a great dearth[3]"; and in con-

[1] 5 El. c. 5 § 26; 6s. 8d. had been the previous limit.

[2] 13 El. c. 13. There are recurring complaints of the decay of husbandry. See the Proclamation 1st March 1569 (Dyson, 113), "And forasmuch as her Maiestie is geven to understande, that notwithstandyng the saide good and profitable statutes and lawes, diuers and sundry of her subiectes in many shires of this realme, upon a greedy and covetous minde, not havyng regarde to obey the sayde lawes, have and do dayly decay Townes and houses of husbandrye, and inclose their groundes, and conuert the same from tyllage into pasture, and kepe not such hospitalitie as by the saide lawes they ought to do, to the great displeasure of almightie God, the provocation of idlenesse and destruction of her Maiesties people, wherby her realme is in some part weakened and more is like, if speedy reformation be not had therein."

[3] Dyson, 146, *A proclamation for restraint of transportation of grayne beyonde the seas.* These proclamations do not appear to have attracted the attention of Dr Faber as they are not mentioned in his admirable monograph.

sequence, export was prohibited till the end of October, A.D. 1558
when it might be possible to judge what the effect of this —1603.
restriction had been upon prices[1]. Special provision was
made for the continuance of the coasting trade; though care
was to be taken that there should be no export to foreign
parts, under the pretence of taking grain to another English
town. There is, however, less evidence of interference with
export, in the interests of the home consumer, than we
might have expected to find; but in the latter part of the *and during*
reign, precautions were taken, again and again, to prevent *several years care*
the shipment of corn or other victuals to the dominions of *was taken to prevent*
the King of Spain. The principle, that corn was not to be *export to Spain*
exported to the enemies of the realm, had been recognised
from time immemorial[2], but it had been insufficiently attended to; and there was reason to believe that the Spanish
forces, collected for the invasion of England, had been partly
victualled with English corn[3]. Elizabeth and her advisers
fully recognised the advantages they possessed, in the great
contest, from the deficiency of Spanish supplies of cereals.
The situation is admirably reviewed in a proclamation
which was issued in 1591 *straightly commanding that no*
Corne nor other Victuall nor any Ordonance nor furniture
for shipping be caried into any of the king of Spaines
countries[4]. " For this purpose, considering that our Realmes
and dominions are plentifully blessed by Gods singular
favour, with the plentie of Corne and all other Victuall, and
with furniture of sundrie kindes of munition, meete for the

---

[1] According to Thorold Rogers' averages, the price of wheat rose from 13s. 6¾d.
in 1572 to 26s. 3¾d. in 1573. See IV. p. 290.

[2] *Rot. Parl.* III. 320, No. 39, 1393—1394 A.D.

[3] Dyson, 267, " *A Proclamation for the restraint of transportation of graine,*
Nov. 1588, "Whereas the Queenes Maiestie is giuen to understand, that divers
of her subiects of this Realme, under the colour and pretence of carying of
Corne to certaine partes of Fraunce, being in good amitie with this Crowne:
(but neere to the partes of Spaine) have caused the said Corne to be transported
and caried by colourable means into Spaine, and there vented and sold the same,
whereof a great part was this last yeere past imploied in the victualling of the
late Armie and Fleete set foorth to the seas by the King of Spaine, for the
Invasion of this Realme, and directly against her highnesse person and crowne."
The export of corn is wholly forbidden.

[4] Dyson, 296. Compare the proclamation of 1597, Dyson, 351. See also below
p. 237.

A.D. 1558
—1603.

sustentation and defence of our owne people against all
Forreine enemies, and also for maintenance and furniture
of our Armies both by Sea and Land, which we are constrained to prepare and hold against his violence. And that
it is most manifest that the sayd king, though he have
abundance of treasure by his Indian Mines, yet he hath in
his owne Countrey great wants of such kinds of Victuall,
specially of Corne and munition for the warre . . . . as
whereof our dominions have by Gods goodnesse, plentie; for
the recoverie whereof, he is forced to expend great treasures
to get Corne." No corn is to be exported to Spain, and
none exported to any country without licence. "And because it hath pleased almightie God, to graunt this yeere to
our countrey such plentie of Corne, as it is likely that divers
of our people neere the Sea coasts shall be desirous to have
cause to vent some parte of that which they shall haue of
their owne growth, for lacke of sale within our realme: For
remedie thereof, we doe first aduise, and earnestly require,
the principall persons of wealth, both in Townes corporate
and other places (in such a time as this is, so needefull to
restraine caryage of graine to our enemies, or out of our
Realme, whereby our enemies may be relieved) to buy in
the markets of the countries neere the Sea-coast, such
quantitie of graine as the owners cannot forbeare, but
shall be constrayned to sell for their necessitie: And the
same to keepe in store to serue the markets in the latter
ende of the yeere, before the comming of new Corne to use.

"And if by such good meanes (which we desire greatly to
be used) the necessitie of them that shall be constrained to
sell their graine cannot be satisfied without such venting
out of our Realme, upon certificate to be made to our
Counsell, from those which shall have commission, as hath
bene accustomed, to restrayne the carying of Corne out of
the Realme, of such necessitie to have the same vented out
of the Realme . . . . that such as be the proper owners of
such Corne, and not Marchants, shall passe by sea with such
quantitie onely as shall manifestly appeare, may be spared
to be transported in English shippes into the Countreys,
with whome we are in good amitie and not into any other,

so as to
cripple
that
power,

with as
little incon-
venience as
possible to
English-
men.

with such bonds and conditions as the enemie may not be A.D. 1558
—1603. relieued thereby."

The Proclamation is specially interesting not merely *The agrarian policy was proving successful.* from the fact that the government realised the valuable asset England had in her corn as compared with Spain, but also as showing that the Elizabethan agrarian policy was proving successful, and that corn was fairly plentiful. Subject to the occasional restrictions, in time of dearth, and owing to political exigencies, the policy of permitting export, so long as the price within the country was moderate, was persisted in throughout the reign[1]. There can be little doubt that it gave a considerable stimulus to tillage[2]; though it is also true that English agriculture was not sufficiently developed to afford a surplus for exportation[3] in any but exceptional seasons[4], and that the occasions of importing corn for home consumption were not infrequent[5].

It is far more difficult to appreciate the merits of the *Specially licensed bodgers* regulations which affected the internal trade in corn. The necessity of permitting a certain amount of trade was ob-

---

[1] The price of 20s. was fixed as a limit at which restraint should begin by 35 El. c. 7, § 33.   [2] See below, p. 98.

[3] In times of scarcity there was a danger of tumultuous assemblies to oppose the transportation of corn, as in 1629. *Hist. MSS. Comm.* I. Ap. 57.

[4] The home demand and price appear to have been increasing, apart from the facilities for export. Complaints of the increase of population, which is ascribed to the infrequency of war, the decrease of continental employment, the cessation of pestilence, the marriage of the clergy and access of strangers, will be found in an interesting paper, Abstract of a discourse on *The radicall cause of sondry offences that are happened withyn our state*, dated January, 1581, in Brit. Mus. *Lansdowne MSS.* CXXI. 17.

[5] For a full recognition of this occasional dependence see the proclamation of 20 Jan. 1565, Dyson, *op. cit.*, 92. The Queen "havyng sundry earnest requestes" made to her "by dyvers of townes belongyng to the kyng of Spayne her hyghnes good brother in the Lowe Countreys, to have licence for buying and carying out of certayne quantitie of Wheate, and other grayne for theyr necessitie: Her Maieste thought best neyther fully to graunt not flatly to denye the same, untyll it myght be fyrst understande howe the same might be done without hurt to her owne Countrey." Enquiry was accordingly instituted, the Queen "meanyng if it should appeare, that a convenient quantitie myght be provyded at reasonable pryses and without enhaunsyng of pryses or other damage to the Realme, then her Maiestie woulde gratifie her neyghbours therewith, in lyke sort as this her Realme hath been oftentymes of late yeres, from the other partes beyond the seas, in tyme of scarcitie here." Also in regard to an importation of Dantzig rye into Portsmouth (1577), *Acts of the Privy Council*, IX. p. 286. For later instances see Naudé, *op. cit.* 89.

A.D. 1558
—1603.

were allowed to carry on an internal trade;

but this was constantly watched, in the interest of poor consumers

vious; and an endeavour was made to control and restrict it, by insisting that none should engage in buying up corn unless they were licensed by the justices of the peace[1]. The "inordinate" granting of licences, out of "special or partial favour" in every shire[2], led to a development of the trade, however; and complaint arose that the dealers, who bought up corn for export, were denuding the country of food. Steps had to be taken to protect the local consumer, and especially the poor consumer, from engrossers. In some counties, the dealers were not allowed to come into the market till a second bell had rung, so that the poor might have the first chance of purchasing the small quantities they required[3]. The orders issued by the Privy Council appear to have been devised in the interest of the poor consumer[4], and to have been aimed at the capitalist farmers and the dealers in corn. Indirectly, however, a farther purpose was served; as by restricting the operations of these traders, a check was put on the export[5] of grain in times of dearth. The scarcity orders, issued by the Privy Council, seem to have been fairly[6] successful in giving the poor full advantage of an existing stock of grain; but they would tend to reduce the regular profit of corn-growing, and they lay down principles of equity and fair dealing, which were hardly consistent with the continued prosperity of agriculturists[7]. A proclamation in 1586 threatens to re-inforce the Statute of 1534, which must have fallen into disuse; this measure had given powers for settling the price of victuals by authority; and the government, when they contemplated the necessity of reviving it, denounced the uncharitable covetousness of the great cornmasters, who apparently were holding stocks of

---

[1] 5 El. c. 12, § 7.

[2] C. Cox, *Three Centuries of Derbyshire Annals*, II. 186.

[3] For Derbyshire see Cox, *op. cit.* II. 191; for Devonshire, Hamilton, *Quarter Sessions Records*, p. 103.

[4] Compare Mr E. Green's paper *On the Poor and some attempts to lower the price of Corn*, in *Proceedings of Bath Nat. Hist. Club*, IV. 6.

[5] The proclamation of 2 Jan. 1586 refers to a general dearth in many lands, but is content to enforce stricter measures against engrossers and bodgers. Dyson, *op. cit.* p. 241.

[6] Leonard, *op. cit.* 319.

[7] *Ib.* 193.

corn in hopes of a further rise of price, and to the pinching A.D. 1558 of the poorer sort[1].   A later Proclamation insists that, $-1603.$ though the season had been bad, that fact did not justify *in bad years* men, who had old corn, in asking a higher price for it[2]. From the standpoint of the Privy Council, the profit of

[1] Dyson, *op. cit.* 241. "Yet it is manifestly knowen the sayd Dearth to have bene wilfully encreased in very many places of this Realme, not onely by and through the covetousnesse of many engrossers of Corne and Cornemasters, but also by unlawful transportation of Grayne, and lacke also of preservation of store in time requisite. Her Highnes acknowledging this maner of Gods mercy and favour in a more favourable measure towards her Countrey and people, then to other forrein partes neere adioyning, hath thought good and necessary, for a further remedie against the uncharitable covetousnesse of the Cornemasters, as cause shall require, to notifie, that if such as be the great Cornemasters and owners of Grayne, or of other necessarie victual for foode of the poore, shall not be willing, or doe not performe these orders, whereby the poorer sort may be relieued in the markets at reasonable prices, or that it shall appeare that other needefull victuals shall by covetousnesse of any persons growe to excessive prices, to the pinching of the poorer sort: Then her Highnesse doth hereby signifie, that she wil not onely severely punish the offendors for their cruel covetousnes and offences against her orders, but will also for redresse of the excessive prices of other needefull victuals, give order that reasonable prices shall be set both on Corne and other victuals to be solde for the reliefe of her Maiesties poore Subiects, according both to her Prerogative Royal and to the order of Justice as by speciall lawe of Parliament thereof made in the five and twentieth yeere of the raigne of her late Noble and deare Father King Henry the eight, is specially in such cases provided." 2nd January, 1586.

[2] July 31, 1596. Dyson, *op. cit.* 338, *A proclamation for the dearth of Corne.* " The Queens Maiestie hearing by report out of sundry Countries in the Realme, of the unreasonable encrease of prices of Graine, to the Griefe of her poorer sort of people that have no living by Tillage: And though the sellers of Corne, as rich Farmers and Ingrossers, do pretend to raise the prices by colour of the unseasonableness of this Sommer: yet that being no just cause to raise the prices of their olde Corne of the last yeeres growth, but that the farmers and Ingrossers of Corne, of meere covetousnesse have very lately, even within two moneths, most uncharitably haunced up their prices, not tollerable to be suffered. For remedie whereof, to the reliefe of the great multitude of her poore loving Subiects, lacking Corne for their foode, and also for reformation of many other abuses committed by such covetous and uncharitable persons, being voide of all naturall compassion towards their neighbours: Her Maiestie calling to her remembrance the good orders by her Maiesties commaundement published the last yeere....the good observation whereof would remedie these disorders of the yll and wealthy sort, and to the reliefe of the good and needie" gives the following orders: the Justices are to assemble and "diligently to peruse the said orders" published in 1595, "and diligently to consider all such points of those Orders, as may tend to the reformation of all persons that by their disorder and covetousnesse, and breach of the said Orders, are the causers directly or indirectly to encrease the prices of Graine in this lamentable sort beyond reason, and foorthwith to proceede to the execution of all such orders, as may with good reason give remedy to the furniture of Markets, and to abate such unreasonable encrease of prices." The making of starch is also strictly forbidden.

speculation was regarded with something more than suspicion, as it seemed to be mere private gain which accrued
to individuals who did not render any obvious service to
the public[1].

It would hardly have been possible for the government
to attempt to exercise such far-reaching and minute control,
if they had not been able to rely, not only on the justices,
through the but on the Clerks of the Market, who had an independent
Clerks of
the Market, jurisdiction[2], and held courts for the regulation of weights
and measures and the punishment of all market offences.
A very full account of the duties of these officials occurs in
a Proclamation of 1618, for *Reformation of the great abuses*
in Weights and Measures and for the due execution of the
Office of Clerke of the Market of Our Household and through-
out Our Realme of England. "Whereas .... there should
be but one Weight and one Measure throughout the whole
Realme, yet neverthelesse .... there are at this day ....
especially in the Northerne and Westerne parts, and in our
Counties Palatine of Lancaster and Durham and Dominion
of Wales false and deceitful Weights and Measures of different contents one from another, and all disagreeing from
Our Standard, and whereas wee are also informed that many
unconscionable persons haue and doe use severall Weights
and Measures with the greater to buy, and with the lesser
to sell; and doe also use false and deceitfull beames and
ballances to the great losse etc. of our Subiects.

whose duty "And whereas the Clerke of Our Market .... ought to
it was to
set prices, punish and reforme" the said abuses, and to "set reasonable and indifferent Rates and Prises upon Victuals and
other provisions chiefly in times of Our Progresse," and
see that victuals be "wholesome and of good condition,
and whereas complaint hath been made of the great
negligence used in the execution of the said office ....

---

[1] See above, p. 16.

[2] Cox, *op. cit.* II. 196. The duties of the court are clearly brought out in the
articles of the charge to the Warwick jury as given in *The Book of John Fisher*
(1580—1588) (ed. Kemp), p. 141. See 17 C. I. c. 19 in Scobell *Acts* I. 18; also a legal
treatise by W. Sheppard, *Of the office of the clerk of the market* (1665). Under
James I., the collection of fines imposed by the Clerk of the Market was farmed.
Hist. MSS. Comm. III. Ap. 21.

because divers of these have been very careless and remisse A.D. 1558 —1603.
and respecting only their own private gaines .... we have
thought fit to make known what should and ought to be
performed by the Clerke of Our Market and his deputies,
and what fees they may justly require and take, and what
courses they should hold for the better execution of their
service, and what accompt wee expect and have determined
to require at their hands concerning this Service hereafter.
The office of the Clerk of the Market ought to enquire of *regulate weights* all abuses in Weights, Beames, Ballances and Measures and *and* ought also to enquire of all Falsities, deceipts and abuses *measures,* in the Trades of Millers, Bakers, Brewers, Vinteners, Inn-
keepers, Alehouse-keepers, Cookes, Victuallers, Fishmongers,
Butchers, Chandlers, Grocers, Mercers, Clothiers, Cloth-
workers, Weavers, Tailours, Brokers, Tanners, Shoemakers,
Smiths, Glovers, White Tawers, Malsters, Corn Masters,
Colliers, Woodmongers, and generally of all other Artificers,
Tradesmen and other persons whatsoever having or using
Weights or Measures, as well to prevent deceipts and frauds
as to punish the same.

" Also he ought to search and inquire that all victuals and *supervise the quality* other things put to sale by them for the sustenance or use *of products and goods* of mans body and al provisions for their Horses or their *exposed for* Cattel be wholesome and of good qualitie and that their *sale,* manufactures be well and workemanlike made and wrought
and that they sell at and for reasonable and moderate gaines
and not at unreasonable and excessive prices.

" And further that he ought especially to inquire of, and *and punish* punish all Forestallers, Ingrossers and Regrators who by *offences in* their inordinate desire of gaine do inhaunce the prices of all *connection with* things vendible." The Proclamation goes on to give instructions as to the times and places at which the Clerk of the
Market should hold his court, and make his enquiry by the
" oaths of twelve men at the least to be impanelled " by him.
It also insists that he should receive constant assistance from
the Justices in the Counties and the constables in every
parish. There was more difficulty in the towns, since it
was reported that the greatest deceits were committed by
the chief officers—" men who ought to reform themselves
and others within their Jurisdiction." Special care was to

A.D. 1558
—1603.
be taken on this point, and the names of refractory persons were to be reported to the Council.

The interest of the poor consumer was the chief object to be kept in view by this elaborate administrative system. The Crown had been informed that "the Buyers (the poorer *buying and* sort especially) were much pinched by slights and deceipts *selling* used in measuring," and the clerk of the market and his deputies were to make enquiries of all such deceits. Travellers were also cared for; no inn-keepers were to use any measure not sealed by the clerk of the market or to neglect to have such a sealed measure "continually hanging by a chaine at the doore of their hosterie so that the traveller may not be deceived[1]." With the assistance of the clerks of the market,

---

[1] *Proclamations* (Soc. Ant., VII. 112). Under Charles I. patentees were appointed to travel and sit in their courts with the Clerks of the Market, so as to keep them up to their duties which were no better attended to than before. This new administrative machinery was also employed to exercise supervision over the conditions of production, in the staple industry of the Country. *A proclamation for the due execution of the office of Clarke of the Market.* Brit. Mus. 506. h. 12 (61). (1636).

"Whereas severall complaints haue beene heretofore made, as well unto Our late dear and Royall Father King James of ever blessed memory in his lifetime and unto Us since Our accesse to the Crowne, as unto the Lords and others of Our Privie Councell and to divers of Our Justices of Assize in their Circuits and Justices of Peace of sundry Counties of this Our Realme at their Sessions, of the great abuses, deceipts and falsities frequently used by and among Weavers, Combers, Spinsters and other Workers and Makers of Woollen Cloth and Yarne by the dayly falsifying their Yarne as well in the length of the Reele-staffe as in the number of the threds and of the differences growne among themselues, concerning a constant Reele for the reeling of Yarne to be kept, and for the increase of the Wages for the Poore according to the Statutes of quinto Eliz. and primo Jacobi. For remedy and reformation whereof and for setling of a constant course for the said Reele and increase of the Poores wages, it hath beene upon great advice thought fit, that the said course of keeping of a constant Reele throughout all the Clothing Counties of this Our Realme of England and Dominion of Wales: and the increase of the Wages for the Poore might proceed and go on for the generall good of the whole Commonwealth: And that in regard the reel-staffe had beene lately increased a fifth or sixth part longer then had beene accustomed, all Spinsters should haue for the Spinning and Reeling of sixe double Knots on the double Reele or twelve on the single Reele, a peny, which is more by two pence in the shilling then formerly they have had. And that all Labourers and other Artificers imployed about the Trade of Clothing and Yarne making should have the like increase of Wages. And for establishing the same Wee have by our Letters Patents bearing date the two and twentieth day of January now last past, for Us, Our Heires and Successors, willed, ordained, and appointed, as well for avoiding of all future deceit in making of Cloth and Yarne and for preservation of peace betweene Buyer and Seller, Workemaster and Servant....

"The surveying, searching, sealing and oversight whereof as of the increase of the wages of the poore we have by Our said Letters Patent committed and appointed unto our well-beloved Servant John Etherington, one of the yeomen of

it was possible to keep a check upon the constables, and in- A.D. 1558 directly on the justices; and the Privy Council had an —1603. organisation ready to their hands, by means of which they *The local* could attempt to administer the food supply of the nation *require-* *ments of* to the best advantage. The government were prepared to *different* control prices, and wages, with the view of economising the *were also* stock of corn, so that it should suffice till the next harvest; *by the* they were not as yet willing to rely on the operations of *Council.* speculative dealers, as an easy means of securing this result[1].

In all probability these corn bodgers did something to equalise the price throughout a larger or smaller area; but this might involve the inland counties in unnecessary distress. It was probably better that the citizens of London[2], or Bristol[3], should be forced to make special arrangements for importing corn from abroad, rather than that a scarcity should be turned into a famine in country districts, by dealers who transported corn to the towns. A limited trade in corn was officially permitted[4]; but, on the whole, the government preferred to provide a machinery for estimating, when necessary, the food supply available in the neighbourhood of each market town. They insisted that a fair proportion of corn should be thrown on the market, to be retailed in small quantities, and sometimes at special rates

our Chamber and to Henry Stracey for the tearme of 31 years," and a schedule of fees was annexed. "And that the Poore imployed about the making of Cloth and Yarn have the said increase of wages, after the rate of two pence in the shilling more than heretofore they have they had paid and continued unto them." This system could not be satisfactorily carried out, and it was accordingly abandoned in Dec. 1636. [Brit. Mus. 21. h. 1 (44)] The attempt at regulation seems to show that the trade was expanding and taking a form in which market spinning was common. S. P. D. C I. ccxliii. 23 and cclxxxii. 81. See below, p. 510.

1 Compare Adam Smith, *Wealth of Nations*, Bk. iv. c. 5.

2 E. M. Leonard, *Early History of English Poor Relief*, 123. It long continued to be a matter of civic regulation. Roger Ascham in a letter dated 11 Aug 1551 holds up the cities of Madgeburg and Nuremburg as an example to London in this matter. Quoted by Millos, *Customers Apology* (Bodleian Library), last page Malyne's *England's View*, 1603, holds up Venice as the example of a well-regulated corn trade (p. 90); see also E. Lamond, *Discourse of Common Weal*, p. 163, on the sale of imported corn in London. Compare also Prideaux, *Memorials of the Goldsmiths Company*, Vol. i. 355.

3 E. M. Leonard, *op cit.* 122.

4 Its advantages are discussed by the Gloucestershire Justices, S. P. D. El. clxxxix 50. On the whole subject see E. M. Leonard, *op. cit.* 88 and 320 n., and Harrison's *Description* in Holinshed's *Chronicles*, i. 340.

A.D. 1558
—1633.

to poor purchasers[1]. The system was intended to act as a preventive of desperate poverty, and of the outbreaks and riots in which starving men might be ready to join.

In the time of Elizabeth

During the reign of Elizabeth, the parliamentary regulation of the corn trade by legislation seems to have been chiefly undertaken in the interest of the producer; while the Privy Council exercised scrupulous care in order to see

revenue was obtained from exported corn, by taxation

that consumers should not suffer. In addition to this, the fiscal side of the subject was not ignored. A duty of 1/- per quarter was levied on all corn exported, under the Act of 1571[2], and this was doubled in 1593[3]; the receipts of the Crown were thus drawn from the regular export trade, to whatever extent it occurred, and not merely from permission to make occasional shipments. It appears that,

and by occasional licences under Charles I.

under the personal government of Charles I., there was a return to the fiscal method which had found favour in the fifteenth century and under the Tudor Kings. The export of corn was forbidden; and large sums were paid by dealers for permission to send out special cargoes[4]. The constitutional character of the practice of issuing such licences had been called in question in 1371[5]; and Charles's action in this matter doubtless had something to do with the alienation of the maritime and shipping interests from the King's cause.

Considerable success had attended

On the whole, it appears that the agricultural policy of Elizabeth was exceedingly successful[6]; King James came to the conclusion that the laws against the conversion of arable land into pasture were quite unnecessary, and that they were misused so as to give rise to considerable grievances. The King was "assured by well weighed consideration of some of his most Honorable priuie Councell, and Judges, and his Councell learned, That the Lawes, or branches of the Lawes, touching the conuerting and turning of tillable lands into pasture, and keeping and using the same in pasture, are rather of late become a meanes to molest some innocent

---

1 Compare the Scarcity Orders of 1586, printed from Burleigh's copy of the draft, among the Lansdowne MSS. E. M. Leonard, *op. cit.* 318.

2 13 El. c. 13, § 3.

3 35 El. c. 7, § 23.

4 Faber, *op. cit.* 97; Naudé, *op. cit.* 96.

5 Faber, 78.   6 See above, p. 91.

subiects, whom it concernes not, as well as others, by the A.D. 1558 practise and connivancie of Informers, then to cause any —1603. reformation of the abuses in the offendor, as it is found by daily and generall experience, and in the execution thereof for the most part it hath happened, for that the innocent and guiltlesse persons, being free by the provisions and exceptions therein, are neverthelesse sued and troubled by reason of the doubtfulnesse and exposition thereof: And the nocent and great offendors, by the practise and agreement of the Informers for some private gaine, escape unpunished[1]." This proclamation[2] affords us some insight into difficulties *royal efforts* which had to be faced in attempting to carry out the *rural pro-* State regulation of tillage, but it also shows that agri- *sperity both in* cultural affairs were becoming more prosperous; it seems to *connection with tillage* confirm the view of those who held that there were good

---

[1] An interesting case in 1611 of malicious prosecution by an encloser who had compensated the tenants is given by Miss P. Wragge, *Victoria County History, Sussex,* II. 191.

[2] It proceeds " And forasmuch as upon due consideration of the conveniencie of this Lawe, and the state of this Kingdome in that point it doeth not appeare: but that, as there is much arrable land of that nature become pasture, so is there by reason thereof, much more other lands of old pasture, and waste, and woodlands where the plough neuer entred, as well as of the same pasture lands, so heretofore conuerted, become errable, and by husbandrie made fruitfull with corne, and so will daily be increased if the price of corne shall arise, whereof yet (God be thanked) here hath beene no want, insomuch as the quantitie and qualitie of errable and Corne-lands at this day doth much exceed the quantitie that was at the making of the said Lawe. And that there is rather want of pasture for breed and feed of Cattell and sheepe, as appeares by the scarcitie and dearenesse of Beeues and Muttons. Wherein there is also a common and generall necessitie and usefulnes as well as of Corne, which as the want thereof shall appeare, or the price thereof increase, all or a great part of those lands which were heretofore converted from errable to pasture, and have sithence gotten heart, strength and fruitfulnesse, will be reduced to Corne lands againe, to the great increase of graine to the Commonwealth, and profite to each man in his private."—The king " understanding that some persons of his subiects not truly offending or not thinking they doe offend herein, as beeing meere purchasers of such lands, upon great and valuable considerations as auncient pasture lands, long after the conuersion thereof.... And others of his subiects hauing conuerted and continued such lands have put in tillage others in lieu thereof" are daily at the mercy of informers and that others though having offended "cannot for the present time, without great damage in their estates alter and change the same againe"...his Majesty hath granted his Commission to consider "offences and offendors of that kind." "And that thereupon his gracious pardon and licence for such offences as are past (with some restraints and cautions therein necessarie ") may be granted as to such persons as shall seem good to the Commissioners, "the rest to bee left to the rigour and more severe prosecution of the Lawe for future offences of that kinde." *Commissioners for considering the ... offenders to whom license shall be granted for arrable lands converted from tillage to pasture* (1619). *Proclamations* (Soc. Ant.) VI. 88.

A.D. 1558
—1603.

and with cattle-breeding.

grounds for looking back to Elizabeth's reign as the era when the period of improvement began[1]. The Act of 1563 had tended to give some regularity to the supply of labour on the land; and the facilities for export enabled the agriculturist to dispose of his crop on profitable terms in plentiful years. When sheep-farming ceased to offer the chief attraction to rural enterprise, cattle-breeding and tillage flourished together[2]; and the English producer seems to have had an excellent demand in foreign parts for butter and cheese[3].

The most remunerative estate management in the seventeenth century

174. The opening of the seventeenth century is marked by a decided alteration in the ideas of profitable estate management which had been in vogue in the sixteenth century, and also in the tone of public opinion in regard to the changes which were proceeding in rural districts. The men in Tudor days, who tried to turn their land to its most profitable use, had been engaged in producing wool for sale; while seventeenth century improvers found that the producing of food stuffs of various sorts was more remunerative.

was no longer sheep-farming but the production of food stuffs,

Since this scheme of using the land provided an increased food supply for the nation, even though it might not everywhere offer as much employment for labour as in the old days, it appeared to be advantageous to the community. In one part of the country after another[4] this new system

---

[1] Dymock writing in 1650 remarks that in Queen Elizabeth's days good husbandry began to take place. Samuel Hartlib, *His Legacie* (1651), p. 52.

[2] It may seem strange that under the Tudors an increase of pasture should have been accompanied by a decline of dairy farming; but there was at all events a general impression that the two changes had gone on together. And this is not unlikely; sheep-farming enabled the landlord or tenant to dispense with labour and to depopulate his farm; for dairy farming and poultry farming constant care and attention was requisite; when the households of husbandmen were broken up there was no one left who could manage the cows, or the poultry; these were really bye-avocations which were actually combined with arable farming. It was commonly asserted that eggs and dairy products had become specially dear, even though other things were rising in price also. A statute of Philip and Mary insisted that a cow should be kept and a calf reared for every sixty sheep (2 and 3 Philip and Mary, c. 3); this regulation was continued under Elizabeth (13 El. c. 25).

[3] S. P. D. El. cv. 61, 1575; cclxii. 101, 107. See also Proclamations of Charles I. in 1634 and 1637, *Proclamations for reforming and preventing the fraud so frequently practised ... in the false packing of butter*, Brit. Mus. 506. h. 12 (30) and 1851. b. 3 (16).

[4] The area of change at different times is discussed by Dr Slater, *The Inclosure of Common Fields considered Geographically*, in *The Geographical Journal*, Jan. 1907.

of management came in, and it sometimes involved social difficulties[1] that were similar to those that had previously arisen in connection with the extended sheep-farming of Tudor times. We get some glimpses of the accompanying evils from Aubrey's complaints of what he observed in Wiltshire[2]; but the new system of land management was generally regarded as a public boon, and not merely as a gain to certain private persons at the expense of their neighbours. Attempts were made to render forest and wastes more remunerative, either for corn growing or as pasturage; and the existence of common fields and common waste was beginning to be regarded as an obstacle to real improvement. Hence the Tudor and Elizabethan policy of legislating against sheep-farming[3] dropped into abeyance.

A.D. 1558 —1603. even though this involved enclosure,

The differences between county and county or district and district are so great that it is hardly possible to speak very definitely about the country as a whole; but we may at any rate take the year 1592 as marking a turning point[4]. Bacon, writing at that date, speaks of the abundance of grain, so that "whereas England was wont to be fed by other countries from the east, it sufficeth now to feed other countries.... Another evident proof thereof may be, that the good yields of corn which have been, together with some toleration of vent, hath of late time invited and enticed men to break up more ground and convert it to tillage, than all the penal laws for that purpose made and enacted could ever by compulsion effect. A third proof may be that the prices of grain and of victual never were of late years more reasonable[5]." This optimistic view seems to have been a little premature; the great scarcity of 1593—1597 called attention to the insufficiency of the corn supply, as a danger which resulted from the turning of tillage to pasture. Bacon

---

[1] See below, p. 552.

[2] J. Aubrey, *Natural History of Wiltshire*, 103, *Introduction to Survey of North Wilts.*, in *Miscellanies*, 33.

[3] See Vol. I. p. 529. Mr Gay notes that 423 entries of proceedings occurred under Henry VIII., 50 under Edward VI., 51 under Philip and Mary. and 83 under Elizabeth; the last of these is in 1599 (*The Inquisitions of Depopulation in 1715*, in *Royal Hist. Soc. Transactions, N. S.* xiv. (1900), 239).

[4] 35 El. c. 7.

[5] Spedding, *Life and Letters*, I. 158.

A.D. 1558
—1603.

public opinion favoured putting the land to its most profitable use.

himself introduced a bill on the subject, with a speech[1] which shows that he had found it necessary to modify the opinion he had expressed five years before. This measure[2] enacted that in specified counties all land, which had been in tillage at the beginning of Elizabeth's reign, should be broken up again; its employment for arable purposes was to be continued, though it might be laid down in grass temporarily, in order to recover strength. Care was taken that the Act should not be so enforced as to interfere with the course of husbandry which the owner found convenient. This Act embodied the substance of former measures, but made allowance for the changes which were requisite, if scope was to be given for agricultural progress. The progress of agricultural improvement was incompatible with the maintenance of the traditional husbandry and the customary village life, and still more with the habits of those who secured their livelihood in forest and fen. Enclosure proceeded and gave rise to considerable riots in 1607[3], and to occasional complaint at other times[4]; but on the whole the

---

[1] *Parliamentary History*, I. 899. For the distress at this time in Oxfordshire see S. P. D. El. cclxii. 4 (Jan. 1597), for Durham, *ib.* 10.

[2] 39 El. c. 2.

[3] There were riots in Leicestershire, Warwickshire and Northamptonshire about enclosures in 1607 (J. G. Nichols, *History and Antiquities of Leicestershire* (1807), Vol. iv. Pt. i. 83). A proclamation on the subject, treating the outcry about enclosures as a pretext, was issued on May 30 (Brit. Mus. 506. h. 10 (72)); the Council apprehended trouble in other counties (*Hist. MSS. Comm.* iv. 367). A proclamation explaining the policy of the government and promising further enquiry in regard to depopulation was issued June 28. The paper printed in Appendix C. shows the points which were taken into account, and a pardon to offenders in regard to enclosures was proclaimed on 24 July (*ib.* p. 146). The Council then sent commissioners of enquiry to several shires (Aug. 20), with instructions to report before the end of October. The returns are in the Record Office, *Petty Bag. Depopulation Returns*. Mr Hubert Hall, who has examined the returns of the Commission in 1607, informs me that there were more recent and extreme cases of depopulation in Warwickshire than elsewhere (*Petty Bag. Depopulation Returns*, Record Office). These returns have been carefully analysed by Mr Gay, *The Midland Revolt of* 1607 in *Trans. Royal Hist. Soc. N. S.* xviii. 220.

[4] Compare the account (1609) of the country in Symond's *Sermon* (Gen. xii. 3), quoted by Anderson, *History of the Church of England in the Colonies*, 2nd ed. i. 197. Coke in 1620 speaks from his own experience of the "Depopular who turns all out of doors and keeps none but a shepherd and his dog" as one that never prospers, *Parl. Hist.* i. 1198. A bill on the subject was drafted in 1624, *Hist. MSS. Comm.* iii. Ap. 29, *C. J.* i. 748, and commissions were issued about the same time, *Hist. MSS. Comm.* i. Ap. 34, S. P. D. C. I. cxcii. No. 24, 93, 94, cxciii. 55. In his inaugural dissertation (*Zur Geschichte der Einhegungen in England* (1902)) Mr Gay shows reason for thinking that depopulation continued

authorities approved of turning the land to its most pro- A.D. 1558 —1603.
fitable uses, and were at all events confident that there was
no longer cause for public alarm in the increase of sheep.

A new era had begun in rural districts, for sheep- *Sheep-*
farming[1] was no longer so profitable as it had been. *farming was no*
Possibly some of the land employed was not really suitable *longer*
for grazing, for there are complaints of a decline in the *specially profitable.*
quality of wool[2]. The high price of wool, of which we
hear in 1576, seems to have been due to a deficiency in
the clip, and to have occasioned great distress among the
weavers. As a remedy, the export of wool was temporarily
prohibited[3], but careful measures were taken by the Privy
Council to prevent the engrossing of wool[4]; such interference would prevent the graziers from profiting through
occasional high prices. But, on the whole, prices were not

---

during the seventeenth century, in the inland counties (p. 56) to a much larger
extent than has been commonly supposed, and Miss Leonard has accumulated a
great deal of evidence as to the precise grounds of the complaints, *Inclosure of
Common Fields* in *Trans. of Royal Hist. Soc. N. S.* XIX. 123. But there were conflicting currents of opinion. Compare the *Acts of the Privy Council* for cases of
enclosure which gave rise to dispute, but were not illegal, e.g. 1579, Vol. XI. p. 178.
In the 17th century both Burton (*Anatomy of Melancholy*, 1800 pref. p. 89) and
Fuller (*Holy State*, Bk. III. c. 13) advocate enclosure, though they protest against
depopulation. A bill for the better ordering commons and dividing into severalty
was drafted in 1621 (*Hist. MSS. Comm.* III. Ap. 19); and one for improving waste
grounds and regulating commons and preventing depopulation was introduced in
1656. *C. J.* VII. 470. See p. 552 below.

¹ Blith (*English Improver*, 1649, p. 34) regards the grazier who never grew
corn as behind the times.

² Prothero in *Social England*, III. 533.

³ Proclamation, Nov. 1576. "Forasmuch as upon the lamentable complaynt
made unto the Queenes most excellent Maiestie by sundrye her loving subiectes,
the Clothiers of divers partes of the Realme and of a multitude of other people
mainteined in their hand labours by them: It appeareth that partly through the
great death of sheep which of late yeares hath happened in sundry partes of the
Realme and partlye through the great abuse of some which have obteyned (upon
reasonable consyderations) licence to buy and sell wool within this Realme,"
they by their "unsatiable greedinesse" bought up great quantities of wool "so
that the Clothiers can buy litle or none, but suche as is very course, or els at such
excessive prices, as they cannot make theyr principal thereof agayne." The
consequence would be the "decay of divers good townes whiche are cheefely
maynteyned by the Clothiers." All buying of wools "other than suche as by the
lawes of this Realme are appoynted and permitted" is forbidden. The Company
of the Merchant Staplers is not "to buy or bargayne" for "any woolles growyng
within this Realme untyl the latter ende of Februarie next ensuing," Dyson,
op. cit. 166. There was a similar proclamation on April 30th, 1579, *ib.* 188.

⁴ *Acts of the Privy Council*, x. pp. 8, 24, 25 (1577). Compare also S. P. D. El.
CXIV. 25—43. On further regulation of the trade in wool see below, p. 298.

high; according to Thorold Rogers' calculations, an extraordinary rise had taken place in the value of wool about the
middle of the sixteenth century, when it trebled in price;
but the high level, thus reached, was not wholly maintained
during the succeeding decades[1], and the price remained
stationary during the seventeenth century[2]. In the Midland
counties, especially in districts which had no navigable rivers,
the cost of carriage rendered corn-growing unprofitable, while

*Tillage
and cattle-
breeding
were re-
munerative*
the soil was well suited for pasture farming[3]; but in the
country generally it would seem that tillage and cattle rearing[4]
could quite hold their own. The policies pursued in the sixteenth and seventeenth centuries with regard to wool and corn
are in strong contrast. Wool producing was regarded with
more than suspicion; the increase of pasture was prohibited,
and the export of wool was restricted, so that the material for
the cloth manufacture might be as cheap as possible. On
the other hand corn-growing was stimulated by the permission of export, and even by the granting of bounties in 1689.

There seems to be good reason to believe that the rural
districts generally had entered on a period of prosperity, in

*as was
evidenced
by the
increase of
building
in rural
districts*
spite of the difficulty caused to landed men by the fall in
the value of silver[5]. The increase of building is an unmistakeable sign of wealth; and during the Elizabethan age,
there were numbers of nobles and gentry who were able to
erect new mansions. Nor was this the only form of fashionable expenditure; for there are numerous proclamations
extant which impose restrictions on extravagance in dress[6].

---

[1] *Agriculture and Prices*, IV. 328.   [2] *Ib.* v. 407.

[3] *Consideration of the cause in question before the Lords touching Depopulation*,
1607. See Appendix C. Compare also *A defence of Inclosure and of Converting Arable in the Inland shires to pasture*, 1608. Brit. Mus. *Cotton MSS.*
Faustina C. f. 165.

[4] In an interesting tract dated 1612, it is pointed out that fenced land gave
much better shelter for cattle, and that the enclosure of waste was advantageous
for cattle rearing. *Of fishing the Seas and converting waste into wealthe* by A. D.
(Trin. Coll. Camb. O. 5. 21) f. 5.

[5] Those who had let their land on leases, or whose incomes were relatively
fixed, had difficulty in maintaining their establishments. Rogers, *Agriculture and
Prices*, IV. 739, 750; Norden, *Surveyor*, 17.

[6] See the proclamation of 1579 in Nichols' *Illustrations of manners and
expenses of ancient times*, Appendix, Sumptuary Proclamations; also Dyson,
343 (6 July, 1597). "In regard of the present difficulties of this time, wherein
the decay and lacke of Hospitalitie appeares in the better sorte in all Countreys,
principally occasioned by the immeasurable charges and expences which they are

This was said to be one cause of the decay of hospitality which was frequently deplored; it was therefore necessary to take additional measures against absenteeism[1]. When *and the changes in* the country gentry were compelled to reside on their estates, *the habits of the* they could both assist in keeping order, as well as in or- *gentry* ganising defence[2], and also do their part in relieving the necessitous poor[3]. The evidence of increased wealth not only impressed foreign visitors to England[4], but seems to have been a frequent subject of remark within the country[5].

It is easy to understand that the gentry were able to *who obtained* make so much display, as rents, not only of grazing but of *higher* corn land, were rising in the latter part of the sixteenth *rents.* century[6]; and this movement went on rapidly in the early

put to in superfluous apparelling their wives, children and families, the confusion also of degrees in all places being great, where the meanest are as richly apparelled as their betters, and the pride that such inferiour persons take in their garments, driuing many for their maintenance to robbing and stealing by the hiewaye." Also Oct. 1559, Dyson, 14; 7 May 1562, *ib.* 52; 12 Feb. 1566, *ib.* 94; 18 June 1574, *ib.* 154; 16 Feb. 1577, *ib.* f. 168; 12 Feb. 1579, *op. cit.* 196; Harrison, in Holinshed's *Chronicles*, 289.

1 Absenteeism had been first noticed as a serious evil in connection with sheep farming (Townsend Warner, *Landmarks*, p. 137); but when arable land also could be let for large money rents, there was still less inducement for the landowner to stay at home and attend personally to his estate. One typical example may be quoted from the Proclamation of 29 July 1603. "The Solemnities of our Corona-tion being now performed according to the usages and customes of this our Realme of England and with mutuall contentment, as well of us in the zeale and love of our people at the performance thereof expressed, as of them in the expectation of our government; we have entred into consideration of the state of the seuerall parts of the body of our Realme, And therein do finde, that the absence of the Noblemen and Gentlemen, which are used to reside there in seuerall quarters, is accompanied with great inconvenience, as well in the want of reliefe which the poorer sort did receiue by their ordinary Hospitalitie, as also chiefly in the defect of Government; whereby, besides other inconveniences, through lacke of order, the infection of the Plague spreadeth and scattereth itselfe into diuers places of the Realme, and is like further to increase, if by the presence and care of such as are in authority and credit amongst our people, they be not contained in some good course, for the preuenting of that contagion." [Brit. Mus. 510. h. 10 (23).] See also Proclamations in May 1603 [Brit. Mus. 506. h. 10 (12)], 1622 [Brit. Mus. 21. h. 1 (12)], 1623 [506. h. 12 (105)], 1624 [506. h. 11 (30)], 1626 [*ib.* (83)], 1627 [*ib.* (101)], 1632 [506. h. 12 (8)], 1639 [1851. b. 3 (24)], 1640 [21. h. 1 (52)].

2 *Proclamation*, 2 Nov. 1587, Dyson 246.

3 2 Nov. 1596, Dyson, *op. cit.* 340. Compare the proclamations in 1622, Leonard, *op. cit.* 145.

4 W. B. Rye, *England as seen by Foreigners*, p. 110.

5 Harrison, in Holinshed, I. 317, and J. Hall, *Satires*, III. 1.

6 That rents would not conform immediately to the rise of prices is perfectly true, but the change was noted by Harrison (Holinshed, I. p. 318). In the face of this contemporary observation, it is difficult to accept Prof. Thorold Rogers' con-

part of the seventeenth century[1]. This increase of income
would certainly render land an attractive investment to
merchants and others, who had made their money in commerce, and would thus tend to recruit the landed gentry
with a body of *nouveaux riches*[2].

Nor was it only the landlord class who had the means of
*The im-
provement
was also
seen in
the condi-
tion of
yeomen
farmers,*
increased luxury and display. Harrison remarks on the improved condition of the yeoman[3], and the furniture and
plenishing of his house[4], and Norden some years later gives
confirmatory evidence of a change in their habits[5]. He was

clusion as to the suddenness of the change at the opening of the seventeenth century (*op. cit.* v. 804). It seems more probable that the corporations, from whose
accounts his facts are drawn, were comparatively easy-going landlords; we know
that they were trying to avoid loss by bargaining for the payment of rent in corn,
which was rising in value, rather than by insisting on an increased money payment.

[1] Thorold Rogers, *Agriculture and Prices*, v. 803, also among contemporaries:
Best, *Rural Economy in Yorkshire* in 1641 (Surtees Soc.) p. 129. "The lands in
the pasture weere (att my father's first cominge) letten to our owne tenants and
others for 2*s.* a lande; afterwards for 2*s.* 6*d.* a lande, and lastly for 3*s.* a lande;
but nowe, being inclosed they will let for thrice as much." Norden (*Surveyor's
Dialogue*, 1607, p. 9) had "seene and observed" among the tenants "a kind of
madnes, as I may call it, but in the best sence it is a kind of ambitious, or rather
auaricious emulation, wherein they striue one to outstrip another in giuing most:
as where myself haue had businesse of this nature, namely of letting, of letting
setting, or selling of land for yeeres or lives, being or neere being determined in
farmes or other like, whereby the Lord hath bin at liberty to dispose thereof at
his will, for best aduantage, by choice of a new tenant. Proclamation to that
effect has been made in open court, where I haue seene, and it is dayly in use,
that one wil outbid another, as at an outcry in London, in so much as I haue
wondred at their emulation, and could not have asked what they haue raysed it
unto themselves, and should any that is in authority in this case (who in duty is
not to hinder the Lord, or the Lord him selfe) inhibit such hot spirits to clyme as
high for the Lords aduantage, as the ladder of their own will, and supposed
ability will reach? This is not as one Swallow in a Summer, but they are many
and euerywhere Winter and Summer, and yet are other men accused and condemned for them and their faults, if these will be a fault in itselfe: but I should
thinke it greater madnes for a Lord, wilfully to refuse what is so voluntarily
offered, and so willingly giuen. Now who is the cause of raysing rents and fines?"
Glanville's assertion as to the difficulty of collecting rents and the fall in the
price of land in 1620 is difficult to reconcile with these facts. *Parl. Hist.* I. 1188,
also Sir E. Sandys, p. 1194.

[2] Harrison, in Holinshed, I. 274, and Brodrick, *English Land*, p. 46.

[3] This sort of people ... commonlie liue wealthilie keepe good houses and
trauell to get riches ... "with grasing frequenting of markets and keeping of
servants" they "do come to great welth, in so much that manie of them are able
and doo buie the lands of unthriftie gentlemen, and often setting their sonnes to
the schools, to the universities, and to the Inns of the Court." Harrison, *op. cit.*
275.

[4] *Ib.* 317.   [5] *Surveyor's Dialogue* (1607), 81.

of opinion that there was little to choose between the A.D. 1558 —1603. comfort of the leaseholder and that of neighbouring freeholders. That there were many cases of hardship and oppression, as between the rich man and his neighbours[1], or the landlords and tenants, is probable enough; but there is more complaint of excessive fines on copy-holders[2], and of arbitrary eviction from small tenancies[3], than of harsh treatment of tenants or leaseholders; so far as they were concerned, the chief subject for dispute appears to have had reference to the value of improvement[4].

Though it is true that the rise of wages was comparatively small, there is no reason to believe that the agricultural labourer altogether failed to share in the general improvement. The revival of tillage would give greater frequency of employment, and this would in itself be a considerable gain; while the diffusion of the clothing trades, and increased demand for yarn and employment of spinners, must have brought an additional source of income within the reach of many peasant families[5]. Even apart from this new source of income, the agricultural labourer was probably

and probably extended to the rural labourers, who obtained income from by-employments

---

[1] *Social England*, III. 354.

[2] Harrison, in Holinshed, I. 318.

[3] There seems to have been some encroachment by lords upon the tenants, who paid fines to the Crown to have their ancient customs (Hunter, *Doncaster*, I. 158, 7 J. I. c. 21). I should gather from Norden that the chief tenants' grievance was when the lord insisted on forfeiture on insufficient grounds (*Surveyor*, p. 60). According to Thorold Rogers similar harsh treatment was extended to freeholders under the Statute of Frauds, 29 C. II. c. 3. *Agriculture and Prices*, V. 87.

[4] It was said however that tenants were unwilling to improve, because if they did the landlords were likely to raise their rents to the full value of the improvement. In this difficulty Dymock again got a suggestion from the Low Countries. "According to the usual custome in Flaunders, a Law may be made of letting and hiring Leases upon Improvement; where the manner is, That the Farmer covenanteth on his part, to improve the land to such or such a greater Rent, by an orderly and excellent management of Husbandry as well as Building. The Landlord on the other side covenanteth on his part, at the expiration of the said Lease, to give so many years purchase of the Improvement (according to the agreement) which is 3 or 4 years or some times more, or, to give out of it such a parcel or moity of Ground. As if land formerly going for 6s. an Acre be upon Improvement worth 10s. or 13s. 4d. an acre. The Landlord is to give 4s. or 5s. upon every Acre, more or lesse according to the agreement" (*Hartlib's Legacie*, 1651, Preface; S. Taylor, *Common Good*, 1652, p. 15, regards 3s. 4d. per acre as a typical rent, and unenclosed downs as worth 1s. 8d., p. 36).

[5] See above, p. 97. The change affected some artisans; the wives and children of Kentish iron-workers found employment in spinning. S. P. D. C. I. 1631, CXCII. 99.

A.D. 1588
—1603.

*and some
subsistence
from their
holdings,*
sure of obtaining a large portion of his subsistence, without relying on his earnings at all. There seem to have been few cottagers[1] in any village, who had not got some acres of land to work; in all probability, the agricultural labourer of the day was either a small farmer, who was willing to do an occasional day's work, or a grown-up son, who had not yet obtained a holding for himself, and who either helped his father or hired himself out for regular service by the

*while many
of the
weavers
were econo-
mically
dependent.*
year. These men were much better off than such weavers[2] as were economically dependent on the merchants or capitalists for employment[3]; some of these wage-earners were, even at this time, divorced from the soil, so that they had no other source of income than their earnings[4]. The agricultural labourer, on the other hand, had a holding, from which he could procure a living for his family; and his service with a neighbouring employer was of the nature of a by-employment. The labourer had not lost the economic independence which he had secured at the Black Death, even though subsequent legislation had limited his opportunities of bargaining[5]. In many parts of Europe the policy pursued in regard to the food supply had been dictated in the interests of the consumer only; the English labourers had forced the Government to adopt another scheme, and at all events to take account of the interests of the producer. After the Black Death they had refused to work unless for adequate wages; and the agricultural system of the country had been gradually revolutionised in accordance with their demands. The legislature had been successful in checking the depopulation of rural districts; the Statute of Artificers endeavoured to provide that the labourers should

---

[1] By 31 El. c. 7 four acres were to be assigned to every cottage; the gradual formation of a landless class of agricultural labourers is admirably traced by W. Hasbach, *Die englischen Landarbeiter*, p. 71, etc.

[2] Leonard, *op. cit.* pp. 147, 149. Compare also Elizabethan proclamations about Essex weavers, March, 1590, Dyson, 280, 7 Feb. 1601, 379.

[3] That many weavers and other artificers had small holdings is probably true (see below, pp. 502, 616), but their severance from the land had begun apparently 18 El. c. 16.

[4] Compare the Statute 2 and 3 P. and M. c. 11, where complaint is made of clothiers letting out looms at such "unreasonable rentes as the poore artificers are not hable to mayntayne themselfes, muche les their Wyefes Famulie and Children."　　[5] See above, p. 38.

have reasonable wages; and the policy of permitting export *A.D. 1558 —1603.* gave the agriculturist additional opportunities of securing a profit, even when he paid a living wage. It is obvious that the fall in the value of silver and rise of prices tended to affect all mere wage-receivers severely[1]; but the journeyman in the towns, who depended entirely on his earnings, was far less able than the agricultural labourer to hold his own and maintain his independence.

175. These alterations, in the condition and circumstances *Tillage was no longer chiefly practised* of the different classes of the rural population, were closely correlated with the changes that had occurred in the aims of those who were concerned in the management of estates. The scheme, which was recommended in the *Husbandry* of the thirteenth century, no longer held good[2]. The great landowner of Tudor times was not merely concerned to obtain supplies from his land for his own household; he expected that the produce of his estate would be sent to market by his tenants, and that his rent would be paid out of the money they realised. There were doubtless many places *for subsistence,* where subsistence-tillage still survived, especially among the yeomanry and small freeholders; but, in so far as the cultivation of the soil came under the cognisance of the authorities, they appear to have assumed that tillage was *but with a view to the market, so* carried on, as it is in modern times, with a view to profitable sale, either for use at home or for export. Economically, the business of the agriculturist had come to be closely analogous to the employments of tradesmen, who manu- *that it was analogous to other trades.* factured wares for sale; the receipts from tillage depended on the state of prices and the conditions of demand; the work was no longer done by a special class under compulsion[3], but by a body of labourers whose training and terms of employment were provided for in the code that regulated all other industrial conditions. Just as in the cloth trade we find a marked distinction between the domestic weaver, who was an independent workman, and the capitalist clothier,

---

[1] See below, p. 169.

[2] In *Walter of Henley*, edited by E. Lamond, p. 59, Vol. I. p. 239.

[3] Hasbach, *op. cit.* p. 70, note 2, points out that servile tenures continued in England till late in the seventeenth century.

A.D. 1558
—1603.
who employed many hands, so we may mark the contrast
between the yeoman, who worked the land on his own account, and the capitalist, who employed labourers to cultivate
Landlords a large farm. But, so far as the progress of agriculture is
found it re-
munerative concerned, it is necessary to take account of the body of
men who were not mere tenants, but owners of the soil. It
is hardly possible to exaggerate the beneficial influence which
has been exercised on English tillage by 'spirited proprietors'[1]
in modern times. This trait of the economic life of the country
has comparatively little analogy in other lands; and it is
worth while to pay some attention to the indications of this
tendency that may be noted in the Elizabethan age. Before
to sink this date we do not get instances of wealthy men sinking
capital in
the land, capital in the land in expectation of finding it a remunerative investment. There had been very little inducement
for the mediaeval proprietor to improve those portions of his
land which were worked by tenants, who paid him customary
rents; his receipts would often vary with the number of
tenants on his estate[2], or, so far as his domain was concerned,
with his success in securing an increased amount of service
from his dependents[3]; there was no direct inducement to
make permanent improvements on the estate. In the revolutionary days of the fifteenth and sixteenth century, when
so much land was devoted to sheep farming, large sums
must have been invested in stocking the pastures with
flocks; but there was comparatively little expenditure on the
land itself, except in the way of fencing. There were frequent
complaints that the buildings were allowed to decay, and
that large areas had reverted to mere prairie. With the introduction of the system known as convertible husbandry,
by which land was used for alternate periods of tillage and
pasture, all this was changed; it became clear that improvements in the estates would bring about increased rentals.
as is shown Fitzherbert[4], writing in 1529, calculated that an estate of
by the ex-
perience of 20 marks could be rendered worth £20 if it were enclosed
Fitzherbert with a view to better tillage; and landlords began to aim,

---

[1] See below, p. 540.   [2] Vol. I. 5, 170
[3] N. Neilson, *Economic Conditions of the Manors of Ramsey Abbey*, 45, 50.
[4] *Surveyenge*, f. 58.   Vol. I. p. 527.

not merely at collecting customary dues, but at so managing A.D. 1558 —1603. their property that they might fairly obtain an increased rent roll. An excellent illustration is supplied by the account which Rowland Vaughan gives of the irrigation *and of* *Vaughan.* he carried out, on his estate in Herefordshire in 1610[1], with very profitable results. That his was no solitary instance is shown by the language in which a writer in the last decade of the sixteenth century refers to the effects of the influx of American silver, in raising the value of land and encouraging the owners to utilise waste ground for tillage and pasture[2]. Moneyed men were not slow to realise *Moneyed* *men saw* the importance of this change; the purchase of rents had *that land* always been recognised as an allowable and secure employ- *was a* *profitable* ment for money; but in Elizabethan times, it became obvious *investment* that the purchase of land might be an improving investment. The landlord found it worth his while to take an active part in promoting better tillage, both by personal expenditure and by the effective supervision of his tenants. The ranks of the country gentry were increasingly recruited[3] with city men, who were desirous, not merely to climb to a higher grade in social status, but to have a safe and profitable in- *and infused* *new blood* vestment for their money. There were plenty of new men, in many parts of the country, in the early part of the seventeenth century; their readiness to break with old traditions gave rise to some of the discordant elements of the times. The class into which they had entered was charged, as we

---

[1] *Rowland Vaughan His Booke*, edited by E. B. Wood. *Most approved and Long experienced water-workes containing the manner of Winter and Summer drowning of Medow and Pasture...thereby to make those grounds (especially if they be drye) more Fertile Ten for One.*

[2] *Rowland Vaughan*, p. 120. "It's not unknowne to my neighbourhood my demeasues at New Court was set and forsaken at 40 pound by year, besides my Parke, I set it so my selfe, and let any man, that hath an upright judgment and equall eyes in his head view and review it, hee will say it will yeild within three yeares, three hundreth pounds yearely besides my Parke." He further says that one meadow for which he got £5 yearly now yields £15 in hay and aftermath alone (p. 134); that if after "laying out of five hundred pound at the end of foure yeares you make it not two or three thousand pound your choyce is bad and lucke worse" (p. 129). He says he was requested by many gentlemen "to putt their Water Workes in Print" because "it would bee very profitable to the kingdome to be put in execution: being of late a common thing in Devonshire; but not in so ample manner," p. 142.

[3] See below, p. 126.

have seen, with varied and difficult functions; it served as
the very backbone of the social system and supplied administrative organs for every possible purpose. Whatever
the subject of a proclamation may be, the justices were to
see to its execution. They had to administer the poor law,
apprentice pauper children, regulate the relations between
master and servant, restrain pirates, see to the food supply
of the county, license or restrain export of corn, as the case
might be, see to the supply of wool, have a care for the
coinage, give employment themselves to a certain number
of men, suppress all rioting and keep order generally. As
the land was the great 'fund' from which taxation was
drawn, it was by the good management of landed property
that the available sources of public revenue might be maintained or increased. It is only when we notice this state of
affairs that we can appreciate the extent to which the welfare
of the country was then bound up with the prosperity of the
landed interest.

*Permanent
improve-
ment at this
time chiefly
took the
form of
reclaiming
land from
inundation
or flood.*
176. The reclaiming of waste land was a favourite form
of improvement in the sixteenth century; the attempts
made at that time appear to have promised so well, as to
encourage the extraordinary development of enterprise,
similar in character, but on a much larger scale, which took
place during the seventeenth century. Considerable portions of the land on the east coast of England lie very low,
and are exposed to inundation, either from the sea itself, or
from the sluggish rivers which drain the Midlands. Their
channels were apt to be silted up with sand at the mouth,
and there was danger that they would overflow their banks
on the occasion of specially high tides, or in wet seasons
when they failed to carry off the additional rainfall[1]. Some
of the most important works had existed time out of mind;
the great embankments which guard Romney Marsh in
Kent[2], and protect the marshland of Norfolk from the Wash[3],

---

[1] The channels in the fens were important, not merely for drainage, but as
waterways for traffic. Dugdale, *The History of Imbanking and Drayning* (1662),
305, 397. See also title of *Private Act*, 13 El. c. 1. W. H. Wheeler, *The Fens of
South Lincolnshire*, p. 32.

[2] Dugdale, *op. cit.* 17.

[3] Smiles, *Lives of the Engineers*, i. 19.

are probably of Roman origin; and some of the channels in Lincolnshire[1] appear to have been excavated at the same period in the history of Britain. There is frequent evidence, all through the Middle Ages, of the care which was exercised in the maintenance of these works[2]; occasional commissions[3] were issued, from time to time, to ensure that repairs were properly executed. In the reign of Henry VI. the powers and duties of these Commissioners of Sewers were defined by Statute[4]; it was their business to maintain such public works, by means of contributions compulsorily levied from the proprietors, whose land was benefited by being protected from flood. Despite the efforts of these Commissioners, and the increased powers they obtained under Henry VIII.[5], the low lying grounds in Cambridge, Lincolnshire and Yorkshire appear to have been more hopelessly subjected to inundation than ever[6]. It seems probable that, owing to the decay and dissolution of the great monasteries[7] at Ramsey and Crowland, the necessary repairs of the dykes and cleansing of the drains were seriously neglected; and it became apparent that it was not only necessary to put the old banks and channels in a satisfactory state, but to undertake a general scheme, on a large scale, for dealing with each of these districts as a whole, and especially with the Great Level of the Fens. With this view, a Statute was passed in 1601[8],

A.D. 1558
—1603.

The Romans had carried out some works with this object;

the Commissioners of Sewers had been appointed to see to their maintenance, and the monasteries had given attention to the matter, but it was necessary to take up the work afresh.

---

[1] Wheeler, *op. cit.* 10.

[2] Dugdale, *op. cit.* 17 seq.

[3] *Ib.* 23 seq.

[4] 6 H. VI. c. 5.

[5] 23 H. VIII. c. 5.

[6] Dugdale, *op. cit.* 144. "Well I know that these xx. yeres was not doon so moche for the cleansyng of sewers as is doone and shall be doone this present yeare (1552)." Rich. Ogle writing to Cecil, S. P. D. Ed. VI. xiv. 52.

[7] Dugdale, *op. cit.* 216, 335, 375. Elizabeth was appealed to for £500 to be expended on the embanking of the Welland, "in respect of her monasteries of Crowland and Spalding." Apparently £100 was all that the Crown afforded for the purpose. Brit. Mus. *Lansdowne MSS.* lxxi. 61.

[8] 43 El. c. 11. The Act requires the consent of the major part of the commoners, and thus prohibits such action as that of the Earl of Lincoln who carried out drainage works in disregard of his neighbour. "The first notorious undertaker was the Earl of Lincoln, in Queen Elizabeth's dayes. His covetous Lorship by bribes to some Courtiers, and mis-information by pretending what a glorious work drayning would be to the Publick, and that he had the consent of the Country (which indeed were but an inconsiderable party of his own faction) procured a Pattent or Commission for the drayning of the Fens. But his private

which gave a legal basis to the action of adventurers in different parts of the kingdom, and rendered it possible to undertake works on the necessary scale.

The powers of the Commissioners were insufficient to bring pressure on local proprietors,   Large as the powers of the Commissioners had been, they were never in a position to initiate the new undertakings that were needed. It was difficult to force particular persons to contribute for the general good[1]; the Commissioners could only obtain funds by means of an assessment levied with reference to the prospective gain, which each landholder would receive from the improvement[2]. Much discussion had taken place on the subject in 1578; but the Commission, that was then issued, had no success in dealing with the problem, apparently for lack of money to begin their operations[3].

or on commoners,   A still more serious difficulty arose from the manner in which vested interests were affected by new works; there was

ends were to drain his own surrounded foul lands at the Public charges; and he so packed his Commissioners by making them Judges and Parties, that they made a Level and took away the poor Country-mens lands (which were never drowned, or bettered by overflowing) for melioration. The Queen being informed how her good Subjects were abused and that the said Commission was contrary to the Law of Sewers, She thereupon made that just and equitable Law, so consonant to nature and reason, for the most strict preservation of propriety called the Stat. of Improvement, etc. in 43 of her reign." *Anti-Projector* (1651), p. 2. The principal works that were commenced about this period were the costly and unsuccessful scheme of Thomas Lovell's for draining Deeping Fen. Dugdale, *op. cit.* 207. He was said to have lost £12,000 in the attempt. Wheeler, *op. cit.* 316.

[1] According to the decision of Popham and Anderson in 1612 they had the necessary powers (Dugdale, *op. cit.* 371), but it must have been hard to act upon them, especially as the local tradition was against this view. Compare the disclaimer of the Abbot of Crowland. At a commission of Sewers held 17 H. VI. at Waynfleete there was a presentment exhibited against the Abbot and Convent of Crowland charging him with neglect to repair certain banks "to the great damage of the Country." The Abbot attended the Court and said "that he himself and some of his Predecessors, with their Tenants and Fermours in the Towns and places adjacent to those banks had for their own Commodity and benefit, often repaired divers parts of them, but not at all for the advantage of the Country." He affirmed this upon oath before a Jury, "wherefore the said Abbot was discharged from that Presentment." Dugdale, *op. cit.* 218.

[2] The Commissioners complained in 1620 that they had no power to take any man's land without his voluntary assent; and that "the authority which they had by their commission (to which they were strictly bound) was only to rate the charge of every particular man towards any such general work, according to the profit which every person should receive from the same. And forasmuch as t'was impossible to be discerned, before the work were finished, who should have profit thereby, or how much, they could not legally procure any such assurance beforehand." Dugdale, *op. cit.* 406.   [3] Dugdale, *op. cit.* 376.

a considerable population that subsisted principally on the A.D. 1558
—1603. fish and wild fowl of the marshes; these men objected obstinately to any drainage schemes which would change the character of the country[1]. The Commissioners of 1605 did consider the probable effect of their proposed schemes on the condition of the poor, and took an extremely sanguine view of its operation[2]; but the fen men themselves were persistently obstructive, and, as many of them were commoners, they could assert legal rights to prevent the inception of new works, till almost the close of the reign of Elizabeth. The *and to carry out* vehemence of their opposition was shown in the riotous pro- *new works* ceedings which broke out, especially in Lincolnshire, in the *in the face of opposi-* middle of the seventeenth century. The Commissioners of *tion.* Sewers were neither able to raise capital, nor to disarm local hostility; public works of the kind contemplated could not, as a matter of fact, be carried through by the mere pressure of authority[3] urging neighbours to co-operate for the common good.

[1] The *Anti-Projector, or the History of the Fen Project,* gives a good statement of the case against drainage. "The Undertakers have always vilified the Fens and misinformed many parliamentary men that all the Fen is a meer quagmire, and that it is a level hurtfully surrounded, and of little or no value. But those who live in the Fens and are neighbours to it know the contrary. For first, the Fens breed infinite numbers of serviceable horses, mares and colts, which till our lands, and furnish our neighbours. Secondly we breed and feed great store of young cattle, and we keep great dayeries, which afford great store of butter and cheese to victual the Navy, and multitudes of heyfers and Scots and Irish cattle have been fatted in the Fens, which afford hides and tallow. Thirdly, we mow off our Fens fodder, which feeds our cowes in winter, which being housed we gather such quantities of compost and dung that it enriches our pastures and corn ground, half in half, whereby we have the richest and certaintest corn land in England, especially for wheat and barley, wherewith by sea we do and can (if our navigable rivers be not made unserviceable by the undertakers pernitious new ditches) abundantly provide London and the northern parts in their necessities. Fourthly, we keep great flocks of sheep upon the Fens. Fifthly, our fens are a great relief not only to our neighbours the uplanders, but to remote countries, in which otherwise, some years thousands of cattle would want food. Sixth, we have great store of osier, reed and sedge which are such necessaries as the countries cannot want them for many uses, and sets many poor on work. Lastly we have many thousand cottagers, which live in our fens, which otherwise must go abegging." p. 8. (Brit. Mus. 725. d. 35.)

[2] Dugdale, *op. cit.* 385. It was contended that enclosure was a protection to the poor man, as there was a danger that the rich would not give his fair share of pasturage to the poor commoner. A. D., *Of fishing the Seas and converting waste into wealthe* 1612 (Trin. Coll. Camb. O. 5. 21) f. 4. b.

[3] The Privy Council occasionally took cognisance of the matter and brought pressure to bear, *Acts of the Privy Council,* Vol. x. p. 321, 7 Sept. 1578.

A.D. 1558
—1603.

Fresh schemes were chiefly due to the enterprise of individual proprietors

or associated undertakers.

Some attempts were quite unsuccessful,

while others answered all expectations,

The failure of local effort, even when stimulated by all the pressure which the Royal Commissioners could bring to bear, rendered it necessary to fall back on private enterprise, as the best instrument for carrying through these large schemes. Small pieces of land had been successfully reclaimed by individual proprietors[1]; Sir William Russel had organised a considerable undertaking at Thorney in Cambridgeshire, and had planted a colony of Walloons to execute the works[2]. But the great schemes, which were seen to be necessary at the close of the sixteenth century, were far too vast for any single person to carry through; there was need of associated enterprise, and in 1605 several wealthy individuals came forward to risk large sums of money in the enterprise. Sir John Popham, the Lord Chief Justice of England, and Sir Thomas Fleming, the Chief Baron of the Exchequer, together with an alderman and a clothier of London, undertook to carry out and maintain the drainage of the Great Level of the Cambridgeshire fens, amounting to more than 300,000 acres, at their own cost, on the understanding that they were to obtain possession of 130,000 acres when drained[3]. Despite the excellent auspices under which they started, their project turned out to be a failure; it was noted in 1619, that "Sir John Popham and others had ventured much money therein, with much loss and disadvantage to themselves and little effect[4]." In the Lincolnshire fens, near Witham, Sir Anthony Thomas obtained a temporary success; he commenced operations in 1632, and completed the work in three years. The outbreak of the Civil War, however, gave the fen men an opportunity of reasserting their views; and the fields, which had been cultivated for seven years, were entirely destroyed, together with the houses built on the drained land. The undertakers failed

---

[1] Irrigation was practised as a means of improving the land in the valley of the Wye by Vaughan, who held that 'drowning was cousin-germane to draining.' *Rowland Vaughan, His Booke* (1610), reprinted 1897 by E. B. Wood.

[2] Brit. Mus. *Lansdowne MSS.* cx. 4; also S. P. D. El. xcix. 38.

[3] Dugdale, *op. cit.* 383.

[4] Brit. Mus. *Lansdowne MSS.* clxii. 12. The similar project sanctioned by 4 J. I. c. 13 for draining 6000 acres in the Isle of Ely appears to have been more successful. Dugdale, *op. cit.* 390.

to obtain any redress from the parties then in power[1]. The dislocation of government, in 1642, was equally favourable to the rioters who objected to the draining of Hatfield Chase[2]; this had been successfully carried out by the Dutch engineer Cornelius Vermuiden, and cereals were cultivated on ground that had recently been mere marsh. Early in 1643 the fen men pulled up the flood gates of Snow Sewer, "which by letting in the tides from the River of Trent soon drowned a great part of Hatfield Chase; Divers persons standing there with Muskets; and saying, that there they would stay till the whole levell were drowned, and the Inhabitants forced to swim away like Ducks: and so continued guarding the said Sluse for the space of seven weeks together, letting in the tides at every full water, and keeping the Sluse shut at an ebb. And about that time, likewise, some of the Inhabitants of Millerton, pulled down another Sluse, neer that Town; which occasioned the River of Trent to break down the Banks and overflow the whole levell, so that the Barns and Stacks of Corn were drowned a yard high, at the least.

"And thinking this not to be mischief enough, the Inhabitants of the Isle of Axholme, did about Michaelmasse in the year 1645 tumultuously throw down a great part of the Banks, and filled up the Ditches, putting in Cattel into the Corn, and Pastures of those that had been Adventurers for the drayning[3]." Cromwell, who probably recognised the importance of the drainage schemes[4] endeavoured to restore order; but the agitators had a formidable spokesman in the person of Colonel John Lilburn[5], and the damage does not seem to have been redressed. James I. and Charles I. had both been keenly interested in the progress of such works,

A.D. 1558 —1603. but the works were destroyed during the Civil War,

---

[1] Wheeler, *op. cit.* 207. There were complaints in 1641 from the authorities of Charterhouse as to the highhandedness of the proceedings in these Lincolnshire improvements. *Hist. MSS. Comm.* IV. Ap. 95; also see *ib.* 94 for the commoners' complaint.

[2] Hunter, *The History and Topography of the Deanery of Doncaster*, I. 166.

[3] Dugdale, *op. cit.* p. 146.

[4] The names of his father Robert Cromwell and his uncle Oliver Cromwell occur in the Commission of Sewers in 1605. Dugdale, *op. cit.* 379. He had had opportunities of noting the results of draining in Cambridgeshire according to the *Mystery of the Good Old Cause* in Cobbett's *Parliamentary History*, III. 1595.

[5] Lilburn, *Case of the Tenants of the Manor of Epworth*, 1651.

A.D. 1558
—1603.

*which also
interfered
with royal
plans for
draining
the Great
Level.*

and as the undertakers had enjoyed royal countenance, there can be little surprise at the reverse they sustained during the Great Rebellion[1]. The draining of the great Cambridge-shire fens was a work which Charles himself had greatly at heart; he had given every encouragement to the Earl of Bedford and his partners, in carrying out Vermuiden's plans for this district[2]. They proved only partially successful, since the reclaimed land, though available for summer pasture, was flooded in winter; and Charles I. undertook at his own expense to carry out such further works as should render the district dry at all times of the year[3]. The out-break of the disturbances in Scotland, however, rendered it impossible for him to supply the necessary funds, and the affair was left to drag on in an unsatisfactory fashion[4] till it was carried through[5] by the corporation which was re-con-stituted at the Restoration[6].

*But
associated
enterprise
triumphed
eventually.*

The ultimate triumph of associated enterprise, in com-pleting these great undertakings[7] for the good of the realm and the benefit of the investors, is an interesting illustration of the possibility of directing private interests for the common weal. Patriotic moneyed men supplied the means of executing the works, in the expectation of profit for

---

[1] The Bishop of Lincoln's enclosures at Buckden in Huntingdon, which seem to have been made without reference to drainage, were broken down in 1641; the House of Lords endeavoured to protect him as a member of their house and made an order on the subject (L. J. IV. 281). The justice who went to estimate the damage done on the Bishop of Lincoln's land found there a crowd of about a hundred persons, chiefly women and boys, who had broken down the fences, made gaps in the hedges and turned in their cattle and done damage to the amount of £10; and when he asked them with fair speeches, to drive out their cattle until the matter should be lawfully determined, they only answered him with contemptuous words, and refused to obey the order of the House though three times read out to them. *Hist. MSS. Comm.* IV. Ap. 85; see also 62.

[2] Dugdale, *op. cit.* 408. Compare also S. P. D. C. I. cccxc. 89, 1637—8.

[3] S. P. D. C. I. ccclxxxii. Feb. 13, 1638, p. 252. Dugdale, *op. cit.* 412.

[4] Scobell, *Acts* II. p. 33 (29 May, 1649).

[5] Even so, it seems to have been imperfectly successful, or possibly in-sufficiently maintained. J. Armstrong, *The History of the Ancient and Present State of the Navigation of the Port of King's Lynn and of Cambridge* (1725), pp. 99, 100. *Journal of Royal Agricultural Society,* III. Series ii. 125.

[6] 15 C. II. c. 17, *An Act for settling the dreyning of the Great Levell of the Fenns called Bedford Level.*

[7] Many additional works remained to be carried out at the close of the eighteenth century under the stimulus of the high price of corn. Smiles, *Engineers,* II. 153.

themselves and with the hope that general advantage would A.D. 1558
accrue to the realm. The direct exercise of royal influence, —1603.
through the Commissioners of Sewers, on the inhabitants
of the districts affected, had proved a failure; but the
delegation of powers to privileged corporations answered the
purpose. In the Elizabethan age little was actually accomplished, but public opinion was being rapidly formed as to
the only method[1] in which this necessary task could be
pursued with success.

177. The Elizabethan age must also be credited with *The enter-*
the inception of other schemes, which were destined to be of *prise of landed men*
far-reaching importance in developing territorial resources. *in establish-*
The reclaiming of marsh land was very well in its way; still, *ing planta-*
this improvement could only be undertaken in particular *tions*
districts, and over a limited area; but the efforts of Englishmen to carve out estates for themselves in other countries,
were the first steps in a movement that has changed the
entire character of distant parts of the globe. English
colonisation was, in its beginnings and in its growth, the

---

[1] The statute of 1601, as a general act empowering concessions to undertakers,
gave a great impulse to the movement. There had been a previous attempt to
legislate, and a summary of the Act presented in 1585, intitled "An Act for the
recovery and inning of drowned and surrounded grounds" will be found in
S. P. D. El. clxxvi. 74. Much activity was shown in connection with the matter
in the last decade of the sixteenth century:

1592. Guillaume Mostart to Lord Burghley. Has undertaken to drain the
fens of Coldham in Cambridgeshire, bought by John Hunt, of London, on assurance that they can be drained. The work will be a great encouragement and
example to the draining of other fens in the kingdom, &c. S. P. D. El.
ccxli. 114.

1593. Humfrey Bradley to Lord Burghley. Sends a project for draining the
fens......Considering the diversity of the tenures and leases of the fens, and the
opinions of men, the most expedient way will be by Act of Parliament, &c.
S. P. D. El. ccxliv. 97.

1598. Note of the course to be taken for recovering surrounded grounds until
the late intended Act is established. Information is to be made by the Attorney
General in the Star Chamber of the loss to the Commonwealth by continuing
those grounds under water, and the loss and decay of outfalls to the sea; of the
rich profit which would arise from their recovery, and the multitude of people
which might be relieved and nourished thereby. S. P. D. El. cclxviii. 102.

The number of subsidiary proposals made in Elizabeth's reign show how much
hold these speculations had on the public mind. Compare Golding's patent for
an invention for draining marshes (S. P. D. El. cxxvii. 57), also Engelbert (Brit.
Mus. *Lansdowne MSS.* cx. 7). Many of the engineers and workmen employed
were foreigners. Cunningham, *Alien Immigrants*, 209.

A.D. 1558
—1603.
expansion of the landed interest. It certainly included
other elements and was influenced by other motives; but it

was the special character- istic
was carried through by men who went beyond the sea, to
make new homes and manage estates in accordance with
English ways. The plantations were not established by merchants and shipowners to serve as trading stations, like the
factories of the Dutch or of our own East India Company;
still less were they organised by capitalists with a mere
view to mining speculation, as was so much the case in the

of English colonisa- tion.
Spanish possessions. The English colonies have a character
of their own; because men, who loved the soil and lived on
it, were found ready to go abroad, not only to make their
fortunes, but to settle and rear families in a new country.

An attrac- tive field was offered by Ireland,
Ireland was an island which, both from its fertility and
position was specially attractive to men who were fired with
this ambition. The distracted condition of the country
rendered English immigration desirable from the point of
view of the government, as little progress had been made
in introducing law and order into the sister isle or in developing its resources. In the fifteenth century[1], Ireland
had been for commercial purposes a foreign country, and an
entirely undeveloped country; its principal products were
obtained from its wastes and rivers, and the surrounding seas.
Rabbits and deer, otters and squirrels and martins, salmon
and herrings, were objects of merchandise; while there was
also some cloth[2] and hides and woolfels. The author of the
Libel urges in impassioned language that the lordship of
such a country should be made a reality, that the wild Irish
should be reduced from barbarism, and that its rich resources, both in mineral wealth and in the fertility of its soil,
should be developed. Even while he wrote the fatal effects
of the Hundred Years War were telling on the ranks of the
English nobility, and the 'wild Irish' were becoming bolder
and recovering some of the ground they had lost[3]. When
the Wars of the Roses drew still further upon the English
gentry resident on their Irish estates, the wild Irish de-

---

[1] *Libel of English Policy* in *Political Songs*, II. 186.
[2] See below, p. 368, n. 2.
[3] *Libel of English Policy*, *Pol. Songs*, II. 189.

scended from the mountains, and lands which had been A.D. 1558
occupied by settlers were "shortly displanted[1]." And where —1603.
the 'wild Irish' encroached, the possibility of industrial life *which had*
was lost. They reverted at once to the nomadic type, moving *long con-*
tinued in a
from place to place to pasture their cattle, and subsisting *disturbed*
chiefly upon their milk[2]. This roving mode of life gave *condition,*
abundant opportunity for the harbouring of thieves or the
retaining of stolen cattle and for disorders of every kind.
The chief article of their attire was a mantle or plaid, which
served as a "fit house for an outlaw, a meet bed for a rebel,
and an apt cloak for a thief[3]." The feuds of different septs
rendered the country a constant scene of civil war, and gave
excuse for the maintenance of galloglasses and kerns whose
"common trade of life[4]" was to oppress all men. "They
spoil as well the subject as the enemy, they steal, they are
cruel and bloody, full of revenge and delighting in deadly
execution, licentious, swearers and blasphemers, common
ravishers of women and murderers of children." The general
uncertainty of life was particularly inimical to tillage; as
among the border reevers[5], so among the Irish, corn was
only to be had in small quantities[6]: neither the landlord
nor the tenant would have long leases,—the tenant because
the "landlords there used most shamefully to rack their
tenants, laying upon them coigny and livery at pleasure,
and exacting of them (besides his covenants) what he
pleaseth. So that the poor husbandman either dare not
bind himself to him for longer term or thinketh by his
continual liberty of change to keep his landlord in awe from
wronging of him[7]." Such continual disorder and uncertainty rendered industry and commerce impossible, and
the work of civilisation had to begin over again. It is
unnecessary to examine the precise reasons of the failure
of the various monarchs who, from the time of Henry II.
onwards, had endeavoured to evolve order from this chaos;
it is enough to mark the chequered success which attended
subsequent efforts.

[1] E. Spenser, *View of the State of Ireland, Works* (ed. Todd), VIII. 315.
[2] *Ib.* 363.   [3] *Ib.* 367.   [4] *Ib.* 392.
[5] Scott, *The Monastery*, c. 23.   [6] Froude, *History* (1870), x. 220.
[7] Spenser, *View, Works*, VIII. 404.

A.D. 1558
—1603.

in the hope
of reducing
the country
to order;
Either of two distinct policies might have been pursued ; one was the Roman method of establishing a strong military rule and forcing the natives to abstain from constant pillage so as to give the opportunity for the development of some sort of civilised life, for settled homes, and at all events for tillage. This was the scheme of Spenser, as of the author of the *Libel.* Had it been followed, a real Irish nation might have at last grown up out of the rival septs, under this protecting and civilising despotism; the Brehon laws might possibly have given birth to an Irish common law, and the poetry of the bards to a wealth of Irish literature. This was the statesmanlike scheme, and the scheme which is being now followed in India ; but it appeared to involve an enormous expenditure in maintaining a military establish-ment, and Elizabeth could not be expected to adopt it.

On the other hand it might be possible to establish successive bodies of settlers who should be strong enough to hold their own in a considerable territory, and thus bit by bit plant the whole country. A scheme for encouraging such enterprises had been talked of as early as 1560 when and planting was
attempted
by Gilbert
in Ulster, Sussex, who was then Deputy, proposed[2]. In 1567 a definite plan was arranged; Sir Humphrey Gilbert and other west-country Englishmen undertook to plant Crown lands in Ulster; and an elaborate plan was drawn up by which every two parishes in England were to provide a man, and £9. 2s. to keep him[3]. It was also suggested that some of the numerous refugees from Flanders should be sent there[4]: the project, however, fell through.

in Munster, Two years later, the Devonshire men offered to plant Munster, a proposal of which Cecil did not altogether ap-prove[5]. The Earl of Desmond had surrendered his large territory in Munster, and it was suggested that the whole should be declared forfeit, and granted to these gentlemen of Devonshire, who would endeavour to carry England into

---

[1] The difficulties and the fortunes of this colonisation in Ireland have been carefully treated by Dr M. J. Bonn, *Die englische Kolonisation in Irland,* i. 265.

[2] *Calendar of the Carew Manuscripts* (1515—1574), p. 302.

[3] Froude, *History*, x. 225.   [4] *State Papers, Ireland,* xxi. 48, July 1567.

[5] Froude, x. 232. *State Papers, Ireland,* xxviii. 2, 3, 4, 5, 9.

Ireland , they were ready to transport labourers and artisans from their own neighbourhoods, and they were prepared to proceed to extremities with any of the native Irish, who would not suffer themselves to be absorbed in the new social system : they hoped, after three years, to be able to pay a regular rental to the Queen. The scheme was too heroic and drastic to commend itself either to Elizabeth or to Cecil; and any prospect of its being carried into effect was wrecked by Sir Peter Carew, and others of the projectors, who attempted to enforce claims to landed possessions, to which they had legal claims under ancient deeds[1], though the area had been re-occupied by the Irish during the fifteenth century. The whole of Ireland was set in a blaze by their proceedings, and the project of planting the Desmond estates was deferred. It was revived in 1584, under specially favourable circumstances, as the country was so entirely waste that there was no reason to fear difficulties with the native inhabitants[2]; but between the dilatoriness of the commissioners, who surveyed the estates, and the recklessness of the undertakers, who occupied them, the whole proved a miserable failure.

Meanwhile, the scheme for planting lands in Ulster[3] had *and by Sir* been kept in view; Sir Thomas Gerrard undertook it in *T. Smith in Ulster.* 1570[4]; but the attempt was first really made by the son of Sir Thomas Smith[5]. When the Irish heard of the scheme, the country was in an uproar[6], and Thomas Smith the

---

[1] Froude, *op. cit* x. 234.

[2] Dunlop in *English Historical Review*, III. 250.

[3] Camden, *Elizabeth*, 190.   [4] *State Papers, Ireland*, xxx. 32.

[5] (Sir Thomas Smith) has "sithens his returne tolde me divers times, that he thought Irelande once inhabited with Englishe men and polliced with Englishe lawes, would be as great commoditie to the Prince as the realme of England, the yerely rent and charges saved that is now laide out to maintaine a garrison therein, for there cannot be (sayeth he) a more fertile soile thorowe out the worlde for that climate than it is, a more pleasant, healthful, full of springs, rivers, great fresh lakes, fishe and foule, and of moste commodious herbers, England giveth nothing save fine woole, that will not be had also moste abundantly there, it lacketh only inhabitants, manurance and pollicie.... To inhabite and reforme so barbarous a nation as that is, and to bring them to the knowledge and law, were bothe a godly and commendable deede, and a sufficient worke for our age." Letter of T. B. Gent to his friend Master R. C. in Hill, *An Historical Account of the Macdonnells of Antrim*, pp. 406, 409.

[6] *Calendar of the Carew Manuscripts*, 1515—1574, p. 419.

younger was killed in a fray soon after his arrival[1]. Sir Thomas Smith did not relinquish the effort, however, to which he had given much thought; and his nephew, William Smith, endeavoured to carry on the undertaking after his death; but he had no success, and his heirs failed to establish a claim to the lands on which so much had been spent[2]. About the time when Sir Thomas Smith was planning the undertaking, Essex obtained a grant of Clandeboy, and many gentlemen joined with him to establish a settlement[3], but after a fruitless attempt he gave up the enterprise and resigned his grant.

Plantations were also projected in America as When so much difficulty had to be encountered by settlers in Ireland, it is all the more surprising that men should have been found who were venturesome enough to emigrate across the Atlantic. Still, this great undertaking appealed very strongly to patriotic men[4], who desired to rival *a menace to Spain,* the achievements of the Spaniards, and to check their arrogant claims to undisputed possession of the newly-discovered lands. The possibilities of mining and trading seem to have operated, as additional incentives, to these arduous *and with a view to mining and fishing,* endeavours; the first English attempt at settlement was made in connection with the fisheries of Newfoundland. From Parkhurst's memoir, on the subject, it appears that the English authority was recognised among the fishing fleets off that coast in 1578[5], though they only sent some fifty sail, while the Spaniards had over a hundred, and the French a hundred and fifty. They could obtain sea-salt in plenty and become the lords of the fishing, if they were settled there; while there was always a chance of mining, and furs might be had from the adjoining mainland. Others were in the field, *by Sir H. Gilbert,* and just before the Bristol merchant[6] urged his scheme, a patent had been issued to Sir Humphrey Gilbert[7] "for the inhabiting and planting of our own people in America." The

---

1 Strype, *Life of the learned Sir T. Smith*, 133.
2 Strype, *op. cit.* 137.
3 *State Papers, Ireland*, XL. 59—71 (May 1573).
4 See below, p. 335.
5 Hakluyt, *Voyages*, III. 134, also III. 150.
6 Nov. 13, 1578.
7 June 11, 1578. Hakluyt, *op. cit.* III. 135.

grant was couched in the widest terms and empowered Gilbert A.D. 1558 —1603. to settle in America, to take out subjects there and to exercise jurisdiction over them. The difficulties which attended this *whose scheme* ill-fated expedition "in which Sir Humphrey consumed *was too* much substance and lost his life at last," have been related *ambitious,* in detail by Mr Edward Hayes, one of his companions. In sending it out, Elizabeth had evidently been actuated by the hope of obtaining precious metals, for she had reserved a right to one-fifth of all the minerals discovered; the Saxon refiner, who accompanied the expedition, declared that certain ores they discovered in Newfoundland contained silver, but this proved to be an error. The chief cause of failure, however, lay in the vagueness of the enterprise; it was Sir Humphrey's intention to take possession of the whole coast from Florida to Newfoundland, and grant assignments to settlers who chose to occupy some particular points. But in order to found a colony, it was necessary to fix on some definite place of settlement which should be chosen for clear and intelligible reasons, and to concentrate the enterprise on that point[1].

Sir Walter Raleigh[2], who received a very similar patent *and by Sir W.* in 1584, did not fall into the same error, but expended his *Raleigh,* efforts on special points in Virginia. The settlers wrote enthusiastically of the fertility of the soil, and the excellence of the grapes and maize it produced, but they had to contend with many difficulties. Their stores failed them before they reaped their harvest, and after ten months' residence they returned to England, with the assistance of Sir Francis Drake[3]. Raleigh shortly afterwards sent out another expedition; fifteen men, with stores for two years, were left in the deserted colony, and in 1587 an expedition was sent *but without* out on a much larger scale. Raleigh obtained a charter *success.* of incorporation for the Virginia company, and appointed Mr John White, governor, with twelve assistants, to carry on the affairs of the colony[4]. But disaster still dogged the attempt; it was found necessary to move the colony inland,

---

[1] Hayes in Hakluyt, *op. cit.* III. 160.
[2] Hakluyt, *op. cit.* III. 243.
[3] *Ib.* III. 264.   [4] *Ib.* III. 280.

and the vessels, which came from England after a long delay, were unable to follow the settlers to their retreat, where they at last perished miserably.

Such schemes had become possible because the landed interest was closely in touch   The distance from the mother country, and the lonely and defenceless position of colonists in America, were certainly grave disadvantages; Camden remarks[1] that such undertakings were too much for private persons to attempt; and the first permanent settlements were carried out under the auspices of a corporation of London merchants[2]. None the less is it true that the practice of making a grant of territory to some man of property and title, who might be able to plant it with the help of his dependents, continued to be a favourite expedient for developing the English possessions in America. The landed gentry and the yeoman of the seventeenth century were not so rooted to their native soil as to be unable to endure the prospect of migration across the ocean.

The venturesomeness and vigour, which characterised so many classes in the Elizabethan age, are possibly connected with the fact that there was a greater solidarity throughout the nation than ever before. Provincial feeling and civic enthusiasm were giving place to a keen sentiment of nationality; the classes of society were more closely blended than had been possible in feudal times; and the cleavage, which became so marked at a later date, between the landed and moneyed interest had hardly begun to show itself[3]. A large *with commercial enterprise.* proportion of the London apprentices were drawn from the homes of rural gentry. "It was a great matter," as we read, "in former Times to give £10 to bind a Youth Apprentice; but in King James the First's Time they gave 20, 40, 60, and sometimes £100 with an Apprentice. But because the Apprentices of London were often Children of Gentlemen and Persons of good Quality, they did affect to go in costly apparel and wear weapons[4]." And the merchant who had made his fortune in trade was eager to invest it in land[5].

---

[1] *Elizabeth*, anno 1583, p. 287.

[2] The London Goldsmiths contributed to these attempts at the instance of the Lord Mayor in 1611. Prideaux, *op. cit.* Vol. I. pp. 111, 119.

[3] See, however, below, p. 160, n. 3.

[4] Stow, *Survey*, v. 329.   [5] See above, p. 111.

There was at least such intercourse between the merchants A.D. 1558
and the rural population that schemes of plantation, which $\overline{1603.}$
involved the cooperation of both, could be started, and
eventually carried to a successful issue.

V. THE MONEYED INTEREST.

178. The first years of Elizabeth's reign were marked *On the*
by a financial operation of unexampled magnitude; she was *accession of*
Elizabeth
able to carry through a scheme, which had been in considera- *immediate*
steps were
tion for several years[1], and restore the coinage to something *taken for*
restoring
like the old standard of fineness. There was real courage in *the silver*
coinage,
facing this difficult task[2]; it was not easy to estimate beforehand the probable expense of the undertaking[3]; the mere
work of turning out such a mass of coinage with the desired
rapidity strained the resources of the Mint; a special Commission was appointed, and a temporary mint was organised[4];
speculators were ready to take advantage[5] of any oppor-

---

[1] Ruding, *Annals of the Coinage*, I. 319. There are numerous proclamations
on the subject in the years from 1545 to 1556. Several have been preserved in
the Society of Antiquaries Library, and a list will be found in the Earl of Crawford's *Handlist of Proclamations (Bibliotheca Lindesiana)*.

[2] The Commission which was appointed in 1560 to enquire into the organisation of the Mint, the state of the coinage, and the best methods of effecting
a change (S. P. D. El. XII. 67) included Lord North the Treasurer, Mr Carr,
Mr Peckham, Mr Mildmay, Mr N. Throckmorton, as well as Cecil himself, who
recorded the names.

[3] We have some recorded examples of expert advice on the subject, e.g., Mr
Humfreys' scheme (Brit. Mus. *Harleian*, DCLX. No. 25 f. 76), Mr Stonley's opinion
(S. P D. El. XIII. 27), also Mr Burd's (*ib.* 34). Compare also the elaborate
scheme preserved among the *Cottonian MSS.* Julius F. VI. 86, and Fitzherbert's
proposals, *Lansdowne MSS.* IV. 19.

[4] The Marquis of Winchester, Cecil, Parry, Sackville and Mildmay were the
Commissioners appointed for carrying out the work (S. P. D. El. XIV. 33). Two of
them were to visit the Mint and inspect the refining and recoining twice each week
or oftener It was found necessary to establish a temporary mint in consequence
of the great increase of work. *A Breife Collection of the Alterations which have
been made in the monies of this Realme* (1611). Brit. Mus. *Lansdowne MSS.*
DCCVI. f. 17. The accounts in the *Lansdowne MSS.* (IV. No. 58) distinguish the
Upper and the Lower Mint.

[5] Proclamation of Edward VI. entitled "*A proclamation set furth by the
kinges maiesty with the aduise of his most honorable priuey counsail, declaring
his graces determinacion, concerning the amendement of his highnes coyne and
also to admonish such of his subiectes as be engrossers of fermes, victualles and
other thinges and the inhauncers of al prices of the same, and for the amendemente*

A.D. 1558
—1603.

*and public
suspicion
was roused*

tunities for gain, while the public were not fully convinced of the necessity of the measure, and were suspicious that the change would only cause them loss of one kind or another. As a matter of fact this suspicion was justified; the men who held base money[1] were mulcted by the difference between the actual value of the coins in their possession, and the value the coins would have had if they had been minted of pure silver. The Crown had gained at the expense of the public by debasement; and at this re-issue, the moneyed men were forced to sacrifice themselves in the public interest. The government undertook the expense of the actual minting[2] and organised the machinery

of their gredy and insaciable doinges, the xi day of May in the v yere of his moste prosperous reigne.

"Yet neuerthelesse, suche is the malice and naughty nature of a certain kinde of people that liue onely for themselves, and as it semeth by their doinges, neither respect God, King, the suertye of his Maiesties Croune, nor any other Christian creature, but goyng about to eate and denoure, aswel the state of Nobilitie, as the lower sorte, beyng Seruing men, Artificers, Handicraftes, poore Husbondemen, laborers and such like, and further maliciously ouerwharting and hindering all good purposes of the kinges maiestie, and his counsaill, trauailing to do to the common wealthe good, and especially when they perceaue anything purposed, to amend the unreasonable prices of victuall, and suche necessary thinges for mens sustenance, that as it is come to his Maiesties knowledge, and his counsaill, by the information of diverse credible persons from sundry partes of this his Realme, since the aforesaid proclamation was published, whiche was the very ordinarye and necessary beginning of a manifest amendement of the coine, the prices of victualles, wares and such like thinges, be purposely inhaunced beyond all expectacion, and the gratious meaning of the Kinges Maiestie and his counsaill utterly peruerted, and sinisterly abused, the same most manifestly comming of the deuelishe malice, and slight of the foresaide kinde of naughty people, iniurious to the whole common wealth: which thinges considered, his Maiesty having the Swearde not in vaine committed to him of God, and with the same as a minister of the almighty, the very indignacion and plages from heaven to fall where his Swearde shall strike, cannot, ne may not, without thoffence of God, se and suffer suche lewde persones as wilfully be the causers hereof remaine unpunished to their own dampnations, and the distruccion of others." Brit. Mus. 1851. b. 3 (2). Compare also Milles on the action of the Merchant Adventurers in the time of Edward VI. (*Customers Reply*, p. 20).

[1] "The cheff greff wilbe to them that shall have there substance in mony and not in wares; Likewise such wilbe greved as have payd great fynes for there firmes, consydering the prycees of thyngs growing uppon the same firmes wilbe cheper than they thought when they toke the firmes." *Reasons ageynst the decryeng of Monny*, Brit. Mus. *Cotton MSS.* Julius, F. vi. 54. f. 84.

[2] Proclamation, Dyson, p. 25, 1560. "And for the reliefe of such persons as shall possesse any of them Her Maiestie is pleased of her mere goodnesse to susteyne the burden, and cause not onely to be delyuered at her Mint in London at any time within the sayd space of the sayde foure monethes, for every one of

by which this important change was effected[1]; that it was A.D. 1558
—1603.
carried out so successfully reflects great credit upon the
Queen's advisers[2]. Some preliminary investigation had been
made in the time of Edward VI.[3]; but the scheme, as even- *and the*
tually carried through, was entirely organised under Eliza- *scheme*

the sayd testons so marked, the summe of two pence farthyng of good new sterlyng
monyes of fine sylver, or so much more as the same shalbe proued to conteyne in
good syluer: But also for every pounde of the same beying brought to her Mynt
ouer and aboue the sayde rate, three pence of good sterlyng sylver....And for
the more spede to be used also in the conversion thereof and thereby the full
abolishing of all maner of the sayde base monies; Her Maiestie is pleased to
beare the charge, and to geve further in rewarde to the bryngers thereof, for
every twenty shyllynges of them so brought to the sayde mynt and exchaunged
three pence of lyke good fine monyes."

[1] German capitalists undertook much of the work of refining (S. P. D. El. xiv.
43, also 55). This stimulated the competition of Englishmen, and Peter Osborne
undertook to refine 18 cwt. of base money at a less charge than the Alymayne
refiners in the Tower (*ib.* 57). We hear also of the competition between English
and German workmen in a letter from Stanley to Cecil (S. P. D. El. xiv. 8), "We
do coyne £7000 a weake and I trust we shall corn to £10,000 yf we might have it
speadelye refyned, my Lorde Tresorer hath promysed to healpe us with some more
rome with the bowyers. His lordshipe wilbe ther tomorrowe, and set the fyners of
London in hand to trye what thay ar able to doo, and how good chepe thay will
take it upon them to serve the quene, for it greveth them muche that Strangers
shulde do it better cheape than thaye, but for anyethinge that I have seane as yet,
yf the Stranger will doo it for 10*d.* a lb., one with another, it shalbe a good
bargayne for the Quens Majestie, and better than we shalbe able to doo it in the
mynte. I shall advertisse your honor within this iii dayes howe our fynors will
undertake to doo it." Sir John Yorke writing to Cecil, Oct. 5, 1560 (S. P. D. El.
xiv. 11), considers the Almayns could save the Queen £20,000 at the least.
According to the accounts in the *Lansdowne MSS.* (iv. 58, f. 213), the Englishmen
coined 96,500 lbs. for which they received £5,015, and the Almaynes 535,405 lbs.
at a cost of £22,308. 10*s.* 10*d.*

[2] In completing Miss Lamond's notes to the *Discourse of the Common Weal*
(p. 160, note 1. 22), I remarked that Sir Thomas Smith (unlike Gresham) was not
convinced of the evils of debased currency (see also Vol. i. p. 561). My attention
has since been called to a note in Strype's *Life of Sir Thomas Smith* (1820), p. 36,
which does not occur in the edition of 1698, which I had habitually used; it
states that "according to the advice of Smith for good sterling money to be
coined, those coarse testoon pieces were forbidden to be coined." In Sir Robert
Cotton's speech in the Oxford Parliament of Charles I., the credit of advising
the return to the old standard of fineness is given to Sir Thomas Smith, jointly
with Burleigh; I thus learn to my regret that I have done that "grave and
learned man" an injustice. *Cottoni Posthuma* (1679), 287. That he had given
great attention to monetary questions is seen from his treatise, dedicated to Cecil,
on the value of Roman coins. See especially Chapter VI. where the changes in
the number of English coins minted from an ounce of silver are noted, and the
history is carried down to 1562. Brit. Mus. *Harl. MSS.* dclx. 35, and *Lansdowne
MSS.* iv. 25.

[3] Ruding, *Annals*, i. 321.

A.D. 1558
—1603.

was care-
fully
planned.
beth. It seems that she took a keen personal interest in the matter, and drafted some papers on the subject with her own hand. A mass of base money, amounting to 631,950 lbs., was collected, and yielded 244,416 lbs. of pure silver; this was re-coined into £733,248, and as only £638,113. 15s. 6d. had been paid for it[1], the Crown appears to have been a gainer by the transaction. After the cost of collection had been paid, together with the expenses of refining and re-coinage (£40,306. 15s. 3d.), a handsome balance remained to the Queen, as the profit of the transaction; though the interest on borrowed capital would reduce this considerably[2]. Such successful management reflects the greatest credit on those who accomplished this difficult work. The chief refiner employed was Daniel Wolstat of Antwerp, who was engaged by Sir Thomas Gresham, on the understanding that he would receive five per cent. on the value of the reissued coinage[3]. The work was executed more rapidly than would otherwise have been possible, through the command of 300,000 dollars which were borrowed about this time by the same financier[4].

*It was
necessary
to call
down the
base money
to its
value in
silver.*
So many proclamations were issued, that it is possible both to follow the course pursued, and the steps that were taken to reassure the public[5]. The first action of the Government was to issue, on 27 September, 1560, a succinct statement of the evils that arose from the circulation of base moneys, and to call down these coins to their actual value in silver[6]; the testoon of 6d. was not to pass for more than 4½d.;

---

[1] Froude (vii. 9) calls attention to the accounts in *Lansdowne MSS.* iv. 58, which Ruding had not the opportunity of studying at first hand.

[2] See below, p. 147.

[3] Burgon's *Life and Times of Sir Thomas Gresham*, i. 354.

[4] *Ib.* i. 343. Elizabeth also granted a warrant to the Lord Treasurer to melt down royal plate for this purpose. S. P. D. El. xiv. 4, 12.

[5] On the grievances of the poor, in 1552, through the tampering with the currency, see T. Cooper, *Chronicle* (ed. 1565), f. 351.

[6] Dyson, 25, *Proclamation for the valuation of certain base monies currant in this realme called testons.* "The Quenes most excellent Maiestie, amongst other great and wayghtye consultacions had at sundry tymes with her counsayle, and somtymes with other wise and expert men, for the reformation of such abuses as be thought hurtfull to the commonweale of this her Realme, hath founde by consente of all sortes of wyse men, that nothyng is so greuous, ne lykely to disturbe and decaye the state and good order of this Realme, as the suffraunce of the base monies, being of dyvers standardes and mixtures, to be so aboundantly currant within this Realme, which have ben coyned in the same, before her

though the worst examples of this coin, in number about one- A.D. 1558
—1603.
sixth of the whole, were only to be reckoned at half that figure
($2\frac{1}{4}d$.). This preliminary step,—the reduction of current *This gave*
money to lower denominations,—apparently created great *rise to*
some
alarm. No one seems to have known which were the good *discontent,*
and which the bad testoons. Accordingly the Queen sent out
directions that these last should be stamped. The reason is
given in a letter to the Lord Mayor[1]. "Forasmuche as we *and*
measures
perceyve that notwithstanding your travayle in our Citie of *were taken*
London, for the quyeting of our Ignorant people, in the discerning of the bassest testons from the better, wherin we com-
mende you, yet ther needith furder ayde therin." Several
places were to be appointed, where people could go and have
their coins stamped with the portcullis or the greyhound, according to their value. We know, from the letter-books of the
City of London, that the halls of the city companies were

Majesties raigne, and no parte sence: Nor contrarywyse anye one thyng so
profitable, or in short tyme to be so comfortable for al maner of people, as to
have in place of the same base and copper monies, fine and good sterlyng monyes
of siluer and golde. For her Maiestie well perceiueth, by the long sufferaunce of
the sayde base and copper monyes, not onely her Crowne, Nobilitie, and subiectes
of this her Realme, to be dayly more and more impouereyshed, the auncient and
singuler honour and estimacion, which this Realme of Englande had beyond all
other by plentye of monies, of golde and syluer, onely fine and not base, is
hereby decayed and vanyshed away: but also by reason of these sayde base
monyes, greate quantitie of forged and counterfaites haue ben and be dayly made
and brought from beyonde the seas, for the which the auncient fine golde and
syluer, and the rich marchaundise of this Realme is transported and dayly caryed
out of the same, to the impoueryshyng thereof, and enryching of others. And
finally hereby all maner of prices of thynges in this Realme necessarye for
sustencacion of the people, growe dayly excessiue to the lamentable and manifeste
hurte and oppression of the state, speciallye of Pensioners, souldyers, and all
hyred seruauntes, and other meane people that lyue by any kynde of wages, and
not by rentes of landes or trade of marchaundyse."

The longer statement, of which a summary is printed by Ruding (I. 334), does
not appear to have been formally proclaimed; a draft of it exists in the Record
Office (S. P. D. El. XIII. 42), and is largely corrected by Cecil. Sir Thomas
Gresham gets the credit of insisting on the necessity of recalling the base
money—as good and bad coins would not circulate together. It is clear, however, that Cecil was convinced of the importance of taking action; "He held a
position (which undoubtedly is true), viz. that 'That realme cannot be rich whose
coigne is poore or base.' And he would also saye *Opportet patrem familias magis
esse vendacem quam emacem* (That a prince ought rather to be a seller than a
buyer). Seeing that realme must needs be poore that carrieth not out more than
it bringeth in." Peck, *Desiderata Curiosa*, I. 11.

[1] S. P. D. El. XIV. 5.

used for this purpose.   Stanley, writing in October 1560, says that he fears the stamping will quiet the people very little, as it is so easy to counterfeit the stamp of the better sort[1].   It was a comparatively easy matter to get the testoons marked *to distin-guish the different sorts of base coin* in London, and much more difficult in the country.   There is a very interesting letter, drafted entirely by Cecil[2] writing in the name of the Queen.   "We have ordeined that in sondry placees of our realme there shuld be certen trusty persons appoynted, not onely to informe our people herin, but also to stamp the sayd testons."   The letter directs the recipient : "On the receipt of these letters, ye shall imme-diately assemble your brethren, and if there be any gentle-man dwelling in that towne, or within one myle of the towne, being a Justice of Peace in any part thereabout, ye shall also send for hym and in your hall, or tolbothe, or other commen place of your assemblees . . . In the oppen presence of them all ye shall rede this letter, and then unseale a bagg, which this messengar shall delyver unto you, conteining in it twoo stamping yrons"; and then "choose to yourself iiii moo of the wisest and metest persons of the towne, whereof the Justice of Peace to be one, to sitt with you."   These were "to sitt in the sayd oppen place or at the market cross, calling to you some goldsmith of the best knowledg that ye can gett, or some other person having best knowledg in the matter of monyes, and shall there be redy to judg and discerne of all manner of testons, that any our subiects shall bryng unto yow, which be of the vallue of 2¼ and which 4½."   These were to be stamped.

"But in casees very doubtfull, ye shall rather forbeare such doutful testons, and permitt them to pass without any stamp, and so be brought to our mynt, where the just tryall shalbe made and the very vallue payd for the same.

with the aid of experts "Ye shall also, by authorite hereof, sweare the Goldsmyth to judg and discern trewly betwixt the one monneys and the other to the uttermost of his knowledg.   And for the Con-tynuance of your sitting, at one tyme or for your dayes of sitting, we doo referr that to your discretion, as ye shall see cause gyven to you by confluence of our people to you with

[1] S. P. D. El. xiv. 7.   [2] S. P. D. El. xiv. 17, Oct. 10, 1560.

there monnyes, so as ye nether sitt before ix of the clock in _A.D. 1558_
the fornoone nor after iii in the afternoon, nether uppon any _—1603._
hollydaye, nether that fewer of you sitt at one time than iiii
beside the Goldsmyth, if any such can be had." When done
with, the irons were to be put into the bag and sealed till
next time, and never to be used except in the open place.
After a month they were to be sent back to the Mint. No
fee was to be taken for stamping. " Before one month shall _till new coin was_
pass, we trust to cause a quantite of fyne monnyes to be sent _ready to be_
into these partes for the use and comfort of our subiects[1]." _issued._
Great pains were taken to reduce the incidental evils to a minimum, and to carry out the change as rapidly as possible;
the Queen undertook of her "mere goodnesse to susteyne the
burden," and supply good silver at the proclaimed rates to
those who brought base money to the mint[2]. The goldsmiths
were the agents by whom the base money was collected[3];
and a small bonus of 3_d._ in the pound was offered by the
Crown, in the hope of inducing the holders to bring it in[4],
so that the conversion might proceed quickly.

[1] This letter was to be sent to Canterbury, Salisbury, Exeter, Bristol,
Gloucester, Coventry, York, Lincoln, Norwich, Durham, Chester, Ipswich,
Warwick; to Wales, also to Newcastle, Hereford, S. Albans, Bury, Shrewsbury,
Nottingham, Northampton, Chichester, Oxford, Cambridge, Worcester, Hull,
Boston, Bedford, Colchester, Winchester, Launceston, Lancaster, Stamford,
Reading, Stafford, Leicester, Huntingdon, Derby and Carlisle.

[2] Dyson, _op. cit._ 25, Sept. 1560.

[3] S. P. D. El. XIV. 7, 11, 54. The Mayor of Bristol gives a detailed account of
the proceedings in that city (XVI. 10) when £1000 was sent down to be exchanged
for base testoons, by two goldsmiths, Robert Wells and Francis Eton.
"I and my bretheren the aldermen of this Citie did not onlie appoint a verie
discrete citezyn here to accompany the said Goldsmithes in the tyme of the said
exchange of the moneys aforesaid but also we ourself had ernest regard that they
said Goldsmithes did not receve for the exchange of the said base monyes above
viid in the pounde and that they received no pece of the base moneyes of 4½ or 1½
in exchaunge of the said ffyne monyes so longe as the said peces of 2¼ were
brought in to be exchanged for new monyes. During the whiche tyme of exchange notwithstanding we caused proclamation to be made that all persons
shold repayer unto the place of exchange with their base monyes of 2¼ where they
shold have ffyne monyes in exchange for the same . . . . yet litle more then the
somme of £400 of the peces of 2¼ were brought unto the said place of exchange,
any somme of the base money, were it never so little, not being refused." Then a
proclamation was issued saying that 4½ and 1½ pieces would be exchanged, 4_d._ in
the £ being taken. So few were brought in that for the better despatch the goldsmiths were afraid to take the 4_d._ in the £.

[4] This allowance was calculated to defray the expense of portage. Proclamation 12 June, 1561.

A.D. 1558
—1603.
*Pains were
taken to
provide
against
disputes*

*and
against
trading in
the debased
coins.*

The Government endeavoured to guard by anticipation against two obvious practical difficulties. They feared it was likely that disputes would arise about the value of particular coins, especially in the case of the various issues of base testoons; and provision was made for the speedy settlement of disputes[1]. There was also considerable danger that the base money might be engrossed, and transported to some other country, or to Ireland, where a better rate, than that now proclaimed, might be obtained for the coins[2]; apparently this traffic occurred to some extent[3], for there are repeated prohibitions of the export of bullion[4]. It is obvious that if this practice had been permitted, the effect

---

[1] Dyson, 25. "And by cause it may be, that the knowledge and understandyng of the foresayd base testons, being marked with the sayd markes, may be so doubtfull, by reason the markes be but small and may be partly worne out, It is ordered that upon any controuersie thereof arrysyng within any citie or towne corporate, or within any market towne not corporate, or within any other paryshe, the same shalbe thus ended and determined. That is, in euery Citie or towne corporate, by the Maior, Alderman, Provost, Baylyffes, or any other that is, by the same corporation, the principall officer of the same. And in every market towne not corporate, by the Justices of the peace there resydyng, yf any such be, or els by the Curate of the principall Church, and the chiefe officer or baylyffe of the toll of the same market. And in every other paryshe, eyther by the Justice of the peace, yf any resyde within one myle, or elles by the Curate of the parishe and the two Constables, or headborowes, or any two of them, to whose iudgement it is ordered both the parties which shall pay and receive, shall stande and abyde, concernyng the valuacion of the sayde base Testons."

[2] There was danger that they might be sent to Ireland, and special precautions were recommended on this point. S. P. D. El. xiv. 59.

[3] Dyson, 28. "The Quenes Maiestie understandyng, that aswell before as sythens the late Proclamation made, for reducyng of the base monies to theyr equall values, sundry people, both straungers and Englyshe, have bought and gathered together great summes of the Testons (as it is to be doubted) to make some perticuler gayne by meltyng, or carrying the same out of the Realme, whereby the good entent of her Maiestie to reduce the same to fine monies, shalbe greatly hindered, and consequently the common weale of this Realme, shall lacke the fruite long desiered."

[4] Compare the proclamations of Sept. and of October 1560 (Dyson, 26, 28), also that of 1 May, 1559, *A Proclamation for the Marchunt Aduenturers and against transportation of money, gold or bullion*, re-enforcing the statute 17 Edward VI., Dyson, 8. Also *An order how to avoyde the stealing of the quenes maiestie's customs and to provide that no golde shalbe caried oute of the weste partes of England*. Brit. Mus. *Lansdowne MSS.* cx. No. 48 f. 148. A bullionist policy of refusing to allow the export of the precious metals was carefully maintained at this time. An exception was made for Merchant Adventurers, and other "notorious marchauntes," who were permitted to take as much as £4 out for their personal expenses; also 18 March, 1600, Dyson, 371, *A Proclamation concerning coyne, plate and bullion of gold and silver*.

would have been to denude the country of the metal in the A.D. 1558 —1603. base money, so that the silver it contained would not have been available as material for the reissue.

January 31st, 1561, had been fixed on as the date when *The withdrawal and demonetisation of the base money* the worst testoons (2¼d.) were to be brought in to the Mint; as the time drew near, however, it became obvious that the Mint could not cope with all the mass of base money sufficiently fast. The public inconvenience of the transition was considerable[1], but it was necessary to grant an extension of the interval when these testoons would be received at the Mint till April 1st; while the public were assured that the better testoons (4½d.) would continue to be legal tender, and that no man might refuse to take them[2]. By the middle of February it was becoming clear that the operation could be successfully carried through, and that it was possible to proceed to demonetise the better, as well as the worse species of base coin[3]; and the 9th of April was fixed as the date when 4½d. testoons should cease to be current coin of the realm. By this time the Mint was working so well, that the Queen could assure her subjects that there was no fear they *and reissue of fine silver* would have to submit to an unreasonable delay in waiting for the new silver to be issued, in exchange for any base money brought in[4]; as an extra inducement to prompt action on the part of those who had the old testoons in their possession, it was announced that the bonus of 3d. in the £

---

[1] Compare the Earl of Bedford's report from Exeter (S. P. D. XIII. 48) and the letter from the Earl of Huntingdon in regard to Leicester (S. P. D. El. XIV. 49). The Archbishop wished to have a mint set up at York (S. P. D. El. XIX. 7) on account of the scarcity of coinage in his diocese in August 1561.

[2] Proclamation of 23 Dec. 1560 (Dyson, 30). The 2¼d. testoons ceased to be generally current on 31 Jan. 1561.

[3] Proclamation 19 Feb. 1651, Dyson, 31.

[4] Dyson, 31. Proclamation 19 Feb. 1561, "Furthermore her Maiestie thynketh meete to admonyshe her Subiectes that although in the begynnyng of this refining and coynage, such difficulties happened, as the expedition of exchaunge coulde not be so speedely made as was meant. Yet for that it is manifest that use and experience hath taken away all those difficulties, and that nowe the ministers of her Mintes be hable to make speedy retourne of fine monies for the base: Her Maiestie woulde that her Subiectes shoulde not forbeare to come to her sayde Mintes, without doubte there to be satisfied, for small summes at syght, or within two or three dayes, and for greater within viii or x and at the furthest not to continue above xx for so her Maiestie understandeth the habilitie of her officers nowe to do it and so hath directed them to execute the same."

A.D. 1558
—1603.
would not be given after 20th April; while the $4\frac{1}{2}d$. testoons would not be taken at the Mint after the 20th May, 1561. When these coins, which had presented the greatest diffi- culty, were once got out of the way, it was possible to give more serious attention to the pennies, three-farthing pieces and other coins of small denomination. These ceased to be legal tender on July 20th, though the holders were encouraged to bring them to the Mint for exchange at a later date[1]. The whole change was accomplished within a year from the date of the first proclamation (Michaelmas, 1560), and her Majesty congratulated herself on having "atchieved to the victory and conquest of this hideous monster of the base money."

were gradually carried out,

The withdrawal of the debased coinage had not been accomplished, however, without causing some inconvenience. There was in many places a deficiency of small change. A Proclamation[2] speaks of the base money being re-coined into "fine sylver moneys ... in greate peeces of shyllinges, and but a small quantitie in grotes and pence or halfpence, in respecte of haste and expedicion to auoyde the base moneys. There is rysen great anoyaunce amongst the poorer sort of her subiectes for lacke of small moneys of fine sylver. Whereupon her Maiestie hauing a perpetuall care from tyme to tyme, and from one degree to another to relieue the common hurtes or griefes of her subiectes, as they maye be perceiued: hath presently ordered, that in her Myntes no more peeces of shyllynges shoulde be coyned," but instead "half shyllynges of six pence, quarter shyllynges of three pence the peece, and a half piece called three half pence. And because a half peny cannot be made of such finenesse to beare any conuenient bulke, another small peece shall also be coyned of three farthynges. All which peeces her Maiestie assureth her subiectes shalbe of meere fine starling sylver." The Queen claimed that she had found the coinage

despite some consider- able incon- venience,

---

[1] Proclamation, 12 June 1561, Dyson, 35. The allowance of 3d. per £1 was to be given till August 25th, and the acceptance at the proclaimed rates to cease on Sept. 20.

[2] Dyson, 42, 15 Nov. 1561. Compare also Stow, *Annals*, 656. He says "the citizens of London were plagued with a three fold plague pestilence, scarcitie of money, and dearth of victuals, the miserie whereof were too long here to write."

"to be for the more parte copper, and hath nowe recouered A.D. 1558
—1603.
it to be as fine, or rather finer sterlyng sylver, then euer it
was in this Realme by the space of these two hundred yeres
and more, a matter worth markyng and memory."

There was doubtless some disappointment that the re- *but the re-coinage* coinage did not bring about an immediate cessation of the *did not* " dearth," or dearness of goods of every kind, which had been *realise all public ex-* rightly ascribed to the issue of base money. All sorts of *pectations.* rumours were in the air, about the Queen's intention to make further changes in the currency[1]; and these were made the excuse for holding back stocks of corn, and other sorts of victual. The difficulty was so great that it was necessary for the Justices to intervene, so as to ensure that the markets should be well supplied with food stuffs at a reasonable rate[2]. This practice was systematically developed in the periods of scarcity later in the reign[3].

179. By the great re-coinage the silver currency was *Current* restored to purity; but there were serious difficulties with *gold coins were* regard to gold coins. The amounts of this metal, which had been minted in England, had never been large[4], and there seems in consequence to have been a considerable quantity of foreign gold in circulation. Her Majesty was compelled *chiefly of foreign* to warn her subjects generally to " beware howe they shall *issue* receyve any maner forrayne coyne of golde or syluer, not beyng valued by publike aucthoritie and well knowen[5]." An improvement in the English silver standard necessarily involved a change in the 'rating' of. this gold currency by an *and after the re-* authoritative statement of the amount of English silver money *coinage of silver*

---

[1] Proclamations 30 Jan. 1562, Dyson, 44, and 13 March 1562, Dyson, 46, *A Proclamation against such as falsely report that the Queene intended to decrease her monies: and commanding that the markets may be supplied with corne and other victuals.*

[2] Proclamation 10 March 1562, Dyson, 45. Miss Leonard points out that similar instructions had been sent out in 1561 (*Early History of English Poor Relief*, p. 51), and refers to the Stowe MSS. CLII. f. 16. See also Proclamation of Ed. VI., 30 April 1551.   [3] See above, pp. 92, 97.

[4] The angel of Henry VI. and the royal (or rose noble) of Henry VIII. appear to have been the most ordinary coins in use; see the figure, Dyson, 42. For the amounts coined by Elizabeth see *Brief Collection* (1611) in Brit. Mus. *Lansdowne MSS.* DCCVI. f. 31.

[5] Proclamation 1st June, 1565, Dyson, 85.

A.D. 1558
—1603.

*it was
necessary
to change
the rating
at which
they were
to be
accepted in
England.*
for which the coins should pass. As soon as the re-coinage began, it had been necessary to call down the foreign gold crowns—French, Kaisers and Burgundians—from 6s. 4d. to 6s. in English silver[1]; the gold pistoles of Spain, Venice and Flanders were rated at 5s. 10d. instead of 6s. 2d.[2], and no other coins of this denomination were to be current[3]. Complaints were also made about the introduction of foreign coins, which bore a very close resemblance to the angel; but, whereas the English coin was valued at 10s., these imitations were not worth 9s. 3d.[4] at best, and some were hardly the equivalents of 7s.[5] A few months later, it was found that

*The
forging of
English
coins*
another coin—the royal of Henry VIII.—which was also worth 10s., was being imitated at foreign mints, and that great quantities of light and debased gold were getting into circulation; active steps were taken to insist that such gold should not continue to be current, but should be paid into the English mint; and the sheriffs and mayors were warned to be on their guard against "any lyke deceypt to be used to the preiudice of other current moneys of this Realme[6]."

It was very much harder to deal with the gold than with the silver coins, for the latter were the ordinary circulating

*and traffic
in coins
were causes
of com-
plaint*
medium within the realm, and gold was to a considerable extent an international currency[7]; it contained great value in small bulk, and was in consequence more easily smuggled than silver. The chief causes of complaint on this score are fully stated in a proclamation of 1587[8]. "Forasmuch as a great part of our moneys of Gold of our Realme of England, and such Gold of forraine countries, which are now currant within our said Realme, are by the sinister and unlawfull dealings of wicked persons, not onely caried out of our Realme to forraine countreys, and there by divers meanes diminished of their value, and from thence returned hither, and payed in lieu of lefull coyne for the commodities of our countreys, and some other of them embased by clipping,

---

[1] Proclamation October, 1560, 29. [2] *Ib.* 29.
[3] Proclamation 2 Nov. 1560, Dyson, 28.
[4] Proclamation 15 Nov. 1561, Dyson, 42.
[5] Proclamation 1 June, 1565, Dyson, 85.
[6] Proclamation, 1 Dec. 1565, Dyson, 88.
[7] Compare above, Vol. I. p. 328. [8] 12 Oct. 1587, Dyson, 244.

sowthering and other unlawfull practises of their due fines, A.D. 1558 —1603.
so that both the one sort and the other (by the meanes
aforesaide) are brought much inferiour to their first true
value and goodnesse. And beside that many false peeces
be counterfeited in forraine parts of the said coynes, whereby
great and intollerable losse and diminution of the riches of
our Realme doeth daily growe and encrease."

The only means of remedying the evil, that the govern- *and government insisted that gold payments should be made by weight,* ment could adopt, was to insist that payments of gold should be made by weight. The authorities of the Mint were in- structed to supply good balances and standard weights[1]; and a table was annexed of the deficiency which might be allowed for, in various coins. Any that were still lighter were not to be passed, but were to be taken to the Mint to be re-coined. This may have gradually proved fairly satis- factory for transactions within the realm[2], but the export of *but the prohibition of export could not be enforced* gold for payments abroad was not easily checked; and in 1600, a further attempt was made to re-enforce the pro- hibition which had been embodied in numerous statutes from the time of Edward III. onwards[3]. There would of course, under any circumstances, have been difficulty in pre- venting the occasional export of gold in connection with commercial transactions; but the temptation to evade the regulations was all the greater, because in England gold was rated at a lower value relatively to silver than in Scotland, or on the Continent[4]. There was a definite gain to be made by employing silver to buy up English gold, for export to other countries, where it would fetch a higher sum than had been paid for it. The attempts at fixing the ratios of gold and

---

[1] 12 Oct. 1587, Dyson, 244. On the 19th March in the following year we get a declaration about these cases of weights; they were made at the Mint and vended by the Wardens of the Goldsmiths' Company. The prices range from 3*s.* 5*d.* to 4*s.* 6*d.* Dyson, 258.

[2] As late as 1588 however, Sir Richard Martin, writing to Cecil, says that very few balances had been sold, and that coins of gold still passed in payment without weighing. Stow, *Survey*, Bk. I. 291.

[3] *A Proclamation concerning Coyne, Plate and Bullion of Gold and Silver*, 18 March, 1600. Dyson, 371.

[4] Proclamation 8 April, 1603, Ruding, I. 362. On the currency difficulties of the seventeenth century, the raising the value of money, and the rating of gold coinage, see below, pp. 435, 438 on the re-coinage of 1696; also W. A. Shaw, *The History of Currency*, 134; Lord Liverpool, *Treatise*, 60.

A.D. 1558
—1603.

*since the
variations
in official
rating*

silver, so as to keep both metals in circulation, were a source of constant trouble till the demonetisation of silver was accomplished in 1816. We are unfamiliar with the idea of official ratings, and fail to recognise that during the time when they were in constant operation, extraordinary opportunities arose for obtaining a profit, by transferring bullion from one place to another[1]. In all the great marts of Europe there was a variety of coins in circulation[2], and each was supposed to pass at an authoritatively established rate; any alteration of the recognised rate in a particular mart would probably render it profitable to export coins that had been called down[3], or to import any that had been enhanced from some other place, where the official rates were different. A community, that had a deficient supply of coinage, might be able to draw to itself the currency of other places, by the simple process of enhancing the rating[4]. It might be possible for the Prince of one land to do serious mischief

*might
induce a
flow of the
precious
metals*

[1] An illustration from the time of Henry VIII. is given by Malynes, *England's View*, pp. 61, 62. "Now before we conclude, it is worthie the noting, that when in this King's time the angel was woorth under the Archduke of Burgundie, 9 shillings 7 pence; the King did send unto the Duchesse (whiles her husband was in Germany) desiring her to value the angell at 10 shillings Flemish: but he could not obtaine the same. Which seemeth very strange, considering that the aduancing of the price of money, doth cause the money to be transported to the places where it is aduaunced: whereby all the angels might have bin caried into her dominion. But she like a wise and politike Duchesse, caused the matter to be examined and considered of, sending men skilfull in mint causes into England. And finding that the golden fleece, alias Toison d'or was the money then most currant with her: and the same was worth both in regard of weight and finenesse as much as the angel, and was also valued at 9 shillings 7 pence: She could not graunt the kings requests without altering also her money, unless shee would have suffered the English merchants to bring angels unto her for 10 shillings, and to carie away the golden fleeces for 9 shillings 7 pence to be conuerted into angels, to the great losse of her dominions, both in the money, and to leaue the Commodities of her country unvented: so long as there were a gaine upon the mony, which abated the price of commodities."

[2] Some insight into the difficulties which it caused in the xvth century may be obtained by reference to Mr H. E. Malden's Introduction to the *Cely Papers* (Camden Society, 3rd Series, Vol. I.), p. xlix.

[3] It would also affect the trade in commodities; it was alleged that it paid the merchant better to export gold from England rather than any of our commodities. Malynes, *England's View*, 181.

[4] Interesting illustrations of this fact may be drawn from the eighteenth century history of the North American colonies, where English reckoning was used, but the actual currency consisted of Spanish and Portuguese coins assessed at an official rate. See my article on *American Currency Difficulties in the*

to his neighbours by using his right of rating the coins current in his realm[1], but the evil became more serious, in so far as this power was usurped by private individuals. It was alleged that the continental bankers obtained a practical monopoly of the circulating medium and were able to rule the rates of exchange in their own interest[2]. During the sixteenth and seventeenth centuries, when a monetary revolution was in progress, and the masses of American silver were being gradually distributed throughout Europe[3], there would be great variations in the purchasing power of bullion in different localities, and the leading financiers must have had unexampled opportunities of manipulating the foreign exchanges. In England, many of those who were engaged in this occupation were aliens[4], and they were constantly

A.D. 1558 —1603. and bankers were able to manipulate the rates of exchange.

Eighteenth Century in the *Economic Review*, xi. 17 (1901). For a proposal on similar lines in 1580 see S. P. D. El. cxlvi. 98. Compare also Sir Walter Cope in 1613, "Populer states, whoe raise when they paie and advise when they receave monies, and make theire art of improvinge theire coine a matter of infinite gayne and plentie." *Certen breef Remonstrances offered to His Maiestie* (Trin. Coll. Camb. R. 5. 4), p. 10. See also R. Vaughan, *Discourse of Coin and Coinage* (1675), p. 32.

[1] "The way to retayne Gold and Silver within a Kingdome, and draw more unto it, is to hold a perfect and steddy Standerd at home, and call all Forraine coynes currant, one penny in an ounce of Siluer, and xij pence in Gold above their owne," Milles, *Customers Alphabet*, fol. G. 2 b. Compare also *An abridgment of a Treatise concerning the undervaluation of gold and silver in Englande, whych is proved to have beyn hurtfull unto our State; the reformation whereof, as yt shalbe needfull nowe above former tymes for Commonwelthe, soe shall yt bringe a present Masse of Treasure into her Majesties coffers, by a course very plausible.* Brit. Mus. *Lansdowne MSS.* cxxi. 16.

[2] Malynes, *Canker*, 20 seq. Milles, *Customers Replie*, p. 8, complains of the Bankers of Antwerp for setting their own rate which was different from the Princes'.

[3] Wiebe shows that England was affected by the influx of precious metals less quickly than the other lands of Western Europe. *Zur Geschichte der Preisrevolution des 16 und 17 Jahrhundert*, 317. See below, p. 160, n. 1.

[4] "Forasmuch as there are so great abuses of late yeeres groune by the corrupt dealing of sundry Merchants and Brokers as well strangers as English upon bargaines of exchanges and rechanges of Moneyes to bee payed both out and within this Realme as not onely the good laudable and profitable use of naturall Merchandizing is greatly decayed, the true values of the moneyes of this Realme much abased, and her Maiesties Customs and Subsidies that are the ancient inheritance of this Crowne diminished and withdrawne with sundry other inconveniences to the notable damage of this Realm." Proclamation 20 Sept. 1576, Dyson, 162. There were many wealthy aliens at London at this time. See the List in Stow, *Survey*, Bk. v. p. 303; also James' Proclamation, 23 Nov. 1611, raising the unite of gold to pass for 22 shillings instead of for 20. Brit. Mus. 506. h. 12 (72).

A.D. 1558
—1603. suspected of pursuing their own gain to the disadvantage of the realm[1].

180. The real or alleged misdeeds of wealthy men, in treating coins as merchandise, were a subject of constant discussion and care in the sixteenth and seventeenth cen-

Banking business was being regularly practised

turies. To us, who look back on the Elizabethan age from a distance, it is more interesting to try and trace the beginnings of modern English banking. The subject is very obscure ; much financial business was conducted by bankers in foreign cities, or by resident aliens, and we cannot easily follow the process by which the conduct of such transactions

by English citizens

passed into the hands of English citizens, especially as the naturalisation of wealthy aliens, so that they became English citizens, seems to have been a common occurrence. We have ample evidence, however, that the London Goldsmiths at the time of the Civil War, were in the habit of receiving deposits. *The Mystery of the New fashioned Goldsmiths or Bankers*[2], published in 1676, gives an interesting account of the matter.

in the middle of the XVIIth century.

" About Thirty years since, the Civil Wars giving opportunity to Apprentices to leave their Masters at will, and the old way having been for Merchants to trust their Cash in one of their Servants' custody, many such Cashiers left their Masters in the lurch and went to the Army, and Merchants knew not how to confide in their Apprentices ; then did some Merchants begin to put their Cash into Goldsmiths hands to receive and pay for them, (thinking it more secure) and the trade of Plate being then but little worth, most of the Nobility and Gentry, and others melting down their old Plate rather than buying new, and few daring to use or own Plate, the Goldsmiths sought to be the Merchants Cash-keepers, to receive and pay for nothing, few observing or conjecturing their profit they had for their pains. . . . Some of them who had the highest Credit, undertook to receive

Land-owners

Gentlemens Rents, as they were returned to Town, and indeed any Man's money, and to allow them some interest

---

[1] In 1576 the Goldsmiths' Company were to be cautious to prevent the withdrawal of gold from the country, as large sums had been recently exported by merchant strangers trading here. Prideaux, *op. cit.* p. 81.

[2] This rare tract has been reproduced in facsimile in J. B. Martin's *Grasshopper in Lombard Street*, 285.

for it, though it lay for a month only, or less, the Owners A.D. 1558 —1603. calling for it by a hundred or fifty pounds at a time, as their occasions and expences wanted it; this new practice giving hopes to everybody to make Profit of their money, until the hour they spent it, and the conveniency as they thought, *found it convenient* to command their money when they pleased, which they *to open* could not do when lent at interest upon personal or reall *accounts with* Security; These hopes I say, drew a great Cash into these *goldsmiths,* new Goldsmiths hands, and some of them stuck to their old Trade, but every of them, that had friends and credit, aspired to this new Mystery to become Bankers or Casheers; and when Cromwell usurped the Government, the greatest of them began to deal with him to supply his wants of Money upon great Advantages, especially after they had bought those Dollers whereof he robb'd the Spaniards to about the value of 300000£.

"After the King's return he wanting money, some of these Bankers undertook to lend him not their own but other mens money, taking barefaced of Him ten pound for the hundred, and by private contracts many Bills, Orders, Tallies, and Debts of the King's, above twenty, and sometimes thirty in the hundred, to the great dishonor of the Government[1]."

These bankers not only lent money to the Government, but were also in the habit of making advances to merchants. "Having thus got Money into their hands, they presumed upon some to come as fast as others was paid away, and upon that confidence of a running Cash (as they call it) *who were also ready* they begun to accommodate men with moneys for Weeks *to discount* and Moneths, upon extraordinary gratuities, and supply all *merchants' bills.* necessitous Merchants that overtraded their Stock, with present Money for their Bills of Exchange, discounting somtimes double, perhaps treble interest for the time, as they found the Merchant more or less pinched[2]."

We have reason to believe that this banking system had

---

[1] See the excellent account given by W. A. Shaw, *Beginnings of National Debt* in *Owens College Historical Essays*, 408; also Clarendon, *Continuation of Life*, III. 8—10, and T. Violet, *An Appeal to Caesar* (1660), p. 22. People continued however to hide their money in the Civil War period and afterwards. Pepys' *Diary* II. 159, IV. 222, ed. Braybrooke (1848).

[2] *Mystery of New Fashioned Goldsmiths*, 4.

A.D. 1558
—1603.

*As early as
the reign
of
Elizabeth
trading on
borrowed
capital
was
common ;*

grown up gradually.   There are various incidental references to particular transactions, which show that Englishmen, in the Elizabethan period, had both the means and the capacity to engage in finance[1].   It seems probable too that the lending of money, and trading in borrowed capital, had become fairly common in fact, before the legislative prohibitions which placed restrictions on such transactions were formally abolished by statute.   The change of opinion, on the subject of the permissibility of usury, may be taken as evidence of an antecedent change in commercial practice.

*the increase
of bank-
ruptcy*

There is incidental evidence that new habits were coming into vogue.   Keen competition and speculative trading seem to have had their natural result in an increase in the number of bankrupts[2].   The first Act on this matter[3] seems to be directed against men, who indulged in very prodigal expenditure, and then disappeared; and the curious statute, which insists on cash payments for foreign apparel and wares, except in the case of purchasers who had £3000 a year[4], was probably aimed at the same class of dishonest but "delicate livers."   The Act of 1571, however, is specially intended to apply to traders[5] and ordains that anyone who exercised his trade by way of bargaining, exchange, rechange, bartering or otherwise, in gross or retail, and who fled the country, or took sanctuary should be reputed bankrupt, and that his estate should be administered for the benefit of his creditors by commissioners appointed by the Lord Chancellor. It is not unlikely, too, that the increase of bankruptcy was due to other causes also.   As the practice of lending money

*may have
been
connected
with this
practice
and with
the decline
of*

for usury became common, those who were in temporary difficulties would be less likely to obtain gratuitous loans from their friends.   All the literature of the day is full of complaints about the decline of this kind of charity[6], while the resources of the gilds were no longer available for

---

[1] There must have been some English merchants, who were dealers in bullion at the time of the re-coinage and later. See above, p. 134, n. 2, also S. P. D. El. LXXVII. 21, Feb. 1571, and cases of loans by Englishmen to the King of France (*Lansdowne MSS.* CIV. 50), and the Ambassador of Muscovy, *ib.* CLX. 71.

[2] Wilson, *Discourse on Usurie,* f. 31 b.   [3] 34 and 35 H. VIII. c. 4.

[4] 5 Eliz. c. 6.   [5] 13 Eliz. c. 7.

[6] Harrison, in Holinshed, *Chronicles,* I. 189.

helping men to live down some unexpected misfortune. In the present day people are inclined to doubt whether such gratuitous lending was ever done, even by charitable people, and such may esteem Sir Thomas Whyte's benefaction a real curiosity. He died in 1592 and provided a sum of money which should afford every year a free loan of £25, to each of four young freemen and occupiers, to set them up in trade; they were to find sureties for the return of the money at the end of ten years, when it could be lent out to others. Twenty-four towns were to share in the benefit of this fund in turn, but if the burgess of any town and his sureties failed to repay the loan, that town was to be struck out of the list for the future[1]. There were very many similar benefactions for gratuitous loans, and parochial authorities endeavoured to grant temporary assistance, under the powers given them by the Act of 1601, by loans out of the parish stock. The accounts, for thirty-five years, of the fund at Steeple Ashton in Wilts, where loans were made at 10 per cent., have been printed by Mr Toulmin Smith[2], and give an excellent illustration of the working of such a public friendly society. This must have been a real boon to many young traders, and the change of circumstances, which rendered such loans less frequent, and enabled them to try and start with capital borrowed at 10 per cent., was a doubtful boon, and one that may have had something to do with the increased number of bankrupts.

A.D. 1558 —1603.

gratuitous lending,

but benefactions were left for this purpose.

Several transactions which had been on the border line, according to the old habit of thought, now became quite common. From time immemorial there had been a method of relieving merchants from the sole responsibility for losses

Insurance

---

[1] Brit. Mus. *Cole MSS.* xii. 124, 121. On the mismanagement of this charity by the Corporation of Warwick, see Parkes, *Charter of Warwick*, p. 26. See also Stow, *Survey*, ii. Bk. v. pp. 62, 263. Similar benefactions occur in many towns.

Rose Bloyze left £20 at Ipswich, to be employed in loans. *Hist. MSS. Com.* ix. Ap. 247, and John How entrusted the Corporation of Plymouth with money for the use of indigent and worthy persons. Loans were made in the years 1567, 1570, 71, 81, 83, 84, 86, 87, 88, and 1613. *Ib.* 263. On difficulties in administering a fund of the same kind at Chippenham, see Goldney, *Records of Chippenham*, 45.

[2] Toulmin Smith, *The Parish*, p. 626.

A.D. 1558
—1603.
at sea by loans on bottomry[1]. An investor would lend a merchant a certain sum to fit and freight his vessel[2] or purchase a return cargo, on the understanding that he would receive his money back when the ship came in, together with a definite sum to reimburse him (or a *premium*). This had been regarded as a fair transaction, because the lender undertook a considerable risk and was entitled to a profit; he did not bargain for a certainty. In the sixteenth century, the more

in modern forms modern form of insurance seems to have become common; the premium was paid in advance, and the principal sum only changed hands if the ship was lost, and a claim arose.

had become possible. This mode of insurance became possible, when merchants had large capitals of their own, or could borrow on their personal credit, but it lent itself to frauds more readily than transactions of the older type. Bacon alludes to it, as a familiar practice, when he asks, "Doth not the wise merchant in every adventure of danger, give part to have the rest assured[3]?"

Antwerp was the monetary centre of the world, In the sixteenth century, the great financiers, whose principal establishments were at Antwerp, were quite accustomed to watch the principal money markets of Europe, and to transfer large sums to those places where the rate of interest was attractively high. In their capacity as lenders, they were frequently appealed to by the monarchs of different countries; and the men who thus held the purse-strings had no little influence in controlling the destinies of different realms[4]. Sir T. Gresham is said to have succeeded in delaying the sailing of the Armada for a year by a successful corner in bills[5]. Financiers did not act out of pure benevolence, and

[1] Hendricks, *Contributions to the History of Insurance*, p. 7.
[2] For an excellent account of the practice in regard to fitting fishing vessels, see Hitchcock's *Politic. Plat.* in Arber, II. 165.
[3] *Parl. Hist.* I. 1558.
[4] See above, Introduction, p. 2, n. 1, also p. 8.
[5] H. Parker, *Of a Free Trader* (1648), p. 10. The story is thus told by Burnet. "Orders were given to make all possible haste with a fleet. Yet they were so little provided for such an invasion, that, though they had then twenty good ships upon the stocks, it was not possible to get them in a condition to serve that summer: and the design of Spain was to sail over in 1587. So, unless by corruption, or any other method, the attempt could be put off for that year, there was no strength ready to resist so powerful a fleet. But, when it seemed not possible to divert the present execution of so great a design, a merchant of London, to their surprise, undertook it. He was well acquainted with the state of the revenue of Spain, with all their charge, and all that they could raise. He

they could sometimes count on obtaining useful concessions A.D. 1558
from princes whom they had assisted. Queen Mary, like —1603.
Edward IV., had relied chiefly on the good offices of the
Hanse League; the favour shown to the merchants of the
Steelyard had been one cause of her unpopularity in the
City[1]. Elizabeth, on the other hand, gave her hearty support *but*
to native merchants, and was able in turn to look to them *Elizabeth ceased to*
for assistance. She did, indeed, find it convenient to ne- *be dependent on*
gotiate a loan of £75,000 in Antwerp in order to undertake *loans*
the re-coinage[2]. At the beginning of her reign, she had *negotiated abroad,*
difficulty in raising money even on the joint credit of the
city of London, and she was forced to try to get the city of
Hamburg to act as her security in negotiating a loan[3]. The
Merchant Adventurers appear at first to have hesitated
about lending to her[4]; but Elizabeth soon established a
character for paying her debts within a reasonable time[5],
and her credit in the City was good[6]. Political events were
altering the monetary centre of gravity. After the failure
of Alva's administration, to which Elizabeth had contributed

knew all their funds were so swallowed up, that it was impossible for them to
victual and set out their fleet, but by their credit in the bank of Genoa. So he
undertook to write to all the places of trade, and to get such remittances made on
that bank, that he should by that means have it so entirely in his hands, that
there should be no money current there, equal to the great occasion of victualling
the fleet of Spain. He reckoned the keeping such a treasure dead in his hands
till the season of victualling was over would be a loss of £40,000. And at that
rate he would save England. He managed the matter with such secresy and
success, that the fleet could not be set out that year. At so small a price, and
with so skilful a management, was the nation saved at that time." Bishop
Burnet's *History of his own Time* (ed. 1823), Vol. I. § 313, p. 544.

    [1] Sharpe, *London and the Kingdom*, I. 475.

    [2] Burgon's *Gresham*, I. 343. Hume [*Hist. Eng.* (1788), v. 764] has apparently
mistaken dollars for pounds.

    [3] Ehrenburg, *Hamburg und England*, 62. At one time she hoped to get
money in Hamburg at 6 %, *Hist. MSS. Comm.* II. Ap. 95. She borrowed both
in Hamburg and Cologne in 1576. *Ib.* II. Ap. 95.

    [4] Stow, *Survey*, Bk. I. p. 283. They had found that Mary was not punctual
in repaying loans (S. P. D. Mary, XII. 66), and might wish for additional security.

    [5] She repaid a large part of a loan which Mary had negotiated in the city.
Sharpe, *op. cit.* I. 482, n. 4. Half of the £30,000 borrowed from the citizens in
1575 was repaid within the year, and she was at pains to see that the money
assigned for the purpose really reached the hands of the original creditors. *Ib.*
519.

    [6] See Gresham's note of the moneys borrowed in 1569. Brit. Mus. *Lansdowne
MSS.* XII. 14.

very materially, by seizing treasure destined for the payment of his soldiers—under the pretence that it was being preserved from French pirates and that it belonged to Genoese Merchants[1]—Antwerp declined rapidly, and London came to be more and more of an important trading and monetary

and borrowed from her own subjects

centre. The Queen was able to borrow easily, not only from merchant strangers, but from her own subjects, in the year of the Armada and on other occasions. Considerable sums were raised for her by the City authorities[2], through the liveried companies, and by regulated companies[3] or private individuals. Among those who were able to assist in this fashion were the Goldsmiths[4], some of whom were English,

or resident aliens.

while others were resident aliens[5]. One of the merchant strangers, Gerard Malynes, who wrote many pamphlets on

Malynes has described

financial subjects, has given us a full description of the methods of continental bankers before 1600; and even if the system was not so fully developed in London at that time, there is reason to believe that it did not lag far behind[6]:

---

[1] Elizabeth did not however let this money lie idle, but minted it into English coin, at a profit of £3,000 or £4,000. Sharpe, *op. cit.* I. 512. See Gresham's Letter to Cecil, *Lansdowne MSS.* XII. f. 16 b.

[2] Stow, *Survey*, Bk. I. p. 283. The practice seems to have been for the city to assess each company with its share; and, according to the practice of the Goldsmiths' Company, the shares were then allotted among the members, according to the status of each man. Prideaux, *op. cit.* I. 58, 88, 91, 103.

[3] It is still more curious to find the Turkey Company borrowing £10,000 from her Majesty 'for the better Maintenance of their Trade.' Stow, *Survey*, Bk. I. p. 284.

[4] The ostensible business of the Goldsmiths both English and foreign, in 1622, was the manufacture of plate [S. P. D. James I. (1622), CXXVII. 12]; but the anxiety of the Company about the proposed revival of the office of Exchanger, in 1627, is difficult to understand if they confined themselves to this craft. Prideaux, *op. cit.* I. 143.

[5] On loans obtained from Dutch strangers compare S. P. D. El. 1600, CCLXXIV. 28; CCLXXV. 143; CCLXXVIII. 8—15, 27, 124.

[6] Trading on borrowed capital is spoken of as a common practice of young merchants in 1564 in the *Report of the Commission on the Exchanges*, Brit. Mus. *Harleian MSS.* DCLX. f. 113. T. Wilson, in his *Discourse upon Usurie* (1569), writes as if there was a considerable amount of banking business in the city (f. 14 b). See also Milles: "As a steady standard and store of coyne in the Princes Treasury makes all things else to be cheape, holds trade in request, shows kings to be powerful and subjects wealthy, so as the Standard falls uncertayne and money engrost into private hands all things grow deere, the king becomes weake and his subjects poore, whilst coin itself by usury in merchaundizing exchanges eats out industry and trades, and merchaundizing merchants by monopoly conspire to stifle traffic." *Customers Alphabet*, f. G. 2.

"It behoveth us to speak somewhat of the commanders A.D. 1558
—1603. or rulers of this exchange through all Christendom, which *the banking* in effect are the bankers, and therefore shall we declare *system of the* what the nature of a bank is, from whence the name banker *day* is derived.

" A bank is properly a collection of all the ready moneys of some province, city, or commonwealth, into the hands of some persons licensed and established thereunto by public *as it* authority of some prince, erected with great solemnity in *existed on the con-* the view of all the people and inhabitants; and with an *tinent,* ostentation in the open market place upon a scaffold, of great store of money, of gold and silver as (belonging unto the persons so established) which is unto them an attractive matter to persuade and allure the common people to bring their moneys into these bankers' hands; where, at all times they may command it and have it again at their own pleasure, with allowing them only a small matter of five upon every thousand ducats or crowns, when any man will retire or draw his money into his own hands again: which although it be once but in twenty years, yet during all that time they are to have no more: so that these persons or bankers do become (as it were) the general servants or cashiers of that province, city, or commonwealth.

" These bankers, as they have their companies, factors, or correspondents in the chief places of trade in Christendom, so must they also keep account with every man, of whom they have received any money into their bank, out of which number no man of that jurisdiction is almost exempted. But generally, all men are desirous to please them, and to bring their ready money into their bank, as also such money as they have in foreign parts: in regard whereof these *where the* bankers do give them great credit: for if any man have *con-venience of* occasion to bestow in merchandise, or to pay in money, three *obtaining* or four thousand ducats, and have but one thousand ducats *credit,* in the bank, the bankers will pay it for him more or less, as the party is well known or credited, without taking any gain for it, although it be for three, four, six or more months.

" This seemeth to be a great commodity (as no doubt it is to men in particular:) but being well considered of, it will be found a small friendship, and no more in effect than if a man did participate the light of his candle unto another man's candle: for what is this credit? or what are the payments of the banks: but almost, or rather altogether, imaginative or figurative? As for example: Peter hath two thousand ducats in the bank, John hath three thousand, and William four thousand, and so consequently others more or *the* less. Peter hath occasion to pay unto John one thousand *facilities* ducats; he goeth to the bankers at the hours appointed, *for* *payment* (which are certain both in the forenoon and afternoon), and requireth them to pay one thousand ducats unto John; whereupon they presently make Peter debtor for one thousand ducats, and John creditor for the same sum. So that Peter having assigned unto John one thousand ducats, hath now no more but one thousand ducats in bank, where he had two thousand before. And John hath four thousand ducats in the same bank, where he had but three thousand before. And so in the same manner of assignation. John doth pay unto William and William unto others, without that any money is touched, but remaineth still in the bankers' hands; which, within a short time after the erection of the bank, cometh to amount unto many millions. And by their industry they do incorporate the same, which may easily be understood, if we do but consider what the ready money and wealth of London would come unto, if it were gathered in some one man's hands; much more, if a great deal of riches of other countries were added thereunto, as these bankers can cunningly compass by the course of the exchange for moneys: the ebbing and flowing whereof, is caused by their motion from time to time, as shall be declared.

" But some will say or demand, Cannot a man have any ready money out of the bankers' hands, if he have occasion to use it?

" Yes that he can: but before he have the same, they will be so bold, as to know for what purpose he demandeth the same, or what he will do with it.

" If it be to pay any man withal, they will always do that for him, as having account almost with all men, for he

is accounted to be of no credit, that hath not any money in A.D. 1558
—1603.
bank.

" If he do demand it for to make over by exchange in some other country, they will also serve his turn in giving him bills of exchange, for any place wheresoever, because they have their companies or correspondents in every place.

" If he do demand it for his charges and expenses, it will be paid him forthwith, because it is but a small sum, and in the end the money cometh into their hands again.

" If they pay out money to any man, that having money in bank, will bestow the same in purchase of lands, they will still have an eye to have it again in bank one way or another, at the second and third hand. So that they once being possessed of moneys, will hardly be dispossessed. And their payments are in effect all by assignation and imaginative.

" And if they have any money in bank, belonging unto *and the possibility* orphans or widows, or any other person, that hath no oc- *of receiving* casion to use the same, they will allow them interest after *regular interest* four or five upon the hundred in the year at the most, and upon especial favour; for every man seeketh to please them, as in matters where *commodum privatum* beareth the rule: for they can easily please men in particular, in giving them *rendered the system* some credit, of that great credit which they have obtained *popular.* in general[1]."

The practice of relying on borrowed money appears to have spread from the highest personages to the humbler ranks of society. Modern banking began with the accom- *In lending to princes* modation afforded by the wealthy to princes[2]; the next phase *or to* is seen in temporary advances to prosperous men of business. *prosperous men of* It was generally felt that such merchants were able to look *business* after themselves, and that there was little danger of their being oppressed, especially as the money borrowed was obtained in comparatively small sums from persons who were not familiar with business, or was drawn from trust funds[3].

---

[1] Malynes, *A Treatise of the Canker of England's Commonwealth*, p. 20. The manuscript copy in the British Museum (*Cotton*. Otho E. x. f. 65) is dated 159-.

[2] Cunningham, *Western Civilisation*, II. 168.

[3] The great practical difficulty in the old days had been that of making provision for a family in case of death. It was not easy to find trustees, and trustees could not find suitable investments. Public bodies assumed the guardianship of orphans; this system was in operation under Richard II. in London

A.D. 1558 —1603. Throughout the seventeenth century the Crown, and rich merchants who had the means of offering good security, *there was little risk of extortion* were the principal borrowers. There was, under these circumstances, no question of such oppression as had occurred in Norman or Angevin times, when the moneyed men lent to those who had no means of paying the royal or papal demands, and thus gained at the expense of temporarily *and deposit banking* necessitous persons. Deposit banking was usurious, according to all the old definitions of that offence; the depositor bargained for interest for certain, and for the return of his

(Stow, *Survey*, Bk. v. p. 372), and a similar practice is mentioned in the Custumel of Rye (J. Lyon, *The History of the Town and Port of Dover*, II. 367). So long as the City acted as a trustee, and took charge of the orphans' inheritance, it was an obvious boon; but a practice seems to have been in use in Elizabeth's time about which casuists were more doubtful. "A merchant lendeth to a corporation or company an hundred pound, which corporation hath by statute a grant that whosoever lendeth such a summe of money and hath a childe of one yeere, shall have for his childe, if the same childe doe live till he be full fifteene yeeres of age, £500 of money, but if the childe die before that time, the father to lose his principall for ever. Whether is this merchant an usurer or no? The law saith, if I lend purposely for gaine, notwithstanding the perill or hazard, I am an usurer" (Wilson, *Discourse upon Usurie*, f. 104 b).

In the reign of Edward VI. the city of London made elaborate ordinances (Stow, *Survey*, II. Bk. v. p. 322) chiefly intended to prevent the orphans of freemen from marrying vain and light persons who squandered their portions; but the whole system was called in question in 1586, and the Mayor and Corporation wrote in defence of the custom to the Privy Council. "The Court of Orphans" (Stow, *Survey*, Bk. v. p. 372) they said, "taketh care for their reasonable Maintenance and virtuous Education, foreseeth that they be not defrauded by the Executors, by Concealment, or mispraising the Goods or by false Account; nor abused by Disparagement in Marriage; provideth Safeguard for their Portions. So that neither themselves nor others may misspend the same: And in the behalf of the Orphans do prosecute Suits for Recovery or Defence of their Right.... Which provident Care had of th' Orphans, as aforesaid, doth not only extend to their Benefit, but stretcheth further to the good of the Widows, Creditors and Legatories of the Dead, who might (by sinister Practice of the Executors) be greatly prejudiced if such exact Care were not had. And that which is more, there be a great number of young and towardly Merchants and Occupiers within the City, relieved and profited by the Use of Orphans' Portions, yielding but an easy Allowance to the Orphans for their competent Maintenance." On this method of managing the orphans' money Wilson spoke with no uncertain sound. "Neither doe I allow of your order in London for orphanes money, bicause it hath no ground upon Gods word, but rather utterly forbidden" (Wilson, *Discourse upon Usurie*, f. 70). The system appears to have continued in successful operation till the time of the Great Fire, when the fund became bankrupt; the wrongs of these widows and orphans were at length redressed by Parliament (Stow, *Survey*, Bk. v. p. 373, 5 and 6 W. and M. c. 10). The Speaker of the House obtained a gratuity of a thousand guineas on this occasion, and was expelled in consequence (*Parl. Hist.* v. 906).

principal also[1]; but, under changed circumstances, there A.D. 1558
—1603. was no sort of oppression in the practice. The goldsmith was able to make a large gain by lending to the Crown, or *enabled* by trading; when he received deposits at a lower rate of *the men of small* interest he managed to thrive, and his intervention enabled *means to be lenders.* the man of comparatively small means to obtain a return on his money. As a necessary consequence, the old doctrine *The old doctrine of* in regard to the immorality of usury came to lose its appli- *usury* cation to practical life and was gradually set aside. *ceased to appeal to*

The first sign of this change, so far as the law is con- *the conscience,* cerned, is to be found in a Statute passed in 1545. This follows the regular tradition in such matters, and condemns all usury or payments for the mere use of money, while it specifies one of the most common evasions of the law[2]. But the main object of the new Act was to limit the rate of 'interest' which was allowable ; that is to say, the payments which might be received on the definite pleas that had always been recognised,—such as delay in repayment (*poena conventionalis*). According to the old view, there might be special grounds for claiming more than the money lent, and it was fair to take something (*id quod interest*) under such special circumstances, but unfair to claim payment for the mere use (*usuria*) if no such special circumstances could be proved. The practical effect of this Statute was to abolish this distinction; it aimed at limiting exorbitant claims, though made on good grounds, but it resulted in giving lenders facilities for claiming a moderate rate in cases where, according to the old way of thinking, none should have been paid. By limiting excessive 'interest' this Act opened the *and the law* way for moderate 'usury.' That this was its effect may be *recognised* gathered from the Statute of 1552 which prohibits interest *that moderate* as well as usury[3]; but this Act cannot have worked satis- *'interest'* factorily, for it was repealed in 1571, and the Act of 1545

---

[1] Compare the Apprentice in Wilson's *Discourse upon Usurie*, "I will use one trade that shall without all doubt bring me certaine gaine, although I sleepe upon the one side, and that is with putting my money foorth for interest and taking good assurance," f. 14 b.

[2] By the fictitious sale of goods which were repurchased at a later date for less money. 31 H. VIII. c. 9, § 2.

[3] 5 and 6 Ed. VI. c. 20.

A.D. 1558 —1603.

was permissible.

Some of the Puritans took a very stringent view;

was revived[1]. Despite the strong verbal condemnation of usury, there can be little doubt that the practical effect of the Elizabethan measure was to render usury legal, so long as it was moderate. This becomes perfectly clear in the Statute of 1624; although entitled *An Act against Usury,* it is really directed against excessive rates, and 'usury' is explicitly permitted so long as it does not exceed eight *per cent.*[2] There is a mere tribute to the older opinion in the final clause which forbids that this Act shall be construed so as to "allow the practice of usury in point of religion or conscience."

The principle, which was implied in this measure, slowly obtained acceptance, not only with lawyers, but with moralists; though a considerable number of writers and preachers endeavoured to maintain the old distinctions[3]. Henry Smith[4] was one of a small section of the Puritans who insisted on

---

[1] 13 El. c. 8. This statute makes an exception in regard to the Orphans' Fund in London. Mosse, *Arraignment* (1595), 159.

[2] 21 J. I. c. 17.

[3] Thomas Rogers, who published translations of P. Caesar, entitled a *General Discourse against the damnable sect of usurers* and of Nicolas Hemming's *Lawful use of Ritches* (1578), deplores the change of sentiment. "If but a probable suspicion rose of a man to occupie that filthie trade, he was taken for a devill in the likenesse of a man * * * But goode Lorde, how is the Worlde chaunged? That which Infidels cannot abide, Gospellers allowe, that which the Jews take onlie of straungers, and will not take of their owne Countreimen for shame, that doe Christians take of their dear freindes, and thinke for so doing they deserve greate thankes" (Epist. Ded.). Richard Porder in his *Sermon* (1570) connects the growing practice of lending money to the rich with engrossing, as this could be done by men who had the use of large capital (p. 59). Miles Mosse in dedicating his *Arraignment and Conviction of Usurie* (1595) to Archbishop Whitgift assigns as one of his reasons, "your Grace is reported to be one who neither lendeth, nor taketh upon usurie, which is not in this age every such mans commendation." The men who opposed all usury, on theological and legal grounds, in the seventeenth century write as if they were conscious that public opinion is against them. Among them we find Bishop Andrewes, who maintained the thesis *Usuras legitimas esse illicitas* when proceeding to his degree as Bachelor of Divinity (*Opuscula Posthuma,* 119), Sanderson, Blaxton and Holmes. Fenton's *Treatise of Usury* was the most celebrated; and called forth a reply from Sir Robert Filmer, *Quaestio Quodlibetica* (1653), which came to be the classical expression of the opinion then current among well-doing men that only 'biting' usury was unlawful. Before the close of the century, however, the controversy was practically over, and though Mr David Jones, *Farewell Sermon* (1692), p. 34, at S. Mary's Woolnoth, roused passing excitement, it was treated with contemptuous ridicule; see *The Lombard Street Lecturers late Farewell Sermon answered, or the Welsh Levite toss'd De Novo* (1692) [Brit. Mus. T. 752 (2)].

[4] Henry Smith, the most important of these extremists, was known as the

taking a stronger line than that laid down in mediaeval A.D. 1558
times, but the influence of Puritanism generally was against ―1603.
the restrictions; it was strongly affected by Calvin's pronouncement. The Marian exiles were in many cases reduced to great want, and those who had escaped with their
possessions were fain to make the most of them. Some of *but when*
these refugees, during their residence in Geneva and else- *appealed*
where, had been therefore drawn into transactions that had *to, Calvin*
hitherto been stigmatised as usurious[1]; and Calvin, Bucer,
and others were forced to appear as their apologists. The
former expressed an opinion hesitatingly and reluctantly;
for he evidently regarded usury as an evil, but felt unable
to draw the line between transactions that were admittedly
fair, and those that had hitherto been condemned. He saw
dangers on both sides[2]; and it seems strange that his very
hesitating pronouncement should have attained such celebrity,
as a justification of money-lending. But it had a very real
importance, not as a learned discussion of the difficulties in
the light of patristic teaching and ecclesiastical decisions, *had not*
but because it gave no countenance to the new-fangled *endorsed*
Puritan doctrine, with the overstrained interpretation of the *opinion.*
Bible, which had made itself felt under Edward VI.[3]

'silver-tongued' lecturer at S. Clement Danes. He inveighs strongly against any
evasion of the Scriptural prohibition by men who bought an interest in some
estate or lent money on mortgage, or gave advances in partnership with merchants, or were concerned in other transactions to which no exception had been
taken by mediaeval moralists [Henry Smith, *Examination of Usury* (1591), p. 17].

The immediate effect of the new doctrine however must have been very
serious, especially on conscientious Englishmen who sought to do their duty.
They were now told by preachers that practices which had been approved in all
ages, and which they and their fathers had practised without scruple, were condemned by God's law; that no true distinction could be drawn between fair
increase and heinous usury, because the Old Testament made none. Their overstrained interpretation of these texts brought the Puritans into direct conflict
with the old Christian opinion as to right and wrong in these matters; they held
that all modes of obtaining increase were equally wrong, but they forged a
weapon for those who were ready to argue that all were equally right.

[1] Wilson, *Discourse*, f. 179; Fenton, *Treatise of Usurie*, p. 60.

[2] " Si totallement nous defendons les usures nous estraignons les consciences
dun lien plus estroict que Dieu mesme. Si nous permettons le moins du monde
plusieurs aincontinent soubs ceste couverture prennent une licence effrenée dont
ils ne peuvent porter que par aulcune exception on leur limite quelque mesure "
("Corpus Reformatorum," Calvini, *Opera*, x. i. 245).

[3] Calvin regarded the passage in S. Luke as rhetorical and as referring to an
excellent ideal, not to actual practical life. He took much the same view as

A.D. 1558
—1603.
Calvin agreed with men like Henry Smith in disregard-
ing the old distinctions in this matter; but he completely
He justified undermined the position from which they had so solemnly
transac-
tions warned citizens against evading God's law by lending on
which mortgage. Calvin held that lending on mortgage was ob-
others
regarded as viously fair and right; and the differences of opinion between
not
allowable, these teachers produced their necessary result, and, by rendering men doubtful as to the right and wrong of the matter,
tempted them to regard the whole discussion with indifference, and to enter on any contract that gave them a prospect
of gain.

Subsequent Puritan writers[1] appear to have followed the
line which Calvin took, and to have trusted to the private consciences of interested dealers to decide aright on cases which
proved too hard for learned doctors in their studies. Nor is
there any attempt to reconstruct a fresh doctrine of fair dealing
out of the ruins of the Puritan prohibition, on the space
from which the canon law had been cleared away. The
preachers were a great power in all the reformed countries,
and they do not appear to have made much use of their
influence in upholding a new standard of commercial morality.
and when The "Pope's laws" were treated with contempt, as con-
the Canon
Law was taining much that was evil, in all the regions where the
abandoned Reformation had made any way; and, when the leaders of
the Calvinistic and Zwinglian parties explained away the
Scriptural prohibitions, no firm ground was available for
reproving any usurious practices that were permitted by

Molina who argued that it prohibited such rates of interest as were oppressive,
but that it enjoined lending as an act of charity, and without expecting even the
return of the principal, *Tract. Contract. et Usurarum*, 11; it gives a counsel of
perfection. Again, the command in Deuteronomy was treated as binding on
us, only so far as equity and human reason reiterate it; and the denunciations of
the prophets were viewed as directed against the Jews, because usury was
forbidden to them, while all usury is not forbidden us.

Calvin takes his stand on the fairness of such transactions as the buying of
rents; it is as fair to lend a rich man money on interest, as to take his estate on
pledge and profit by it; and to condemn the one and allow the other is mere
playing with words. On the other hand, the danger of oppression and of covetousness, the duty of doing as one would be done by, the necessity of being guided
by public good not by our own gain, are all noted; and the custom of the country
is not to be taken as relieving our own consciences; moreover, he could not allow
that anyone should practise usury as a calling.

[1] Pearson, *Theories of Usury*, p. 79, and Haweis's *Reformation Sketches*, c. 12.

civil or municipal law; this is the gist of the celebrated *A.D. 1558* *—1603.* treatises of Salmasius. The strict ecclesiastical discipline, *no new* which was reared in Scotland, does not appear to have been *doctrine of* *fair* much concerned with attempting to check extortion or greed *dealing* *took its* of gain: its authors were so eager to root out witchcraft[1] *place.* that they had little time to attack covetousness, and were more ready to put down promiscuous dancing[2] than to prevent usurious contracts.

The common-sense judgment of business men only con-*Business* demned 'biting' usury as oppressive; they held that if you *men con-* *demned* lent to a merchant who made gain with your money, it was *usury when* *it was* fair to charge him for the use of it, but if you lent to the *oppressive,* poor husbandman, it should be as a gratuitous kindness[3]. There was indeed some difficulty about obtaining any measure to decide what was biting and what was not[4]; and the distinction seemed to ignore the fact that evil lies in the motive and not merely in the effects. Still, oppressiveness is a convenient test of what should be condemned; to condemn gaining at the expense of a neighbour, is not to say that all other transactions are clearly right. This line of argument was taken by Peter Baro[5], who for a long *and as this* time was Lady Margaret Professor at Cambridge: *view was* *accepted by* "The last verse containeth yet two things, whereof the *Baro* first is, that he giveth not his money to Usurie: touching which pointe, many thinges were to be spoken, if the time would suffer: but we must be content with a fewe. This then is the meaning of the Prophet, that albeit in the Common weale, by reason of the sundry affaires and dealings of men among themselves, and the use of money so manifold,

---

[1] *Acts of Assembly*, 44. 216.

[2] *Ib.* 201, 311.

[3] Malynes, *Lex Mercatoria*, Pt. II. c. 11. Wilson puts this line of argument into the mouth of his lawyer, *Discourse*, f. 42.

[4] The preciser sort held that all usury was more or less biting, and that it was only a question of degree. "There is difference indeed betwixt the biting of a dogge and the biting of a flea, and yet, although the flea doth the lesse harme, yet the flea dooth bite after hir kinde, yea, and draweth blood too. But what a world is this, that men will make sinne to be but a flea biting, when they see God's word directlie against them." Wilson, *Discourse*, f. 66 (b).

[5] For an account of him see Fuller's *History of the University of Cambridge*, Section vii. 10, 21, 22.

and necessary for the trafficks of men, and that almost in every contract and bargaine: albeit, I say, for these and such other like causes, it is plaine and evident, that all gaine, which is gotten by money, is not to be condemned, yet a godly man must take diligent heed sith there is also so great and many abuses of money, lest he abuse his moneye to the hurt of his neighbour: as it is a usual practice among rich men, and some of the greater sort, who by lending, or by giving out their money to usurie, are wont to snare and oppress the poore and needier sorte: as they commonly are wont to do, who sitting idle at home make marchandise only of their money, by giving it out in this sort to such needy persons, altogither for gaines sake, without having any regard to his commoditie, to whome they gave it, but onely of their owne gaine. For by this craft they easily get many into their snares, whom they do not only bite, which is meant by the noune נשׁך naschac, which David useth, but also devoure and spoyle. But the true worshippers of God are far from this wickednes, seeing they embrace others with true brotherlye love, neither will they do that to any which they would not have done to themselves. Which rule in human affaires and contractes, is diligentlye of us evermore to be observed, if we will live uprightly as becometh us[1]."

Baro was not the only French divine who took this view of the subject: Molina had advocated it, and it was clearly put by Henri Holden, who wrote in 1642, "Ubi praeceptio lucri ex mutuo proximum non laedit illicita forsitan et injusta non erit, quamvis propriam cujusdam usurae naturam participet[2]." The doctrine which was then somewhat of a novelty has come to be very generally adopted by Roman divines since that time[3]. This, too, appears to be the ordinary English view in the present day; as we find, the word usury in common conversation implies oppressive interest, and has

---

[1] *Fowre Sermons and two Questions as they were uttered and disputed ad clerum in S. Maries Church and Schools in Cambridge.* Sermon II. on Ps. xv. p. 419. Appended to *Special treatise of Gods Providence.*

[2] Quoted by Marin-Darbel, *L'usure, sa définition*, p. 178.

[3] Mastrofini, *Discussion sur l'usurie*, and compare Funk, *Zins und Wucher*, p. 6.

lost the signification which attached to it, when there was A.D. 1558
no real market for capital. It had then meant payment for —1603.
the use of money, when the charge was not justified by any
real risk undertaken or inconvenience sustained by the
lender. Perhaps it already bore this modern and popular
sense rather than the ancient and technical one when it
was condemned by the CIX. Canon of 1604.

It appears that by this time the revolution in public *the revolu-*
opinion was complete, and that the practice of lending *public*
money for moderate interest was at length regarded as en- *opinion*
tirely reputable. Changes in the circumstances and con- *complete*
ditions of business transactions had brought about a modification of public opinion; and it was possible for men of
high standing to engage openly in transactions, which would
have been regarded as disreputable in the fifteenth century.
It is likely enough that the facilities, which were available
under these circumstances, for trading on borrowed capital *and new*
were abused[1]; at all events, they enabled new men to enter *methods*
into competition with the old established traders[2], and caused *were*
not a little annoyance to the members of the privileged com- *adopted.*
panies and others, who desired to preserve a 'well ordered'
trade. The new finance, of the Elizabethan and Jacobean
periods, was not remotely connected with the rise of the
interlopers, who succeeded in revolutionising the traditional
methods of British commerce before the seventeenth century
closed.

The political agitations, and wars of religion, which affected Flanders, France, and Germany in turn, were favourable to the commercial prosperity of England. Amsterdam
was the chief heir of the business which had centred at
Antwerp; but London secured a considerable share. The *London*
increased quantity of silver, which was available in business

---

[1] It was said that apprentices were able to borrow money and deal on a large
scale before they had learned their business properly; the opportunity of borrowing "causeth many apprentises to become untimely maisters, when as swim-
ming with other mens bladders, they are soone drowned" [Malynes, *S. George for
England* (1601), 39]. Some of them were sharp enough to take good care of
themselves, and to prosper at the expense of easygoing masters. Hall, *Society
in the Elizabethan Age*, p. 50.

[2] J. Wheeler, *Treatise of Commerce* (1601), 73. Cf. Bagehot, *Lombard Street*, 9.

A.D. 1558
—1603.

circles[1], favoured the rapid progress of industry and commerce, in more ways than one.   Prices were rising rapidly, so that all transactions could be conducted at a very high rate of profit[2]; the expectations of manufacturers and merchants, in regard to the terms they might secure, could usually be fulfilled or exceeded.   Business was attractive, because it was so successful; and the formation of capital was rendered easier by the mere fact that so much money was in circulation.   As commercial and financial business developed, the capitalists, who were engaged in prosecuting it, attained to much greater status and importance than they had ever before enjoyed[3].   Though it was on the landed interest that the monarchs chiefly relied for the 'fund' from which revenue was ultimately drawn, it was to the moneyed interest that they looked for prompt assistance in any emergency.   In the seventeenth century, when the Crown had become dependent on taxation for the ordinary expenses of government, it was usual to obtain assistance from the moneyed men, as a regular thing, in order to get prompt command of money that Parliament had voted.   In this way, the royal creditors, who were for the most part the merchants and goldsmiths of the City of London, exercised an extraordinary influence on the course of public events[4].   They seem, on the whole, to have been genuinely attached to the principle of representative government, both in ecclesiastical and civil affairs,

became an important monetary centre,

and City bankers exercised an important political influence,

[1] England would not at once share in the silver which came from the new world. It had been asserted that England received large payments in bullion from abroad by Henry of Huntingdon (*Historia Anglorum*, I. 5) in the twelfth century, and by Sir John Fortescue in the fourteenth [*Comodytes of Englond*, in *Works* (1869), I. 551]. The development of the cloth manufacture ought to have tended to the increase of the balance in favour of England. But the debasement of the coinage would effectually prevent merchants from bringing pure silver to England, so long as base metal served to make their payments: it was not till the coinage was restored in 1561 that trading relations could re-adjust themselves.

[2] Compare F. A. Walker (*Money*, p. 79), who discusses the opinions of Hume and Alison on this topic.   See also Hall, *Elizabethan Society*, 41.

[3] As early as 159- Malynes points out as "the unknown disease of this politique body of the Englishe common wealth," that "there is no mony or substanc in the land answerable therunto as it ought to be, the land being still the same that alwayes it hathe bene; so that if we doo seeke to ballance the valewe of thynges uppon this beame, we must in this poynt laye the lands on the one side, and the mony or thynges monye worthe in value on the other." *Canker*, Brit. Mus. *Cotton.* Otho E. x. f. 65.

[4] For instances see Sharpe, *London and the Kingdom*, II. 127, 147, 152, 165.

and to have objected alike to the episcopal government of A.D. 1558
—1603. the Church, and to interference by the army with parlia- mentary institutions. At all events, the power of the purse, as held in London, was effectually brought to bear through- out the country to check the extending claims of royal pre- rogative, and to maintain the ascendancy of what were after- wards called Whig principles. The fact that the Crown was dependent on citizens with democratic sympathies was of primary importance for the constitutional progress of England throughout the seventeenth century[1].

in the time of the Stuarts.

181. The greater frequency and magnitude of monetary transactions also tended to a clearer understanding of the nature and functions of money. The events of the sixteenth century gradually exposed the unsatisfactoriness of the old theory; this had treated money as artificial riches, which had a conventional value, assigned by common estimation and declared by the Prince. It was clear that he could not arbitrarily rate his coin 'at his pleasure,' but that he must take account of 'the value of the metal that is in it[2]'; but there was still much misunderstanding as to the causes which affected the value of the metal. Many years after the output of the American mines had been first regularly imported to Europe, the world was inclined to attribute the general 'dearth' to the greed of those who engrossed com- modities, and not to a change in the value of the precious metal. Men were slow to apprehend that a fall in the value of silver ore entailed a decrease in the purchasing power of silver coins, and thus necessarily brought about a general rise of prices. The point was clearly put, however, by an English[3] writer in 1581:

These changes reacted favourably on monetary science,

and led to a clearer apprehen- sion of the cause of the rise of prices

" Another reason I conceive in this matter, to be the great store and plenty of treasure, which is walking in these partes

---

[1] In Spain, the alien financiers who supported the monarchy, were quite out of touch with the native population and their institutions, and this favoured the growth of absolutism.

[2] Compare the paper on coinage by John Pryse (1553) printed by W. E J. Archbold in the *English Historical Review* (1898), XIII. 709.

[3] It had been previously noted in the *Discours sur les causes de l'extrême cherté qui est aujourdhuy en France* (1574). Cimber et Danjou, *Archives*, Série I. vi. p. 429. This was probably written by Bodin. Compare his *Discours sur le rehaussement des monnoyes* (1578).

A D. 1558
—1603.

in the
importa-
tion of
silver
from the
new world.

of the world, far more in these our dayes, than ever our forefathers have sene in times past.   Who doth not understand
of the infinite sums of gold and silver, whych are gathered
from the Indies and other countries, and so yearely transported unto these costes ?   As this is otherwise most certain,
so doth it evidently appeare by the common report of all
auncient men living in these daies.   It is their constant
report, that in times past, and within the memory of man,
he hath beene accoumpted a rich and wealthy man, and well
able to keepe house among his neighbors, which (all things
discharged) was clearely worth xxx or xl li.; but in these our
dayes the man of that estimation, is so far (in the common
opinion) from a good housekeeper, or man of wealth, that
he is reputed the next neighbor to a beggar.   Wherefore
these ii reasons seemed unto me to contain in them sufficient
probability for causes of the continuance of this generall
dearth."

Knight.   " Yea, but (Sir) if the increase of treasure be
partly the occasion of this continued dearth : then by likely-
hood in other our neighbors nations, unto whom yearely is
convayghed great store of gold and silver, the pryces of
victayles, and other wars in like sort, is raysed according to
the increase of their treasure."

Doctor.   " It is even so, and therefore to utter freely
myne Opinion (as I accoumpt it a matter very hard for the
difficulties above rehersed), to revoke or call backe agayne al
our Englishe wares unto their old pryces : so doe I not take
it to be either profitable or convenient for the Realme, excepte
wee would wishe that our commodities should be uttered
good cheape to straungers and theirs on the other side deare
unto us : which could not be without great impoverishinge
of the Common weale, in a very short time[1]."

[1] From the matter inserted by W. S. when he published the *Discourse of the
Commonweal*, p. 187.   Within the last few months I have had an opportunity of
examining two manuscripts of this dialogue, with which I was unacquainted when
I prepared Miss Lamond's edition for press, though they are mentioned in the
Reports of the Historical Manuscripts Commission, II. 43 and IV. 201.   The text
of both of these MSS. is closely similar to that of the Bodleian copy, and in the
case of Lord Salisbury's MS. the writing is very similar to that of the earlier
part of the Bodleian book.   Neither of these MSS. has, however, been transcribed
from the Bodleian copy, as both have the few concluding lines which it does not

It was at last recognised that the value of money was closely related to the cost of producing the precious metals at the mines, and the consequent plenty or scarcity of bullion in the world.

The fact that silver has a different purchasing power in different countries was gradually recognised,

There were writers at the beginning of the seventeenth century who held that this was a sufficient account of the matter, and who therefore believed that money, of the same fineness, ought everywhere to have the same purchasing power[1]. It was, as they described it, of the nature of a constant, by which all other things were measured, and any apparent variations were due to the self-interested machinations of individual monopolists. But common experience shows that this is not the case, and that the purchasing power of money in one country is greater or less than that which it has in another; this fact cannot be accounted for by the relative dearness or cheapness of one commodity or another, it is directly connected with the circulating medium itself[2]. When bullion is plentiful, its purchasing power will be relatively low; it is likely to be plentiful in the commercial world as a whole, when there are good opportunities for procuring gold and silver from the mines. The value of money in a particular country, however, does not merely depend on the possible supplies, but also on the effective national demand. This really consists of the wares available for export; these enable a country to obtain a larger or smaller share of the bullion in

contain. Lord Calthorpe's MS. gives the pagination of the MS. from which it was transcribed, both in side-notes and in the table of contents.

[1] Malynes, *Canker*, p. 14.

[2] The exceedingly interesting and acute paper on the phenomena of exchange, dated 1564, suggests various remedies for the mischiefs connected with the exchanges. It advocates first of all the export of English products and reduced consumption of foreign imports as the principal means of preventing the exchange from becoming adverse (f. 112), and also suggests that if English money were rendered current in France and Flanders the "ventinge of moneyes out of England will save treasur withein the Realm" (f. 112 b). A third remedy was the establishment of an English bank of £10,000 in the hands of the Queen's factor at Antwerp, as a means of checking the fluctuations caused by the market operations of the bankers there. A fourth plan was to move the English factories from Antwerp to Embden, as this would modify the course of trade in commodities, and consequently of exchange (f. 113). This document is the Report of a Commission consisting of Winchester, Knowles, Mildmay and Cordall, who were appointed to consider the conveniences and inconveniences resulting from exchanges. Brit. Mus. *Harl. MSS.* DCLX. No. 38.

A.D. 1558
—1603.

the mercantile world. The countries, that arê rich in commodities, tend to become rich in the precious metals, so that the range of prices in them is high. There is a real difference in the purchasing power of the same coin in different countries; but their ignorance of this fact vitiates the criticism of some of the Elizabethan and Jacobean writers, who discussed the phenomena of the foreign exchanges, and renders it impossible for us to trust to their observations implicitly.

and the attempt to maintain definite rates of exchange

Malynes, among other experts, advocated the authoritative establishment of fixed rates of exchanges; he believed that foreign trade and internal prices would alike adapt themselves to the conditions thus imposed, and that it would be for the good of the State[1]. The government made careful enquiries and took expert advice[2], and Charles I appointed an official to regulate the exchanges[3], but public opinion was against this scheme. The Goldsmiths' Company treated

was abandoned.

the proposal as quite out of date in 1627; "such office being obsolete and long out of use although endeavoured to be revived two several times in the reign of the late King James[4]." Leading English merchants generally appear to have regarded the proposals with indifference, and to have set themselves to acquire increased skill in the conduct of business and the management of finance.

182. At this distance of time, there can be no doubt that the influx of precious metals from the New World caused a very serious fall in the value of silver and rise of prices in England, as well as in other countries of

There was an immensely increased supply of silver

continental Europe. From the middle of the fourteenth till the sixteenth century, the trend had been in the opposite direction. The value of silver had been steadily rising[5]; there was a drain of silver to Asia[6] and to Africa[7]; the

---

[1] The same view is taken by Sir W. Cope, who held that we should have a treaty with Flanders and France as to the rates at which our money should be reckoned, and if they broke faith and tried by art to "exhaust the treasure of our Kingdomes" we should "staie our entercourse with them." *Certen breef Remonstrances*, p. 10.

[2] Proclamation of 20 Nov. 1611, Brit. Mus. 506. h. 12 (72).

[3] Proclamation 25 May, 1627, Brit. Mus. 21. h. 1 (19).

[4] Prideaux, *op. cit.* I. 143.

[5] Wiebe, *Zur Geschichte der Preisrevolution*, 104.   [6] *Ib.* 277.

[7] Mas Latrie, *Relations et Commerce de l'Afrique Septentrionale*, 365.

interruption in the working of the Bohemian mines, during A.D. 1558
a great part of the fifteenth century[1], tended to render —1603.
the scarcity more serious, though this was to some extent
counteracted, by an increased rapidity of circulation[2]. But *available*
their first contact with the West Indies revealed to the *in the*
sixteenth
Spaniards the possibility of opening up fresh sources of *century,*
supply; and the amount of the precious metals they acquired
was quite unprecedented[3]. The Islands supplied annually
increasing quantities, till 1516; in 1522, the exploitation
of Mexico began.   Silver was obtained in greater and greater
masses; and the discovery, in 1557, of a simpler process
of reduction of the ore, by means of Spanish quicksilver,
diminished the cost of production, and still farther augmented
the yield of bullion.   In 1553, the Spaniards had obtained
access to Peru, from which additional supplies of silver could
be obtained.   Despite the efforts of the Spaniards[4] to retain
this treasure in their own hands, it soon began to circulate
in Europe; and a share of it was brought to England[5],

[1] Soetbeer, *Edelmetall-Produktion*, 25.

[2] Helferich, *Von den periodischen Schwankungen in Werth der edeln Metalle*, 71.

[3] There was great mining activity in Germany during the last decade of the
fifteenth and beginning of the sixteenth century, and the American supply was
not so especially important till about 1545 (Helferich, *op. cit.* 69). On the total
supply from Mexico and Peru see Soetbeer (*op. cit.* 51, 65). A careful discussion
of various estimates of the quantities of gold and silver obtained from the New
World has been given by Humboldt (*Essai Politique*, II. 519, 616). The results
of Humboldt's enquiry have been summarised by Jacob, who places the average
annual importation of treasure from 1492 to 1521 at £52,000, from 1521 to 1545 at
£630,000, from 1556 to 1578 at £440,000, and during the rest of the century at
£280,000 (*History of Precious Metals*, II. 53, 58, 60). Mr Jacob thinks Humboldt's
estimate for 1545 to 1556 too large, and that the rate during these years was
similar to that from 1556 to 1578. To estimate the difference the treasure made
in European prices is however a very different matter: the attempt made by
Mr Jacob (cc. XVIII. and XIX.) is not so successful as to deserve special attention.
The quantity of coinage in Europe in 1490 is wholly unknown, though Mr Jacob
hazards an approximation; his estimates of the quantity used in manufacture
and sent to India are, as he allows, "in the absence of precise data," quite hypo-
thetical; his conclusion that before 1543 the mass of bullion in Europe had
increased not quite 50 per cent. on the amount in 1490, and had in 1599 quadrupled, is perhaps as good a guess as any other—but not obviously any better.
According to Roscher, the quantity of bullion which got into circulation before
1545 was inconsiderable (*Political Economy*, I. 408).

[4] On the colonial and commercial policy of the Spaniards, see Cunningham,
Western Civilisation, II. 191, and references there.

[5] Our main supplies of treasure had been from Spain in the earlier part of
Elizabeth's reign. Abstract of treatise on *Undervaluation of Gold and Silver*
(1581). *Lansdowne MSS.* CXXI. 16, f. 129 *b*. See above, p. 71.

A.D. 1558
—1603.

especially, as we may believe, for the purchase of wool and cloth. We see clearly enough that there was an immense change in the value of silver; but it is by no means easy to measure the extent of the fall, or to trace out its precise social and political effects.

but it is not easy to estimate the effect of this influx on prices.

The most attractive method of attempting to estimate the rise of prices is to select one single commodity, and to compare the variations of its value, in terms of silver, over a considerable period. No commodity can be so conveniently chosen for this purpose as corn; the variation of price, which might be due to exceptional seasons, can be sufficiently allowed for, by taking decimal averages; while the fact that corn is an article of very common consumption, renders it particularly suitable as a type: the demand is not likely to vary seriously, with mere change of fashion, but may be assumed to be fairly regular. On these grounds Adam

Corn appears to afford the best standard,

Smith[1] has argued that corn is the best measure of value for long periods; and the price of ordinary food has been adopted by Fleetwood[2], Eden[3], and Thorold Rogers as the basis of their calculations; according to the last authority, if we take grain of all sorts[4] into account, the ratio of the rise

[1] *Wealth of Nations*, Bk. I. c. 11.

[2] *Chronicon Preciosum* (1745), p. 48. Fleetwood endeavoured to take account of other commodities, but relied mainly on corn.

[3] Eden was aware of many of the uncertainties in the quotations of the price of grain which were accessible to him. *The State of the Poor*, III. Ap. I. p. v.

[4] During some part of this period Wheat was not the chief food of the poorer classes. "The bread through out the land is made of such graine as the soile yeeldeth, neuerthelesse the gentilitie commonlie prouide themselues sufficientlie of wheat for their owne tables, whilest their household and poore neighbours in some shires are inforced to content themselues with rie, or barleie, yea and in time of dearth manie with bread made either of beans, peason, or otes, or of altogither and some acorns among, of which scourge the poorest doo soonest tast, sith they are least able to prouide themselues of better. I will not saie that this extremitie is oft so well to be seene in time of plentie as of dearth, but if I should I could easilie bring my triall. For albeit that there be much more ground eared now almost in euerie place, than hath beene of late yeares, yet such a price of corne continueth in each towne and market without any iust cause (except it be that landlords doo get licences to carie corne out of the land onelie to keepe vp the peeces for their owne priuate gaines and ruine of the common-wealth) that the artificer and poore laboring man, is not able to reach vnto it, but is driuen to content himselfe with horsse-corne, I meane, beanes, peason, otes, tares, and lintels: and therefore it is a true prouerbe, and neuer so well verified as now, that hunger setteth his first foot into the horsse manger." Harrison, *Description of England* in Holinshed's *Chronicles*, I. 283.

appears to have been as 1 to 2·40 for the period from 1540 A.D. 1558
—1603.
to 1582[1], and as 1 to 2·22 for the period from 1583 to 1642[2].
The price of wheat shot suddenly upwards in 1549[3]; only in
exceptional years did it fall back to anything like its previous
level; and during the century preceding the Great Rebellion,
the ordinary price of cereals seems to have quadrupled[4].

There are good reasons, however, for hesitating before we *but the
market for
this com-
modity was*
accept this result as conclusive; we are not at liberty to
assume that the market conditions were so far similar,
throughout the whole period, as to render the comparison
reliable. There was, as we know, occasional interference
with the market rates of corn, in the interest of local
purchasers, and of poor consumers in times of scarcity[5];
and, even though we may be justified in neglecting the
possible effects of such measures, we are not at liberty to
ignore the policy, which was deliberately pursued, of foster- *affected by
legislative
inter-
ference,*
ing the agricultural interest by favouring the producer[6]. It
was the desire of the legislature, under Elizabeth, to render
corn-growing more profitable than it had been in the reign
of Henry VIII; and with this object considerable liberty was
given for export. Under these circumstances, it seems highly
probable that the price of cereals would rise more rapidly
than can be accounted for by the mere fall in the value of
silver; the influence exercised on the price of corn, by the
agricultural policy of the day, cannot be fairly left out of
account. We have, as has been shewn above, confirmatory
evidence that the policy was successful; this surely means that
the price of wheat rose disproportionately[7]. Harrison[8] notes
that in his time a larger area of soil was "eared" than had formerly been the case: if, as seems likely, it had become worth
while to have recourse to worse soils, the contemporary rise of

---

[1] Thorold Rogers, *History of Agriculture and Prices*, iv. 725.

[2] *Ib.* v. 789.   [3] *Ib.* iv. 290. From 8s. 1¾d. to 16s. 4d.

[4] It is convenient to remember that as, during this time, the weight of the
silver penny was reduced to one-third of what it had been, the nominal prices of corn
rose about 12 times between the time of Henry VII and the Civil War. For the
purpose of purchasing cereals at the later date, a shilling was about as useful as a
penny had been at the earlier period. See my article on *The Value of Money* in
the (Harvard) *Quarterly Journal of Economics*, June, 1899, p. 379.

[5] See above, pp. 51, 92.   [6] See above, p. 87.

[7] On the change in the relative value of wheat and other cereals see Nicholson,
Principles, iii. 70.   [8] Harrison in Holinshed, *Chronicles*, i. 283.

rents[1] becomes easily intelligible, without our being forced
to suppose that it was wrung by tyranny out of a down-
trodden peasantry. During this period, then, this particular
commodity was affected by special causes, and cannot be
trusted as an accurate measure of the fall in the value of silver.

*and it is
only
possible
to compare
groups of
commodi-
ties*
It would be more satisfactory if we could obtain the
prices of a group of commodities of common consumption,
and compare them at two different dates. It is tempting to
try and construct a family budget for the labourer, and see
what increase, on the necessary income of 1540, would have
been needed to meet similar requirements a century later; but
sufficient data are not available[2]. We do not know in what
proportions the English labourer assigned his income to food,
to clothes, or to shelter ; nor do we even know what might be
the ordinary apportionment of his money, between beef and
bread and beer. So far as the rural labourer is concerned,
we are left in much doubt whether he habitually purchased
such articles, or raised them from his own holding. Even if
we had all this information, we should still be uncertain as
to whether there might not have been some change, in the
habits of the population, that would seriously affect the
demand for one or more of the commodities selected, and
thus render it an unsatisfactory measure of the fall in the
value of silver.

[1] W. S. writing in 1581, holds, as Ricardo did not, that rent enters into the
cost of production. "Thys therefore being taken as most true, the Gentlemen
desirous to mayntaine theyr former credite in bearing out the Parte of theyr
Predecessors, were driven of necessity as often as whensoever any Leases devised
for terme of yeares, by themselves or their Auncestors were throughly expyred
and fel into theyr handes, not to let them out agayne for the most part, but as
the rents of them were farre racked beyond the old: Yea, this reckynge and
hoyssing up of Rentes hath continued ever since that tyme, untill this present
day: Hereupon the husbandman was necessarily inforced, whereas his rent was
now greater then before (and so continueth unto this day) to sel his Victaylls
dearer, and to continue the dearth of them: and likewise other artificers withall
to maintaine the like proportion in theyr wares, wherefore as this dearth at the
fyrst time (as I said before) sprange of the alteration of the coyne, as of his firste
and chiefest efficient cause: so doe I attribute the continuance of it hitherunto
and so forwarde, partely to the racked and stretched rentes which have lasted,
yea and increased ever since that time hetherunto, and so are like to continue I
know not how long." *Discourse of Commonweal,* 186.

[2] For discussion of the similar problem in other countries see Hanauer,
Etudes économiques sur l'Alsace, II. ix; G. d'Avenel, *Histoire Économique,* I. 3;
Lamprecht, *Deutsches Wirthschaftsleben im Mittelalter,* II. 601; Inama Sternegg,
Deutsche Wirthschaftsgeschichte, III. ii. Vorwort viii.

There are, however, a few cases where we shall not be far
wrong in assuming the approximate similarity of demand;
and where the quotations of the prices for a group of *in isolated cases.*
commodities afford a useful basis of comparison. There is
no reason to believe that there was any considerable change
during this period in the standard of comfort that would be
expected in providing for the maintenance of the impotent
poor; quotations of the expense for this purpose, in the
same place at different dates, might help us to estimate the
rate of change. We do not in such cases have a series of
data, nor can we strike averages; but information of this
kind may help to check the conclusions, which are based on
the study of the variations in the quotations for particular
commodities[1].

To whatever extent the fall of silver and the rise of general *Though we cannot*
prices may have occurred, there can be no doubt about the *measure its*
nature of its influence on society. Merchants and moneyed *extent, there is no*
men would be able to recoup themselves at once[2] by selling *doubt about the*
the goods they bought dear, at still higher rates; but the *direction of changes.*
change would tend to depress the position of those who had
fixed incomes. The landed gentry would pass through a time
when their circumstances were severely strained; but, on
changes of tenancy, or when leases fell in, they would be able
to obtain increased fines, or to raise their rents. In their
circumstances, and with the general agricultural progress of
the time, their troubles would only be temporary, and were
probably over in the latter part of the reign.

Wage-earners, too, were in receipt of an income which *Those with*
would not easily re-adjust itself to the changed conditions. *relatively*
In so far as wages were settled by competition, there would *fixed incomes,*
be great obstacles in the way of securing a rise; the practical *including*
restrictions on freedom of movement, which were laid down *wage-earners,*
by the Act of Artificers and the Poor Law System, would
seriously interfere with the fluidity of labour, and the

---

[1] Uncertainty as to the quality of the goods supplied at the price is another
serious difficulty. This is particularly noticeable in the case of a commodity like
wool. Professor Thorold Rogers' instances seem to show that it trebled in value
about 1540, and was practically unaffected during the century when grain was
rising in price. *Agriculture and Prices*, iv. 328.

[2] These phenomena are well discussed by Hales in the *Discourse of the
Commonweal*, 19. See Vol. i. 562.

A.D. 1558
—1603.

consequent freedom for the individual to bargain; while the combination of labourers would not have been tolerated. The man, who was solely dependent on his earnings, was in a position of great economic weakness; and we hear, at times, of starvation rates paid to weavers by their employers. In so far as the machinery for assessing wages failed to secure an adequate increase in the labourers' income, he would have little prospect of obtaining a rise. It is not easy to see, moreover, how the men employed by capitalists, *suffered severely,* especially in London, could eke out their subsistence; and on one occasion, in 1629, the justices came to the relief of the Essex weavers, and insisted that they should enjoy better terms than those which were afforded them by competition[1].

The most serious difficulties were felt by the Government, as the income of the Crown was inelastic. The rents and *and the Revenue of the Crown gave no margin for meeting fresh demands.* fines from the Crown lands might be slowly raised indeed, and increasing trade would bring in a larger revenue from customs; but the land was the principal source from which taxation was obtained; and the tenths and fifteenths, and general subsidies, had alike become fixed payments[2], so that there was hardly any possibility of increasing the royal income, except by obtaining larger and more frequent parliamentary grants. Elizabeth's parsimony enabled her to carry on the affairs of State, even under these difficulties, but the Stuarts were less successful. They may have been guilty both of extravagance and of bad management; but after all, the financial troubles of Charles I were partly his misfortune and not wholly his fault. It is practically certain that the constitutional crisis of the seventeenth century, and the parliamentary disputes which led to the Civil War, were greatly embittered by the fall in the value of silver and the consequent poverty of the Crown.

---

[1] Leonard, *op. cit.* p. 160. Even if the remedy was effective the case shows that the system was not working so regularly as to prevent the evil from arising.

[2] Vol. I. p. 547. The general subsidy soon became a sort of fixed charge of £80,000; indeed, though personal property was increasing the accounts of the subsidies to some extent declined through the fault of collectors. Dowell, *Taxation,* I. 198.

II. THE STUARTS.

VI. The Necessities of State.

183. It was the misfortune of James I and Charles I *The Stuarts did not limit their projects* that they were idealists; they had definite views as to what ought to be done for the good of the realm. It may be doubted whether, under any circumstances, they were the men to rally popular enthusiasm and induce their subjects to accept their policy. They were probably doomed to disappointment in any case, but they were certainly hampered for lack of means. Elizabeth had been content to limit her political endeavours by considerations of her income; she earned a deserved reputation for frugality, not, as is sometimes thought, by niggardliness in her outlay[1], but by her unwillingness to embark definitely on any large scheme of policy. The first Stuarts were extravagant, for they entered *with due regard to their resources.* on a course and pursued it, in the hope that the money would be forthcoming somehow. Supplies might have been voted readily in recognition of success, but they were doled out grudgingly in condemnation of royal failures.

James had a high sense of the dignity of his office as *James's policy* king of both England and Scotland, and desired to take a leading part in the politics of Europe. Had he been willing to place himself at the head of the Protestant interest, he might have counted on a considerable measure of popular support; but he aimed at filling a more difficult *rôle* and constituting himself arbiter between the great monarchies of *was ambitious* the continent. Wolsey, with his extraordinary powers and

---

[1] Laughton, *Defeat of the Spanish Armada* (Navy Records Society), i. pp. lvii, lxiv, lxvii.

A.D. 1603
—1689.

*but un-
popular,*

*and in
pursuing it*

*he neglected
to main-
tain the
navy
adequately.*

*Under
Charles I
the admin-
istration
continued
to be bad,*

exceptional opportunities, had been able to attain this position for a time[1]; but even he could not hold it. Despite his
temporary success, the great Cardinal alienated the regard
of his countrymen, who could not understand his friendliness
to France. No lesser master of statecraft could hope to
succeed where Wolsey failed. James' diplomacy proved to
be futile; and his desire to enter into alliance with Spain
was viewed with the deepest suspicion by men who had
memories of the Armada. Not only was his policy unpopular, but his efforts to keep up kingly dignity at home,
and maintain the state that was suitable to his position,
exhausted his resources. At his accession, he probably
regarded them as so large that he could afford to use them
lavishly; and he never learned to restrain his royal generosity
to his favourites. As a consequence, he never had money to
spare for the proper maintenance of that maritime power
which would have afforded a solid basis for prestige. When
once the importance of the sea power was recognised by the
country, a criterion was established, in accordance with which
the permanent reputation of successive governments has been
framed.

With all their faults, the Duke of Buckingham, and
subsequently Charles I., did realise the importance of the
navy for the defence of the realm and the protection of
English shipping; but they lacked capacity to recover the
ground that had been lost during twenty years of negligence.
The royal ships and arsenals, which had been provided and
managed on Burleigh's initiative, and under the supervision
of Hawkins[2], had been less efficiently cared for, after the
decease of the latter in 1596[3]. With the peace policy of
James, the administration of the Navy Office became more
lax; and, during the period when Sir Robert Mansell held
the office of Treasurer, it was utterly and hopelessly corrupt.
The appointment of Naval Commissioners to act along with
the Lord High Admiral[4], or to hold that office jointly[5], was

---

[1] M. Creighton, *Cardinal Wolsey*, p. 81.
[2] Oppenheim, *Administration of the Royal Navy*, 145.
[3] *Ib.* 189.
[4] 12 Feb. 1619. *Ib.* 195.
[5] 20 Sep. 1628. *Ib.* 279.

of little avail in bringing about any remedy; despite all A.D. 1603 —1689.
their efforts, the maritime power of England[1], which stood
so high, as compared with that of her rivals, at the close of *and the navy was quite unable to protect English shipping*
Elizabeth's reign, had fallen considerably before 1625, and
had sunk still lower in 1642[2]. Yet during all this time the
need of a well organised royal navy was becoming more and
more apparent. Not only were the French preparing to compete with England[3], but the pirates of Dunkirk and of Algiers
were a constant menace to her shipping, in spite of the efforts
of the Government to provide convoys[4]. It appears that the

---

[1] On the condition of English shipping at the time of the Armada compare
Burleigh's memorandum 25 Feb. 1587 (Brit. Mus. *Cotton MSS.* Vesp. C. viii.
f. 12). He writes, "The Realms of England and Irland cannot from Spayn or
the Low Contreys be assayled but by sea. Therfor hir Majesty's speciall
and most proper defence ageynst the Ennemys Navy must be by shipps. * * *

"For shipps of England hir Maiesty is of hir own proper shipps so strong as
the enemy shall not be hable to land any power wher hir Maiesty's Navy shall be
neare to the Ennemys Navy. The shipps of hir subjects ar also, at this daye,
both in nombre, in strength, in hable captayns and marryners stronger than ever
they war in the memory of any man.

* * * "The Navy of England may be so devyded as the on[e] part may be
here in the Narrow Seas on the est part of England and another part on the west
towards Irland and Spayn by which meanes the Spanish Navy shall not be hable
to come to the low Contreys to joyne with the flemish Navy for the English
western shall follow them if they come to the est and they shall be intercepted
by the English Est Navy. It shall also be to a great purpose to provyde a
nombre of shipps that may mak a voyadg to portyngale to put comfort in the
portyngales * * * If also in tyme of the yere convenient, shipping may be redy to
pass to the Islands to intercept some of the Indian flete the exeqqution thereof
will be very proffitable for the mayntenance of the charges of the warrs "—and he
suggests that it may draw off some of the Armada.

[2] Oppenheim, *op. cit.* 218. Its ineffectiveness was all the more felt, as there was
a much larger amount of shipping which required protection. See below, p. 176, n. 1.

[3] Richelieu organised a navy with great rapidity; it took part in the defence
of Rochelle; but the foundation of the French navy on a permanent basis was
due to Colbert. *Ib.* 264.

[4] The convoy system, which is sometimes spoken of as part of the Cromwellian policy, was well developed under Charles I. We hear, in 1636, of the
True Love and the Roebuck convoying a fleet of merchants to Ostend (S. P. D.
cccxxvii. 114). The convoy money in 1636-7 came to £999 (S. P. D. cccxliii.
72). There is frequent mention in the State Papers of arrangements for affording
protection to shipping. "Sir John Pennington has been over to Dunkirk with a
convoy" (S. P. D. 1637, cccliv. 73). "Admiral Van Dorp lies to again between
Dunkirk and this place with 20 sail of stout men of war but meddles with none of
our convoys" (S. P. D. 1637, ccclv. 22). "Before our going to Holland the Nico-
demus was sent over by the Admiral and Captain Johnson with a convoy for Dunkirk,
and in his going over (Buller) lost one of his convoy, an Irishman" (S. P. D. ccclxiii.
99). See also ccclxiv. 29 on a convoy for Dunkirk. "I have given order to Sir Elias
Hickes to stand away with his ship for Rouen, to convoy some ships from Dover"

Turkish seamen had some provocation[1]; they retaliated fiercely, and made occasional raids on the English coasts[2]. This was a most discreditable state of affairs; and the best

(S. P. D. ccclxv. 64). "Since my last I have sent Capt. Slingsby, of the Royal Defence, to convoy some barks for Dunkirk, and Capt. Donald of the First Whelp, with vessels for Ostend. I have appointed Capt. Burley, of the May-flower, to convoy vessels of Dover for the Tassell (Texel) and Sir Elias Hickes, of the Richard and Mary, to convoy barks to Rouen" (S. P. D. ccclxvi. 60). "I will be very careful of all your commands concerning Sir Henry Mainwaring, etc., and for the time of the winter convoys beginning, about hastening which I will send you in my next his lordship's answer" (S. P. D. cccxcvii. 94). "I am sorry I cannot give you so good an account of the convoy as I would wish, but all things are so dead here amongst the merchants that there are scarce any vessels stirring." "All the convoys that we have made this year come as yet but to £300 and there are no goods at Dover, for here have not been two Spanish shipes since I came hither, and besides the convoy has been neglected ever since the Lord Admiral's last order for keeping ourselves together" (S. P. D. ccccxxiii. 18). "The second Whelp is gone for the Seine head with a convoy" (S. P. D. ccccxxv. 62). "Capt. Carteret having taken care of all the convoys this summer, I conceive will be the fittest man still to perform that service" [S. P. D. ccccxxv. 76 (1).]

[1] A Proclamation declaring the kings Majesties Royall Pleasure touching the inhabitants of Algiers, Sallie, Tunis and Tituan in the parts of Africa, 20 Oct. 1628 [Brit. Mus. 506. h. 11 (111).]

[2] "Four sail of Turks have taken 5 fisher boats of Looe as they were fishing between England and Ireland, and in them 30 people; three more are suspected lost in the same way; at St Keverne and Helford near Falmouth seven more fisher boats taken on Thursday last" (S. P. D. 1636, cccxxvii. 12). The Mayor of Plymouth reports two fishing boats and eight fishermen taken in view of the port and island by a Turkish man of war whereof the coast is now full and they receive daily relations of Newfoundland ships and other vessels and captives taken by them and of 200 Christians brought into Sallee in April last in one day (S. P. D. 1636, cccxxix. 29). The State Papers and Appendices to the Reports of the Commission in Hist. MSS. teem with these complaints. Indeed the inhabitants had got to such a state that they "fancy the crescent in all colours," and ran away from the royal ships (S. P. D. 1637, cccxlv. 70). The destruction of Baltimore, a corporate town in County Cork, in 1631, made a deep impression, "All of them English most of them Cornish, suddenly surprised in the silence of the night" (Fitz Geffrey, Compassions towards Captives, 1637—46). Some instances of plucky resistance and escape from Algiers pirates will be found in A relation of a ship of Bristol, 1622 (Camb. Univ. Lib. Bb. 11. 39). The Cinque Ports were called upon to contribute towards sending a fleet against them in 1619 (Hist. MSS. Comm. iii. Ap. 346 and ii. Ap. 92); it appears to have sailed in the following year (ib. iv. Ap. 277). In 1626 an expedition was fitted out under Captain John Harrison; attempts were to be made to effect an exchange of prisoners, and by giving the princes and governors of Barbary and Sallee presents, to induce them to deliver up English captives (Rymer, Foedera, xviii. 793, 807). The mission was so far successful that Harrison was employed in a similar voyage in 1628 (ib. xix. 27). At this latter date it was computed that there were no fewer than 15,000 English captives at Algiers (Hist. MSS. Comm. iv. Ap. 14). Another expedition to Algiers was planned by Charles I. in 1636, when the Lords of the Admiralty

hope of suppressing the evil lay in equipping a navy which A.D. 1603 —1689. should be capable of attacking them in their strongholds. In the first years of his reign Charles was forced to rely on the use of hired merchantmen for naval convoys[1], and there were few additions to the royal ships; but, between 1632 and 1634, six vessels were built, each of from 478 to 875 tons, and carrying from 34 to 48 guns[2]. Ships of still larger burden were added in 1637; the most extravagant *despite the* was the *Sovereign* of 1522 tons and 100 guns; but she proved *money* unwieldy. Indeed, some of these ships seem to have been *spent on it* badly designed, badly built and badly equipped; though the most serious of all the administrative defects lay in the gross tyranny and culpable neglect which was meted out to the seamen[3]. It was not, however, through lack of personal *and the* interest in the matter[4] that Charles failed to secure efficient *the govern-* administration and to get his money's worth. He and his *ment in promoting* colleagues on the *Committee for Trade*, which was organized[5] *trade.*

conferred, with the officers and the Trinity House, concerning the choice of the Leopard and the Bonaventure, two Whelps and two frigates, to go to Sallee against the Turks (S. P. D. C. I. cccxxxvi. 31). This expedition sailed under the command of Rainborough (S. P. D. C. I. cccxlvii. 32), but it did not accomplish very much when it got there (Gardiner, *History of England*, viii. 270). The English could not take the place, though quarrels occurred among the Moors, and 271 captives were surrendered. H. Robinson urged that a blockade of Constantinople with forty ships would force the Grand Turk to give redress (*Libertas* or *Reliefe to the Englishe captives in Algiers* (1642), p. 8). On the treatment to which captives were subjected compare S. Lane-Poole, *The Barbary Corsairs*, 236. The evil continued to engage the attention of the charitable; compare Andrews, *Sermons*, ii'. 230. Bishop Cosin devoted money to the relief of captives in his will (Anderson, *History of Church of England in Colonies*, ii. 100). See also Dean Sherlock's *Exhortation* in St Paul's, 11 March, 1702.

[1] Oppenheim, *op. cit.* 252.   [2] See table, *ib.* 254.
[3] *Ib.* 231—236.   [4] *Ib.* 252.
[5] "The generall heads for a Comission for Trade" were specified as follows (S. P. D. C. I. xliv. 19), "(1) To advance home Commodities, (2) To repress the ungainefull Importacion of forraigne Commodities to the end Trade maie bee ballanced, to the advauncement of the generall proffitt, and that in such a waie a good Correspondencie may be held with Neighbour States." There is a list of "Commissioners thought fitt for this Imployment. (*Of his Majesties learned Councell and Clarkes of his Privie Councell*) Mr Atturney Generall, Mr Sollicitor, Mr Trumball, Mr Whitacre, Mr Wm. Boswell. (*Gentlemen of Qualitie*) Sir Thomas Savage, Sir Stephen Leizure, Sir Thos. Ffanshawe, Sir Thos. Middleton, Sir Wm. Russell, Sir George Goringe. (*Farmers of the Customes*), Sir Wm. Cockaine, Sir Paul Pyndar, Sir John Wolstenhome, Mr Abraham Jacob, Mr Sackvill Crow. (*Merchants of all sorts*), Mr Phillip Burlamochi, Alderman Freeman, Mr Thos. Munn, Mr Clement

in 1626, took an immense amount of pains in developing English commerce; and their efforts in this direction appear to have been very successful[1], till trade was disorganised by the Civil War. The Council might be excused for thinking that the failure, in connection with the royal navy, was due to circumstances they could not control; and that things could not go well, unless they had the command of a larger amount of money.

It was necessary to procure money It was under the stress of this necessity that Charles issued writs for the collection of ship-money[2]. The constitutional aspects of his action do not specially concern us, but we cannot fail to note its economic significance. Money was the commodity which the Government needed above all else. Burleigh had set himself to develop the sources of maritime *not merely to develop maritime resources;* strength; much had been accomplished, both in procuring the requisite stores and in fostering a seafaring population. Still, money was essential to purchase material and victual the ships. The loyalty of the sailors was not such that they would continue to imperil their lives, without food or clothes, and without pay[3]. It was obvious that money must be had somehow, if the government of the country was to be carried on.

In the sixteenth century, comparatively little attention had been given to the question of treasure, or to the best means of attracting the precious metals to the country. Even in earlier times this object had not been wholly ignored; and

Harvie). It is not thought fitt that there shonld bee anie of his Maiestie's priuie Councell in this Comission but that theis Commissioners should bee as a Sub Comittee under the graund Councell." This was apparently a permanent body, which was actively engaged in the regulation of trade (S. P. D. C. I. cclxxxiii. 13 and numerous other references, also *Hist. MSS. Comm.* iii. Ap. 71). There are notes of the business transacted at some of its meetings (S. P. D. C. I. cclxxxiii. 13, 46, cccxv. 141, cccxxi. 19 and cccxxvi. 6), which show that the King was occasionally present; it appears to have ceased to meet about 1640. The attempt which was made to resuscitate it in 1649 (Cal. S. P. D. p. 417, 1 Dec.) does not appear to have been a success, but it was revived by Cromwell and maintained by Charles II. See below, p. 199.

[1] In 1639, the authorities of Trinity House explained that the "navigation of his Majesty's kingdoms is increased, within these thirty years, ten to one." *Hist. MSS. Comm.* iii. Ap. 79. Lewis Roberts, writing in 1641, estimated that the annual receipts from customs had increased from £14,000 to £500,000 in the preceding fifty years. *Treasure of Traffike,* 86.

[2] See the writ in Dowell, *A History of Taxation and Taxes in England,* i. 241 (1888).

[3] Oppenheim, *op. cit.* 241.

the preambles of many statutes acknowledge the necessity A.D. 1603
—1689. of attending to it; still, the practical measures that were taken, in regard to the transfer of bullion, do not necessarily imply that their authors had any other aim than the regulation of the currency[1]. But in the seventeenth century all this is changed; the amassing of treasure becomes the *and efforts were di-* principal aim of economic policy; and the expedients of the *rected to* bullionists and mercantilists, for effecting this result, were *the amass-ing of* hotly debated. The bullionists had been content to insist *treasure* that foreign merchants should pay, in money, for English products; and that they should 'employ' the coin they received, by the sale of their wares, in purchasing English goods. As old-fashioned financiers, the bullionists relied chiefly on the means they devised for regulating the exchanges, so as to check the export of the precious metals once introduced. But such regulations were very inconvenient to traders; they involved fussy interference; and, after all, they were often ineffective. The mercantilists were of a newer school, and maintained that it was unnecessary to legislate directly in regard to the transmission of silver; they held that it was possible, by enforcing wise measures for the transference of goods, to induce a constant influx of the precious metals. The mercantilists urged that the *by regu-lating the* encouragement of export trade, and diminution of imports, *balance of* would leave a balance in favour of the country; this would, *trade.* as they insisted, be necessarily paid in bullion. This doctrine of the balance of trade obtained general acceptance in the earlier part of the seventeenth century, and exercised a considerable influence on practical legislation[2].

The new prominence given to monetary questions is *Pecuniary straits* brought out in the parliamentary history of the times. The eager debates, in Elizabeth's days, had turned on questions of religion, or privilege, or freedom to trade. But the troubles of James I. and Charles I. were all directly connected with *were the cause of the* the levying of taxation. They arose with regard to the revision of custom rates and impositions, or the levying

[1] See Vol. I. p. 329.

[2] It is clearly indicated in the Report on Exchanges in 1564 (see p. 163, n. 2 above), but the policy was not systematically carried into effect in our tariff regulations till the time of Walpole. See p. 428 below.

of tunnage and poundage, or ship money, or attempts at indirectly imposing an excise. The rise of prices had had its full effect in crippling the resources of the Crown, before the Civil War broke out; and the efforts of the Stuart kings, to recoup themselves, had been worse than useless.

That pecuniary difficulties, aggravated by the exhaustion of royal credit in the City[1], were a determining factor in the reign of Charles I. is sufficiently obvious; it is equally true that the fiscal and monetary straits, to which the subsequent governments were reduced, contributed not a little to their fate. The failure of the Commonwealth was doubtless due to the fact that the political ideas of the parliamentary party had such a slight hold upon the community. Their enthusiasms had neither cohesive force nor constructive power; the country was involved in constant military operations, and learned by costly experience[2] that some farther change was necessary. Despite its success in some departments, the weakness of government by a legislative assembly was demonstrated by the inability of Parliament to control the Army; capacity for rule seemed a sufficient test by which to judge the claim to authority. The Long Parliament was unable to provide for the payment of the soldiers who had fought in its behalf; and the irritation, thus created, gave an excuse to the Army to seize the reins of power and to establish a military despotism. Cromwell preferred a government with "somewhat of a monarchical power in it[3]"; he came to be more distrustful of parliamentary encroachment[4], and his success in reconstructing a personal authority paved the way for the re-introduction of Monarchy. This change was also facilitated by the play of material interests. The intense relief which the nation experienced, when a stable government was once more constituted at the Restoration,

is easy to understand. There was a natural revulsion from the disgust that had been roused by the mismanagement of national resources during the Interregnum. "The Long Parliament people had £120,000 a month, they had the

---

[1] See below, p. 411.

[2] *London's Account, or a Calculation of the Arbytrary and Tyrannical Exactions, etc. during the four years of this Unnaturol Warre* (1647). Trin. Coll. Camb. Y. 1. 56 (16).   [3] Gardiner, *Commonwealth*, ii. 2.   [4] *Ib.* iii. 100.

Kings, Queens, Princes, Bishops Lands; all Delinquent A.D. 1603
—1689.
Estates, and the Dean and Chapter Lands which was a very
rich Treasure[1]." They had, however, run through it all, and
incurred a debt of £700,000 besides, before Cromwell dismissed
them. With diminished resources, he embarked on a heroic
policy, and retrenchment was impossible. Taxation was high,
but it did not serve to defray current expenses. Not only was
the government gravely embarrassed[2], but private interests of *and the*
every kind were seriously affected by the exigencies of public *irritation of various*
affairs. The landed men had, on the whole, been attached to the *classes of the com-*
Crown, or at any rate to parliamentary government; and they *munity*
were completely alienated. The confiscation of ecclesiastical
property, the mismanagement of sequestrated estates, and
the treatment of compounders, had given occasion for a deep-
seated sense of insecurity; and the prohibition of the export
of wool caused considerable loss[3]. Widespread irritation was
felt at the changes in local administration which were introduced by the establishment of military rule under Majors
General[4], while both internal and foreign trade were subjected to unusual difficulties. Cromwell possibly hoped that
the Spanish war might be so conducted as to pay its own
expenses, but it proved very costly in itself, and its indirect
consequences were ruinous[5]. Under these circumstances there *undermined*
can be no reason for wonder that the government found great *the credit of Crom-*
difficulty in collecting the taxes. Hence the credit of the *well.*
government in the City suffered[6], so that the means for
conducting the business of State could hardly be procured.
Moneyed men turned their backs on the Protectorate, and
treated it as a spendthrift that had no assets.

[1] Carlyle, *Oliver Cromwell's Letters and Speeches*, ii. 453.

[2] The fleet alone cost £120,000 a month, the whole of the money received from monthly assessments, at the time when the Little Parliament was summoned (Carlyle, *op. cit.* ii. 272). See also Cromwell's statement in 1657 (*ib.* ii. 582).

[3] Scobell, *Acts* 1647, c. 103. "The Government of that time having been assisted in the Civil Wars by great Numbers of the Wool-Workmen who liked much better to rob and plunder for Half-a-Crown a-day than toil at a melancholy work for Sixpence a-day, to encourage and reward them, I say, and to weaken the Gentry, they made this prohibition." *Reasons for a limited Export of Wool* (1677), p. 8. Brit. Mus. 712. g. 16 (14).

[4] Rannie, *Cromwell's Major Generals* in *English Historical Review* (1895), x. 500.

[5] There was a large accumulation of debt (Prideaux, *op. cit.* i. 277, ii. 17), and credit was low (Oppenheim, *op. cit.* 369). Shaw, in *Owens Coll. Essays*, 392.

[6] Compare the petitions in Appendix E.

*There is a
striking
contrast
between the
high aims
of the
Stuarts,*

184. The predominance of pecuniary motives gives a somewhat sordid character to all the great struggles of the seventeenth century. There is an irony in the contrast between the high claims of the Stuarts to govern in their own way, with no responsibility to earthly critics but only to the God from whom they derived the right to rule, and their inability to check the grossest abuses and most flagrant peculation on the part of their officials. The evil was of long standing, and it was almost necessarily inherent in a system which did not provide adequate salaries for the remuneration of government servants, or satisfactory means of checking the receipts of tax-collectors. The customs, as a varying source of revenue, were ordinarily farmed, an arrangement which presupposed that the officials would remunerate their services to the best of their ability, out of the money which passed through their hands. Even a trusted servant of Queen Elizabeth, like Sir Thomas Gresham, showed himself entirely unscrupulous in handling public money[1]. The evil was notorious in the time of James I., when Bacon's reputation was clouded, and the dishonest practices of certain patentees were exposed. But the worst frauds, in these days as in our own, were in connection with contracts for the army and navy. The men, who undertook to provide clothing for Elizabeth's troops in Ireland, only delivered half the quantity of goods for which they were paid[2]. Burleigh had wrestled with these evils; and the tradition he established, in regard to the navy, was maintained for a time; but James was culpably lax in overlooking the gross misconduct of his favourites; the enquiries of 1608[3], of 1618[4] and 1627[5] proved that the whole organisation of this branch of the public service was utterly corrupt.

*and the
notorious
corruption,*

*against
which
Burleigh
had strug-
gled,*

---

[1] By successful use of his influence he obtained the Queen's signature to his unaudited accounts (Hall, *Elizabethan Society*, 68). Sir Thomas Smith, who had helped to detect the goldsmiths' frauds in 1574 (Stow, *Survey*, Bk. v. p. 184), was forced to refund some of the money which had passed into his hands when he farmed the revenue (Dowell, *History of Taxation*, i. 167). Sir George Carey appears to have been even more unscrupulous in abusing his position (Hall, *op. cit.* 124).   [2] Hall, *op. cit.* 126.

[3] Gardiner, *History of England*, iii. 203. *Report by Sir Rob. Cotton on the abuses detected in the government of the Navy* (S. P. D. J. I. xli. 1).

[4] Gardiner, *History of England*, iii. 204.

[5] Oppenheim, *op. cit.* 229.

The government was defrauded by charges for seamen, who *A.D.* 1603
only existed on paper; and the seamen were cheated by the —1689.
non-payment of their wages, as well as by the miserable *in naval*
adminis-
quality of the supplies which were scantily doled out to them. *tration.*

Puritan politicians were even more unfortunate in their
record; it was hardly possible that they should all emerge
from such a struggle with untarnished reputations. The *As the*
popular
victors did, as a matter of fact, obtain the spoils of the conflict. *party were*
Their attachment to their principles was not adequately *successful,*
their disin-
tested by a contest which was the occasion of improving the *terestedness*
was never
fortunes of so many[1]. The disinterestedness of their conduct *tested;*
must either be taken on trust, or proved by the examination
into their private characters. Ample material has been
preserved to establish the magnanimity of particular men,
such as Cromwell or Ludlow, but the question whether they
are to be regarded as typical, or as exceptional, remains
open. We know, from Cromwell's scathing words, how
public opinion judged the persons who were in power in
1645. "Without a more speedy and effectual prosecution of
the war, casting off all lingering proceedings like soldiers of
fortune beyond the sea, to spin out a war, we shall make the
kingdom weary of us, and hate the name of a parliament.
For what do the Enemy say? Nay what do many say that
were friends at the beginning of the parliament? Even
this—That the members of both Houses have got great *grave doubt*
was thrown
places and commands, and the sword into their hands, and *upon the*
what by interest in parliament, and what by power in the *honesty of*
army, will perpetually continue themselves in grandeur, and
not permit the war speedily to end, lest their own power
should determine with it[2]." We can see, too, that the
parliamentary leaders cherished no illusions as to the public-
spiritedness of their fellow citizens; they recognised that
three-fourths of their countrymen were 'worldlings' who
were ready to embrace anything that made for their profit[3].

---

[1] On the contrast between the two parties in this respect see Winstanley, *The Loyall Martyrology*, Preface, also p. 99.

[2] Rushworth, *Collections*, Part IV. Vol. I. p. 4.

[3] As Needham was rewarded by Parliament with a gift of £50 and a pension of £100 a year for writing it, (Gardiner, *Commonwealth*, I. 285), his *Case of the Commonwealth of England Stated* may be regarded as a semi-official

A.D. 1603
—1689.
Under these circumstances, it was natural for Parliament to appeal to the interest of citizens, rather than to their loyalty or their duty, and to bring the meaner aspects of patriotism into relief.

When we look at the leaders who rose to prominent positions in public life, we do not find evidence of a much higher tone of conduct than that which they attributed *prominent* to ordinary citizens. The Long Parliament attained an *members of* *the Long* unfortunate notoriety for the worst forms of political cor-*Parliament* ruption. Dishonest administration is an evil that can be remedied by a proper system of checks and audit, and effective supervision; but the unscrupulous use of legislative power is more difficult to detect, or to punish. Parliament, by the confiscation of Crown and Ecclesiastical Lands, threw an immense amount of real estate into the market, and some of the members were able to become purchasers at very low rates. Lenthall, the Speaker of the House of Commons, did not set an example of uprightness[1]; and in the case of Harvey, when formal enquiry was made[2], under the Protectorate, the allegations of rumour[3] seem to have been supported. The

publication. He was confident that he would make many proselytes among the worldlings, "the greater part of the world being led more by Appetites of Convenience and Commodity than the Dictates of Conscience; and it is a more current way of Perswasion, by telling men what will be profitable and convenient for them to do than what they ought to doe." Preface. See above, p. 16.

[1] Lady Verney writes, "Everybody tells me there is no hope of doing anything in the House of Commons except by bribery," and she offered £50 to the Speaker's sister-in-law, as she was told it was the best way to take (Gardiner, *Civil War*, IV. 76). On the articles of impeachment against the Speaker drafted in 1649 see Walker, *History of Independency*, II. 211.

[2] Edmond Harvey was charged in 1655 with abusing his opportunities as Commissioner of Customs and sent to the Tower (*Dictionary of National Biography*, s.v.).

[3] The contrast between the wealth of the leaders and their agents and the distress in the country generally must have been very galling. The dissatisfaction in the City in 1647 found expression in a tract entitled *The Mournful Cryes of many thousand Poore Tradesmen who are ready to famish through decay of Trade.* " The merchants have already kept back from the Tower many hundred thousand pounds, and no bullion is brought into the Tower, so that money will be more scarce daily....You may, if you will, Proclaime Liberty for all to come and discover to a Committee of disengaged men, chosen out of every County, one for a County, to discover to them what Monies and Treasure your owne Members and your Sequestrators have in their hands, and you may by that meanes find many Millions of money to pay the Publique debts. You may find £30,000 in Mr Richard Darley's hand, £25,000 in Mr Thorpe's hands....And thus you may take off all Taxes

pretensions of such men to continue indefinitely in power
were intolerable, and Oliver Cromwell earned the gratitude
of honest citizens by evicting the gang of unscrupulous politicians, who were plotting to prolong their tenure of authority.
Their characteristics have been graphically pourtrayed by
Milton[1], a man who moved in a sphere which showed the

A.D. 1603
—1689.

before its
dismissal
by Crom-
well,

presently and so secure Peace, that Trading may revive and our Pining, hungry,
famishing Families bee saved.

"Note. Mr William Lenthall Speaker of the House, to cover his cozenage,
gave two and twenty thousand pounds to his servant Mr. Cole to purchase Land in
his own name, though for his use; which hee did, and then dyed suddenly and the
land fell to his Sonne, and the Widow having married, a Lawyer keeps the Land for
the child's use, saith he knows not that his predecessor received any monie from
the Speaker, and now Master Speaker sueth in Chancery for the Land. A hundred
such discoveries might be made.

"And O yee Souldiers, who refused to Disband because you would have Justice
and Freedome, who Cryed till the Earth echoed, *Justice, Justice*; forget not that
Cry * * * there is a large Petition of some pitifull men that's now abroad, which
containes all our desires, and were that Granted in all things, wee should have
Trading againe, and should not need to begge our Bread, though those men have
so much mercy, as they would have none to cry in the streets for Bread." [Brit.
Mus. 669. f. 11 (116), Jan. 1647.] On other evidence of distress in the City
during the Interregnum see below, p. 186.

1 "For a Parliament being call'd, to addres many things, as it was thought the
People with great courage, and expectation to be eas'd of what discontented
them, chose to thir behoof in Parliament, such as they thought best affected to
the public good, and som indeed men of wisdom and integrity; the rest, (to be
sure the greater part,) whom Wealth or ample Possessions, or bold and active
Ambition (rather than Merit) had commended to the same place.

"But when once the superficiall zeal and popular fumes that acted thir New
Magistracy were cool'd and spent in them, strait every one betook himself (setting
the Commonwealth behind, his privat ends before) to doe as his own profit or
ambition ledd him. Then was justice delay'd, and soon after deni'd : spight and
favour determin'd all: hence faction, thence treachery, both at home and in the
field: ev'ry where wrong, and oppression: foull and horrid deeds committed
daily, or maintain'd, in secret, or in open. Some who had bin call'd from shops
and warehouses without other merit, to sit in Supreme Councills and Committees,
(as their breeding was) fell to huckster the Commonwealth. Others did thereafter as men could soothe and humour them best; so hee who would give most,
or, under covert of hypocriticall zeale, insinuat basest, enjoy'd unworthily the
rewards of learning and fidelity; or escaped the punishment of his crimes and
misdeeds. Thir Votes and Ordinances, which men looked should have contained
the repealing of bad laws, and the immediat constitution of better, resounded
with nothing else, but new Impositions, Taxes, Excises; yeerly, monthly, weekly.
Not to reckon the Offices, Gifts, and Preferments bestow'd and shared among
themselves: they in the meanwhile, who were faithfullest to this Cause, and
freely aided them in Person, or with thir Substance, when they durst not compell
either, slight'd and bereev'd after of thir just Debts by greedy Sequestrations,
were toss'd up and down after miserable attendance from one Committee to
another with Petitions in thir hands, yet either miss'd the obtaining of thir

A.D. 1603
—1689.

but there was an immense improvement in administrative efficiency.

Commonwealth and Protectorate at their best; for during this period, there seems to have been extraordinary success in improving the vigour of official life[1]. The administration of the navy was admirable[2]; the farming of the customs was discontinued; and it is probable that other departments were also well managed, and formed a good school for training the excellent public servants who proved so assiduous under the Restored Monarchy[3]. Cromwell's success in organising and maintaining a vigorous and honest system of administration was his most lasting achievement.

The chiefs of the Army

Even in the Army, however, the claims of self-interest were not wholly laid aside[4]. In the first campaign, the parliamentary forces had been largely recruited from men who had nothing to lose, and much to gain, by disturbance

suit, or though it were at length graunted, (meer shame and reason oft-times extorting from them at least a show of Justice) yet by thir Sequestrators and Sub-committees abroad, Men for the most part of insatiable hands, and noted disloyalty those Orders were commonly disobeyed: which for certain durst not have bin, without secret compliance, if not compact with som superiours able to bear them out. Thus were thir Freinds confiscate in thir Enemies, while they forfeited thir Debtors to the State, as they call'd it, but indeed to the ravening seizure of innumerable Thieves in Office: yet were withal no less burden'd in all extraordinary assessments and oppressions, then those whom they took to be disaffected: nor were wee happier Creditors to what wee call'd the State, then to them who were sequested as the States Enemies.

"For that faith which ought to have been kept as sacred and inviolable as anything holy, "the Publick Faith," after infinit Summs receav'd, and all the Wealth of the Church not better employed, but swallow'd up into a privat Gulph, was not ere long ashamed to confess bankrupt. And now besides the sweetnes of Bribery, and other Gain, with the love of Rule, thir own guiltiness and the dreaded name of Just Account, which the People had long call'd for, discover'd plainly that there were of thir owne number, who secretly contriv'd and semented those Troubles and Combustions in the Land, which openly they sat to remedy; and would continually find such worke, as should keep them from being ever brought to that Terrible Stand of laying down thir authority for lack of new business, or not drawing it out to any length of time, though upon the ruin of a whole nation." *History of England*, Book III. in *Works* (1851), v. 95.

[1] The history of Tammany in New York City shows that a high degree of effectiveness may be obtained, though on costly terms, under a government which its enemies stigmatise as corrupt.

[2] Oppenheim, *op. cit.* 347.

[3] Sir George Downing and Mr Povey were men, with great knowledge of trade affairs, who were public servants both under the Protectorate and the Restored Monarchy. With others, this was not the case; Williamson and Petty began their careers in 1660.

[4] According to Walker (*History of Independency*, II. p. 4), "the Independents were the greatest dilapidators of the Commonwealth."

and the chances of war[1]. Cromwell had spoken in sufficiently
strong terms[2] of the quality of the soldiers, with which his
party were trying to oppose the gentlemen who rallied round
the King. He saw the necessity of organising the Army on *as re-*
a new model, so that there might be a real enthusiasm in *organised*
the ranks; but as time passed, it seemed as if the evil of
self-seeking had not been completely exorcised. It must be
remembered that, however high the spirit of the leaders
might be, the rank and file of the new model could not be
recruited without the aid of the press-gang[3]. Even the *were not*
leaders were hardly above suspicion; they had neither the *unwilling to receive*
simplicity of a Cincinnatus, nor the scruples of a Washing- *rewards for their*
ton[4]; they were patriots of another type. They had hazarded *personal services,*
their lives for the cause, and were fully conscious of the deep
obligations under which England lay to the saviours of the
country[5]. The Protector and his supporters had the opportunity of remunerating themselves, according to their own
valuation of their services; they would have been exception-
ally fortunate, if they had escaped the criticism of opponents
who held that their activities had been mischievous from
the first.

The public of the day would doubtless have accepted the
new order with complacency, if the country had enjoyed a

[1] The Royalists appear to have been particularly to blame for requisitioning
supplies, but the country suffered more or less from both armies. "Chill zell my
cart and eke my plow, And get a zword if ich know how, For ich mean to be
right; * * * Ich had six oxen tother day, And them the Roundheads vetcht away,
A mischief be their speed. And chad zix horses left me whole, And them the
Cabbelleero's stole: Cheevoor men be agreed." *The Western Husbandman's
Lamentation*, Brit. Mus. 669. f. 10 (19). A portion of the army in 1647 lived at free
quarter, *Parl. Hist.* III. 805, 813.

[2] Speech, 13 April 1657, Carlyle, *op. cit.* II. 223.

[3] "There was no zeal among the men thus forced into the ranks." Firth,
Cromwell's Army, 36.

[4] P. L. Ford, *The true George Washington*, p. 304. An exception may be
noticed in the case of Ireton, who showed something of this spirit (Gardiner,
Commonwealth, II. 58).

[5] Cromwell held that merit was the only ground for promotion or reward, and
"he had certainly no objection to see rewards conferred upon himself." Gardiner, *Civil War*, II. 529. Lilburn reports, "I pinched him [Mr Hugh Peters]
a little, particularly upon his great masters large fingering of the Commonwealth's
money..." "I, but," saith he, "Ireton hath got none." "Then," said I, "former
Reports are false; and besides, if he have not, what need he, when his father-in-
law gets so much for them both, as 3, or 4000*l. per annum* at one clap, with well
nigh twenty thousand pounds of wood upon it, if Parliament mens relations may be
believed." *Discourse between Lt.-Col. John Lilburn and Mr Hugh Peters*, 25 May 1649.

A.D. 1603
—1689.

*while the
trade of the
country*

period of prosperity. It has been often assumed that this
was the case, on the general grounds that the powerful navy
would protect shipping, and that, as there was a large
increase of the customs duties, there must have been an
increase of trade[1]. But the inference is quite unwarranted;
under the Commonwealth a new system for collecting the
customs was organised, and the practice of farming this
branch of the revenue was abandoned[2]. Allowances on re-
exportation were discontinued, and the exaction was much
more strict than it had been[3]; so that there was room for an
immense increase of receipts from this cause alone and apart
from any development of trade. The demands of the government pressed much more seriously on the merchants than
had hitherto been the case. As the merchants and tradesmen of London pointed out, in 1654, "All who understand
trade know that the best expedient to attract and enlarge it
is to make the ports free, while these acts[4] would contract
home trade, and almost extinguish foreign; whereas the
enlarging the freedom of the ports, for import and export,
would make this country the magazine of both eastern and
western nations[5]." The governments of the Interregnum
were too much pressed to adopt this far-seeing policy, or to
imitate the Dutch in this matter; and under the circumstances, the increase of customs revenue cannot be taken as
good evidence of an increase of the volume of trade. It
may be admitted that there had been a development of
the commerce with France, but the advantage derived from

*was suffer-
ing under
heavy
customs
duties*

*and was
greatly
distressed;*

---

[1] Oppenheim, *op. cit.* 343.

[2] H. Hall, *History of Customs Revenue,* I. 189.

[3] "The surveyor generall had opened diuers pokes of cloth, and weighed all
half clothes, and made stopage of what he found overweight, till they had entred
bound to stand such order as the Parliament should make touching the same.
The Merchants at Hull say no custom has been paid for the last 30 years for
overweight, and further that the surveyor general hath given orders to the other
officers not to passe any entries for the future, till the Merchants have paid for
over weight, and for default to make seizure." Letter of Alderman Will. Dobson
of Hull, March 26, 1650. York Eastland Merchants' *Record Book,* f. 12. For this
and other references to documents in York, I am indebted to Miss Maud Sellers.

[4] The practice of repaying the excise charged on imported goods, when they
were subsequently exported was partially discontinued in March 1654 (Scobell,
Acts, 1653, cc. 14, 15). Some relief was granted after the merchants' petition (*Ib.*
1654, c. 13). On the pressure of excise see also the *Petition of the inhabitants of
the North Riding of the County of York,* 1656.   [5] S. P. D. 1654, April, 117.

traffic with our nearest continental neighbours was much A.D. 1603
questioned[1]; in any case it seems unlikely that the increase —1689.
in this branch made up for the serious losses in other trades.
Roger Coke's review of the situation is worth quoting, as it is *as we may*
amply borne out in its main features by other evidence, and it *the state-*
was not the expression of irritation at recent embarrassments. *ments of*
Roger
"We have lost the Trade upon the matter by Sea and *Coke,*
Land at home; but before we demonstrate from what causes,
or propound any Expedients by which we may be relieved,
let us see how it stands abroad: We have lost the Trade to
Muscovy, so have that to Greonland, the trade to Norway
possessed by the Norwegians, and the Reasons given in to
the Parliament last Sessions. The Trade to Guinney driven
by a few, and exclusive to other men: The Spanish and
Turkey Trades abated, and in danger: So that unless it be
in the French and Canary Trades, wherein we undo ourselves,
we are making hast to betake ourselves to our Plantations
only, yet shall not be long able to continue that trade for want
of shipping.

"It is true indeed, that England of late, under King
James, but more especially under King Charles, did flourish
by Trade[2], and was more Rich than any other Kingdom in
these Western Parts of the World; but this was by an
Accident of the Times, not to be again hoped for: For the
Austrian Family under Maximilian the Second, and Philip
the Second, attained to that Power and Riches when the
Netherlands made their defection from the Crown of Spain,
that it was not only formidable to the Great Turk, but to all
Christian Princes of Europe: Queen Elizabeth therefore and
the French Kings successively openly assisted them in their
defection. But Philip the Second dying, and Queen Elizabeth
soon after, King James and Philip the Third in the beginning
of their Reigns made Peace, which continued neer 40 years
with little Interruption. During which the Warrs continued
between the United Netherlands and Spain, with little Intermission; whereby the English became Proprietors of the

---

[1] S. P. D. C. II. xxi. 108—110. See below on the jealousy of French competition, pp. 406, 458.
[2] See above, p. 176, n. 1.

Trade with Spain, and by consequence Great sharers in the
Wealth of the West Indies. And this Benefit, moreover,
the English reaped by these Warrs, that the Merchant supplied the Spanish Netherlands with Commodities; and both
Spanish and United Netherlands were supplied with Souldiers from England, whereby many of them on both sides,
especially Officers, acquired much Wealth.

"But the Nation, not content to enjoy Peace, Riches and
Plenty above any other Nation, brought upon itself all the
miseries and Calamities incident to a Civil Warr, so that
Regal Power, as to the exercise of it, for neer 20 years
together was suspended; during which, in the year 1648
the Dutch made Peace with Spain, and Oliver in the year
1654 brake with it[1] (which was a folly never to be forgiven
in his Politicks, nor the losses this Nation susteined thereby
ever again to be repaired) whereby the Condition of the
English and Dutch in reference to the Trade with Spain
became quite inverted; and this continuing neer seven years,
the Dutch are so good Masters of Trade, that little hopes is
left the English of enjoying it as before[2]."

*the diffi-
culties
about
piracy,*
It is, moreover, quite illusory to suppose that the navy
was able to give adequate protection to British shipping;
for greatly as the maritime force of the country had been
augmented, the dangers to English shipping had increased
still more. The old evil of the Algerian pirates remained
unabated; the Earl of Derby and other royalists had fitted
out numerous privateers[3]; the French were ready to prey on
English commerce in the Mediterranean[4], and the Spaniards
and Dutch rendered the Channel and the coasting trade most
insecure[5]. Parliament endeavoured to provide gratuitous

---

[1] An interesting account of the Spanish trade and its importance will be found
in a Remonstrance addressed in 1655 to Cromwell by English merchants. Thurloe,
State Papers, iv. 135.

[2] R. Coke, *Discourse of Trade* (1670), Preface to Reader, pp. 4, 5. See also
T. Manley, *Present State of Europe Examined* in *Harleian Miscellany*, i. 196.

[3] Gardiner, *Commonwealth*, i. 330.   [4] *Commons Journals*, vi. 489.

[5] "The trade of the West of England is almost ruined since the War with
Spain, most of their vessels being taken and carried to S. Sebastians by Spanish
Frigates, which wait daily about Lands End, so that a merchant vessel cannot
stir, there being sometimes no convoy for three or four months. Bristol has lost
250 sail." S. P. D. 1658, CLXXIX. 15. On the Dunkirk privateers see Gardiner,
op. cit. III. 477.

convoy to France[1], and to the Netherlands[2]; but the Levant A.D. 1603
—1689. trade had suffered immensely[3], and the Company endeavoured to secure protection by offering to pay an advance of 20 per cent. on the customs[4]. Blake's raid on the nest of pirates at Tunis was a gallant exploit, but it does not seem to have done much to improve the conditions of trade; there is even some reason to believe that it provoked reprisals and changed things for the worse[5]. The complaints of the loss of shipping continue throughout the whole Interregnum; indeed, it seems that the authorities were so conscious of their inability to protect commerce[6], that they were forced to alter their trade policy. Under the Council of State, and in the early days *the resuscitation of* of the Protectorate, the privileged companies had been *privileged* practically set aside[7], and the African trade and East India *companies,* trade had been open to interlopers. This policy was of doubtful wisdom on other grounds, and it greatly increased the difficulty of arranging for convoys. The resuscitation of such companies as the Merchant Adventurers, the East-land Company and the East India Company—the last with far larger military and judicial powers than it had had before—was a confession of the Protector's inability to defend the property of British subjects on the high seas.

It is difficult to trace any sign of recovery from the mischief that accrued during the Civil War[8]; the effects

---

[1] In 1643. *Commons Journals,* III. 431, 509.

[2] In 1648. Compare the *Humble petition of divers well-affected English Masters and Commanders of Ships. Commons Journals,* VI. 18. Also *ib.* 310.

[3] The merchants had lost diverse great ships within two years past valued at nearly a million of money. They feared that trading would be in time utterly lost. S. P. D. (1650), IX. 34; see also S. P. D. 25 Ap. 1650, p. 121.

[4] *Commons Journals,* VI. 489.

[5] Gardiner, *Commonwealth,* III. 384. In 1657 the Levant Company complained that "their trade was never before in so languishing a condition as it now is, by reason of the swarms of Turkish and Spanish pirates pestering those seas, and the several ships we have lately lost by their means." S. P. D. 1657, CLVI. Sept. 10, p. 95; see also CLVIII. 109.

[6] In 1653 the Merchant Adventurers point out that they have not presumed to ask for a convoy and so could not send any ships to Hamburg during the preceding twelve months. They urge that the interruption of exportation of cloth had given opportunity for the development of a native manufacture in Germany and thus caused irreparable loss to English trade. S. P. D. 1653, XXXIV. 64.

[7] See below, pp. 218, 264, 273.

[8] A possible exception may be noticed in the development of the postal service. The post office, which had been organised by a patent from Charles I. (Rymer, *Foedera,* XIX. 649), became a source of revenue under the Commonwealth (it was farmed for

of that contest on trade and industry were clearly summarised by Violet when called to give evidence before
a Parliamentary Committee in 1650.

"The first and principal reason of the decay of trade has
been the late unhappy wars; before then trade was free and
flourishing at home and abroad; but immediately after, fell
into a consumption, under which it has languished ever since.
Our golden fleece, which is our Indies, was devoured by the
rapine of the soldiers, and great quantities of the remainder
transported" to the Netherlands. Clothiers and workmen
were discouraged and many of them forced either to take
up arms or to emigrate. "The merchants were discouraged,
and many undone, by confiscation of their ships and goods,
in foreign parts, by Princes and States[1] that favoured the late
King's designs, and many more were spoiled at sea, under
pretence of the late King's commissions, for want of sufficient
convoy, which never being wanting to the Hollanders and
Jutlanders they carried the trade from the English merchants
and seamen and more especially since they have concluded a
peace with Spain....Our money employed in trade was either
belonging to strangers or to our nation; that of strangers,
which was employed by exchange, or let out at interest, was
soon drawn in and returned from whence it came, upon the
first breaking up of the war; our merchants had upon their
credits made use of it for enlarging of their trade, and many
of our nation disposed of a great part of their estates into
foreign parts, and some also transported their persons and
families, fearing the issue of the sad distractions....The
money belonging to our nation has been very much exhausted
in the war, not only by losses and diminution of trade, but
by the excessive charge the Commonwealth has been put
to in maintaining the war....The materials of war for our
armies and navy, bought in foreign parts, has also much
diminished the stock of the nation." He adds that owing to
the dearth of corn it had been necessary to import food[2].

£14,000 in 1659. *Commons Journals*, VII. 627), and was farmed out at the Restoration for £21,500; the monopoly was strictly reserved and no one but the Post-
master General was to presume to carry letters for hire (12 Charles II. c. 35 § 6).

[1] On the difficulties at Leghorn compare J. Battie, *Merchants Remonstrance*, 14.
See p. 240 below on the interruption to the Russian trade.

[2] S. P. D. 1650, p. 178, No. 61.

In such disastrous conditions it was inevitable that there should be a large number of bankrupts[1]; public opinion evidently regarded them as the victims of circumstances and desired that debtors in prison should be treated with leniency. The statutes of Henry VIII. and Elizabeth had dealt with the bankrupt as a criminal, who through carelessness or fraud cheated honest men of their dues; he was liable to imprisonment by the Lord Chancellor. The first parliament of James I. took a similar view of the case; and rendered the machinery for realizing the bankrupt's assets, and making payments to his creditors, more stringent than before. The practices of bankrupts were said to be so secret, and so subtle, that they could hardly be found out, or brought to light[2]; and the Commissioners for Bankruptcy had enlarged powers for imprisoning offenders, especially if they were endeavouring to evade full enquiry into their possessions. But while the law was becoming stricter, there are signs of a change in public opinion; it was obvious that in some cases the bankrupt might be an object of commiseration; while it was also clear that the unlimited incarceration of the debtor did not tend in any way whatever to re-imburse the creditor. The case is strongly put in a *Declaration and Appeal*[3], which was drawn up in 1645, and signed by a hundred debtors confined in the Fleet. They were the spokesmen of a considerable class, as they estimated that there were 8000 debtors, thus confined, throughout England and Wales, and they urged that, as they were neither villains nor slaves, the treatment they had received was unconstitutional; the high-handedness of Sir John Lenthall was a special subject of complaint[4].

No public action appears to have been taken in the matter, however, till September 1649[5], when an Act was passed for discharging from imprisonment poor prisoners unable to satisfy their creditors; an additional Act, for the

A.D. 1603 —1689.

the increase in the number

and change in the public attitude toward bankrupts

---

[1] According to Neal (*History of the Puritans*, IV. 246), "there was hardly a single bankruptcy to be heard of in a year, and in such a case the bankrupt had a mark of infamy upon him that he could never wipe off": but this statement cannot be easily reconciled with other evidence.   [2] 1 James I. c. 15.

[3] Brit. Mus. 669. f. 10 (17), and (40).

[4] Whitelock, *Memorials*, 555.

[5] In 1648 when prices were high the sufferings of the prisoners were notorious. Cooke, *Unum necessarium*, 42.

further relief of poor prisoners, was passed in December 1649.

Prisoners, who had no possessions worth more than £5 and their clothes and tools, were to take an oath to this effect before the justices; and after due notice was served on the creditors, so as to allow of their taking objection on sufficient grounds, the prisoners were to be discharged[1]. Further facilities were given in April 1650; and additional measures were passed in April 1652, October 1653[2] and in 1656. As in other matters, the Restoration parliament adopted the measures devised under the Commonwealth, and there were additional acts on behalf of Insolvent Debtors in 1671[3] and 1678[4]. It must not be supposed, however, that the prisoners were always the victims of relentless creditors. In some cases they were 'politic bankrupts[5]' who remained in prison by preference, as a means of evading the just claims that might be made on them. The committee appointed in 1653 ordered the debtors in the Upper Bench to "show cause why their estates should not be sequestered for payment of their just debts[6]"; and a clause in an Act of 1661 facilitates proceedings against 'many persons' who 'out of ill intent to delay their creditors from recovering their just debts, continue prisoners in the Fleet[7].'

The constant attention given to the subject seems to show that bankruptcy was frequent. Little is said in the statutes about the causes of failure, though the Act of 1671 specifies the late unhappy times, and the sad and dreadful fire, as the causes of much misfortune[8]. The conditions of life which make for steady economic progress were conspicuous by their absence, during the Civil War and the years which

succeeded it. The depletion of capital and interruption of the old-established lines of commerce could not but have serious results on the industry of the country, especially in the case of workmen who catered for a foreign market. We have ample evidence that the cloth manufacture fell into a most depressed condition; there was much lack of employment and a marked decline in the quality of the goods

---

1 Scobell, *Acts*, 1649, cc. 56, 65.　　2 Scobell, *Acts*, II. 265.
5 22 and 23 C. II. c. 20.　　4 30 Ch. II. c. 4.
6 Dekker, *Seven Deadly Sins* (1606), p. 1.　　6 Whitelock, *Memorials*, 555.
7 13 Charles II. st. ii. c. 2, § 4.　　8 22 and 23 Charles II. c. 20.

produced[1]. The new model had conquered in Great Britain and Ireland; but the privateers of the royalists, and the other enemies of the new government, were able to sap the sources of English prosperity on the sea, and to compass the fall of the Protectorate.

A.D. 1603—1689.

185. It is pleasant to turn from the intestine struggles and general distress during the Civil War and Interregnum, to the exuberant development of national life which occurred under the restored Monarchy. There has been a tendency lately to ante-date this movement, and to associate the great commercial expansion of the seventeenth century with the name of Cromwell[2]. Though Ranke[3], Gardiner[4] and Schulze-Gaevernitz[5] have lent the weight of their authority to this view, it is difficult to see that any evidence can be adduced in support of it[6], while there is much to be said against it. In regard to colonisation and trade, Cromwell was for the most part content to follow the lines of policy laid down by James I. and Charles I.[7]; where he struck out a line of his own, as in the project for forming a commercial staple at Dunkirk[8], he was retrograde. His whole character

The great develop-ment of commerce,

which is sometimes ascribed to the initia-tive of Cromwell,

---

[1] "The generality of English exports are bad, and this being discovered by other nations causes them to get into disrepute and thus not to sell. . . . Two thirds of the nation depend upon manufactures of one kind or another, and the complaints of the people are grounded upon the deadness of trade and want of employment caused by such malpractices. In one port of Spain alone, within these few years, we used to vent 12000 pieces of says, serges and such like woollen stuff, but now scarcely 2000, and so in other parts, the Dutch having taken up a truer way of making them. We also formerly sent a great store of darnix draft-work and other like work but, on account of its badness and falseness, it has become totally disused. The same may be said of our cloth and several other commodities; through the want of care and inspection, they come into disrepute, and to abatement in value, and at length are refused to be bought at all....It is impossible to regulate a foreign trade, or to exact the performance of articles agreed upon with other nations for the encouragement of our commerce, without such reformation, as they cannot be obliged to traffic with our people if we will cozen them." S. P. D. Dec. 1651, xvi. 139 (*Cal.* p. 88).

[2] G. L. Beer, *Cromwell's Economic Policy* in the *Political Science Quarterly*, xvi. 582 and xvii. 46; Hunter, *History of India*, ii. 107; L. Wolff, *Manasseh Ben Israel's Mission to Oliver Cromwell*, Introduction, p. xxviii. See also Cunningham, *The Imperialism of Cromwell* in *Macmillan's Magazine*, 1902.

[3] *History of England principally in the Seventeenth Century*, iii. 68.

[4] *Commonwealth*, ii. 87.

[5] *Britischer Imperialismus*, 53.

[6] On Cromwell's alleged interest in the Navigation Act and the East India Company, see below, pp. 210 n. 3 and 261 n. 9.

[7] See below, pp. 211 and 335 n. 6.

[8] Ranke, iii. 386. Some of the French opponents of the cession of Dunkirk in 1658 appear to have regarded Cromwell as less actuated by commercial motives

C. 13

becomes unintelligible[1], and ceases to be consistent, if he was at heart an Empire-builder. It was only when his despotism was broken, and his ideal of a great protestant alliance was abandoned, that England entered on the career of colonial and commercial expansion, which has rendered her a world power.

It may, of course, be true that this was to a very small extent due to the influence of the king. Charles II. seems to have been lacking in that sense of kingly duty, which had given a dignity to his father's bearing, even in the most pitiable plights. We shall hardly do the son injustice if we take his cynicism as genuine, and regard him as frankly opportunist in playing for his own hand. Had Charles been a better man, he would have strengthened the Stuart succession in the affections of the country, but it is not clear that his reign would have been more beneficial from the economic standpoint. The interest of the prince and of the people do coincide to a very large extent ; and several of the causes of friction, which had existed in the early part of the century, had been removed. Provision had been made for the Crown by the Restoration Parliament, and Charles would probably have preferred to play the part of a constitutional monarch, if the moneys which were voted him had really been at his disposal. As a matter of fact, the actual receipts fell far short of the estimated revenue[2], and Charles was driven to depend on the subsidies he received from France. But however much he might disregard the sentiments of his subjects, he never played fast and loose with their material interests. He was a man of considerable mental acuteness and power of observation; he had had unusual opportunity of improving his abilities by means of

harmonised with the interests of the Crown.

than by the desire of political aggression on the continent. " These projects which came to nothing in the Indies, but to his own confusion doth certainly turn his restless and ambitious imaginations to other parts nearer home, which are more exposed to his Tyranny. He feeds his soul with these Soaring Ideas of the ancient Brittans, . . . and without doubt when he considers that the first of his Conquests cost him but so little pains, he sooths up his ambitious thoughts, which Ferries him over our Seas and represents unto him at one time Guienne revolted under his Standarts and another he fancyeth Normandie reduced under his Laws." *France no friend to England* p 14, Royal Irish Acad. *Halliday Tracts*, Box 74 (3).

[1] Seeley, *Growth of British Policy*, II. 75; Morley, *Oliver Cromwell*, 447.

[2] W. A. Shaw, *Beginnings of National Debt* in *Owens College Historical Essays*, 392.

foreign travel, both in France and in Holland, and he was prepared to take a sympathetic attitude towards wise schemes of internal improvement, and of commercial and colonial development. He was quite aware that the increase of national prosperity was beneficial to the Crown, as well as to the subjects; and it is remarkable how immediately the new government took in hand the improvement of the convoy service[1] and the better administration of the affairs of trade.

The marriage of Charles II. marks a stage in the expansion *The Portuguese* of England; for it brought this country into close economic *marriage,* relations with Portugal, and enabled Englishmen to reap the permanent advantage of the extraordinary enterprise that kingdom had previously displayed[2]. The success of the Portuguese, in throwing off the yoke of Spain in 1640, was followed by a revolt of the Portuguese colonists in Brazil from their subjection to the Dutch. These changes offered a great chance to English traders, as the Portuguese were unable to provide the requisite shipping for intercourse with their dependencies, and Charles I. concluded an important commercial treaty in January 1642[3]. Englishmen were glad to take advantage of these facilities[4]; but their status was rendered uncertain during the Civil War. When the quarrel with Portugal broke out, 'trade ceased,' and the "evil consequences of that war were many and considerable[5]"; but Cromwell was eventually able to obtain a restoration of valuable privileges in 1654[6]; and Charles II., by his marriage with Katharine of Braganza, established a dynastic connection with Portugal, and did not a little to revive the commercial relations which had existed at an earlier time[7]. The alliance seems to have given the English a decided advantage, as compared with the Dutch, and led to the development of a considerable trade with the Azores, Madeira and other Portuguese possessions.

[1] 13 C. II. St. i. c. 9.

[2] Cary, *An Essay on the State of England in Relation to its Trade*, 118.

[3] Dumont, *Corps Diplomatique du Droit des Gens*, VI. i. 238.

[4] There were English vessels in the Brazil fleet which Blake stopped, while watching for Prince Rupert at Lisbon (1650). Gardiner, *Commonwealth*, I. 334.

[5] Carlyle, *op. cit.* II. 265.

[6] The Brazil Company of Portugal had been erected in 1649, and the rights allowed to Englishmen in the Brazil trade were strictly limited. Dumont, *op. cit.* VI. ii. 83, art. xi.　　　　　　[7] Vol. I. p. 414.

A.D. 1603
—1689. The injury which had been done to English commerce
and industry by the breach with Spain has been already
alluded to. The matter came before the Council of Trade
immediately after the Restoration[1]; and the government
and the of Charles II. was successful in re-establishing the trade on
treaty
with Spain, more satisfactory lines than had ever been secured before.
The English merchants in Andalusia had obtained privileges
for themselves from Philip IV. in 1645, by the payment
of 2,500 ducats[2]; these privileges were now restored, and
extended to the whole of Spain. Englishmen were henceforth to be free to trade in any part of the king's dominions[3],
and were to pay no higher duties than those levied from
other nations[4]; they were to enjoy liberty of conscience, so
long as they did not cause public scandal[5]. In this way the
trade with Spain, and with the Netherlands[6], was thrown open
to Englishmen again. It was perhaps even more important
that the King of Spain agreed that English merchants
should enjoy "in all places whatever the same Privileges,
Securities, Liberties and Immunities, whether they concern
their Persons or trade, with all the beneficial clauses and
circumstances that have been granted or shall be hereafter
granted ... to the States General of the United Provinces,
the Hanse Towns, or any other Kingdom or State whatever
in as full ample and beneficial manner, as if the same were
strengthen- particularly mentioned and inserted in this treaty[7]." English-
ed the
English in men were thus placed in a position to compete with the
their com-
petition Dutch on even terms, as they had not been since 1648; but
with the
Dutch, they were also allowed a privilege which was of the greatest
importance, with the view of developing a carrying trade.

[1] They appointed a Committee on Spanish petitions, 18 and 21 Dec. 1660
(S. P. D. C. II. xxiv. 21).

[2] *Copy of a Patent* in *Articles of Peace, Commerce and Alliance between the
Crowns of Great Britain and Spain concluded in a Treaty at Madrid* (1667), p. 36,
Brit. Mus. 6915. b. 4.

[3] Art. 4, p. 5.   [4] Art. 5, p. 6.

[5] Art. 28, p. 23. Charles II. thus obtained a concession which the Spaniards
refused to discuss with Cromwell. Carlyle, *op. cit.* II. 98.

[6] Art. 20, p. 19. All the Acts prohibiting the importation of dyed and dressed
English cloth into Flanders were revoked. The chief point which the Spaniards
gained was in article 25, by which England agreed not to regard wheat and other
cereals as contraband, but as goods which might be transported to towns and
places of enemies.

[7] Art. 28, p. 29.

The King of Spain consented to permit goods which had A.D. 1603
—1689.
paid duty on entering the country to be re-exported within
twelve months without being charged any duty outward[1].
These provisions must have struck a much more severe blow
at the Dutch carrying trade than the Act of 1651 had done,
and would tend not a little to the revival of English commerce
from its long depression.

There were several other treaties which Charles negotiated *and piracy*
at the beginning of his reign[2]. Among the earliest were *abated.*
those intended to protect the Levant trade from the Turkish
pirates[3]. The conditions were sufficiently humiliating politically[4]; but so far as shipping was concerned, it seems to have
been more favourably circumstanced than had been the case
in the era before the Civil War. We hear far less of the
ravages of pirates in the Restoration period.

The Portuguese connection not only gave English mer- *England*
chants a better status in European commerce, but effected *obtained*
a firm
a great change in the position of English traders in the East. *footing in*
the East,
The dowry which Charles received with his bride included
the fortress of Tangier[5], which controlled the access to the
Mediterranean, and the island of Bombay; this became
a most valuable basis for the operations of the East India
Company[6], to which it was leased in 1668. This side of

---

[1] Art. 12, p. 13.

[2] A collection is in the British Museum, 6915. b. 1–4: it contains treaties with
the United Provinces, Louis XIV., and Frederick III. of Denmark, and with
Spain, all concluded in 1667 or 1668. On earlier negociations see S. P. D. C. II.
xxiv. 22.

[3] Treaties in (1662) with the Bassa of Algiers, the Bassa of Tripoli, and the
City of Tunis, in Dumont, *op. cit.* vi. ii. 420, 431, 432.

[4] R. L. Playfair, *Scourge of Christendom*, p. 80.

[5] On plans for developing this port as a place of trade see S. P. D. C. II.
cxx. 38.

[6] An important step in the position of English traders in the East is marked
by the twelfth article of the treaty which Charles I. concluded with Portugal in
1642. It confirms the agreement which had been made between the Viceroy of
Goa and Methwold, the Governor of Surat, for three years, and directs the appointment of Commissioners to examine the question a fin que par ce moyen, une Paix
et Alliance perpetuelle puisse être etablie et confirmée par les deux Roys entre
leur Sujets de part et d'autre. In 1654 the Portuguese agreed that Englishmen
might sail to and trade with the Portuguese settlements in India (Dumont, *op.
cit.* vi. ii. 83, art. xi); John IV. was probably glad to strengthen the English
interest in the East, in order to have help against the Dutch in those waters.
This was the motive which led to the cession of Bombay in 1661 (Hunter, *History
of British India*, ii. 190).

commercial development had received little encouragement
from Cromwell, who had been prepared in 1653 to leave most
of it to the Dutch[1]. The work of settlement on the American
continent had also suffered from the apathy of the Protector[2];
he had tried to induce the New Englanders to migrate to the
Island of Jamaica[3], or to come back to Ireland[4], but they
and secured preferred the country where they had established their homes.
the basis
for Anglo- Under Charles II. and his brother, the work of plantation and
Saxon pre-
dominance trade was organised[5] and pushed on with vigour; there was
in America. continued settlement on the Atlantic coast of North America,

[1] "That the trade of all Asia, the Great and Little, shall henceforth belong
unto the United Provinces; and that the State of England, Scotland and Ireland,
nor any of their inhabitants, Shall not, nor have nor may trade there any more,
the places in Asia, which do join on the Middle Sea only excepted. And that there
shall be given unto the English Company of East India, by the Company of the
East India of the United Provinces the sum of [*left blank*] and thereupon shall the
English Company and all others leave trading there and return home and go no
more." *A collection of the State Papers of John Thurloe*, II. 125. On Cromwell's
personal part in this proposal see Gardiner, *Commonwealth*, II. 351 n. In the
face of this statement as to his attitude on the subject, I am unable to accept Sir
W. W. Hunter's view (*op. cit.* II. 124) that Cromwell took an active part personally in reconstructing the East India Company on a national basis and with
enlarged powers in 1657. See below, p. 261.

[2] He had doubtless been interested in the attempt of the Pilgrim Fathers to
find an asylum from Laudian coercion, but with the triumph of Puritanism in
England there was no longer the same reason for the emigration of men of this
type. The religious rather than the economic motives for plantation were those
that appealed to Cromwell.

[3] Gardiner, *Commonwealth*, III. p. 455. Cromwell does not appear to have
advanced beyond the Elizabethan ideas of English policy, despite all the changes
that had taken place in the first half of the seventeenth century. His chief
desire was to cripple Spain, and he tried to attack her in the American possessions from which she drew her supplies of treasure. He was anxious to get the
Dutch to join him in this scheme, and was apparently prepared to make any
sacrifices which were involved in pushing it forward. Gardiner, *op. cit.* II. 350.

[4] Egerton, *A Short History of British Colonial Policy*, 64.

[5] See the arrangements for the Council of Plantations, S. P. Col. XIV. 59,
1 Dec. 1660. The spirit of enterprise and the desire for colonisation appear to
have been almost as strong at that period as in the days of Elizabeth and James
"Look at the efforts of the Lord Proprietors Albemarle, Ashley, Berkeley,
Clarendon and others to colonise Carolina, which turned out, after a little experience, eminently successful ... the love of adventure of Lord Willoughby, who
at his own expense of £20,000 settled a colony of 4000 inhabitants in Surinam,
though it was afterwards taken from him by the Dutch during the war. In
Africa, too, Englishmen secured a footing, and made settlements in many places in
spite of the hostilities of the Dutch. In the West Indies there were Lord Francis
and then his brother Lord William Willoughby devoting their best energies to
consolidate the settlement of the Leeward Isles of Antigua, Montserrat and
Nevis and that 'rare pearl in the King's Crown,' Barbadoes. See also what
D'Oyley, Lord Windsor and Sir Thos. Modyford did for Jamaica and how these

till the chain was completed by the planting of Pennsylvania A.D. 1603
—1689. and the capture of New York. The bases for the English conquest of India[1], and the Anglo-Saxon predominance in America, were laid in the time of Charles II.

Charles II. had no single counsellor who could compare in assiduity and judiciousness with Lord Burleigh; but Clarendon was fully alive to the importance of trade *Clarendon was fully* interests. He had fully appreciated the importance of the *alive to the* American colonies. "At his majesty's return and before, *interests of* he had used all the endeavours he could to prepare and *plantation,* dispose the king to a great esteem of his plantations, and to encourage the improvement of them by all the ways that could reasonably be proposed to him. And he had been confirmed in that opinion and desire, as soon as he had a view of the entries in the custom house; by which he found what a great revenue accrued to the Crown from those plantations, in so much as the receipts from them had upon the matter repaired the diminution and decrease of the customs which the late troubles had brought upon other parts of trade from what it had formerly yielded."[2] He maintained the practice[3] which had been established under Charles I., and to which Cromwell had reverted[4], of organising a permanent committee for trade; so that the *and a* government should regularly have the benefit of expert *permanent committee* opinion[5]. In August 1660 an order was addressed to the

islands, in spite of the attacks of both French and Dutch on some of them, developed in wealth and prosperity.... Surely it may be said with truth, that in the early years of Charles II.'s reign some glory was reflected upon England through her Colonies, and that in these eight years of our Colonial History shine forth some brilliant examples of Englishmen in the persons of the Governors appointed by Charles II." *Calendar of State Papers Colonial*, America and West Indies (1661—1668), Preface by W. N. Sainsbury, lxxxi.

[1] As Sir W. Hunter writes "Charles II. found the Company a trading body; he left it a nascent territorial power, with the right of coinage, the command of fortresses and of English and Indian troops, the authority to form alliances and to make peace or war, the jurisdiction over subjects, and other attributes of a delegated sovereignty." *History of British India*, II. 185.

[2] *Life of Edward Earl of Clarendon* by himself (1827), III. 407.

[3] The need for permanent supervision is strongly expressed in king James's Commission, 23 Jan. 1624. Brit. Mus. *Add. MSS.* 12,496 f. 113. See Appendix.

[4] Thurloe, *State Papers*, IV. 177, S. P. D. 1655, p. 1 (Nov. 1). This body had members from the outports.

[5] Sir George Downing had a great reputation in regard to finance, but according to Clarendon, he did not altogether deserve it. W. A. Shaw, *op. cit.* 415. Clarendon,

A.D. 1603
—1689. Lord Mayor of London[1] requiring him "to give notice to the Turkey Merchants, the Merchant Adventurers, the East India, Greenland and Eastland Companies, and likewise to the unincorporated trades for Spain, France, Portugal, Italy, *of experts was organised* and the West India Plantations, of the King's intention to appoint a committee of understanding able persons to take into their particular consideration all things conducible to the due care of trade and commerce with foreign parts. And the king willed them, out of their respective societies, to present unto him four of their most active men, of whom his Majesty might choose two of each body, and to these merchants added some other able and well experienced persons to be dignified also with the presence and assistance of some of his Majesty's Privy Council. Together they were authorised by a Commission under the Great Seal to be a standing committee to enquire into and rectify all things tending to the advancement of trade, and insert into all treaties such articles as would render this nation flourishing in commerce." A separate Commission was also established to deal with the affairs of the Plantations[2].

to advise the Council on Economic policy, The business of the Committee of Trade was considered by sub-committees[3], and the result of the deliberations was embodied in a report or recommendation delivered to the King by a Privy Councillor. The bold policy which was inaugurated during this period in regard to the export of precious metals[4], and the real decision about such disputed matters as the Navigation Acts, probably lay with this body[5]. The very important tariff questions which were dealt with in the new Book of Rates, as well as the charges for convoy,

Life, ii, 289. Possibly Clarendon was likely to be a severe critic of a man who had been scoutmaster-general of the New Model. Frith, *op. cit.* 65.

[1] Bannister, *Life and Writings of William Paterson*, ii. 252.

[2] Dec. 1, 1660 (S. P. Col. xiv. 59).

[3] I am indebted to Mr Hubert Hall for calling my attention to the Instructions to the Committee of Trade and the Minutes which record their action. See Appendix.

[4] The Council was specially summoned for November 22nd to consider the Report of the Committee on Trade on this subject (S. P. D. C. II. 1660, xxi. 84, Dec. 12, 1660, xxiii. 85). See Macculloch *Select Tracts on Money*, p. 153, also below, p. 432.

[5] See the interesting report *Cal. S. P. Col. America and W. I.* 1664, 947; S. P. D. C. II. xxi. 27.

must certainly have been considered by some such body of experts[1].   De Witt bears testimony[2] to the excellence of these arrangements.   " The English, anno 1660, settled their Rates of Customs and Convoy money so well, according to these maxims, to favour their inhabitants as much as they could, and to burden all foreign Masters of Ships and Merchants, that if we continue charged in this Country (i.e. Holland) so unreasonably as at present, and there too, and the English on the other hand continue to be so favourably used, both here and at home, they will bereave us of much of our Trade."

The authorities in the Restoration period endorsed the opinion, which had been formed by the Council of Trade during the Interregnum, for they discouraged open trading. With a view to the development of English commerce and colonisation, and to the improvement of English industry, special privileges for trade and jurisdiction were conferred on individuals or companies.   The experiments of the Commonwealth in dispensing with company trading[3] had not been successful, and the work of pioneers in the Indies and in Hudson's Bay was carried on by bodies which enjoyed chartered privileges from the Crown.   Plantation and settlement were also authorised by royal grants to the Duke of York and to Penn, and to the Lords[4] who erected a proprietary government in the Carolinas.   In regard to internal affairs, however, a change of method is noticeable; companies were still erected to supervise some particular department of industry; but these for the most part obtained their powers by Act of Parliament and not by letters patent from the Crown[5].

while the prosecution of particular trades was organised by Companies.

186.   The rate of the advance of commerce and colonisation was much more rapid in the years which followed the

Though commerce

---

[1] S. P. D. C. II. xxxii. 57.

[2] De Witt, *Interest of Holland*, p. 97.

[3] Hunter, *History of British India*, ii. 123.

[4] J. H. Wheeler, *Historical Sketches of North Carolina*, p. 29.

[5] See in regard to the Tapestry manufacture, S. P. D. C. II. xliii. 54; the Council of Trade recommended that this industry should be vested in a Company under royal control, but the king gave instructions that a bill should be prepared empowering His Majesty to settle the trade as a Corporation.   S. P. D. C. II. l. 61 (15).

Restoration than in the previous part of the century, but it is true to say that the progress was unbroken, and that the methods pursued were similar, throughout the whole era.

was continuously advancing in the seventeenth century,

The laying the foundations of the commercial and colonial empire of England, widely and firmly, was the great and lasting achievement of the seventeenth century. But there was no steady development in the internal life of the country; that was marked by violent changes. The fall of such a highly organised and actively administered government as the monarchy of Charles I. not only resulted in a great constitutional upheaval, but had lasting effects on industrial conditions of every kind. The importance of

there was a violent crisis in social life within the realm.

the Civil War, as a crisis in the social history of the country, is not obvious at first sight. The Restoration gave us back a monarchy, but it did not bring back the governmental machinery[1] which had failed to meet the wants of the country in previous days. The Civil War had destroyed the traditional financial and military systems, and left room for improved schemes of administration. The money obtained from the grants of tenths and fifteenths, along with the general subsidies, had proved insufficient for the needs of the government; hence the fiscal arrangements which had been suddenly called into being by Parliament to meet the exigencies of the Civil War, were perpetuated at the Restoration. Similarly, the traditional methods of maintaining order against riot and insurrection had proved a failure; Charles had issued commissions of array to call together the armed citizens under the lords lieutenant; but they had been unable to resist the onslaught of an army drilled and disciplined in accordance with the best examples of conti-

The fiscal and military systems were reconstructed,

nental organisation. And this had come to stay. The history of British regiments begins with Coldstream Guards, who survived the disbanding of the New Model and formed the nucleus of a standing army.

It was, of course, necessary that the fiscal and military systems, which had collapsed, should be promptly replaced;

---

[1] Very insufficient stress was laid upon this in previous editions of this book. The real importance of the Restoration as a crisis in social history is well brought out by Hasbach, *Die Englischen Landarbeiter*, 3.

but in industrial and social life the case was different. Immense pains had been taken under Elizabeth to organise the means by which prices should be assessed, and wages regulated, for the whole country; and great efforts had been made by James I. and Charles I. to maintain the quality of English manufactures. This elaborate system depended on *but the machinery* the co-operation of central and local authorities; the Civil *for social* War and Interregnum gave it a shock from which it could *regulation was render-* not recover. The machinery, which had lain to the hands of *ed useless.* Elizabeth's advisers for the regulation of social and industrial conditions, was no longer available. The change in the habits of the landed gentry[1], against which Elizabeth had striven, as well as the alterations which had been brought about by the war, had rendered a breach in the traditions of local government inevitable. The political disorder of the times paralysed the central authority. The vigour of the Elizabethan rule had been due to the power of the Privy Council, backed as it was by the Court of Star Chamber. When these powers were shattered, the supervision, which had been exercised over the magistrates by the Council, was withdrawn. Parochial and county officials were left to their own devices, till the period of the reformed Parliament, when the Charity Commissioners, the Poor Law Commissioners and the Local Government Board were instituted[2].

There can be little doubt that the elaborate system of search, which the earlier Stuarts had instituted, fell to pieces, *The system* *of search* and that the government abandoned the attempt to exercise *was not* an effective supervision over the quality of goods. The *main-* *tained,* growth of capitalist industry, and the organisation of such centres of trade as Blackwell Hall, may have rendered State interference in the matter less necessary; the maintenance of quality, as well as the terms of prices, were henceforth left to be determined by the action of skilled wholesale buyers. Still, there is some reason to believe that the standard of English manufacture was not altogether main-

---

[1] See above pp. 104, 111. The changed character comes out in many ways. Burton (*Anatomy*, I. 51, 109) speaks very bitterly of the graspingness shown by patrons in their dealings with the clergy. [2] See below, pp. 772, 809.

tained for a time, and that English industry suffered in consequence in the commercial world[1]. It was by no

[1] " The debasing and falsifying our Manufactures hath been a great hindrance to their consumption; hereby we have given away that excellent Advantage (that Providence hath afforded us) whereby we are capable of exceeding the whole World, and suffered the Dutch and other Nations to out-do us in Trade. And I can see little hopes of good Success in Trade, whilst there is Error *in fundamento*, and the sinister practices of straining and falsifying our Goods are the chief wheels that brings our Gain, which for some time may answer private Ends, but will soon be prejudicial to the Publick; which is no way to be prevented but by fixing our manufactures to a certain length, breadth and weight, and preventing the great abuse of straining." *The languishing State of our Woollen Manufacture, Humbly Represented to Parliament* [Brit. Mus. 816. m. 14 (80)]. This volume has numerous broadsides on the subject apparently of about the date 1677—78. *A narrative of the whole proceedings in the last two sessions of Parliament concerning the Transportation of Wool*, contrasts the well regulated trade of Norwich and Colchester with that of other parts of the kingdom and suggests that the statute of 1563 should be amended so as to insist on apprenticeship in the Worsted manufacture [Brit. Mus. 816. m. 14 (91)]. Compare S. P. D. J. I. 1622, No. 78.

The complaints of other pamphleteers are worth quoting. "The ready way to rectifie abuses about Cloathing were to compare them with the rules of Law provided for them. * * * For instance, the Law empowers the Merchants and Drapers to be their own searchers and to punish the Cloathiers' Purse as they find his works to be faulty; and so they do, to the no small grief of the Cloathier: but the Retayling Buyer is not hereby at all relieved; the Draper selling to him these faults for which he was before paid by the clothier; the merchants do the same by causing their clothiers to bring their manufactures into the merchants private Ware-houses, where their own servants are judges, who upon searching the cloth do make and marke faults enough, for which they have reparable abatements, but themselves again do practise all fraudulent wayes they can to barter and exchange those faults away without giving any allowance for them. * * * It doth undeniably follow that Cloathing must be purged from its corruption or England must be poor. * * * For a true Reformation and Regulation of those damages that have befallen England by the false and deceptious Manufacturing of Wools we must rightly understand the cause." The bad manufacturing "is by that division in Trade both in Merchant and Cloathier, by which meanes it falls out that by the consequence of one man's single Act, a thousand persons may be undone." The Author suggests "incorporating the manufactures." *England's Interest* (1669) *asserted in the Improvement of its Native Commodities and more especially the manufacture of Wool*, Brit. Mus. 712. g. 16 (4) p. 29. Compare also *The humble petition of Wm. Smith on behalf of the Clothiers* [Brit. Mus. 816. m. 14 (111)]. No date. "That the Workmen in each preparation and manufacture of the said materials are (through want of legal Visitations and Searches into the respective Trades thereunto appertaining) run into great Abuses, Frauds and Deceits insomuch as no less than Your most Wise and Grave inquiries thereinto together with a speedy Reformation, will give encouragement or hopes that their Trades, with the Merchandize and Commerce thereupon, will long continue in these His Majestie's dominions. That the Woole winding, Combing, Spinning, Dying, Weaving, Dressing and continual Interloping in the making of Cloaths hath encouraged and almost licensed such a multiplicity of Abuses and Offences practised against the known Laws as the Cure seems almost desperate. That through want or neglect

means easy, however, to devise any system of authoritative A.D. 1603 —1689. supervision that should be effective and should not hamper trade unduly. The Interregnum and the Restoration period *and there* approached more nearly to *laissez faire* conditions than had *was a nearer* ever been deemed wise before; and in so far as public *approach to industrial* authority interfered, the initiative was taken, not by the *laissez faire;* Crown, but by Parliament. We hear no more of patentees for industrial purposes, though a certain number of companies with powers for regulating some branch of trade were erected by statute.

While this side of the economic activity of the Crown came to an end at the Civil War, it seems unlikely that the economic functions of the Clerks of the Market or the Justices of the Peace were vigorously discharged. Cromwell found it necessary to institute an entirely new set of officials for dealing with weights and measures, and the repression of vagrancy, under the control of his Majors General[1]. When this experiment was abandoned, the Justices of the Peace were free to resume their functions; and Charles II. appears, both in his legislation[2] and proclamations, to have assumed that they could be counted upon to discharge them as before. But this was not the case. The wisdom of attempting to regulate prices had been occasionally called in question[3] under James I. and Charles I.; from the time of the Civil *little syste-* War, the local authorities, who disapproved of the practice, *matic regu- lation of* would be free to abandon it, and there would be great *wages and prices took* difficulty in re-introducing it after it had been allowed to *place,* drop. Similar difficulties would be felt about the authoritative assessment of wages, and we cannot be surprised if the regular publication of rates should have fallen into desuetude in many districts. There would also be changes in regard to poor relief, as there was much greater opportunity for a variety of local practice to spring up, than would have been at all

or miscarriage of due visiting defective Manufactures, the Domestique and foreign Chapman and Consumers of the Cloathing are exceedingly Oppressed, the Trade Disgraced, the Kingdome Dishonoured and the Manufacturers Ruined," etc.

[1] Rannie, *Cromwell's Major Generals* in *English Historical Review*, x. 492, 496.

[2] See above, p. 40, n. 2.

[3] Leonard, *op. cit.* p. 193.

A.D. 1603
—1689. possible under Elizabeth or Charles I. There cannot have been any effective means of meeting the disorganisation caused by the war; it was only natural that there should be complaints in connection with the unemployed, at the close of the seventeenth century, when the problem of pauperism and the pressure of the poor rates created alarm.

If this view of the changes in local administration is *and there was less State interference in view of local conditions* correct, it is obvious that the central authority could no longer attempt to be constantly modifying local action according to circumstances, after the manner of Queen Elizabeth's Council. The result was an immense development of economic freedom, both as regards the practice of various callings and the conduct of internal commerce. But this step in progress was purchased at a heavy price; loss arose as well as gain in the changes of the time. Under these altered conditions no room was left for authoritative *or moral obligations.* insistence on moral, as distinguished from legal obligations; the success of Puritanism meant the triumph of the new commercial morality, which held good among moneyed men[1]; capitalists had established their right to secure a return for their money, and there was no authority to insist upon any correlative duty, when they organised industrial undertakings and obtained a control over the means of production. There are still examples of manufacturers who continue to carry on business at a loss in bad times, in order to provide employment for their hands, but the time has passed when government could insist on such conduct as obligatory[2].

English development was affected by the conscious imitation of **187.** There were two neighbouring nations that were ever present to the minds of English statesmen in the seventeenth century as examples of economic development. The rise of the United Provinces, and the success of the Dutch[3], in defending themselves against the Spaniards and attacking their supremacy in distant parts of the world, moved the admiration of contemporaries, and made them eager to analyse the causes of this remarkable growth of

[1] See above, p. 50.

[2] See above, p. 93. The interest of the Elizabethan government at such times was not purely philanthropic; they were aware that if people were both hungry and idle there was considerable danger of riot.

[3] John Keymor's *Observations made upon the Dutch fishing about the year* 1601 in the *Phenix* (1707), I. 222; also his *Booke of Observations consisting of Five*

maritime power. Equally striking, in its way, had been A.D. 1603
the recovery of France from the devastation caused by the —1689.
wars of religion; the resuscitation of prosperity had begun
under Henri IV., and though progress was not uninterrupted,
considerable advances were made in the time of Richelieu,
and still more under the administration of Colbert. Each of *continental*
these countries was a model which Englishmen were trying *models.*
to copy more or less faithfully.

A system of industrial control, similar to that which *France pre-*
prevailed under Elizabeth and the early Stuarts, but much *sented an*
more highly organised, had gradually grown up in France. *example of*
The initiative in the revival of French industry after the *industrial*
Hundred Years' War, as well as in the development of *system,*
internal commerce, had come from the Crown; there were
few signs of the tendency which we note in Elizabeth's
Parliament, to resent encroachments on individual enterprise.
There are many advantages in centralised control; and it
was eminently successful in securing a high standard of
workmanship, and in planting new industries; but it accustomed the people to rely entirely on government initiative,
and this was often injurious. The exhaustion of French
resources under Louis XIV. gave rise to a decided reaction
against the system which Colbert had developed; and it
was certainly more suited to the French than to the English
people. There was, however, a better opportunity of giving
it a trial under Elizabeth, James I. and Charles I. than
there has been before or since. In particular, the attempts
to encourage the manufacture of wares of the best quality
are closely analogous to the expedients that were adopted in
France[1]. There had been officers for the supervision of the
cloth industry in England from time immemorial; but the
system was greatly extended in the early seventeenth century.
Officers were proposed for the regulation of strangers and for

Propositions (Trin. Coll. Camb. O. 1. 24). This last has been attributed to
Sir W. Raleigh, and is commonly printed in his *Works*, VIII. 355.

[1] The French administrative system has perpetuated to the present time many
of the features which characterised the government of England under Elizabeth
and the early Stuarts. The drafting of statutes to be interpreted in detail by the
executive (A. L. Lowell, *Governments and Parties in Continental Europe*, I. 44)
and the establishment of separate courts for dealing with administrative affairs
(*ib.* 57) present interesting analogies.

supervising all sorts of manufactures[1]. In the period after
the Restoration, the direct copying of French practice is less
noticeable, but on the other hand, jealousy of French progress
increased. There was, as we shall see, constant and close
study in the eighteenth century of the secrets of their success,
and the conscious application of French principles, but with
different administrative methods.

While France presented the example of a well-ordered
monarchy, Holland could be quoted as a country which had
prospered, under wholly distinct political and social conditions.

and Holland of commercial greatness and maritime power The fact that the Dutch had developed a great maritime and
trading power marked them out for the imitation of men
who were striving to excel in these very lines. The United
Provinces were, in consequence, a more apposite model than
France. The intercourse between England and the Low
Countries was so frequent[2], that the process of learning from
our rivals and adopting their practice went on steadily in
many departments of life[3]; until the silent Dutch invasion
was completed by the invitation to the Stadtholder to accept
the crown of England. So far as the general lines of economic
policy go, the example of Holland was regarded with admiration by all Englishmen alike, whether royalist[4] or not. The
fact that Holland was a republic, however, rendered its
institutions specially attractive to the parliamentary party,
and they were particularly inclined to introduce financial
expedients which answered well in Holland. Experts had
long seen that the introduction of an excise was a necessary

---

[1] Under Charles I. some of these patents appear to have been granted partly as
expedients for raising revenue, and at all events the tariff of honours, which was
borrowed from France, was introduced as a method of taxation which lay outside
parliamentary control.

[2] On the parallel between the Norman influence before the Conquest and
Dutch influence in the xviith century see my *Alien Immigrants*, 194.

[3] This was especially the case with regard to the fishing industry. John
Smith pointed out that this was the very foundation of Dutch prosperity [*England's
improvement revived* (1673), 262], and Misselden complained of the encroachment
of the Dutch on our herring fisheries [*Free Trade* (1662), 35]. Tobias Gentleman
gave various suggestions on the subject [*Englands way to win wealth* (1614)], and
it was specially pointed out that Englishmen should build ships on the Dutch
model. *Britain's Busse* (1615) and *Politic Plat* in *Arber's Reprints*, II. 142.

[4] The Tory policy of the later seventeenth century follows the lines of the
Burleigh tradition and Dutch example. The Whigs on the other hand were more
inclined to outdo France by following French principles, though in new forms.

step in order to tap a new source of revenue ; the royalists A.D. 1603 —1689. had not dared to venture openly on this unpopular expedient ; and it may be doubted whether Pym would have succeeded in forcing it on the country, if he had not been fortified by the example of the Dutch. The Parliamentary party and *secured under* their successors were always inclined to call attention to *popular* those features of political life in Holland which were favour- *government.* able to commercial development. They made much of the general toleration, and of the ready welcome which was held out to aliens of all sorts ; while they criticised such English conditions as the methods of exclusive companies, and denounced the high rate of interest permitted by statute. There is abundant evidence of the conscious effort to accept Dutch principles and imitate Dutch practice all through the seventeenth century.

Englishmen of all parties were eager to outrival the *Jealousy of* Dutch by copying their methods ; and they were ready to *the Dutch gave rise to* adopt other expedients which might tend in the same *the Naviga-* direction. A measure, which gave rise to much controversy *tion Act,* at the time and has attracted most attention in subsequent periods, was the celebrated Navigation Act of 1651[1], and

---

[1] The Act of 1651 (Scobell, *Acts*, p. 176) declared that no goods " of the growth, production, or manufacture of Asia, Africa or America" should be imported into England or any of her possessions except in ships " that do truly and without fraud belong to the people of this commonwealth or the plantations thereof." The master and mariners of such ships were to be for the most part English. Goods from Europe might be imported in two ways, either by English or colonial vessels as above, or by the ships of the country which actually produced or manufactured the goods imported. This was expressly aimed at the Dutch, who did not themselves manufacture or produce, but who distributed corn, timber, East Indian and other goods. An exception was allowed in the case of silk goods, which might be brought from Holland and Flanders if the owners made oath that they had been brought overland from Italy. No alien moreover might engage in the English coasting trade or bring in fish for sale. The penalty of contravening the Act was forfeiture of the ships and goods, one-half to go to the informer.

The Act of 1660 (12 C. II. c. 18) re-enacted this statute, but made it more stringent. The vessel was to be English-built and the crew were to be three-fourths English. All goods brought in vessels of the country of origin had moreover to pay higher customs. But the regulations as to the plantation trade were made much stricter. The Act of 1651 had only considered the importation of goods into the plantations, the Act of 1660 took account of their export and internal trade. The colonies might only henceforth export in their own or English ships, and no alien might be a merchant or factor in any English plantation, and the governor received a third share of any forfeited ship to increase his vigilance. Moreover a proviso was inserted for the first time in a statute that certain colonial products,

C. 14

for this no precedent could be quoted from Holland. This Act was directly aimed at the maritime power of Holland[1]; and, according to common opinion, it was largely instrumental in accomplishing its object. This view is plausible, since the maritime supremacy of the Dutch has been superseded by that of the English; and this measure seems to give an adequate explanation of a patent fact. There were some contemporary observers who appeared to believe that the Act was exerting its intended effects, and that English shipping was increasing at the expense of Dutch[2], but the matter deserves more careful consideration. Historians have been so ready to give Cromwell[3] and the Council of State the credit for initiating the line of action which is alleged to have undermined the sea-power of Holland, that *which was not new in principle* it is, at all events, worth while to note that this piece of policy was not in any sense a new departure. Navigation Acts of one kind or another had been passed from the fourteenth century onwards[4]; the wisdom of such measures had not commended itself to Burleigh[5], but the grounds on which he had taken exception to them were less weighty in the changed circumstances of the seventeenth century. Under James I. some attempts were made to re-enforce the Acts[6];

while allowed a free circulation within the colonies themselves, must be sent, when exported, to England first, and not to continental countries direct. The commodities enumerated were sugar, tobacco, cotton, wool, indigo, ginger, fustick and other dye-woods, and bonds were to be taken of all ships that these should be brought straight to England.   [1] Gardiner, *Commonwealth*, ii. 83.

[2] Child held that it was "one of the most prudent Acts ever made" (*New Discourse of Trade*, 112), and Sir W. Temple thought the Dutch trade had already "passed its meridian," *Works*, i. 180. In the second edition of this book I felt justified in following the ordinarily received opinion, but further consideration has caused me to modify my view.

[3] There is no evidence that Cromwell had anything to do with the Navigation Act. While he was writing his famous despatch about the 'crowning mercy' at Worcester, the House of Commons were sitting in committee on the Bill, and it had already passed its second reading (*Commons Journals*, vii. 4 Sept. 1651). He did not become a member of the committee on trade till a month later (2 Oct. 1651. *Cal. S. P. D. Inter.*, p. 462). Contemporary opinion did not connect him with the measure. Roger Coke, who regarded the Navigation Act as mischievous, and denounced Cromwell's French policy severely, yet makes a grudging admission that "Old Oliver entertained this Law but coldly" (*Discourse of Trade*, 22). See also p. 360 n. 2 below.   [4] Vol. i. p. 394.   [5] See above, p. 193.

[6] Compare the bill which was introduced in 1614 (*Hist. MSS. Comm.* iv. Ap. 119). A proclamation was issued 17 April, 1615 (*Soc. Ant.* vi. 49) *Prohibiting the bringing in of any Commodities traded from the Levant, into this Kingdome, as well by Subiects as Strangers, not free of that Company; also containing a*

he instituted a careful enquiry in 1622 as to the expediency A.D. 1603
of exercising greater stringency in the matter[1], and Charles I. —1689.
took definite action on more than one occasion with the
view of preventing the Dutch from engaging in trade with
the English colonies[2]. Writing in 1637[3] to the Governor *or in its*
and Council of Virginia he enjoined them to "strictly and *application
to the*
resolutely forbidd all trade or trucking for any Merchandize *plantations.*
whatsoever with any Dutch shipp that shall either purposely
or casually come to any of your plantations. And if that
upon some unexpected occasion and necessitie the Governor
and Councell shall thinke fitting to admitt such intercourse
(which wee admitt not but upon extremity) that good caution
and bond bee taken both by the Dutch Master as alsoe of
the Owners of the said Tobacco and other commodities soe
laden That they shall (dangers of the Seas excepted) bee
brought without fraude to our Port of London, there to pay
unto us such duties as are there due upon the same." It
is clear on the face of it that the policy which was laid
down by the Statute of 1651 was substantially the same as
that which had been devised by the councillors of Charles I.
Nor is there any evidence to show that Cromwell attached
much importance to the measure, or insisted on enforcing it
vigorously; on the other hand it is clear that the Act of
1651 was habitually disregarded in the plantations[4] or set

*publication of certain Statutes for the restraint of All His Maiestie's Subiects from
Shipping any Commodities in Strangers' Bottoms either into the Kingdome or
out of the same."* It concludes with the following paragraph: "Furthermore,
whereas there hath bene in Ancient time divers good and politique lawes
made against the Shipping of Merchandizes in Strangers' Bottomes either
inward or outward, as namely the Statute of 5 Rich. 2, 4 Hen. 7, 32 Hen. 8, &c.,
which Lawes have of late yeeres bene much neglected, to the great preiudice of
the Navigation of Our Kingdome: We doe straightly charge and command, that
the saide Lawes bee from henceforth duely put in execution, upon the great and
grievous paines therein contained, and upon paine of Our high indignation and
displeasure toward all Our Officers and Ministers which shall be found slacke and
remisse in procuring and assisting the due execution of the said Lawes." A subsequent proclamation dealt specially with the French trade. See also on the
Virginia and Somers Island trade (*Cal. S. P. Col.* 4 March, 1623, p. 40).

[1] Rymer, *Fœdera*, XVII. 14. See also in 1629, *Ib.* XIX. 130.

[2] The charter for Maryland in 1632 insists that the products should be sent to
England; the colonials were allowed to tax imports from England. Fisher, *Men,
Women and Manners*, II. 155.

[3] *S. P. Col.* (America and the West Indies), IX. 47.

[4] See p. 343 n. 3 below on the beginning of Dutch trade with English
plantations, and the first attempts to prevent it, which seem to have had
some success (*S. P. Col. C. I.* VIII. 3), though there were some cases of

14—2

aside[1], and it is alleged that the Protector connived at this negligence[2].

It was not strenuously enforced, Even though the Navigation Act was somewhat more strictly enforced[3] after the Restoration, it can scarcely have affected Dutch commerce severely, so long as the Dutch retained their hold on New York and used it as a depot for clandestine trade with the English colonies[4]. After 1664 the opportunity for evasion ceased, and the Acts pressed more heavily on the colonists[5]; but even though the Dutch were ousted from their footing in America, it does not appear that their commercial progress was really checked. Indeed, in one branch of trade the measure recoiled upon its authors; the English had not sufficient supply of ships of such burden that they could be employed in the Baltic and Scandinavian trade; and the restrictions imposed on them forced English merchants to abandon this line of commerce altogether[6]. As a consequence the Dutch obtained a more complete monopoly than before in the Baltic trade, which was the

evasion (*ib.* viii. 6). Parliament took the same line in 1645 (Macpherson, *Annals*, ii. 430), but in the articles which were agreed to, on the reduction of Virginia, a right to trade with any country was included (Hening, *Statutes of Virginia,* i. 364). The colonists were somewhat aggrieved when the old restrictions were re-imposed after the Restoration (*Virginia and the Act of Navigation* in the *Virginia Magazine of History and Biography* (1893), i. 141). There was similar laxity in 1652 about the shipment of tobacco from the Somers Islands. *S. P. Col.* xi. 49, 50.

[1] Applications for dispensations from the action of the Navigation Acts in connection with the Baltic and other trades frequently engaged the attention of the Council in 1653 (*Calendar S.P.D.*, Item 25, May 21, p. 344; also 413, 442). On the Leghorn trade, *Ib.* p. 116.

[2] Brewster, *Essays on Trade*, 1695, p. 101. See below, p. 360 n. 2.

[3] It was entirely set aside by Proclamation, 23 March, 1664 [Brit. Mus. 1851. c. 9 (13)] in spite of the petition from the House of Commons in favour of more rigorous enforcement (July 10, 1663). *Commons Journals*, viii. pp. 521-2. There were also suspensions, with a view to the northern trades, by order of Council (28 April, 1670), S. P. D. C. II. 1670; *Calendar*, p. 188, and (1 May, 1672), S. P. D. C. II. 508, No. 1; *Calendar*, p. 518.

[4] Miss R. B. Mory has informed me that there is good evidence that this was a common practice so far as Maryland is concerned. The trade with New Amsterdam (or as we call it New York) was considerable. The growth of this trade, and consequent evasion of the Navigation Act, seems to have been one motive for the reduction of New Amsterdam by the English. On this subject compare *Calendar S. P. Col.* 1661—8, p. 172; also O'Callaghan, *Documents on New York*, iii. 43, 50. The loss it caused in Customs was estimated in 1663 at £10,000 a year.

[5] *S. P. Col.* 1676, No. 923.

[6] The Greenland trade also had decayed (25 C. II. c. 7, preamble). Relaxation was allowed for the sake of obtaining naval stores from Norway and Sweden by 7 and 8 W. III. c. 22. Child (*New Discourse of Trade*, p. 117); Coke (*A Discourse of Trade*, 1670, p. 23); Brewster (*Essays on Trade*, 1695, p. 4); and Davenant (*On*

very foundation of their maritime power[1], and they could A.D. 1603
—1689.
afford to relinquish the plantation trade, which was at that
time a somewhat small affair[2]. On the whole it seems
that the Dutch did not suffer perceptibly during the seven- *and does*
teenth century; their industry was reinforced to an even *not appear
to have*
larger extent than that of England by religious refugees, and *seriously
affected*
it was not till the first years of the eighteenth century that *the Dutch.*
Holland attained the zenith of her commercial greatness[3]. At
that time she was still far ahead of England in the shipping
and maritime resources at her command[4]. Though England
had not overtaken her rival she had been gaining in the race.
English shipping had developed enormously during the later
part of the seventeenth century[5], and it is, of course, possible
that the Navigation Act contributed along with other causes
to this result. Had it been entirely ineffective, it could not
have roused so much controversy or called forth such strangely
conflicting opinions. Public opinion favoured it, and strenuous
efforts were made to enforce it in the plantations after 1696[6],
but there is no sufficient proof of any direct connection between
this celebrated measure and the decline of Holland.

the Protection and Care of Trade; *Works*, Vol. I. p. 396), are all agreed as to the
decline of the northern trades.

[1] Cary writes in 1695 "The Trade of the Dutch consists rather in Buying and
Selling than Manufactures, most of their Profits arising from that and the Freight
of their Ships, which (being built for Burthen) are imploy'd generally in a Home
Trade for Bulky Commodities." *Essay on the State of England*, 123.

[2] Even as regards trade with England a comparison is instructive. According
to Whitworth, *State of the Trade of Great Britain*, p. 1, the English exports in
1696 to Virginia and Maryland amounted to £58,796, while those to Holland were
£1,462,415, four times as large as to any other European country.

[3] Pringsheim, *Beiträge zur wirthschaftlichen Entwickelungsgeschichte der vereinigten Niederlande*, p. 11. In 1751 the question as to a positive decline of Dutch
commerce was under discussion; it was alleged to have begun some 25 years
before. *Proposals by his late Highness the Prince of Orange for redressing and
amending the Trade of the Republic*, p. 10. C. Owen in 1721 wrote of Holland as
if it were continuing to make progress. *Danger of the Church and State from
foreigners*, 641.

[4] Gülich, *Geschichtliche Darstellung des Handels*, Vol. I. p. 93 n.

[5] Sir J. Child writes (*New Discourse of Trade*, 10), "I can myself remember
since there were not in *London* used so many Wharfs or Keys for the Landing of
Merchants Goods, by at least one third part as now there are; and those that
were then could scarce have Imployment for half what they could do; and now
notwithstanding one third more used to the same purpose, they are all too little
in a time of peace, to land the goods at, that come to *London*." According to
Macculloch (*Dictionary of Commerce and Navigation*, s.v. Ships), the English
mercantile marine doubled itself between the Restoration and the Revolution. It
rose from 95,266 tons to 190,533 tons. See also p. 361 below.

[6] *S. P. Col. A. and W. I.* 1696–97, No. 1007 and Preface p. ix.

VII. PRIVILEGED COMPANIES FOR COMMERCE.

The State frequently interfered   **188.** It is a commonplace in the present day to deplore the evils which tend to arise when every individual is free to pursue his own advantage in his own way, subject to the general law of the land. All sorts of projects are on foot for introducing some system of state or municipal socialism, or of co-operative organisation, which shall limit the field of competition and minimise its mischievous results. This feeling is a not unnatural reaction from the thoroughgoing application of the doctrine of *laissez faire*, which characterised the early part of the nineteenth century; but it is well to remember that the state-organisation of industry has already had a considerable trial in this country, and that the system has *in the direction of industry,* been discarded. It is, of course, true that state direction of industrial and commercial life is in many ways different from the state ownership of the means of production, which is proposed in the present day. It is also possible that attempts at controlling the conditions of production and exchange, which failed to answer under one form of government, might be successful in different political conditions; and that a democratic state-socialism might achieve results which were not feasible under a monarchy[1].

The story of the Stuart period is not directly analogous, but still it is very instructive; whatever may be our expectations for the future, we are hardly justified in neglecting our own national experience in the past. The history of the seventeenth century is particularly worthy of study, as we may gather from it the causes which contributed to bring about the break-down of a complex system of commercial and industrial organisation.

Intercourse between distinct political communities presents the greatest difficulties to the working of any such scheme. It was not possible for the monarchs to exercise minute control in regard to foreign trade, such as they

---

[1] It is extremely unlikely, however, that the organisation of industry and commerce would be so efficient under a democracy, as it may be under a monarchy; or that there would be more sense of responsibility in pursuing the public, as compared with private interests, under a popular than under a personal government. On the various forms of corruption under different governments see above, p. 19.

attempted to carry out, by means of proclamations in regard *A.D.* 1603
—1689. to internal trade in corn. There were few consuls at foreign ports ; and in any case they would not, like justices of the peace, have had authority over both buyers and sellers. The *and the ordering of commerce was delegated to Companies* simplest expedient for maintaining a hold upon foreign commerce, so as to regulate it on wise lines, was to confer special trading privileges on a body of merchants who should be responsible for conducting the traffic in the manner that was most advantageous to the realm. This was one reason for the organisation of commercial companies, which were much more extensively developed among English traders than among those of any other nation[1], and the practice of merchant vessels sailing in fleets for mutual safety also rendered some organisation among traders desirable[2].

These companies were of two distinct types ; several of *either regulated or joint-stock,* them were regulated companies. Each member of such an association, though he traded separately on his own capital, was bound to observe certain rules which were laid down for all the fellowship. The Stock Exchange at the present day may serve as an illustration of a regulated company ; for each member conducts his business independently, though all are bound to settle fortnightly with the other members, to refrain from advertising, and to abide by the other rules imposed upon the whole body. On the other hand, the joint stock company is a single corporation with one capital, which the members hold jointly : they trade as one individual, and subsequently divide the profits. The London and North Western Railway is a modern instance of a joint-stock company ; the shareholders do not compete against one another at all, but hold shares in a single undertaking. If the corporation has the sole right to deal in a certain class of goods, or to trade in a given area, the joint-stock company *which were stigmatized as mono- polies* is of the nature of a monopoly ; and no one can have any part in the business unless he succeeds in buying stock from one of the shareholders. The regulated company, on the

---

[1] There is some reason for thinking that the Dutch copied English practice in the matter. Misselden, *Free Trade*, 82. On the Dutch East India Company see below, p. 267 n. 3 ; also on the difference between the English and the French Levant Companies, pp. 252, 253.

[2] Compare the detailed instructions for the fleets of the newly-founded Turkey Company. S. P. D. El. ccxli. 12, 13.

other hand, permitted limited competition between its members; as any subject could join it and take his chance in the trade, by paying the entrance fee and complying with the accepted conditions. The regulated companies were not monopolies in form; but the constant complaint, to which they gave rise, seems to show that they tended to become monopolies in fact, and that the rules they made often had the effect of putting the whole of some important line of trade into the hands of a narrow clique[1]. The regulated companies were subjected to frequent attack by *by inter-lopers.* the outside traders, who were stigmatised as interlopers. These merchants set the privileges of the companies at defiance, and maintained their right to try their fortune in some chartered trade and to conduct it on their own terms.

When we read the polemical pamphlets of the seventeenth century, and take note of the mutual recriminations of the Staplers, the Merchant Adventurers, the East India and other Companies, as well as the grievances of the Customers and the Interlopers, we are inclined to condemn the whole system as utterly bad and corrupt; and this view seems to be confirmed by the fact that these institutions *The Companies appear to have served a useful purpose,* have gradually passed away. It is none the less true that companies were generally believed to serve a useful purpose. The question was carefully examined[2] by Commissioners of

---

[1] Hewins, *English Trade and Finance*, 44.

[2] "Whereas we have understood, by the generall Complaints of our loving Subjects from all the Parts of this our Realme of England, as also by Information from our Ministers imployed in Parts beyond the Seas, that the Cloth of this Kingdom hath of late Yeares wanted that Estimation and Vent in Forraign Parts which formerlie it had, and that the Wolls of this Kingdom have and are fallen much from their wonted Values, and Trade in generall to be so far out of Frame, that the Merchants and Clothiers of this Kingdom are greatlie discouraged, so that great Nombers of People ymployed by them, and depending on them, want Work, the best meanes of their Livelihood, the Landlords fail in their Rents, and Revenues wherewith to maintain their ordinarie Charges, and the Farmors have not so good means whereby to raise their Rents as heretofore they had, and our selfe also finde the Defects thereof by the Decaie of our Customes and other Duties, and generallie the whole Commonwealth suffereth, so as it is high time to look into the cause of this great Decay of Trade and the Commodities of this our Kingdom, as alsoe how to have fit Remedies applied for the restoring the same to their former florishing Estate. * * * We have therefore, by the like Advise of our Privie Councell, thought fit and resolved to have a standing Commission for theis Causes, and to make choice of a convenient Nomber of Persons of Qualitie, Understanding, Experience and Judgment, to be our Commissioners, to whose Judgement, Industrie and Care we might commit the further

Trade in 1622. At that date the government seems to have come to the conclusion that the companies should be searching out and better discerning of the true Causes of the Decaie of Trade, and the findeing out of fit and convenient Remedies to be applied to the same; and that after they shall have with mature deliberation prepared the same, they might from tyme to tyme certifie us and the Body of our Privie Councill of their Opinion, to the end that thereupon we might give such order for Remedies herein as may be for our own Honour and the Wealth and Prosperitie of our People....

"And whereas a suspition hath been raised uppon the Societies and Companies of the Merchant Adventurers and other Merchants, and of some Companyes of Handicrafts Men, that for their private Gaine and particuler Advantage they make and put in Execution divers Ordinances amongst themselves for ordering their Trades and Mysteries, which tend to the hurt of the publique, we will and command you, and hereby give you Power and Authoritie, uppon any Complaint to be made unto you thereof, to enform your selves of the Ordinances Orders and Constitutions of such Companies and Societies of Merchants and others for the ordering of their Trade, to the end that if it shall appeare that any thing therein contayned be unfitt to be contynued, as tending to the generall hurt of others, either in making the Cloth, or other Merchandize and Wares of this Kingdome over deare or otherwise, that the same may be laid down, and that no new Orders or Ordinances be hereafter made and executed by the said Companyes or any of them, before they be first perused and allowed by Us and our Privie Councell, or so many of them as we shall thereunto especially appoint.

"And because it is conceived by many, that by reason of the Discouragements happened to Trade, the number of Merchants now applieing themselves in course of Merchandise are of too small a nomber to manage the same and that if the Nomber of Traders were enlarged, Trade itself would be enlarged, which is now said by some to be ymprisoned, being for the most part confined to Companies and Societies of Marchants, and others excluded which are not Members of those Companies, we will and require you to take into your considerations, whither it be necessarie to give waie to a more open and free Trade or not? and if it be, then in what manner it is fittest to be done? wherein we would alwaies have you take care that Government and Order in Trade may be preserved, and Confusion avoided, and that to be done which may be best for Us and our People; and, amongst other things which we conceive to be Hinderances of a fair and free Trade, we will and require you to consider how farr it shall be fitt to admitt of a Joint-stock in Companies or Societies of Marchants?

"And also whether it be at all fitt to allow any Marchant to be also a Retayler, at least of those sorts of Merchandise which himself retorneth from beyond the Seas?

"And because the Life of Commerce and Trade is Mony, whereof a greater Scarcitie is now found in this our Kingdom then hath been in former tymes, we will and require you with all Diligence and Care to take into your considerations, what are the Principall Causes and Occasions thereof? and by what means Coyne or Bullyon may be hereafter more plentifully brought into this Kingdome? and how the same may be here kept and preserved from Exportation unles it be only in cases necessarie and profitable for the State?

"That to prevent an apparent Consumption and Confusion, which cannot otherwise be avoided, ye diligently observe the true Ballance of the Trade of this Kingdom, least the Ymportation of Merchandise from forraign Parts, exceed the Exportation of our own native Commodities, and consider of some fitting courses to reduce the same to more equalitie, and to think uppon the Gain or Losse that comes to our Kingdom by the course of Exchange now used by our Marchants....

"And generallie our Will and Commaud is, that with all Care and Diligence yee apply your selves to enform us and our Privie Councell, from tyme to tyme, of

A.D. 1603
—1689.

and were
main-
tained
by the
various
forms of
govern-
ment

maintained[1], but twenty years later there was a brief period when the advocates of open trade obtained their own way. Though a trade commission appointed in 1650 was instructed to "take care that government and order in trade may be preserved and confusion avoided[2]," this principle seems to have been set aside in practice, as the opponents of monarchy were not inclined to favour the privileged bodies which had obtained exclusive powers from the king. After a few years' experience of unregulated trade, however, it seemed necessary to abandon or limit it. The regulated companies were re-established, and after protracted consideration it was decided to grant the new charter to the East India Company, by which it became a permanent institution erected as a Joint-stock[3]. The contest between the supporters of the Companies and the advocates of open trade took place at somewhat different dates in regard to the Hamburg trade[4], the Turkey trade[5], the African trade[6], the East India trade[7] and the rest, but the result was everywhere the same; public opinion in the City was in their favour at the Restoration[8], and

theis and all other things which in your Experiences, or out of your Jugements, ye finde or conceive may be a means to advance and quicken Trade, raise again the native Commodities of our Kingdom, encourage Traders Clothiers and the Woll-growers and Manufactors, or to remove the Ympediments or Discouragements thereof, and to that purpose we hereby give you Power and Authoritie, to send for such Persons to attend you, and to have viewe of all Records and Writings, as you shall finde needfull for your better Information in any thing concerning this our Service.

"And our Pleasure and Command is, That when, and as soon as ye shall maturely have considered and resolved upon any material parts or points of theise our Instructions, that ye certifie the Body of our Privie Councill thereof from tyme to tyme, that by their Advises wee may proceed to a present Reformation of the same as occasion shall require, without the expectation of a total and absolute Reformation of every part of theis our Instructions all at once, for that of necessitie must be the Worke and Labour of a long tyme, when tymely Redress may happily be given to some while others are in handling; And this our Commission to stand and be in force until our Pleasure be signified, under our Privie Seale or Great Seale, to determine and declare the same to be voide." Rymer, _Foedera_, xvii. 410—415 (Oct. 20, 1622).

[1] Some notes of the discussion seem to have been preserved. _Hist. MSS. Comm._ iv. Ap. 312.   [2] _Parl. or Const. Hist._ (1751), xix. 316.

[3] Hunter, _History of British India_, ii. 120—131.
[4] See below, p. 229.   [5] See below, p. 253.
[6] See below, p. 275.   [7] See below, p. 266.

[8] _Petition of Lord Mayor, &c. to the Parliament for the reducing of all Foreign Trade under Government and Proposals of several Merchants of London humbly tendered to the Grand Committee of Trade containing the desired manner and method of such Regulation_, 1662. Brit. Mus. 517. k. 16 (2).

on the whole the regulated companies succeeded in holding A.D. 1603
—1689. their own during the seventeenth century. Unless they had had a strong case they could not have emerged so successfully from the criticism to which they were exposed. The most influential of them all, the Hamburg Company, outlived these controversies and maintained its position as an important trading body in the eighteenth century[1].

The benefits which these companies offered to their *as they gave their members a definite status* members were obvious and highly prized. It was possible for such a body to secure definite privileges, as to tolls and customs for their goods, and a satisfactory status in regard to the recovery of debts and other civil business. Until the government was able to maintain a consular service in foreign ports there was no other convenient means of securing protection for the persons and property of English merchants in the lands they visited; and the system had immense advantages for placing intercourse with Mahommedan or Pagan territories on a satisfactory footing. The political importance of these institutions declined during the seventeenth century, so far as trade with European countries was concerned; but the privileged company, especially the joint-stock company, continued to afford the most convenient form for organising intercourse with half-civilised peoples and far-distant trades.

The members benefited, not only because of the improved status which a company could secure for them, but by reason of the facilities it provided for their personal comfort and convenience in the conduct of business. These organisations had grown up under the old *régime*, when merchants did not do business through commission agents, but visited foreign ports themselves, or had factors of their own to act as their correspondents. It was a matter of importance to them to *and favourable conditions for residence* obtain board and lodging on reasonable terms[2]; the factory of the Merchant Adventurers at Hamburg was organised as a residential college; and the discipline[3] about giving " full

---

[1] *Hist. MSS. Comm.* III. Ap. 248; Postlethwayt, *Dictionary*, s. v. *Hamburgh.*

[2] On the mode of life of the Staplers at Calais compare H. E. Malden's Introduction to the *Cely Papers* (Camden Society), 3 Series, vol. 1, p. xxxix.

[3] Lingelbach, *The Merchant Adventurers of England, their laws and ordinances*, p. 46. The Eastlanders were still stricter, prohibition, not limitation, being their rule. "It is ordeyned that if any brother that is an apprentice or any other

banquets, dinners and suppers " was similar to college discipline at Oxford or Cambridge. No apprentice might play
at cards or dice for higher points than fourpence a game.
This strict discipline, often under Puritan influence[1], doubtless helped to form the high personal character[2] on which the
old fashioned merchants prided themselves. For the rest the
rules were meant to secure fair play among the merchants ; no
one might trade at odd times or in secret places, but fairly
and openly. A minimum price was fixed, and no one was to
spoil the market by taking less ; but if he failed to get the
price, other merchants could be required to take the goods
off his hands ; only when the market was regularly glutted,
and after consultation with others, was a merchant permitted
to lower his price ; no one man was allowed to undersell others.

*and for
sharing
the oppor-
tunities of
trade,* Similarly the "stint" was intended to prevent any one
dealer from engrossing the whole trade[3]; the Merchant
Adventurers had elaborate arrangements for apportioning
this limited amount of business among the different members
of the Company, so that each might have a fair chance of
earning his living by his calling. The Adventurers contended
that these regulations benefited merchants, by ensuring a
steady trade with no violent fluctuations ; and that the rules
really conduced to the public weal. They also denied that
there was any monopoly of the trade, as they managed it ;
since the merchants competed with one another within the
*while the
fact of
their ex-
istence* prescribed limits, and the whole body was subject to competition with the Hanse and other alien merchants[4].

unruly person or persons of our Brethren or any the King's Majestys subjects shall
misbehave themselues or use whorehouses, keepe dishoneste and unlawfull Company, or Ryotinge, or wastefully mis pendinge his or their Masters or Friends
goods, or is missinge out of his hoasts house all night, or after eleven of the clock
in the summer and tenne in the winter (withoute he can prove he hath bin in
honeste company and urged to keepe their company soe late or use cards, dyce, or
any other unlawful games or gaminge for money) he or they so offending shalbe
punished at the discretion of the Deputy and Assistants." Sellers, *Actes and
Ordinances of the Eastland Merchants*, p. 27. The Master is expressly exempted
from being careful in his language when addressing his apprentices, *ib.* p. 26.

[1] Hitzigrath, *Die Kompagnie der Merchants Adventurers*, 15.

[2] Schulze-Gaevernitz, *Britischer Imperialismus*, 45.

[3] *Lawes*, p. 51 (1609). Wheeler, *Treatise* 57, see vol. I. p. 416. A similar
arrangement in the Newcastle coal trade was known as the Vend. Brand, see
below. p. 530.

[4] Wheeler, *Treatise of Commerce*, 113.

It is easy to see that many traders would value these privileges, and a little consideration will enable us to under- A.D. 1603 stand why the government was ready to grant them. The —1689. authorities were inclined to take any step that seemed to tend to the steady development of commerce, and the maintenance of the reputation[1] of English wares; but other reasons weighed with them also. The concentration of trade *simplified* was a matter of public concern, as well as of private *the collec-* advantage, since it gave the best security for the regular *tion of* advantage, since it gave the best security for the regular *revenue* collection of customs. The proper charges on the export of wool and cloth could be easily made and readily checked[2] so long as the Staplers[3] and the Merchant Adventurers formed the two great channels of outgoing commerce. There was administrative convenience of another kind. At a time when it was generally assumed that trade should be controlled in political interests, there was good reason to urge that the existence of companies was very desirable; they gave the best means for attempting to enforce statutes of 'employment[4],' or for regulating the flow of treasure. It *and the* was also possible in periods of depression to force the *regulation of* merchants who exported cloth to come to the assistance of *industry,* the clothiers, and to bear a portion of the loss which might arise from continuing to keep men at work, even on unremunerative terms[5]. Thus the existence of companies for foreign trade provided a machinery for attending to public interests and guarding against social dangers.

The companies served admirably as organs for giving effect to the definite scheme of commercial policy, which had been generally accepted all through the Middle Ages. The habitual aim of statesmen had been to limit the export of English products, so that foreigners should not get our

---

[1] The Merchant Adventurers suffered severely in 1630 from the bad quality of some cloths supplied them, and approached the King as to the best remedy. Lohmann, *Staatliche Regelung der englischen Wollindustrie*, 64, S. P. D., C. I. ccccvii. 78. See below, p. 297 n. 4.

[2] Compare T. Milles, *The Customers Alphabet and Primer*, f. 1 2. The Book of Rates issued by James I. was an attempt to meet the difficulty of collecting customs on a great variety of articles. Compare also Wheeler, *Treatise of Commerce*, 60.

[3] On the difficulties of the Staplers see below, p. 298.   [4] See above, p. 177.

[5] Compare the case of the Merchant Adventurers in 1527. Lohmann, *op. cit.* 16.

thrifty goods on too easy terms, but that we should have them for our own use. This principle has more to commend it in regard to raw products than in connection with manufactured goods; and, as applied by the Merchant Adventurers to the cloth trade, it was a constant cause of friction between the Company and the clothiers[1]. The Company alleged that, by regulating the export, they prevented the overstocking of foreign markets with English goods—with the consequent fall in price. They tried to forecast the probable demand and to meet it with a sufficient supply; but they were afraid that a glut at the factory abroad would react unfavourably on the trade at home. It is quite possible that they did something to check the evils of over-production and *but they were inconsistent with national progress,* speculative trading; but it seems to be certain, from the complaints and eventual success of Interlopers, that their rules interfered with the progress of English trade abroad, and hampered enterprising men who would have pushed it more rapidly. The benefits, which were believed to arise from organisation, necessarily entailed some concomitant disabilities to individuals, and acted as restrictions on independent merchants. The rules of regulated companies with regard to export, which were supposed to mitigate violent fluctuations and serious depression, were one element in what the companies described as "well-ordered trade." But national industry and international commerce were outgrowing a system that had served in city communities. Manufacturers were beginning to realise that it was desirable to push our trade and open up new markets[2] so as to obtain a better vent for our commodities, and that this could be best accomplished, not by well-ordered trade, but by individual enterprise.

Some of their opponents appear to have recognised that the regulated companies were useful in securing political status for Englishmen abroad and to have desired to maintain the companies, but to provide that their privileges should be available for all English subjects, and not confined,

---

[1] An admirable statement of the arguments *pro* and *con* will be found in *Commons Journals*, I. 218 (1604).

[2] See below, p. 611.

as was practically the case, to a ring of London merchants[1]. A.D. 1603 —1689.
There were others, however, who objected to the whole
system of privilege on principle, and held that sufficient
" order " could be obtained in trade by treaties with foreign
powers and general rules imposed on all subjects.   This was
the view of Thomas Milles, the Customer at Sandwich : he *which could be*
held that " the best rules for order to direct Trafficke by, are *sufficiently cared for*
those that beeing precisely squared out, to the Generalitie, *by legisla-*
Certaintie and Indifferencie of the Lawes of our Land, and *tion.*
forraine Contracts, admit no particular, partiall, nor doubtfull deceit, iniury nor disturbance to Master, Persons nor
Place[2]." This appears to have been an exceptional view at
the beginning of King James I.'s reign ; but it seems to
have grown in popularity, and to have become the dominant
opinion in Parliament, after the Revolution of 1689.   At
that date, the privileges of the regulated companies were,
for the most part, opened up very completely ; but even
then trade was not left to take its own course.   Throughout
the seventeenth and early part of the eighteenth centuries
those men who were most eager for the freedom of all
markets, as against exclusive privileges, still recognised the
necessity of " order " in trade, and " rules to direct traffic."
The era of regulated commercial companies, which were at
all exclusive, passed away ; but while they existed they had
served as an expedient for rendering trade subservient to
public objects ; and their advocates alleged that they also
had the advantage of preventing, what we have learned to
call, cut-throat competition and speculative trading.

189.   In the sixteenth century the long-continued *The Hanse League were*
struggle between the Merchant Adventurers and the Hanse *finally*
League was finally decided in favour of the Englishmen. *ousted*
The German merchants had enjoyed preferential tariffs over
natives, both for the export and import of goods[3], since the
Utrecht Treaty in the time of Edward IV. ; and there had
been an ever-growing hostility to their privileged position in
London, as they were no longer indispensable intermediaries

---

[1] This appears to have been the view of the Committee of the House of
Commons of which Sandys was chairman. *Commons Journals*, I. 219.

[2] Thomas Milles, *Custumers Alphabet and Primer*, f. E.

[3] Ehrenberg, *Hamburg und England*, 51.

A.D. 1603
—1689.

from their
preferen-
tial
position,
of commerce. In 1578 the efforts of the Englishmen to oust the foreigners were crowned with success; the Hanse merchants were forced to withdraw from the Steelyard. The Merchant Adventurers suffered some inconvenience from the machinations of their rivals, but they were able to bring so much trade to any locality where their factory was settled that they could count on a welcome from the authorities; they were able to choose between several positions on the Elbe, or in Holland, any of which offered advantages for establishing their factory. This great result had been gradually accomplished. Sir Thomas Gresham, who acted as agent for the English Crown at Antwerp in the time of Edward VI.[1], had cherished the definite aim of undoing the Hanse merchants and promoting the interests of the Adventurers. He was able to obtain the sanction of Queen Elizabeth and of Burleigh[2], and was thus enabled to lay the foundations of ultimate success.

and the
Merchant
Adven-
turers
superseded
them,
The Merchant Adventurers had moved their factory from Bruges to Antwerp in 1494, and the trade they attracted to that port had contributed not a little to its rapid rise. They carried very large quantities of cloth to that part, and much of this was undyed and undressed, so that a considerable industrial population was employed in finishing the goods[3].

---

[1] Compare the very interesting letter printed by Burgon, *Life and Times of Sir T. Gresham*, I. 484.

[2] Compare Cecil's draft of instructions to Sheres on his mission to the Duchess of Parma in 1564. *Ib.* II. 58.

[3] "Poore labouring men and artificers as the dyer, the clothworker, the mather-seller, the Allam and woad seller, the coppres and the gall seller, and a nomber moe that I doe not reckon; and after theis 80,000 clothes be dyed and drest, then the picker gaineth for his worke, then the poore gaineth for carrying 2 or 3 times, then the skynner gaineth for skynnes to packe with, the canvas seller with canvas, the roaper for roapes and thred, then the porter gaineth againe after they be packt, then the waygh master for waying the packes and the carter who carieth them into Germany to the mart of Frankfort Lepsick and Noremborow and other places. So that there is spent by theis petty charges at every cloth at the least 4s. 6d. which amounteth unto 18000*li* that is 72,000 dollers all this is gayned by Artificers and laboring men besid the Marchauntes who gain in every cloth 40s. before it come to wearinge which maketh 160,000*li* which is 600 and 40 thousand dollers. Soe is here gayned by theis 80,000 white clothes by the marchauntes Artificers and poore labouring men 300 and 38000*li*. * * * * Here your grace may see the subjectes of K. Phillip doe gaine yerly by woll and wollen cloth that cometh out of England almost 600,000*li* which is 240,000 dollers." *Letter to Edzart and John, Earls of East Friezeland*, Brit. Mus. Sloane DCCCXVIII. f. 21.

The Englishmen were also considerable purchasers of hardware manufactured in Germany, which passed down the Rhine
to Antwerp[1]. The government of the Company was carried in trade
with
Germany.
on at the mart abroad[2], though there were of course many
members who were resident in London. The Adventurers
appear to have been affected to some extent by the habits
of such a cosmopolitan city as Antwerp, where merchants were
apt to become denationalised. It seems to have been felt
advisable to take special precautions against the marriage of
English merchants with Antwerp families[3]. Political changes
occurred, however, which led to the entire detachment of
the English colony, and eventually to its migration to a
more favourable situation.

This was partly due to very far-reaching plans on the *Owing to*
part of Philip II., who already had command of the chief *Philip's
commercial*
sources of mineral wealth, and seems to have been aiming *plans*
at concentrating the trade of the world in the hands of his
subjects[4]. His possession of Spain and the Two Sicilies,
together with his influence in the north of Italy, gave him
an effective control over the commerce of the Mediterranean,
while the realm of the house of Burgundy included the
most populous manufacturing and commercial district in
the north. He was able to anticipate Napoleon in devising
a continental system, which should ruin the trade of England,
and cut her off from supplies of armaments[5] and treasure ;

---

[1] "Thenglish merchantes buy of them Renysh wyne, fustians, cotton wolf,
copper, copper wyer, Iron, Iron wyer, coprous, latten, brasse, kettles, steele of all
kindes, of wares made in Norenburgh, harnes of all sortes, gonnes, gonn pouder,
feild pikes, running staves for Norsmen, there is no kinde of ware that Germany
maketh or bringeth out, but generally the English merchaunt buyeth, as much or
more of yt as any other nation doe. All which thinges the Germanes merchauntes may
bring to Embden, if they will, as good cheap as to Antwerpe." *Letter to Edzart and
John, Lords of East Friezeland*, f. 23 b. It is noticeable that these were the manufactures which Burleigh was making such eager efforts to introduce into England.

[2] The majority of the merchants abroad elected their governor, his deputies
and the court of assistants, according to the Charter of Elizabeth, recited in
S. P. D. C. II. xxvii. pp. 49, 76, and a similar practice prevailed in earlier reigns.
Ib. 3. See also the careful investigation by Dr Lingelbach, *The internal Organisation of the Merchant Adventurers* in *Royal Hist. Soc. Trans.* xvi. 51.

[3] 2 June, 1563, *Hist. MSS. Comm.* iv. Ap. 207. *Letter to Edzart and John*,
f. 20 b. Ehrenberg, *Hamburg und England*, p. 73. Compare also the anecdote
related by Burgon, *op. cit.* i. 59, and Lingelbach, *op. cit.* 23.

[4] *Letter to Edzart and John*, f. 13.   [5] See above, p. 57.

A.D. 1603
—1689.

the Adven-
turers were
forced to
migrate
from
Antwerp

to Emden

but he was no more successful in carrying it into effect. English trade was prohibited by the Duchess of Parma[1], in retaliation for Elizabeth's protective legislation for English manufactures[2]. The disturbance of commerce gave occasion to a conference at Bruges[3], which had no practical result. Subsequently, more hostile measures were adopted by Alva[4]; but the English merchants, though subjected to considerable loss, were confident that the demand for their wares was so great, that some other mart would be found which would serve their purpose as well. In this they were not disappointed; though the policy of Philip had been chiefly directed against England, it was keenly resented in some parts of Germany. He had obtained control over the mouth of the Rhine, and threatened to govern the course of trade by extending his influence over the whole area between Germany and the North Sea. There were doubtless many merchants, both in the Baltic towns and in the Tyrol, who were attached to Philip's interests; but there were others, who complained of the manner in which "feathers were being plucked little by little from the noble Eagle[5]." At this juncture various courses were open to the Merchant Adventurers; Richard Clough, who had been Sir T. Gresham's secretary, argued that they would be wisest to establish themselves at some English port, such as York, or Hull[6]; an anonymous German writer urged on the Earls of East Friesland that they should invite the English to settle in Emden, and for a brief period the factory was established there[7]. The project of securing their presence was taken up much more keenly, despite some local opposition, by the town of Hamburg. Early in 1564 the Burgomaster and Council

[1] 28 Nov. 1563. The existence of plague in England was the reason alleged for the restrictions on English merchants. Ehrenberg, *op. cit.* 65. Haynes, *Burleigh's State Papers*, 584.   [2] Burgon, II. 46.

[3] *Hist. MSS. Comm.*, II. Ap. 39 (vii. pt. 2).

[4] *Ib.* II. 289; from 1568—1572. The prejudicial effects in Antwerp were noted in the Appendix to the *Letter to Edzart and John* (1572), f. 39.

[5] *Letter to Edzart and John*, f. 13. It is to be noticed, however, that the increased facilities for the importation of English cloth, which occurred when the Adventurers migrated to Hamburg, proved very injurious to the woollen manufacture in many parts of Germany. Ehrenberg. *op. cit.* 124.

[6] Brit. Mus. *Cott. MSS.* Galba, B. xi. f. 264. Burgon, *op. cit.* II. 59.

[7] Ehrenberg, *op. cit.* 69, 72.

wrote to Elizabeth, inviting the English merchants to settle A.D. 1603
in their town[1]; and in 1567 they conferred most ample —1689.
privileges[2] upon the English traders. The Adventurers were
reluctant to leave Antwerp altogether and dallied with the
invitation; but in 1569 they sent a large fleet to Hamburg[3], *to*
and the main stream of their trade never afterwards reverted *Hamburg,*
to its old channel[4]. Despite the opposition of the Hanse
League[5], and the dislike of a considerable section of the
population[6], the English merchants had been able to establish themselves on the Elbe; and the artisans[7], who had
worked up English goods, or produced wares for the English
market, migrated in their wake.

In 1578, however, the Hanse Towns succeeded in bringing
pressure on the Council of Hamburg[8] to withdraw these
privileges, in the expectation that Elizabeth would be forced
to grant them the concessions they desired for the Steelyard.
But they were wofully disappointed; no improvement was
made in their status; the London magistrates were allowed
to disregard their privileged position altogether[9]; and before

---

1 Ehrenberg, *op. cit.* 310.   2 *Ib.* 312.

8 This voyage was a critical experiment, and its success marked the failure of
Alva and Philip to destroy English independence by ruining English trade; it
proved, too, that Elizabeth was no longer dependent on the Antwerp merchants
for financial support, but could afford to go past them. Compare the letter from
Gresham to Cecil in *Lansdowne MSS.* XII. 8, f. 16, referred to by Ehrenberg,
op. cit. 111.

4 There appeared to be a prospect of returning to the old lines in 1573; the
sack of Antwerp by the Spanish soldiery in 1576 was the most important of
several occurrences which rendered it illusory. Ehrenberg, *op. cit.* 132.

5 The Hanse League under the influence of Heinrich Sudermann were always
endeavouring to revert to the terms assured to the Steelyard, after long discussion
[*Hist. MSS. Comm.* II. Ap. 39 (VII. pt. 1)] in London, by the treaty of 1474; they
hoped, by refusing the Merchant Adventurers access to Germany, to coerce
Elizabeth into reverting to that agreement (Ehrenberg, *op. cit.* 134). The
Hamburg authorities admitted the English to trade on more favourable terms
than those actually enjoyed by German merchants in London, and did not join in
boycotting the English traders.

6 This was partly due to the influence of the Lutheran clergy; the English
merchants were inclined to Calvinistic principles, and they eventually obtained
greater freedom for their own worship at Emden, which was not under Lutheran
influence (Ehrenberg, *op. cit.* 115). There was, however, in addition, on the
part of Hamburg tradesmen, some economic jealousy of aliens who dealt with
one another.

7 Ehrenberg, *op. cit.* 128.

8 *Ib.* 140.   9 *Ib.* 146.

A.D. 1603
—1689.

long the Hanse Merchants withdrew from active commerce with England. Trade with Germany was not broken off, however; the Earl of East Friesland was willing to receive the Merchant Adventurers at Emden[1], and they were permitted to transfer their factory from Hamburg, across the Elbe, to Stade; thus the whole of the commercial intercourse between England and the valleys of the Rhine and Elbe came under their control.

and to Stade.

The English had thus succeeded in getting the business of exporting cloth to Germany entirely out of the hands of the Hanse League; but they were not allowed to reap the fruits of their victory without a struggle. The contest entered on its final phase—and an active effort was made to drive the English merchants[2] out of Germany altogether[3].

They were denounced as a monopoly by the Hanse League,

It was urged that the Company, as a monopoly, ought to be banished from the Empire; and the Emperor was induced to concur in this view[4]. At the same time there was difficulty in insisting upon it, or in showing that the so-called monopoly was a grievance to the German consumer. The competition of the Steelyard had come to an end, but the Eastland Company, which had been organised in 1579, exported considerable quantities of English cloth to the Baltic towns[5]. There were also large numbers of interlopers, who had a settlement at Nuremburg[6], and continued

---

[1] See the copies of letters between the Emperor Rudolf and Edzart, Earl of East Friesland, 1580. Brit. Mus. *Cotton MSS.* Faustina, C. II. f. 82 b.

[2] The Staplers were proposing at this time (Dec. 1578) to have the mart for cloth held at Ipswich; compare John Johnson, Brit. Mus. *Lansdowne MSS.* XXVI. 33, 34, 35, 36, 37, 38. In 1588 a mart was held at Westminster, and the Merchant Adventurers gave up trading, to the great inconvenience of the clothiers generally. *Commons Journals,* I. 220.

[3] This is one of the striking proofs of the importance of national unity in connection with the growth of English trade. English merchants were now engaged in internal trade in Germany, just as aliens had been in England before the time of Richard II.: but the separate interests of the various towns and the lack of political cohesion rendered it impossible for the Germans to deal effectively with the strangers.

[4] Ehrenberg, *op. cit.* 160. The negociations to prevent this ban from having effect were ably conducted by George Gilpin; the proceedings are well described by C. Molloy, *De jure maritimo et navali* (1588), p. 302.

[5] S. P. D. J. I. LXXII. 70.

[6] Ehrenberg, 121. Walsingham gave interlopers a licence to export 30,000 pieces of undressed cloth in July 1579. *Ib.* 153.

to carry on business at points which the Adventurers A.D. 1603
had relinquished. It is probable that the Merchant Ad- —1689.
venturers were able to make larger gains than their rivals,
but it is not clear that they could maintain a real monopoly
of English cloth in Germany. The appeal to Imperial *and as*
jurisprudence, about their privileged position, was not very *prejudicial to the*
successful; they were, indeed, forced in 1598 to remove their *Empire.*
main factory from the mouth of the Elbe to Middleburg
in Zeeland, till the storm had blown over and they could
return to Hamburg in 1611; but the temporary migration
to a Dutch town proved to be of no advantage to German
merchants, as the attack on the Adventurers only gave an
opportunity for English interlopers to develop their business
to a larger amount than ever.

The result of the outcry was far more important in *The complaint*
England itself; it seems to have been the occasion for the *of their*
first great attack on these Companies by English subjects *monopoly was taken*
who denounced them as monopolies; the Imperial courts *up in England,*
had furnished the interlopers with a weapon[1] which enabled
them to begin the agitation that lasted all through the
seventeenth century. This has been already alluded to in
general terms, and it is unnecessary to do more than call
attention to some of the more important incidents in the
controversy.

The complaint that the Adventurers had a practical
monopoly was put forward by shippers, who insisted that
their interests were affected by exclusion from the trade;
and it was also urged that the Company was injurious *and it was*
to the maritime power of the country generally. For *also said they did*
shipping to the Elbe vessels of large burden were desirable, *little for English*
but smaller boats would suffice for the voyage to Middle- *shipping*
burg[2]; and hence, in 1601[3] and 1605, when the factory was
at the Dutch town, it was possible to allege that this great

---

[1] See, however, below on English ideas of Natural Liberty in connection with
industrial regulation, p. 286.

[2] Ehrenberg, *op. cit.* 199. S. P. D. El. cclxv. 71, 1597. For Wheeler's defence of the Company on this point see *Treatise*, p. 58.

[3] It was at this time that Wheeler, the Secretary, issued his *Treatise of
Commerce*, which is an apology for the Company. It contains formal attestations
in their favour from Antwerp, Emden, and Stade.

A.D. 1603
—1689.

or naval stores.

body of merchants did little or nothing to encourage the employment, or building, of large English ships. It was also possible to compare the Adventurers to their disadvantage with the men of the Hanse League, who were able to import such naval necessaries as hemp and cordage. These stores were brought from the Baltic and Russia, regions in which the Hanse League had large connections; while the Adventurers[1] had neither right nor opportunity to engage in the trade. These objections sounded plausible, but did not carry conviction to the responsible authorities. The corporation of Trinity House declared themselves in favour of maintaining the privileges of the Company, on the very ground of the encouragement they gave to ship-building[2]. It is not possible to trace the changing currents of opinion with any certainty[3]; the House of Commons appointed a committee in 1604, which was apparently in favour of enlarging the regulated Company[4] rather than abolishing it altogether; but the Bills, which were drafted with this object, were delayed by the House of Lords, and failed to pass in a form that affected the Adventurers[5]. Under the personal government of Charles the privileges of the Adventurers were continued, but the fine for membership

Their privileges were maintained after full discussion in 1604, and

---

[1] Ehrenberg, *op. cit.* 150. When Buckingham came to be Admiral he was at great pains to promote the native manufacture of cordage, so as to do away with our dependence on foreign sources. Oppenheim, *Administration of the Royal Navy*, 280.

[2] S. P. D. J. I. viii. 58 (1604).

[3] The personal bias in the pamphlet literature of the period is apparent. Malynes, the Stapler, criticises the Merchant Adventurers in 1622 (*Maintenance of Free Trade*, p. 50), so does Milles, the Customer at Sandwich, who opposes all monopolising companies, in 1601. Wheeler hints that the support which customers gave to the Hanse League was by no means disinterested (*Treatise of Commerce*, 61). The author of *Trades Increase*, 1615 (Camb. Univ. Lib., Syn. 7. 61 (82)), speaks in favour of the Adventurers (p. 10) and Misselden is an uncompromising advocate (*Free Trade* (1622), pp. 50, 74), who holds that the decay of clothing trades is due to frauds in the manufacture and deficient searching (p. 127).

[4] See Sir E. Sandys' statement in *Commons Journals*, i. 219. "This Act dissolveth no Company, taketh away no good Government; Those Orders in Companies which tend to Monopoly, it abrogateth: Orders for necessary Contribution to publick Charges it establisheth; the rest it leaves as it found them, neither in worse State nor better ' On this incident compare Hewins, *English Trade and Finance*, p. 30.

[5] F. H. Durham, *Relations of the Crown to Trade under James I.* in *Royal Hist. Soc. Trans.* N. S. xiii. 205

was limited to £50 in London, and in the other cities A.D. 1603
—1689. to £25[1]. The discussion broke out again in 1643[2], when *in 1643,* the Company obtained the support of Parliament, and was even permitted to double the fines for entrance which had been settled by Charles I. The same policy was continued *in 1656;* by Cromwell in 1656, and the Mart was fixed at Dordrecht *but ad-mission was* in Holland[3] The agitation was renewed in 1662[4], and the *rendered easier,*

[1] Rymer, *Fœdera*, xix. 583. *A Proclamation prohibiting the Transportation of Wollen Clothes into Germany or the Provinces of the Netherlands*, 1634.

[2] Scobell, Acts i. 58. Compare *A Discourse consisting of Motives for Enlargement and Freedome of Trade * * * engrossed by a company of private men who stile themselves Merchant Adventurers* (1645). Brit. Mus. 712. g. 16 (2). The preface of the book sets out to show how the Patent of the Merchant Adventurers "trencheth upon the native Rights of the free-born subject: which Patent hath been often complaind of and clamord against from time to time, as an universall greevance to Town and Countrey, tending to the diminution of Trade, and of all sorts of Manufactures at home and to the disrepute of the policy of this Nation abroad, the sayd Patent being accounted no lesse amongst all people, then a Monopoly, a word odious all the world over."

The tract gives an interesting account of the way in which the Adventurers agreed to deduct for defects in cloth (1634). No brother was to "buy any white cloth that is made in Gloucestershire, Wiltshire, Oxfordshire, and the Easterne limits of Somersetshire, without abatement for all faults in which they shall be found defective"; every brother who bought cloth contrary to this was to forfeit 20s. on every cloth so bought (p. 33).

The objection is brought forward that the Dutch had taken to cloth making and that to destroy this trade it was necessary to undersell them. The stint of the Merchant Adventurers rendered this impossible, and prevented cheap sales generally. It was said that before 1633 the Dutch "made not above 2000 cloths, but since in some yeares 20,000, and also made Perpetuanoes,...so that trade is insensibly stolen away from us, our workmen by hundreds going over to set up their manufactures in other Countries, because they were discouraged to exercise their ingenuitie at home, and have freedome to make away to their best advantage any new fashioned stuffe, by reason of the said Proclamation of restraint, whereat there was much discontentment abroad as wel as at home, for Amsterdam and other Townes did stomach extremely that his Majestie of Great Britaine should exclude them, and that Rotterdam should be only priviledged to be Mistris of the Trade" (p. 26).

The author of the pamphlet insists on the fact (p. 38) that in view of the competition of the Dutch, it was absolutely necessary to undersell. Therefore "there is no one thing that requires the policie of England more, then to draw the one (Holland) and prevent the other (the Flemings) from making of cloth. Now there is no way under Heaven to doe it, but by devising wayes to sell our Manufactures at cheaper rates, and disperse them more up and downe the Countrey, which cannot be otherwise effected then by a free Trade, and multitude of Merchants, and by fitting all places and remote parts with such kind of Manufactures as are most proper for them." On the Dutch manufacture, see below, p. 233, n. 9.

[3] Proclamation, 30 May, 1656. Brit. Mus. 669. f. 20 (26).

[4] *A Remonstrance proving that confinement of Trade to particular Companies is of general losse to His Majesty and His people.* Brit. Mus. 816. m. 12 (9).

A.D. 1603
—1689.

and after the Restoration, and the abuses seem to have ceased.

fines were reduced to 20 and 10 marks respectively[1]; it seems probable that the abuses, which had been complained of, had been so far amended that there was no longer any reason for attacking the Company as a monopoly *de facto*; for it survived the Revolution[2] and continued to be an important commercial institution till it was broken up by Napoleon in 1807[3].

Thus far the story of the Merchant Adventurers serves to illustrate the principles which were being debated in regard to commercial companies generally; but the fact that those merchants were primarily concerned in the export of cloth, brought them into specially close relations with the leading industry of the country[4]. The interruption to their trade, at the time of the Spanish Armada, had caused serious suffering among the weavers[5]; at later dates, when the reasons for the cessation of the usual demand were less obvious, the Adventurers became the object of attack by the unemployed and their sympathisers. There was a good deal of complaint in 1604[6], and again in 1606[7]; it was alleged that the Company did not push the trade as effectually as they might have done, and that, as a London company, they gave insufficient opportunities for the export of cloth from the West of England[8]. They were much

Their business brought them into difficult relations with the weaving industry,

---

[1] *Newcastle Merchant Adventurers* (Surtees Society), II. 15.

[2] The trade was practically thrown open at this time, and the Merchant Adventurers were anxious to have parliamentary support, so far as the trade to Germany was concerned. They disclaimed any desire to interfere with the trade of the Exeter merchants to Holland and Flanders (*Reasons humbly offered in support of the Company of Merchant Adventurers of England in their trade to Germany*, Brit. Mus. 816. m. 11 (98)), and appear to have successfully disarmed the opposition at the centre of the West of England trade, as the Mayor, Aldermen, Common Councillors, Fullers, and other traders in the woollen manufactures of Exeter petitioned in favour of their Bill in 1699. *Commons Journals*, XIII. 8, 9.

[3] *Narrative of Proceedings* in *Hamburg Correspondence* Ap. G. *Reports*, 1835, XLVIII. 143.

[4] Even in the fifteenth century the clothiers grumbled about the restrictions they imposed. Wheeler, *Treatise of Commerce* (1601), 11.

[5] *Commons Journals*, I. 220.

[6] The arguments for and against the Company will be found in Brit. Mus. *Cotton MSS*. Titus, F. IV. f. 259—285.   [7] S. P. D. J. I. 1606, XX. 10.

[8] This complaint continued as late as 1670. *Reasons humbly offered, that Merchant Adventurers are detrimental to England and especially to Devonshire.* Brit. Mus. 712. g. 16 (8).

criticised during the serious trade depression of 1621—23, A.D. 1603
—1689.
which was attributed to their monopoly[1]; the clothiers of
Berkshire, Hampshire, Kent, Suffolk, Wiltshire and other
manufacturing districts represented that the merchants *especially*
would not pay them ready money[2]; and exception was ap- *when trade was de-*
parently taken to them after the Restoration[3]. This close *pressed;*
connection with the manufacture was not always advantageous to the Adventurers. Their privileged trade consisted
in exporting white cloth, which was subsequently dyed and
dressed in the neighbourhood of their continental factory;
and this right brought them into direct antagonism with
the clothworkers, in a way that did not concern weavers.
Subjects generally were prohibited from exporting undressed
cloth[4], but the Merchant Adventurers had been permitted
to do so[5]; and occasionally other persons obtained a licence
to carry on the same trade. King James I., who was *and their*
anxious to plant the trades of dyeing and dressing cloth *privileges were sus-*
in England[6], showed little respect for the Adventurers' *pended*
privileges; in 1614 he abrogated their charter[7], after constituting a new Company[8] to carry on trade in dressed
cloths, but it had no success. The Dutch retaliated by
refusing to buy English-finished cloth, and by attempting
to develop a weaving industry of their own[9], and in

---

[1] Mr Shaw attributes it entirely to financial reasons which were quite independent of their action. *History of Currency*, 144, compare Malynes, *Maintenance
of Free Trade* (1622) 50, 68, and Misselden's defence of the Company, *Circle of
Commerce* (1623), p. 58.

[2] 6 May, 1641. On the same day the Hanse merchants complained of the
Merchant Adventurers for engrossing trade and asked to be restored to their
former privileges. *Hist. MSS. Comm.* iv. Ap. 62.

[3] *Hist. MSS. Comm.* ii. Ap. 18 (? 1679).   [4] 33 Henry VIII. c. 19.

[5] Misselden, *Free Trade*, p. 63, refers especially to the grant of 6 Elizabeth to
the Company. Compare also 8 Eliz. c. 6, which recognises the export of un-
wrought cloth by special permission as a frequent practice.

[6] In 1606 the clothworkers of Salisbury wished to have the cloth finished in
England, while the Adventurers thought this injurious. S. P. D. J. I. xx. 9, 10.

[7] Proclamation 2 Dec. 1614. *Abolishing the Charter of the Merchant Adventurers'*. Soc. of Antiquaries.

[8] Proclamation 23 July, 1614 (Soc. of Antiquaries).

[9] S. P. D. J. I. lxxxviii. 76 (Sept. 11, 1616). The success which attended
these endeavours was attributed by Roger Coke (*Detection of the Court and State
of England*, i. 358) to the migration of 140 Walloon families from Canterbury and
other towns, where they were aggrieved by Laud's measures. Compare Gardiner (*History*, viii. 121); also the curious poem in J. Trevers' *Essay to the*

1617[1] the King was forced to re-establish the old Company of Merchant Adventurers. The scheme for planting the *when Cockayne's scheme for dressing cloth was being tried.* trades of dyeing and dressing cloth, which had been floated by Alderman Cockayne[2], looked well on paper, but the attempt to introduce it suddenly proved most disastrous to weavers and to merchants alike[3] The whole story serves to bring out the nature of the difficulties with which any Government must contend, in organising foreign trade, and in regulating a manufacture which is directed to meet the requirements of foreign countries.

190. The abrogation of the Hanse privileges in London, and the closing of the Steelyard, had left the Merchant Adventurers in a dominant position, for carrying on com- *The Eastland Company was founded to supersede the Hanse in the Baltic trade,* merce with the valleys of the Elbe and the Rhine. The other great branch of Hanse trade, with the towns on the Baltic, lay outside their chartered limits; and a new Company was created by Elizabeth[4], in 1579, to organise the inter- course with Scandinavia[5], Poland, and the German ports on the Baltic. Like the Merchant Adventurers, the Eastland

---

restoring of our decayed trade (1677). A farther development of Dutch woollen manufacture is spoken of as occurring after the peace of Munster in 1648. (T. Manley, *Usury at Six per cent.*, 15.) It was also alleged that the dislocation of the English clothing trade led to the development of weaving at Frankfort. Battie, *Merchant's Remonstrance* (1648), 3.

[1] S. P. D. J. I. xciii. 23, 12 Aug. 1617. See also Proclamation 12 Aug. 1617, Brit. Mus. 1851 b. 3 (3). The contract between the reconstituted Company and the City of Hamburgh (2 June 1618) is printed in full in *Hamburgh Correspondence* Ap. F. *Reports* 1835, xlviii. 133.

[2] Sharpe, *London and the Kingdom*, ii. 68. A paper with the reasons of the projector and the answers of the Adventurers will be found in Brit. Mus. *Lansdowne MSS.* clii. f. 282. See below, p. 294.

[3] Misselden, *Free Trade* (1622), 41. " In charitie wee may thinke it was Good in the Purpose though it proved Ill in the Practise. For thereby the *Draperies* of this *Kingdom* are much diminished, and the forreine advanced and advantaged." On this experiment see Unwin, *Industrial Organisation*, 182, 186.

[4] Stow, *Survey*, v. 262. A charter had been granted to some English mer- chants in 5 Hen. IV. N. Tench, in *Reasons humbly offered by the Governor, Assistants and Fellowship of the Eastland merchants against giving a general liberty to all persons whatever to export the English Woollen Manufacture* (1689), p. 7. Brit. Mus. 712. 8. 16 (25), but this Eastland Company does not appear to have claimed any connection with that body. Denmark was open for trading purposes both to the Eastland Company and the Merchant Adventurers, as it lay between their spheres of special privilege.

[5] The tolls which the kings of Denmark exacted from all ships passing the Sound were an important factor in the commercial history of the period. They

Merchants exported English cloth, though they do not seem A.D. 1603 —1689. to have been permitted to send it abroad undyed and un-dressed[1]. Their voyages were important to the country, not so much because they kept open a market for our and to im-port naval stores, commodities as because of the products they imported[2]. Tar, hemp, cordage and all sorts of naval stores could be most easily procured from the shores of the Baltic; and as the English woods were in danger of being used up, it was necessary to find some other means of procuring masts, spars and timber of every kind[3]. The Company seems to have carried on a vigorous trade in the earlier part of the seven-

were supposed to be contributions paid for the advantages supplied by the Danes in maintaining lights on the coast, and for the protection from pirates afforded by the Castle of Elsinore. The increase of the tolls in 1553 was one of the causes which led to the decline of the trade of Lubeck and other Hanse towns. Elizabeth endeavoured unsuccessfully, in 1588, to obtain some advantages for English merchants (Camden, *Elizabeth*, s. a. 1588, p. 421), and with no better result in 1602 (Macpherson, *Annals*, II. 224, 228). The Danes were inclined to give a very large interpretation to their claims in regard to ships engaged in the Russian trade. James I. joined, in 1613, with the Dutch and the Hanse towns, in protesting against the sudden raising of the rate, and it was in consequence lowered again to the old terms (*Ib.* 266). Charles I. commissioned Sir T. Roe to open negociations with Denmark, but the tolls at the Sound do not appear to have been a cause of difficulty at the time (Rymer, xx. 285, 338). The whole question entered on a new phase in 1644. The Swedes, with the assistance of the Dutch, invaded Denmark and secured substantial advantages, as the Swedes were granted immunity from the toll, and the Dutch were allowed by the Danes to obtain favourable terms in 1645, and in 1649 to farm the revenue from the toll, which was subsequently collected at Amsterdam, and not at Elsinore (Thurloe, *State Papers*, I. 127, 226). This arrangement came to an end in 1653. In 1654 Cromwell made a treaty with the King of Denmark by which he secured that the English should pay no more toll than was paid by the most favoured nation, other than the Swedes (Dumont, *Corps diplomatique du droit des Gens*, vi. ii. p. 93, § 5). Causes of complaint continued, and a treaty was concluded between England and France in 1657, by which the two countries, in conjunction with Sweden, agreed to insist on keeping the Sound open to trade (Macpherson, *Annals*, II. 475). The definitive settlement was reached in 1659, in the time of Richard Cromwell, when England, France and Holland agreed to insist that the tolls should be levied at an unvarying rate (Dumont, *op. cit.* vi. ii. 253). The entry of France on the field of controversy marks her new importance as a sea power.

[1] They petitioned for this privilege under James I. *Hist. MSS. Comm.* IV. Ap. 302.

[2] Tench, *op. cit.* 8.

[3] In 1623 the Eastland Company, who favoured the Navigation policy, peti-tioned that a certain Rikhaut be not permitted to land his deal boards, because abundance had been imported in English bottoms. *Hist. MSS. Comm.* IV. Ap. 314.

but they were not very successful.

teenth century[1] and it was reinstated at the Restoration[2], though, as in other cases, there is some difficulty in tracing its later history. Its limits were reduced by the statute[3] which declares the trade to Denmark, Sweden and Norway open to any subject, and at the same time the fine for admission to the Company was lowered to 40s. There were various reasons which combined to prevent it from attaining first class importance. Eventually, the Government adopted the policy of looking to our plantations in North America for the supplies of timber and naval stores, which were needed to supplement British deficiencies, so that less care was taken to foster the Baltic trade, while a decrease in the demand for English cloth contributed to their decline[4]. The English failed, owing to the want of proper shipping, to secure the lion's share of the commerce which had been

The Dutch developed the trade with Spain in Baltic corn,

formerly carried on by the Hanse League in this quarter. These German merchants had done an extensive business in supplying corn to other European countries; the Dutch, who were forced to import cereals for consumption in Holland, had special facilities for engaging in this trade on behalf of other countries also. They had great granaries at Amsterdam and very large numbers of vessels suitable for the traffic, so that they became the chief carriers between the wheat-growing districts of northern Germany and Poland, and the Iberian Peninsula and Mediterranean lands, which failed to produce their own supplies of food. This great trade was the foundation and mainstay of Dutch maritime power, and the English Eastland merchants had not succeeded in competing with them in this branch of commerce[5].

[1] Their monopoly for the importation of cordage was confirmed by proclamation in the time of James I. (21 July, 1622), 506. h. 12 (98). See also the proclamation of Charles I., Brit. Mus. b. 11 (116) (7 March, 1629) to the same effect. Both of these enforce the policy of the Navigation Acts not only in regard to the trade of the Company, but generally.

[2] Stow, *Survey*, v. 262. A good statement of the case for the Companies is found in the *Reasons offered by the Merchant Adventurers of England and Eastland Merchants residing at Hull* (1661). Brit. Mus. 816. m. 11 (100).

[3] 25 C. II. c. 7. [4] Sellers, *Acts of Eastland Co.*, lix.

[5] *Discourse of Trade*, 104. The relative failure of the Eastland merchants was one of the subjects into which James I. desired the Commission to enquire in 1622. "And because our Marchants Tradeing into the Eastland Countries were

This Company thus played but a small part in the work of building up the maritime power of England—the object for which it had been instituted by Elizabeth. There are, however, some incidents in connection with its history which are exceedingly instructive. As has been already pointed out, the great contest between England and Spain was not confined to armed engagements, but was fought out on commercial fields as well. The Spaniards had endeavoured to cut off the English from any markets for cloth, and thus from the means of purchasing ordnance and gunpowder; but though considerable privation was inflicted on English weavers, the trade was not destroyed, but only diverted. Towards the close of the sixteenth century, Elizabeth was *which the* strong enough to take the offensive in this struggle, and to *Hanse League* try to cut off the main sources of the Spanish food supply[1], *had been forced to* so as to increase the difficulty of victualling ships and troops. *relinquish.* In 1597[2] a corn fleet of "many ships" destined for Spain was captured by English cruisers; this was a blow from which the Hanse Towns never recovered[3], as their merchants were unable to replace the vessels they had lost. The protests of the injured parties were contemptuously disregarded; they pleaded the rights of neutral traders, and the Law of Nations[4]. Elizabeth retorted by claiming a

wont to make good Retornes by Corn, which they have neglected of late to their own Hurt and the Hurt of the Kingdom, we would have you to consider how to give them Encouragement in that Trade, and to do it so as our own Dominions may be supplied in time of Want, and yet in Tyme of Plenty the Husbandry and Tillage of this Realm not to be discouraged?

"Further, whereas our Eastland Marchants in former tymes did lade their Shipps with Hempe and Flax rough dressed in great Quantities, which did not onlie helpe them much in their Retornes, but did also set great Nombers of our People on work with dressing the same, and converting the same into Lynnen Cloth, which kind of Trade we understand is of late almost given over, by bringing in of Hemp and Flax ready dressed, and that for the most part by Strangers, we commend unto your care, by what meanes this hurtfull Error in Trade may be reformed, to the Help of our Marchants and the Releife of our poor Subjects." Rymer, *Fœdera*, XVII. 414.

[1] See above, p. 89, also p. 196, n. 6.   [2] Wheeler, *Treatise of Commerce*, 66.

[3] The Thirty Years' War and the political conditions of the first half of the seventeenth century were inconsistent with communal prosperity. Naudé, *Getreidehandelspolitik*, 311.

[4] Wheeler, *op. cit.* 68. "For this prohibition was not set forth by the Queenes Maiestie before she was of necessitie compelled thereunto: least the King of Spaine, open enemie to this Realme, should bee furnished with Armes, Ships and

natural right of self-defence, and she got her way. The whole incident presents a curious parallel with the events of a later period; on the one side there was an attempt, like Napoleon's, to close continental ports to English commerce, and on the other, there was the same sort of high-handedness that roused the antagonism of Russia in 1780 and called forth the assertion of the rights of neutral traders[1].

Still, the Eastland Company seems to have

So little complaint seems to have been directed against the Eastland Company, at times when the Merchant Adventurers and Muscovy merchants were the objects of bitter attack, that we are perhaps justified in supposing that this association was really conducted as a regulated company, and did not, in practice and fact, he open to the charge of being a mere monopoly[2]. At the close of the seventeenth century the policy of the Eastland merchants was controlled by their governor, Nathaniel Tench; and on two occasions he came prominently before the public. On the first he took a leading part in arguing in favour of the principle of company trading[3], on the other he criticised the Russian Company, as unnecessarily and injuriously exclusive[4]. The line he

Ammunition with such facilitie, and in such great abundance, as he was from the Maritime parts of Germanie, by meanes whereof he might maintaine long warre against this realme, so that if he could not gett these aides, and helpes, it is manifest that hee should bee forced to leave off warre and offer peace not onely to this Realme, but also to others, against whom he most uniustly maketh war, whereas therefore it is plaine, that this of Spaine, being an enemy to this realm, is furnished, armed, and strengthened to continue this uniust war with ships, victuall, and other warlike provisions out of certain cities under *Polone* and other maritime cities of Germany, in what sort can her Maiesty (being oppressed by the Spaniards with uniust war) tolerate or suffer that such orders, and helpes so openly and so copiously should be carried to the said King her enemie for the continuance of warre against her? And although you many times repeate it, that the said her Highnes prohibitions were contrary to the law of nations, it is straunge, that you would alleagde this against the law of Nature, when as by nature itselfe, it is ordeined, that every man may defend himselfe against force, which law not written, but borne with us wee have not learned, but received and drawen from Nature it selfe, besides it is provided by the ancient lawes to forbid, yea to lett, and hinder, that no man minister armes, victuall, or any thing else, whereby the enemie may bee holpen to make warre, as by this one, wherewith many other agree." Wheeler, *Treatise* 74.

[1] See below, p. 670.

[2] There were, however, many serious charges brought against the Eastland Company by the seamen of Hull, in 1641. *Hist. MSS. Comm.* IV. Ap. 76. Sellers, *Acts of Eastland Company*, lxxxii.

[3] Tench, *op. cit.* 4.   [4] Stow, *Survey*, v. 261.

maintained in both cases was perfectly self-consistent, and A.D. 1603
—1689. was exactly what might have been expected from a fair-minded man, who regarded company trading as a useful expedient in the circumstances of the day.

An incident, which served the supporters of companies as a stock illustration of the evils of unregulated trade, had occurred at Narva in Russia, on the Baltic coast, but not *justified its* within the limits assigned to the Eastland merchants by *existence as a regulated* their charter. "The Englishe had at the Narve in Liefland *Company,* a profitable trade, and good sales for their Countreis commoditie a good while together, till at length in the year 1565 a number of stragling merchaunts, resorting thither out of this Realme, the trade was utterly spoiled, insomuch that many of them went about the Towne with Cloth upon their armes and measures in their hands, and sold the same by *Arsine*, a measure of that Countrey, to the great imbasing of that excellent Commoditie, the discredite of our Nation and the finall empoverishing and undoing of manie of the said straglers, which being made knowne to her Maiestie and Her Highnes Right Honorable privie Counsell order was taken at the next Parliament that the Towne of Narve should be comprized within the Charter of the Muscovie Companie, to prevent the like pedlarlike kinde of dealing ever after, and the making vile of the principallest commoditie of the realme[1]." Such a mishap served as a warning to men like Tench, and confirmed them in the opinion that in the "ungoverned single trade the first comer marreth the market for him that cometh after," while it was also believed that the supervision regulated companies were able to exercise over the quality of cloth exported, was an additional safeguard against the frauds of manufacturers and the carelessness of searchers[2], and helped to maintain the reputation of English goods in foreign markets[3]. It was on these grounds that Tench and the Eastland merchants argued[4] that the abolition of all companies would tend to

---

[1] Wheeler, *Treatise of Commerce*, p. 55.

[2] See above, p. 204 n. 1.   [3] Lohmann, *op. cit.* 50.

[4] Tench, *Reasons humbly offered by the Governor, Assistants and Fellowship of the Eastland Merchants* (1689), p. 6.

throw the commerce of England back again into the hands
of foreigners, as it had been before these bodies were erected;
while there was a danger that the reputation of English
cloth abroad would be diminished, so that the change would
react unfavourably on the clothing trade.

On the other hand, Tench was perfectly alive to the
evils of a practical monopoly, such as the Muscovy Company
while the
Muscovy
Company
had become. The career of this body had been most dis-
appointing; it had been organised after the remarkable expedition of Sir Hugh Willoughby, partly at least in the
hope of finding a north-east passage and planting settlements upon the route[1]. The hopes of the traders had been
frustrated, however, as the Czar had become less favourable to them in the reign of Elizabeth. The management
of the company was severely criticised in the Commons
report of 1604. "The Muscovy Company, consisting of
eightscore persons or thereabouts, have fifteen directors,
seems to
have been
a practical
monopoly
who manage the whole trade; these limit to every man the
proportion of stock, which he shall trade for, make one purse
and stock of all, and consign it into the hands of one agent
at Moscow, and so again at their return, to one agent in
London, who sell all, and give such account as they please.
This is a strong and shameful monopoly, a monopoly in a
monopoly, both abroad and at home, a whole Company by
this means, is become as one man, who alone hath the uttering of all the Commodities of so great a country[2]." In 1615
the trade was practically extinct[3], and though there was
some subsequent revival, the English interest suffered a
severe blow at the fall of the monarchy in 1649[4]. The
Dutch were able to undersell the English merchants, but
a few men continued to prosecute a trade in the opening up
of which many losses had been incurred. This little knot of
merchants were anxious to enjoy the full benefits of their
privileges; they charged very heavy sums for licences to

---

[1] Compare the preamble of 10 W. III. c. 6, *An Act to enlarge the trade to
Russia*, also vol. I. p. 505.

[2] *Commons Journals*, I. 220.

[3] *Trades Increase*, p. 4.

[4] Postlethwayt, *Dictionary*, s.v. *Russia Company*. Charles II.'s efforts to
re-establish it were not very successful.

trade, and they injured English enterprise by standing on A.D. 1603 —1689.
their exclusive rights in the whale fisheries[1]. According
to Tench, the only remedy for the condition of the trade *which hindered the develop-ment of the Russian trade*
was to throw it more widely open, so as to attract a sufficient
number of men, with adequate capital, to develop the commerce properly. There was, he contended in a speech to
the Council, a very good market for English cloth in Russia,
if it were brought in larger quantities and sold at lower
rates; he pointed out that many of the valuable products
of Russia were bulky goods, so that a considerable fleet of
shipping might be advantageously employed in importing
them. There was, at the close of the seventeenth century, *in the seventeenth century.*
a prospect of greatly increasing the trade, as the Czar, on
a visit to England, in 1697, had conceded a tobacco monopoly
in Russia to the English merchants; but Tench contended
that unless more capital was brought into the trade, it would
be impossible for the members to take advantage of this
great opportunity. His argument was so convincing that
the claims of the Muscovy merchants were set aside; the
Company was not dissolved, but the fine on admission was
reduced from £60[2] to £5[3]. This measure seems to have
answered its purpose; the Company was no longer a mono--
poly in fact, and the management of the regulated companies in the northern trades ceased to give rise to complaint
before the seventeenth century had closed. *The exist-ence of companies, even if beneficial to the nation,*

191. The formation of these great companies, which
regulated particular branches of commerce, might be advantageous for the nation as a whole, but it seems to have

---

[1] See the proclamations in their favour in 1613, Rymer, XVI. p. 747, and again on 18 May, 1619 (Brit. Mus. 1851. b. 3 (6)); also by Cromwell (9 March, 1658), Brit. Mus. 669. f. 20 (78). They appear to have pressed their exclusive rights, as against Scotch whalers, and to have prevented the sending out an expedition from the Northern Kingdom (*Hist. MSS. Comm.* IV. Ap. 5). Papers containing the charges brought against them in 1628 are mentioned in the *Hist. MSS. Comm.* IV. Ap. 18. Among other things the Company had "sold the Greenland trade by a candle two years since to some of themselves at a court where few were present." On the whole story compare Hewins, *English Trade and Finance*, 36.

[2] Stow, *Survey*, Bk. V. p. 265. Compare *Reasons humbly offered for passing the Bill for encouraging Trade to Russia*, and *Some Considerations relating to the enlarging the Russian Trade*. Brit. Mus. 8223. e. 1 (19, 20).

[3] 10 and 11 W. III. c. 6.

C.   16

A.D. 1603
—1689.

*was disad-
vantageous
to the
out-ports,
which were
the strong-
holds of
Interlopers.*

proved prejudicial to the merchants who traded from the smaller ports[1]. London would have a larger proportion of members than any other port; and, in the arrangements for common sailings, it would be natural to take their convenience into account. Under these circumstances, it is not surprising that there should have been a great deal of controversy between the Londoners and the provincial townsmen. These local merchants were generally independent traders, who objected to the existence of the companies altogether; they were stigmatised as interlopers. In other cases, however, the traders at a provincial port constituted a gild, or court, which stood in definite, but not always cordial, relations to the members of the Hamburg or the Eastland Companies[2] who resided in London.

A curious illustration of these difficulties is found in connection with the French and Spanish trade. An attempt

---

[1] Sandys, *Instructions*, in *Commons Journals*, I. 218.

[2] From 1663 to 1680 the York Eastland Merchants were constantly in dispute with the London Company. The whole quarrel is summed up in a letter from London, read 17 Feb. 1669. " Your Commissioners have here moved for the Restoration of certain ancient privileges, which they allege you have formerly had, namely, a certain number of assistants at that place, and for collection of impositions by your own deputy, to both of which we should willingly agree, if we could find it convenient and feazible; but for the former of these we find no hint or power in our Charter (which is the foundation of our proceedings) to constitute assistance in any other place than London, and in our residence beyond the seas; and as for the latter, we doubt whether impositions could be with ease and certainty collected elsewhere than where the entries are made, which was doubtless the reason why that was, by our ancestors, put into the posture it now stands." *Acts of Eastland Company*, 90.

The merchants of York had grounds for dissatisfaction, for cloth for the Baltic was shipped in their names without their knowledge. In order to obviate "these indirect practices," the Deputy at Hull was ordered not to admit any entries, unless the Deputy at York had signed or affixed the seal of the Company to each entry. York, Eastland Merchants, *Record Book*, f. 44 b. The controversy came to a climax in 1677 when York refused to send commissioners or accounts to the General Meeting. London retaliated by refusing to appoint a deputy at York, "We do not conceive ourselves obliged *ex officio* to choose you a deputy, after you break off your brotherly correspondence with us, and have refused to treat with us in the same manner as you yourselves and all the other residences have of a long time used to do, denying to send us either commissioners or accounts, when in ours of 16 Dec. last, to prevent differences, we expressly desired both, which you were by duty as well as custom but now especially by oath bound to do, it is no wonder, if you have a mind to leave us, that we should easily content to let you be left." York, Eastland Merchants, *Record Book*, f. 61. Miss Sellers informs me that the quarrel covers about 80 folios and is not finished when the records end.

to commit these branches of commerce, in which the West of England was largely interested, to a regulated company had roused violent opposition; and in 1604 this trade was declared open to all Englishmen[1]. In the following year, however, the Governor and Merchants of the Company of Merchant Adventurers of Exeter, who had been incorporated by Elizabeth in 1560[2], had their privileges confirmed[3] by

A.D. 1603
—1689.

The
Merchant
Adven-
turers

---

[1] 3 J. I. c. 6. "*An acte to enable all his Maiesties loving subjects of Englande and Wales to trade freely into the Dominions of Spaine, Portugal and France.*"

[2] Cotton, *An Elizabethan Guild of the City of Exeter*, 3, 25.

[3] This Company's powers were intended to check the intrusion of artisans into trade. "Whereas it pleased our late Soveraigne Lady Queene Elizabeth of famous memorie, by her Highnes Letters Patents under the Great Seale of England, bearing date the seaventh daye of June in the second yeere of her Highnes Reigne (in consideracion of the good, true and faithfull obedience and service done by the Maior and principall Citizens of the Cittye of Exeter, as well in the time of Kinge Henrye the Seaventh as of Kinge Edward the Sixt, against dyvers Treasons and Rebellions moved and stirred in those dayes, as also for the takinge awaye abolishinge and moovinge of many and sundrie absurdities and inconveniences which within the said Citie and Countye did increase, by reason of the excessyve number of Artificers, and other inexpert, ignorant and unworthie men, which did take uppon them to use the Arte, Science and Misterie of Merchandize and traffique of Merchant Wares, to the greate detriment of the Commonwealth of this Realme of England, and to the manifest ympoverishment of the said Citye and incorporate certain Merchantes therein named, and their Successors, (beinge Citizens and Inhabitants of the said Citye and Countie) and to give and graunte unto them the perpetuall Name of the Governor, Consuls, and Societye of the Merchants Adventurers of the Citye and Countye of Exeter, traffiqinge the Realme of Fraunce and the Dominions of the French Kinge; (2) which said Incorporacion or Companye of Merchants are found to be of greate use, honour and service to the State in general, as well in the Advauncement of his Majesties Customes, as alsoe for that the said Incorporacion for the space of Fourtie and fyve yeeres have releeved Twelve poor Men with Gownes, Money and other Necessaries, to their greate Comforte, and doe still yeerelye soe apparell and comfort them, and by their said Charter they are bounde to contynue and keepe the same for ever: (3) and lykewise they have and doe not only charitably from tyme to tyme set up sundrye young Merchants with the loane of Money at their first entrance into the Trade, but alsoe have raysed, and alsoe doe raise divers auncient Merchants, who by Losses at the Sea have beene decayed by meanes whereof they have afterwardes profitable both to the Kinge in Custome and other payments, and good Members to the Commonwealth of the said Cytie: And for that many particuler Merchants of the said Corporacion, have in the tyme of dearth and scarcitie of Corne adventured greate sommes of Money out of their owne private Stockes for Corne into foreigne Kingdomes, for the Reliefe of the Poore as well of the said Citye, as of the Countye of Devon, to whome they have sold the same Corne in tyme of great Dearth and Necessitye, sometimes for Twoe Shillings Six Pence, Three Shillings, and Three Shillings Foure Pence lesse in everye Bushell, then the Prices in the Marketts have then beene." 4 J. I. c. 9.

Parliament, and their claim to an exclusive trade with
France was admitted. They seem to have had close relations
with the London Company of Merchant Adventurers, but
their powers did not prove very profitable; for it is said
that, in 1661, only one member of this body remained[1].
*were op-
posed*
The West of England appears to have been a stronghold of
interlopers; the clothiers there had objected, as early as the
time of Henry VII.[2], to the practical necessity which compelled them to send their drapery to Blackwall Hall in
London, so that it might be shipped from there by the
Merchant Adventurers, who had the exclusive rights of
exporting it to the Low Countries. Complaints were made
*by Exeter
merchants*
by some Exeter merchants in 1660; but the answer of the
London Company seems to have impressed the Government
favourably, and the interlopers got no satisfaction[3]. The
*and Bristol
traders;*
traders of Bristol took the lead in a similar agitation in
1669, and endeavoured without success to get the merchants
of Newcastle to join with them in their efforts; but the
Tyneside men were in favour of well-ordered trade, and had
little sympathy with interlopers, though they had grievances
of their own[4], of which some record has been preserved in
the papers of the Newcastle branch of the Merchant Adventurers.

It is by no means easy to follow the precise story of the
relations between the main body of Merchant Adventurers
who resided in London, and the members who traded from

---

[1] Macpherson, *Annals*, II. 501. As I read the evidence, the Exeter Company of
Merchant Adventurers, with special privileges for France, had also a side as a
court of the Merchant Adventurers of England; it seems unlikely that there were
two bodies in the City with the same name. The point is not cleared up by
Cotton; he says (p. vii.) that the Guild probably collapsed during the Civil War,
but he gives no hint of any connection with Londoners.

[2] 12 H. VII. c. 6.

[3] The terms in which Anderson, writing in the later part of the eighteenth
century, recounts the incident are remarkable. Anderson, *Historical and Chronological Deduction of the Origin of Commerce* (1787), II. 466.

[4] "Although the Marchants Adventurers have dealt very unkindly with us * * *
yett in this case wee doe hold it more conduceing to the common good of trade,
and the mainetayning of our generall priviledge to joyne with the Marchants
of London rather then with these interlopers ... and if you find them (the London
branch) desirous of it (petitioning) if York and Hull will doe the like, wee shall
joyne our force against those enemies of our trade." *Newcastle Merchant Adventurers* (Surtees Society), II. 137.

the out-ports on the North Sea. In the time of Henry VII. the London Company of Merchant Adventurers had been thrown open to all Englishmen, and so many of the citizens of Hull and York took out their freedom, that separate courts of the Company were organised in each of these ports[1]. The policy of the whole society was determined by a governor and assistants, elected by the residents in the mart town abroad; and the Hull and York courts were apparently organised under deputy governors, like the London court[2]. There were occasional causes of dispute, as *and the Courts at Hull and York had many disputes with the London brethren.* to the responsibility of the Hull court for debts contracted by the Merchant Adventurers in London[3], and in regard to the conditions on which the factors of York and Hull merchants were to be accredited to the authorities at the mart town; but the constitutional relations of these courts to one another appear to have been clear[4]. The main

---

[1] Lynn, Norwich, Ipswich, Exeter and Southampton are also specified as ports from which the Adventurers traded in 1603 (S. P. D. El. CCLXXXIII. 61). James I. assured, to the inhabitants of the out-ports, the right to deal in the new draperies at the marts of the Merchant Adventurers. (Proclamations, 10 July, 1621, Brit. Mus. 506. h. 12 (87).)

[2] Strype's *Stow*, Bk. v. 260. See also above, p. 225, n. 2.

[3] In 1662 there was a great dispute about a sum of £80,000, which had been borrowed from Widows and Orphans Fund, and which the London members of the Company could only hope to pay by putting a new imposition on goods. After an expensive suit the companies of Hull and Newcastle obtained a decision that they were not liable for this money. *Newcastle Merchant Adventurers*, II. xvi.

[4] There were similar relations between the Eastland merchants at these outports and the original company. Pains were taken to draw a line firmly between the artisan, or retailers, and the merchant; but the merchant might apparently join in any of the regulated companies he chose, and be free of more than one. There was a special rate for Merchant Adventurers and Spanish Merchants, who were admitted to the Eastland Company by a fine of 40 marks, whereas people free of no other company paid £20. (Sellers, *Acts and Ordinances of Eastland Company*, p. 87.) Miss Sellers points out that the two companies in York had some connection, for occasionally items in the Eastland Book are mentioned as having been entered also in the Adventurers' Book; when money was left to the Merchant Adventurers to be loaned, "Merchants of the old Hannce if qualified shall be preferred, and Eastland Merchants next." In 1674, the Eastlanders may possibly have felt that the Adventurers were getting too much control over their affairs, for on the death of their beadle, they refused to share a beadle with the Adventurers, "The Court have also now declared that they ought not to have the same person, chosen by the Company at Trinity Hall as their beadle, imposed upon their Company, but that they ought and will make choice of such a person for their servant in that place as they themselves shall approve and like of." *Ib.* p. xxxv.

business of these branches at the out-ports was doubtless
to charter the necessary vessels, and arrange the times of
sailing[1] and the proportions in which goods might be
exported by different merchants[2].

*The
Newcastle
Adven-
turers
claimed*

The Newcastle Adventurers, however, claimed to have a
very different status to that of the merchants at York and
Hull, and their relations with the General Court of the
Merchant Adventurers, at the Mart Town, were in consequence severely strained. The Tyneside Adventurers
would not admit that they were a mere localised court of
the Merchant Adventurers of England, for they claimed
that they were an older and independent body; they insisted
that Newcastle merchants should be subjected only to their
ancient payment, and therefore to lower charges than were
levied on the other members of the Company. The Newcastle men obtained decisions in their favour both in 1630[3],
and 1657[4]; but they got little satisfaction out of their
victories. The turn of the quarrel at different times is
unimportant; how the Newcastle court returned the letters
of the General Court unopened, because their Governor was
not addressed by his proper style[5], or how the London
Adventurers intrigued with certain Newcastle drapers to
engage in the export of cloth, in disregard of the privileges
of the Newcastle Adventurers[6]. Incidentally, however, it
supplies information of considerable interest. The facts,
which were put on record in connection with this controversy, give us a unique means of tracing the changes in
one commercial community, and of seeing how the civic
institutions of mediaeval times were gradually modified, so
as to meet the requirements of an age when a system of
national commercial regulation had come into vogue.

At this time the more important office of Deputy Governor was held by the same
man in both companies,—a practice which was maintained from 1646—1698.
There was also a branch of the Eastland Company to which some of the Merchant
Adventurers of Newcastle belonged (*Newcastle Merchant Adventurers*, Surtees
Soc. II. 140), and members of the Eastland Company also took out freedom of the
Russian Company after 1699.

[1] *Newcastle Merchant Adventurers*, I. 180.
[2] *Ib.* I. 39.   [3] *Ib.* II. 30.   [4] *Ib.* II. 62, 71.
[5] *Ib.* II. 34.   [6] *Ib.* II. 103.

A gild merchant had been granted to the men of New- A.D. 1603 —1689.
castle by King John; its membership, like that of other gild
merchants, included artisans, retailers, and other inhabitants
who had occasion to buy and sell[1]. This general privilege *that they*
was confirmed by Edward III. in 1342; but at that date, *were the representa-*
twelve distinct misteries had been specialised within the *tives of the ancient*
Merchant Gild; the trades of the Drapers, the Corn dealers *gild mer- chant,*
or Boothmen[2], and others, were separately organised, and *from which*
the choice of civic rulers was placed in their hands. The *the mis- teries*
members of those misteries did not forfeit their privi-
leges as gildsmen, in regard to the purchase of materials or
sale of goods, but the Merchant Gild had endless difficulty
in pursuing its policy of restricting each man to his own
branch of business, and of not allowing him to engage
in another calling, and especially in foreign commerce of
some form or other. As the coal trade developed in the
fifteenth century, a new specialised organisation of traders
arose; the export seems to have been chiefly conducted
by Normans, Bretons, Gascons, Flemings and other aliens[3]
who came in their own ships. The hosts, with whom *and the*
these men lodged, had a responsibility for their conduct[4], *hostmen had sprung*
both personal and commercial, and naturally acquired
supervision over their transactions; and the hostmen were
formed by Elizabeth into a regular company[5], charged
with authority to regulate this branch of commerce.
The members of the misteries had a right to become
free of this new company[6], but not to engage in the traffic
independently. From 1600, the date of this charter, onwards, the merchants of Newcastle left the management

---

[1] Every burgess whether poor or rich to have the liberty of going on board
the ships, either of foreigners or fellow subjects, and of buying merchandize
necessary for himself and family at prime cost. Nor were any goods to be sold in
such ships till a plank was laid on board, on pain of forfeiture. Brand, *History
of Newcastle*, II. 156.

[2] The small amount of corn grown in the northern counties rendered an
import trade in corn very important at Newcastle.

[3] *Trades Increase* (1615), Camb. Univ. Lib., Syn. 7. 61 (82), p. 11; also Brand,
II. 277.

[4] Cunningham, *Alien Immigrants*, 92.

[5] *Newcastle Merchant Adventurers*, I. xxxii.

[6] Brand, *History of Newcastle*, II. 274.

of this large trade[1] to the Hostmen[2]. At this point we can see the nature of the claim of the Newcastle Adventurers; they insisted that their body was the parent stock, from which the misteries, and the company of Hostmen, had

and that they did not derive their privileges from the Merchant Adventurers.

sprung; they repudiated the idea that they derived their powers from the Merchant Adventurers of England, or any comparatively recent grant, since they claimed to inherit the rights of the old Gild Merchant of the town. Their ordinances of 1480[3], and the grant of 1506[4], certainly seem to show that they had a continuous existence, and had good reason for refusing to admit the right of any newly constituted body to tax them.

Their principal business, at the beginning of the sixteenth century, appears to have been the export of wool and the other staple commodities of the realm. In 1519 they made an agreement with the General Court of Merchant Adventurers, that the Newcastle Company should pay £8 annually at the mart abroad, and that this should be a composition for the payments that would otherwise have been due from Newcastle merchants, individually, on their goods. In the seventeenth century, when their commerce had increased, and the General Court was in difficulties, traders at London and Hull may well have felt aggrieved at the exceptional terms which had thus been secured for Newcastle merchants. The latter were able to hold their own, though they were put to much expense in the repeated effort to assert their rights.

Their exports differed from those shipped from London,

The commodities in which the Newcastle Adventurers dealt were so different from those of their London brethren, that they were probably little affected by Cockayne's patent, or other attempts to protect English cloth-workers. They had their own troubles however; the export of wool to the

---

[1] Brand, II. 277. In 1615 there were 400 sail of ships employed, one half of which supplied London. The French came in fleets of 50 sail to fetch fuel, while Hanse ships took coal to Flanders.

[2] Acts regarding the Hostmen had been previously entered in the Merchants' Book (*Newcastle Merchant Adventurers*, I. 51). Bertram Anderson, a 'Merchant-venturer,' had taken an active part in coal mining and the coal trade. Brand, II. 266 n.

[3] *Newcastle Merchant Adventurers*, I. 1.

[4] *Ib.* p. xxv.

Low Countries was forbidden in 1618[1], and some years later, when they had developed a considerable business in the export of coarse cloth to Holland, the passing of the Navigation Act (1651) caused an interruption to their trade[2]. The troubles consequent on the Civil War also landed them in considerable difficulties, and Parliament grudged their shipping the protection they desired[3]; the London merchants would appear to have far greater claims, and were certainly in a better position for urging them.

The jealousy, which the merchants at out-ports felt of *and it was* London traders, seems to have had some justification; at all *difficult to bring both* events, we can see that the commerce of Newcastle and *branches of trade* Hamburg was so far distinct from the trade of the London *under one system of* Adventurers, that there must have been difficulty in bringing *regulation.* them all under one set of rules. Where the provincial merchants were admitted, their demands would tend to introduce complications into the orders of a regulated company; but from the joint-stock companies they were practically excluded altogether. The joint-stock companies were, for the most part, London undertakings; and the shipowners at other ports, if they desired to have employment for their own vessels in the particular branch of commerce assigned to any of these monopolies, could only find it as interlopers. During the period when company trading was vigorously maintained, London merchants had a preference as compared with those of the other ports[4]. On the one hand the decline of the regulated companies synchronised with the greater prominence of parliamentary

---

[1] *Newcastle Merchant Adventurers*, I. 119.

[2] *Ib.* I. 179.

[3] *Ib.* I. 156.

[4] Compare the argument on the African trade. "By this Exclusive Scheme, all the Out Ports of Great Britain which now depend Intirely on the Plantation Trade, and are already excluded from any Part of the Trade of Asia, by means of those Companies already on foot will also be excluded from that of Africa and America, whereby they must all decline by degrees, when this Trade falls to London, and the greatest Part of Great Britain confin'd to the Trade of Europe only. Which the said Out-Ports are very sensible of, as appears by the many Petitions, on this Subject, from time to time, wherein those of North Britain among other Reasons, set forth, that such a Monopoly would be a direct Breach of the Articles of Union." *Reasons against establishing an African Company at London*. Brit. Mus. 816. m. 11 (30).

legislation in regard to commerce, and on the other it allowed freer scope for the energies of the provincial traders.

The Levant Company survived as an exclusive body   **192.** The difficulties and inconveniences, which arose in connection with the system of regulated companies, are illustrated very clearly in the history of the Turkey Company; this was founded later, and continued to maintain its exclusive practice longer, than other similar companies. The principal factories were at Smyrna and Aleppo, which was the depot for trade with Persia[1]. There was a large demand at these points for English cloth; while raw silk, drugs of many sorts, and Eastern produce generally, formed valuable return cargoes. This traffic had been carried on by the Venetians and other Italians, until Englishmen obtained a footing in the time of Elizabeth[2]. The Company, which was authorised to regulate this trade, preserved its exclusive *through the* powers, and enjoyed a practical monopoly till 1753, that is, *first half of the eighteenth century.* till ninety years after the time when the chief complaints against the management of the Hamburg Merchant Adventurers had been set at rest.

The successful establishment of this Company followed some tentative experiments. Attempts had been made by Englishmen, during the sixteenth century, to obtain a share in the commerce of the Eastern Mediterranean; indeed, we hear of English ships trading with Scio as early as the reign of Henry VII.[3] The indefatigable Anthony Jenkinson was successful in obtaining some concessions in 1553[4]; and, in 1581, Elizabeth granted an exclusive patent, for seven years, to Edward Osborne and other merchants who adventured in *The Turkey merchants* this trade[5]. There were occasional trading voyages, but it was not till 1606, when the Turkey Company was re-constituted[6],

---

[1] Newberry, Fitch and Leedes, members of the Turkey Company, made their way to Bagdad, Ormuz and India. Cawston and Keane, *The Early Chartered Companies*, 73.

[2] S. P. D. El. ccxxxix. 40 to 44, and 80. Compare Hawkins' opinion on the advantage of a joint-stock in the Turkey trade. *Ib.* 124. On the scheme Burleigh adopted see *ib.* 140. See also *Calendar S.P.D.* 1592, p. 58, and above pp. 148 n. 3 and 215 n. 2. Common hostility to Spain drew England and Turkey together. P. Masson, *Histoire du commerce français dans le Levant*, xvii.

[3] Hewins, *English Trade and Finance*, 44.

[4] *Dictionary of National Biography*, s.v. *Jenkinson*, by Professor Laughton.

[5] P. Masson, *op. cit.* xvii.   [6] *Ib.* 120.

that regular trading intercourse was established between England and any part of the dominions of the Sultan.

A.D. 1603 —1689.

It was in connection with this trade, that Englishmen were first brought into direct competition with France,—the power with which they were to wage such a keen commercial struggle, in all parts of the world, during the eighteenth century. In the latter half of the sixteenth century, the French had succeeded in establishing factories at Constantinople, Alexandria, and Beyrout, and in securing a large share of the trade which had hitherto been carried on by the Venetians[1]. French statesmen and merchants have often dreamed of the East as a field for extension; one monarch after another tried to strengthen his hold upon Italy; and memories of the enterprise associated with the Crusades, and of the brilliant achievements of Jacques Cœur, shaped the commercial ambitions of Frenchmen in the sixteenth century. With the exception of the seamen of Rouen and Dieppe, who got but little encouragement, they seem to have been willing to leave the newly-discovered lands to Spain and Portugal, and to have preferred to confine themselves to Mediterranean trade. The 'Franks' had obtained exclusive privileges in 1535[2], which gave them a preference over all other Christian traders; but during the Wars of Religion, their manufactures were ruined, and their commerce languished for a time, so that the English and Dutch were able to obtain a firm footing in the trade[3]. The chief difficulties with which all Mediterranean traders had to contend were due to piracy; and it might have been expected that the exploits of Blake would have resulted in a great development of English trade. This anticipation was not realised, for the Company, which had received very extensive powers from Parliament in 1644[4], complained in 1657 of a complete declension of the trade[5]. In 1661, however, a new charter was granted; the affairs of the Company improved, and they were able to defray the salaries of the ambassador and

were brought into direct competition with the French,

who had preceded them in trade; but during the Wars of Religion, the French lost ground,

---

[1] P. Masson, *op. cit.* xv.

[2] *Ib.* xii.

[3] *Ib.* 118.

[4] Scobell, *Acts*, c. 33, Vol. I. 65.

[5] See above, p. 189 n. 5.

A.D. 1603
—1689.

*which they
more than
regained in
the time of
Colbert,*

*since the
Govern-
ment main-
tained
consuls*

*and
granted a
subvention
to the cloth
manu-
facture.*

consuls[1], but they also found themselves exposed anew to French competition. Colbert[2], on his accession to power, set himself to reform abuses and to re-organise this trade; under his fostering care, a very elaborate system of political and commercial privilege was gradually built up, to the admiration and envy of the less fortunate English traders.

The political expenses of the consular establishment in Turkey were borne by the French monarchs from the first, but no such assistance was given to the English Company, as it was not till 1803 that our Government assumed the appointment of representatives in Turkey[3] The charges thus involved must have been very heavy; and it was impossible to dispense with the existence of the Company, in some form or other, till public arrangements were made for discharging such duties[4]. But the French monarchs did not limit their care for their subjects to securing them a political status; they granted valuable assistance in the actual conduct of the trade. The chief article of export from France was woollen cloth, and this could not have been delivered in Turkey at such a moderate price, if it had not been for the liberal subvention accorded to the manufacturers in Languedoc[5]. Just as in recent years the French bounties on sugar have done serious injury to the English producers, so in the seventeenth century, the English advantage, for procuring materials used in the making of cloth, was discounted by the assistance rendered to the French manufacturers.

---

[1] Masson, *op. cit.* 121.   [2] *Ib.* 138.

[3] Hewins, *op. cit.* 54.

[4] The charter of the Company was surrendered in 1825.

[5] " 'Twas by thus giving Credit to Traders out of the Royal Treasury that the celebrated Monsieur Colbert first enabled France to rival England in the Woollen Manufactory; for after he had brought the French to furnish their own people, and clothe their own Nobility and Gentry and even the King himself, with their own Woollen Manufactures, and exclude the English manufacturers from France by a Law, they turned their Thoughts upon supplanting us at foreign Markets. To which End that great Statesman caused Credit to be given to Exporters, even till the Returns of their Woollen Goods came from abroad. This was done particularly to the Turkey Merchants at Marseilles, who had credit for the Woollen Manufactures of Nismes till the Return of their ships from Smyrna and Scanderoon, by which wise Encouragement the Marseillians first supplanted the English in the Levant trade, in which, we are too sensible, they have greatly increased ever since." M. Postlethwayt, *Considerations on the Revival of the Royal British Assiento* (1749), 18.

The companies' factories provided suitable places of residence for merchants and their agents, and membership con-
ferred many advantages. There were complaints, however, *The policy of the Turkey Company*
especially in the eighteenth century, as to the exclusive
practice of the Company. The point, on which the controversy chiefly turned, was as to the advisability of organising
one annual fleet to export English goods, instead of allowing
English merchants to send out ships as they liked. Trade
had been 'open' for four years previous to 1717, but at that
time it was determined to revert to the 'well-ordered'
system of annual fleets; and this practice was maintained *in or- ganising*
till 1743[1]. Those who criticised the Company pointed to *annual fleets was*
the success of the French, as compared with the chequered *much dis-*
career of the English Company. This was scarcely con- *cussed,*
clusive, however, as the methods of organising French trade
differed from time to time; though it seems to have been
most prosperous when it was not conducted on a joint-stock
basis, but was regulated by the Chamber of Commerce at
Marseilles[2]. The adherents of the Company urged that the
French system involved much more restriction than had
been forced on English traders[3], and that it was by imitating
the exclusive methods of the French that there was most hope
of success[4]. In view of the condition of trade, the Company *and the*
suspended all sailings for many months, and roused much *restrictions*
complaint among the merchants who were unable to ship
the cargoes they had purchased for export. At length, after
much discussion[5], Parliament was forced to intervene, and a

---

[1] The history of the changing policy, in regard to general or particular ships, from 1625 onwards will be found in some detail in Postlethwayt, *Dictionary* (s.v. *Oriental Trade*), iii. 380.

[2] Bonnassieux, *Les Grandes compagnies de Commerce*, 179.

[3] The advocates of the Company argued that the French trade was strictly a monopoly, while there was no real hindrance to prevent any English subject who desired to do so from engaging in the trade. *Some remarks on a late pamphlet* (1753) [Camb. Univ. Library, Dd. 23. 40]. For the whole history of this trade see Sir James Porter, *Observations on Religion, &c. of the Turks* (1771), p. 361.

[4] The great risks attending the trade gave some force to the contention that men of little capital should not be encouraged to enter it. Compare the story of the loss of the greater part of the Turkey fleet in 1693. Luttrell, *Brief Relation of State Affairs*, iii. 136—141.

[5] There was a long debate in 1744, but no action seems to have been taken at that time. *Parl. Hist.* xiii. 895.

*were set
aside in
1753,*

Bill was passed in 1753[1], which practically threw the trade open; the Company was thus brought into line with the Hamburg Merchant Adventurers and the Eastland Company, and there was no further complaint against it as a practical monopoly.

*under cir-
cumstances
which gave
rise to an
anti-
Semitic
agitation.*

The opening of the Company, in 1753, was of some interest, as it synchronised with a remarkable outburst of anti-Semitic feeling. The Jews had been, from time immemorial, the principal brokers in the Levantine ports[2]; and the proposal to naturalise the Jews alarmed the Turkey merchants, who feared that these brokers would compete with them in the business of shipping Eastern products to England. In this, as in other matters, they were following the example of the French, as an ordinance had been passed in 1727, carefully limiting the privileges of the Jews in connection with trade to France[3]. In England the opposition was not sufficiently strong to prevent the Bill for the Naturalisation of the Jews from becoming law in 1753[4], but an agitation immediately arose, which could only be allayed by the repeal of the measure in the following year[5].

*The
Turkey and
East India
merchants
competed
for the
Persian
trade,*

The Turkey Company was brought into competition, not only with the French merchants, but with the English East India Company; as both commanded access to supplies of Persian products, especially raw silk[6]. For many reasons public sentiment was inclined to favour the Mediterranean shippers. None of the objections, which were most commonly urged against the East India Company, held good of the Turkey merchants. They did not export bullion, so that they did not run counter to seventeenth century opinion; and they could claim that their trade reacted favourably on several branches of English industry, the test to which

---

[1] 26 G. II. c. 18. An Act for enlarging and regulating the trade into the Levant seas.

[2] *Parl. Hist.* xv. 98.

[3] Postlethwayt, *op. cit.*, s.v. *Levant Trade*, III. 66.

[4] 26 G. II. c. 26. Compare *Parl. Hist.* xiv. 1365; also Tucker, *Letter concerning Naturalisation* (1753).

[5] 27 G. II. c. 1.

[6] A statement of the two sides will be found in *The allegations of the Turkey Company and others against the East India Company* (1681). Brit. Mus. 522. 1. 5 (8).

eighteenth century publicists attached so much importance. A.D. 1603
—1689.
But though their criticism of their rivals was damaging, the
and the
Levant merchants did not make out a case for the main- regulated
tenance of their own privileges. Regulated companies, in Company
went to
any form in which they could control and restrict trade, were the wall.
becoming an anachronism, and the Turkey Company was
forced to succumb.

193. Important as these regulated companies were in *The first*
voyages of
their own day, their story is tame and insignificant when *the East*
India
compared with that of the East India Company. The career *Company*
of this association of traders, and the steps by which it
rendered English influence dominant in India, make it an
important factor in political history ; and in view of recent
developments, a great deal of economic interest attaches to
the first great trading company which was organised on the
principle of a joint-stock[1]. Not only so, but the long and
acrimonious controversies, which arose at different periods in
its history, are particularly instructive, as they turned on
broad issues, and throw much light on different phases of
contemporary opinion.

The East India Company was really a monopoly, in form *were made*
as separate
and according to its constitution, not merely practically and *ventures,*
in fact. The shareholders had one common purse ; no one
could enter into the trade by merely paying a fine ; he had to
purchase a share from one of the merchants who were in the
business already, and who might not always be ready to sell.
The Company was the sole seller of the goods it imported,
and there was nothing to prevent it from setting arbitrary
prices and making exceedingly large gains. The Company
had indeed been founded in 1600[2] as a regulated company[3],
and there is considerable interest in tracing the steps by
which it changed its form and established the type of joint-

---

[1] The joint-stock trading of the Muscovy Company appears to have been
earlier ; see above, p. 240.

[2] The materials for the history of the Company during the period when
separate voyages were organised will be found in Birdwood, *First Letter Book of
East India Company*, xiv.

[3] The undertaking was due to a sudden rise in the price of pepper, from 3 to 6
or 8 shillings a pound, owing to the monopoly of Dutch intermediaries. Birdwood, *op cit.* xliii.

A.D. 1603 —1689.

though each was on a common fund.

stock company which has become so common in all branches of trade. From the very first, this principle had been kept in view[1], and each of the separate voyages, organised by members of the Company, had been undertaken on a joint-stock; though some of the merchants, who were free of the Company, had subscribed for one venture, and some for another. The distance and risk of the enterprise were so great, that no one merchant attempted to trade on his own account, and the members of the Company were very particular in framing rules against private trading by any of their factors[2] or seamen[3]. In 1612 a change took place which increased the importance of the directors[4]; instead of having different funds, separately subscribed and managed for each voyage, the directors determined to have one joint-stock for all the purposes of the Company for a limited period, and that this aggregate fund should be officially administered by the Governor and directors. This course was forced upon them, not merely by difficulties in their accounts, and the impracticability of assessing establishment

Steps were taken in 1612

---

[1] Compare the petition of 1599 quoted by Hewins, *English Trade and Finance,* 56.

[2] "It is ordayened and decred that all the preparation of moneis, merchandizes and other provisions for this present voiadge, and all commodityes, moneis, Jewells and other merchandize retourned in the saide voiadge shalbe holden, reputed and accompted, and be carried, maunaged, ordered and handled as one entyre Joynte and Common Stock of adventure wherein no private traffique, barter, exchaunge or merchaundizinge shalbe used, practized or admytted by any particuler Governor, Capten, Merchaunte, Agent factor, master marinner, officer or other person whatsoever imployed in the saide voiadge, or permitted to goe in the same vppon payne of the losse and forfeiture to thuse of the Generall Companie and Adventurers in this voiadge of all sommes of money, Jewells, warres goodes or merchandizes which shallbe founde in the saide shippes or els where, carried forthe or retourned home by any private or particuler man, and not contayned and brought into generall and common accompte and joynte adventure of the saide voiadge. And to thend this prejudice of private traffique may the better be avoyded it is alsoe ordeyned and appointed yt due inquisicion be made in all and everie the severall shipps of the saide voiadge and elswhere by serche of all such Chestes, boxes, Packes, Packetts, books, wrytinges, and other meanes whereby discoverie may be made of the breache of this present ordinauuce." H. Stevens, *The Dawn of the British Trade to the East Indies,* p. 130.

[3] The Government discountenanced private trade, as it was apt to lead to smuggling: it could not be wholly suppressed, and it appears from the Proclamations 15 Feb. 1628, Brit. Mus. 1851. b. 3 (10) and 19 Feb. 1632, Brit. Mus. 506. h. 11 (2) that private trade to a limited amount was permitted.

[4] Mill, *History of British India,* I. 22.

charges satisfactorily, but by the trouble they had experienced in calling in the quotas of capital contributed
for separate voyages. In 1657 a further step was taken, *and 1657, which*
and the capital then raised was treated as a permanent *transform-*
fund, which was not destined to be divided among the *ed it into a joint stock*
subscribers[1]. *company.*

In spite of the hostility of the Dutch, and comparative
indifference at home, the Company was fortunate in forming
many important connections in the first century of its
existence. It founded factories[2] at Surat (1609[3]), Madras *They established*
(1639[4]), Hooghly near Calcutta (1650[5]), and Bombay (1665[6]), *several*
and its power gradually extended over the whole of *factories*
Hindustan; but Englishmen were not equally successful
in maintaining themselves in the Spice Islands; the Dutch
had been before them, and eventually drove them out
altogether. The massacre at Amboyna[7] in 1622, and the
loss of Poleroon in 1664[8], were two incidents which marked
the rivalry of English and Dutch merchants in the East,
and greatly embittered the feeling between the two nations.
There were also the disputes at Bantam, by which the
English were forced to retire, and establish themselves at
Bencoolen in 1682. But if they were confined in this one
direction, their trade was opened up in many others: they

---

[1] Hunter, *op. cit.* II. 150. The subscription list for shares of £200 and upwards
in the first voyage amounted to £30,133. 6s. 8d. and the first call was 1s. in the £100.
(Stevens, *Dawn of British Trade*, pp. 4, 17). This volume is a careful reprint of
the minutes of the Company, and gives most interesting details of the purchase,
fitting and victualling of the ships for the first voyage. Very great trouble was
involved in getting the subsequent calls paid, and the Lords of the Privy Council
were requested to put pressure on the members to pay up their promised shares
(*ib.* 165) while some additional capital was obtained by borrowing a *pro rata*
contribution from the members of the Company (*ib.* 110). Altogether there was
great difficulty in financing the scheme, though the promoters calculated on a
return of from 100 per cent. to 400 per cent. on the capital employed (*ib.* 152).
There were many delays before the ships could actually start, and much uncertainty as to the best cargo with which to lade them; a considerable amount
was taken in *reals* and they also took some handsome presents in plate (*ib.* 151)
to propitiate oriental princes.

[2] An admirable account of the organisation and history of the Madras factory
will be found in Penny, *Fort S. George.*

[3] Hunter, *History of British India*, I. 296.

[4] *Ib.* II. 80.   [5] *Ib.* II. 96.   [6] *Ib.* II. 193.

[7] Gardiner, v. 242.   [8] Macpherson, *Annals*, II. 530.

had obtained privileges in Persia in 1622, and had a factory in Japan from 1613 to 1623[1]. The rivalries of Europeans resulted in their taking different sides in the quarrels of native princes; and in this way, the East India Company had occasion to make use of its enlarged privileges after the Restoration, and to become a great political power, as well as a company for carrying on foreign trade.

*but they
had to
face much
hostile
criticism
as to the
effect of the
trade on
shipping,*
The company found on the whole that it was easier to propitiate princes abroad than to disarm the prejudices which their trade excited at home. Their opponents argued that these distant voyages had an injurious effect on the maritime power of the country. The vessels which sailed away for many months at a time could not be counted upon to render any assistance in the defence of the realm, as the ships of the Hamburg or Eastland Company might do; while the dangers of the Indian seas were so great, that many ships, and the lives of many seamen, had been lost. This objection was more especially heard in the early days of the Company, when the total shipping of the country was but small, and when the length of the voyage and the losses that occurred seemed to some to be out of all proportion to the gain[2]. The Company did indeed provide for the wives and children of those who were lost in its service, and "a thousand widows and some hundreds of blind and lame" joined in petitioning Parliament against the suppression of the Company[3]. The case in its favour could also be argued on more general grounds; as it was asserted that the Company, by providing employment for shipping and seamen, was giving an encouragement to all maritime trades and was thus indirectly promoting the maritime strength of the realm.

*and in
regard
to their
exportation*
Another objection, and one which it was much more difficult to meet, arose from the fact that the Company could not expect any large demand for English products in the East; they were forced to carry on their trade, as the Mediterranean peoples had done from time immemorial, by

---

[1] *Cal. S. P. Col. E. I.* 1513–1616, p. lxx.

[2] Compare the objections and answers printed in Sir D. Digges' *Defence of Trade* (1615), p. 16.

[3] *Petition of Margaret Walker*, Brit. Mus. 8223 e. 1 (47).

exporting bullion to India, and thus drawing upon the A.D. 1603
—1689.
supply of treasure at home. This difficulty was very *of bullion.*
strongly felt from the first, and the committee of governors
were ready to listen to any proposal for obviating it.
Mr George Waymouth[1] had inherited the enthusiasm for
forcing a north-west passage to the East, and it was argued
that in northern climates it would be possible to find a
market for English cloth, and that therefore trade could
probably be carried on with China, without any export of
bullion. "Wheras this society, in the setteing forth of their
late viage by the Cape of Bona esperansa towards the Islands
of Sumatra, Java, and other the parts therabouts, entendinge
to trade those Islands and places for Pepper, Spices, gould
and other merchandizes which are likest yeald the most
profitable returne for the Adventurors in the same viage, have
sett forth the greatest parte of their adventure in English
money Coyned of purpose for the said voyage, and other
forreine coine Current in those Islands, which moneyes and
coyne they could not prepare but with great difficultie and
trouble, and not without some mislike of the transportation
of treasure out of land. They therefore, beinge desirous to *This they*
use the priviledges to them graunted rather for the good of *endeavour-*
ed to
the Commonweale of theire Countrie then for theire private *obviate by*
opening a
benefite, and to maintayne the trade of the East Indies, if it *North-West*
passage,
be possible, by the transportation and vent of Cloth and other
the native Commodities of this Realme, without any money
at all or eles so litle as may be conveniently tollerated, Do
resolve to attempt the discovery of a Passage by seas into the
said East Indies by the Northwest thorough some parte of
America, which if they shall fynd navigable, Then shall they
by that passage arrive in the Countries of Cataia and China
beinge the Eeast parts of Asia and Africa, Climates of that
Temperature which in all likelihood will aforth a most

---

[1] Stevens, *op. cit.* 184. Compare an earlier attempt by John Davis (Camden,
Elizabeth, anno 1585, p. 324). A similar idea struck the Dutch and led to a north-
east passage expedition being sent out by merchants of Amsterdam (Davies,
History of Holland, II. 291). On the north-west passage, see A. Markham, *Voyages
and Works of John Davis*, 197. The subject seems to be fully discussed by
Sir W. Monson in *A yearly observation of the English and Spanish fleets from
1585 to 1603*; see *Hist. MSS. Comm.* III. Ap. 52; also *Ib.* IV. Ap. 251.

17—2

A.D. 1603
—1689. liberall vent of English clothes and kersies, to the generall advancement of the trafficke of merchandize of this realme *but without* of England[1]." The scheme for forcing a north-west passage *success;* was therefore originally taken up from a desire to save the export of bullion, and to find a new market for English goods. There were some difficulties with the Muscovy Company, who claimed that their existing patent for river trade with the East, gave them a prior claim to the fruits of the north-west trade also; eventually the voyage took place under the joint management of the two companies; but its failure contrasted strongly with the success which attended the Cape of Good Hope voyage, and the Company wisely threw their strength into this route.

As a consequence, the necessity for the export of bullion, in order to carry on the Company's trade, continued, and the advocates of the trade had difficulty in showing that it was *the ad-* not ultimately hurtful, and did not really deplete the country *vantage* of treasure. The classical piece on the subject was written *accruing* *from the* by Sir Thomas Mun, and entitled a *Discourse of trade from* *Company's* *trade* *England unto the East Indies*[2]; he argued that the export of gold and silver[3] was justified, since the spices taken in return were got with far less outlay than when they were obtained by an overland route, and through the intervention of Venetian and Egyptian merchants; while there was also a vent for some English goods in the East, and a profitable coasting trade to be done there. But the principal point was that by the sale of Indian products in Europe, England obtained far more of the precious metals in return than the

---

[1] Stevens, *Dawn*, 198.

[2] Published in 1621 and printed in Purchas' *Pilgrimes* (1625), i. 732.

[3] After the first voyage the Company were obliged to bring into the realm as much gold and silver as they had transported (John Shaw, *Charters relating to the East India Company*, p. 30). They were also permitted to re-export any foreign bullion which they themselves had introduced; but this permission did not give them the liberty they desired. This point is much discussed in a contemporary controversy on the course of the foreign exchanges. Misselden argues for the reality of the gain which accrued through the East India trade as a balance from the sale of Eastern goods in Europe (*Circle of Commerce*, 1623, p. 34), while Malynes held that this gain was illusory, unless there were a statute enforced for actually bringing in bullion in return for spices exported to other parts of Europe (*Center of Circle*, 1623, p. 114). The argument for the Company on this point is well put by Robinson, *England's Safety in Trades Encrease* (1641), p. 24.

sum that was needed to purchase them in the East; the A.D. 1603 —1689. coin sent to India was but the seed which brought back a large balance in coin by the sale of spices to other European nations[1]. These arguments proved convincing in the long *became* run; but the Company[2] can hardly be said to have emerged *more obvious,* from the experimental stages of its existence during the first half of the seventeenth century. The treatment their merchants received at the hands of the Dutch[3] roused widespread indignation, but James was so anxious to accept such terms as he could secure by peaceful means[4], that he neither obtained adequate redress for the Amboyna massacre[5] nor succeeded in securing a satisfactory status for the English *but it enjoyed* traders in the East. Under Charles I. the Company fared *little royal* little better; the Crown desired that the trade should be *patronage* controlled, but not that it should be monopolised in such a fashion as merely to enrich a coterie of merchants. . King Charles was on the one hand willing to grant licences to Sir William Courten and other interlopers, to engage in independent trade to Goa and any places where the Company had no factories[6], and on the other, demanded support from the chartered company[7]. During part of the Interregnum, the trade with the East was practically open[8]; but in 1657, after protracted discussions in the Committee on Trade[9], it was determined to re-establish the Company on

---

[1] An official statement of the case will be found in the *Petition and Remonstrance of the Governor and Company of the Merchants of London trading to the East Indies, exhibited to the Honourable the House of Commons assembled in Parliament*, 1628 (Camb. Univ. Lib.) Bb. 11. 39 (12).

[2] Its condition in 1620 was most unsatisfactory. *Hist. MSS. Comm.* III. Ap. 64, 65.

[3] *An Answer to the Hollanders Declaration concerning the occurrents of the East India Company*, 1622 [Camb. Univ. Lib. Bb. 11. 39 (7)]; also the official *True Relation of the Unjust, Cruell and Barbarous Proceedings against the English at Amboyne* (1624).

[4] Gardiner, *History*, IV. 408.

[5] This Cromwell obtained after the Dutch war in 1654. Hunter, *op. cit.* II. 110.

[6] Rymer. *Foedera*, XX. 146. Hunter, *History of British India*, II. 34, 37.

[7] The so-called Pepper Loan was a case in point. *Ib.* 30.   [8] *Ib.* 121.

[9] Sir William Hunter argues that Cromwell took a keen personal interest in fostering and establishing the Company's trade in the East (*op. cit.* II. 125—127). The evidence does not seem to me conclusive. Taken in conjunction with his willingness to relinquish so much of the East India trade to the Dutch (p. 198 above), his action only becomes self-consistent on the supposition that he thought,

a more permanent basis than it had ever enjoyed before[1]. It received a fresh charter when Charles II. came to the throne, and from this time forward it derived considerable advantage from royal patronage[2]. The special favour bestowed upon it roused the jealousy of other English merchants[3], and as the Company had become possessed of large powers of jurisdiction[4], it was able to indulge in most high-handed proceedings against its competitors in trade. From 1661 onwards, the East India Company was not only a trading monopoly but a political and judicial power.

Exception was also taken to the Company and its pro- This trade
was also
regarded
as a mis-
direction
of capital, ceedings from a more strictly economic standpoint. There was no plethora of capital[5] at that time, and there seemed to be reason to believe that the money employed in this branch of trade, might have been more usefully invested in developing the resources of the country[6]; it was thought that, even though the profit to the shareholders might not be so high, yet the advantage to the community would be greater. All sorts of projects for the improvement of

that if the trade was allowed to go on at all, it should be organised in the form of a joint-stock company, so that the government might be relieved as much as possible of any responsibility in regard to it. The possibility of obtaining financial assistance from wealthy companies was a consideration which Cromwell could not afford to neglect. *Cal. S. P. D.* 1655, p. 240.

[1] Hunter, *op. cit.* II. 129.　　　　[2] *Ib.* 185.　See below, p. 265.

[3] *An essay towards a scheme or model for erecting a National East India Joynt Stock* (1691), 9. Brit. Mus. 522. 1. 5 (9). The Crown specifically relinquished the power it had hitherto exercised (Hewins, *op. cit.* 66) of giving licences to subjects to trade without the company's consent. Shaw, *op. cit.* 41.

[4] Shaw, *op. cit.* 37, 45.

[5] The discussions on the high rate of interest bring out the fact that it was difficult to obtain capital for business purposes; see below, p. 384.

[6] Misselden, who was ready to defend the East India Company at other times, writes, "The special remote cause of our want of money is, the great want of an East India Stock here at home: for the stock of the East India Company, being of great value, and collected and contracted from all the other particular trades of the Commonwealth; and a great part thereof having been embargued and detained now for more than five years past; * * * this loss I say * * * is the more intolerable, in that the Commonwealth hath lost the use and employment of the stock itself, and all the increase of Trade which the same might have produced in the several trades of the subjects, whereby abundance of treasure might have been brought into this land in all this time." *Free Trade*, 1622, p. 13. The frequent discussions as to whether the Merchant Adventurers possessed sufficient capital to develop their trade is another illustration of the difficulty which was felt from the scarcity of capital in these times.

internal communications were being suggested, but they could not be carried into effect for want of money[1]. Canals were non-existent, roads were bad, much land was waste that could be drained and tilled, and many manufactures could be set agoing, if there were funds for the purpose; such was the general cry, and as banking was in its infancy, the capital which did exist was not so fully utilised as would now be done under our modern system of credit. As the Company became more successful, and was able to borrow money to a very large amount at three per cent., there were serious forebodings that any mischief which happened to the Company would entail ruin on large classes throughout the nation; just as eventually occurred through the failure of the Scottish Darien Company, and the bursting of the South Sea Bubble.

Still more serious grounds for objection lay in the fact that the East India Company exercised little, if any, beneficial effect upon the industry of the country[2]; it did not open up any considerable market for English cloth, nor introduce materials other than raw silk, of which a supply was already obtainable from the Levant. The importation of saltpetre, for the manufacture of gunpowder, was of course a matter of immense importance[3], and in this branch of commerce the East India Company had no rivals; but, so far as the ordinary manufactures of the country were concerned, it conferred little benefit. Spices and drugs were the chief commodities the Company imported; but after

A.D. 1603 —1689.

and as failing to stimulate English industry.

---

[1] The *Report on the Decay of Trade* (1669) shows that large sums of foreign capital were in the hands of Goldsmiths for investment in England; English capital was also sent abroad to Venice where a still higher rate of return could be obtained. *Hist. MSS. Comm.* VIII. Ap. 134.

[2] See below, p. 463. Compare the complaints in *England's Almanack showing how the East Indies Trade is prejudicial to the Kingdom*, 1700. Brit. Mus. 816. m. 11 (92). This sheet has engravings of weaving, wool-combing and spinning, as practised at the time.

[3] It was one of the conditions on which the Charter of 1693 was granted that the Company should deliver 500 tons of saltpetre annually to the officers of the Ordnance. John Shaw, *Charters relating to the East India Company from 1600 to 1761*, p. 111. Compare also the powers given in 1626 empowering the Governor and Company to erect Mills and manufacture gunpowder (Shaw, *op. cit.* IV.). Also the payment to the Company in July 1683 of £40,463. 10s. for 1,051 tons of saltpetre (*ib.* IX.).

the Restoration, when they obtained permission to export bullion without a licence[1], their trade increased enormously, and they began to import considerable quantities of textile goods, which were said to exercise an injurious influence on English manufactures. Commerce, which did not have a healthy reaction on the industry of the country but really brought foreign competition to bear upon it, was, in the point of view of many writers, gainful to the merchants engaged in it, but injurious to the community[2]. The most bitter controversy on this point arose in the decades succeeding the Revolution[3], when the development of the Company's trade seemed incompatible with the economic policy which had been adopted by Parliament.

The inter-lopers who resented the monopoly of the Company The great accession of business which occurred in the latter half of the century offered an inducement to many interlopers to enter into competition with the Company. They resented the monopoly of the Company; and found themselves in a worse position than ever. Licences were no longer granted; and the liberty they had obtained by agitation[4] in 1652 was withdrawn; the trade, which had been practically left open from 1653 to 1657[5], was lost to them. After the Restoration, when the Company was securely based on a joint stock, and the relations of the Company and the interlopers became more and more embittered, the merchants who had engaged in private shipping were inclined to take their stand on their constitutional rights[6].

---

[1] In 1663. 15 C. II. c. 7, § 12.

[2] The balance of trade in any particular line of traffic was taken as a criterion to show whether it was 'gainful' or 'losing' from the point of view of the community.

[3] See below, p. 463.

[4] Compare J. Darell, *Strange News from th' Indies* (1652), for a statement of the interlopers' case at that date.

[5] Hunter, *op. cit.* II. 121, 122.

[6] One case "was rendered famous by the altercation which it produced between the two houses of parliament in 1666. Thomas Skinner, a merchant, fitted out a vessel in 1657. The agents of the Company seized his ship and merchandise in India, his house and the Island of Barella, which he had bought of the king of Jambee. They even denied him a passage home; and he was obliged to travel overland to Europe." The Lords took up Skinner's cause, but the Company would not acknowledge their jurisdiction, and appealed to the Commons, who sent Skinner to the Tower. He obtained no redress, though the Lords had awarded him £5000. Mill, *History of British India*, I. 70.

The struggle was complicated by disputes that arose, about
1680, as to the management of the Company[1]. The principal
influence in the direction of the Company's affairs at home
lay with Sir Josiah Child, who threw in his lot heartily with
the Court party[2], and by his magnificent presents was able
to secure the patronage of the King and the Duke of York.
His brother, Sir John Child, co-operated with Sir Josiah
in his direction of affairs at Bombay: he showed himself
masterful and high-handed in putting down a rebellion in
the fort[3], and in making demands which brought about a
costly war with Aurungzebe. Had James II. maintained
his position on the throne, Sir Josiah might have weathered
the storm without much trouble; but the Revolution, by
depriving him of court influence, upset all his plans and
left him to face the opposition of .the interlopers, who
obtained unexpected support from Child's opponents in the *combined with the opponents of Sir Josiah Child*
government of the Company. Papillon and other Whigs,
who objected to the course which Child was taking with
the support of the Court, had been forced from their
responsible positions in the Company. They entered into
temporary alliance with the interlopers; but there was
no strong bond of union between the parties. The Whig
merchants were more eager to upset the autocracy of
Sir Josiah, and to prevent the possibility of its recurrence,
than to carry out the schemes of the interlopers, and throw
the trade open to the public generally, but this was the
aim of the merchants of the out-ports, and other interlopers.

It is by no means easy to form an opinion as to the

---

[1] *Some remarks upon the present State of the East India Company's Affairs* (1690). Brit. Mus. 522. l. 5 (1).

[2] Macaulay, *History of England*, IV. 136. Hunter, *op. cit.* II. 286. Child's writings on commercial subjects are interesting; he was an opponent of regulated companies, though he insisted so strongly on the advantages of a joint-stock Company. His low opinion of parliamentary wisdom came out in his refusal to accept the terms proposed to him in 1693 for an accommodation between the two companies. The following phrases are attributed to him, "I expect my will and orders shall be your rule, and not the laws of England, which are a heap of nonsense compiled by a number of ignorant country gentlemen who hardly know how to govern their own families, much less the regulating companies and foreign Commerce." James Macpherson, *History and Management of the East India Company*, 18.

[3] A very severe indictment of him will be found in Hamilton's *New Account of the East Indies* (1727), I. p. 213.

precise position and grievances of the interlopers at this time. The Company had been supported in its claim to possess exclusive rights to trade with heathen lands in the East[1], but in face of the Declaration of Right, there would have been great difficulty in continuing, on the strength of a royal charter, to exercise the judicial powers by which the Company attempted to enforce its claims. On the other hand, it was easy to contend that the intrusion of the independent merchants into territory, where the Company had secured privileges at great trouble and expense[2], was both unfair *to thwart* and unwise. Since arrangements with native powers were *and harass* *the Com-* inevitable, the formation of a corporation, to conduct both *pany* commercial and political intercourse, appeared advisable. The intense irritation of the Company against the interlopers becomes intelligible, when we see that independent commerce was scarcely possible, except at the points where the Company's agents were already established. It appears, too, that much of the interlopers' trade was mere piracy, and that the Company suffered severely, in their relations with native princes, because of outrages committed by Englishmen for whom they were in no sense responsible. Thus, in 1695, one of the interlopers, who had failed to make a profit on his cargo, seized some native ships, including one belonging to Abdul Gophor, a leading merchant at Surat, and one belonging to the Mogul, which was carrying pilgrims to Mecca. As the natives could not distinguish between one English ship and another, the Company was held responsible for these outrages, and very serious complications ensued[3].

The power which the Company had of dealing with these abuses was directly derived from the Crown. On the accession of William III., the English merchants had regarded him with considerable suspicion, as they feared he might subordinate their interests to those of the Dutch East India Company[4]; but William's necessities in connection with his

---

[1] Shaw, *Charters*, vi. (13 Charles II.).

[2] Sir Thomas Roe, who was sent in 1614 as an ambassador to Jehangir, obtained a promise of liberty to trade and establish factories at Surat, Bengal and Sinde, or any part of the Great Mogul's dominions. Mill, *History of British India*, i. 23. On the successful negociations a century later, 1716, see *Ib.* iii. 23.

[3] Bruce, *Annals of the Honourable East India Co.*, iii. 187 sq.   [4] *Ib.* iii. 5.

continental wars, rendered him not unwilling to grant privi- A.D. 1603
—1689.
leges to English merchants who were able to assist the
Government. The Company had been empowered to execute martial law, and to exercise Admiralty jurisdiction at
Bombay[1], and under these powers they carried out very
severe sentences upon their competitors in trade. Still the
Company could not but feel that their position was somewhat insecure; and the chief object of their policy at home
was to procure a confirmation of their privileges, not merely
by Charter but by Act of Parliament. In this, however, they *which*
were foiled, and the Company had to be contented with re- *failed to obtain par-*
ceiving two additional charters in 1693[2]; by the latter of *liamentary sanction*
these their monopoly was granted for twenty-one years; the *for its*
constitution of the Company was carefully defined, and it *privileges,*
was provided that the dividends must be paid in money
only[3]. There was also a provision that the Company should
export[4], each season, £150,000 worth of English manufactures[5]; this might help to satisfy the critics who objected
that the trade was not beneficial to English industry.

The directors were by no means content with their
position, however; and the fact that the Scotch (East India)
Company had obtained Parliamentary powers[6]—the only
success which attended the ill-fated Darien Company—en-

---

[1] *Ib.* II. 497. [2] *Ib.* III. 133, 134.

[3] This was one of the points in which the East India Company differed from
the Dutch, which paid its dividends partly in produce. Another point lay in the
constitution of the Dutch Company in "Chambers" which were representative of
the different states. Its close relations with the Government enabled the Company
to exert a more complete influence in Holland than our Company ever succeeded
in doing in the English Parliament (Bruce, III. 135). The constitution is described in detail by Raynal (I. 249), *A Philosophical and Political History of the
Settlements and Trade of the Europeans in the East and West Indies.* Its
peculiarities were due to the fact that the Company was formed by fusion of
several private associations. Hunter, *op. cit.* I. 334.

[4] This was a stroke of policy which had been entirely neglected by the Portuguese. The effort to garrison their foreign possessions drained the mother
country of its population and industrial resources, while the trade gave no
stimulus to Portuguese agriculture or manufactures; it was the object of William
to insist that the Company should give a vent for English products and not
merely serve as a means of enriching the official class (Raynal, *op. cit.* I. 153).

[5] Norfolk camlets and certain West of England serges were expressly manufactured for this trade. See below, p. 795, n. 4.

[6] *Acts of Parliaments of Scotland,* IX. 377 (June 26, 1695).

A.D. 1603
—1689.

*despite
liberal
bribery,*

couraged them to hope that they would meet with similar favour[1]. Although their resources were somewhat crippled, they spent large sums in corrupting[2] public men. The House of Commons ordered an enquiry into this matter, and found that in 1693 the amount expended had reached £90,000, of which it is said that £10,000 was traced to the King[3]. The feeling of the House of Commons was thoroughly hostile to the existing Company, which they regarded as utterly corrupt. They passed a resolution "that all the subjects of England have equal right to trade to the East Indies unless prohibited by Act of Parliament[4]"; and in a subsequent session, they inflicted a very serious blow on the existing London Company by passing an Act, which enabled the Whig dissentients and the interlopers to float a new, or

*and a new
General
Company
was erected.*

General, as distinguished from the London Company[5]. The Company so formed was a regulated company, and each of the members was able to trade on his own account; but they were not restricted to this method of doing business, as the majority were also empowered to trade together on a joint stock.

*After a
period of
rivalry*

For these rights the merchants and interlopers, who floated the new Company, were forced to pay exorbitantly. They advanced £2,000,000 to the Government at 8 per cent.[6], on the understanding that they should have an exclusive right

---

[1] Bruce, III. 177 n.

[2] This was not a new thing; the Long Parliament had a bad reputation in regard to bribery. See above, p. 182. Nor was the Restoration Parliament exempt from this blot. "It was moved at this Court (10 Jan. 1664) that it was necessary some gratification should be made to the Northern Members of Parliament that had been very active to hinder an Act of Parliament that was endeavoured to be passed to lay an imposition upon all foreign iron imported. After a learge and serious debate thereof it was agreed that in regard it was generally known that the Residents at Hull had already gratified some particular members for their service in this business that Mr Deputy (Bryan Dowson) should chardge the sum of £5 for this purpose in his accompt but to keepe it in his own hands till his account was passed and allowed of." *Acts of Eastland Company*, 88.

[3] Mill, *India*, I. 93.

[4] *Parl. Hist.* v. 828.

[5] 9 and 10 W. III. c. 44, § 52.

[6] Bruce, III. 252—5. This offer was preferred to that of the old or London Company, who were willing to provide £700,000 at 4 per cent., but the exigencies of the European war made Parliament prefer the larger and more expensive loan.

to trade after 1701. This new Company was from the first A.D. 1603
—1689. hampered by want of capital. They had difficulty in getting their calls paid, and no ready money was available until the interest was obtained from Government. The London Company not only endeavoured to maintain its advantages during the three years that remained to it, but also subscribed to the new Company; so that the old body might be able to carry on operations as an independent trader within the new society, even after its own exclusive rights had come to an end. The position, which was thus created by the rivalry of the two Companies, both in the East and in England, was soon found to be quite intolerable. After lengthy negociations, Lord Godolphin was empowered by Act of Parliament[1] to ar- *the two* bitrate between them. As a result of an arduous investiga- *Companies were united* tion, the United Company of Merchants of England trading to the East Indies was established in 1708. By this means, the exclusive rights of the combined Company were guaranteed not merely by the Crown but by Act of Parliament till 1726, and by a later Act till 1733[2]. It may be said that the view of policy, for which the directors of the old or London Company had contended, was now endorsed by Parliament. The experience of the English Company[3], the members of which at one time opposed the principle of trading on a joint stock, *on a joint* had after all told in its favour. Parliament accordingly *stock basis.* accepted the principle of giving a corporation of traders exclusive rights, as against other English subjects; and in 1718 they sustained the objection to interlopers, so far as to empower the Company to punish their competitors when trading under foreign commissions[4]. The cost of obtaining these privileges had been so great that the Company was placed at a serious disadvantage in prosecuting its proper business. So much money had been employed for political

---

[1] 6 Anne, c. 17. [2] 10 Anne, c. 28.

[3] A second charter dated 5 Sep. 1698 (quoted 6 Anne, c. 17) empowers the majority of the members of the newly created Company to trade as a joint stock. This joint-stock branch of the General Company was technically the English Company referred to in the text. Bruce, III. 258.

[4] 5 G. I. c. 21. A proclamation to this effect had been issued by the Crown in 1716. Mill, III. 18. These powers were further enforced and extended by 7 G. I. c. 21; 9 G. I. c. 26.

purposes, at home and abroad, that the directors were constantly hampered for want of capital to carry on the trade[1].

In 1730, three years before the expiry of the United
Company's privileges, the struggle was renewed by the
interlopers. It was now admitted by the opponents of the
Company that it was necessary in the interests of trade to
Subsequent maintain considerable establishments abroad. Under the
agitation
on the part existing *régime* the expenses of these establishments were
of the
Interlopers defrayed out of the gross profits of the joint-stock Company.
The new proposal was that these charges might be met by
the interest on £3,200,000, which was owing to the Company
by the Government, together with customs on the trade[2];
and it was argued that if the factories were maintained in
this fashion, it would be possible to dispense with the joint
stock, and throw the trade open to the public. This scheme
was supported by petitions from merchants in London, Bristol
and Liverpool. Public opinion, which exaggerated the gains
to be derived from the East India trade, was strongly in
favour of the new project; and the Company could only
secure the renewal of their exclusive powers till 1766, by
consenting that the rate of interest paid by the Government
should be reduced to 4 per cent., and by contributing a fine
of £200,000 for the continuance of their privileges[3]. In
failed 1744, however, they gave additional assistance to the Govern-
to break
down the ment, during the war of the Austrian Succession, by lending
monopoly
of the them £1,000,000 at 3 per cent.; and they thereby obtained
Company, an extension of their exclusive privileges till 1780[4]. Before

---

[1] An attempt was made to remedy this by 7 G. I. c. 5, § 32, which authorised
the Company to borrow to the amount of the sums due to them from the public.
This fact also explains the extraordinary difference between the profits of the
English and of the Dutch Company. The latter divided 25 per cent. from
1732—36, when the English could only pay 7 per cent. (Mill, III. 35). Of course the
money sunk in diplomatic and judicial expenses at home and abroad was unremunerative. The capital of the Dutch Company was only £565,236 (Raynal, I.
259), while that of the English Company at the same period was over £3,000,000
(Mill, III. 18, 359). The extraordinary fortune of the Dutch in capturing Portuguese vessels and supplanting them in foreign states enabled them to obtain a
footing with this very small capital; they confined their political ambitions
abroad, and owing to their constitution, secured a large interest in the Councils
of State at home.

[2] Mill, *op. cit.* III. 27.   [3] *Ib.* III. 34.
[4] 17 G. II. c. 17.

that time arrived, the magnitude of the interests involved, and the discreditable rumours which were afloat, had roused a storm of indignation. The House of Commons appointed a committee of inquiry in 1766, and the Company was re-constructed in 1773.

A.D. 1603
—1689.

Time after time, and under one Government after another the principle of joint-stock trading to the East was re-affirmed, despite the persistent efforts of merchants at the out-ports to have it thrown open. There were Englishmen, however, on whom the Company's system of trading pressed more heavily than it did on the inhabitants of Great Britain. The colonists of North America felt the grievance of being debarred from a direct trade with the East, and they showed scant respect to exclusive privileges conferred by a Parlia-ment in which they were not represented. Though they were prohibited from having a part in legitimate trade, they could not be prevented from taking their chance of plunder. The extent to which piracy was developed by the colonists, with the connivance of some of the authorities, would be incredible, if it were not established by abundance of docu-mentary evidence. The Earl of Bellomont reported to the Council of Trade in 1698, "I find that those pirates that have given the greatest disturbance in the East Indies and Red Sea, have been either fitted from New York or Rhode Island, and manned from New York[1]." The business was ingeniously organised. When the pirates "had taken prizes in the Indian or Red Sea they brought the spoils to Mada-gascar, and then merchant ships from this port were fitted out by the owners of such pirate's ships and others, who landed here publickly with goods usefull to the Pirates, as Liqur, Arms and Gunpowder, and these ships returned back to this port with East India goods, either purchased from the pirates or belonging to them[2]." Such precautions were hardly necessary at the time when Fletcher was Governor of New York. He "commissioned these vessels and granted individual protections to their crews. One hundred dollars

which the American Colonists were ready to defy.

---

[1] *Documents relative to the Colonial History of the State of New York,* edited by E. B. O. Callaghan, iv. 306.

[2] *Ib.* 323.

per man was the price asked for this official indulgence[1].
His council consisted of merchants generally interested in
the expedition. The governor, his wife and daughter, all
received presents from the pirate chieftains. He sold a
vessel given him for £800[2]. Hore, a famous privateer or
pirate, was commissioned in *The Fortune* from New York for
the Red Sea, and brought home a rich cargo of East Indian
Commodities, which was partly shared among the members
of the council[3]." The grievances of the colonists in connection with the East India trade were similar to those
which were experienced by the English interlopers, or by
the merchants of the out-ports who engaged in the Hamburg trade. So long as regulated trade was maintained,
there was a danger of such conflicts; but the merchants at
home do not seem to have organised such lawless schemes
in order to participate in the commerce of a chartered
company.

194. While the history of the East India Company
illustrates the triumph of the principle of joint-stock trading,
for distant intercourse and for an undertaking on a very
large scale, other experiments, on the same lines, were less
successful. There was, for a time, a joint-stock bank to carry
The joint-stock principle was also applied on commerce with the Morea[4], in connection with the Levant
Company, and the whale fishery gave rise to some attempts
of a similar kind. There is more interest, however, in the
repeated schemes for establishing an African Company with
exclusive rights of trading. This body, in its various forms,
received hearty support from royalty, and it was favourably
regarded by the nation; but in spite of this, the interlopers
managed to hold their own, and to frustrate all attempts to
oust them from the Guinea trade.

---

[1] Callaghan, *op. cit.* 307.   [2] *Ib.* 480.

[3] Weeden, *Economic and Social History of New England*, I. 344. The account
of Thomas Few is also worth quoting; this pirate was well known both at New
York and Newport R. I. "He flitted often to the Red Sea and was on the Black
List of the East India Company. Fletcher entertained him, exchanged gold
watches and carried him in his coach; when the Lords of Trade remonstrated,
the artless governor replied that he wished to make Captain Few a sober man.
In particular he wished to reclaime him from a vile habit of swearing." *Documents
relating to the colonial history of the State of New York.* IV. 447.

[4] Macpherson, *Annals*, under 1593, II. 202.

The beginning of an organised trade to Guinea from London[1] has been usually assigned to 1618, when a patent for a joint-stock company was granted by James I. to Sir Robert Rich and others[2]; but the private traders would not give way, and after a brief existence, the Company was dissolved. In 1631, Charles I. granted a similar patent to Humphry Slaney[3] and others; and serious attempts were made to establish factories and to build forts, in the hope of obtaining a footing in a trade which had fallen into the hands of the Dutch[4]; but no permanent success attended the undertaking. In 1651 the privileges thus granted were confirmed to Rowland Wilson[5]; but the principal business, so far as English trades were concerned, was done by the East India Company[6], which was allowed to use the Guinea factories; its ships exported English cloth to Africa, and obtained in exchange the gold which enabled the Company to drive a trade in India. During the Interregnum, little pains were taken to support a privileged body[7] and the trade was practically open; there were, in consequence, the usual complaints that the interlopers sold inferior goods which injured the repute of English wares[8], and spoiled the market

A.D. 1603 —1689. in the African trade.

Several Companies were organised in succession,

---

[1] A patent had been granted for this trade to some Exeter Merchants, with one or two London members as well, by Elizabeth in 1588. It was to last for two years, and at least three voyages were made, with considerable success. Macpherson, *Annals*, II. pp. 189, 193, 200.

[2] Macpherson, *op. cit.* II. 292.

[3] Rymer, *Fœdera*, XIX. 370. *Certain Considerations relating to the Royal African Company of England* (1680), p. 3.

[4] *Reflections upon the Constitution and Management of the Trade to Africa* (1709), p. 5

[5] *Certain Considerations relating to the Royal African Company*, 3.

[6] Compare *Answer of Company of Royal Adventurers trading to Africa* (1677), p. 7. Macpherson, *Annals*, II. 370.

[7] Cawston and Keane, *Early Chartered Companies*, 103. "By the many Revolutions of Government here the Trade of Guiney fell into great disorders, and the stock of that Company was much impaired by the intrusion of Interlopers; which the Dutch and Danes observing, encreased their Number of strong Forts, Factories and Ships of War on the Coast of Guiney, and thereby did not only defend and encourage their own, but during these times took also the ships and goods of the English private Traders to the value of £300,000 or thereabouts as was made appear to his Majesty after his happy Restauration." *Certain Considerations relating to the Royal African Company of England* (1680), Camb. Univ. Lib. Bb. 10. 5 (1), p. 3.

[8] Stow, *Survey*, Bk. V., p. 269.

C.

18

A.D. 1603
—1689.

under
princely
patronage
by reckless competition[1]. At the Restoration, when there seemed to be an opportunity of securing a large share of the commerce with Brazil[2], the work of developing the African Trade was taken up by the Duke of York and Prince Rupert, and a third attempt was made to start a joint-stock company[3], with exclusive rights; all trade was prohibited except by the Company in vessels it authorised[4]. But this new scheme hardly had a fair chance; as their constant conflicts with the Dutch involved the merchants in serious losses both of shipping and stations[5]. The opponents of the Company attributed its misfortunes to its fault, and pleaded for an open trade[6]; but the advocates of the joint-stock principle were successful in floating a more ambitious experiment than ever, when the Company was re-constructed in 1672[7].

and with
popular
support;
The trade was generally viewed with favour by the public; it offered a fair vent for English goods; it supplied gold and ivory, as well as materials for dyeing and other industries[8],

---

[1] The Act 12 C. II. c. 24 establishes a principle of limited liability for share-holders in the East India or Guinea Companies, while private traders who were unsuccessful might of course be declared bankrupts. See below, p. 817.

[2] *A detection of the Proceedings and Practices of the Directors of the Royal African Company* (1749) 2. Brit. Mus. T. 788 (5).

[3] S. P. Colonial America (1663), No. 408.

[4] Stow, Bk. v. p. 268.

[5] S. P. Colonial (1663—1668), Nos. 618 and 903.

[6] The arguments on each side will be found in the *Answer of the Company of Royal Adventurers of England trading to Africa to the Petition exhibited by Sir Paul Painter*, 1667, Camb. Univ. Lib. Bb. 4. 16 (3).

[7] S. P. Colonial America (1672), No. 934. The financial history of the Company has been worked out with great thoroughness by Dr W. R. Scott in the *American Hist. Review*, VIII. 244.

[8] Macpherson, *Annals*, II. 569. "They introduced and encouraged the making of several Sorts of Woollen and other Goods, proper for the Trade of *Guinea*, not formerly manufactur'd in *England*, and reduced the making thereof, to a staple and settled Goodness; they exported yearly upward of Seventy Thousand Pounds worth of the said Wollen, and other Manufactures; and gave far better Prices for the same, than what usually is now given for the like; they furnish'd the *Western* Plantations with frequent Supplies of considerable Numbers of Negroes, at very moderate Rates; and in so encouraging a manner too, that they sometimes trusted the Planters, to the value of a Hundred Thousand Pounds and upwards, till they could conveniently pay the same; They imported (beside *Elephants' Teeth, Red wood* and other Goods fit for being manufactured at Home) such Quantities of *Gold Dust* from the Coast of *Africa*, that they frequently Coin'd Thirty, Forty or Fifty Thousand Guineas at a time, with the Elephant upon them, for a Mark of Distinction." *Reflections upon the Constitution and Management of the Trade to Africa* (1709), p. 6. Brit. Mus. 712. m. 1 (19).

while it afforded facilities for the supply of labour to the A.D. 1603
—1689. West Indian islands and American plantations[1]. It seemed necessary[2], too, that it should be conducted on a joint stock, so that the charges for the forts and other establishments might be most conveniently defrayed. But the princely initiative and royal patronage were of little avail; the Company dragged on a chequered existence[3], and as it had no parliamentary status[4], there must have been difficulty *but they* *could not* in enforcing its regulations. As the interlopers had no *compete* expense in maintaining forts and factories, they were *against the* *interlopers,* able to outbid and undersell the Company, and in 1698 Parliament was forced to interfere. The Act then passed definitely declared the trade open, but insisted that the traders should pay a 10 per cent. duty to the Company, which might provide for the maintenance of the necessary fortifications and establishments[5]. The Company continued their joint-stock trade, but failed in their attempts to secure a monopoly[6]; while the interlopers were equally unsuccessful

[1] The slave trade had become an accepted fact, though the Spaniards had been opposed to it at first. Ximenes did his utmost to prevent the King of Spain from permitting the trade. Robertson, *America* (1808), I. 319. The opinion of a canonist is worth quoting: "Quod si libere veneunt non est cur mercatura illa crimine ullo denotetur. Veruntamen si, quae jam percrebuit, vera est fama, diversa est ferenda sententia. Sunt enim qui affirmant fraude et dolo calamitosam gentem seduci. * * * Quae ei vera est historia, neque qui illos capiunt, neque qui a captoribus co-emunt, neque illi qui possident, tutas habere unquam conscientias possunt quousque illos manumittant, etiam si pretium recuperare nequeant." D. de Soto, *Libri X de Just. et Jure*, l. iv. q. ii. a. 2, p. 103.

[2] *Certain Considerations*, p. 7.

[3] It was attacked by Roger Coke, *Reflexions upon the East India and Royal African Companies* (1695), a tract in which the case against monopolies is forcibly stated.

[4] Parliament so far recognised its existence in 1692 as to lay a contribution of £1 per share on the shareholders. 4 and 5 W. and M. c. 15, § 11.

[5] 9 and 10 W. III. c. 26. *An Act to settle the trade to Africa.*

[6] Macpherson, II. 702 and III. 17. In 1711 a great effort was made by the Company to secure the sanction of Parliament to the erection of a Joint Stock Company in this trade. "If the present Company's Charter had been confirm'd by Act of Parliament, so as to have prevented the many Obstructions and Difficulties, which they have been forced to struggle with, these twenty Years last past, the *British* Interest on the Coast of *Africa* had been, by this time, in a much more flourishing Condition. * * * However, it so happened that soon after the Revolution, the Interlopers, breaking in upon the Privileges of the Royal African Companies' Charter, and thereafter the Parliament being in the year 1697 induced, for an Experiment, to grant a Permission to all His Majesty's subjects, as well as the

in obtaining admission to the Company[1]. But the affairs of the Company did not prosper; the duties paid by the interlopers did not cover the expenses of the maintenance of the forts. In 1711, the Company were forced to get a special Act to enable them to make an arrangement with their creditors[2], and were obliged to make a call of 5 per cent. on the shares in 1722. Like the East India Company, the African Company were weighted because they had wasted much of their capital, or sunk it in forms which were not directly remunerative; and in 1727 they attempted to cut down their nominal capital[3], so that each proprietor of a nominal £800 should be credited with only £100 of actual capital[4]. Despite the serious state of things, the Company was not allowed to collapse. As the nation was determined to maintain trading settlements in Africa, Parliament granted them £10,000 a year annually from 1730 onwards[5]. Even this liberal aid proved insufficient; *and a* *regulated* *Company* *was or-* *ganised,* and affairs became so desperate, that Parliament interfered[6], and passed a measure[7] in 1750, which wound up the joint-stock African Company and incorporated all merchants trading to Africa as a regulated Company. The fine for

Company, to trade to and from Africa for the span of 13 years, they paying to the Company a Duty of ten per cent. upon their Exports towards defraying the Charge and Expences of their Forts and Settlements in those Parts, the Trade has ever since fallen into great Disorders and Confusions." *The Case of the Royal African* *Company.* Brit. Mus. 816. m. 11 (14). The Company appears to have dealt very hard measure to the interlopers. "Many have been robb'd of their Ships and Goods, divers have been Imprison'd, and some have lost their Lives. These things have been done by the African Company, by colour of an illegal Patent they call their Charter. Which Company have carried on their Oppressions with a high hand and in contempt and defiance of the Law. If their Patent were Legal, they would have no need of an Act of Parliament, for none would or could oppose a Legal Patent." *The Case between the African Company and the People* *of England.* Brit. Mus. 816. m. 11 (15). A large number of broadsides on the African trade will be found in the same volume; compare also the tracts in Brit. Mus. 8223. e. 4.

[1] Macpherson, *Annals*, III. 9.   [2] 10 Anne, c. 27.

[3] The want of success which attended the operations of the African Company is reflected in the price of their stock, which was selling at £4. 10s. per £100 share in 1711 when the East India Company shares were at £124. 10s., the Bank shares at £111. 5s., and the South Sea shares at £77. 10s. (Macpherson, III. 22.)

[4] Macpherson, III. 136.

[5] In 1744 £20,000 was granted. Macpherson, III. 154.

[6] See the debate and petitions, *Parl. Hist.* xiv. 564.   [7] 23 G. II. c. 31.

admission was fixed at 40s., and the members of the A.D. 1603 —1689.
Company[1], in London, Bristol and Liverpool, were entitled
to choose members of a committee who were to manage *in the management of which the outports were represented.*
affairs, subject to the approval of the Commissioners for
Trade[2]. The public compensated the old Company for their
forts and other possessions with £112,000; and the new
Company obtained all their property, and secured powers
to arm military forces, to punish offences, and to decide
mercantile cases[3]. Under this new arrangement, the expense
of maintaining the forts was borne by the nation, but the
public funds were administered by a committee of merchants[4];
all British subjects were practically able to join in the trade,
and to have a voice in the election of the committee. The
experience of a few years, however, showed that this method
did not answer better than the old one, so far as the maintenance of the forts was concerned[5]. The total public money
which passed through the hands of the committee between
1750 and 1776 amounted to £343,400; while the fortifications had become ruined and useless, and the officials
of the Company took advantage of their position to carry on
private trade, on much more favourable terms than could be
done by ordinary traders[6]. This branch of commerce had been *The inter-lopers were successful*
organised in three distinct forms; as an exclusive and joint-
stock Company, and this had failed several times; secondly as
a joint-stock Company trading alongside of private traders
who paid it duties; thirdly as a regulated Company; but at no
time had it been able to work at a profit, and in both of its
later forms it had been largely subsidised by Government[7].

The failure of the Company to hold its own, either as
a joint-stock or regulated Company, despite the strong case

---

[1] On the working of this scheme, compare *Parl. Hist.* xix. 301.

[2] Macpherson, III. 280.   [3] *Ib.* 290.

[4] 4 G. III. c. 20. By this Act the fort of Senegal and its dependencies, which had been recently acquired, were handed over to the Company.

[5] The trade appears to have been very profitable. Hippisley, *Essays on the trade, populousness etc. of Africa* (1764), p. iii.

[6] Report of Commissioners of Trade to House of Commons, summarised by *Macpherson*, III. 603. See the debate in *Parliamentary History*, xix. 1.

[7] In 1765 (5 G. III. c. 44) some of the forts and settlements were vested in the Crown, but restored to the Company in 1783. Finally the Company was dissolved (1 and 2 G. IV. c. 28) and its possessions were vested in the Crown.

A.D. 1603 —1689.

as they had advantages for prose-cuting the same trade

it was able to present, was chiefly due to the character of the most profitable branch of its trade. The interlopers were supported in their demands for an open trade by the planters, who complained that the Company engrossed the supply of labour, and thus raised the price of negro-slaves[1]. The private shippers, engaged in this trade, regarded the apparatus of forts and factories as quite unnecessary; they did not desire to frequent a secure centre of commerce, but merely to carry on slave-raids on the coast as opportunity offered[2].

and were favoured by

The controversy between the Company and the combined interests of the planters[3] and the interlopers broke out again

[1] There is an early and very interesting protest against Negro Slavery in *A Letter from a Merchant at Jamaica to a Member of Parliament in London touching the African Trade, to which is added A Speech made by a Black of Guadaloupe at the Funeral of a Fellow Negro* (1709) [Brit. Mus. 1061. g. 17 (2)].

[2] "The said Guinea trade for Negroes was formerly Free to all Adventurers, and that without prejudice to the gold trade there which was heretofore managed by the East India Company, for that same cannot be well maintained without a great and general Charge as the building of Forts, settling continual Factories, etc.; which the trade for negroes in no wise requires; It being the most usual way for the said Adventurers to procure their Negroes, by ranging or coasting it along those vast Territories, without intrenching up or assistance of the said Factories and Forts." *An Answer*, &c. p. 6.

[3] It was originally raised by the petition of Sir Paule Painter and Ferdinando Georges, which was referred to the Committee on Trade by the House of Commons on Friday, 15 Nov. 1667 (*Commons Journals*, IX. p. 21). An *Answer of the Company of Royal Adventurers of England trading to Africa* was compiled and put in, and was printed [Camb. Univ. Lib. Bb. 4. 16] with the heads of the arguments adduced by the petitioners and the reply of the Company on opposite pages. See also *Groans of the Plantations*, 1689, and reprinted 1698, p. 5. "Heretofore we might send to *Guiney* for *Negroes*, when we wanted them, and they stood us in about seven pound a Head. The Account is short and plain. For they cost about the value of forty Shillings a Head in *Guiney*; and their freight was five pound for every one that was brought alive, and could not go over the Ship side. But now we are shut out of this Trade: and a Company is put upon us, from whom we must have our *Negroes*, and no other way. A Company of *London* Merchants have got a Patent, excluding all others, to furnish the Plantations with *Negroes*: some great Men being joyned with them, with whom we were not able to contend. But those great Men might have had some better Exercise for their Generosity, than the pressing too hard upon (we must not say oppressing) industrious People. And now we buy *Negroes* at the price of an Engross'd Commodity; the common Rate of a good *Negroe* on Ship-board being twenty pound. And we are forced to scramble for them in so shameful a Manner, that one of the great Burdens of our Lives is the going to buy *Negroes*. But we must have them; we cannot be without them, and the best Men in those Countries must in their own Persons submit to the Indignity." The Guinea negroes were preferred, as they worked better than men from other parts of Africa. *Alarm Bell* (1759), p. 8. Brit. Mus. T. 13* (4).

and again[1]. The success of the South Sea Company in ob- *A.D. 1603* *—1689.* taining the *assiento*, for the supply of negroes to the Spanish *the* colonies, introduced another powerful interest into the Guinea *planters.* coast; and the well-organised trade of the French from Senegal[2] was held up as an example[3]. In the middle of the eighteenth century there was every reason to fear that the success of the French, in developing the resources and trade of the West Indies, would be pushed on, till the English position in the transatlantic plantations was completely outflanked.

195. The Hudson's Bay Company has been able to *The* maintain its constitution and character, with but little modi- *Hudson's* *Bay has* fication, since its foundation, and it thus serves as a monu- *been a very* *successful* ment of the remarkable outburst of trading activity which *joint-stock* *Company.* characterised the era of the Restoration. Like the East Indian and the African Companies, as re-established at that time, it was organised upon a joint-stock basis. Despite the difficulties with which they had to contend and the criticism they had to face, the Hudson's Bay Company continued to exercise exclusive rights in a lucrative trade, long after the time when other branches of commerce were thrown open to all subjects[4]. The favour they enjoyed was largely due to the fact that the existence of the Company and its forts was a constant menace to the French fur trade, and checked the extension of French influence in the north of Canada.

The earlier history of the Company does not redound to *The enter-* the credit of English enterprise; its inception was due to *prise was* *opened up* two Frenchmen[5], Groselliers and Radisson, who were anxious *by French-* *men,* to push the commerce in furs with greater activity than the Canadian authorities were prepared to do. As Huguenots,

---

[1] The discussion was carried on with special vigour in 1711, at the time when the separate traders prevented the formation of a Joint-Stock Company with powers of exclusive trading conferred by Parliament.

[2] M. Postlethwayt, *The African Trade the Great Pillar and support of the British Plantation Trade* (1745), 8.

[3] M. Postlethwayt, *Considerations on the Revival of the Royal British Assiento* (1749).

[4] The Hudson's Bay Company surrendered their political and exclusive trade rights to Canada in 1869, but continued to trade in a corporate capacity. Willson, *The Great Company*, 492.

[5] B. Willson, *Ib.* 26.

A.D. 1603
—1689.

they were viewed with some suspicion by their compatriots, and they were forced to turn to the subjects of a rival power for the means of giving effect to their scheme of organising a fur trade on the shores of Hudson's Bay. At Boston, where the importance of this branch of commerce was well understood and the difficulties of navigation were not over-estimated, they were able to interest a ship-captain in their undertaking; and through this connection they came to *and organised by Prince Rupert.* appeal for patronage in England. They were fortunate in securing the attention of Prince Rupert; who, though not in high favour at court, managed to obtain an ample charter[1], and presided as governor over the fortunes of the Company from 1670 to 1683, when he was succeeded by his nephew the Duke of York. The two Frenchmen, who had contributed so materially to the inception of the Company, and who assisted the English in founding factories and establishing trading relations with the tribes, did not remain *The English traders were exposed to constant French hostility,* faithful to their new masters[2]. They attempted to oust them altogether, and to bring the trade of Hudson's Bay completely under French control. The Englishmen showed a certain tenacity, however, in holding on where they could, and in even recovering positions from which they were driven; they were able to maintain an effective competition with their French rivals, till the downfall of Quebec disorganised the trading system of the French, and left the Hudson's Bay Company in an admirable position for profiting by the increased number of Indians who began to frequent their factories[3].

The economic advantages which the Englishmen possessed for conducting this commerce were very considerable; they had the command of shipping; and the navigation of Hudson's Straits, with all its dangers, was a very preferable route *but they had the advantage of better shipping facilities,* to the long land journeys, on which the French were thrown back by the insufficiency of their marine. Much of the distance could be traversed by canoes on rivers, but there were long portages; and the Indians would not convey in this

[1] B. Willson, *The Great Company*, p. 50. This is the event with which it seems most natural to associate the medal reproduced on the title-page.
[2] *Ib.* 111.   [3] *Ib.* 287.

manner any but very valuable furs, which were of course *A.D.* 1603 relatively less bulky than the others. The heavy trade came *—1689.* naturally into English hands[1], and the Indians, in some cases, *and their merchan-* preferred to deal with the Company's officials on account of *dise was more ac-* the goods they offered in exchange. From the first, the *ceptable to the* Company thought it desirable to increase the possibilities *Indians.* of their trade, by supplying the Indians with weapons which enabled them to prosecute the chase to greater advantage. This practice of arming the Indians had disastrous results of many kinds upon the tribes; as it rendered them dependent on continued intercourse with civilised people, for carrying on the hunting by which they procured their supplies of food[2]; but at least it made them feel that the English commerce was more remunerative than that which they had hitherto practised with the French[3]. The French had difficulty, after a time, in carrying on their trade except with European merchandise obtained in the American plantations; and when the governor of New York prohibited the sale of such goods to the French they were very seriously hampered indeed[4]. Though the French had been first in the field, there were many economic advantages which lay with the English.

Politically the English were less fortunate, and at the *Political* conclusion of the Peace of Ryswick they were hardly entitled *complica- tions* to maintain themselves in any position on the Bay. That agreement had been intended to restore the *status quo*, as it had existed before the first War of Spanish Succession; but as a matter of fact, the English were now prevented from attempting to recover forts of which they had been forcibly deprived by the French, because these places had been captured by the French at a time when the two nations were supposed to be at peace. The military operations between French and English Companies, which were waged intermittently and without much direct relation to hostilities in Europe between the two countries, had taken an unfavourable turn for the London merchants. A Canadian expedition, together with *endangered the exist- ence of their* a French fleet, had driven the English from all their factories

---

[1] Willson, *op. cit.* 274.   [2] See below, p. 856.
[3] *Ib.* 64.   [4] *Ib.* 214.

save one, and the English title to retain Fort Albany—the
most southerly of their stations—under the terms of the Treaty
was more than doubtful[1]. The affairs of the Company were
at a very low ebb during the next sixteen years, but they
were once more successful in regaining court influence under
Queen Anne; and the treaty of Utrecht[2], though it failed to
settle the exact boundaries of their territory, gave them the
whole of Hudson's Bay, and thus established their claim to
exclusive navigation against the French. The confirmation
of their Charter by Parliament in 1690[3], though only for a
period of seven years, had already put them in a stronger
position as against English subjects who might desire to
break down their monopoly; so that the political safeguards
of their exclusive commerce were at last rendered effective.

The profits were undoubtedly very large, and public
opinion exaggerated them still farther; it seems to have
been commonly believed that they were as high as 2000 per
*but the
trade was
so managed
as to be
very profit-
able,*
cent. The parliamentary enquiry of 1749 elicited figures
which showed that at that time 40 per cent. was nearer
the mark[4]; the original capital had only been £10,500; but
the Company had been successful in procuring ships and
building factories, even while they were dividing large
profits, and the actual value of their possession in 1720
was taken as £94,500[5]. The proprietors thought that a
propitious moment had come for re-organising the Company,
by watering the stock, and throwing a large number of
shares on the market when the fever of speculation was at
its height. They missed the opportunity, however, as the
South Sea Bubble burst before they were ready to float
their scheme; and the Company continued to carry on
a sound and profitable business for the benefit of the "smug
ancient gentlemen" who were fortunate enough to hold its
stock.

---

[1] Willson, *op. cit.* 168, 187. It had been re-taken by the English during the
period of war in Europe, 153.

[2] Willson, *op. cit.* 199.

[3] *Commons Journals*, x. p. 369, 7 April, 1690. Private Acts 2 W. and M. Sess.
i. c. 15.

[4] Willson, *op. cit.* 274. Compare the Report (1749) in *Reports to House of
Commons*, Vol. ii. p. 215.   [5] Willson, *op. cit.* 68, 210.

The parliamentary committee of 1749 rendered it abun- A.D. 1603 —1689.
dantly clear that the Company had shown little enterprise
of any kind; the Liverpool and Bristol merchants united *though the policy of*
with some Londoners, to demand that the trade should be *the Company was*
thrown open to men who could conduct it with more energy. *restrictive,*
Especial complaint was made, by Mr Arthur Dobbs, of the
neglect of the Company to prosecute such voyages of discovery as might lead to the opening up of a North-West
Passage through the Bay. As we now know that these
dreams were chimerical, we are inclined to smile at the
indignation of those who were influenced by them; more
substantial reasons were alleged by the Skinners and
Hatters for adopting a new policy in regard to the trade.
They urged persistently, that the Company's methods un- *and limited*
necessarily limited the quantities of skins and beaver wool *the supply of mate-*
imported; and that they maintained a high rate of profit *rials for*
for the merchants, but provided an insufficient supply of *home industry.*
materials for the manufacture of their wares. This was
probably perfectly true, and it was the back-bone of the
opposition to the Company both in 1690[1], and 1698[2], and
again in 1752[3], since there was some reason to urge that
French manufacturers were better served than their English
rivals and could therefore undersell them[4]. The decline of *With the*
the French power and French trade, however, took some *decline of French*
of the force out of this objection. Curiously enough, the *power the political*
same victories which did away with much of the political *excuse for the*
reason for maintaining the Company, as a menace to the *Company ceased,*
French trader, gave new weight to the economic reasons
for preserving its mode of trading. It was engaged in
transactions with wild tribes; and the arguments for
organised commerce, and well-ordered trade, as opposed to
the competition of Englishmen against each other, were
particularly strong. Under these circumstances, the survival
of the Company was the exception which proved the rule;

[1] *Commons Journals*, x. 392, 28 April, 1690.

[2] Willson, *op. cit.* 174. *Commons Journals*, 12 and 19 March, 1698, xii. pp. 155, 165.

[3] In 1752 they attempted to form a new company. Willson, *op. cit.* 278.

[4] *Reports, House of Commons*, ii. 372. Upon the petition relating to the manufacture of hats.

A.D. 1603
—1689.
in the unusual circumstances of this business, the monopoly of a joint-stock company still appeared to be the best arrangement.

but it survived as an exception to the rule that
The joint-stock companies survived, in spite of the fact that they were real monopolies, but the regulated companies, which were less exclusive in character, had much greater difficulty in justifying their existence. The change in public opinion on this point during the seventeenth century is very remarkable. In the earlier part of the seventeenth century it appeared to be assumed that the organisation of trade, by persons who were concerned in it, was essential, and the only discussion was as to the form in which this was to be carried out. In the time of the Georges, new exclusive companies were not formed, and the real question was as to how far the old ones should be maintained. In the case of distant trades, where forts and armaments were necessary to protect the merchants, the company might have its privileges continued, in order that these forts might be retained without public expenditure; this course was adopted in the case of the East India Company. On the other hand the African Company was maintained as the most convenient instrument for managing the public funds devoted to this purpose. But,

the era of well-ordered trade had passed away.
so far as purely trading interests were concerned, the very idea of maintaining a "well-ordered" trade, where the company attempted to secure that its members should deal in goods of sound quality and should not spoil the market by eager competition, had passed away. The evils of the competition of interlopers were notorious and patent, but the companies had not been able to control their own servants, or to justify the retention of their privileges. A well-ordered trade meant an exclusive and confined trade; open trade, with all its faults, meant expanding trade; and Parliament, as representing the English public, decided in favour of expanding rather than of exclusive trade.

VIII.   THE REGULATION OF SOCIAL AND INDUSTRIAL CONDITIONS.

196.   The English Government under James I. and Charles I., attempted to realise a very high idea of duty with regard to the internal condition of the realm.   We are satisfied in modern times with trying to check or limit definite evils—to prevent the adulteration of food and the overworking of children; but in the earlier part of the seventeenth century the Stuart kings endeavoured to maintain positive standards of what appeared good and fair. They were not content to put down abuses, but aimed at so ordering the economic life of the country that every man should have opportunities of practising his calling, and that he might be able to count on obtaining the necessaries of life at reasonable prices and of a good quality. *A.D. 1603 —1689. James and Charles endeavoured to regulate the whole economic life of the country,*

It was almost quixotic to attempt to carry out a system of positive economic regulation for England in the seventeenth century.   The only conditions, under which such a scheme could have succeeded, were wanting at that time, though they had been more or less present in the civic communities of the Middle Ages.   The effort to maintain definite standards of industrial and social well-being, is hardly compatible with progress[1], or with changes in the arts of life and the organisation of industry; but the Stuarts tried to introduce improvements[2] and also to render each man's position stable and secure.   It was impossible, for any ruler who was not omniscient, to take full account of the varieties of local conditions in considering the general welfare, or to mediate with absolute wisdom between the conflicting interests of producers and consumers, who were not in close contact with one another.   The effort to *but this was more impracticable in England.*

---

[1] See below, p. 617.

[2] Compare the language of the (suppressed) proclamation on Cockayne's project.   "Where Wee see an apparent meanes of doing Our people further good, not to tie Ourselues to the simple and positiue degree of their Welfare, but to proceed from good to better." *Proclamation Conteyning his Maiesties Royall pleasure concerning the project of Dying and Dressing of Broad Cloathes within the Kingdome, before they be exported.*   25 May, 1614, Vol. VI. (35), (Soc. Ant.)

maintain and enforce the best conditions practicable for the welfare of each and all, throughout such a large area as England, may have been heroic, but the inherent difficulties of the task were insuperable; it was destined to fail.

Such an experiment might have been made with better
*than in
France.*
success in a country like France, but in England it could hardly have a fair trial. Detailed national regulation necessarily involved habitual and constant interference with ordinary business transactions; this was wholly alien to a sentiment which was at all events widely cherished. There was a very general feeling that the Englishman should enjoy the liberty of buying and selling as occasion offered, and that definite and sufficient grounds must be shown for any
*The tra-
ditional
Economic
freedom
of the
English-
man had
been esta-
blished*
restrictions on his rights. The claim to this economic freedom underlay all the complaints of the interlopers against the chartered companies for commerce; but it comes out much more explicitly in the agitation, which was raised on behalf of consumers, against the practice of conferring special powers on individuals, or companies, with regard to industrial avocations. In the face of all the restrictions on natural liberty which had been maintained in civic communities, in the later middle ages, it is somewhat surprising to find evidence that the claim to economic freedom should be so strongly asserted in the seventeenth century. We may, however, easily over-rate the importance and thoroughness of exclusive trade organisation in mediaeval times.

The systematic attempt to enforce a national scheme of social and industrial regulation involved a vast amount of interference in areas which had been hitherto left to them-
*in rural
districts*
selves. The rural districts, and the suburbs, had been regions in which craftsmen established themselves, when the rules of the gilds pressed heavily upon them; there had been very little industrial supervision in country places or market towns; and even in some of the corporate towns, such as Cambridge, there do not appear to have been any craft gilds. These areas were much more important economically, as compared with the large towns, than they are to-day. In fairs it
*and at
fairs,*
would appear that the liberty, of all those who frequented them, to buy and sell was fully preserved; and the fact that pedlars

were allowed to perambulate the country freely[1], proves that there was no restriction on internal trade, so far as a large part of the population were concerned. The principle of an Englishman's liberty, in regard to buying and selling, finds full expression in the statute of 1497[2], and its bearing on ordinary occupations is brought out by Sandys in his paper of *Instructions towchinge the Bill for Free Trade*[3]: "all free Subiects are borne inheritable as to ther Lands, soe alsoe to the free exercise of ther industrie in those trads wherto they applie themselves and wherby they are to live. Merchandise being the chiefe and richest of all other, and *and was asserted in regard to foreign trade.* of greater extent and importance then all the rest, it is against the naturall right and liberty of the Subiects of England to restrain it into the hands of some fewe."

Those who felt aggrieved by the industrial patents of Elizabeth, James and Charles, were thus able to take their stand on a great constitutional principle which the ministers of the Crown did not call in question. The opponents of *Patents which trenched on the liberty of internal dealing* patents insisted that the encroachment on this natural right was an evil which was only justified by clear proof that each particular grant of special privileges really tended to the public good.

Under these circumstances we can easily understand that there should be a great deal of parliamentary criticism, in the time of Elizabeth and of James, both of the grants themselves[4] and of the manner in which the patentees

---

[1] They were licensed for definite circuits under Edward VI., 5 and 6 Ed. VI. c. 21.

[2] 12 Hen. VII. c. 6.

[3] Cotton MSS. Titus, F. IV. f. 261. *Commons Journal*, I. 218.

[4] The nature and extent of the admitted evils comes out in James' Proclamation of 10 July, 1621, announcing the revocation of many grants [Brit. Mus. 506. h. 12 (87)]. He revoked patents for "gold and silver foliat, the licensing of Pedlars and pettie Chapmen, the sole dressing of common Armes, the exportation of Lists, Shreds and other like things, the sole making of Tobacco pipes, the hotte Presse, the manufacture of playing Cardes, and brogging of Wooll." The following Commissions were also revoked: "for pardoning and dispensing with Tradesmen for not serving a Prenticehood, for pardoning or dispensing with the conversion of arrable Land into Pasture, for licensing of Wine Caske, for making of Denizens, granting of Leetes, passing of Parkes and Free Warrens, for granting of Faires and Markets, granting of Tols, tallages and other like dueties, leasing of Tithes, for Passing or Leasing of Concealements, Intrusions, Incroachments, Lands

A.D. 1603
—1689.

*were viewed
with great
suspicion,*

*but they
promised a
convenient
means of
procuring
revenue*

exercised their rights[1]. To show that certain privileges had been given, in the hope of securing a public object, was not enough; the Commons wanted to see that the common weal had actually been advanced. It was clear that private individuals gained by the powers of search, or the special rights that were conferred upon them[2]; and the suspicion was aroused that the alleged public boon was illusory. During the personal government of Charles, the feeling that the interests of the public were not the primary object of certain grants was very general, and the King and his immediate advisers bore the blame. There can, indeed, be little doubt that one of the motives, which influenced the Crown in the granting of patents and monopolies, lay in the fact that they offered a probable means of obtaining supplies[3]. This comes out very clearly in a most interesting letter from Strafford[4] in regard to the Irish revenue; he suggests that the King should take the business

out of Charge and other Lands of like nature. Other licenses and privileges revoked. Gilding and printing of Leather, printing upon Cloth, the making of pauing Tyles, Dishes, Pots, Garden poasts and vessels of earth, making of Stone pots, Stone jugs, and the like; the importing of Pikes, Carpes, Eeles, and Scallops, making of Racket hoopes, Rackets and cloth balls, the making and selling of Oyle for keeping Armour, the importation of Sturgeon, the making of Garments of Beaver, making of hard Waxe, making of Chamlets, making of backe Screenes, making of sortage and lineage for Paper, the measuring of Corne, Coale, and Salt, the printing of Briefs and other things upon one side of the paper, the weighing of Hay and Straw, the discouerie of annoyances in the Thames and Ballasting ships."

[1] The chief grievances were at the hands of the agents, or substitutes, of the men who held the royal letters patent. Mr Martin in 1601 spoke of the burden of "monstrous and unconscionable substitutes to the Monopolitans of Starch, Tinn, Fish, Cloth, Oyl, Vinegar, Salt, and I know not what, nay what not? The principallest commodities both of my Town and Country are ingrossed into the hand of those blood-suckers of the Commonwealth." (Simon D'Ewes, *The Journals of all the Parliaments during the reign of Queen Elizabeth*, p. 646.)

[2] According to James I.'s proclamation, Elizabeth "at the importunitie of her scruants, whom she was willing to reward with little burden to her estate (otherwise by necessary occasions exhausted)" had granted several patents which he thought it right to revoke. 7 May, 1603, Brit. Mus. 506. h. 10 (8). The same sort of evil appears to have occurred on a much larger scale under the personal government of Charles, when necessity forced many of the ladies and gentlemen of the royal household to become project mongers. Mr Bruce's Preface to the Calendar S. P. D. 1635—6, p. xxvi.

[3] Laud in particular appears to have looked at the matter from this point of view. Cal. S. P. D. 1635—6, Preface, p. viii.

[4] *Letters and Dispatches*, edited by W. Knowler, I. 193.

of importing salt into his own hands, and that he would thus get a payment like the French *gabelle*; by similar arrangements for malt, he meant to pave the way for an excise, on the model of those in Holland. He was sanguine enough to hope that he could get parliamentary authority for these arrangements, while he thought it would be rash to try to effect them without.   In England, Charles pursued a similar course during his personal government.   Salt was *from such* an article which was largely imported[1]; it was, from the *commodi-ties as salt* point of view of contemporaries, undoubtedly desirable to introduce the manufacture into England, rather than to continue to depend on foreigners for a necessary commodity. A company was formed at Shields for the production of salt[2], and another company was licensed to carry on the manufacture by a new process, while the importation of salt from the Bay of Biscay was forbidden.   To these measures little exception could be taken.   It was certainly plausible, too, to urge that a payment should be made by the manufacturers of salt to reimburse the Crown for the diminution of the customs obtained on this article when it was no longer imported[3].   All readjustments of economic life necessarily affected the revenue; and it is interesting to see the principles which Charles laid down in 1626, as instructions given to the Commissioners of Trade.   They were ordered to overhaul the Book of Rates "to the end that some particulars, which are conceived to be over-burthened, might be eased and yett that it might be done without diminution (if not without increase of our revenue) by laying more upon some other particulars imported from foraigne parts tending rather to superfluitie than necessitie." They are out of their "owne experiences and judgments and by the assistance of such marchants and others as you shall thinck fitt to call unto you" to overhaul the customs.   They were to inform the king of their opinion, "whereupon wee are resolved to establish such a settled and constant course for that part of our Revenues as maie best advance the

---

[1] See above, p. 77.   [2] See below, p. 309.
[3] Gardiner, *History*, VIII. 285.

A.D. 1603
—1689.
Trade of Marchandize and not hinder us in our just profitts[1]."
The tariff could be used as an instrument for influencing
consumption ; it was not yet deemed sufficiently powerful to
be relied on for stimulating production. For calling new
branches of industry into being, or improving the old ones,
it seemed necessary to take more direct measures; and the
and soap efforts to provide a better quality of soap, and other articles
of common consumption, may certainly have been made with
the genuine desire to benefit the citizens generally, though
they were liable to be interpreted as an indirect attempt to
levy an excise and thus obtain additional revenue for the
Crown[2]. It is probable that Charles and his advisers believed that the steps they were taking, with regard to the
manufacture of soap[3], would be beneficial to the public and
to the Crown as well. If this was his view, his action was
not only plausible but perfectly defensible; at the same
time, the fact that there was some prospect of gain accruing
to the Crown, renders it impossible to prove that Charles
was as wholly disinterested in his industrial as he was in his
colonial policy[4].

Some other cases arose in which it was easy to show
that there were sufficient political grounds for inter-
*Political
reasons
could be
pleaded* fering with private rights and convenience. Saltpetre was
needed for the manufacture of gunpowder, and various
expedients were adopted for securing an increased supply
of a good quality. Queen Elizabeth had taken the matter
under the direct control of the Crown[5]. King James, in

---

[1] Brit. Mus. Add. MSS. 12496, f. 339.

[2] The proceedings by which the Crown obtained considerable sums from the
Vintners' Company, who reimbursed themselves at the expense of the public,
gave colour to this view (Gardiner, viii. 286). An attempt was made to throw the
whole blame of this transaction on the Vintners' Company [*A true discovery of
the Proiectors of the Wine Project* (1641), Brit. Mus. E. 165 (13)]; but the part of
the Court in the matter is brought out in the *Vintners' Answer* (1642), Brit. Mus.
E. 140 (1), and *A true Relation of the proposing threatening and perswading the
Vintners to yeeld to the Imposition upon Wines* (1641), Brit. Mus. E. 171 (5).

[3] See below, p. 306.

[4] See below, pp. 357, 358.

[5] See above, p. 61. The precise limits of the royal prerogative in assuming
exclusive rights over the production and sale of any commodity were the subject
of much difficulty. Compare the argument of Pollexfen in his defence of Sands,
an interloper in the East India Trade, as to what the Crown might grant to a

1622[1], appointed a sworn proof master, who had the exclu- A.D. 1603
sive right to the purchase of saltpetre, and was responsible ―1689.
for testing the quality of gunpowder.   Though the House of *for taking*
Commons acquiesced in the action of the Crown, the English *measures in regard to*
public were less complacent, and seem to have resented and
obstructed the operations of the saltpetre-men[2].   King James

subject [*Discourse of Trade, Coyn, etc.* (1700), Ap.].   But the Commons do not
appear to have been much inclined to raise this point directly, either under
Elizabeth or James, or to have questioned the royal wisdom in assuming the
immediate responsibility for certain trades, that admittedly required some sort of
regulation.   No exception was taken in regard to the tin in Cornwall, which came
from royal lands; in regard to goods that came from new colonies, such as tobacco,
a similar claim was allowed.   "And lastly, whereas it is agreed on all Sides that
the *Tobacco* of those Plantations of *Virginia* and the *Summer Islandes* (which is
the only present Meanes of their subsistinge) cannot be mannaged for the good
of the Plantations unless itt be brought into one hand, whereby the Forraigne
Tobacco may be carefullie kept out, and the Tobacco of those Plantations may
yealde a certayne and ready Price to the Owners thereof, Wee doe hereby declare,
That to avoyde all Differencies and Contrarietie of Opynions, which will hardly
be reconcyled betweene the Planters and Adventurers themselves, We are resolved to take the same into Our own Hands and, by Our Servants or Agents for
Us, to give such Prices to the Planters and Adventurers for the same as may give
them reasonable Satisfaction and Incouragement but of the manner thereof we
will determine hereafter at better Leisure." Rymer, *Fœdera*, xviii. 72.
   [1] 16th January, 1623, Brit. Mus. 506. h. 12 (96).
   [2] *A Proclamation for the Preservation of Grounds for making of Salt Peeter,
and to restore such Grounds which now are destroyed, and to command assistance
to be given to his Maiesties Salt-Peeter-makers.* 26 Dec., 1624. Brit. Mus.
1851. b. 3 (8).   "Yet we are credibly giuen to understand, that this great blessing
of God unto this Kingdome is abused, and like to be utterly lost, by the euill
dealings of many ill disposed persons (who respecting more their own then the
publike good) and having Douehouses for breeding of Pigeons, being in some
measure a grieuance and an inconuenience, and an offence to our Subiects in
generall, in destroying their Corne, and other Graine, much more then the profit
which it any way bringeth, either to the publike, or owners thereof, might therefore well, without grudging, be contented to affoord the dung thereof for the
increasing of so necessary a prouision, as concernes both the safety of themselues,
and of the whole Kingdome; yet being not sensible of the great danger and
inconuenience that the want of these prouisions may bring upon the Kingdome in
generall, and themselues in particular, doe take liberty unto themselues daily to
use and practise many wayes and deuices purposely to spoile, kill and utterly to
destroy the Mines of Salt-Peeter, and the growth and increase thereof, as well in
such Douehouses and Dovecoats, as in Cellers, stables, and other places in their
possessions and occupations (wherein the same Mines are naturally apt to breed
and increase, and which are allowed to be wrought and used for Our service) by
carrying out of such places the ground or earth that is naturally good for that
service, and laying the same upon their land, and by pitching, paning and laying
of such places with Brickes, Stones, Planckes, Boardes, Lime, Sand or Grauell,
by which meanes a great part of the best and most sufficient grounds, which
heretofore have been good, and wrought for Our service, are now spoiled and

A.D. 1603
—1689.

denounced this lack of public spirit, and Charles issued several proclamations on the subject[1]. He endeavoured to

the supply of salt-petre, obtain a supply from the East Indies, but the quantities the merchants introduced in his time were inadequate, and in 1626 a patent was granted to Sir Thomas Russell and others for the sole use of an invention they had devised for the manufacture of saltpetre[2]. Care was taken that this new process should not be made an excuse for resisting the saltpetre-men who relied on the old methods[3]. The results were not satisfactory, however, for in 1634 there was need for further attention to the home supply[4]; while the hindrance that had been placed on the importation of gunpowder[5], with the tendency to engross the manufacture, were declared void by statute in 1640[6].

There were many other cases in which the ordinary manufacture and sale of commodities was interfered with for

the suppression of tobacco planting, and the manufacture of gold thread. political objects. Examples in point are the prohibitions of tobacco planting in Ireland, which might prove inimical to colonial development[7], and the various attempts that were made to supervise the manufacture of gold and silver thread; this was viewed with suspicion, as it tended to exhaust the

destroyed, and the like practises are daily used upon those grounds that yet remaine good, although the same hath been forbidden by Our expresse Commandement in our Commission granted for that service from time to time, for the space of these Tenne yeeres, upon paine of Contempt in that behalfe."

[1] *Proclamation for the maintenance and encrease of the Mines of Salt peter.* 13 April, 1625. Brit. Mus. 506. h. 11 (38).

[2] *A Proclamation for the better making of Saltpeter within this Kingdome.* 2 Dec. 1626. Brit. Mus. 506. h. 11 (84).

[3] *For the maintaining and increase of the Mines of Saltpeter and the true making and working of Saltpeter and Gunpowder.* 23 July 1627. Brit. Mus. 506. h. 11 (95).

[4] *For preservation of grounds for making of Saltpeter and to restore such grounds as are now destroyed and to command assistance to be given to his Majesties Saltpeter Makers.* 14 Mar. 1634. Brit. Mus. 506. h. 12 (37).

[5] *Proclamation prohibiting the importation of forraine Gunpowder* 20 Feb. 1636. Brit. Mus. 506. h. 12 (50).

[6] 16 C. I. c. 21. *An Act for the free bringing in of Gunpowder and Salt-peter from forraign parts, etc.*

[7] This is explicitly stated in the preamble of 12 C. II. c. 34, the first statute on the subject; but the policy was of long standing at that time. The tobacco monopoly was one of the grievances alleged by the Irish Parliament against Strafford. (Cox, *Hibernia Anglicana*, II. 62.) See also the twelfth article of impeachment in Rushworth, *Historical Collections*, VIII. 66.

treasure of the kingdom.   The claims of the Goldsmiths' Company were set aside, and the trade was conferred on patentees, who undertook to import bullion for the purpose. Subsequently, under Bacon's advice, it was taken into the king's hands to be exercised only by his agents[1].   The same *and of alum.* course was taken with regard to mining for alum in Yorkshire.   Burleigh had recognised that it was of great importance to develop the home production[2] of a commodity which was so necessary in the cloth trade.   This was now attempted under Government management[3], and protection against imported supplies[4] was accorded to the enterprise.

There were reasons of a strictly economic character which *Though some attempts were made* were generally recognised as good grounds for the granting of patents.   Encouragement was constantly given to men

---

[1] Oct. 10th, 1619, Gardiner, IV. 18. This does not appear to have proved satisfactory, and a special company for this branch of trade was subsequently created. Proclamation 16 June, 1623. Brit. Mus. 506. h. 12 (108).

[2] The alum necessary for the cloth trade was practically a papal monopoly, Beckmann, *Hist. of Inventions*, I. 194, and Cecil was at pains to furnish a native supply. A grant is made to Cornelius de Vos, who had discovered alum in the Isle of Wight. "Whereas he hath found mines and intendeth at his owne proper costes and charges to work for the benefit of the realm" (S. P. D. El. XXXVI. 72, June, 1565). In this Cecil was financially interested (S. P. D. El. XL. 50; Aug. 1566, S. P. D. El. XLII. 24, Mar. 1567). Lord Mountjoy the assignee of the patent hoped "to supply the whole realm at ⅔ less than the present price to the benefit of the whole realm and the annoyance of the Pope" (S. P. D. El. Add. XIII. 49). In 1571 the British merchants complain of the decay of their trade, for the alum and iron which had formerly come from Spain were made better and cheaper in this country (Hulme, *op. cit.* XII. 147). We find Burghley, May, 1581, S. P. D. El. CXLIX. 11, directing an imposition of 3s. 4d. on every cwt. of alum imported from the dominion of the Bishop of Rome.

[3] The Crown was badly served by its agents and the experiments were not successful. Price, *English Patents of Monopoly*, 100. "Whereas that great and commendable Worke of making Allome of the Native Mynes of this our Kingdom not many yeeres since discouered within our County of Yorke is by the disbursement and expense of sundry great summes of money made by our most deare and Royall Father ... brought to such perfection as there is now no doubt or question but sufficient quantities of good, well roached and merchantable Allome may be made, as well for supply of our owne Dominions of so necessary and usefull a Commoditie, as also for forreine vent and sale of great quantities thereof with other neighbour Kingdoms." Charles I., Proclamation 13 April, 1625. Brit. Mus. 506. h. 11 (39).

[4] Proclamation 19 June, 1609, Brit. Mus. 506. h. 10 (106). Also 10 Oct. 1614, *A Proclamation prohibiting the Importation of Allome.* Soc. Ant. VI. (42). The King pointed out that the course he was taking involved loss of customs. Charles I. continued this action. Proclamation 13 April, 1625. Brit. Mus. 506. h. 11 (39).

A.D. 1603
—1689.
who really introduced and practised[1] arts, which had not previously existed in the realm; it is hardly necessary to enumerate additional illustrations, besides those already noted in connection with Burleigh's efforts to develop the resources of the realm and render it economically in- *to plant* dependent. The most important grant of this kind, under *new indus-* James I., was the patent, already alluded to, which was *tries, as by Sir W.* obtained by Sir W. Cockayne. The English did not excel *Cockayne,* in the dressing and dyeing of cloth, and a large part of the products of English looms was exported by the Merchant Adventurers, under special permission[2], to be finished in Holland[3]. To this the clothworkers and dyers of London took exception, and they carried their point in 1614. Sir William Cockayne obtained a patent for the sole right of dyeing and dressing cloth by an improved process. He hoped after three years to be able to render the export of any undressed cloth unnecessary[4] but the project was un- successful, and in the mean time the staple trade of the country was thrown into confusion[5]. The whole business of the weavers was very seriously affected[6]; the manufacture was so important and so wide-spread that it was hardly a *anything* fit subject for experiment. The connections of different *that inter-* branches of trade were so complicated, that it was scarcely *fered with* possible to attempt the improvement of one without doing *existing trades* injury to others. The concomitant mischief in such a change for the better as the attempt to substitute the use of coal for wood as fuel in smelting[7] could be easily reckoned, but it

---

[1] The undertaking to work the grant was the essential consideration in these patents. E. W. Hulme, *On the Consideration of the Patent Grant* in the *Law Quarterly Review*, XIII. 314, July, 1897.

[2] Spedding, *Letters and Life of Bacon*, v. 169. See above, p. 233.

[3] No fewer than 600,000 poor were said to be employed in dyeing and dressing English cloth in Holland. S. P. D. J. L xc 24 Jan. 1617.

[4] S. P D. J I. LXXX. 112.   [5] *Ib.* 108.

[6] Alderman Cockayne was ordered (Aug. 1616) to buy up the Gloucestershire cloth in London, and such as shall be widely brought in (S. P. D J. I. LXXXVIII. 51). But the export trade, as well as internal traffic, was seriously disorganised, and Cockayne must have lost heavily (S. P. D. J. I. xc. 24 Dec. 1616).

[7] On Sturlevant's patent, see Hulme, *Law Quarterly Review*, vol. XIII. p. 315. There were various ways in which new industries involved a fresh demand on the diminishing supply of timber The glass-manufacture was checked on this account in 1615. Proclamations, Soc. Ant. VI. 51, 23 May, 1615.

was more difficult to gauge the prospective results of such A.D. 1603 labour-saving appliances as an engine for needle making[1]. The inventor of an improved process did not find much favour, from our point of view he would have deserved encouragement, as he was doing something for industrial progress; but if his invention interfered with an existing *was viewed* trade, and put his neighbours to a disadvantage in the *with dis-* *favour.* exercise of their calling[2] he was left to take his chance, and he was not treated as a man who deserved patronage of any kind. Machinery was viewed with suspicion not only on account of the quality of the work done[3], but because of its injurious effect upon handicraftsmen[4] The common-sense opinion of the sixteenth and seventeenth centuries was in sympathy with the view of those who objected to the introduction of any engine which, by doing work better and cheaper, took the bread out of some handicraftsman's mouth. The patent system afforded a means for protecting progress, so far as that consisted in planting arts not hitherto practised, but it did little or nothing under Elizabeth and the early Stuarts, for the modification of existing arts.

197. The chief object which James and Charles set *With the* before themselves in regard to the industry of the country *view of* *maintain-* was not the introduction of new forms of skill; they were *ing the* *quality of* much more occupied in providing for the supervision of *goods,* the existing industries, so that the wares produced might be of good quality. This was of the first importance with regard to goods manufactured for export; according to common consent, the best means of promoting commerce lay in maintaining the reputation of English cloth in foreign markets. So far as articles produced for home consumption

---

[1] S. P. D. J. I. CLVIII. 38.

[2] E. W. Hulme, *History of the Patent System* in *Law Quarterly Review*, XII. 152. Compare however the dispute in 1624 (?) with regard to the patent for the alleged invention for printing linen cloth. *Hist. MSS. Comm.* III. Ap. 35.

[3] Compare Charles's Proclamation re-enforcing the Statute of 5 and 6 E. VI. against the use of Gig or Mosing Mills. Proclamation, 16 April, 1633 [Brit. Mus. 506. h. 12 (19)] See below, p. 661.

[4] Compare James's Proclamation which prohibited the use of a machine for making needles. 20 Jan. 1623, Soc. Ant. VIII. 209. Also Charles's Proclamation prohibiting brass buckles because "those who cast the brasse buckles can make more in one day than ten of those that make the iron buckles can do." 506. h. 12 (5).

were concerned, there was a strong tradition for inspecting them minutely and carefully. The organisation of craft gilds, and the whole machinery of the assize of bread and ale, had been primarily concerned with caring for the interest of the consumer, in every town and village. Under *arrangements were made for industrial supervision* the Stuarts, strenuous efforts were made to organise a system of industrial supervision on national lines, and thus to maintain a high standard of quality for goods of every kind, manufactured for sale either at home or abroad.

There were two possible expedients by which a system of supervision might be carried out, and there was abundant precedent for both of them; it might be desirable to erect *through officials* an office and confer the responsibility of detecting bad workmanship on some individual[1], or it might be wiser to establish a company, the members of which would exercise mutual supervision over each other.

The former expedient had existed in the English cloth manufacture from time immemorial. The official, who *in the cloth trade,* searched the cloth prepared for sale, was known as the aulnager. We find most interesting details as to his functions in the seventeenth century, and see the difficulty of adapting the old institution to the requirements of a growing trade, after the incursion of the Walloons[2]. The new drapery, which had been introduced under Elizabeth, did not conform to the rules laid down for the broad cloth of the realm; and the aulnager, whose business it was to view the old drapery, had no standing in regard to these lighter goods. It was, however, a recognised principle that all manner of woollen cloth should be searched, measured and sealed, so that no person should be deceived by buying deceitful woollen cloth and that woollen cloth should be truly made, and Elizabeth

---

[1] This was a favourite system in France, and it seemed the natural method to adopt, after the Restoration, when some attempts were made to encourage the woollen industry in Ireland. See below, p. 275 n. 2. The same system was introduced in the province of New Jersey with regard to commodities for export. In 1676, a packer of meat was appointed to seal barrels, with the right of charging a fee, and at the same time the office of sealer of leather was also created. *Grants, Concessions and Original Constitutions of the Province of New Jersey*, pp. 116, 117.

[2] The immigrants had organised a good system of search of their own, J. May, *Declaration of Estate of Clothing* (1613), p. 7, but the levying of customs was a difficulty.

had endeavoured to carry this into effect [1]. She had created the office of Aulnager of the New Drapery [2], who was to be remunerated by the fee he was entitled to charge on each cloth examined. In 1605, however, King James was obliged to define the terms of the office more fully, so as to bring all the new branches of the weaving industry under proper supervision. The proclamation by which he announces the appointment of the Duke of Lennox to this office points out that divers other new sorts of stuffs and draperies and commodities, not mentioned in Queen Elizabeth's patent, were being manufactured   It goes on to say that " diuers clothiers heretofore using to make broad Clothes, have changed their Loomes, and spinnings to the making of the same new inuentions,......the gaine and returne of such new Draperies and late inuented stuffes, and Commodities, made of Wooll or part of Wooll and comparing weight to weight, being farre greater and quicker, and the trade thereof exercised with lesse stocke and charge then is requisite to the making of broad Clothes [3]." The proclamation gives a long list of the fabrics which were being made, and insists on bringing them within the scope of the aulnager's office [4], both for the purposes of proper search and for the collection of the subsidies on cloth exported from the realm.

A.D. 1603 —1689.

which had developed greatly,

A similar course was adopted with regard to some of the staple products of the realm. The extraordinary change, which had taken place in the industrial condition of England during the three centuries which succeeded the accession of Edward II., is strikingly brought out by the contrast in the arrangements which were adopted for disposing of the

---

[1] Proclamation, 16 Sept. 1605, reciting Elizabeth's Grant, Soc. Ant. vi. 7.

[2] 13 July, 1594. The searching of the old drapery at Blackwell Hall was also the subject of complaint during this reign, *Hist. MSS. Comm.* iii. Ap. 37. See also for Eastern Counties, *Ib.* 51.

[3] Proclamation, 16 Sept. 1605, Soc. Ant. vi. 7. For an instance of the action of the Duke of Lennox under these powers in 1612 see *Hist. MSS. Comm.* iii. Ap. 59.

[4] In 1630 Anthony Wither was appointed a special commissioner for the reformation of abuses in the West of England cloth trade (S. P. D. C. I. clxxiv. 97). He appears to have endeavoured to put down the use of gig-mills (S. P. D. C. I. ccxv. 56), and this was prohibited by Proclamation, 16 April, 1633. The attempt to enforce this order brought about a serious dislocation of trade (S. P. D. C. I. ccxliv. 1).

annual production of wool[1]. The organisation of the Staplers had been a matter of difficulty in the time of Edward VI.[2]; and with the loss of Calais under Queen Mary, the scheme for forcing the export trade into a definite channel appears

while the occupation of the Staplers was gone.
to have come to an end. The merchants of the Staple did not readily acquiesce in the new conditions; and one of them pointed out how seriously the Crown lost through the non-payment of customs, since the trade was no longer under proper supervision[3]. The merchants themselves were in serious difficulties; the export trade was dwindling, especially after the introduction of the new drapery caused an increase in the home demand for wool[4]; and the Staplers endeavoured, on the one hand to exercise a control over the internal trade in wool, and on the other to compete with the Merchant Adventurers in the export trade in cloth[5]. Despite repeated efforts[6] the Staplers failed to get any substantial encouragement. Under changed circumstances there was no room for them. The Stuart kings preferred that internal trade should be regulated by officials[7] rather than by companies[8]; and the English drapery manufacture had developed to such an extent that the Government could aim, not only at giving a preference to native producers in the purchase of materials, but at starving out continental competition altogether. The policy of prohibiting the export of wool was mooted in the reign of James I.[9], it was to

---

[1] Vol. I. pp. 316 and 415 n.   [2] Vol. I. p. 496.

[3] J. Johnson, *A device to increase her Majesty's customs and to maintain the Ancient Company of the Staplers* (1582?). Brit. Mus. *Lansdowne MSS.* xxxiv. 68, 69, also (1579) xxviii. 27.

[4] Lohmann, *Die Staatliche Regelung der Englischen Wollindustrie*, 69, in Schmoller's *Staats und Socialwissenschaftliche Forschungen*, xviii.

[5] J. Johnson, *Lansdowne*, xxxiv. 68. Also *Hist. MSS. Comm.* ii. Ap. 40.

[6] See the draft Act in 1614 *Hist. MSS. Comm.* iii. Ap. 15. *Commons Journals*, i. 505; also in 1621 (*Hist. MSS. Comm.* iii. Ap. 25, *Lords Journals*, iii. 174).

[7] Sir Edward Hoby had a patent under Elizabeth and James I. for dealing in wool in certain counties of England, *Hist. MSS. Comm.* i. Ap. 124. S. P. D. J. I. viii. 115.

[8] Traders might be good judges of quality, but they were always under the suspicion of manipulating the markets in their own interests and to the detriment of the public. Compare the complaint in 1621 by the wool growers against the staplers for combining with the clothiers to keep down the price of wool, *Hist. MSS. Comm.* iv. Ap. 277.

[9] James by Proclamation (24 March, 1616) caused the staples approved by

receive attention from Charles I.'s Committee on Trade[1], and A.D. 1603 —1689. it became a burning question in the years which succeeded the Restoration. It brought into clear relief an antagonism between the landed and the manufacturing interests.

The same system was adopted with regard to other staple articles of export. Sir Walter Raleigh had a patent for tin, and defended his management of the business when it was attacked in Parliament. He asserted that he had so conducted the business as to give full employment and good wages, to all the miners who liked to apply for work, however the price of tin varied[2], and that the monopoly was therefore a real benefit to the producers generally, and not for his private advantage. There were also complaints under King James of the abuses in smelting, which caused a "great disgrace to the lead of this realm"[3] and were likely to injure the trade in foreign parts, and he accordingly

Officers were also created for supervising the trades in tin, lead,

Queen Elizabeth at Middleburg, Bruges, and Bergen-op-Zoom to cease, and appointed towns within the realm for the staple of wool (*Soc. Ant.* VI. 80). This appears to have been aimed at the recently developed weaving abroad (see above, p. 233). Compare also Proclamation 28 July 1622 [Brit. Mus. 506. h. 12 (99)].

[1] See below Appendix C. ii. Also Petition to House of Commons, 3 March, 1641. *Hist. MSS. Comm.* IV. Ap. 55.

[2] *Parl. Hist.* I. 928. There are proclamations supporting the system for assaying tin in Cornwall and prohibiting the illicit export of tin, 22 Jan. 1634 [Brit. Mus. 506. h. 12 (15)] and 19 Feb. 1638 [1851. b. 3 (26)]. In 1646 a *Declaration of Sundry Grievances* [Brit. Mus. 669. f. 10 (45)] blames the patentees for the decay of trade, but a later writer asserts that the quality of tin and pewter suffered when the restrictions were removed. W. Smith, *Essay for Recovery of Trade* (1661) 31.

[3] On the patent for surveying lead in 1619, see *Hist. MSS. Comm.* III. Ap. 35. Also in 1624 "The Copy of the King's Maiesties Letters Patents concerning the reformation of the Abuses used in melting and making up of Lead And the Sealing of the same,...holding it in our Princely Judgment a thing most fit and properly belonging to our Regall Office, by the best and most speedy meanes wee may, to preuent subuert and extinguish fraudes and practises attempted and put in use, for uniust and priuate ends and particular lucre and gaine, to the generall detriment and prejudice of the Commonwealth of this our Kingdome, attended with the disgrace and discredit of the Marchandizes of the same and the hindrance of the trade and Traffique of our Subiects in Forrayne parts, which hath been famous throughout all Nations, And finding no better way for the effecting thereof then by ymploying some person or persons of trust and skill who may survey and see to the melting and making up of the said Lead into Pigges or Sowes of Lead, before it be sent from the melting houses, or by other convenient meanes may try and proue the goodness and well making of the said Pigges and Sowes of Lead" ..a mark is to be set on "whereby the buyer of the same Lead may be assured of the goodness and well making up and melting of the same." Proclamations (Soc. Ant.) VIII. 227.

created a Surveyor of Lead. A similar official was appointed to have charge of the iron trade, which was regarded
as needing special supervision, because of the manner in
which it consumed the timber of the realm[1].

The principle of official supervision was applied in other
directions, and the story of the changes in the regulation of
silk-dyeing, brings out the practical difficulties which were
felt in connection with these efforts to regulate the quality
in the
manufac-
ture of silk,
of goods. The main abuse in silk-dyeing arose through the
addition of gum in the dyeing process; this increased the
weight of the silk, but interfered with its quality. In 1606
King James issued a proclamation against this practice and
imposed heavy fines, but with no good result; and in 1632
King Charles incorporated the silkmen to have supervision
over one another. As, however, the Company "upheld
abuses" instead of correcting them, he revoked the charter,
and gave the responsibility over them to the London Company
of Dyers, who were empowered to seize all silks impro-
perly dyed; this company was apparently content to exact
quarterly payments and connived at the frauds the members
were expected to prevent. In 1639, accordingly, Charles
finding that no search was sufficient to detect the mischief,
erected an office and insisted that all persons in London
should bring their silks to be viewed and registered, both
before the process of dyeing and after. This scheme, it was
said, had worked well, and Charles II. was petitioned to take
similar order[2].

This method of supervision was also employed in regard
the supply
of coal,
to certain articles of common consumption. There is considerable interest in the institution of a royal surveyor of
coal[3]; this form of fuel was coming into common use in

---

[1] Proclamations, 29 July, 1637. Brit. Mus. 1851. b. 3 (18).

[2] *Reasons for Renewing the Office for finding out and punishing the Abuses in
Silk Dyeing.* Brit. Mus. 816. m. 12 (96).

[3] The Kings most Excellent Maiestie...hauing beene very credibly informed
of the great abuses and wrongs daily committed in mingling, amongst coales
commonly called Newcastle coales, much Blacke Earth, Dirt, Slate and other bad
stuffe not fit to burne or serue for firing, and so mingled, are brought and uttered
within the Realme of England, and thereby for the most part the same Newcastle
coales are made unmerchantable, to the great hurt and preiudice of the buyers

London as the woods in the neighbourhood were being cut A.D. 1603 —1689. down, and billets were scarce. A much more difficult task was that of supervising the alehouses in all parts of the *the manage- ment of ale- houses,* kingdom, this was desirable not only for the sake of the consumers but in the interest of public order. From what- ever cause it may have arisen, there was, especially in the early part of the seventeenth century, an immense amount of complaint as to the increase of drunkenness[1]. The chief outcry was in regard to alehouses[2]; there had been, as the records of manorial courts show, immemorial efforts to control the breweresses; but ale-conners and ale-tasters were chiefly interested in securing ale of the proper quality and strength, as laid down in the Assize. Parochial officers were not efficient agents in putting down tippling; the constables were inclined to connive at it, or visit a house " under colour of search " in the hope of getting beer from the company[3]; while the penalties were so excessive in the first statute on

---

thereof, as well Noblemen, Knights, Gentlemen and other his Maiesties louing subiects who partly for the preseruation of woods and partly for the scarcitie of woods, doe for the most part burne of the same. With a view "to prohibit and suppresse such wrongs and abuses aforesaid" a surveyor is appointed "to be Sur- veyor of the said coales who or his Deputie or deputies are to be attending and attendant in and about the searching, viewing, seeing and surveying of the said coales. And are appointed to informe and complaine against such as shall offend in such mingling or uttering of unmerchanteable coales as aforesaid. And to have a Seal of office under which to certify what coales and of what sort of goodnesse of coales any Master, Owner or Shipper, doe or shall take in, fraight or lade into their Ships or Barkes at the places abovesaid to be brought to the Citie of London or otherwise to bee spent within this Realme of England, to the end that the buyers of the same coales may the better know and be informed of the goodnesse or badness of them." Anyone having "cause of complaint" is to go to "Andrew Boyde Esquier his Maiesties Surveyor" and then in writing "without charge to such as shall so complaine" to leave his complaints, when the matter shall be attended to 26 Feb. 1616. Soc. Ant. VI. (60). See also *the Proclamation touching the Surveying of the Sea Coals of Newcastle,* 16 Feb. 1625. Brit. Mus. 506. h. 11 (20).

[1] Hall, *Society in Elizabethan Age,* 76. Camden definitely dates the intro- duction of this vice from the Netherlands in 1581. *Elizabeth,* p. 263.

[2] In large towns there was an excessive number of taverns where wine was drunk; and in the reign of Charles II. we hear of the increasing consumption of French brandy, as a habit which was both deleterious and unpatriotic (*Grand Concern,* in *Harleian Miscellany,* VIII. 559. The substance of this and the following paragraphs appeared in the *Contemporary Review,* Nov. 1886.

[3] Lupton, *London and the Countrey carbonadoed,* in *Harl. Misc.* IX. 330.

A.D. 1603 the subject[1] that they could not be enforced. The Act[2] in
—1689.
the first year of James was intended to restrain " inordinate
haunting and tippling in Innes and Ale-houses"; it declares
" the true and principall use of ale-houses" to be for the
relief of wayfarers and not for the "entertainment of lewde
and the and idle people." There was to be a penalty of ten shillings
repression
of drunken- for permitting "unlawful drinking," and all drinking was
ness.
unlawful except by *bona fide* travellers, by the guests of
travellers, and by artisans and labourers during their dinner-
hour. The licensed ale-house was only to be open to
residents in the locality for one hour in the day, for the
consumption of liquor on the premises. An additional
measure was passed in 1607[3], and these Acts were made
perpetual in the last Parliament of James[4]. Besides en-

---

[1] The Act of Edward VI. (5 and 6 Ed. VI. c. 25) gave power to the justices to
suppress unnecessary tippling-houses, but it was chiefly directed against disorder,
and not against excessive drinking.
[2] 1 J. I. c. 9.   [3] 4 J. I. c. 5.
[4] 21 J. I. c. 7. The fines on unlicensed ale-houses were so high that offenders
could not pay them, nor "bear their own charges of conveying them to gaol"; so
that constables were "much discouraged" from presenting them (3 C. I. c. 4)
Accordingly the penalties were somewhat relaxed under Charles I., but the evil
seems to have gone on increasing. The Brewers' Company in 1647 were much
aggrieved about the laxity of the magistrates in neglecting to put down "unlicensed ale-houses, which are the only receptacles of drunkards." They hoped
that a consideration of the heinousness of the brutish sin of drunkenness would
" move the hearts of the pious magistracy of these times to have a more vigilant
eye over these irregular unlicensed private houses," and to show a just appreciation of the merit of the Company of Brewers. But the evil does not seem to
have abated, for in the year preceding the Restoration a French Protestant wrote
from London, "there is, within this city, and in all the towns of England (which
I have passed through), so prodigious a number of houses where they sell a
certain drink called ale, that I think a good half of the inhabitants may be
denominated ale-house keepers.... But what is most deplorable, where the gentlemen sit, and spend much of their time drinking of a muddy kind of beverage, and
tobacco, which has universally besotted the nation, and at which, I hear, they have
consumed many noble estates.... And that nothing may be wanting to the height
of luxury and impiety of this abomination, they have translated the organs out
of the churches (Thursday, May 9, 1644. Scobell, *Acts*, I. 70) to set them up in
taverns, chanting their dithyrambics and bestial bacchanalias to the tune of those
instruments which were wont to assist them in the celebration of God's praises,
and regulate the voices of the worst singers in the world, which are the English in
their churches, at present " (*A character of England* in *Harleian Miscellany*,
x. 193). This language might seem to be mere exaggeration, but it receives considerable confirmation from other sources. The Newcastle magistrates asserted
that out of 200 inhabited houses in Shields no fewer than 140 were ale-houses

deavouring to legislate on the subject, the Government A.D. 1603
—1689. appointed officers to see to the execution of the law[1]. The patent for alehouses was intended to restrict their numbers and promote temperance: it did not have this result, but gave rise to scandalous exactions and abuses; and was withdrawn by proclamation in 1621[2].

The creation of a Company to exercise a supervision over some branch of trade was an expedient which had been in vogue from time immemorial. The revival of Industrial Associations under Elizabeth was partly due to the desire to provide for the maintenance of quality; though such bodies served other purposes as well. They could be employed as agents for enforcing industrial legislation[3], and they seem to have been used as a means of protecting townsmen from alien competition[4]; still, the reason, which is put prominently forward in the patents or Acts which conferred on them their exclusive powers, is the necessity of securing a better quality of wares. *In other cases the Companies were utilised to exercise supervision*

There were several cases in which the wardens of long-established companies received extended powers under Elizabeth and the Stuarts. The wardens of the London Haberdashers[5] were to have a right of search in regard to the hats and caps which required so much oversight. So *both in London*

(*Conservatorship of Tyne* in Richardson's *Reprints of Rare Tracts*, III. p. 46), and the vice certainly seems to have affected many classes of society. Norden describes the habits of the squireens (see below, p. 544), while Puritan ministers made the "great pains they were to take or had taken in preaching" an excuse for smoking and drinking in the vestry (Scrivener, *Treatise against Drunkenness*, 83).

[1] Like Sir Walter Raleigh's patent for taverns (Hall, *Society in Elizabethan Age*, 79), it helped to secure a sort of police supervision, and the same motive was at work in other cases; great abuses were found to exist in common bowling alleys, dicing houses and tennis courts, erected and frequented by many persons of mean quality; and the whole responsibility for the supervision and regulation of such places of amusement in London and the neighbourhood was given in 1620 to Clement Cotterell, who held the office of groom-porter (Rymer, *Fœdera*, XVII. 236). Another courtier, Sir S. Duncombe, sued for a patent for the sole right of hiring covered chairs and litters in London and other towns. *Hist. MSS. Comm.* III. Ap. 191.

[2] 30 March, 1621. Brit. Mus. 21. h. 1 (9).

[3] See above, p. 35.

[4] See above, p. 81.

[5] 8 Eliz. c. 11.

A.D. 1603
—1689. too, in regard to the trades which worked on leather; all
men living within three miles of the city of London and
working at these crafts were to make their payments to
the London Companies, and to be under the survey of the
wardens. The Companies of the Curriers, Saddlers and
Shoemakers were recognised as the proper authorities for
seeing into these matters[1]. In a similar fashion, when a
series of disgraceful frauds was discovered on the part of
Goldsmiths in 1574[2], the wardens and fellowships of the
Company were made liable for any loss that occurred, if
plate which bore their mark was not of the proper touch[3].

In some cases, indeed, the gilds had urged that they
could fulfil this duty, but were not entrusted with it: thus
*and other
towns.* the drapers of Shrewsbury complained that certain dealers
infringed their privileges, and that as a consequence the
public were defrauded by having defective Welsh cloth
brought for sale[4]: their privileges were at first reaffirmed,
but no real gain accrued to the public from establishing
the restriction, and the measure was rescinded after a short
experiment[5]. Still more curious was the petition of the
London house-painters, who had long been a brotherhood,
but had never been incorporated, and who were annoyed
by the way in which plasterers "intermeddled with their
science." The consequence was that "much slight work
went off, as Pictures of the Queen and other Noblemen
and others; and all manner of Works which shewed fair
to sight: And the People bought the same, being much
deceived; for that such Pictures and Works were not
substantially wrought: a Slander to the whole Company
of Painters, and a great Decay of all Workmanship in the
said Science; and also a great Discouragement to divers

---

[1] 5 Eliz. c. 8, § 31. There was a very severe struggle shortly after the passing
of this Act, as to the respective rights of the London Company and the Westminster
Company of Cordwainers. Stow, *Survey*, vol. II. bk. v. p. 213. In 1622 the office
of searching buff and chamois leather was granted by patent to Sir T. Glover, who
was empowered to search vessels in the ports. *Hist. MSS. Comm.* III. Ap. 27.

[2] Stow, *Survey*, v. 184.

[3] 18 Eliz. c. 15.

[4] 8 Eliz. c. 7.

[5] 14 Eliz. c. 12.

forward young Men, very desirous to travel for Knowledge in the same[1]." The painters did not get supervision in this matter of portraits, however; perhaps the Queen had no desire that her pictures should be substantially wrought unless they were also fair to see. There was a similar revival of company organisation in Hull, Coventry, Newcastle, Carlisle, and Winchester during the reign of Elizabeth, and a very large number of new companies were constituted by Charter or Act of Parliament under the Stuarts. Of these the Cutlers' Company[2] of Sheffield has obtained the greatest celebrity.

Charles and his advisers seem to have relied on the *Though Charles* whole on inspection by officials rather than on supervision *usually* by companies[3], but in some cases they had recourse to this *relied on officials* latter method of regulation[4], and in one instance at least they seem to have tried to combine the two expedients. There was a great deal to be said for controlling the manufacture of starch, especially as it was a new business and there were no vested interests to be considered; the corporation to which the regulation of this industry was assigned, was enjoined to see that good wheaten flour was not wasted in the manufacture of a new-fangled luxury[5].

[1] Stow, *Survey*, v. p. 214.

[2] 21 J. I. c. 31. Repeated pains were taken to organise one such company during the Interregnum. The trade in Norwich goods was much interrupted, and the manufacturers were greatly distressed. Parliament was forced to try and do something to mitigate the evil, and a new corporation of weavers for this district was the result. Scobell, *Acts*, 1650, c. 36; 1653, c. 24. Similar bodies were erected under Charles II. for carpet-weaving at Kidderminster (22 and 23 C. II. c. 8) and for the silk-throwers (14 C. II. c. 15).

[3] The patentees and the companies were not infrequently in conflict. See in regard to the Vintners in 1594 (Stow, *Survey*, v. 196), the Brewers in 1580 and 1586 (*ib.* 202), the Distillers in 1596 (*ib.* 237) and the Fletchers in 1570 and 1576 (*ib.* 217).

[4] The supervision of the making of bricks for the city of London was intrusted to the Brickmakers Company by James I. Proclamation, 7 Nov. 1622 [Brit. Mus. 506. h. 12 (103)], and Charles I. appears to have erected a new corporation for carrying on the industry in 1636 (Gardiner, VIII. 283). The beaver makers of London were also incorporated by Charles I., and were accorded protection against foreign competition. Proclamation, 26 May, 1638. Brit. Mus. 1851. b. 3 (29).

[5] James I. issued various proclamations on the subject, 23 August, 1607, Brit. Mus. 506. h. 10 (76), also 5 July, 1608 (*ib.* 89) and incorporated a Company; Charles I. gave them exclusive powers in the manufacture, and appointed a Surveyor of Starch to oversee them. Cunningham, *Alien Immigrants*, p. 148,

C.

In attempting to interfere with the manufacture of soap the government was on more delicate ground, as the industry had been practised in the country from time immemorial. Under existing conditions, however, the supply was inadequate, and the country was forced to pay largely for the importation, not only of materials for the manufacture, but of the soap itself. There seemed to be a good case *he erected a* for interference. In 1631, Charles incorporated a London *Company* Society of Soap-boilers to work patents for a new method *of Soap-* *boilers* of manufacturing soft soap which had been granted by James I.[1] A few months later a Westminster Company was started which bought out the rights of the London patentees, and undertook to pay a substantial commission to the Crown on all the soap produced, and to use native materials in the process. Charles also endeavoured to insist on a high quality, by erecting an office for the assay of soap and by giving the new Company powers of search over other manufacturers[2]. This project roused the opposition of the existing soap boilers, who refused to have anything to do with the Company and thwarted the scheme of the government in every way[3]. Proceedings were instituted against them in the Star Chamber[4] and other drastic measures were taken to force all the trade into the hands of the privileged body, though there is evidence, both in the rise in the price of old soap and in the large importation which occurred, that it was unable to meet the demand in a satisfactory fashion[5]. The opinion of the official inspector did not convince the public mind, and even after a formal competition before the Lord Mayor[6] there was no disposition to accept his decision that the White Soap manufactured by the Westminster Company was really good. In 1637 the Westminster Company surrendered their

on the introduction of starch. Proclamation, 30 June, 1629. Brit. Mus. 1851. c. 11 (1).

[1] *A Short and True Relation concerning the Soap busines* (1641), p. 4 [Brit. Mus. E. 156 (6)].

[2] Proclamation, 26 June, 1632. Brit. Mus. 506. h. 12 (12).

[3] Proclamations, 13 July, 1634, Brit. Mus. 21. h. 1 (40), and 25 Jan. 1635, Brit. Mus. 506. h. 12 (24).   [4] *Short and True Relation*, p. 7.

[5] Proclamation, 13 July, 1634 [Brit. Mus. 21. h. 1 (40)].

[6] Proclamation, 26 Jan. 1633 [Brit. Mus. 506. h. 12 (17)].

charter, after receiving £43,000, which was paid by the independent soap boilers, who were in their turn erected into a corporation, on promising to pay a commission of £8 a ton to the Crown on all the soap they manufactured[1]. The project seems to have given rise to much distress among the soap boilers[2] and inconvenience to the public; legal proceedings dragged on till 1656, when a judge in the Court of Exchequer decided that the grant of 1637 held good[3].

The attempt to confer the manufacture of an article of common consumption on a small body of patentees, who were using a new process, and who had to fear no competition from abroad, appeared to be straining to the utmost the permission which had been allowed by the Act of 1624 for the granting of exclusive rights to companies. This *which caused* soap patent, more than any other, seems to have caused the *serious* smothered indignation to break into flame; it had been the *grievance,* occasion of much difference of opinion within the council[4], but there was a singular unanimity in the outcry which was raised when public opinion found expression at last. At the Council of York, Charles was obliged to declare many of the industrial patents void; but enough remained to call forth an indignant declamation from Sir J. Colepeper[5] in the Long Parliament. "I have but one Grievance more to offer unto you; but this one compriseth many; it is a nest of wasps, or swarm of vermin, which have overcrept the land, I mean the monopolers and polers of the people. These, like the frogs of Egypt, have got possession of our dwellings,

---

[1] Gardiner, VIII. 284. Proclamation, 28 Dec. 1637, Brit. Mus. 1851. b. 3 (21).

[2] A contemporary writer asserts "That many Citizens of London were put out of an old Trade, in which they had beene bred all their time, and which was their only lively-hood, by Knights, Esquires, and Gentlemen, never bred up to the Trade, upon pretence of a Project and new invention, which in truth was not so. Their prosecution of the Soape-makers of London in Star chamber, being beyond example, both in respect of the manner of proceedings, and of the Sentence itselfe, who for using fish-oyle, and not obeying their searchers, were fined at great summes; imprisoned at three severall times about twenty moneths; their goods extended; their Pannes, Fats, etc., broken and destroyed, their houses of a great yearely value made unusefull; their families dispersed and necessitated; and their estates almost ruined." *A Short and True Relation concerning the Soap busines*, 1641.   [3] W. H. Price, *The English Patents of Monopoly*, 127.

[4] *Cal. S. P. D.* 1635—6, Preface, ix.

[5] He subsequently suffered on account of his attachment to the royal cause. Peacock, *Index of the Names of those royalists whose estates were confiscated.*

and we have scarce a room free from them; they sip in our cup, they dip in our dish, they sit by our fire; we find them in the dye-vat, wash-bowl, and powdering tub; they share with the butler in his box, they have marked and sealed us from head to foot. Mr Speaker, they will not bate us a pin; we may not buy our own cloaths without their brokage. These are the leeches that have sucked the commonwealth so hard, that it is almost become hectical. And some of these are ashamed of their right names; they have a vizard to hide the brand made by that good law in the last Parliament of King James; they shelter themselves under the name of a corporation; they make bye-laws, which serve their turns to squeeze us, and fill their purses; unface these and they will prove as bad cards as any in the pack. These are not petty chapmen, but wholesale men[1].'

Considering the storm of indignation which had been roused by these experiments in industrial supervision, it can *and the system was abandoned at the Restoration,* hardly be a matter of surprise that little, if any, effort was made to revive the system after the Restoration. Inclination and policy alike would render Charles II. disposed to refrain from meddling in such delicate matters. In so far as the prospect of obtaining revenue indirectly had weighed with his grandfather or his father, in their interference with the brewers and sellers of ale, there was no longer the same reason for special action, after the Excise was formally voted[2]. The army of officers, who had held patents from the Crown for particular classes of wares, had ceased to exist, and the Companies must have had increasing difficulty in exercising

---

[1] *Parl. Hist.* II. 656.

[2] The introduction of this change in the taxation of the country under the Commonwealth gave government new status for dealing with the matter. The imposition of an excise brought the whole trade directly under the supervision of revenue officials (14 Aug. 1649, c. 50. Scobell, II. 72); there were heavy penalties, for fiscal reasons, on unlicensed houses; and the loss of a licence was a severe punishment to hold over the head of an ale-house keeper The Commissioners for Excise thus came indirectly to be concerned in putting down the worst classes of houses; and by a curious arrangement, the Commissioners of Customs were empowered to deal in a summary manner with the most frequent offenders. These were the watermen on the Thames and the carmen and porters at the quays, and such persons were liable to be arrested without warrant, and dealt with summarily for drunkenness or disorderly conduct (1654, c. 38. Scobell, II. 320).

their authority effectively. In those cases, where they had A.D. 1603
—1689. been superseded by royal patentees, they would not be likely to recover effective control of the trade when the officials ceased to act The regulation of industry in England generally was left to Parliament, and though in some cases the legislature erected new companies[1], it was more inclined on the whole to adjust tariffs and lay down *in favour* conditions which would be favourable to some branch of *of methods of fostering* industry and leave those who embarked on it to do their *industry* best. An illustration of the different methods of encouragement adopted before and after the Civil War is supplied by the treatment of the salt trade. Salt-works had been promoted in England under Charles I., as the fishing interests were very insufficiently supplied with foreign salt, especially in 1628 and 1629. It therefore became a matter of great importance to develop the native production; salt-pans were erected in the neighbourhood of Shields, and a corporation was formed, against which the familiar complaints were brought in 1641[2]. The chief competitors of the Shields manufacturers appear to have been the Scotch makers, who were charged with a higher imposition than the English makers, but had more favourable terms than the foreigners[3]. The men of Shields argued that "coales, labour and diet, being above one-half cheaper in Scotland (especially dureing the troubles and heavy taxes in England) a much heavier imposition on their salt than on our own was necessary[4]." In 1647 Parliament accepted this view, and removed the excise on English salt, leaving the imposition on Scotch salt as before[5]; but the makers still found that "the English salt could not keep market with the Scottish"; and in 1649 the imposition on Scottish salt was raised to the same figure as that on other foreign salt; but almost at the same time an excise was laid on English salt, at the

---

[1] See above, p. 305, n. 2.

[2] John Davies, *An answer to those printed papers, published in March last,* 1640, *by the late patentees of Salt,* 5.

[3] *Ordinance of Parliament,* 9 Jan. 1643. Scobell, I. 60, c. 29.

[4] *Narrative concerning Salt-works of the North,* in Richardson, *Reprints,* III. p. 13.

[5] 11 June, 1647.

request of the importers of Scottish salt[1].   Under Cromwell
Scotland was united to England for commercial purposes,
and the salt-pans at Shields were demolished.   The tract
from which this information comes is an appeal to Charles II.
to give the salters better encouragement by insisting on the
use of English salt in the fishing trades ; it urges on general
grounds, that it is the "wisdom of a kingdom or nation to

*by means of
the tariff.* prevent the importation of any manufacture from abroad
which might be a detriment to their own at home, for if
the coin of the nation be carried out to pay for foreign
manufactures and our own people left unemployed, then in
case a war happen with our potent neighbours, the people
are incapacitated to pay taxes for the support of the same.'
These were exactly the objects which Parliament had in
view in legislating for particular industries as it did so
fully during the eighteenth century.   Attempts to foster
the manufacture of salt in salt-pans ceased to be of such
pressing importance in 1670, when rock-salt was accidentally discovered near Droitwich.   "A person that searched
with an auger for Coles lighted upon a Rock of Salt ; that
which the instrument brought up was as hard as Allom,
and as pure, and when pulverised became an excellent sharp
salt.   Out of the Augur-hole Brine flew up more fierce than
if it had been squirted out of a London Water Engin used
for quenching Houses on Fyre.   This Bryne proved very
vigorous and sharp, beyond any of the Springs in other
Salt-works[2]."   It was the most fortunate solution of the
difficulty, and appears to have had a useful effect in stimulating other producers to aim at turning out a high quality,
—a result which could never have been obtained either
by the grants of exclusive privileges or the imposition of
protective tariffs.

*The aban-
donment of
systematic
supervision* So far as we can judge, the collapse of the personal
government of Charles I. involved the abandonment of

---

[1] *Narrative,* in *Reprints,* III. 16.

[2] John Collins, *Salt and Fishery* (1682) 4.   Collins was a Fellow of the Royal
Society and several members appear to have interested themselves in these
discoveries and in new processes for the manufacture.   *Phil. Trans* III. 1060,
XI. 1059.

attempts to organise a national system for the supervision A.D. 1603 —1689. of industry[1]. It is probable enough that there was at least a temporary injury to English manufacture[2] from the *synchronises with complaints* cessation of constant attempts to search, but the system of trade-marks[3] seems to have established itself, at all events *as to the quality of* in the cloth trade[4], before very many years had elapsed. *goods.*

[1] On this point it is worth while to refer to the evidence of W. S. in the *Golden Fleece* (1656). He complains bitterly of the carelessness in regard to apprenticeship and the general industrial disorganisation of the break-down of the system of search; he says (p. 91), "Out of townes Corporate there is no Searcher appointed, but all is left at liberty to the Clothier, who useth his liberty so much to his own advantage, as should a Searcher be there established by a Justice of Peace, as the Law requires, he shall assuredly be affronted, sued and imprisoned by such secret helps as the Clothier can procure in the Exchequer, carrying therewith such abusive countenance of the Law, as a single and simple Officer dares not resist.

"Secondly, in Townes Corporate, where this office ought to be attended with numbers, there is sometimes none, but never above one, and that an ignorant man, as also both nominated and sworn by the Magistrate, who undoubtedly is ever a Clothier, and as likely by his power to be an offender, whom such a worthlesse officer as himselfe puts in, dares not controule, much lesse correct or seize his Clothes: Adde to this also, that as he is an abject person, and the creature of the Magistrate, so he is wanting in knowledge to judge of good and true worke * * * If in Villages there be a Searcher established by the Justice (as the Law enjoynes) then such seizures come to the Quarter Sessions, where by favour and friendship the offender escapes and the State is the sufferer." He goes on to say no fines ever reach the Exchequer, "but the abuses continue, increase and are maintained, the Commonwealth and foreigners are generally wronged, the State deprived of its Revenue even to vast summes, the Nation is dishonoured over all the world." The distress in the cloth trade at the close of the Protectorate may have been partly due to this disorganisation, as well as to the effects of the Spanish war. Compare also an *Essay for Recovery of Trade*, 1661, p. 7. "The charge of true making Cloaths and finishing them, rests upon the trust of the Searcher and Measurer which Trust in these dayes is very weakly discharged, even where there are any such officers (for generally there are none) * * * But in Villages and out of Corporations there are no such Officers established, because no body takes upon him to present fit persons (qualified to those Services) to the Justices of Peace, who are by the Law appointed to administer the Oath nor are any such Persons forward to seek the Imployment because the Sallary is very small and the work lies scattering and dispersed and will not acquite his paines and charge who shall undertake the same."

[2] See in regard to the Taunton trade, in 1617 (?), *Hist. MSS. Comm.* III. Ap. 63.

[3] Trade-marks were familiar enough in the wool trade in the fifteenth century. Duke, *Prolusiones Historicae*, 581.

[4] The official sealing, and the trade-marks, probably existed for a time as a double security. In 1632 a London cloth-worker was punished for affixing the seals of Colchester bays to inferior qualities (*Hist. MSS. Comm.* III. Ap. 71); while in a proclamation (16 April, 1633) on abuses in the cloth trade of the Midlands and West of England, Charles insists that every clothier shall have

During the later part of the seventeenth century, however, there is a constant outcry about the preference of the public for French goods. This may have been a mere vagary of taste; but it is a tempting suggestion to connect it with the fact that there was much more effective supervision of the quality of goods manufactured under the *régime* of Colbert, than was at all possible in England in the time of Charles II.[1]

*The Com-
mercial
progress of
London
reacted*   **198.** The rapid growth of English commerce which occurred in the latter part of the sixteenth and the seventeenth centuries affected the port of London very favourably: indeed, there was a general feeling that this centre was increasing at the expense of the out-ports. This commercial progress reacted on industry in many ways; the Londoners had the best facilities for procuring imported materials, and *on its
industry* the best access to foreign markets. As London was the centre of the Turkey trade, and the East India trade, it offered special advantages to silk-manufacturers; soap-boilers also could procure the oils they required from the Muscovy and Greenland Companies, or from the Mediterranean; it was an appropriate centre for the ship-building and other maritime trades, which relied for materials on the products imported by the Eastland Company. There were few if any trades that could not be conveniently localised in London.

*and led to
the rapid
growth of
population,*   The opportunities of industrial development would probably have attracted a large population to this city under any circumstances. Even during the fifteenth and sixteenth centuries, when we hear so much of the decay of other English towns, London appears to have flourished: it certainly was re-inforced by a number of aliens who settled and worked in the neighbourhood. The labour legislation of Elizabeth's reign, which was intended to be favourable to

one several mark for his cloth and should continue to use it without change so long as he practised the trade. [Brit. Mus. 506. h. 12 (19).]

[1] "With regard to the deceit in manufactures Mr Child says Colchester baize was sold by the credit of its seal; but since the siege of Exeter it is not so good by 15 or 20 per cent., Mr Papillon thinks every manufacturer ought to have a particular trade mark." *Report of Committee on Decay of Trade*, 1669. *Hist. MSS. Comm.* viii. Ap. i. p. 134 b.

corporate towns[1], would give an additional stimulus to the *A.D. 1603 —1689.* industrial growth of London, and men who had served a seven years' apprenticeship in any part of the country would be ready to try their fortunes in the one great city which England possessed. The rapid growth of London was an almost inevitable result of the economic conditions of the Elizabethan and Stuart periods; but it caused constant surprise, not unmingled with alarm, at the time. There *so that it was diffi-* was the greatest difficulty in maintaining any effective in- *cult to organise* dustrial and social regulation in such a rapidly increasing *regulation* centre of population, and the machinery of municipal institutions, which had been very highly developed, proved insufficient to grapple with the situation. The Mayor and Common Council were no longer able to arrange for the adequate supply of water, food and fuel without assistance, and the Livery Companies were ceasing to be effective agents for supervising industry. Municipal control needed to be supplemented or superseded by national regulation; and during the seventeenth century both royal intervention and Parliamentary legislation were brought to bear in turn, on the problems of London life. The City was an immense political power, and the influence it exerted in the constitutional struggles of the seventeenth century was decisive. It did much both with men and money to contribute to the victory of the Parliamentary forces; but there was some danger that the crowds of citizens and other inhabitants would be able to interfere with the freedom of Parliamentary debates, and to put an undue pressure upon the members[2]. Dislike of agitation by women and apprentices, either on the part of the kings or Parliament, was quite compatible

---

[1] A Proclamation of James I. asserts that the growth of London was at the expense of other towns. "The other good Townes and Borrowes of his kingdome, by reason of so great receit for people in and about the said City, are much unpeopled and in their trading and otherwise decayed." 12 Oct. 1607. [Brit. Mus. 506. h. 10 (79)]. Sir Thomas Roe (1641) asked, "Whether, indeed, London doth not monopolise all trade? In my opinion it is no good state of a body, to have a fat head and lean members." *Harl. Misc.* IV. 436. But some provincial towns like Manchester, Leeds and Halifax were growing too (Inderwick, *The Interregnum*, 93).

[2] On the incidents connected with the women's petition in 1648 see *Parl. Hist.* III. 161; see also the apprentices. *Ib.* 717 (1647), 887 (1648).

with respect for the political influence of the City. The proclamations which were intended to check the growth of the suburbs, were not inimical to the interest of the old corporation, and seem in several instances to have had its approval. There is no reason to suppose that jealousy of the wealth and power of the City of London, as a real political influence, had anything to do with these measures, though no political party could view with perfect equanimity the presence of large numbers of human beings, who were under no effective control.

in the suburbs, A fundamental difficulty arose from the fact that there was no one body which was able to exercise direct authority throughout the whole area over which London was extending. Suburbs were springing up outside the limits of City authority. Spitalfields was beginning to be occupied by weavers, and Whitechapel was fast being built upon, while houses were being also constructed in S. Giles'. But all these districts lay outside the area of the City and of its corporations. The city fathers appear to have favoured a very drastic method of dealing with this problem; they would appear to have been anxious to confine the growth of the town within the limits of their jurisdiction, and to have approved the policy of preventing the erection of new houses. As early as 1580, Elizabeth issued a proclama-
or to prevent overcrowd-ing tion in regard to the overcrowding of London houses. "There are such great multitudes of people brought to inhabite in small roomes whereof a great part are seene very poore, yea, such as must live of begging or by worse meanes, and they heaped up together and in a sort smothered with many families of children and seruantes in one house or small tenement." The plague was the special danger feared; but the remedy seems unsatisfactory. Her Majesty by "good and deliberate advise of her Counsell, and being also thereto mooved by the considerate opinions of the Lord Maior, Aldermen and other the graue wise men in and about the Citie, doeth charge and straightly command all maner of persons * * * to desist and forbeare from any newe buyldings of any house or tenement, within three miles from any of the gates of the sayd Citie of London, * * * and

also to forbeare from letting or setting, or suffering any A.D. 1603 more families then one onely to be placed or to inhabite —1689. from henceforth in any house that heretofore hath bene inhabited[1]." The 'undersitters' were to be turned out and set to find places for themselves in decayed towns in any part of the country. In this Elizabeth was acting with the consent of and through the Mayor, but she contemplated the fact that the good government of such multitudes could " hardly be done without devise of mo newe jurisdictions and officers for that purpose." After an outbreak of the plague James reiterated similar orders and enjoined the disinfecting of houses[2]. The Crown and the civic authorities acted together and, in 1633, they were jointly responsible for demolishing some houses that had been recently built[3]; the City urged the same policy on the House of Commons[4] when the period of personal government had come to an end.

The inevitable result of such restrictions appeared in the overcrowded and insanitary condition of the City itself. *in the City.* Ample evidence of this is afforded by the special outbreaks of the Plague as well as by the ordinary death-rate. In 1593 it raged in a very alarming fashion, and Bartholomew Fair was not held as usual[5]; the excitement which these successive visitations occasioned gave rise to a useful institution; as the first steps were taken for compiling statistics of deaths by the weekly bills of mortality[6]. There can be no doubt that the whole City was in a most unhealthy state; *The conditions of* the water-supply was poisonous in the extreme[7]; the houses *life were* were overcrowded; and there were frequent encroachments on the remaining open spaces. There were also many

---

[1] Proclamation, 7 July, 1580. Brit. Mus. G. 6463 (205).

[2] Proclamation, 16 Sept. 1603. Brit. Mus. 506. h. 10 (25).

[3] Gardiner, VIII. 289.   [4] *Ib.* 288 note.

[5] Rymer, XVI. 213. On the whole subject see Creighton, *A History of Epidemics in Britain,* Vol. I. cc. VI. X. and XII.

[6] Macpherson, *Annals,* II. 231 (1603).

[7] Thames water formed the chief supply, and was laid on to houses in 1594, but the first great improvement began in 1605, when an Act was passed for bringing in a stream of running water to the northern part of the City of London (3 J. I. c. 18), and the New River Company was formed. Clutterbuck, *The History and Antiquities of the County of Hertford,* II. 5.

elements of risk owing to the manner in which houses
were built, especially from the number of wood buildings;
and most of the proclamations and acts which deal with
the subject, and limit or regulate the building in London
and its suburbs[1], were concerned with the question in its
sanitary aspects. The Act of 1593 may be quoted as sum-
marising the evils which had been observed even at that
time: "For the reformynge of the great Mischiefes and Inconveniences that daylie growe and increase by reason of
the pesteringe of Houses with diverse Famylies, harboringe
of Inmates, and convertinge of great Houses into severall
Tenements or Dwellinges, and erectinge of newe Buyldings
within the citties of London and Westminster and other
*most
insanitary,* Places nere thereunto adjoyninge, whereby great Infection
of Sicknes and dearthe of Victualles and Fewell hathe
grown and ensued[2]"; it ordains that no new buildings
shall be erected within either city or within three miles of
them unless for "inhabitants of the better sort," that houses
shall not be broken up into tenements, and that no commons
shall be enclosed. The last provision had reference rather
to the practice of archery than to the healthfulness of open
spaces. Similar reasons were alleged in subsequent proclamations[3], though under James some stress was laid on
the unsightliness of the "noisome pestes of bulkes, stale-
sheds, cants, jutties wherewith our streets are in all places
so much cumbered and amazed that it taketh away the

---

[1] King James was concerned that wood, which might be available for ship-
building should not be used for houses, and issued several proclamations in favour
of brickbuilding in London, 1 March, 1604, Brit. Mus. 506. h. 10 (51). Also 22 July,
1611 (Soc. Ant. vi. 18). He advocated brickbuilding partly on aesthetic considerations; it was his ambition to have it said that he found London houses "of stickes
and left them of Bricke," Proclamation, 16 July, 1615 [Brit. Mus. 21. h. 1 (1)].
He also objected to unsightly additions to old buildings. In support of his
action he was able to refer to the building regulations of Harry FitzAllwyn
in the time of Richard I., Proclamation, 17 July, 1620 [Brit. Mus. 21. h. 1 (5)],
and to count on the support of the municipal authorities [14 July, 1624, Brit.
Mus. 506. h. 11 (26)]. Charles the First issued very complete building regulations
(2 May, 1625), Brit. Mus. 506. h. 11 (40), and instructed commissioners to see that
there was a supply of good bricks at moderate prices, 16 July, 1630, Brit. Mus.
506. h. 11 (137).

[2] 35 El. c. 6.

[3] Rymer, *Foedera*, xvii. 107 (1618).

benefit of air, sweetness and decency of the same[1]," and A.D. 1603
—1689. special regard was had to appearances in laying out a new district like Lincoln's Inn Fields[2], under the advice of Inigo Jones. In the time of Charles I., there were very precise directions as to the character of all new buildings erected; every whole storey was to be ten feet high, and the walls of three-storey houses were to be two bricks thick[3]. A similar measure[4] was passed in 1656; a fine of one year's *but some improve-* rent was imposed on all houses, with less than four acres of *ment took* ground, which had been erected since 1620 in the City of *place,* London or within ten miles of it; and a fine of £100 to the State, £20 per month to the poor, was imposed on all houses erected after 1657 on new foundations. Any house rebuilt was to be of brick or stone, and straight up without jetting or butting out into the street[5]. The limitation and regulation of building in the City, in sanitary interests, and for the sake of security, was kept steadily in view from the time of Elizabeth to the Restoration.

The disaster of the Great Fire showed that the measures *especially after the* we have discussed had been introduced too late to render *Fire.* the City free from the risk of conflagration; but advantage was taken of the opportunity thus offered to try and remedy the old defects. Not to the full extent indeed; order and proportion were but little regarded; the beautiful plan devised by Sir Christopher Wren was set aside, and the streets were rebuilt on the old lines[6]. But an honest effort was made by the Long Parliament of the Restoration to see that the houses of different classes should all be fairly substantial, and that the worst evils in the old city should be avoided.

The impracticability of providing shelter for the largely *Care was taken to* increased population was only one of the problems to be *obtain* faced. There were considerable difficulties in obtaining a sufficient supply of corn; King James had encouraged the erection of granaries for the storing of foreign corn, to be

---

[1] Rymer, *Fœdera*, 143 (1619). [2] *Ib.* 119 (1618).

[3] *Ib.* xix. 179 (1630).

[4] Compare petition of Brickmakers. S. P. D. 26 March, 1652, xxiii. 132.

[5] Scobell's *Acts*, ii. 484 (1656), c. 21.

[6] Loftie, *History of London*, i. 373.

used for home consumption or re-exportation[1], and at a later
time an ingenious projector named Yarranton[2] proposed the
formation of granaries, similar to those which served the
requirements of continental towns, at which corn might be
collected in Oxfordshire and Northamptonshire, and brought
by river to London. No effort seems to have been made
to put this scheme into effect, and there is reason to believe
that municipal attempts to set the price of bread were falling
into abeyance. The problem appears to have been becoming
insoluble[3], and it was commonly believed that the difficulty

[1] Proclamations, 1623, *For the Well Storing and furnishing of the Realme with
Corne*, Brit. Mus. 21. h 1 (14).

[2] *England's Improvement*, 114—138 (1677).

[3] John Powell, Clerk of the Market, testifies to the difficulties that had arisen
in 1600. "Forasmuch as divers Officers, by reason of their unskilfulness and
want of knowledge, do not afford the bakers such sufficient allowances therein as
are answerable unto all the Charges of baking at this day whereby some Questions
are made between the said Officers and Bakers concerning that matter; I have
therefore at this present thought it good not only to revoke my said book (in
respect of the said assize of bread only) and to my great pains and travel to
publish this new book for the good and true Assize of all sorts of Bread." His
new book seems to have been found useful, for it was reprinted in 1621, 1626,
1630, 1632, 1636 and 1671. But further changes were needed; the terms in which
the settling of the assize of bread were enjoined, were found to be no longer
intelligible, and in 1709 (8 Anne, c. 18) a measure was passed which was more
adapted to the times. In particular it arranged that the price of bread should
vary with the price of corn, and not, as in former days, that the weight of the
bread should be always changing. There was a further regulation in 1757, at a
time of very great scarcity, when all sorts of other cereals are mentioned besides
wheat, and prices of bread, of oatmeal, rye and pea-flour are promulgated
(31 G. II. c. 29). On the working of this Act compare the Report of 1772 (*Parl.
Hist.* XVII. 555). This statute, however, only affected places where the assize
was set; as there were many where this practice had been discontinued, and the
magistrates were at no pains to revive it, another statute had to be passed a few
years later for regulating prices in places where the assize was not set (3 G. III.
c. 11). The wisdom of the magistrates who did not attempt to carry out this
mode of regulation was certainly confirmed by the experience of the London
magistrates. During the great scarcity of 1757 they cut the price of bread
as fine as possible, and made it follow every symptom of the diminished price
of corn (see C. Smith, *Three Tracts on the Corn Trade*, 28). In some cases, even,
they set it in anticipation of a further decline. The result was that the greatest uncertainty prevailed among those who had stocks of corn and flour; and
as a consequence the corn-factors and meal-merchants actually were at the
expense of withdrawing their stocks for sale elsewhere. In fact if the assize was
set too high, the bakers had an unnecessary profit; if it were set too low, the
factors did not bring corn and flour to the town; in either case there was a
distinct disadvantage. The only countervailing advantage was that the public
were somewhat reassured by this authoritative declaration that the price they
were paying was not altogether unreasonable, and were less likely to join in riots

of procuring goods would sooner or later set an insuperable A.D. 1603
obstacle to the further increase of the city; but Petty[1], who —1689.
made this forecast, did not foresee the immense improvements of communication which have been brought about
by modern applications of steam power. The insufficiency *of water,*
of the London water supply has been already alluded to[2];
but there was also a very real difficulty in procuring fuel.
The scarcity of wood was being felt more and more all over *and of fuel.*
the country; the Londoners had been gradually forced to
take to burning coal, not only in bakeries and workshops,
but for domestic fires. As a result a very great trade sprang
up with the Tyne, since Newcastle was by far the most
important coal-field then opened. It was asserted early in
the eighteenth century that "the Colliery trade brings up
a greater number of Seamen, than all our navigation elsewhere[3]"; most of these vessels coasted between the Tyne
and the Thames. This trade formed a favourite source of
revenue, and the charge of re-erecting public buildings after
the Great Fire was defrayed by an additional custom on
coals[4]. The Londoners did not readily reconcile themselves
to this form of fuel[5], but as the new fashion established
itself, the gain of Newcastle proved to be the loss of other
places. There had been one district in Kent, which supplied
kindling for the large faggots in common use for fires; but
as Defoe remarks "since the taverns in London are come to
make coal-fires in their upper rooms that trade declines;
and though that article would seem to be trifling in itself,
it is not immaterial to observe what an alteration it makes

(11 G. II. c. 12) against corn-factors and bakers. See also *House of Commons
Report,* 1795, Vol. IX.

[1] Hull, *Economic Writings of Sir W. Petty,* II. 471.

[2] See above, p. 315, n. 7.

[3] C. Povey, *A discovery of indirect practices in the coal trade* (1700), p. 43.

[4] 18 and 19 C. II. c. 8, § 34.

[5] The use of coal for fires had been prohibited in 1306. Stow, in his *Annals*
for that year, draws an interesting contrast with the habits of his own day (1612).
In 1624 a bill against using coal west of London Bridge was passed by the House
of Lords, but rejected by the Commons. *Hist. MSS. Comm.* II. Ap. 29. The
'fine-nosed city dames' complained, "Oh Husband wee shall never bee well, wee
nor our children while we live in the smell of this Cities Seacoale smoke"
[*Artificial Fire* (1644), Brit. Mus. 669. f. 10)]. Locke, who suffered from asthma,
was unable to reside in the City in 1679 (*Reports,* etc., 1871, XVIII. 828).

A.D. 1603 —1689.

Industrial regulation presented greater difficulties,

but neither the extension of the powers of the City

nor the incorporation of the suburbs provided the needed authority.

The power of the City Companies

in the value of those woods in Kent, and how many more of them than usual are yearly grubbed up, and the land made fit for the plough[1]."

While so much attention was given to the conditions of life, the supervision of industry was not neglected. Indeed it seems to have been chiefly with a view to the exercise of effective control over the quality of wares produced and exposed for sale, that the question of bringing the whole area of London under civic jurisdiction was mooted. In Henry VIII.'s time, attempts had been made to increase the powers of the citizens for purposes of industrial regulation[2]; and this was undoubtedly one element in favour of trying to restrict the growth of the town. In 1632 the Mayor and Aldermen petitioned the Council in regard to the growth of suburbs; but the suggestion of the Council that the ungoverned area should be divided between the cities of London and Westminster, fell to the ground[3]. When the attempts to strengthen and enlarge municipal authority had thus failed, the only hope of reducing the suburban population to governance, lay in the direct exercise of royal authority, and King Charles erected a new corporation[4] for this purpose. This experiment was, not unnaturally, viewed with much suspicion by the Londoners, and it does not appear to have had more than a brief existence.

In cases where the Stuart Kings felt it advisable to appoint royal officials for the supervision of a particular branch of industry, they were sometimes brought into conflict with the London Companies and forced to override their claims. King James had not respected the privileges of the Goldsmiths, while the appointment of surveyors and other officials by royal authority weakened the power of the Companies for industrial and trade purposes; and they do

---

[1] Defoe's *Tour*, I. 138.

[2] 14 and 15 Hen. VIII. c. 2.

[3] Gardiner, *Hist.* VIII. 288.

[4] Proclamations, 24 Feb. 1637. Rymer, xx. 173. "Upon the earnest and frequent complaints of our loving subjects the inhabitants of the places as well within the City of London exempt from the freedom thereof, as without our said city and within three miles of the same of the great grievances by them sustained, through the intrusion of aliens and foreigners into those parts, and by the ungoverned exercise of trade there."

not seem to have regained effective authority under the <i>A.D. 1603
—1689.</i> Commonwealth. Parliament was inclined to disregard <i>was weakened,</i> privilege of every kind; there was occasional legislation on industry, but this did little or nothing to re-establish the authority of municipal institutions. After the Restoration, Charles II pursued a similar course; he did confer powers on the companies for foreign trade, but he was very chary of interfering in any way with industrial affairs, and left this matter entirely to Parliament[1]. The legislature seems to have preferred to adopt the course, which became habitual in the eighteenth century, and to lay down general conditions <i>and though some companies received fresh powers from Parliament,</i> for manufacture, rather than to create special machinery for one locality; but there are various cases where special companies were created by Parliamentary authority[2],in the time of Charles II.[3], and legislative support was occasionally given to local industrial corporations in the eighteenth century. The Bricklayers' Company were employed to maintain the standard of the building materials chiefly used in London[4]. The use of logwood, instead of woad, in producing certain dyes was unsatisfactory, and Parliament gave the Dyers' Company the right of search within a considerable area round the metropolis[5]. There was another case in which two new corporations were erected; the silversmiths and plate-workers of Birmingham and Sheffield suffered greatly in the exercise of their trade for want of assayers "to assay and touch their wrought plate," and an Act was passed by which guardians of the standard of wrought plate were incorporated in each town, to secure the quality of these wares[6]. A company of workers in glass was also created in 1773[7]. These were mere exceptions <i>they were dying out</i>

---

[1] A comparison between the proclamations in the Earl of Crawford's *Handlist*, before and after the Civil War, is very instructive.

[2] On the facilities for forming joint stock companies in Scotland, and the part they played in the industrial revival after the Restoration, see Scott, *The Records of a Scottish Cloth Manufactory*, xxxix.

[3] See above, p. 201, n. 5, also 305.

[4] 12 G. I. c. 35. The appeal of the Stationers' Company against Interlopers in 1710 (Stow, *Survey*, v. 225) led to the first copyright act (8 Anne, c. 19). On the ineffectiveness of monopoly in maintaining accuracy of production, see Erskine's speech on the University monopolies of Almanacks. *Parl. Hist.* xx. 609.

[5] 13 G. I. c. 24.   [6] 13 G. III. c. 52.   [7] 13 G. III. c. 38.

to the common practice. Though the civic trade corporations continued to exist both in London and other towns, during the eighteenth century, they appear to have been falling into disrepute[1]; and the books of some of the Companies, both in Coventry and Hull, show that few apprentices were entered in the latter half of the century, and that there was
in England generally.
but little regularity in their ordinary proceedings. In many centres of industry they had already ceased to be of practical importance, and where they continued to exist they were looked on with disfavour. The author of the *Interest*
In Scotland where municipal trade institutions persisted later
of *Scotland* is especially severe upon them[2]. "This well deserves the Consideration of the Royal Boroughs, who grone under a heavy Burden of paying a sixth Part of all the Land-tax for the seclusive Privilege of Trade, and yet by the indiscreet Exercise of these Monopolies and seclusive Privileges of their Tradesmen, Trading is forc'd from amongst them. How many Towns, once wealthy and flourishing, are by this become mere Deserts, as if they groned under the Oppression of Tyranny, like those ancient ruinous Cities under the Dominion of the Turk and See of *Rome*? So that this heavy Burden lies now upon a few, and these not well able to bear it. They know, from Experience, the unfree Trade, as it is, and ever will be managed, can yield them but small Relief; but if the Trade and the Freedom of handicraft Imployments was laid open, as the *African* Trade

---

[1] There were several strong expressions of opinion in regard to the mischief they wrought during the earlier part of the eighteenth century. In particular, Lord Molesworth [*Franco-Gallia* (1721), Preface] urged that the backward condition of many of the old towns was due to the unwise regulations which were framed by the trade corporations. A country gentleman writes in 1753, "In the City of London, where by making the Residence of *Strangers* difficult, the Suburbs are grown ten times as big as the *Corporation; where* oftentimes 300 or 400 Houses stand vacant in a Parish within the City Walls; and where likewise many do not let at so high a Rent as they would, if situated in some *Country* Towns? But that we may be more sensible of the bad Influence of these *Exclusive Priveleges*, and the Injury they do their very *Abettors*, we need only take a Survey of all the *Kingdom*, and see how the antient *Corporations* and Cities dwindle into *Villages*, whilst our open *free Towns* have grown up into populous *Cities*. Among many Instances I will give only one, viz. the Town and Parish of *Hallifax* in *Yorkshire*, which about forty years ago contained only 25,000 Souls which are now increased to 120,000 Inhabitants." *Reflexions upon Naturalisation, Corporations and Companies* (Brit. Mus. 111. e. 18), p. 25.

[2] Lindsay, *Interest of Scotland*, pp. 51—57.

was, the Royal Boroughs would reap as great Benefit by the one, as the Nation in general gains by the other. Many of those unfree Traders, who are now disperst thro' the Country, would come and reside in Burghs, where they could carry on their Business to greater Advantage; the best Tradesmen, the most ingenious Artificers, Mechanicks, and Manufacturers would, in like Manner, settle in the great Towns; and the small Burghs of Barony and Regality[1], where they now live, would, in this Event, become Nurseries for Persons of narrow Fortunes, and those who begin to trade, to stock the Royal Boroughs with wealthy Inhabitants, their Proportion of the Land-tax would then prove an easy Burden to them; when, as we are of one Country, under the Dominion of one Prince, and governed by the same Laws, every Person should be intitled to the same Privileges, Freedoms and Immunities,

A.D. 1603 —1689.

they were not favourable to national development.

---

[1] These various classes of burghs (Gross, *Gild Merchant*, I. 200) existed side by side in Scotland till 1856; we find them at the capital of the country. Under a charter of David I. the Abbot of Holyrood erected the burgh of *Regality* of Canongate in 1128 (Mackay, *History of Canongate*, 1), while Edinburgh was a *Royal Burgh*. There were also burghs of *Barony*, where the burgesses had no part in the election of baillies. The merchants of Royal Burghs had exclusive privileges for foreign trade (*Memorials for Government of Royal Burghs*, 1685, by Φιλοπολιτεῖος, p. 18), and the craftsmen seem to have been free to ply their craft anywhere throughout the realm. The respective rights and functions of the *Gilda Mercatoria* (Guildry) and Town Council, which are problems for the student of English municipal history in the thirteenth century, gave rise to questions of practical importance, and to litigation in Edinburgh in the nineteenth century. The relations of the Guildry and the Town Council were adjudicated on by Lord Cringlety in 1820 (Colston, *Guildry of Edinburgh*, 71). The relation of the Guildry with the crafts (incorporated trades) also gave rise to litigation; the right of members of the Guildry to import and sell jewelry was successfully maintained by my grandfather Alexander Cunningham, when it had been attacked by the Goldsmiths (1802); on the other hand the Guildry were said to encroach on the rights of the Hammermen when they repaired watches (1793). Shaw, *Digest*, I. 214.

In Scotland till 1846 (9 and 10 Vict. c. 17) there were real craft gilds maintaining the old relations with the municipalities. Instances of attempts on the part of these incorporated trades to assert their ancient and exclusive privileges were not infrequent; e.g. lorimers (1829); the Canongate Hammermen (1807); there was a very difficult point as to the right of men, who were not free of the weavers, to set up looms and weave cotton cloth (1778, 1804, 1829). *Ib.* I. 215.

Lindsay, writing in 1733, contrasts the trade restrictions in Scottish towns with the comparative freedom in London. In his time it appears that a man who was free of one company (say the Fletchers) might practise any other trade, and be e.g. a joiner. But he appears to have been mistaken in supposing that this was due to some one act of the Common Council. See above, 34, n. 3.

21—2

upon this sole Condition, Residence, and Subjection to
the Rules, Customs, Services, and Duties of the Burgh in
common with the other Inhabitants." From the numbers
which still survive in the northern kingdom we should
suppose that they were specially powerful there, but Adam
Smith regarded the actual rules of Scotch corporations as
less mischievous than those of similar institutions in the
south[1]. On the whole the tendency of the times was
against such bodies. The method of supervising industry
by erecting companies, which had suited mediaeval times
and had flourished in civic communities, was not compatible
with the requirements of national life and progress. Parliament preferred to encourage industrial pursuits by granting
premiums and bounties to those individuals who earned
them, rather than by conferring special privileges on particular groups of citizens.

*London
offered
opportuni-
ties to alien
merchants
to invest
their
capital, or
to come
and reside;*
199. London, as a growing commercial centre, was
proving attractive to provincial Englishmen, and was also
once more becoming a resort for merchants from continental
towns. There were considerable opportunities for the remunerative employment of capital; and large sums, belonging
to moneyed men in Amsterdam and other towns abroad, were
transmitted to England for investment[2]. These wealthy
men not only sent their money, but came to settle themselves[3]. There are traces of alien capitalists in Elizabeth's
reign, and the English moneyed men had reason to fear
competition, such as they had hardly experienced since
the fall of the Bardi, in the time of Edward III. The
Queen obtained considerable sums of money as loans from
naturalised Dutch residents[4], and the Goldsmiths complained
bitterly of the intrusion of strangers in their trade[5]. Once
and again during Elizabeth's reign there had been a great

---

[1] *Wealth of Nations*, Bk. I. ch. xii. p. 50.

[2] Much of the capital used in the re-building of London was said to be Dutch
[*Hist. MSS. Comm. Report*, viii. App. p. 134], and a large part of the capital of
the Bank of England came from similar sources.

[3] *Parl. Hist.* vi. 782.

[4] S. P. D. El. (1600), cclxxiv. 28; cclxxv. 143; cclxxviii. (1601), 8—15, 27, 124.
The connection of these men with finance is brought out by the proposal made by
Erasmus Vanderpere for establishing a bank of Money. Brit. Mus. *Lans.* xxx. 37.

[5] S. P. D. J. I. (1622), cxxvii. 12.

outcry about these foreigners, and the manner in which they conducted some branches of foreign trade[1]. The commerce with Spain, and the Spanish Netherlands, was said to be entirely in their hands, and attempts were made to revive and enforce the statutes of employment[2], so as to restrict the business in which they engaged of importing foreign manufactures. The proposal to control and restrict their dealings by appointing an English broker, through whom all their business should be transacted, was not favourably received[3], and on the whole it appears that the foreign merchants in London continued to flourish in the reigns of James I. and Charles I. No inconsiderable number applied for naturalisation at that period, and though they were excluded from various branches of trade by the regulated Companies, their foreign connections must have enabled them to do a profitable business in those lines of traffic which were open to them.

Peculiar interest attaches to one section of the foreign merchants who settled in London during the reign of Elizabeth. A few families of Marranos or Spanish Crypto-Jews who, despite the care with which they conformed to Christian worship and practice, were liable to be detected by the Inquisition and persecuted in Spain, established themselves in London[4]. They had been extensive traders in their old homes, and maintained their relations both with the Iberian peninsula and with Brazil; and their experience of the Inquisition led them to sympathise with the extreme protestant opponents of the English Crown. They gave pecuniary support to the Parliamentary party on the outbreak of the Civil War[5]; indeed there is according to Dr Gardiner reason to believe that some of them were introduced into the country, in 1643, with the specific object of assisting the new administration[6]. The triumph of Puritanism seemed for a time to open up the prospect

A.D. 1603 —1689.

and they were accused of engrossing some branches of trade.

Among them were a body of Crypto-Jews,

whose influence strengthened the parliamentary party.

---

[1] Strype's *Stow*, v. 295.   [2] See Vol. I. pp. 396, 401.   [3] Stow, *Survey*, v. 296.

[4] L. Wolf, *Menasseh Ben Israel's Mission to Oliver Cromwell*, p. xiv. One of them, Roderigo Lopez, was court physician to Queen Elizabeth, and is probably the original of Shakespeare's Shylock.

[5] *Hist. MSS. Commission*, VII. 401, 403.

[6] Gardiner, *Academy*, 4 March, 1882, Vol. XXI. 158.

of a welcome being extended to the Jews to come and
settle in England[1], and a conference, which discussed
the matter in 1655, arrived at the conclusion that "there
was no law which forbad the Jews' return into England[2]."
Still, the persons whom Cromwell consulted showed no
disposition to smooth the way for the return of the Jews,
and proposed that they should only be admitted to trade at
the out-ports, and should be charged double customs and
Cromwell favoured the recognition and enlargement of the colony,
duties on all their transactions[3]. Cromwell appears to have
been particularly eager for the formal recognition and enlargement of the Jewish colony in London[4], and this was
not unnatural under the circumstances. The government
found it difficult to collect the taxes, the City magnates
were not very ready to make advances, and Jews might be
expected to render assistance on easier terms. According
to a contemporary writer "Oliver Cromwel's design to bring
in the Jewes amongst us, was to make them Farmers of the
Customs and Excise, and to have naturalized them, by that
means to have drawn into this Nation the principal Jewes
in the World, with their Estate and Credit which, if death
had not suppressed the Tyrant, he would have made these
Jewes very instrumental to carry on his designs of furnishing
Cromwel with vast sums of treasure; Anthony Fardinando,
the great Jew, told me the Jewes were to advance one
Million of Money[5]." At all events it is clear that, despite
the hostile sentiments which had found expression, the Protector gave the Marranos his personal support, and permitted
them to practise their religion privately[6]. The Anti-Semites,
who had successfully thwarted Cromwell's plans for giving
more public recognition to the Jews, were not contented
with this result, however, and, by pressing on the attack,
and the position they obtained
they over-reached themselves. On the outbreak of the
Spanish War, an attempt was made to treat the Marranos
as subjects of the King of Spain, and to confiscate their
goods. They boldly took the opportunity of throwing off

[1] This feeling was particularly strong about 1649 and 1650. Wolf, *op. cit.* xix.,
xxvii.

[2] *Ib.* xlix.   [3] *Ib.* lii.   [4] *Ib.* liii.

[5] T. Violet, *Petition against the Jewes*, p. 7

[6] Wolf, *op. cit.* lviii.

their disguise, and pleaded that they had been the victims of Spanish tyranny who hoped to find an asylum in England[1]. As a result the authorities refused to treat the Marranos as Spanish subjects, and the failure of this scheme, for ousting them, gave them a firmer position in their capacity as Jews[2]. Despite the vigorous attack which was made on them after the Restoration[3], their position was not changed for the worse. Charles II. had received so much assistance from the Dutch Jews, who for the most part cherished royalist sympathies[4], that he was not inclined to institute any rigorous action towards their co-religionists in London.

It is not easy to say how far the Jews, and other aliens resident in London at this period, were prevented from taking a part in foreign trade. They seem to have been excluded from the regulated Companies, and therefore from commerce with the Levant, the Baltic and Hamburg; but the trade to France, Spain and Portugal was apparently open to them, and they could take shares in joint-stock Companies, if they desired it. The Navigation Act rendered it impossible for them to take up the business of shipping, but they would have considerable opportunities, as interlopers and for illicit trade, if they were inclined for maritime ventures. Under Charles II. they were relieved from the burden of paying additional customs[5], and they seem on the whole to have occupied themselves as brokers and intermediaries, and not to have taken a prominent part in developing the maritime trade of the country.

Towards the close of the seventeenth century, London received a considerable incursion of alien immigrants of another type. The Huguenots seemed to have obtained a secured position in France, and emigration from the country had practically ceased, when Louis XIV. entered on a fresh

A.D. 1603 —1689.

was not changed by Charles II. who had been aided by Dutch Jews,

but they were still excluded from several mercantile occupations.

There was also a large immigration of Huguenots

---

[1] S. P. D. Interregnum, cxxvi. 105, April 25, 1656.

[2] Wolf, *op. cit.* lxvi. They obtained a cemetery of their own, and were allowed to worship publicly in their synagogue. Violet, *Petition against the Jewes* (1661), p. 2.

[3] See below, p. 386, n. 1.

[4] Wolf, *op. cit.* xli., lxxiii.

[5] 25 C. II. c. 6, *An act for taking off aliens duty upon commodities of the growth, product and manufacture of the nation.*

campaign for the suppression of heresy[1]. From 1680 onwards the emigration of Huguenots commenced on a very
large scale, and considerable numbers round their way to
England[2]. They were able to count on a warmer welcome
than that which had been extended to their Walloon predecessors in the time of Elizabeth. The organised opposition
to alien settlers had had its strength in municipal powers
and institutions, but these had been so far weakened[3] that
who were they could no longer offer an effective resistance. Public
generously
welcomed opinion, too, had veered in favour of the refugees; there
by the
public was a magnificent outburst of public generosity, which found
expression in the ready response to the briefs appointing
collections in the churches. Five separate appeals were
made between 1681 and 1699[4], and funds were also contributed from the Privy Purse and by a Parliamentary
grant[5].

The government were fully aware of the advantage
which might accrue to England if these refugees were
attracted to settle in this country. Sir Henry Savile, the
ambassador at Paris, had written strongly on the subject[6]
as soon as the signs of Huguenot unrest became very
and the marked; in 1681, Charles issued a proclamation[7] which
Crown.
promised a ready welcome and letters of denization to those
who settled in England, and James took action on their

[1] Cunningham, *Alien Immigrants*, 224.

[2] It has been calculated that 17 out of 20 of those who left France by sea
came to England, and that the total number who arrived was about 80,000;
though many of these were passed on to Ireland, Scotland and America   *Ib.* 229

[3] The antagonism to men who were foreign to the town was maintained in
1652 (*Records of the Burgh of Reading*, IV. 292, 460). In 1709, when the naturalisation of foreign protestants was under discussion, the difficulty of admitting them
to trade corporations was pointed out (*Parl. Hist.* VI. 780) The hostile influence of
the trade corporations had also been felt in 1681 (Agnew, *Protestant Exiles*, II. 44).

[4] W. A Bewes, *Church Briefs*, 208 f. Povey refers to this as a proof of the
generosity of the public when their sympathies were roused, "We have no
reason to call in question the bounteous liberality of so many hundreds, if not
thousands, of well-disposed people, who gave to the Brief of the French Protestants 5, 15, 20, 30, 40, 50 and some an 100*l.*, and few of any repute less than
5, 10, 15 or 20*s*. By which means a very large sum of money was raised; for the
second brief brought in between 40 and 50,000*l.*, and the last 25,000*l.*, there being
five briefs on that occasion." Povey, *Unhappiness of England as to its trade*, 58.

[5] Cunningham, *Alien Immigrants*, 231

[6] Cooper, *Savile Correspondence*. Camden Society, Vol. LXXI. p. 210.

[7] Cooper, *List of Foreigners*. Camden Society, Vol. LXXXII. p. xviii.

behalf in 1685[1]. At the beginning of the century there was *A.D. 1603 —1689.* a great opportunity for remedying the chief deficiencies in *They proved a* the industrial system by planting new trades. Before the *great ac-* days of machinery, skilled labour rather than capital[2] was *quisition to* the primary element that was requisite for improving the *the indus-* *trial force* industry of a country. A new art could only be introduced *of the* *country* by inducing some of those who possessed it to migrate[3] and the persecution of the Huguenots gave the opportunity for starting the manufacture of goods that had been greatly in demand, and for which this country had been hitherto indebted to France. It was a case where England gained at the expense of her great rival[4], and Parliament was *and re-* *ceived par-* eager to foster the newly introduced industrial arts. The *liamentary* Royal Lustring Company obtained exclusive rights for the *encourage-* *ment.* manufacture of certain classes of silks in 1692, and a protective measure was enacted in its behalf[5].

---

[1] Baird, *The Huguenots and the Revocation of the Edict of Nantes*, II. 96.

[2] It was of course necessary that there should be capital too, if the work was done on a large scale. A few of the Huguenots succeeded in saving their effects; some of them were able to organise manufacturing in this country, while others had the necessary stock-in-trade, and some of the arts which the new comers practised were domestic in character. The account of Louis Crommelin's method for establishing the linen industry at Lisburn is instructive: he brought seventy persons, who had their own looms, they were credited with capital in the company which carried on the undertaking according to the worth of the stock-in-trade they contributed. W. R. Scott, *The King's and Queen's Corporation for the Linen Manufacture in Ireland*, in the *Proceedings of the Royal Society of Antiquaries of Ireland*, XXXI. 377.

[3] On the labour difficulty in connection with the introduction of a new art see W. R. Scott, *Records of a Scottish Cloth Manufactory*, XXXV, lxv.

[4] The economic loss to France was very great, and it was of various kinds. Many of the refugees succeeded in emigrating with their households and their property, though some of them had been reduced to a temporary abjuration of their faith in order to make good their escape (Poole, *History of the Huguenots*, 31); not a few were able to bring their property and household goods with them. The amount of capital which was taken from France at this time appears to have been enormous. There was also a large emigration of skilled artisans of different sorts; and in other cases a loss of business connection and access to foreign markets (Poole, *op. cit.* 170; Macpherson, *Annals of Commerce*, II. 616—7). The emigration of artisans and mariners was noted early, and eager efforts were made by the French ambassador to secure their return (Macaulay, *History of England* (1858), II. 51; Agnew, *Protestant Exiles from France* (1886), II. 17). The extent of the influence of the various causes of decay came out fully and clearly in the reports of trade, which were sent from various provinces (Baird, *The Huguenots and the Revocation of the Edict of Nantes*, II. 77) about fifteen years after the Revocation.   [5] 8 and 9 W. III. c. 36.

A.D. 1603
—1689.

Though chiefly concentrated in London

The strangers in Elizabeth's time had settled in separate colonies in different parts of the country; and there are signs that the government would have been glad if the Huguenots had followed a similar course[1]. By far the largest number of the new immigrants, however, preferred to be in London: the silk trade was concentrated, during the earlier part of the eighteenth century, in Spitalfields, and a great variety of skilled trades were carried on by refugees in Soho and Long Acre. There were indeed

some of them were diffused in many parts of the country as well as in Scotland and Ireland,

certain callings which could be more conveniently practised in other districts. The manufacture of sailcloth was started at Ipswich[2], and calico printing was established at Richmond[3]. The linen manufacture was successfully developed both in Ireland[4] and in Scotland[5]. Paper-making was

---

[1] In the distribution of the funds, a very disproportionate sum was allotted to the out-ports for the erection of churches, " 3 in London, 12 in several counties." Stow, *Survey*, Bk. v. p. 303.

[2] T. Gimlette, *French Settlers in Ireland*, in *Ulster Journal of Archaeology*, IV. 206.

[3] Burn, *History of French, Walloon, Dutch and other Foreign Protestant Refugees*, 259.

[4] The Irish Parliament under Charles II. had been making considerable efforts to foster the linen manufacture (17 and 18 C. II. c. 9). This Act was repealed in 1705, and another passed in the same year for the improvement of the hemp and flaxen manufactures. In 1695—6 the English Parliament were ready to encourage the linen manufacture of Ireland (7 and 8 W. and M. c. 39), especially after the repression of the woollen trade in 1696, and they were cordially willing to welcome foreign Protestants. Acts were passed by the Irish Parliament for the encouragement of the settlement of Protestant strangers (14 and 15 C. II. c. 13, and 4 W. and M. c. 2); but little success attended their efforts until they obtained royal patronage and secured the services of Louis Crommelin. He was a Frenchman from Picardy, who had settled in Holland, and he was enabled to bring over an industrial colony of Frenchmen from Holland, and to settle at Lisburn, C. N. de la C. Purdon in *Ulster Journal of Archaeology*, I. 211. This was the foundation of the success of the North of Ireland linen manufacture; and a few years later he also organised the manufacture of sailcloth at Waterford. There were other sailcloth factories at Cork and Rathkeale, and the trade continued to receive support from Government for many years (*Irish Commons Journals*, 4 October, 1721). Other colonies of refugees were founded at Dublin, Dundalk, Cork and Kilkenny (*Ulster Journal of Archaeology*, I. 211). There appear to have been a few settlers at Belfast, *ib*. IX. 142.

[5] The linen manufacture had existed in Scotland before the Union (*Scots Acts*, 1641, c. 101), and received much Parliamentary encouragement from the fund, which became available at that time for the promotion of Scotch industries. It was in a very backward condition in 1727 when a Linen Act was passed (Lindsay, *Interest of Scotland*, 170); but the immigrants from Picardy who settled in the burgh of Broughton, between Edinburgh and Leith, were successful in giving it

another trade which was greatly improved[1], if not freshly A.D. 1603 introduced, by the Huguenots. Indeed it is hardly an —1689. exaggeration to say that almost every kind of industrial *and they* *did much* art[2] was invigorated in consequence of the new standards *to stimulate* *local* of skill and of taste which these refugees brought with them *industries.* from France.

IX. THE BEGINNINGS OF EXPANSION.

200. Much had been done, before the seventeenth century *During the* *XVII cen-* opened, in developing the maritime power of England, but *tury the* the process of settling in distant lands had hardly begun. *founda-* *tions were* The foundations of our colonial empire were laid during the *laid for* reigns of the Stuarts. At the accession of James I., English-men had not established their footing either in Asia, Africa, or the American continent. Their hold upon Newfoundland, with a share in the fisheries off its coast, gave them their only sphere of influence in distant regions; for their attempts to plant in Virginia had not so far been crowned with success. But within ninety years there was a marvellous change. At the Peace of Ryswick England was secure in

a considerable impetus (see p. 521 below). The Huguenots at Moultrie's Hill abandoned the manufacture of silk for that of linen; and foreign linen-weavers, who may have been French refugees, are said to have settled at Drumsheugh (A. W. C. Hallen, in *Huguenot Society Proceedings* (1887), II. 175—6. The Dun-fermline manufacture was an offshoot from this centre. From Edinburgh the trade spread west to Glasgow and the district around, through the medium of the French settlers who were sent to instruct the weavers (Agnew, *Protestant Exiles from France* (1886), II. p. 520). In the eighteenth century several manufactures in Scotland were developed by alien skill. Certain Paisley merchants induced a Frenchman and his wife to come from Lisle to start thread- and lace-making in Renfrew, in 1710 (G. Crawfurd, *History of the Shire of Renfrew*, 1782, p. 17). Dutch linen-weavers were brought over to Glasgow in 1725 (J. Gibson, *History of Glasgow*, 1777, p. 243), and in 1732 a workman from Holland began the tape manufacture (*ib.* p. 241). About forty Frenchwomen were introduced by a Glasgow merchant for the weaving of fine yarn in 1768 (*Glasgow, Past and Present*, 1851, III. 318). There appears also to have been a French potter in Glasgow in 1779 (*ib.* III. 505—6).

[1] Cunningham, *Alien Immigrants*, p. 242.

[2] On the variety of trades practised by the immigrants in Scotland see Colston, *Incorporated Trades*, p. 15. The introduction of sugar-boiling, dyeing, and the advance in pottery during the seventeenth century appear to have been chiefly due to Dutch settlers. Cunningham, *op. cit.* 216, 219.

A.D. 1603
—1689.

*English
Empire in
America,
Africa and
India.*
the possession of more or less extensive territories in Africa, in North and in South America[1]. The East India Company, and Hudson's Bay Company, had several valuable factories for trade, and St Helena, the Bahamas, Bermudas, Jamaica and other West Indian Islands had also been acquired. There is no side of economic life in which the progress during this period was so marked as in colonisation; it is the new and characteristic contribution of this century to the development of England's material greatness.

[1] The dates and agents of acquisition and settlement of the principal English possessions were as follows (*Calendars S. P. Colonial*):

PLANTATIONS IN AMERICA AND THE WEST INDIES.

Newfoundland	1583	Sir H. Gilbert.
Barbadoes	1605	
Virginia	1607	Company.
Bermudas	1614	Company.
New England	1620	Company.
Nova Scotia	1621	Sir W. Alexander.
Guiana	1627	Duke of Buckingham.
Antigua, &c.	1627	Earl of Carlisle.
Trinidad, &c.	1627	Earl of Montgomery.
Carolina	1629	General Heath.
Bahamas	1630	Company.
Maryland	1632	Lord Baltimore.
Long Island	1635	Sir W. Alexander.
Jamaica	1655	
New York, &c.	1664	Duke of York.
Hudson's Bay	1670	Company.
Pennsylvania	1682	W. Penn.

FACTORIES AND POSSESSIONS OF AFRICAN COMPANY.

Gambia	1631
Gold Coast	1660
Lagos	1661

FACTORIES AND POSSESSIONS OF EAST INDIA COMPANY.

Surat	1609
Madras	1639
Hooghly	1650
S. Helena	1651
Bombay	1665

Before the close of the seventeenth century England had already withdrawn from several regions in which settlements had been attempted. She had rendered Canada up to French, and Darien to Spanish influence. In the East she had relinquished her position in the islands, for the commerce of which she had struggled with the Dutch, but she had established her hold on various points of the main-land.

There has been much discussion at various times as to A.D. 1603 —1689. the benefit which colonies confer on the mother country; Whigs in the eighteenth, and the Manchester School in the nineteenth century, were inclined to disparage them as a mere encumbrance, and would not have been unwilling to be rid of them altogether[1]. We have completely out-lived that feeling; but the fact that the advantage or disadvantage *The advantage of* of developing colonies abroad continued for so long to be a *developing* subject of dispute, makes it necessary to enquire carefully *colonies was in* into the reasons which weighed with the men who acted as *dispute and the diffi-* the pioneers in the expansion of England. The difficulties *culties were* which they had to face were enormous; the distance of the *enormous,* colonists from the mother country, and the irregularity of communication, exposed them to serious perils; while their ignorance of the climate, and the uncertainty of their relations with the natives, proved nearly fatal to more than one enterprise. We must also bear in mind that there was in many quarters a feeling not merely of indifference, but of positive antagonism to these undertakings. Like the distant trade of the East India Company, these settlements seemed to divert labour[2] and capital[3] that could be usefully employed on English soil, without conferring any compensating advantage. The decrepit condition of Spain, despite her enormous American possessions, gave some colour to the opinion that colonies were a drain on the mother country rather than a source of wealth. If Philip II., *but there* it could be asked, had derived so little benefit from the *was a* richest lands of the New World, what advantage was there *variety of strong* in spreading over the less coveted regions which she had *motives for under-* left untenanted[4]? There were, however, various motives, *taking it.*

---

[1] Tucker posed as a moderate man, and maintained the economic tradition of the Whig party in 1774, though he denounced 'Republican Whiggism' (*A Review of Lord Clive's conduct* (1775), 2). He wrote: "America ever was a millstone hanging about the neck of this country to weigh it down, and as we ourselves had not the wisdom to cut the rope and let the burden fall off, the Americans have kindly done it for us." *Four Letters*, 7. See also below, p. 850.

[2] *Britannia Languens* (1680), 176.

[3] This objection is stated and effectively answered by William Penn, *The benefit of Plantations* in *Select Tracts relating to Colonies* (Brit. Mus. 1029. e. 16).

[4] The promoters of English colonisation were ready to argue that the mineral wealth of the Spanish colonies was of doubtful advantage. "But what are those riches where we heare of no Gold nor Silver, and see more impoverished here than thence enriched, and for Mines we heare of none but iron? Iron mindes!

political, religious and economic, which combined to induce
undertakers and emigrants to engage in colonial enterprise,
and influenced the government to view it with favour.

*Political
aims were
at work in
schemes for
planting
Ireland*
Political aims were obviously operating in the various
schemes of plantation which were floated during the reign
of James I. The task was undertaken in Ireland, with the
hope of introducing some sort of stable government into that
unhappy country, where the Crown had entirely failed to
establish effective authority over the native population.
The statesmen of the day came to the conclusion that the
only hope of reducing the island to order lay in abandoning the attempt to adapt Irish institutions to the purposes
of government, and in seriously attempting to create a
new system. They came to the conclusion that this could
be best accomplished by settling it with Englishmen, who
would hold the land on some secure form of tenure[1] and

Iron age of the world! who gave Gold or Silver the monopoly of wealth, or made
them the Almighty's favourites? Precious perils, speecious punishments whose
originall is neerest hell. * * Penurious mindes! Is there no riches but Gold
Mines? * * But let us consult the wisest Counsellour   *Canaan, Abraham's*
promise, *Israel's* inheritance, type of heaven and joy of the earth! What were
her riches? Were they not the grapes of *Eshcol*, the balme of *Gilead*, the Cedary
neighbourhood of *Libanus*, the pastury vale of *Jericho*, the dewes of heaven,
fertility of soile, temper of climat, the flowing (not with Golden Sands, but) with
Milke and Honey (necessaries, and pleasures of life, not bottomeless gulfes of
lust), the commodious scituation for two seas and other things like (in how many
inferior?) to this of *Virginia*. * * That then is the richest land which can feede
most men, Man being a mortall God, the best part of the best earth, and visible
end of the visible World. What remarkable Gold or Silver Mines hath *France*,
Belgia, Lumbardig, or other the richest peeces of *Europe?* * * The *Spaniards* old
Mynes made them the servants of *Rome* and *Carthage:* and what their Mynes and
mindes doe now I leave to others. * * Neither let any thinke that I pleade against
the sournes of the grapes like the fox which could not reach them: but I seriously
shew that they are calves and not men, which adore the Golden Calfe, or *Nabu-
chadnezzars* great golden statute, as if the *body* were not *more than raiment*, and
those thinges to be preferred to money, for whose sake mony (the creature of Man;
base Idolatry where the Creator worships his Creature!) was first ordained and
still hath both use and being." *Virginias Verger* in Purchas's *Pilgrimes*, IV.
p. 1814. See also *Nova Britannia* by R. I., f. 23. "The abundance of King
Solomon's gold and silver did not rain from heaven upon the heads of his subjects,
but heavenly providence blessed his navigations and public affairs, the chief
means of their wealth." Compare John Smith, *Advertisements* in *Works*, 929, 915
and *History of Virginia* III 3 in *Works* 407; also Bacon, *Essay on Plantations*.

[1] Sir Toby Caulfield, who was employed by the Crown to collect Tyrone's
rents after his flight in 1607, has left a report which gives curious insight into the
management of an Irish estate. The rents were paid partly in money and partly
in oats, oatmeale, butter, hogs and mutton. Rent was not levied on the land, but
on the milch cows, and the proper enumeration of these was a matter of no little

would maintain their own language and laws uncontami- A.D. 1603
—1689. nated by contact with Irish neighbours[1]. It was necessary to deport many septs[2] in order to give this scheme a trial, and only to admit a small portion of the native population[3]. Sir Arthur Chichester and Sir John Davies hoped that by promoting immigration they might diffuse a respect for the *and sub-jecting the* authority of the Crown in all parts of the island, and secure *whole* the presence of men on whose help they could rely for the *country to the Crown;* various purposes of local government. Under James I. and Charles I. the settlements had a highly military character, as it was not merely necessary for the colonists to be able to hold their own against Irish raids, but also to be ready to defend the country, in the not improbable event of a Spanish invasion[4]. From the time of Cromwell there was less need for fortifications and strongholds; he subjugated the island so entirely that English law and language became dominant, and material progress on English lines seemed possible. The native Irish were collected in Galway, between the Shannon and an inhospitable coast, where they could do little to assist the Spaniards or French in any attack they might make[5]. In the early part of the seventeenth century, plantation was necessary as a step towards consolidating the political and administrative system of the British Isles. Immigration to Ireland was encouraged, with the object of improving the efficiency of government in an island that had long formed part of the dominions of the Crown.

Political aims were also kept in view in all the schemes *and also in attempts to* for colonising beyond the Atlantic. It was hoped that these *plant in* plantations would tend to restrict the overweening power of *the West Indies* Spain in the New World, and might even serve as a basis for attacking it[6]. Deep-seated hostility to the Spanish type

---

difficulty; another element of uncertainty arose from the fact that, as Caulfield wrote, "the tenants may remove from one lord to another every half year, as usually they do." *Calendar of S. P. Ireland*, 1608—10, p. xxvi.

[1] *Ib.* p. 358.   [2] *Ib.* Preface, lxxiv.

[3] Compare Sir Arthur Chichester's account of the effects of the opposite policy in the plantation of Munster. *Ib.* No. 587, p. 357.

[4] The flight of the Earl of Tyrone seemed to show that Irish rebels might hope for countenance and support from Spain.

[5] Pocock's *Tour* edited by Stokes, p. 5.

[6] Compare Sir John Coke's project in 1625 (S. P. D. C. I. i. 59; also S. P. Col. v. 18 and 111). Sir T. Roe argued for founding a West Indian Company in

and raise up a barrier against Spain.

of civilisation was combined in the minds of many English-men with dread at finding so much wealth and power concentrated in a single monarchy. The sense of antagonism to the Spanish system first awakened in the minds of Englishmen a consciousness of their duty and destiny to plant free institutions in the lands beyond the sea. Till the seventeenth century, no serious effort had been made to anglicise Ireland; Englishmen had been satisfied to live their own life in their own island. The discovery of America, and the development of maritime power under Elizabeth, had, however, provided an opportunity for diffusing English civilisation in the New World. The men of the seventeenth century threw themselves eagerly into the task. England recognised and accepted her vocation.

Religious views were blended with political motives in opposing the Spaniards

The inner reasons for the antagonism to Spain, which had so much to do with shaping the colonial ambitions of Englishmen, were rather religious than political. The rule of the most Catholic Majesty, with the scope it gave for the Inquisition, was abhorrent to Protestants. Interference in America was a defiance of the authority claimed by the Pope[1] to partition out the newly discovered lands between Portugal and Spain. The planting of a new England across the seas was an idea that appealed strongly to men of a religious temperament, as well as to those who were moved by considerations of political expedi-ency. Religious and pecuniary motives had been inti-mately blended in the Crusades; and in this respect English colonisation resembled them, at the outset. The plantation of Virginia was regarded by Hakluyt[2] and some other

1637 (S. P. Col. IX. 61), "There is no other way advantageous and profitable to make war upon the king of Spain, but in the West Indies" (*Hist. MSS. Comm.* III. Ap. 74). The scheme for taking Hispaniola was apparently devised by Sir John Watts in 1637 (?), (*Hist. MSS. Comm.* III. Ap. 75), but laid aside till Cromwell attempted to carry it out, with disastrous results.

[1] G. L. Beer, *Cromwell's Economic Policy* in *Political Science Quarterly*, XVI. 584.

[2] Richard Hakluyt in his dedicatory letter to Sir W. Raleigh writes as follows: "A wise Philosopher, noting the sundry desires of divers men, writeth, that if an oxe bee put into a medowe hee will seeke to fill his bellie with grasse, if a Storke bee cast in shee will seeke for Snakes, if you turne in an Hound, he will seeke to start an Hare; So sundry men entring into these discoveries propose unto them-selves severall endes. Some seeke authoritie and places of commandement,

men[1], who formed a London company with this object in 1606, as not only a commercial but also a missionary enterprise[2]. They set about their adventure in the hope that it would "hereafter tend to the Glory of his Divine Majesty, in propa- *and in the* gating of Christian religion, to such People as yet live in *arrangements of the* Darkness and miserable Ignorance of the true Knowledge and *Virginia* *Company* Worship of God, and may in time bring the Infidels and Savages living in those Parts to human Civility, and to a

others experience by seeing of the worlde, the most part worldly and transitorie gaine, and that oftentimes by dishonest and unlawfull meanes, the fewest number the glorie of God, and the saving of the soules of the poore and blinded infidels. Yet because divers honest and well disposed persons are entred already into this your businesse, and that I know you meane hereafter to sende some such good Churchmen thither, as may truely say with the Apostle to the Sauages, *We seek not yours but you:* I conceiue great comfort of the successe of this your action ; hoping that the Lorde, whose power is wont to bee perfected in weaknesse will blesse the feeble foundation of your building." Hakluyt, III. 302. The same views are expressed in *Nova Britannia* by R. I. (1609): "We purpose to pro- claime and make it knowne to them all, by some publike interpretation, that our coming thither is to plant ourselves in their Countrie, yet not to supplant and roote them out, but to bring them from their base condition to a farre better: First, in regard of God the Creator and of Jesus Christ their Redeemer, if they will beleeue in him. And secondly, in respect of earthly blessings where of they have now no comfortable use but in beastly and brutish manner, with promise to defend them against all publike and private enemies." f. 6.

[1] Peckard's *Life of Nicholas Ferrar* (1852), 86, 107; Purchas, *Pilgrimes*, IV. 1777.

[2] Compare also *A true and sincere declaration of the purpose and ends of plantation begun in Virginia,* 1610 (Brit. Mus. C. 32. d. 13, p. 2): "The Prin- cipall and Maine Ends ... weare first to preach, and baptize into Christian Religion, and by propagation of that Gospell to recover out of the armes of the Divell, a number of poore and miserable soules, wrapt upp unto death, in almost invincible ignorance ; to endeavour the fulfilling and accomplishment of the number of the elect, which shall be gathered from out all corners of the earth ; and to add our myte to the treasury of Heaven, that as we pray for the comming of the kingdome of glory, so to express in our actions, the same desire if God have pleased to use so weak instruments, to the ripening and consummation thereof.

"Secondly to provide and build up for the public Honour and safety of our gratious King and his Estates ... some small Rampier of our owne in this opportune and generall Summer of peace, by transplanting the rancknesse and multitude of increase in our people; of which there is left no vent, but age; and evident danger that the number and infinitenesse of them, will outgrow the matter, whereon to worke for their life, and sustentation, and shall one infest and become a burthen to another. But by this provision they may be seated as a Bulwarke of defence, in a place of advantage, against a stranger enemy, who shall in great proportion grow ritch in treasure, which was exhausted to a low estate; and may well indure an increase of his people long wasted with a con- tinuall warre."

C. 22

settled and quiet Government[1]." The Company endeavoured to be careful in the selection of the men who were to emigrate and to refuse "idle and wicked persons such as shame or fear compels into this action: and such as are the weeds and rankness of this land": they issued a *True and Sincere Declaration* to show what settlers they would accept, both as regards religion and conversation, and faculties, arts and *for emi-* trades[2]. They also made careful provision for the main-*grants,* tenance of the religious habits they prized so highly; churches were built with such elaboration as their means allowed[3], and the practice of attending the daily services

[1] King James's first Charter, 10 April, 1606; Stith, *Virginia*, Ap. p. 1.

[2] An advertisement was issued in 1609, which is of interest as showing the class of persons whom the Company desired to attract, and the terms it offered. "Whereas (if God permit) for the better settling of the Colony and Plantation in Virginia, there is a voyage intended thither by many Noblemen, Knights, Marchants and others, to bee furnished and set forth with all conuenient speed: And for that so Honorable an action pleasing to God and commodious many waies to this Common Wealth should be furthered and furnished with al meanes and prouisions necessarie for the same, wherein both Honorable and Worshipfull personages doe purpose and prepare to goe thither in their owne persons: This is therefore to intimate and giue notice to al Artificers, Smiths, Carpenters, Coopers, Ship Wrights, Turners, Planters, Vineares, Fowlers, Fishermen, Mettell men of all sorts, Brickmakers, Brick-layers, Plow-men, Weauers, Shoe-makers, Sawyers, Spinsters and all other labouring men and women, that are willing to goe to the said Plantation to inhabite there, that if they repayre into Phillpot Lane, to the House of Sir Thomas Smith, Treasurer for the said Colony, their names shall be Registred, and their persons shall be esteemed at a single share, which is Twelve pound ten shillings, and they shall be admitted to goe as Aduenturers in the said Voyage to Virginia, where they shall haue houses to dwell in, with Gardens and Orchards, and also foode and clothing at the common charge of the Joynt stocke, they shall haue their diuident also in all goods and Merchandizes, arising thence by their labours, and likewise their Diuident in Lands to them and to their Heyres for euer: And if they shall also bring in money to Aduenture in the Joynt Stock their shares both in goods and lands shalbe augmented accordingly. And likewise al other that wil bring in Twenty fiue pound or more by the last of March though they goe not in their persons shall be accepted for Free men of the Company, and shall haue their Billes of Aduenture, as all other Aduenturers haue in the same Action." Brit. Mus. C. 18. e. 1 (63).

[3] "The Captain Generall," says Strachey, writing in 1610, "hath given order for the repairing of it (the church at Jamestown), and at this instant many hands are about it. It is in length three score foote, in breadth twenty foure, and shall haue a Chancell in it of Cedar, and a Communion Table of the Blake Walnut. and all the Pewes of Cedar, with faire broad windowes, to shut and open as the weather shall occasion, of the same wood, a Pulpet of the same, with a Font hewen hollow, like a Canoa, with two Bels at the West end. It is so cast, as it be very light within, and the Lord Gouernour and Captaine Generall doth cause it to be kept passing sweete, and trimmed up with divers flowers, with a Sexton

there was carefully enforced[1]. The whole work of colonisa- A.D. 1603
tion was treated as an enterprise in which it was a work —1689.
of piety to engage[2], and collections were made in parish
churches for the college that was planned, for English and *and for*
Indians, at Henrico[3]. The work continued despite many *natives.*
difficulties of every kind. Notwithstanding the efforts of
the Company, the colony had been the refuge of a certain
number of dissolute adventurers from the first; there had
been much difficulty in keeping them in order, and in
preserving friendly relations with the natives, while there
had been many quarrels among the officials. On the whole,
the colony prospered more in its material life than as a
missionary enterprise; but it was not in a very flourishing
condition at the close of King James's reign.

The religious impulse was also strongly at work in the *The desire*
first settlement of New England, not merely as affecting *to found a*
the spirit in which the enterprise was planned, but also as *Theocracy*
affording the main motive of those who actually emigrated. *the*
The Pilgrim Fathers were not much concerned in planting *Puritans*
the existing English type of Christian civilisation in the
New World; but they desired to secure the opportunity of
founding a society for themselves, which should be thoroughly
scriptural in character; they hoped that this would serve as
a bright example to the rest of mankind. They established
a very strict ecclesiastical discipline, but one which was
entirely unlike the system they had found so galling in
England. Under their scheme temporal privileges were
dependent on church-membership. "Most of the persons
at New England are not admitted of their Church and
therefore are not Freemen; and when they come to
be tryed there, be it ıor life or limb, name or estate, or

belonging to it; and in it every Sonday wee have Sermons twice a day, and every
Thursday a sermon, having true preachers, which take their weekely turnes: and
every morning at the ringing of a Bell about ten of the clocke, each man ad-
dresseth himself to prayers, and so at foure of the clocke before Supper."
Purchas, iv. 1753.
    [1] Smith, *Advertisements, or the Pathway to Experience to erect a Plantation*,
c. xiv., *Works*, p. 957. Also on Bermuda, see Purchas, *Pilgrimes*, iv. 1746.
    [2] Sermons by Crashaw and Whitaker, quoted by Anderson, *op. cit.* i. 194, 237.
    [3] Anderson, i. 255.

whatsoever, they must bee tryed and judged too by those of the Church, who are in a sort their adversaries[1]." The enthusiasts for Theocracy sought out witches, and banished Antinomians; they even expelled and shipped off two members of the Council who were in favour of using the *in New* Prayer-Book[2]. In a community of men of this type there *England.* was much intense individual earnestness, but little sense of corporate duty to their neighbours, except in the way of furnishing them with a model to copy. Though they had traded with the Indians, they had made no serious efforts to civilise them[3], and had been careful to keep them at arm's length. The war of extermination, waged against the Pequod nation[4], alarmed all the neighbouring tribes; and some of the colonies found it wise, in 1643, for their own security to consolidate themselves into "The United Colonies of New England." Massachusetts, Plymouth, Connecticut

[1] Lechford, *Plaine Dealing* (1642), 23 (*Mass. Hist. Soc.* iv. p. 81).

[2] Anderson, I. 362. These acts contrast curiously with the professions they made before leaving England (Baird, *Religion of the United States*, 107) and were inconsistent with the obligations implied in the terms of the Massachusetts Charter (Story, *Commentaries on the Constitution* I. 34, 36). The attitude the colonists assumed must have been a disappointment to Capt. John Smith and other English sympathisers who had regarded them, not as Brownists, but as " Good Catholic Protestants according to the Reformed Church of England," *Works*, 926.

[3] Lechford seemed to think that the form of Church government which existed in New England was incompatible with systematic efforts for the conversion of the natives (*Plaine Dealing*, 31—35). There were, however, some heroic and earnest individuals who did what they could; Henry Dunster, a schoolmaster of Cambridge (*ib.* 53), Roger Williams (Neal, *The History of New England*, I. 160), and Eliot (*ib.* 242), were remarkable examples of what might be done by men who gave themselves to this work. Compare also *A despised Virgin beautified* by O. Ll. [Trin. Coll. Dublin, P. gg. 40 (9)]. This proposal (1653) to unite the line of colonies from Florida, Carolina and Maryland to New England is imbued at once with a Puritan and a missionary spirit. A Society which was formed in 1649 (Scobell, *Acts*, II. c. 45) to publish Eliot's translation of the Bible, was reorganised through Boyle's influence by charter (7 Feb. 1662); and led to the foundation of the Society for the Propagation of the Gospel in 1701. Anderson, II. 410, 496.

[4] Bancroft, *Hist. of the United States*, I. 400. The Puritan settlers were inclined to think of themselves as the divinely-favoured conquerors of a new Canaan. "The heathen are driven out, and we have their lands in possession; they were numerous and we are few; therefore hath the Lord done this great work, to give his beloved rest," *General History of Connecticut*, attributed to Rev. Samuel Peters (1781), p. 31. The same writer calculates that within fifty years from this time the English had killed 86,000 Indians. See also *News from New England*, 1676. Hooker, *History of New England*, pref., 117, also 17, 51.

and New Haven were the first members of this Union[1]. It A.D. 1603
—1689. was the beginning of that federation which has proved such a convenient system for governing a growing nation. Both in the nature of the impulse which gave them birth, and in the character of the settlements themselves, there is a marked contrast between the history of the northern and southern colonies on the American coast.

Religious convictions of different kinds exercised a considerable influence in connection with the planting of other English settlements in North America. Maryland was taken *Civil toler-* in hand by Sir George Calvert, a Romanist, in 1632; through *ation was* *practised* the personal connections of the proprietor, this territory *in Mary-* *land, and* became the resort of such of his co-religionists as emigrated. *adopted as* *a principle* It was a district where English Romanists obtained toleration[2], *in* till the aggressive action of the Jesuits called forth the inevitable reaction. Liberty of conscience was adopted, as a matter of conviction, by Roger Williams at Rhode Island, the *Rhode* settlement which he founded in 1636, after he had been *Island* obliged to withdraw from New England[3], and a similar course was pursued by the Quakers in West New Jersey and Pennsylvania. No serious effort was made to enforce religious uniformity after the Restoration[4], and the principle of civil toleration was formulated, on grounds of expediency, in the *Constitutions* which Locke drew up for Carolina. *and* *Carolina.* He hoped that peace might be maintained among the diversity of opinions, "and that Jews, heathen and other dissenters from the Christian religion might not be scared away from the new colony[5]." When the Puritan Theocracy succumbed before the storm which was raised by the trials of witches in New England, there was no longer any effective obstacle to the diffusion of Whig principles in regard to religious liberty. They found a congenial soil, and have so deeply impregnated American life and thought that there is some excuse for the mistake of regarding them as an original element in its composition.

---

[1] Bancroft, *History of the United States*, I. 420.

[2] C. Ernest Smith, *Religion under the Barons of Baltimore*, 148, 202.

[3] Bancroft, *op. cit.* I. 375.

[4] Osgood, *England and the American Colonies*, in the *Political Science Quarterly*, XVII. 214.   [5] Locke, *Constitutions*, cap. XCVII. in *Works*, IX. 194.

A.D. 1603
—1689.

Economic
motives
were the
chief force
at work;

Virginia
and the W.
I. Islands
attracted
capital to
grow pro-
ducts for
export;

these
colonies
were not
self-sus-
taining,

201. Religious motives had much to do in shaping the character of particular settlements, but the main impulse in the work of colonisation was economic. The plantations offered a field for the profitable investment of capital. While many of the London merchants were eager to establish themselves on English soil[1], others were ready to develop colonial resources, and to promote the cultivation of products, such as tobacco and sugar, which were in demand in European lands. The development of the southern colonies and the West Indian islands was promoted by moneyed men in England, who directed the energies of the planters into raising commodities for export. These traders were not specially concerned to foster communities which should be self-sufficing; they preferred that the planters should manage their estates with a view to the requirements of outside markets. As a consequence, there was little subsistence farming in these regions. The land was mostly held in large estates by men who carried on their business, either with their own capital, or through the help of the credit extended to them by the merchants who were interested in the trade. The course which these London capitalists pursued did not always commend itself to the government; King James, while he sympathised with their enterprise[2], was somewhat afraid of pushing it too vigorously, and involving himself in a dispute with Spain[3]. Charles I. was eager for the prosperity of Virginia, and was anxious that the colony should at least provide its own food supply[4]; he feared that the future of the territory was being sacrificed to the immediate gain of the planters. It was clear, however,

---

[1] "In ancient times Merchants and Tradesmen were very careful to provide and lay up a stock of money for the building of ships, and buying of commodities to trade with. But in these latter years, as within 40 or 50 years, they have disbursed much money in purchasing land, and building stately Houses, minding pleasure more than profit, to the undoing of many of them, and that great cause of the decaying of Trade." J. Smith, *Trade and Fishing of Great Britain Display'd* (1662). It appears that after the Fire, when money was required for the rebuilding of London, the market for real estate was seriously affected and the price of land fell considerably.

[2] A. Brown, *First Republic in America*, 588.

[3] Beer, *Pol. Sci. Quarterly*, XVI. 588 and refs. The Spaniards were jealous of Virginia on economic grounds, as till it was founded they had supplied England with tobacco.   [4] See below, p. 357.

that the development of these settlements was of advantage to the realm, and successive Commissions gave careful attention to their affairs[1]. For one thing, the plantations served to sup- *but they* plement the resources of the realm, and to furnish supplies of *supplemented* commodities which had hitherto been procured from abroad, *English resources,* so as to diminish the commercial indebtedness of the country and to influence the balance of trade in our favour[2]. Again, *gave* the trade with the colonies opened up a field for the employ- *employment to English* ment of our shipping; and efforts were made, both by the *shipping,* Crown and Parliament, to restrict this newly established line of intercourse to English vessels[3], in the interest of the

---

[1] Council for New England (1622—35). Lords Commissioners for Plantations (1635). Council for Foreign Plantations (1660) *Calendar S. P. Col.* 1574—1660, pp. 32—35, 492, and *passim*.

[2] Sandys, *Parl. Hist.* I. 1196, 1197.

[3] It appears that from 1621 onwards the Privy Council, and the Commissioners they appointed, consistently ordered that goods from Virginia should be unladen in England (S. P. Col. I. 55, II. 20). Dutch trade with the English tobacco colonies had commenced in 1624, but it was regarded as an intrusion (S. P. D. J. I. CLXIX. 5, 6, 7.). The planters, who were anxious to secure a monopoly of the English market, seem to have been quite willing, in 1630, to forego intercourse with Holland (S. P. Col. V. 84). The Privy Council maintained this line of action in 1633 (S. P. Col. VI. 74), but referred the matter to commissioners, who were to consult farmers and planters. The report of these commissioners is an interesting statement of the case for restriction. "According to your Lordships order of the 7th of this present August, Wee haue had meetinge with divers of the cheefe Planters of Virginia and have considered of the proposicions therin mencioned Wherunto (in all humblenes) wee present our opinions as followeth. That this plantacion hath bene maintained and supported for many yeeres by the Planters and Adventurers of the Virginia Company; and they have lately peticioned his Majestie for renewinge their Antient Charter, And do hope his Majestie wilbe gratiously pleased to graunt it unto them, forbiddinge all others, And it hath beene often moved unto your Lordships by us, that the Trade should be carryed wholly by the English, and the retournes to be made wholly into England only. And therupon your Lordships haue heertofore given order, to the Governors to take bondes of all shippes, that they bringe and land all their ladings in England By performance whereof it will follow that

His Majesties Customes and duties shalbe wholly receaved,

Our owne men and shippinge Imployed,

The Navigacion of the kingdome encreased,

The Plantacion duly and sufficiently supplyed,

Our Merchantes and Planters benefitted and encouraged by the Transportacion of that surplus which now strangers carry to their owne Marketts

All which benefitts to his Majesties kingdome, and people, are wholly loste if Strangers be permitted to trade and transporte the Comodities of that Plantacion into fforayne partes as now they do.

And for the same reasons (as we conceave) in all the Kinge of Spaines Plantacons in the West and East indies, all Strangers are prohibitted to trade and

maritime power of the country. After the Restoration, when the plantations were firmly established, a third economic advantage to the mother country came more and more clearly into view[1]. The colonists demanded considerable

and eventually afforded a large market for manufactures.
quantities of European goods, and the progress of the settlements opened a larger market, the advantage of which English manufacturers endeavoured to retain for themselves. On these various grounds English moneyed men were inclined to promote the plantation of new areas, and the English Governments were ready to approve of the undertaking.

The plantations also attracted the sons
202. There must also have been a very large class who looked eagerly to the plantations, in the hope of finding a sphere where they could engage, as independent men, in rural occupations. They may have had little capital of their own, but they were confident that if they obtained a

transporte, and their owne subjects are prohibitted to trade and transporte, and theire own subjects constrained to make all retournes into Spain and Portugall only. All which we humbly submit to your Lordships graue wisdomes." (S. P. Col. 1633, vi. 80.)

Wolstenholm, in what appears to be a covering letter sent with this report, urges that immediate action should be taken to stop the Dutch trade (S. P. Col. vi. 81).

[1] Pollexfen, *Discourse of Trade and Coyn* (1697), p. 86. "Our *Trade* to our Plantations or *West-India* Collonies takes off great quantities of our Products and Manufactures, as well as Provisions and Handicraft Wares, and furnishes us with some goods for a further Manufactury, and others in great abundance to be Exported to Foreign Nations, especially of *Sugar* and *Tobacco*. And although some Objections may be made against the use and necessity of those Commodities, yet being so introduced amongst us as it may be impossible to prevent our having them from other Countries, and being a *Trade* which imployes vast numbers of Ships and Seamen, ought to be incouraged; for having lost so great a part of our *Fishing Trades*, these *Trades*, and that to *Newcastle*, are now become the chief support of our Navigation, and Nursery for Seamen. And if all back doors could be shut, that all the Products Exported from those Collonies might without diminution be brought to *England*, that what are not spent here, might be Reexported from hence; and those Collonies, as the proprietors are *English*, made to have their whole dependence on *England*, the fruits of their labours to be as much for the advantage of *England*, as of those that stay at Home, then all incouragement by easie Laws, Regulations and Protection, should be given to them, they having more opportunities, and being under a greater necessity of gaining more laborious People (from whence Riches must arise), to help to make great improvements than *England*, or any other of the Dominions belonging to it: And if it be considered what Forests and Deserts have been improved, and Riches acquired, in some of those Collonies, in so short a time, as the Age of a Man, it must be agreed what hath been asserted, *That the Original of moveable Riches is from Labour*, and that it may arise from the Labour of Blacks and Vagrants, if well managed.

start, they could make a living by their labour. There is ^{A.D. 1603} reason to believe that the material prosperity, and the ^{—1689.} comparative peace, which England enjoyed during the Elizabethan and Jacobean periods, had resulted in a considerable increase of population[1]. The growth of trade *of substan-* afforded openings for the younger sons of country gentle-*tial men in* men; but there must have been a large number of young *rural dis-* men who greatly preferred an outdoor life, and who had *tricts,* difficulty in raising the premium that was required in order to be apprenticed to any branch of commerce. The fact that the competition for farms was so keen[2], is an incidental proof that there were a number of men who desired to follow this avocation; and if they had no opportunity at home, they would be ready to look for one abroad. Such men would be prepared to devote their own labour to the arduous work of clearing and tilling the ground for a livelihood; they desired to have a holding which they could work on their own account[3]. Those plantations, which did not raise suitable products for export, offered a poor prospect of profit to the capitalist, but they would attract the classes of the *and offered* community who were prepared to engage in farming for *a field for* subsistence. It was almost inevitable that the colonies, *subsistence* which were suitable for the growth of cereals, should be *farming.* settled with small homesteads, and not with large plantations managed by men who were catering for distant markets.

There have been many periods of English history when the Government would have looked askance on schemes for drawing off large numbers of adult men to distant countries, where they could not be called upon to play a personal part in defending England against invaders. More pressing *Govern-* anxiety was felt in the seventeenth century as to the best *ment did* means of utilising the able-bodied population in times of *not dis-* peace; and the Government was quite prepared to give *courage* active assistance in promoting emigration[4]. The statute of *gration,* 1563 had doubtless done much to bring about the absorption

---

[1] See above, p. 91 n. 4. Also Ap. B below.   [2] See above, p. 105.

[3] See p. 556, n. 3, below.

[4] Some restrictions were imposed, however, by Charles I. on the emigration of subjects to foreign parts (20 July, 1635) [Brit. Mus. 506. h. 12 (40)], and a proclamation was also issued (30 April, 1637) *Against the disorderly Transporting*

A.D. 1603
—1689.
of vagrants in industrial pursuits, but, despite the excellence
of the London system for dealing with the poor, there appears
to have been a considerable body of the unemployed in the
City, during the earlier part of the reign of James I. Among
*and
favoured
schemes for
transport-
ing the un-
employed to
Ireland;*
the motives and reasons, which the King urged with the view
of inducing the City to promote the Ulster Plantations,
it was pointed out that, if a body of inhabitants were
to hive off from London to Derry, the evils of overcrowding
would be reduced, and there would neither be the same risk of
infection nor as great a pressure of competition[1]. The City
was not easily induced to take active steps in response to
this invitation. In the subsequent story we hear more of
the King's endeavours to obtain contributions in money, than
of any great success in securing emigrants from London.

The City merchants were much more keenly alive to the
advantage of developing trade, by planting in Virginia, than

His Maiesties Subiects to the Plantations within the parts of America. "The
King's most Excellent Maiestie being informed that great numbers of his subiects
haue bin, and are euery yeare transported into those parts of America which haue
been granted by patent to seuerall persons, and there settle themselues, some of
them with their families and whole estates: amongst which numbers there are
also many idle and refractory humors, whose onely or principall end is to liue as
much as they can without the reach of authority: His Maiestie hauing taken the
premises into consideration, is minded to restraine for the time to come such
promiscuous and disorderly departing out of the Realme: And doth therefore
straitly charge and command all and euery the Officers and Ministers of his
seuerall Ports in England Wales and Berwick, That they doe not hereafter permit
or suffer any persons, being Subsidie men, or of the value of Subsidie men, to
embarque themselues in any of the said Ports, or the members thereof, for any
of the said Plantations, without Licence from His Maiesties Commissioners for
Plantations first had and obtained in that behalfe: Nor that they admit to be
embarqued any persons under the degree or value of Subsidy-men, without an
Attestation or Certificate from two Justices of the Peace living next the place
where the party last of all, or lately then before dwelt, that he hath taken the
Oaths of Supremacie, and Allegiance, and like Testimony from the Minister of the
Parish of his conuersation and conformity to the Orders and discipline of the
Church of England. And further His Maiesties expresse will and pleasure is,
That the Officers and Ministers of his said seuerall Ports, and the Members
thereof, do returne to his Maiesties said Commissioners for Plantations euery
halfe yeare a particular and perfect List of the names and qualities of all such
persons as shall from time to time be embarqued in any of the said Ports for any
of the said Plantations. And of these His Maiesties Royall Commands, all the
Officers and Ministers of His said Ports and the Members thereof are to take
care, as they will answer the neglect thereof at their perils." [Brit. Mus.
21. h. 1 (45)].

[1] *S. P. Ireland* (1608—10), p. 209.

to the wisdom of schemes for prosecuting subsistence farming A.D. 1603
in the north of Ireland.   The colonists, who were managing —1689.
large estates and raising tobacco for export, were in constant *Labourers*
need of labour; the Virginia Company and, after its disso- *were much in demand*
lution, the agents of the planters, were willing to pay a good *in Virginia*
price for servants of every class; a large business sprang up,
both at London and Bristol, in the shipment of labourers to
the plantations.

There can be no doubt that a preference would be given
to persons who had been brought up in the country and
were accustomed to out-of-door employment.   The young
and active men in any parish, who saw little prospect of
getting a holding of their own, would possibly feel that they
could better themselves by emigration; though it is not
probable that many adult servants in husbandry had either
the inclination[1], or the opportunity[2], to go so far afield.
There was more chance of drawing on the surplus population *where the surplus*
of the towns, and on those artisans who were thrown out of *population could be*
work by the fluctuations of their trade.   It has already been *absorbed;*
pointed out that the arrangements, which were made for
the relief of the poor, prove how very easily the well-doing
and industrious persons of this class might be reduced to
destitution[3]; the rigidity of the Elizabethan system, which
told alike against change of residence and change of

---

[1] Bullock, *Virginia impartially examined* (1649), p. 44, remarks with some
contempt on his poor-spirited countrymen.   Brit. Mus. E. 417 (24).

[2] If hired for a year from Michaelmas the labourer would not be free to avail
himself of the annual September sailings of the regular emigrant vessels.
Compare also Captain Baylie's project.   S. P. D. J. I. CLXXXIX. 36.

[3] See above, p. 50, also 577 below.   An account given in 1615 of Sheffield,
which was a growing centre, is instructive.   "By a survaie of the towne of
Sheffield made the second daye of Januarie 1615 by twenty foure of the most
sufficient inhabitants there, it appearethe that there are in the towne of Sheffelde
2207 people; of which there are 725 which are not able to live without the
charity of their neighbours.   These are all begging poore.   100 householders
which relieve others.   These (though the best sorte) are but poore artificers;
among them is not one which can keepe a teame on his own land, and not above
tenn who have grounds of their own that will keepe a cow.   160 householders not
able to relieve others.   These are such (though they beg not) as are not able to
abide the storme of one fortnights sickness but would be thereby driven to
beggary.   1222 children and servants of the said householders; the greatest part
of which are such as live of small wages, and are constrained to work sore to
provide them necessaries."   Hunter, *Hallamshire*, 148.

occupation, must have put great obstacles in the way of any man obtaining employment when once he was thrown out. Recruits could also be obtained from less desirable elements of the population, as there was a constant desire on the part of the judges and the Government to mitigate the severity of our penal code, and to inflict sentences of transportation in *criminals,* many cases where the penalty of death[1] had been incurred. The colonists did their best to protect themselves against the intrusion of criminal elements[2], as the Virginia Company had done in its day. They insisted that each emigrant should be provided with a guarantee of character and respectability, but these regulations could not be maintained in the face of the great demand for labour.

*and prison-
ers of war
were trans-
ported*
The openings afforded by the colonies must have done much to relieve the country from the after-effects of the disturbance caused by the Civil War. It is in the case of Ireland that we get the fullest evidence; Cromwell's campaign was ruthless enough; and those of the garrison at Drogheda, who escaped with their lives, were transported to the Barbados[3]. The scheme in which Parliament then engaged, for the wholesale planting of Ireland by Cromwell's soldiers, was an ingenious endeavour to get rid at once of a political danger and of the arrears of pay. It could not be carried out, however, until a wholesale deportation of the existing population had been effected, and numbers of them seem to have been compulsory immigrants to the plantations. Similar measures were taken with regard to the royalist prisoners after the battle of Worcester[4], and the possibility

---

[1] Bruce, *Economic History of Virginia in the Seventeenth Century,* i. 605.

[2] Bruce, *op. cit.* i. 603, and references to State Papers there. Also with regard to Quakers in 1662, *S. P. Colonial* (America and West Indies), 1661–8, No. 394. A great deal of information on this subject has been collected by Dr J. Davies Butler, *British Convicts shipped to American Colonies,* in *American Historical Review,* ii. 12.

[3] Carlyle, *Cromwell,* i. 459. On the systematic capture of Irish youths and girls for export to the plantations at this time see Prendergast, *Cromwellian Settlement,* 89. H. Cromwell writes, "I did hope to have given your lordship an account of this port of the buissines of causinge younger wenches and youths in Ireland to be sent into the West Indies; but I could not make thinges readye. The comittee of the Counsell have voted 1000 girls and as many youthes be taken up for that purpose." Thurloe, *State Papers,* iv. 75. See also pp. 23, 40.

[4] Bruce, *op. cit.* i. 609.

of getting rid of restive or dangerous elements in the A.D. 1603
—1689. population, must have contributed immensely to the establishment of civil order once more[1]. When the supply of prisoners and conquered persons fell off, however, there were no legitimate means of keeping up the stream of immigration or meeting the requirements of the planters[2], and *and many persons were spirited away* a systematic practice of kidnapping[3] sprang up, by which large numbers of persons were spirited away to work as servants in the colonies. The extent to which this shameful traffic was carried on is very remarkable[4], and interesting evidence about it is afforded by the mention of occasional and unsuccessful attempts to put it down. In 1660, John Clark petitioned for letters patent empowering him to keep a register office, to which all servants and children might be brought before being transported to Virginia and Barbados, so as to prevent the abuses of forcible transportation of persons without their own or their parents' consent[5]. A similar proposal was made in 1664[6], and the complaints of merchants, planters and masters of ships[7], as well as of the Lord Mayor and Aldermen of London[8], show how greatly some such institution was required.

Of the servants who emigrated to Virginia, some were protected by definite indentures, similar to those of an *to be servitors in Virginia* ordinary apprentice; by far the larger number, however, set sail without any precise engagement with any particular master, and on their arrival in Virginia they were auctioned off to the planters who attended at the quay side[9]; but they

---

[1] Bollagh, *White Servitude in the Colony of Virginia* (Johns Hopkins Studies, XIII. 6, 7), p. 35.

[2] Col. Byrd wrote in 1739 about the possibility of making good arrangements for disposing of Palatines in Georgia. *American Hist. Rev.* I. 90.

[3] Bruce, *op. cit.* I. 614. The evil was not new, but it was immensely extended. In 1623 the condition of the English emigrants who were bondmen to the Company seems to have been very miserable. *Manchester Papers*, nos. 318, 325 in *Hist. MSS. Commission Report*, VIII. Ap. ii. pp. 39, 40.

[4] Some account of the trade with some notice of Baltimore, Philadelphia and northern colonies will be found in E. Eggleston's *Social Conditions in the Colonies*, in *Century Magazine*, N. S. (Oct. 1884), XXVIII. 853.

[5] S. P. D. C. II. XXII. 138.

[6] *S. P. D. Colonial, America and West Indies*, 1661-8, No. 772.

[7] *Ib.* 769.   [8] *Ib.* 770.

[9] Servants who had been in the country for some years were liable to be sold by auction by their masters for the remaining years of their service.

were by no means without legal status. The colonists were perfectly aware that they could not expect to attract a regular stream of immigrants unless the conditions of labour were favourable, and the " custom of the country " gave on the one hand precision to the rights of the employer, and on the other a considerable measure of protection, and possible redress to the servant. The custom of the country was amended in 1661, on the lines of the English labour legislation of 1563[1]; after five years' servitude, or in other cases at the age of twenty-four, the labourer became a free man: if he was unable to attempt to work land on his own account, he would be quite likely to obtain a very comfortable position as an overseer[2]. Such prospects were more attractive than those of the English labourer; even during the period of servitude, the emigrants seem to have fared as well, or better, than they would have done at home. Not only was there frequent legislation in Virginia on their behalf[3], but absconding servants found such easy opportunities of obtaining employment[4], that masters who wished to retain their servants must have been
or the West Indies. forced to treat them well. The conditions of servitude in the West Indies do not appear to have been so favourable[5], and the amount of individual suffering[6] and misery in connection with the whole system must have been frightful; at the same time it transferred a large number of labourers to areas where they could be profitably employed, and it relieved the congested districts in England.

The starting of these distant plantations   203. Some kind of government was necessary for protecting the persons and property of Englishmen who settled

---

[1] Bruce, *op. cit.* II. 4.
[2] *Ib.* II. 18.   [3] *Ib.* II. 10.
[4] *Ib.* II. 20.
[5] N. Darnell Davis, *Cavaliers and Roundheads*, p. 82.
[6] Compare e.g. the story of the seventy Englishmen who had been shipped to the West Indies from Plymouth and sold for 1550 pound weight of sugar apiece, more or less. M. Rivers, *England's Slavery* (1659), p. 5. He continues: "being bought and sold still from one Planter to another, or attached as horses, and beasts for the debts of their masters, being whipt at their whipping posts, as Rogues, for their master's pleasure, and sleep in styes worse than hogs in England, and many other wayes made miserable, beyond expression or Christian imagination."

in these distant regions[1], as well as for guiding the progress A.D. 1603
—1689.
of their undertakings. There were two different methods of
administration which commended themselves to the statesmen of the time. Allusion has been already made to one *was either*
of these systems; a grant of a considerable tract was made *committed to noble*
to a proprietor, who endeavoured to settle it with farmers *proprietors*
to whom he allotted suitable estates[2]. In the time of
James I. there must have been a considerable number of
such grants which were never successfully taken up, as the
whole of the Atlantic seaboard seems to have been allotted
to different adventurers[3]. Few of them in all probability *who had*
had sufficient capital even to make a beginning in the *not always sufficient*
work of colonisation, or at any rate to carry it through. *capital*
Sir G. Calvert had to abandon his settlement at Avalon
in Newfoundland, and the Earl of Stirling lost large sums
in attempts to plant Nova Scotia[4]. The command of much
money was necessary in order to succeed in colonial enterprise, and this need could be most easily met by organising
a company which should be responsible for the development
of unoccupied lands. In 1606, powers for the colonisation
of the great stretch of territory, which was then spoken of as
Virginia, were granted simultaneously to a Plymouth and a *or to companies.*

[1] *A Proclamation prohibiting interloping and disorderly trading to New
England* (6 Nov. 1622). "Wherefore hauing receiued certaine information of
many and intolerable abuses offered by sundry interlopers, irregular and dis-
obedient persons, that seeking principally their present and priuate profits, haue
not only impeached some of the Planters there, of their lawfull possessions but
also taken from them their Timber without giving any satisfaction, as in justice
they ought to haue done: and not therewith contented haue rined whole Woods
to the utter ruine of the same for euer after; as also by casting of their ballast
in the harbors of some of their Islands, haue almost made them unseruiceable.
And yet not so contented, by their promiscuous trading as well Mariners as
Masters with the Sauages, haue ouerthrowne the trade and commerce that before
was had to the great profit of the Planters, and which were indeed their principall hopes for the aduancement of that plantation next unto the commodities
that that coast affords of Fishing * * * but as if they resolued to omit nothing
that might be impious and intolerable, they did not forbeare to barter away to
the savages swords, Pikes Muskets Fouling pieces Match Powder Shot and other
Warlike Weapons and teach them the use thereof * * * to the hazard of the liues
of our good subiects already planted there, no one to trade to or frequent those
coasts without licence." Brit. Mus. 506. h. 12 (102).

[2] This is the method which Fuller had in view, *Holy State* III. c. 16. He lays
stress on the need of large capital on the part of the prime undertaker.

[3] See *the Mapp of New England* in Sir W. Alexander's *Encouragement to
Colonies* (Prince Society, Boston), 216.

[4] *Sir W. Alexander and American Colonisation* (Prince Society, Boston), 107.

A.D. 1603
—1689. London company. The northern portion of the Atlantic
seaboard was assigned to the Devonshire men, who made
some unsuccessful efforts to colonise[1]; eventually a portion
of this territory was occupied, without their formal permission[2], by the emigrants in the 'May Flower,' who preserved
a memorial of the connection in the name they conferred on
The Vir-
ginia Com-
Plymouth rock. The London company was more vigorous;
pany over-
came the
it did succeed in planting Virginia, and in overcoming the
initial dif-
ficulties,
initial difficulties; but its administration of affairs was not
and formed
altogether satisfactory. The colony had so far increased in
a represent-
ative gov-
1619 that it was possible to entrust the settlers with a large
ernment,
measure of self-government, and a representative assembly
was formed of the boroughs and townships in Virginia[3], which
were to carry on the government of the settlement in conjunction with the council of the company at home. This
divided responsibility, however, did not answer well[4], and
before long the Crown interfered directly with the undertaking. In 1620 James determined to turn the plantation
into a penal settlement to which dissolute persons might be
transported[5], and in the same year a Dutch vessel introduced
the first cargo of negro slaves. The attempt to maintain the
high character of the immigrants was abandoned, and there
was also serious trouble with the natives. In 1622, when
all appeared to be on a friendly footing, the English were
massacred by the Indians; but for the warning given by a
convert, hardly one would have escaped; in the consequent
disorganisation, there must have been grave difficulties in
carrying on the government of the plantation, and the
management in London did not cope with them success-
during its
brief
fully. In 1624 the Virginia Company was dissolved[6]; and
career.
the affairs of the colony were left to be governed by the

---

[1] John Smith, *General Historie of Virginia* (1624), 203. These expeditions
seem to have been organised with a view to mining rather than plantation. See
the Introduction to the Reprint of Sir W. Alexander's *Mapp of New England.*

[2] This was accorded by the Company in 1629 but not confirmed by the Crown.
Story, *Commentaries on the Constitution,* I. 29.

[3] Stith, *op. cit.* p. 160. W. N. Sainsbury, *On the first Parliament in America,*
in the *Antiquary* (July 1881), IV. 8.

[4] Smith, *Advertisements,* in *Works,* 927.   [5] Stith, 168.

[6] An interesting account of this enterprise has been preserved in *S. P.
Colonial,* II. 40. It is printed in full in the *Virginia Magazine of History and
Biography,* I. 156.

Assembly in Virginia, subject to the approval of the A.D. 1603
—1689. Crown.

The principle of association was also adopted as the best expedient for introducing some sort of cohesion into the scattered settlements on Massachusetts Bay[1]. This Company *The com-* was formed in 1629, and in 1630 its government was estab- *pany prin-* *ciple was* lished, not in London, but in the new territory[2]. By this *applied in* *a new* means the colonists were relieved from the annoyance which *form to* *Massa-* arose from divided management; but the arrangement was *chusetts* by no means satisfactory from the point of view of the Crown, as there was no practical means of enforcing compliance with the terms of the charter[3], or of preventing encroachments on the proprietary colonies[4] in Maine and Connecticut. The formation, in 1643, of a confederacy among the New England colonists for self-defence against the Indians, tended to render the settlers still more self-reliant, and less inclined to submit to control by English authorities. The struggle became acute in 1685, when the Company's charter was annulled; and in 1691 a new system was constituted, and a governor was sent out to maintain the authority of the Crown and the interests of the realm in the whole Province.

The application of the company principle to planting may have been said to be justified by its results, since Virginia was founded, and Massachusetts developed, by joint-stock associations; but it was more frequently adopted with reference to the management of trade than to the work of colonisation. In Scotland, where capital was scarce, *and by the* this method of organisation continued to find favour; in *Scotch* *colonists* 1682 an association of twenty-four proprietors bought out *in New* *Jersey,* the original founder of New Jersey[5], and the ill-fated Darien

---

[1] Gardiner, *History*, VII. 155; Smith, *op. cit.* 931. Charles was not able to keep to the opinion he had laid down that a company was a body "to whom it may be proper to trust matters of Trade and Commerce but cannot bee fit or safe to communicate the ordering of State affaires be they of never so meane consequence." *Proclamation for setling the Plantation of Virginia*, 13 May, 1625. Brit. Mus. 506. h. 11 (11).

[2] This arrangement had been already adopted in the case of a commercial company by the Merchant Adventurers (see above, p. 245).

[3] Anderson, *History of the Church of England in the Colonies*, II. 139.

[4] *Ib.* 143, 147, 148, 175.

[5] *Grants, Concessions and original constitution of New Jersey*, p. 141. The

C.   23

Scheme[1] was started with a view to settlement as well as to trade. But, during the Restoration period, the English colonial system was developed rather by grants to individuals, than by the formation of new companies.

The system of proprietary colonies was not, however, altogether satisfactory from the point of view of the government at home. Vast stretches of territory had been assigned *the central authority had no effective control.* to men who were practically independent[2]. It was hardly possible for the Crown, or Parliament, to interfere effectively in the administration of these colonies, or to insist on the enforcing of the Act of Navigation. At the close of the seventeenth and beginning of the eighteenth century, there was a general movement in the direction of buying out the proprietors, and sending out governors who should be the immediate representatives of the Crown[3]. The duty imposed on these men was by no means easy; the colonists resisted any restriction of the freedom they had possessed under the lax administration of the proprietors, and cherished a tradition of independence, which made them ready to chafe at the imposition of a Stamp Tax, or any other unaccustomed burden.

Local government was based on the county system in the capitalist colonies The well-being of the colonies depended far less on their administrative connection with the mother country than on the skill they had shown in adapting English habits of local self-government to their own requirements. The institutions of one colony differed considerably from those of another; the system, which was most convenient to the settlers in New England, who occupied small homesteads and practised subsistence farming, was unsuited to the planters who owned large estates and cultivated them with the labour of

---

company had a common stock for purposes of trade, p. 172, but each proprietor received allotments of land to dispose of, p. 192.

[1] See below, p. 416, n. 1.

[2] The danger of rendering any one subject too powerful was apparently kept in view by Sir A. Chichester in schemes for the planting of Ireland, but does not seem to have been considered in connection with American colonisation. Lord Baltimore threw the weight of his influence on the parliamentary side, and Maryland was the only colony outside New England that was not forcibly reduced. C. Ernest Smith, *op. cit.* 336.

[3] The Constitution which Locke devised for the government of Carolina was modelled on that of a County Palatine, such as Durham.

dependents. The Virginians kept up the traditions of the English landed gentry who were responsible for county affairs[1]. The New Englanders were grouped in townships[2], and busied themselves primarily about the needs, spiritual and physical, of each little community[3]. It was only by a gradual process of federation that the original settlements united to form a state, and were subsequently combined in a province. The difference in the political system of the northern and southern states was closely connected with the fact that, while the southerners had occupied large estates[4], the northerners had planted their homesteads in close contiguity with their neighbours.

A.D. 1603 —1689.

and on the township among the subsistence farmers,

The records of the town meetings have sometimes been carefully preserved; they are full of matter of economic interest. Much of the business was devoted to agricultural affairs, the working of common fields[5], or the allotting land in severalty, or the regulation of meadow rights. On the other hand, there is singularly little reference to any organisations for internal trade; markets hardly existed, and fairs seem to have been unknown. The colonists might have to buy goods imported from England; but each household was so far self-sufficing, that there was little opportunity for frequent or regular interchange within the community. Doubtless there was much individual bargaining, especially bartering between neighbours, but no need seems to have been found for laying out a market-place in the first New England towns.

who reproduced somewhat primitive economic institutions.

---

[1] Wodrow Wilson, *The State*, 445; Ingle, *Local Institutions in Virginia*, in Johns Hopkins Studies, III. Ser. p. 97.

[2] The 'township' was recognised as an administrative unit in the sparsely peopled northern counties of England in 1662. 13 and 14 C. II. c. 12 § 21.

[3] Channing, *Town and County Government in the English Colonies of North America*, in Johns Hopkins Studies, II. Ser. p. 36.

[4] The Southerners were less able to protect themselves against attack, and were forced to show more respect to the rights of the natives than was habitual in the north.

[5] Compare the New Jersey rules in 1676 about common lands and the sole responsibility of the man, who improves his holding, for the maintenance of the fencing. *Grants, Concessions and original Constitution of the Province of New Jersey* (1751), p. 113. For instances of common fields and common agricultural life see Weedon, *Economic and Social History of New England*, I. 53, 275, 405; II. 522. An admirable account of the laying out of one New England township will be found in the chapter on allotments and settlements in D. P. Corey's *History of Malden*.

A.D. 1603
—1689.
204. The expense and risk of colonisation in America
was entirely undertaken by private citizens, either in their
individual capacity or as members of companies; but it is a
mistake to suppose that either James I. or Charles I. was
altogether indifferent to these projects. The former was
obliged to proceed with great caution from fear of offending
Charles I. the Spaniards, but Charles was free to give his hearty
gave
cordial approval to plans for the expansion of England. He en-
approval
to schemes deavoured to make common cause with the French monarchy
for coloni-
sation, in these projects, and to come to friendly agreement with
that power as to the boundaries of their respective territories, both in the West Indies[1] and in Canada[2]. His
proclamations show that the government took great pains
to regulate the development of colonial enterprise on wise
lines. He looked on it as "a Worke wherin We hold the
honor of Our deare Father deceased and our owne honour
to be deeply engaged" since it made for "the increase of
Trade and the enlarging of our Royal Empire[3]." The policy
which he favoured for the development of the colony was
perfectly definite, and forms a striking contrast to the views
which were put in practice in the eighteenth century, when
the interests of the colonists were consciously subordinated to
but like his those of certain classes at home[4]. James I. had been clear
father he
was that it was most unwise for the planters to rely, for all
anxious
that the supplies, on the stores they purchased by cultivating tobacco,
plantations
should be and encouraged the settlers to aim at being an economically
self-suf- independent and self-sufficing community. At the time
ficing, and
not merely when the powers of the Virginia Company were withdrawn,
produce
tobacco. James issued a proclamation as to his design for the colony.
"Wee have beene earnestly and often importuned by many
of Our loving Subiects, Planters and Adventurers in Virginia
and the Sommer Islands, and lately by our Commissioners
for Virginia, that we would be pleased to take into Our
Royall care that part of Our Dominions, by Our Royall

---

[1] Macpherson, *Annals*, 1627, II. 350.

[2] See the Treaty of 1631 in Dumont, *op. cit.* VI. i. 31.

[3] *A proclamation for setling the Plantation of Virginia*, 13 May. 1625. Brit.
Mus. 506. h. 11 (41). He instituted a council in Virginia and another Council for
advising the government at home.

[4] See below for the treatment of the colonies in the eighteenth century.

authoritie, and by the industrie of Our loyall Subiects A.D. 1603
added to the rest of Our Empire, for the propagation of —1689.
the Christian Religion, and the ease and benefite of this
populous Realme, and to consider, that those Colonies and
Plantations are yet but in their infancie and cannot be
brought to maturitie and perfection, unlesse we will bee
pleased for a time to tolerate unto them the planting and
venting of the Tobacco, which is, and shall be of the growth
of those Colonies and Plantations[1]." With the view of giving
the colonists the fullest opportunity of turning their advantages to a profit, the importation of foreign tobacco was
prohibited, as well as the cultivation of tobacco in England[2],
so that the plantations had a monopoly of the English
market secured to them[3]; but they were carefully warned *The*
that they were not to continue to devote themselves ex- *planters*
were
clusively to the cultivation of this plant. " For the support *warned*
that the
and incouragement of those Plantations (whose prosperous *encourage-*
ment given
estate We much affect, and shall by all good meanes be *was merely*
temporary,
alwayes ready to cherish and protect) we have beene contented to tolerate the use of Tobacco * * * for a time, untill
by more solid Commodities they be able to subsist otherwise,
which (as We are informed) they cannot as yet by any
meanes doe[4]." King Charles was even more explicit. He
was at pains that the tobacco of " His Majestie's Plantations

[1] Proclamation 29 Sept. 1624. Brit. Mus. 506. h. 11 (28).

[2] Ireland was also brought under this restriction. The tobacco monopoly
was one of the grievances alleged by the Irish parliament against Strafford (Cox,
II. 62). It forms the twelfth article of impeachment in Rushworth (*Collections*,
VIII. 66). A similar policy was pursued after the Restoration, 12 C. II. c. 34;
22 and 23 C. II. c. 26.

[3] Proclamation 2 March, 1625 [Brit. Mus. 506. h. 11 (21)], and 9 Aug. 1627
[506. h. 11 (127)]. "On the whole therefore the conduct of the Crown up to this
date (1627) had been highly meritorious. The most valuable American export
of its cherished ally had been first heavily penalized, then wholly prohibited
(entailing thereby an entire loss of the custom derived from its importation) and
finally farmed at a profit considerably less than the former revenue which it had
brought in; and all this to carry out the strict letter of its responsibility for the
welfare of a tribe of ragged and dissolute colonists. And yet not a particle of
praise or gratitude has ever been bestowed upon its well-meant blundering, but
rather discontent and suspicion were excited in the sordid hearts of those who,
when they were themselves in possession of an illgotten power, were the most
protectionist and extortionate government that the world has ever seen." Hall,
History of the Customs Revenue of England, I. 178.
    Proclamation for the utter prohibiting the importations and use of all

and Colonies may not bee planted and imported hither without limitation or measure" * * * and that the Planters * * * may not "give themselves over to the planting of Tobacco onely to make a present returne of profit, and neglect to applie themselves to solide Commodities fit for the establishing of Colonies, which will utterly destroy these and all other Plantations[1]." The policy of restricting tobacco planting may not have been wise; according to the views of the Manchester School it was well that the planters should devote themselves exclusively to the cultivation of the product for which they had a special advantage, but there was much to be said for the royal view that the colonies should develop various sides of economic life. At all events, the limitations were imposed in the permanent interest of the settlement, as conceived by the authorities in England, and in accordance with the best advice obtainable[2]

though the development of the trade would have brought gain to the Crown.
Virginia was not sacrificed to any interest at home[3], and the line which was taken was distinctly prejudicial to the royal revenue. The payments in customs would have been largely increased, if the colony had enjoyed no protection, and English consumers of Spanish tobacco had been allowed to indulge their taste[4]. It was also to the interest of the Crown that the colonial tobacco trade should be expanded as rapidly as possible, and Charles renounced a present return of profit, in the form of duties on importation, for the sake of enabling the planters to establish the colony on a sound economic basis.

The planters suffered from the Navigation Policy
Other restrictions, which affected all the plantations, were imposed with the public-spirited object of maintaining the maritime power of England; in so far as the pursuance of a navigation policy tended to diminish the total volume

Tobacco which is not of the proper growth of the Colonies of Virginia and the Summer islands, 2 March, 1625. Brit. Mus. 506. h. 11 (21)

[1] Brit. Mus. 506. h. 11 (96), 9 Aug. 1627.

[2] Compare the opinions expressed by John Smith *History*, in *Works*, 616.

[3] On the other hand, repeated and vigorous measures were taken to prevent the cultivation of tobacco in England. See above, p. 357, nn. 2, 3; also Proclamation 19 May, 1634, Brit. Mus. 21. h. 3 (39). Scobell, *Acts*, 1652, c. 2. Some of the inhabitants of Winchcomb were persisting in growing tobacco in 1655. S. P. Col. XII. 43; also 36, 37, 40, 41.

[4] H. Hall, *Customs Revenue of England*, I. 178.

of commerce, it had a prejudicial effect on the revenue[1]. But A.D. 1603 —1689.
Charles decided not merely to make England the depôt for
colonial produce, but also to insist that the trade should be *which was instituted by procla- mation under Charles I.*
carried on in English ships. There is good reason to doubt
whether this measure was really adapted to secure the end
in view. It is not clear that the restrictions which Charles
made, and which were continued by Parliament in 1651 and *and by Statute in 1651 and 1660.*
1660, did as a matter of fact inflict much injury on the
Dutch, or confer much benefit on English shipping. The
policy may have been mistaken; but so far as the Crown was
concerned, at the time of its inception, it was at all events
disinterested, since it involved a diminution of the customs
revenue. The Navigation Act also gave rise to a constant *Even when it was little en- forced it constituted a griev- ance,*
sense of grievance on the part of the colonists, even when
the injury actually inflicted was comparatively slight. In
New Jersey[2], New York and the province of New England[3],
it seems to have been a complete dead letter, during the
seventeenth century. The colonial governors were not
always careful to enforce it[4], and though their occasional
attempts to do so may have caused a good deal of irritation,
they seem to have had little effect on the course of affairs.
The conditions of trade in the tobacco and sugar colonies
were very different; and less difficulty was found in carrying
out the policy there. Still it could only be done at the
cost of inflicting considerable injury on the planters in *and its effects were serious*
these parts. There is evidence of occasional remonstrance
on behalf of the planters of Virginia[5], but the complaints

[1] Compare Charles's Letter to Virginia in 1637. *S. P. Col. America and West Indies*, IX. 47. Later in the century, when the colonies had increased and were consumers of East India goods, they were able by their direct trade to evade the duties which would have been paid if the goods had passed through England. The Navigation Act, if it had been enforced, would to this extent have brought about an increase of customs. S. P. Col. 10 April, 1676, No. 881.

[2] The proprietors gave Governor Lawrie instructions to enforce the Navigation Acts in 1683. *Grants, Concessions and Original Constitutions of New Jersey*, p. 171.

[3] S. P. Col. (19 Jan. 1676), No. 787; (Oct. 12, 1676), No. 1067; (May 6, 1677), No. 218; (June, 1677), No. 295; (11 March, 1681), No. 45; (21 Oct. 1681), No. 264.

[4] S. P. Col. (3 Feb. 1672), No. 748. See also the Report on the working of the Act in 1675, S. P. Col. (12 May, 1675), No. 556.

[5] A very full statement will be found in the Remonstrance of John Bland, a London merchant, in 1663. *Cal. S. P. Col.* 1676, No. 923. Printed in the *Virginia Magazine of History and Biography*, I. 142.

from the Caribbee Islands are reiterated again and again. In one particularly bad season, Lord Willoughby asked for permission to relax the provisions of the Navigation Act temporarily, and asserted that some thousands had migrated from Barbadoes and the other English islands to the French sugar colonies, where there were no such restrictions[1]. The trade in sugar had been introduced and developed by the Dutch in and after 1640; and the attempt to turn it into other channels was disastrous, as the principal commercial connections of the colonists were with Amsterdam[2]. The measure also prevented them from purchasing at reasonable rates the supplies they had been in the habit of using[3]. " The act of navigation lies so heavy on all these plantations that they will lose all commerce from New England and Ireland from whence they have all their provisions; for if they bring but a piece of frieze or anything of their own manufacture not being first had to England, it is forfeiture of ship and goods, when the bare bringing of provisions so long a voyage cannot answer the charge. The merchants of England, not being able as formerly to make 50 or 60 per cent. on sugar, find it scarce worth their hazard, and the want of shipping thereby has raised the freight to £9 the ton, yet can they not get shipping to carry off one-half of their effects this year[4]." The evidence as to the malign effects of the Act of Navigation, not only on the Baltic Trade but on the Sugar Colonies and also on

[1] S. P. Col. 1633, No. 578. See also 25 Aug. 1664, No. 792.

[2] The Jews at Amsterdam had a great deal of the trade in their hands in 1668. Cal. S. P. Col. 1661—1668, 23 Dec. No. 1895, and Cal. 1669—1674, April 21, 1669, No. 48. Sir Francis Brewster writing in 1695 (Essays on Trade, p. 101) says, " For it is to be observed that under Oliver's Government the Act of Navigation had little force, both the Government and the merchants were willing to let it sleep for that during the war with Spain, to avoid their privateers which were so numerous that scarce a ship would stir without a convoy, most of our trade was managed in Dutch bottoms, they being at peace with Spain. This management had almost stifled the Act of Navigation, and the merchants finding their present gain by the cheapness of Dutch sailing did not consider the future conveyance. Immediate gain was what they minded." In 1659 the Assembly of Virginia passed an Act declaring that the Dutch had perfect liberty to trade with that colony (Hening, The Statutes at Large of Virginia, p. 513 note, pp. 535, 540).

[3] S. P. Col. 1676, No. 923, and Virginia Magazine of History, I. 144.

[4] S. P. Col. April 20th, 1675, No. 526. The trade with Scotland and supply of Scotch servants was also cut off. S. P. Col. 24 Nov. 1675, No. 714.

the royal revenue, is such, that we can only wonder at the A.D. 1603
—1689.
persistence with which the Council of Trade adhered to it.
It may have had incidental advantages[1] of which we can *so that there is*
hardly judge, but we are forced to suppose that in the *difficulty*
opinion of experts it was serving its purpose, and did con- *in seeing why it was*
tribute to the rapid increase of the mercantile marine *main- tained.*
which occurred during the latter half of the seventeenth
century[2].

205. The general policy which was kept in view during *The colonial*
the Stuart period, with regard to the development of Ireland, *policy*
was very similar to that which was carried out in the *pursued in Ireland*
Transatlantic plantations. The conditions were so entirely *was similar,*
different in the two cases, however, that the results, which *but the conditions*
accrued during the seventeenth century in the sister-island, *were very*
were very different from those achieved in America and the *different*
West Indies. The settlers beyond the ocean were able to
obtain a definite and secure title to land. When they had
come to terms with the Red Men, or destroyed them, there
was no serious danger of disputes arising, which would interfere with the steady progress of cultivation[3]. But in Ireland *as the country*
this was not the case; the area was not practically unlimited, *was never*
and the native population could not be persuaded to with- *cleared of the natives*
draw altogether. Besides, the object of James I. was to
bring the Celts under English rule; it was not till after the
rising of 1641 that any excuse was alleged for treating them
as savages and exterminating them. The government aimed
at anglicising the native Irish[4]; and the planters, who were

---

[1] See below, p. 472.

[2] Petty, *Political Arithmetic* (1699), pp. 258, 9. "As for Shipping His Majestys
Navy is now triple, or quadruple, to what it was Forty years since, and before the
Sovereign was built; the shipping trading into *Newcastle*, which are now about
Eighty Thousand Tuns, could not be then above a quarter of that quantity * * *
Besides there are employed in the *Guinny* and *American Trade* above Forty
Thousand Tun of Shipping *per Annum*; which Trade in those days was incon-
siderable. The quantity of Wines Imported was not near so much as now; and
to be short, the Customs upon Imported and Exported Commodities did not then
yield a third part of the present value; which shews that not only *Shipping* but
Trade itself hath increased, somewhat near that proportion."

[3] The disputes which arose between different proprietors as to their rights
under charters granted by the Crown may have delayed the progress of some
districts in the plantations, but they were not an abiding source of trouble.

[4] The difficulties are excellently illustrated by the story of Chichester's plantation in Wexford (Gardiner, *History*, VIII. 2; also Prendergast, *Cromwellian*

and political vicissitudes rendered titles to property insecure.

the agents in this Herculean task, lived in constant anxiety from the fact that they were so closely associated with a hostile race. But besides this, the political troubles in England, both during the Civil War and at the Revolution, set in motion more violent disturbances in Ireland, and led once and again to the eviction of English and Scotch proprietors who had recently settled in the country. Owing to the political unrest of the period there was little security for property, so that the first essential for progress was entirely wanting.

A very brief sketch of the vicissitudes which attended the ownership of land in Ireland, during the seventeenth century, will serve to make this evident. The rebellion of the Earl of Tyrone had left the Crown in possession of a large area in the north; and Sir Arthur Chichester set himself to carry out a plan, which had been carefully devised, and in which the City of London had consented to cooperate. At a Common Council in 1611 the Society of the Governor and Assistants of London of the New Plantation of Ulster was constituted, and it received a royal charter in 1613; estates were allotted to the various Companies who undertook the responsibility of developing them[1]. Six counties of Ulster were to be divided into parishes of from 1000 to 2000 acres, a church built and a glebe assigned in each case; there were besides to be three sorts of undertakers,—English or Scottish settlers, who were to plant their proportions with English or Scottish tenants; servitors[2], who might take British or Irish tenants as they pleased; and native freeholders. Both classes of British settlers were to reside on their estates for five years, and to build substantial dwellings,

The City of London cooperated in the plantation of Ulster,

Settlement, 46). The citizens of Bristol declined to follow the example of London, and promote the development of Waterford. S. P. Ireland, 1620, No. 615.

[1] The land in County Londonderry, with the exception of the cities of Derry and Coleraine and some other reservations, was divided into twelve estates, and assigned to the twelve great companies, to each of whom some of the lesser companies were attached. The scheme of apportionment will be found in *A Concise View of the Irish Society*, p. 36. See also the map in G. Hill's *Historical Account of the Plantation in Ulster*, p. 432.

[2] This term Petty understood as applying to anyone who had land given him in reward for his service against a rebellion or insurrection. Petty, *Political Anatomy of Ireland* (1691), 108.

which could be held effectively; but those who were allowed A.D. 1603
—1689.
to take Irish tenants were to pay £8 per 1000 acres, and not
£5. 16s. 0d. as the other undertakers did.   There were also *but though*
to be market towns erected, and a corporation for the *the scheme looked*
regulating of tradesmen and artificers, as well as a free *well on paper,*
school in each county[1].

The whole scheme was one for the foundation of a
military colony, as may be clearly seen from the survey
which was taken in 1619 by Captain Pynnar.   An extract
from Portlough in Donegal[2] may suffice as an illustration of
the whole.

"LXXXV. 1000 acres.   James Cunningham hath a
thousand acres called Moyegh.   Upon this there is a
Bawne of Lime and Stone, sixty Feet square with two
Flankers; the Walls are fourteen Feet high.   Within the
Bawne there is a good Stone House three Stories high,
himself and his Family dwelling therein.

I find planted and estated upon this land of Brittish
Families,

Freeholders 2 viz.	1 having 200 acres 1 having 66 acres	Total twenty-three Families who with their under Tenants are able to make forty-two men armed. He hath good store of Tillage and I saw not one *Irish* family on all the land."
Lessees for years 6 viz.	2 having 100 acres le piece 2 having 200 acres le piece 2 having 240 acres jointly	
Cottagers 15 viz.	Each of these have a House and Garden plott and 6 acres besides Commons for Cows	

From the point of view of the project, this was a model *it was not*
estate, but Nicholas Pynnar was not able to report so *very successful, as*
favourably of the whole scheme.   "Many of the English
Tenants," he said[3], "do not yet plough upon the Lands
neither use Husbandrie; because I conceive they are fear-
ful to stock themselves with Cattle or Servants for those
Labours.   Neither do the Irish use tillage, for that they
are also uncertain of their stay upon the Lands; so that by
this means the Irish ploughing nothing, do use greasing,

---

[1] Harris, *Hibernica* (Dublin, 1770), I. 123—130.
[2] Pynnar's *Survey*, in Harris' *Hibernica*, I. 177.
[3] *Ib.* 236.

A.D. 1603
—1689.

too little
attention
was paid
to tillage
both by
the under-
takers
the English very little, and were it not for the Scottish
Tenants, which do plough in many places of the Country,
those Parts may starve." The Irish graziers paid the best
rents, and the undertakers, or their agents, preferred to have
them as tenants rather than British agriculturists. The
twelve London Companies, each of which had an estate of
over 3000 acres, were subsequently reported to be the
greatest defaulters in promoting immigration. Their agents
found the Irish "willing to overgive rather than remove";
and that they "could not reap half the Profit by the Brittish
which they do by the Irish, whom they use at their Pleasure,
never looking into the Reasons which induced the Natives
to give more than indeed they could well raise, their
assured hope, that time might by Rebellion relieve them of
their heavy Landlords....... So as the Covetousness of the
Londoners, meeting with the rebellious Hopes of the Irish,
has bred the Danger which his prudent Majesty sought to
avoid[1]." Despite the pains which had been taken over the
scheme, there seemed to be little prospect that the country
would settle down and peaceful progress ensue. Great complaints were made of the injustice done by the commissioners
in seizing lands, and of the small proportion they allotted to
the ancient inhabitants[2]. But the conduct of the Irish
who remained was not encouraging; they would not take

to tillage, even on their diminished lands, but continued
pasture farming. An essential part of the scheme had been
omitted, since no attempt had been made to transport the
Irish swordsmen and soldiers into Connaught[3]; and this
unruly section of the population, which could not be absorbed
in civilised employments, was still engaged in robbery and
ready for rebellion. In addition to all these elements of
unrest, there was another cause of uncertainty, as the undertakers had reason to fear that the patents would be revoked,
in the cases of those who had failed to fulfil the conditions
on which they were granted[4]. The statement of those
difficulties makes one feel that if success was to attend

---

[1] Sir T. Phillips' Letter, in Harris' Hibernica, I. 247.

[2] Prendergast, Cromwellian Settlement, 44.

[3] Observations, in Harris' Hibernica, I. 122.

[4] Instructions to Lord Falkland. R. Cox, Hibernica Anglicana, II. 50.

the effort to plant English civilisation in Ireland, it was *A.D. 1603 —1689.* necessary that the execution of the scheme should be thorough.

Strafford was not satisfied that there should be any part *Strafford had no opportunity to put his plans into effect,* of Ireland in which the authority of the King was not fully recognised, but the period of his rule was too short to allow of successful construction. He was preparing for a plantation on the Shannon[1]; he set himself to dispossess the old proprietors of Connaught by asserting ancient and disused rights of the Crown and cancelling the patents granted by a commission under James I.[2] He intended to found a noble English plantation there; but his grand inquisition of 1635 only resulted in sowing the seeds which bore fruit in subsequent rebellions, and the great scheme was soon abandoned[3].

With his fall, the steady prosecution of the work of plantation in Ireland came to an end; the rebellion of *and the rebellion of 1641* 1641, and the reconquest by Cromwell, interrupted all the industrial life that had been beginning to appear; and the scheme for the settlement, which commended itself to the wisdom of Parliament, was different in kind from that which had been adopted by James and Charles. It was devised by Parliament chiefly as a means of getting rid of that pressing difficulty, the victorious army, to which such large arrears of pay were now due; this could be most easily done by giving them allotments of land as 'servitors' in Ireland; and for this purpose a great project of transplantation was carried out. All who had not shown *gave an excuse for the eviction of the inhabitants.* constant good faith to Parliament were to be forced to migrate from their lands to new possessions in Connaught, where they could be hedged in by the rivers and a few forts[4]. This transplantation was to apply to Englishmen who had recently settled, as well as to the men who had Irish blood in their veins; the grandson of Edmund Spenser suffered the confiscation of the estates which had descended

[1] Gardiner, *History*, VIII. 55. [2] Cox, *Hibernica Anglicana*, II. 56.
[3] Gardiner, *History*, X. 44, 45.
[4] They were also cut off from the coast. Stokes, *Pocock's Tour*, Introduction, p. 5. The indignation resulting from these measures caused a stronger trend of Irish feeling in favour of the royalists. Thurloe, I. 562.

A.D. 1603
—1689.

*whether
English or
Irish,*

*to make
room for
new
claimants.*

to him, and failed in his plea for exemption[1]. The project
was devised so as to produce the greatest possible shock to
property; labourers were allowed to remain, that they might
till and herd for those to whom the lands were newly assigned, but the old proprietors were to go[2]; and this ukase
applied not only to landowners, but to the citizens of
Waterford, Kilkenny and Galway. The inhabitants of these
towns were English in every respect, but they had not
shown active sympathy with the proceedings of the Puritan
Parliament; and hence the towns were cleared of English
merchants and artisans. Some continued to pick up a
miserable existence in the neighbourhood, and some were
driven beyond the seas to Ostend, S. Malo and Nantes[3];
but the deserted towns did not attract new settlers, either
from among foreign Protestants or from the American
plantations. The clearing of the country was carried on
ruthlessly; many of those who were not deported beyond
the Shannon, were sent to serve in the West Indies[4]. A
careful survey of the districts, which were evacuated, was
made by Petty[5], but the repeopling was not easily effected,
and at the time of the Restoration, the country was little
better than a wilderness. No social reconstruction of any
sort had been effected, but the claims of the Cromwellian
assignees presented a formidable barrier against any attempt
to replace the former inhabitants in their homes[6]. The
'innocents' and 'ensigns,' who had been dispossessed, were

---

[1] Prendergast, *Cromwellian Settlement*, 116.

[2] *Ib.* 98.   [3] *Ib.* 299.

[4] "Thence the usurped Power proceeded to the execution of those inhumane
designs (long before hatched) of extirpating the Nation by selling so many of
them to Barbadoes and other Plantations, by executing so many (indicted for the
Murther of some unknown persons), by sentence of one of Cromwell's Slaughter-
houses, among whom the Lady Roch will be named in all ages." *Continuation
of the Brief Narrative and of the Sufferings of the Irish under Cromwell* (1660),
p. 8. Royal Irish Academy, *Halliday Tracts*, Box 79 (3).

[5] He was Professor of Anatomy at Oxford and Gresham Lecturer, and was
sent to Ireland to attend to the Army Medical arrangements; but he soon found
other departments which required to be overhauled. His Survey is distinguished
as the 'down' Survey, apparently because everything was measured and laid
down in maps, instead of being roughly estimated. See Weale's *Letter* in Petty's
History of the Down Survey (edited by Larcom for the Irish Archaeological
Society), p. vii.

[6] Prendergast, *Ireland from the Restoration to the Revolution*, 15.

not restored, and gradually sank into utter misery as out- A.D. 1603 —1689. casts, who still hung about the neighbourhood of the lands of which they and their fathers had been deprived.

Ruined though Ireland was, it at least had rest; under Charles II. a semblance of civil order was maintained, and the country showed signs of beginning to enjoy a period of comparative prosperity; though the jealousy of their compatriots at home prevented the English immigrants from having fair play[1]. But this condition of affairs was not to last. At the time of the Revolution, the racial and religious conflict broke out more terribly than ever before, and the progress, which had been made during the Restoration period, came suddenly to an end. As in 1641, so in 1689, *The action* the action of the Celtic inhabitants gave an excuse for the *of the* *Irish Par-* terrible retaliation which followed. James II., who saw in *liament in* *1689,* the Celtic population the means of bringing Ireland once more under the Roman obedience, entered on a series of measures for dispossessing men who had held their lands, by Parliamentary title, for eight and thirty years, and for returning the estates to the representatives of those who had been evicted by Cromwell. Mr Lecky has shown that, from the point of those who regarded James as their lawful king and the upholders of William as guilty of treason, there was little in the confiscatory legislation of 1689 for which ample precedent could not be found[2]. It was a deliberate attempt, on the part of James and his supporters, to destroy the Protestant interest, and thereby to detach Ireland from England. When it failed at the Boyne and Limerick, the Protestants were determined to establish themselves more firmly than ever. They realised, of course, that wealth was a source of power. They deliberately set about *occasioned* securing the whole power of the country, by enacting the *the passing* *of the penal* penal laws which rendered the Romanist proprietors the *laws by the* *victorious* prey of every unscrupulous member of their own families, *party,* or of other informers; they put a premium on the conduct of those who deserted their hereditary faith; and these measures were designed to destroy any remaining influential

[1] See below, p. 372.
[2] Lecky, *England in the Eighteenth Century*, II. 186.

families of the proscribed religion. In the latter part of
William's reign there were other disturbing causes; the
jealousy of the English Parliament forced the King to resume the grants he had made to his Dutch generals. By
these successive measures the whole fabric of society was
reduced to utter chaos, and a most pitiable description of
its condition is given in the address of the Irish House
of Commons to the Crown[1]. The attempt to plant Ireland
with such a number of settlers that they might be able
to assimilate the whole society to English habits and in-
and left the stitutions had proved a failure; and the sole result of all
*English
garrison in* the effort had been to establish an English garrison, which
*command
of the* could only be maintained in power by measures that have
country. left a rankling sense of injustice and disaffection in the
minds of the mass of the population.

Other difficulties, which hardly arose in connection with
the American plantations during the seventeenth century,
occurred in regard to the development of Irish resources.
The danger The economic danger to England from the colonisation of
*of hostile
competi-* Ireland was far greater than in the case of the distant
*tion with
England* colonies. There was some reason to fear that England
*hardly
arose* would be drained of capital and labour, and that the immigrants would become dangerous rivals to English producers. Strafford, in his efforts to plant industries in
Ireland, was careful to avoid all danger of creating fresh
competition with the clothing trade, which provided so much
employment in many parts of England and afforded such
a large revenue; he took credit, in his *Reasons of State,*
for having discouraged[2] the introduction of the woollen

---

[1] *Irish Commons Journals* (20 Oct. 1703), II. pt. i. 341.

[2] "I am of Opinion that all Wisdom advises to keep this Kingdom as much
subordinate and dependent upon England as is possible and holding them from
the Manufacture of Wool (which, unless otherwise directed, I shall by all Means
discourage) and then inforcing them to fetch their Clothing from thence and to
take their Salt from the King (being that which preserves and gives Value to all
their native staple Commodities), how can they depart from us without Nakedness
and Beggary." Knowler, *The Earl of Strafforde's Letters and Dispatches,* I. 193.
Cox, *Hibernica Anglicana,* II. 57. This discouragement did not of course apply to
the domestic weaving of frieze which the people made for their own use. Twelve
sheep sufficed to keep a family in clothing; it was made in widths of about
20 inches, and dyed by the women with madder; very little of it was exported,
but the industry continued to flourish till the rebellion of 1641. There had been

manufacture[1]. He devoted great attention to the develop- ment of the linen trade in Ireland, since this had never obtained a firm footing in England[2]; he reported to the *in connection with the linen trade,* Council that he had sowed £1000 of Holland flax seed, and set up six or seven looms, and that the Irish could undersell France and Holland by 20 %[3]. He tried to insist on a high

a manufacture of frieze by the native Irish from very early times (*Rolls of Parl.* II. 372 a), but it seems to have been made chiefly for home consumption and very little of it was exported. Petty's *Political Anatomy of Ireland* (1691), 81, 98, 112. It is to be noticed however that Pococke (*Tour*, 114) mentions an important manufacture of serges at Limerick; and there seems to have been a similar manufacture for export in the fourteenth century. Fazzio degli Uberti, *Il Dittamondo*, IV. c. 26, l. 28. About the same time the weavers of Catalonia were accused of "basely imitating the serges of Ireland, and clothing the belles of Florence in them to our injury." *Reports*, 1840, XXIII. 521.

[1] In 1615 Mr Talbot moved in the Irish Parliament that "cloth might be made in this realm" [*Irish Commons Journals* (11 May, 1615), I. 52]; and Mr Dallaway followed him with a proposal that cloth workers might be sent for out of England and "every one to be free in each corporation." The subject seems to have been dropped at once and the proposal was not even referred to a committee. Twenty years later the matter was mooted again, and a Bill for freedom for working up native materials was introduced and made some little progress in 1634. [*Irish Commons Journals* (19 Nov. 1634), I. p. 82.] Strafford may have been successful at that time in intervening against the migration of the staple English trade; the new industry could not be planted unless skilled artisans were allowed to leave England; and in 1640 the Council in London gave an unfavourable opinion of the scheme. They did not see how to enforce the seven years' apprenticeship and other rules which were supposed to be necessary for the due regulation of the broad cloth trade [25 March, 1640, *ib.* p. 124].

[2] The linen manufacture is mentioned in England in 1189 (Macpherson, I. 348), and there are several incidental notices of linen weavers in various towns. See above, Vol. I. 309 n. Under King James I. it was reported by the Commission of Trade in 1622 that the Eastland Company had formerly brought in flax and hemp in great quantities which afforded employment for many people in dressing and manufacturing it. They complained that the merchants now brought in finished goods instead, and that the manufacture had declined (*Fœdera*, XVII. 410). Before the Civil War, linen yarn was imported from Ireland to be woven in Manchester. Roberts, *Treasure of Trafficke*, 32. Almost immediately after the Restoration an Act was passed for encouraging the home manufacture and discouraging the importation of foreign linen. The introduction of Indian muslins somewhat interfered with the use of linen, and the chief supply, during the Restoration period, appears to have come from abroad (Macpherson, II. 540). In 1677 the inventor of a spinning engine for the linen trade claimed that by his system one man could be employed to turn fifty wheels, so that the spinners only had to use their hands. *Proposals for building in every county a working almshouse or hospital as the last expedient to perfect the trade and Manufactory of Linnen Cloth* (Royal Irish Soc. Box 88, 14). Hale writing in 1683 speaks of it as in some degree used in Lancashire, Leicestershire and some other places. *Discourse touching provision for Poor*, p. 13.

[3] Cox, *Hibernica Anglicana*, II. 57.

standard of quality in the manufacture, according to the usual practice of the time in the planting of any new industry; and it was made a complaint against him in the Bill of Attainder that he had issued proclamations on this subject "prescribing and enjoining Rules and Methods of making Yarn and Thread, which the unskilful Natives could not Practise," while he seized all badly made linen whereby multitudes were undone and many starved[1]. The attempt to improve the linen trade[2], so that it might provide high class goods for export, broke down completely during the disturbances caused by the Civil War; and does not appear to have been seriously taken up again[3] until the immigration of foreign Protestants after the Revolution[4].

but there was some fear that Irish prosperity might interfere with English resources, During the first half of the seventeenth century the development of Irish resources was restricted by fiscal considerations; it was not allowed to take a perfectly free course, but it was directed on lines which could not prove injurious to the English revenue. The sources of taxation in England and the new plantations in Virginia were allowed the first claims to consideration. The dread of hostile

[1] Cox, *Hibernica Anglicani*, II. 69.

[2] On the early history see *Reports*, 1840, XXIII. 458 and 521.

[3] Some attempts in this direction were made by the Duke of Ormonde, *Carte* II. 343. On the advantages which Ireland possessed for this industry compare V. Gooking in 1663; *Great Case of Transplantation in Ireland discussed* [Royal Irish Acad. *Halliday Tracts*, Box 82 (2)]. "There are few of the Irish Commonalty but are skilful in Husbandry and more exact than any English in the Husbandry proper to that Country... There are few of the Women but are skilful in dressing Hemp and Flax and making of Linnen and Woollen Cloth," p.17. See also Sir W. Temple's *Miscellanea* (1681), p. 114. "The Soil produces Flax kindly and well and fine too, answerable to the care used in choice of seed and exercise of Husbandry; and much Land is fit for it here, which is not so for Corn. The Manufacture of it in gathering or beating, is of little toyl or application; and so the fitter for the Natives of the Countrey. Besides, no Women are apter to spin it well than the Irish, who labouring little in any kind with their hands, have their fingers more supple and soft than other Women of poorer condition among us. And this may certainly be advanced and improved into a great Manufacture of Linnen, so as to beat down the trade both of France and Holland, and draw much of the Money which goes from England to those parts upon this occasion, into the hands of His Majesties Subjects of Ireland, without crossing any interest of Trade in England. For besides what has been said of Flax and Spinning, the Soil and Climate are proper for whitening, both by the frequency of Brooks, and also of Winds in the Countrey."

[4] See above, p. 330 n. 4. Also W. R. Scott, "The King's and Queen's Corporation for the Linen Manufacture in Ireland." *Proceedings Roy. Soc. Ant. of Ireland*, XXXI. 371.

competition by Ireland was not unnatural, nor was it un- A.D. 1603
reasonable to endeavour to prevent its occurrence; in all —1689.
probability this feeling would not, in itself, have affected
Irish development very seriously. Unfortunately, the economic jealousy with which Englishmen regarded Irish
progress was immensely stimulated by considerations of a
constitutional character. The English Parliament were *and furnish*
keenly suspicious of anything that might tend to increase *the king with an*
the royal powers. Charles I., Charles II. and James II. *extra-par-liamentary*
had all suffered from the distrust of their subjects; and *revenue.*
William III., even though he had been invited to come
over, did not succeed in inspiring confidence. As is well
known he bitterly resented the treatment he received.
Since Ireland was an independent kingdom, the English
House of Commons had no direct control over its affairs;
and there was constant uneasiness lest any power, which the
King acquired in Ireland, should be used without the con-
currence of the English Parliament[1], or even against English
liberties. Twice within the seventeenth century serious
attempts had been made to develop the resources of Ireland,
—by Strafford, and under Charles II. and James II.; in
both cases the result had been that the King had found
himself in possession of power that seemed to menace his
English subjects. Under these circumstances, there was the
strongest political reason for dreading any development of
the wealth of Ireland that took place at the expense of
England, since this really implied an increase of the influence of the Crown at the expense of that of Parliament[2].
This political dread of the revival of the arbitrary power *This*
of the Crown, coupled with the economic anxiety as to *political jealousy*
dangerous competition with England, led the English *led to the repression*
Parliament to adopt a hostile attitude to the emigrants
from Great Britain who were settling in Ireland and
beginning to develop its rural and industrial resources.
We see the effects of this feeling both in the measures
which rendered cattle-breeding unprofitable, and in the

[1] *An Answer*, 1698, p. 8, 21. [Brit. Mus. 1029. e. 14 (1).]
[2] Traces of this feeling were found in 1779 and later; as for example in
speeches by Lord Shelburne (*Parl. Hist.* xx. 1163), and in 1781 Fox (*ib.* xxi. 1297).

steps which were taken to restrict the progress of the clothing trade.

The best possibility of turning the depopulated lands in Ireland to good account at the time when it came under the rule of Charles II. lay in the development of cattle raising. For this the climate and soil were alike adapted, as had been proved by the success attained in the time of James I.[1]; and the British settlers in the country threw themselves energetically into the business after the Restoration. But the suspicions of the English House of Commons were roused. There seemed to be some grounds for thinking that this industry was being developed at the expense of the farmers and landlords in certain English counties[2]. The landed interest felt the pressure of hard times[3]; and it might have been impossible to raise the supplies which were necessary for the conduct of war, if there were any further diminution of the available resources at home. The importation of Irish cattle was said to be the chief reason of the fall of rents[4], and though the temporary imposition of a prohibitive duty did nothing for the English farmers[5], the House of Commons persisted in passing a measure which was fatal to the success of the Irish graziers[6] The Lords held out against the Bill for some time, and many parts of England were opposed to it[7], but the Commons forced it on, partly because of jealousy of the Duke of Ormonde personally[8]. Charles was too much afraid of losing the supplies on which he counted, to take a decided stand upon the matter; no similar restriction was placed on Scotland, and the eagerness of the House of Commons can only

---

[1] It was estimated in 1620 that 100,000 head of cattle were annually imported from Ireland and from 40/- to 60/- apiece paid in bullion for them. *Parl. Hist.* I. 1195. On the Trade in 1664 see Petty, *Political Anatomy* (1691), 71.

[2] *Parl. Hist.* IV. 337.

[3] See above, p. 188.

[4] This is discussed and controverted by Temple, *Works*, III. 19.

[5] 15 C. II. c. 7 § 13.

[6] 18 and 19 C. II. c. 2. *An Act against importing cattle from Ireland.* The point which was most keenly debated was as to describing the trade as a 'nuisance': the insertion of this word made it impossible for the King to render the Act a dead letter by granting licenses for occasional shipments. Carte, *Life of Ormonde*, II. 334.

[7] *Parl. Hist.* IV. 345.　　　　　　　　[8] *Ib.* 340.

be accounted for by a fear, that if Ireland became too *A.D. 1603 —1689.* prosperous, or prospered more rapidly than England, Charles would, through the influence of the Duke of Ormonde[1], become practically independent of the English Parliament.

It was bad enough for the settlers in Ireland to be cut *and of the victualling trade,* off from the opportunity of fattening their cattle for the English market, but they were also debarred from competing with English graziers in catering for the requirements of the colonists, or victualling the ships[2] engaged in the plantation trade. The Act of 1660 had indeed permitted direct intercourse between Ireland and the colonies, but this was discountenanced by the Act of 1663[3] and explicitly prohibited in 1670[4]. The outside markets, which had hither-to been available, were completely closed, and cattle-breeding ceased to be profitable. The immediate sufferers, by the restriction on the export of cattle from Ireland, were the English settlers who had devoted themselves to cattle-breeding; but their ruin was probably the salvation of the labourers and husbandmen, who had escaped transportation when the landowners were turned out to make room for the disbanded Cromwellian army. The English in Ireland were sacrificed to the English at home[5]; and as the cattle ranches no longer paid, there was less excuse for driving out the peasantry. Hence it was that those, who were interested in the preservation of the native Irish, looked back with little dissatisfaction on a measure which ruined the great graziers[6], but left room for the humbler cultivators. There were other *and result-ed in an* effects in Ireland which were equally unexpected, and were *increase* deeply deplored by English writers at a later date. Some *of wool growing;* of the Irish graziers, debarred from cattle-breeding, turned their attention to the growing of wool: for this they found

---

[1] Carte, *Life of Ormonde*, II. 317—338.

[2] The author of *Britannia Languens* (pp. 53, 164) regarded the low rates at which ships could be victualled in Ireland as a danger to English prosperity.

[3] 15 Charles II. c. 7 § 6. A. E. Murray, *History of the Commercial Relations between England and Ireland*, 41.   [4] 22 and 23 C. II. c. 26 § 11.

[5] There were strong political, as distinguished from fiscal, reasons against the Acts since they were injurious to English maritime power. J. Collins, *Plea for bringing in Irish Cattle and keeping out fish caught by foreigners* (1680).

[6] Antagonism to graziers in Ireland gave rise to organised agrarian crime in the first decade of the eighteenth century. Lecky, II. 351.

a considerable market on the continent[1]. The main trade
of Ireland had hitherto been with England, but now a
considerable intercourse sprang up with France and other
European countries; and foreigners utilised the materials
so well, that they became formidable rivals to the cloth
manufacture of England[2].

There is reason to believe that the prohibition of export,
among other things, rendered the price of meat and cost of
living somewhat low in Ireland, and served to attract another
class of immigrants to the country. Under Charles II. there
is little sign of the feeling, which Strafford had expressed,
that there was a danger of raising up an Irish rival to
the English clothing trade[3]. We see signs of a steady immigration of clothiers into Ireland and of a development of
the manufacture of drapery during the Restoration period.

*which
favoured
the develop-
ment of
weaving,*
The cheapness of wool, and of living, favoured the experiments which were made at different times; and about 1665,
or a little later, some " Western Clothiers finding, so early,
and upon other Reasons that are now suborned, that Trade
decaying, and many of them reduced to extreme Poverty,
removed themselves and their Families over into *Ireland*,
invited by the Cheapness there of Wool, and of Livelihood.
These erected then a Manufactory (great in respect to
Ireland) at *Dublin* which hath been carried on ever since
and increases daily. There came also over, much about the
same time, sixty Families from *Holland*, setting up another
at *Lymerick*; which, by Occasion of the succeeding Wars
decayed. But, after these, more of the *English* Clothiers
came and fixed about *Corke* and *Kinsale*, where they continue and are grown not inconsiderable. Some *French* have
since resorted to *Waterford* to make Druggets there, and
other Commodities of their Fashion. And about a Year
or two ago, some Merchants of *London* raised another
Manufacture at *Clonmel*, managing it by their Agents....
There is more Cry than Wool in this Matter: For I dare

[1] J. Trevers, *An Essay to the restoring of our decayed trade, wherein is
described the Smugglers', Lawyers' and Officers' Frauds* (1675), p. 19.

[2] Carte, *Ormonde*, II. 337.

[3] Walloon clothiers were introduced by the Duke of Ormonde at Clonmel to
make Norwich stuffs for the Spanish trade. Carte, *Ormonde*, II. 342.

and do assure you that, modestly speaking, the whole A.D. 1603
—1689. Quantity of what we work up in *Ireland* amounts not to the Half of what any one Clothing-County in *England* does[1]." The quantity produced at this time might be small, but the authorities were anxious that the quality should be high. The Irish Parliament was distinctly en- *and at-* deavouring to maintain the character of the newly introduced *tempts were made to* industry and to give a guarantee which might satisfy those *improve this manu-* who purchased Irish cloth for export. If Irish drapery were *facture.* to compete successfully in the English and foreign markets with English drapery, it was desirable that there should be no misunderstanding in regard to size and quality. Accordingly in 1665 a statute was passed, which instituted the office of aulnager[2] and defined the sizes to which the cloth should be woven.

The intention of this Act was evidently to improve and foster the art of woollen manufacture in Ireland; but, as was often the case with similar enactments, it did not serve its purpose. In 1695, the Irish Commons condemned it as "impracticable and prejudicial," and proceeded to prepare "the heads of a Bill for the better making and regulating" of the woollen manufacture[3]. These attempts of the Irish *The* Parliament to regulate the trade were, however, rendered *English were* futile by the fact that the developing manufacture had *alarmed at the* attracted the attention of the English House of Commons; *signs of the* the economic jealousy of Irish progress, in combination with *migration of the cloth* political dread of the independent power of the Crown, broke *trade* out in a new direction. The West of England clothiers asserted that "during the late Rebellion in *Ireland* many of the Poor of that Kingdom fled into the West of *England* where they were put to work in the Woollen manufactures and learned that Trade; and since the Reduction of *Ireland*,

---

[1] *A Letter*, § 4, quoted in Smith's *Chronicon-Rusticum*, i. chapter lix. p. 303.

[2] "For the more orderly managing the trade and mystery of making and working of woollen cloth, and all other sorts of clothes of the natures and kinds aforesaid, and for the better ascertaining of the length breadth and weight of all such clothes to be made within the realm of Ireland......and that the buyers thereof may have just commerce and trade without deceit or fraud, may it please your majesty, that there shall be and hereby is constituted and appointed an office called the Alnage Office, &c." *Irish Statutes* (17 and 18 C. II. c. 15 § 9.)

[3] *Irish Commons Journal* (16 Oct. 1695), ii. i. 95.

Endeavours are used to set up those Manufactures there[1]."
The main attraction of Ireland to weavers was the cheapness
of living and the cheapness of wool, and these advantages
had drawn a considerable number of English-bred workmen
*from
Devonshire
to Dublin.*
to Ireland, so that in 1697 it seemed probable that the
Devonshire industry would soon be transplanted to Dublin.
There does not appear to have been much excitement in
the northern[2] and eastern centres of the clothing trade;
but the West of England clothiers averred that their long-
celebrated manufactures were decaying while the Irish industry increased; labour was attracted away and Irish wool
was intercepted on its way to them.   They were stirred, not
by a mere anticipation of possible competition, but by actual
experience of the migration that had already taken place.
*The duties
and re-
strictions
imposed
on Irish
clothiers*
What they demanded was, that such countervailing duties
should be imposed as would serve to neutralise the advantages in Ireland, and to put both countries on equal
terms, so that the migration of industry from one to the
other should cease[3].   At the same time, they were careful to
guard against any danger of Irish competition in the colonial
markets, and the machinery of the Navigation Acts[4] was
used to prevent the introduction of Irish cloth into the
plantations or foreign parts.   The manufacturers were thus
cut off from all opportunities of an export trade.   Of this
particular grievance inflicted upon Ireland it may therefore
be said, that it had little or no effect upon the native

---

[1] *English Commons Journals,* xii. (Tiverton) 63 b; compare also (Taunton)
37 a, (Barnstaple) 40 b, (Ashburton) 64 a.   Massie, *Observations on the new Cyder
Tax,* p. 2.

[2] They complained at this very date of the export of wool to Scotland.
Commons Journals, xii. 64.

[3] The rate which was actually levied was 20 per cent. on the old drapery and
10 per cent. on the new.   This was arrived at after the Irish woollen manufacturers
had been heard on the subject, and though it actually proved to be a prohibitory
and not merely a countervailing tax, it was obviously intended to be merely
countervailing.   The Commissioners on Trade after going into the matter actually
recommended 43 per cent. and explicitly remarked that they proposed this as
a mere countervailing duty and not as a heavier tax which "would in effect
amount to an absolute Prohibition of the Exportation of that Sort of Cloth from
Ireland, which we humbly conceive can never be intended by that Bill." *Commons
Journals,* xii. 439.

[4] 10 and 11 W. III. c. 10.

population[1] and that immediate sufferers were the Protestant interest in Ireland. There is no sign of jealousy of their prosperity, in the sense in which there was jealousy of the possible prosperity of the native Irish, when the penal laws were passed; the real motive lay in the desire to prevent the Protestant interest in Ireland from undermining the success of an established English trade[2].

A.D. 1603 – 1689.

in the interest of the established English trade

However, even from the English standpoint, it appears that these measures proved hurtful, and failed to secure the object which their promoters had in view; while they did irreparable mischief in Ireland by preventing the development of an industry for which she was admirably adapted.

[1] In legislating about the Irish woollen trades, the manufacture of frieze was specially excluded from the duties that were placed on the export of the old and new drapery. In any case the native cloth was apparently chiefly made for home consumption, and the quantity exported was so small that the new duties might prevent the development of the trade, but would only be a slight injury to those who were already engaged in it.

[2] The action of the Irish woollen manufacturers during this period confirms this view of the case. They were on the one hand anxious to improve the regulation about the quality of cloth, and on the other hand they were anxious to establish themselves in a closer corporation. According to their account the new trade had begun to attract some of the native Irish after 1692 and the Dublin weavers were moving the Irish Parliament to confine the trade more strictly to the Protestant interest for the future. "A Petition of the Protestant Woollen Manufacturers of the City and County of Dublin, as well Freemen as Foreigners, in Behalf of themselves and the Rest of the Woollen manufacturers in Ireland," addressed to the Irish House of Commons in 1698, asserts "that the Papists, in the Year 1692, were but very few in the Woollen Manufactory of this Kingdom, and for six years last they have gotten the third Part of the said Manufactory into their own Hands, for great Numbers of them have left the Trade & Calling they were bred to, viz. Brogue Makers, Mealmen, Bakers etc., and have set up and follow the Woolen Trade, without serving any Time and carry on a greater Trade than most of the Corporation: That the said Papists for Want of Knowledge in the Trade have made much bad Goods, which have gone off by the Lowness of the Rates, and is an absolute Cheat to the Buyer, who cannot always distinguish between good and bad Goods, all which have much damnified the Protestant Interest in this Kingdom, and caused a Jealousy in England that our Manufactory will damnify theirs: for Prevention whereof, and for the Preservation of the Protestant Interest in this Nation, the Petitioners humbly propose to the Consideration of the House the disabling Papists from following or working in the Woollen Manufactory, except spinning, whereby the others may return to their former Trades, or take to the Linen Manufactory, and that no Protestant or Person whatever, may keep above three Apprentices at once, and they to serve full seven Years Time, whereby the goods will be well made, and bear such a Rate as, considering the Dearness of all Necessaries we have from England, we shall not be able to afford them cheaper than they." *Irish Commons Journals* (12 Oct. 1698), II. i. 247.

A.D. 1603
—1689.

gave the opportunity for foreign competition

The Irish were deprived of their home market for wool and exported it in a raw or half-manufactured state to France[1], while the workmen who could no longer earn a living in Ireland found their way to foreign countries where they started industries which became more formidable rivals to the English manufactures than the Irish would have been likely to prove. The single competitor was ousted from the field; but it was a barren triumph, since our statesmen unwittingly called into being new rivals, in the neighbourhood of the best markets.

and checked the development of Irish industry

If the policy was mistaken, even with reference to its professed objects, we who look back from the present day can easily see what was pointed out by pamphleteers at the time, that the scheme of policy was bad, since it was so shortsighted. There were one or two voices which pleaded for the new industry, as a strength, not merely to the Protestant interest, but to Ireland, and indirectly to England too[2]. They held that the development of this trade in Dublin, and the encouragement of Englishmen and aliens to flock there, would give a great impetus to the prosperity of the sister isle, and change her into a new source of strength to the realm. If Ireland enjoyed more plenty, she could do more to support the united power of the two kingdoms. As manufacturing increased, the price of raw products would go up. The Irish peasantry would have a better market both for wool and for food-stuffs; the general increase of plenty, and new intercourse between Protestants and Romanists, might well be expected to give better conditions for the growth of social institutions and for steady political progress. All this was hoped for; all this, so far as

---

[1] [Richardson], *An Essay on the Causes of the Decline of Foreign Trade* (1744). p. 30. Caldwell's *Enquiry*, in *Debates*, 760—769. It was denied however that this occurred on as large a scale as is commonly said (Macpherson, *Annals of Commerce*, III. 182); but others alleged that it seriously affected the profit of the grazier in England. *Graziers' Complaint* (1726), p. 19. Brit. Mus. 712. g. 16 (37). The writer gives a curious estimate of the different expense of production in Ireland and in Lincolnshire.

[2] Arthur Dobbs, *An Essay upon the Trade and Improvement of Ireland* (1729) in *Collection of Tracts* (1861), II. 336, Brit. Mus. 1303. i. 17; *List of Absentees* (1729), *ib.* II. 279. Also *Collection of Tracts concerning State of Ireland* [Brit. Mus. 884. h. 12 (2)] (1729), p. 43.

we see, might have been; but these beneficial results were ^{A.D. 1603} _{—1689.} frustrated by the measures which checked the development of the drapery trade. The fiscal loss would have been very serious if the Devonshire manufacturers had been ruined, but the ultimate gain from an Ireland, that was prosperous and contented, would have far outweighed it.

The chance of securing such prosperity was sacrificed[1]; and no more English capital found its way to Dublin for the establishment of weaving; but even in the narrowest commercial sense the ultimate loss to England was very *and the* *peaceful* great. All those who had attempted to make the most of *settlement* Irish industries had seen that it could be best done by *of the* *country.* attracting British industry and capital to settle there. With the reduction of Ireland by William III. a new opportunity had opened. English enterprise and industry were beginning to find their way to Ireland once more, not now to dispossess men of their hereditary lands, but to give a better market for the produce of each man's lands and labour, and better opportunities of satisfying his wants. Much national benefit might have accrued, even if the drapery manufacture had been developed on the restricted lines which the Dublin weavers suggested; but this great opportunity was thrown away for the sake of an immediate pecuniary gain[2], and because the English Parliament deemed it wise to refrain from improving Irish resources, for fear they should unduly increase the wealth and power of the Crown.

---

[1] On the economic conditions in the eighteenth century see M. J. Bonn, *Die Englische Kolonisation*, II. 218—243.

[2] It has been assumed in the foregoing section that contemporaries were right in believing that Ireland had special advantages for carrying on the woollen manufacture: Miss Murray has shown that, in spite of the restrictions, the trade was maintained in some localities. *History of Commercial Relations*, 105—110. The trade continued to exist but in a depressed condition. The Irish Parliament insisted that the Weavers' Companies in Dublin and other towns should exercise a more effective supervision over the manufacture. *Irish Commons Journal*, II. i. p. 482. The weavers of Dublin complained of the ruin of their trade in 1732 (R. M. Martin, *Ireland*, 39), and there were frequent petitions describing the distress of the woollen and worsted weavers of Dublin and Cork in 1783, 1787, 1788, 1793 and 1800 (*ib.* 49). There was considerable progress about 1801 and for a few subsequent years when machinery worked by water power came into vogue; but hand spinning and weaving seem never to have prospered. This was due partly to difficulties in procuring suitable wool. (Letter to Mr Spring Rice, 3 *Hansard*, XXII. 1257.)

X. ECONOMIC INVESTIGATION AND MAXIMS.

Seventeenth century pamphleteers treated economic questions

206. The prominence which was given to the economic aspects of political life during the seventeenth century is noticeably reflected in the literature of the day. It is true that in formal treatises, like the *Leviathan* of Hobbes[1], or the *Civil Government* of Locke[2], the material well-being of the community is merely discussed incidentally. There was, however, an immense mass of pamphlet literature devoted to contemporary economic problems, and considerable progress was made in formulating suggestions as to the most fruitful means for prosecuting a branch of study that had *according to empirical methods and on biological lines* been hitherto neglected. The writers of the day were greatly influenced by the Baconian enthusiasm for empirical study; they were eager to accumulate and interpret facts, and to apply inductive methods to political phenomena. They therefore concerned themselves with the anatomy of the body politic, and with numerical observations which served as the best available substitute for experiment. They followed the analogy of the biological rather than of the mathematical science of their day, and hence their mode

---

[1] Compare the chapter on the nutrition and procreation of states. According to Hobbes, the nutrition of the commonwealth consists in plenty of materials conducing to life, in the preparation and conveyance of them, and it depends on the natural plenty afforded by sea and land; and also on the labour and industry of men (Hobbes' *Works* (Molesworth's edition) III. 232). In a few pregnant sentences he indicated the two sources from which the prosperity of a people must be obtained. Hobbes was not merely concerned with the income of the prince, but with the wealth of the community from which that ·income must ultimately be drawn, and thus he indicated the main scope of economic art, as it was studied by statesmen; while he avoided the one-sidedness which has been alleged in regard to later schools. The productive power of nature received undue attention from the Physiocrats, while the Mercantilists also recognised the productive power of labour, and set themselves to develop it.

[2] *Civil Government*, in *Works* (1794), IV. §§ 37, 40, 42. Locke's treatise is of great interest from the extraordinary indirect effect which it exercised on Political Economy at a later time. It is a most decided expression of the rights both political and social of the individual, to be governed according to his own ideas of what is right, and to be secured in the free control of his own property. This treatise had a great effect in popularising the doctrines which were implicitly assumed by the English *laissez faire* economists.

of thought has a close affinity with that which has become current, since the decline of the classical school of Political Economy.

There was, some years ago, a good deal of discussion as to whether Political Economy is more properly a science or an art; that is, whether it is primarily engaged in the scientific investigation of the principles according to which the production and distribution of wealth are carried on, or whether its main object is to make practical suggestions for increasing the production and improving the distribution of wealth. It is important to bear in mind that seventeenth century writers approached the subject entirely from the latter standpoint; by far the larger number of contemporary tracts were written by men who were advocating some particular proposal, and who adduced general reasons in favour of the special scheme they had in view. Even when this is not the case, their labour, whether in criticising the proposals of others or in gathering facts, was distinctly and consciously regarded as affording subsidiary helps to the great work of governing the country wisely. The various discussions on coins and money were called forth by a desire to give wise advice in regard to the difficult question of recoinage. The whole subject is approached in its practical aspects by Petty, Locke, and Child, as well as by writers of less note. In so far as contemporary writers discussed economic affairs in another spirit, they treated them artistically in *Utopias*, and *Arcadias*, and *Oceanas*, rather than with any pretence to scientific accuracy. Readers, who thoroughly appreciate the admirable common sense which these men wrote on many intricate matters, will yet miss the clearness of thought and consecutive reasoning, which only became possible after the more purely scientific studies of the followers of Adam Smith. This was indeed inevitable; till the phenomena of wealth were deliberately isolated from other social phenomena, it was not possible to treat them with precision. The seventeenth century economists were so eager about the end they had in view, that they did not concentrate attention sufficiently on the means for attaining it. Their writings are full of acute remark, and many of

Practical objects were kept closely in view,

and economics was not so much an independent branch of study them deal with particular topics in a masterly fashion; but there is a curious disproportion in the space they assign to these special points; and they seem to have had no clear conception of the scope of the subject, or of the divisions into which, according to our habits of thought, it naturally falls. Hence there is an appearance of confusion in the writings of the acutest authors of the period, even when they may be rightly credited with having anticipated Adam Smith on very many points.

as a de-partment of state-craft.
One further indication that the scope of the subject was still very uncertain lies in the fact that Political Economy had not yet attained the dignity of a name[1]; it was but a branch of the art of governing or state-craft. Successive generations of statesmen had been economists without knowing it. One practical expedient had been tried after another, for increasing the power of the nation in this or that direction, or as one occasion or another called forth some special effort. The general result of this long experience had been embodied in the legislation of Elizabeth, and was consciously adopted as the best method for increasing the power of the country. The writers of the seventeenth century were much engaged in comparing English experience with that of other cities and countries, and in thus establishing maxims of more general application, based on a consideration of the actual progress, or decay, of different communities.

The in-cidence of taxation
The fact that the principal constitutional disputes of the seventeenth century turned on questions of revenue, gave the subject great prominence; and writers on political topics busied themselves in discussing the most fruitful forms of taxation. The problem of distributing the burden fairly, and of examining the incidence of taxation, was not overlooked; but the statesmen of the day were chiefly concerned in discovering sources from which a revenue could be regularly obtained. By far the most important work of

---

[1] Petty comes near it: "As wiser Physicians tamper not excessively with their Patients, rather observing and complying with the motions of nature, then contradicting it with vehement Administrations of their own; so in Politics and Oeconomicks the same must be used." *Treatise*, 41.

the time was Sir William Petty's *Treatise of Taxes and* A.D. 1603
—1689.
Contributions[1]; the author's interest in actual problems is *was dis-*
strongly marked, as it was compiled with special reference *cussed by*
to the affairs of Ireland, where Petty held an official position. *Petty,*
He begins by enumerating the charges which ought to be
borne by the public, and discusses some savings that might
be effected in particular departments, and also examines
" how the causes of the unquiet bearing of taxes may be
lessened." He discusses the rival merits and demerits of
every possible manner of raising revenue with much acuteness, and with occasional humour. " A lottery is properly a
tax upon unfortunate self-conceited fools ; * * * now because
the world abounds with this kinde of fools, it is not fit that
every man that will, may cheat every man that would be
cheated ; but it is rather ordained, that the Sovereign should
have the Guardianship of these fools, or that some Favourite
should beg the Sovereign's right of taking advantage of such
men's folly[2]."

It was not possible for a man like Petty to treat of the *as well*
art of taxation, without going back to the more important *as the*
sources of
question of the ' funds' from which each kind of revenue is *wealth in*
labour and
drawn. Like other writers of the day he lays stress on *land;*
human industry and natural resources, as the two principal
factors in material progress. " Labour," he says, " is the
Father and active principle of Wealth, as Lands are the
Mother[3]." A similar opinion is expressed by Samuel Fortrey,
who points out that natural fertility and population are the
two main conditions of prosperity, and shows how France
has prospered by its natural riches, and Holland by the
industry of its people. " Two things therefore appear to be
chiefly necessary to make a nation great and powerfull, which
is to be rich[4] and populous," and England, since it excels in

---

[1] The references are to the edition of 1662. It was reprinted in 1667, 1679 and
1685, also with the title *A Discourse of Taxes* in 1689.

[2] *Treatise*, p. 45.   [3] *Ib.* p. 49.

[4] " Rich " here refers to store of commodities, and not to the accumulation of
treasure, as is obvious from the context. *England's Interest and Improvement* in
Political Economy Club Collection of Early English Tracts on Commerce, 218,
ed. Macculloch. This reprint is from the edition of 1673, but it was originally
published in 1663.

both ways, might confidently expect "to become the most great, and flourishing of all others."

the importance of Capital was recognised, and much attention was given to the effect of the usury laws

There were many authors who were also keenly alive to the importance of an abundance of capital as a factor in national wealth. This comes out most clearly in the numerous tracts which inveigh against the usury laws[1], since the writers believed that the maximum interest allowed by law was apt to be adopted as the rate demanded in practice. Sir Thomas Culpeper[2] may be said to have devoted his life to the task of getting Parliament to lower the maximum it permitted; he succeeded in reducing the legal rate from 10 to 8 per cent. in 1624[3]; subsequently he saw the rate reduced to 6 per cent. in 1652[4], and his endeavours were continued by his son[5], and also by Sir J. Child[6]. The 6 per cent. rate was maintained by the Restoration Parliament, though some men tried to exact the rate which had been legal in the time of Charles I.[7] The precise influence on trade, of authoritatively restricting the rate, is difficult to estimate, without a very full knowledge of the commercial conditions of the times[8]. But it was certainly impossible to force the legal rate below what we should call the market rate. Sir Josiah Child appeared to think that the State could decree as low a rate as 3 or 4 per cent., and showed that these rates[9] were current in Holland. But other writers saw that this was a mistake; Thomas Manley asserted that "low interest is, both in nature and time, subsequent to riches, and he that says low Usury begets riches, takes the effect for the cause, the child for the mother, and puts the cart before the horse[10]." There is

---

[1] See above, p. 153.

[2] His *Tract against Usury* was first published in 1621; it was reissued in 1668 by his son.

[3] 21 J. I. c. 17.

[4] Scobell, *Acts*, 1652.

[5] The preface to the younger Culpeper's *Discourse shewing the many Advantages which will accrue to this Kingdom by Abatement of Usury* (1668) contains an excellent *résumé* of the struggle. See also his *Necessity of abating Usury reasserted* (1670).

[6] *Brief Observations concerning Trade* (1668), p. 7.

[7] 12 Charles II. c. 13.　　　　[8] See below, p. 395.

[9] *New Discourse of Trade*, p. 7.

[10] *Usury at six per cent. examined* (1669), Preface, p. 6. Compare also *Interest*

of course a reciprocal action; riches render low interest possible, and low interest tends in many ways to the increase of riches; but in any case, State action must follow and not precede a change in the market rate. Locke helped to clear the air by insisting that the attempt to fix a maximum rate was illusory, since the want of money is that which regulates its price, and people will pay more if they really need an advance. He admitted that, if all men "consented" to low interest and money could be borrowed at a lower market rate, it would benefit traders; but he regarded the proposal to fix legal interest at 4 per cent. as an attempt to drive the rate down below the market rate. This would, in his view, be hard on those who conformed to the law, it would tempt many to break it, and it would seriously hamper trade, as people would prefer to hoard their capital rather than have the risk of lending on such terms[1]. There is no doubt that substantial men could borrow at less than the permitted maximum; it was commonly said that the East India Company could get loans at 3 per cent., but on the other hand, in special circumstances, money had not been forthcoming at 6 per cent. Sir William *and to the* Petty treated the matter still more fully, as he not only *causes which de-* protested against fixing a legal maximum, but analysed the *termine the rate of* conditions which determined the rate of interest with some *interest,* success. Interest on the best security could not exceed the rent which would come from a similar sum invested in land; but where there was no good security, "a kinde of ensurance must be enterwoven with the simple natural Interest[2]."

The best writing of the day shows much insight into the causes which determined the ordinary rate of interest, and the old difficulties about the morality of usury had come to be regarded as the qualms of specially tender consciences[3].

---

of money mistaken, or a Treatise proving that the Abatement of Interest is the Effect and not the Cause of the Riches of a Nation, and that Six per Cent. is a proportionable Interest to the present condition of this Kingdom (1668), p. 13. Brit. Mus. 1029. b. 1 (5).

[1] *Considerations of the lowering of Interest, Works,* IV. 7, 69.

[2] Petty, *Treatise,* 29. See also *Quantulumcumque,* Query, 32, in *Collection of Scarce and valuable Tracts on Money,* 167; ed. Macculloch.

[3] See above, p. 153.

A.D. 1603
—1689.
Sir William Petty could not see why "usury should be scrupled," when a loan caused, or might cause, any inconvenience to the lender. He was, however, to some extent in sympathy with the mediaeval view, as he did not feel that there was any justification for taking interest in the case of money which was lent on full security to be repaid on demand; to his mind the ground for some charge being made, lay in the *damnum emergens,* or *periculum sortis*; while the rate per annum was determined with reference to the rent of land. He wrote with much severity of many English prejudices, as became a man of the world who had lived much abroad, but it is curious to find how much he sympathised with those who were opposed to the readmission of Jews by the Protector[1].

but not to the morality of usury.

207. The effort to enumerate the chief factors in national prosperity served the very important purpose of providing criteria for judging as to the progress of the country. This was a matter of intense interest, which was sometimes discussed with reference to the changes in England itself, and sometimes with a view of estimating the growth in this realm as compared with that which was taking place in other countries.

The best criterion for gauging the progress of the country

The rough and ready test, which was applied by the ordinary writer, was the prosperity or depression of the landed men as shown in the high or low rentals they were able to obtain, or the rate at which land could be purchased. In this habit of thought there is a curious contrast with our prevailing ideas; it is difficult for us to imagine that any statesman would boldly and officially advocate a measure on the ground that it would raise rentals. A parliament of landlords might have been expected to feel some shame at legislating so palpably in their own interest; but it would hardly have struck these men in the same light. Much of the revenue in the present day comes from an excise, or from the income tax, which were alike unknown in the

appeared to be given by the prosperity of the landed interest,

---

[1] *Treatise,* p. 64. There are some curious suggestions on the desirability of subjecting the newly returned Jews to a strict discipline in *England's Wants* (1667), p. 40 [Camb. Univ. Lib. R. 10. 10 (16)]. Compare also the petition in Stow, *Survey,* v. 243. See above, p. 326.

earlier part of the seventeenth century; at that date, land A.D. 1603 —1689. was the great fund from which taxation was paid. If rents were high, then there was an abundant source from which *as land was the chief source from which taxation was drawn.* revenue could be drawn; if rents were low, even though trade prospered, it made comparatively little difference to the sources of taxation. All through the seventeenth century a rise of rents was treated, not as an especial boon to the landlord class, but as a gain to the public at large, since the fund from which revenue was drawn was amply supplied. Only when we remember this, does the language of the statutes, or of contemporary writers, about high rents, become intelligible to us. If the legislature had been a parliament of landlords deliberately passing enactments in their own private interest, they would hardly have paraded the fact in such a barefaced fashion. As one instance, we may note that Fortrey, in his tract on *England's Interest and Improvement*, advocates the enclosure of commons as a real improvement, because landlords favour it and find it increases the value of their land[1]. The statutes against the importation of Irish cattle and allowing the export of corn, were avowedly intended to make farming more profitable, so that there might be a fund available for paying assessments. The principle that high rents were a sign of national prosperity, was so generally accepted and avowed, that it is unnecessary to do more than quote Locke's statement. "An infallible sign of your decay of wealth is the falling of rents, and the raising of them would be worth the nation's care, for in that, and not in the falling of interest, lies the true advantage of the landed man and with him of the public[2]."

Sir William Petty and others, who attached great im *The importance of population was also recognised* portance to industry as a source of wealth, were inclined to regard the increase of the population as one of the most important tokens of prosperity. The topic was one which lent itself directly to statistical treatment, although Petty

[1] "The land of the common fields, almost in all places of this nation, with all the advantages that belong unto them will not let for above one third part so much as the same land would do inclosed, and always several." *England's Interest*, in *Collection of Early English Tracts*, 228. See also p. 552 below.

[2] *Considerations of the lowering of interest*, *Works*, IV. 69.

did not underrate the difficulties to be encountered, and he
was not allowed to forget them.   In his first essays, he was
met by the objection "that these computations are very hard
and Petty
insisted on
the neces-
sity of ac-
curate nu-
merical in-
vestigation.
if not impossible to make; to which I answer onely this that
they are so, especially if none will trouble their hands or
heads to make them, or give authority for so doing.   But
withal I say that until this be done, Trade will be too
conjectural a work for any man to employ his thoughts
about; for it will be the same wisdom, in order to win
with fair Dice, to spend much time in considering how to
hold them, how much to shake them, and how hard to throw
them, and on what angles they should hit the side of the
Tables, as to consider how to advance the Trade of this
Nation; where at present particular men get from their
neighbours (not from the earth and sea) rather by hit then
wit, and by the false opinions of others rather than their
own judgments[1]."   The ordinary writers argued entirely
from calculations of the very vaguest sort, and the pro-
gnostications of rapid decay often rested on the merest
hearsay.   "It is a hard matter," one writer confesses, "to
put a just Estimate on these yearly Losses, for the present
I shall leave it to be computed by our *Melancholick English
Tradesmen*[2]."

After all it was idle to spend time in explaining the
cause of the decay, if there was no real decline at all;
and the great necessity of the time was the accumulation
of accurate information.   This was fully recognised by
some Fellows of the Royal Society, who set themselves
to collect as accurate statistics as possible.   The first
Graunt set
an example
of statisti-
cal en-
quiries,
example was the work of Captain John Graunt, who
analysed the information which was available in regard to
London; the frequent complaints of the undue growth of
London, and the fears as to the decay of the population
through the drain of the war and the ravages of the plague,

---

[1] Petty, *Treatise*, 34. He notes as one of the causes which aggravate public
changes "Ignorance of the numbers, Wealth and Trade of the people, causing
a needless repitition of the charge and trouble of new additional Levies in order
to amend mistakes," p. 4.

[2] *Britannia Languens*, p. 405, in Macculloch, *Collection of early English tracts
on Commerce.* See also Sir Josiah Child's *New Discourse of Trade*, Preface.

made it desirable that the real condition of the city should *A.D.* **1603** —1689.
be properly investigated, and Graunt claimed that it was a
branch of "natural history" which might fitly engage the
attention of the philosophers who met at Gresham College.
His remarks on the study of statistics are so apposite that it
is worth while to quote them.

"Whereas the Art of Governing, and the true *Politicks*, *with a*
is how to preserve the Subject in *Peace* and *Plenty*; that men *furnishing*
study only that part of it which teacheth how to supplant and *a basis for*
over-reach one another, and how, not by fair outrunning, but *by govern-*
by tripping up each other's heels, to win the Prize. *ment,*

"Now, the Foundation or Elements of this honest harmless *Policy* is to understand the Land, and the hands of the
Territory, to be governed according to all their intrinsick
and accidental differences: As for example; It were good to
know the *Geometrical* Content, Figure, and Situation of all
the Lands of a *Kingdom*, especially according to its most
natural, permanent, and conspicuous Bounds. It were good
to know how much Hay an Acre of every sort of Meadow
will bear; how many Cattel the same weight of each sort of
Hay will feed and fatten; what quantity of Grain and other
Commodities the same Acre will bear in one, three, or seven
years, *communibus Annis*; unto what use each soil is most
proper. All which particulars I call the intrinsick value:
for there is also another value meerly accidental, or ex-
trinsick, consisting of the Causes why a parcel of Land,
lying near a good Market, may be worth double to another
parcel, though but of the same intrinsick goodness; which
answers the Queries, why Lands in the *North* of *England*
are worth but sixteen years purchase, and those of the *West*
above eight and twenty. It is no less necessary to know
how many People there be of each Sex, State, Age, Religion,
Trade, Rank, or Degree, etc., by the knowledge whereof,
Trade and Government may be made more certain and
Regular; for, if men knew the People, as aforesaid, they
might know the consumption they would make, so as Trade
might not be hoped for where it is impossible. As for
instance, I have heard much complaint, that Trade is not
set in some of the *South-western* and *North-western* Parts of

Ireland, there being so many excellent Harbours for that purpose; whereas in several of those places I have also heard, that there are few other Inhabitants, but such as live *ex sponte creatis,* and are unfit Subjects of Trade, as neither employing others, nor working themselves[1]."

The conclusions at which he arrived are very curious; some have reference to the increase of certain diseases, and comparative decline of others; and many of his remarks are suggestive in a sanitary and medical aspect: his main results are summarised in the dedication, in which he calls on Lord Truro to "consider how few starve of the many that beg, That the irreligious *Proposals* of some, to multiply people by *Polygamy,* is withal irrational and fruitless. That the troublesome seclusions in the *Plague time* are not a remedy to be purchased at vast inconveniences[2]; that the greatest *Plagues* of the City are equally, and quickly repaired from the Country[3]; That the wasting of *Males* by Wars and Colonies do not prejudice the due proportion between them and *Females*; that the opinion of *Plagues* accompanying the Entrance of *Kings* is false and seditious; that *London* the *Metropolis* of *England* is perhaps a Head too big for the Body, and possibly too strong; That this Head grows three times as fast as the Body unto which it belongs, that is, it doubles its People in a third part of the time[4]."

and Petty followed the same lines in discussing Irish problems. Sir William Petty, another Fellow of the Royal Society[5] carried on similar investigations in regard to the state of Ireland where he was officially engaged: on economic grounds he strongly advocated everything that should "tend to the transmuting of one People into the other, and the thorough union of Interests upon natural and lasting principles," since he held "that if both Kingdoms now two, were put into one, and under one Legislative Power and Parliament, the Members whereof should be in the same

[1] Graunt, *Natural and Political Observations,* 98, 99.
[2] Since the infection was in the air, not due to contagion, p. 50.
[3] At the rate of about 6000 per annum, p. 59.
[4] Graunt, *Natural and Political Observations,* Dedication.
[5] The opinion that Sir William Petty wrote Graunt's book under an assumed name is carefully discussed and rejected by Dr Hull in his introduction to *The Economic Writings of Sir William Petty,* I. xxxix.

proportion that the Power and Wealth of each Nation are, A.D. 1603
—1689.
there would be no danger such a Parliament should do
anything to the prejudice of the *English* interest in *Ireland* ;
nor could the *Irish* ever complain of Partiality when they
shall be freely and proportionably represented in all Legislatures[1]." Petty was fond of exercising his powers of
prevision on the basis of his definite information: he
formulated a law as to the rate of the progress of London,
and held it would reach 5,359,000 of inhabitants in 1800
and could not increase much beyond that number[2], as from
the area of the country and rate of increase of the rural
population, it would be impossible to supply them with
food. Less ambitious, and therefore more interesting, is
his *Political Arithmetic*[3]. In it he examined the common
complaint of the country's decay, and the rapid progress
of Holland and France; while admitting that there were
mischiefs of many kinds, which he attributed to deep-seated
popular prejudices, he yet was confident that as a matter of
fact England had increased in wealth and power during the
preceding forty years. He also urged that the impediments
to the further progress of the country could be removed, but
that France appeared to be under physical disabilities; she
could not become a maritime power, which would be capable
of holding her own against England or Holland, from the
insufficiency of the harbours on the Channel, and the
difficulty of training a sufficient body of efficient seamen.
In this, as in many other cases, he shows much acuteness,
in stating and analysing the facts, but the course of events
has not confirmed all the conclusions he drew from them.

It was not enough, however, that the population should *The oppor-*
increase, but it was also desirable that it should be well *tunities for*
employing
employed. A large army of vagrants could not possibly be *the popula-*
tion were
an advantage to the realm. It was assumed, as an obvious *estimated,*
maxim, that additional employment would be furnished
either by opening up new markets and thus securing a
vent for our commodities, or by stimulating consumption

---

[1] *Political Anatomy of Ireland* (1691), 29, 31.
[2] *An Essay concerning the multiplication of Mankind* (2nd ed.), 1682, p. 21.
[3] *Several Essays in Political Arithmetic* (1699), p. 141.

at home. Unsound doctrine in regard to the consumption of wealth, rather than any confusion as to the nature of wealth[1], appears to have been the most widely current economic fallacy at the time. It was apparently very generally assumed that "demand for commodities is a demand for labour"; more than one writer criticises the policy of sumptuary laws, and argues that "high living" is advantageous to the nation so long as it takes the form of using luxuries manufactured at home[2]. "Take away all our super-necessary trades, and we shall have no more than tankard bearers and plowmen, and our City of London will in short time be like an Irish hut." The French trade introduced new tastes and "set us all agog, and having increased among us many considerable trades, witness the vast multitudes of Broad and Narrow Silk weavers, Makers of points and white and black laces, Hats, Fans, Looking-glasses and other glasses as I'm told the best in the world, Paper, Fringes and gilded leather." Barbon recognises a difference between productive and unproductive consumption[3], but another writer is more extreme and

with reference to the consumption of native goods

---

[1] See below, p. 594 on Adam Smith. Considering the charge which is commonly repeated about these writers, that they thought money was the only true wealth, and the attempts of modern authors to expose their fallacy and prove that other things than gold and silver are useful and are properly described as wealth, it is curious to find that they considered the value of these metals to be the result of mere caprice or convention. "Gold and Silver," says Locke, "being little useful to the life of man in proportion to food, raiment and carriage has its value only from the consent of men"; "gold, silver and diamonds are things that fancy and agreement hath put the value on, more than any real use, and the necessary support of life." (*Civil Government*, §§ 46—50. *Works*, IV. p. 364.) In similar fashion Graunt argues that the art of making gold would benefit neither the world nor the artist (*Natural and Political Observations*, 97). So long as men had no clear ideas of the conditions on which the value of silver as a commodity really depends, a strong opinion as to the practical importance of amassing treasure for political purposes, was apparently quite consistent with a too depreciatory estimate of the "usefulness" of the precious metals.

[2] *England's Interest and Improvement*, in *Select Tracts*, p. 235. Barbon is almost as paradoxical in his opinion on this subject as Mandeville in the *Falle of the Bees*. "The two Extreams to this Vertue, are Prodigality and Covetousness. Prodigality is a Vice, that is prejudicial to the Man but not to *Trade*. It is living a pace, and spending that in a Year that should last all his Life: Covetousness is a Vice, prejudicial both to Man and *Trade*." *A discourse of Trade*, 62.

[3] "The question which Nation thrives most," is determined "by observing which imports most of such sort of Goods that most increase or lessen the Labour and Industry of the People," and this could not be "discern'd by the value of

seems to hold that every form of demand is alike beneficial A.D. 1603
—1689.
to trade. "I had rather get a thousand pound by lace and
fringes than nine hundred by the best broad cloth that ever
I yet saw[1]." The increase of population was advocated, not
merely as a means of improving the industrial efficiency of
the country, but because the enlarged consumption of food *and*
would create an additional demand for products from the *products,*
soil, and thus raise the value of lands[2]. Opening up a vent
for products, and promoting consumption, appeared the most
obvious ways to increase opportunities of employment and
thus give scope for industrial power[3].

   This policy of promoting home industries, by encouraging
the consumption of native goods, was persisted in through

Goods in the Custom-House Books." *Discourse concerning Coining the New Money lighter*, 50.

[1] *England's Great Happiness or a Dialogue between Content and Complaint* (1677), in *Political Economy Club Collection of Early English Tracts*, 260, 262; ed. Macculloch. This author writes with very little implied reference to national "power," and with a strong appreciation of the advantages of "plenty"; he has no jealousy of other nations but regards dealings with them as exactly analogous to dealings between individuals in a nation. "I'll suppose *John a Noakes* to be a *Butcher*, *Dick a Styles* an *Exchange man*, yourself a *Lawyer*, will you buy no Meat or Ribbands or your wife a fine *Indian* Gown or Fann because they will not truck with you for Indentures, which they have no need of? I suppose no, but if you get money enough of others, you care not though you give it away *in specie* for these things. I think 'tis the same case," p. 261.

[2] *Britannia Languens* (1680), in *Collection of Early English Tracts on Commerce*, 352.

[3] A most curious illustration of the policy of promoting employment by encouraging home consumption is afforded by the expedient put forward in a Proclamation by James I. 1622 (Brit. Mus. 506. h. 12 (99)) and re-enforced by an Act which was passed in 1666 for burying in woollen only, under a penalty of £5 (18 C. II. c. 4); and in 1678 machinery was organised for seeing that this Act was properly enforced (30 C. II. c. 3). Parish registers of the time afford ample evidence of these burials in coffins lined with woollen cloth and in woollen shrouds. The later Act gives a fuller statement of the aims of these measures. They were intended to lessen the importation of linen from beyond the seas (and so to prevent money from going abroad), to encourage the woollen manufacture (by promoting consumption), and to prevent a reckless consumption of linen fibre (so as to assist the paper manufacturers). In Scotland on the other hand there was an Act insisting on the use of Scotch Linen for burying (*Scots Acts*, 1686, c. 26). With the development of a British linen manufacture, many of the reasons for the English Acts for burying in woollen passed away, and the policy of the Acts was severely criticised by Davenant. "Laws to compel the consumption of some commodities and prohibit the use of others may do well enough where trade is forced, and only artificial, as in France; but in countries inclined by genius, and adapted to it by situation, such laws are needless, unnatural, and can have no effect conducive to the public good" (*East India Trade*, in *Works*, i. 99).

A.D. 1603
—1689. the Restoration period and the early part of the eighteenth
century, despite the criticism it received. It is of course
and at- true that the consumer, who pays for any article, replaces
tempts
were made the capital of the man who made it, and that rapid con-
to promote sumption induces the rapid turning over of capital. But it is
it,
also true that the destruction of useful objects is an evil;
and that if goods did not wear out so rapidly, it would be
possible for the consumer to afford other kinds of enjoyment
rather than merely replace his old comforts. There is no
saving at all in encouraging the use of substantial goods,
in cases where flimsy things serve as well and substantial
wares are no better, since this brings about a misuse, and
therefore a waste, of national resources[1]. In this matter of
consumption the Mercantilists appear to have forgotten the
distinction they so constantly drew. Rapid consumption
and reproduction served for the private lucre of particular
manufacturers, but it did not obviously benefit the nation
as a whole[2]. The policy, mistaken as it appears to have
been, was followed with much persistence.

but little   While attention was thus given to providing employment
attention
was given for labour, there is comparatively little consideration of the
to the
formation conditions which were favourable for the formation and ap-
of capital, plication of capital. So far as the matter is discussed, a
considerable difference of opinion becomes apparent. In the
view of the majority of writers, there were great advantages
in a low rate of interest, from the facilities it gave to
merchants to enlarge their business with borrowed capital.
Locke pointed out that a high rate was quite compatible
with a flourishing condition of trade. "High interest," he
says, "is thought by some a prejudice to trade: but if we
look back we shall find that England never throve so well,

---

[1] The American determination to encourage the consumption of coarse native,
rather than fine English cloth, was of a different character, economically; as the
American cloth appears to have been less fashionable but not less durable.

[2] A curious illustration occurs in 1697, when a petition of two manufacturers
of Prunellos was presented; it set forth that the House intended to encourage the
woollen manufacture by insisting that all judges, magistrates and students of the
law should wear gowns made of the woollen manufacture, and that this would be
the ruin of the petitioners and their employés if it was passed. They also urged
that the proposed measure would diminish the export trade of the clothiers, as
Hair and Silk (the materials for Prunellos) were returns obtained in exchange
for cloth. *Commons Journals,* XII. 87.

nor was there ever brought into England so great an increase A.D. 1603 of wealth as in Queen Elizabeth's and King James I. and —1689. King Charles I. time, when money was at 10 and 8 per cent. I will not say high interest was the cause of it. For I rather think that our thriving trade was the cause of high interest, *though* everyone craving money to employ in a profitable commerce. *Locke saw the* But this I think I may reasonably infer from it, that lower- *advantage of high* ing of interest is not a sure way to improve either our trade *profits.* or wealth[1]." In this he anticipated a view which obtained a wide currency at a later date. After the Industrial Revolution, when machinery was largely used, and capital entered more obviously into production than before, the increase of capital appeared to be the great means of rapidly developing industry and commerce, and much attention was given to the rate of profit as a sign of prosperity, since it indicated the effective inducement to add to capital.

208. The students of the day were not satisfied, how- *The rela-* ever, to trace the signs of prosperity at home; they were *tive pro-gress of* anxious to have some means of testing the rate of English *England and other* progress as compared with that of other nations. It was in *countries* this connection that the doctrine of the 'balance of trade' *seemed to be shown* attained its greatest importance. The conception of the *by the balance* country, as one vast estate, was present to men's minds in *of trade,* connection with trade, not merely in regard to the development of resources. They were eager to compare outgoings with incomings, and to see that the dealings of Englishmen with other people were like those of a prudent housekeeper, who found himself at the end of the year with money in hand which could be stored against emergencies.

In the earlier part of the seventeenth century, there *which was* had been much discussion, between the bullionists[2] and the *taken as marking* mercantilists, as to the best means of procuring treasure; *the flow of treasure* and from that time onwards the doctrine of the balance of trade dominated in all commercial legislation. The calculation of the balance of trades, as a whole, and of the balance obtained by particular trades, came to be regarded as a matter of great importance; it was the only possible

---

[1] Locke, *Considerations of the lowering of Interest, Works,* IV. 66.

[2] Especially in connection with the East India Company. See above, p. 260.

means of seeing how far the current expedients for the introduction of treasure were working well, or needed to be re-cast. While the particular balance in each trade was supposed to show which branch of commercial intercourse was beneficial and which was 'hurtful[1],' the general balance served to indicate how much of the precious metals the king might hoard in any given years without withdrawing money from circulation. But the faculty as well as the opportunity was required if treasure was to be amassed, and the Stuarts did not excel in that particular virtue.

and indicating the reaction of particular trades
In the latter part of the Stuart period and during the greater part of the eighteenth century the calculation of the balance of trade began to attract attention from another point of view. It was felt to be important for public men not only to know that the volume of our trade was increasing, but to see that this increased commerce was reacting favourably on the industry of the country. The examples of Spain and Portugal had made it clear that an enormous expansion of colonial and commercial enterprise was compatible with the decadence of the agricultural and industrial life of the mother country; whereas, in the case of Holland, expansion abroad had called forth increased vitality at home. Just as the men of the day asked not merely about the numbers of the population, but also took account of the opportunities of employment, so they endeavoured to use the balance of trade as an index which might show how the commerce of the country was affecting its industry. To what extent did it serve the great purpose
according as they created employment for
of affording a vent for our surplus, and so increasing the demand for labour, or to what extent did it bring foreign competition to bear in the home market, and thus diminish the opportunities of native workmen? According to the ordinary opinion of the day, if foreign industry and agriculture were supported and home products and manufactures were neglected, the prosperity of the nation would be undermined. Where people were buying commodities from abroad and paying for them in bullion, it showed that certain classes at home were not as busily engaged as they

[1] See above, p. 264 n. 2.

might have been. If we brought goods from abroad and sent other goods to pay for them, the producers of the exports were provided with occupation, just as if the results of their labour were used at home. But if we bought these *or injured* things from abroad with bullion, we were exporting the *native workmen.* means of employing our own poor; thus the export of treasure was an index of the subverting of industry at home, on the current assumption as to the relation of demand and employment.

It is of course true that we cannot trade unless we send something from this country to foreigners, and that trade could not continue if the country had nothing to export; but the argument was that it might go on exporting *The argu-ment drawn* bullion for a long while, and that all the time we procured *from the* commodities by so doing, native industry must be in a *balance of trade* depressed condition; and that if this continued long enough the extinction of native industry and ruin of the nation must follow.

"On the other side our Importations must as necessarily be increased, both by the decay of our own former Manufactures at home, and by our modern gawd'ry and affectation of foreign Goods[1]; and as our Trade from Port to Port hath become more impracticable to any advantage, the Exporters of our remaining Manufactures and other home-Commodities, must either come back empty, or else must freight themselves homewards with such consumptive foreign Commodities, as for Gawdry, Novelty, Cheapness, or Lyquorishness, will dazle, tempt and bewitch our People to buy them; in which course of Trade our Merchants may gain considerable proportions of our remaining Treasures as long as there is any in the Nation.

"Nay, rather than sit idle, they will, and do freight themselves outwards with meer Ballast and *Bills of Exchange* (by which the Importation of foreign Bullion or money is prevented): or if Bills of Exchange cannot reasonably be had (as they usually cannot to those Countries where

---

[1] "That *Trade* is certainly best for the Kingdome by which the *Gaine* ariseth from what is exported, and losse by what is imported." Battie, *Merchants Remonstrance*, p. 27.

we are over-ballanced in Trade), then they export Mony and Bullion and buy and import Consumptive Goods which are spent at home; which kind of Trade deserves rather to be called Foreign *Pedling*, than Merchandise.

"It may be remembered here, how much the beneficial part of our Trade may be prejudiced by the loss of 100000 of our Manufactures, and what odds the same loss may produce in our Importations, since if they get but 6 *l. per Ann.* a piece, it must sink the former gain by Trade no less than 600000 *l. per Ann.*

in condemnation of a Consumptive Importing Trade

"And on the other side, that if a *Million* of Families or Persons in a Nation, do one with the other consume to the value of 20*s. a piece* more, yearly in foreign Manufactures, Drinks, &c., than before, this must increase our Importations to the value of a Million *per Ann.* which I observe here to shew how imperceptibly an over-ballance of Importation may creep upon a Nation; and that the Reader may with the less difficulty conjecture at the late and present ballance of Trade in *England*.

"It must also much assist this Importing Trade, if the Merchants shall export Mony, or Bullion; especially in such a Nation as *England*, where a Trade from Port to Port is not ordinarily practicable to any advantage: for in that Case the Goods Imported being spent at home, the Treasure Exported must be lost to the Nation; and as long as the English Merchant can have Bullion or Mony to Export, and can have a vent for his Importations at home, his private gain will never oblige him to complain of the want of Exportable home-Manufactures, or the Clogs upon Trade, especially in *England*, where our Merchants have such a *Monopoly* of their Importations on the rest of the People.

"This Consumptive Importing Trade must be of very fatal Consequence in its Nature; for first, whilst the National Stock is greater, it will exhaust the Treasure almost *insensibly*; but as the Treasure grows less and less, it will work more *palpably and grievously*, because it will consume more and more of that little which remains.

"And as the National Treasure comes to be more and more diminished, the People must generally have less and less, which must cause the price of all home-Commodities, A.D. 1603
—1689. and consequently *Land-Rents* to fall continually, the home Manufactures must be choaked and stifled by Importations, so that both the Farmers and Manufacturers must fling up; the values of their Stocks must be contracted, and will be eaten out by Rent, Wages and other standing charges before they are aware; men cannot provide against misfortunes which have unseen Causes; and as home-trade grows worse and worse, Industry it self must be tired and foiled, to the great amazement, as well as affliction of the People[1]."

This passage I have quoted at length because it is most *showed no misapprehension about the importance of treasure,* important to understand the exact bearing of the doctrine of the balance of trade in its later form. This writer had no over-estimate of the importance of treasure as the only kind of wealth, he was fully alive to the fact that industry was the true source of prosperity, but he objected to the export of bullion, because he held that it indicated the superseding of our native industry, since it meant that we did not obtain markets abroad, while we opened our own to foreign nations.

There are many matters to which exception may fairly *but the difficulty of calculating the balance* be taken in his argument[2]: as prices fell, owing to the

---

[1] *Britannia Languens*, in *Select Tracts*, 372—374.

[2] On the difficulty of calculating see Barbon, *Discourse concerning Coining*, p. 36. "Some men lay so great a stress about the enquiring into this Balance, that they are of Opinion, That a Trading Nation may be ruin'd and undone, if there been't Care taken, by Laws, to regulate the Balance. And yet there is nothing so difficult, as to find out the Balance of Trade in any Nation; or to know whether there ever was, or can be such a thing as the making up the Balance of Trade betwixt one Nation and another; or to prove, if it could be found out, that there is anything got or lost by the Balance.

"For a Nation, as a Nation, never Trades; 'tis only the Inhabitants and Subjects of each Nation that Trade: And there are no set days or times for making up of a general Accompt, every Merchant makes up his own private Accompt; and that's not done at any set time, one Merchant makes it up one week, and another in another week; so that there can be no set time when to begin that Balance.

"Therefore those that rely so much upon finding out the Balance of Trade, do it by taking the Computation from the Trade of several years of one Nation with another, and think it may be done by examining the Accompt of the Custom-House Books, and us'd to give for Instance the French Trade; because the Revenue that arose from those Duties on French Wines, and other Commodities that were imported, were so much greater than the Duties on those Goods that

A.D. 1603
—1689.

renders it useless as a criterion of employment.

export of bullion, merchants would find it was less profitable to import goods from abroad, and the exhaustion of treasure would be most unlikely to continue: and the movements of bullion are affected by so many other matters,

were sent into France, and therefore us'd to cry out very much against the French Trade; Tho', perhaps, if that were throughly consider'd, the French Trade was as profitable to the Nation as any other Foreign Trade; which might be made to appear, if it were proper for this Debate.

"But to make up the Balance of Trade by the Custom-House Books, is a very uncertain way of reckoning: For all Foreign Goods that are imported, pay a greater Duty than the Native Goods exported. 'Tis the Interest of all Trading Nations to lay easy Customs (if any) upon their Native Commodities: that they may be sent cheap to Foreign Markets, and thereby encourage both the making and exporting of them: And to lay high Duties upon Foreign Wares, that they might be dear, and so not lessen by their cheapness the consumption of the Native Commodities: So that there can be no Computation of the Balance of Trade from the difference of the Sum of Money that's paid at the Custom-House for the Foreign Goods imported, and the Native exported.

"But suppose there should be an Allowance made, in casting up the Accompt, for the greatness of the Duties that the Foreign Goods pay more than the Native, yet that can be no advantage in the discovering the Balance of Trade; because they cannot discover by the Custom-House Books, what the Native Goods that are exported are sold for: For the Balance of Trade must arise from the Value of the Goods that are sold, and not from the Quantity that are exported or imported. And that's known only to the Merchant that sells the Goods and 'tis not for his Interest to acquaint others with it, and thereby discover the Profits of his Trade: So that there can be no finding out the Balance of Trade by the Custom-House Books.

"Some are of the opinion, that the way to find out the Balance of Trade, is by the Foreign Exchange. And they reckon that if the Exchange run high upon a Nation, 'tis a sign that there are more Foreign Goods imported, than there are of the Native exported; and therefore there are Bills of Exchange drawn to answer the Effects, and make up the difference in the Value of what the Native Goods were sold for less than the Foreign. This seems to be the nearest way of guessing of the Balance of the Trade of a Nation; but this is altogether as uncertain.

"For Exchanges rise and fall every week, and at some particular times in the year run high against a Nation, and at other times run as high on the contrary. As against a Vintage, a great Mart, or some Publick Sale, the Exchange may run higher to Bourdeaux, Francfort, or Holland, upon an East India Sale: And at other times the Exchange may have run to the same places as much on the contrary; for no Exchange can constantly run high against a Nation; for then the Merchants that trade to that Country, must always lose by their Trade; For if the Goods that they export, don't yield them as much profit as the Goods they import, they must lose by the Return. And it cannot be suppos'd that Merchants will always Trade to a Country, where they must always lose by Trading: therefore there can be no account of the Balance of Trade by Foreign Exchange.

"As to the rise of the Exchange betwixt Holland and England, that's not to be reckon'd as a Rule, because of the extraordinary charge of the War at this time."

On Barbon's importance as an economist compare Dr S. Bauer in Conrad's *Jahrbücher für Nationalökonomie*, N. F. (1890), xxi. 561.

that the balance could never be an accurate index of the A.D. 1603
--1689. increase or decrease of employment; but the matter of importance is, that many of the writers who used it in this way, and condemned one trade as hurtful or consumptive, or approved another as giving a vent for our commodities, were clear on the main point that the development of native industry was the real secret of continued national prosperity.

A survey, however brief, of the literature of the period *Progress in the reasoned* shows what a great advance had been made, during the *reasoned* seventeenth century, in the study of the economic side of *treatment of prac-* national life. The concentration of attention on revenue, *tical questions* rather than on the elements of naval power, was bringing the subject of national wealth and national resources into clear light, as a definite topic for investigation. There was an immense accumulation of data, so that problems were seriously discussed, and not handled in the meagre fashion which had satisfied Bodin or Hobbes. This becomes particularly clear in the discussion which went on as to the best means of calculating the balance of trade. Barbon argued that it was practically impossible to strike this balance with any accuracy[1]. More important was the point insisted upon by Davenant[2], that the only thing that could be gauged was the general balance of trade, and that attempts to estimate the balance with particular countries, and still more to make this the basis of legislative measures, were illusory. The reliance on the particular balance was a refinement on the doctrine of Mun and earlier mercantilists, but it was not a real advance. Indeed it is not easy to say that there was any definite progress in the power of interpreting the evidence. Practical men of business had always had a familiarity with monetary relations; and strong common sense enabled such a statesman, as Burleigh, to deal in a masterly fashion with the difficulties of his day; *prepared the way for* but the writers of the seventeenth century had made little *subsequent* progress in economic analysis, or in the precise definition of *advance* the terms they used. The times were not yet ripe for the

---

[1] See above, p. 399 n. 2.
[2] *Works*, II. 171.

work which was done by Adam Smith in co-ordinating the isolated discussions of previous thinkers into one coherent whole; but these forgotten pioneers supplied the materials on which he was destined to work. Unless considerable progress had been made in the study of Political Economy as a practical art, it would not have been possible for any writer, however able, to confer upon it a scientific form, and to attempt to formulate the causes of the wealth of nations.

III. PARLIAMENTARY COLBERTISM.

XI. THE ENGLISH REVOLUTION.

209. THE withdrawal of allegiance from James II. and accession of William III. were the outcome of the blows which had been struck at the authority of hereditary Monarchy during the Civil War. They mark a veritable revolution in the political life of England, since the changes at this juncture were no mere reform, when improvements were introduced into the machinery of government. The basis on which the whole polity rested was completely altered. The personal rule of the Crown gave place to the power of the people; for it was by popular invitation and Parliamentary approval that William attained the throne. Many constitutional questions were left for subsequent settlement; there was room for much dispute, both as to the precise relation of the king and his ministers to the popular voice, and in regard to the adequacy of the representation of the people of England in the House of Commons. Still, the main result was achieved, since Parliament, in which the House of Commons was a very important element, had attained supreme control over the affairs of the nation. The personal action of the Crown had been of the first importance in economic matters of every kind under Charles I.; the Court had swayed the course of affairs, especially as regards commercial and colonial concessions, under Charles II. From the Revolution onwards, however, it hardly counted as a separate factor, since the influence of the King was exerted through the aid of royal partisans in the Lords, or the Commons.

The new accession of power, which the House of Commons thus attained, involved a tremendous responsibility; the Lower House, containing as it did representatives both of landed men and traders, became the chief authority for

A.D. 1689 —1776.

At the Revolution Parliament became supreme over economic affairs;

but the House of Commons

26—2

discriminating between the claims of different interests, and for determining how far any of them were compatible with, or inimical to, the public welfare. It has already been pointed out that all interference with industry, or commerce, on public grounds must be beneficial to some individuals, and deleterious to others[1]. In all State intervention in economic affairs, there is a constant temptation to subordinate the public good to some private gain. The reasons alleged for favouring particular interests were often extremely plausible; and in any case, the House of Commons of that period was singularly unfitted for the discharge of the delicate duty of promoting the material prosperity of the realm. The men who had come to the front, after the Revolution, do not seem to have been of a better type, morally or socially, than the members of the Long Parliament[2]. In all probability they were less incorruptible; and their temptations were greater, as the resources in the hands of the moneyed interest were much larger than they had ever been before. The East India Companies were the chief sinners in connection with the bribery which went on during the last decade of the seventeenth century. Sir Josiah Child had made large presents to obtain royal favour, and now he was equally lavish in securing Parliamentary support[3]. The promoters of the new Company struck out a line for themselves, and bribed the electors[4] as well as the members of the House. Constitutional changes had brought about a state of affairs in which their privileges rendered Members of Parliament free from the dread of royal displeasure, while there was little danger that their action would be criticised by their constituents[5]. However much William III. and his advisers might regret the necessity, they felt themselves forced to follow the example of Clifford and the Cabal, and purchase support in the Commons. The practice was developed still farther by Walpole, and it was by means of this guilty alliance, between the Crown and a section of the Commons, that the

was not well fitted to exercise this responsibility judiciously.

Trading Companies had recourse to corrupt means of obtaining public support,

---

[1] See above, p. 16.

[2] Davenant, *The True Picture of a Modern Whig*, in *Works*, IV. 128. See p. 183 above.   [3] Macaulay, *History*, IV. (1855), 426, 551.

[4] Bishop Burnet's *History of his Own Time*, IV. 464; Ralph, *History of England*, II. 926.   [5] Macaulay, *History*, III. 544.

King's Government was carried on during the eighteenth A.D. 1689 —1776. century. The existence of such a system testifies alike to *and the Crown* the real power which Parliament possessed, and to the *relied on similar means.* unfitness of the House of Commons to exercise a wise control over economic interests. It is, of course, true that the taint, which attaches to legislative action during this period, does not suffice to prove that the measures adopted were wholly mistaken. Weighty considerations of public good were urged on behalf of the line of economic policy that was adopted during the period of Whig ascendancy. The scheme, which was carried out, contributed to the maintenance of some essential elements of national power. Still, it was pursued at the cost and to the detriment of a considerable body of English citizens, and some of the best contemporary writers were of opinion that the gain, which accrued to the public, was dearly bought[1].

Two different views may be taken as to the nature of the advantage which accrues to a country from its foreign trade. From one point of view we may say that the consumer of foreign products obtains articles he desires to use on easier terms, or of better quality, than would otherwise be the case[2]. On the other hand, we may take a different standard and *The policy* gauge the benefit of trade by its reaction on native industry *of regu- lating* and the benefit which accrues to producers. This latter *trade so that it* standpoint was adopted by Colbert; the principles which *might re-act on* he worked out in France seemed to contemporaries to be *industry* brilliantly successful. Similar opinions as to the benefit of trade, and of the measures which should be taken to promote the prosperity of the country, were dominant in England during the period of Whig ascendancy. "For a hundred years past," as a Dutch writer observed in 1751, "the English have considered exportation, and sale of goods and mer- chandises abroad, as the only profitable and advantageous trade of that kingdom, and on the contrary left it very doubtful whether the importation of goods be beneficial

---

[1] This was the view taken by North, Davenant, Barbon and other Tory writers. Compare Ashley, *The Tory Origin of Free Trade Policy* in *Surveys*, p. 268. At the same time it must be remembered that Davenant and the rest were not Free Traders in the modern sense; they did believe that it was the business of the statesman to foster and encourage trade, not to let it alone. See below, p. 867.

[2] See below, p. 602.

A.D. 1689
—1776.
or prejudicial[1]." There was a close affinity between this economic position and the political aims of the party. The *harmonised with Whig jealousy of France.* Whigs were hostile to France, and bitterly jealous of French influence politically; they were eager to attack the power they dreaded, by protective legislation. French competition was the chief rival which English manufacturers had to fear; and they were able to furnish the Whigs, who were nervously suspicious of French influence, with an excuse for checking intercourse with that country, and for hindering the development of its trade. A similar line of economic policy was adopted by the Whigs in regard to the manufactures imported from other regions. The English producers of textile fabrics alleged that their markets were spoiled by the importation of East Indian goods, and the Whigs were not averse to harass the trade of the great joint-stock Company, which had come under the rule of Tory magnates. There was a close connection between the political affinities of the Whig party and the economic scheme of protecting native industry. During the period of Whig ascendancy, the economic policy of the country became a thoroughgoing imitation of the principles of Louis XIV.'s great minister Colbert[2], though they were put into effect, not by royal mandates as in France, but by parliamentary legislation.

The Whigs in the House of Commons aimed at administrative authority

210. The increasing power of the House of Commons is shown not only in the manner in which that assembly was able to determine the general lines of economic policy, but also in the new attitude which members assumed towards the administration. They were no longer content with criticising the blunders of the King's servants, but attempted to get the control of certain departments into their own hands. Students of the English constitution long believed that it was framed so as to ensure a severance of the legislative and executive powers, and this view appears to have been held by William and his most faithful supporters; but the House of Commons was not prepared to submit to this opinion, and succeeded in setting it aside.

[1] *Proposals made by his late Highness the Prince of Orange for redressing and amending the Trade of the Republic,* 23.

[2] On Colbert's system, compare P. Clement, *Colbert et son administration*; also Sargent, *The Economic Policy of Colbert.*

They passed Acts appointing commissioners[1] to enquire into A.D. 1689 administrative corruption. They had already secured full —1776. control over the collection of the customs[2], and they were on the point of creating a permanent Board of Trade of *over trading affairs.* their own, with the view of maintaining the same sort of supervision over commercial affairs as had been hitherto exercised by the Privy Council. "In the end when all the errors with relation to the protection of our trade were set out, and much aggravated, a motion was made to create, by Act of Parliament, a council of trade.

"This was opposed by those who looked on it as a change of our constitution in a very essential point: the executive part of the Government was wholly in the King: so that the appointing any council by Act of Parliament began a precedent of their breaking in upon the execution of the law, in which it could not be easy to see how far they might be carried; it was indeed offered, that this council should be much limited as to its powers; yet many apprehended, that if the Parliament named the persons, howsoever low their powers might be at first, they would be enlarged

---

[1] 13 W. III. c. 1. A dispute arose between the two Houses over this matter. *Parl. Hist.* v. 1321. The Lords had amended the bill and omitted the name of Edmund Whitaker, the solicitor to the Admiralty, who had failed to give any account of £25,000 of public money. See also Davenant's *Picture, Works,* IV. 165.

[2] "We do not find, after the Restoration, the Crown in possession of a revenue consisting in part of a prescriptive duty on all merchandise, and also of an increase thereof by grant of Parliament known as a subsidy, the whole of which is collected by its own chosen methods, and administered at its own discretion for the public good. On the contrary, this former item of the sovereign's income had come to be regarded as part of the revenue of the State, assessed by authority of Parliament alone in the person of its Speaker, and collected more or less directly by an official department responsible not to the sovereign alone, as heretofore, but to the nation. During the reigns of the two first Stuart kings the Customs at the ports had been collected by farmers, an ancient, obnoxious, unprofitable expedient, and one which bore no resemblance to the lucrative tyranny of the system which prevailed under the same title on the Continent. Under the Commonwealth, however, this plan was completely changed, and the revenue derived from the new Parliamentary Customs was placed under the control of commissioners. Even after the Restoration, the same device (like most other financial reforms of the late *régime*) was continued, and was only changed in 1670 for a still more responsible method. From that date to the Revolution the gross income of the Customs was answered to the country by a Receiver-General, who was associated from the year 1688 with a Comptroller-General; and in this way the most fruitful branch of the ancient revenue of the Crown was converted from a source of royal income into a fund charged with some portion or other of the working expenses of the State." Hall, *History of the Customs Revenue,* I. 189.

A.D. 1689
—1776.
every session; and from being a council to look into matters of trade, they would be next empowered to appoint convoys and cruisers; this in turn might draw in the whole Admiralty to that part of the revenue, or supply, that was appro-

though in this they were foiled,
priated to the navy, so that a King would soon grow to be a duke of Venice; and indeed those who set this on most zealously, did not deny that they designed to graft many things upon it. The King was so sensible of the ill effects this would have, that he ordered his ministers to oppose it as much as possibly they could[1]." The discovery of Charnock's plot against William's life diverted public attention for the time, and the King, by appointing a permanent Board of Trade[2], took away much of the excuse there had been for the agitation in the Commons.

but by their hold on the purse-strings they deter-mined the objects on which money might be spent,
Though foiled in this particular, the Commons had become, as a matter of fact, masters of the situation; they were in a position to exercise a practical control over the spending departments. "The government was plainly in the hands of the House of Commons, who must sit once a year, and as long as they thought fit, while the King had only the civil list for life, so that the whole of the administration was under their inspection[3]." By appropriating the money they voted to particular objects, they prevented the Government from engaging in action of which they disapproved. The Government was so circumscribed that it could not attempt to fit out a man-of-war for Captain Kid to employ against the Madagascar pirates; the expedition was organised at the private expense of Lord Somers and others, and the conduct of the affair was so discreditable as to give ample cause for complaint against those who had undertaken to finance the project[4].

The powers of effective criticism and practical control which had been secured were ultimately of immense advantage, as they tended to purify the administrative corruption which had been the disgrace of the seventeenth century generally[5]. The executive power was not severed

---

[1] Burnet, *History of his Own Time*, iv. 288.
[2] Macpherson, *Annals*, ii. 681 n.
[3] Burnet, *op. cit.* iv. 443.   [4] Id., *op. cit.* iv. 422.
[5] Cromwell's rule appears to afford an exception, Macaulay, iii. 424. The government of Ireland in the eighteenth century seems to have maintained the

from the legislative body and was forced from time to time *A.D.* 1689 —1776. to justify itself to an elected assembly. But this was not all clear gain; parliamentary legislation was a much more *and practi-cally con-* cumbrous instrument for regulating industry and commerce *trolled the* than the administrative machinery which had been in *adminis-trative* vogue in the time of Elizabeth or Charles I. Under these *system.* monarchs the Privy Council had been able to watch the course of affairs from day to day, and to issue temporary orders which were enforced by the justices; Parliament had to be content with more general measures[1], and had no means of adapting them to circumstances from time to time. The Corn Bounty Law took account of an immense variety *The legis-lative* of conditions, and was intended to be a self-acting measure, *method of* under which a useful control might be exercised over the *fostering economic* corn trade, and a steady stimulus given to agriculture. It *life by bounties* was not possible, however, to devise similar means for dealing with the changing circumstances of commercial or manufacturing pursuits. Nor was Parliament in a position to give special concessions to individuals in order to promote any special branch of industry; the favourite expedient of the legislature was that of voting bounties. These rewards were open to all who practised the art which it was intended to encourage, and thus had no exclusive character; but whereas the system of patents had been inexpensive to the Government, this new scheme was very costly, as it *proved* afforded a minimum of advantage to the public at a *cumbrous and costly* maximum of cost to the State[2]. Such grants were only too likely to call forth fraudulent attempts to obtain the bounties, without regard to the conditions on which they were offered. Malpractices of various kinds appear to have occurred in the linen[3], and had to be guarded against in

old traditions. Compare W. G. Carroll, *Life of Hely Hutchinson*, Introduction to the *Commercial Restraints of Ireland*, p. lxviii.

[1] As had been advocated by Milles, see above, p. 223. The English method of settling all details by legislation rendered the system much less flexible than would have been the case if the practice of the French legislature had been adopted. See p. 207 n. 2, above.

[2] Adam Smith, *Wealth of Nations*, 'On Bounties,' Book IV. chapter 5.

[3] " Whereas by reason of the bounty or allowances granted on the exportation of British and Irish linens, evil-minded persons may fraudulently endeavour to export linens of foreign fabrick and manufacture, and to receive the said bounties or allowances for the same, as if the same were of the manufacture of Great Britain and Ireland; and whereas certain stamps are required by law, to be put

A.D. 1689
—1776.
the herring trade[1].   Protection in any form is apt to entail some unsatisfactory results in society, and the increase of smuggling was an evil which sprang directly out of attempts at the national encouragement of industry.   It is impossible to estimate the pecuniary loss which occurred[2], and the demoralisation, which was due to these premiums on evading the law and on dishonesty, brought about a serious lowering of the ordinary respect for the law.

The Whigs, by organising the Bank of England
211.   The establishment of the Bank of England was another economic change which diminished the importance of the monarchy in the realm.   It has been commonly remarked that, by linking the interests of the moneyed men to the revolutionary settlement, it played a great part in extinguishing the chances of a Jacobite restoration; but its constitutional importance lay far deeper than this.   The organisation of this institution brought the power of the *circumscribed the power of the Crown* Crown to borrow still more completely under parliamentary control.   When the taxes were assigned[3], and the Crown lands[4] administered by Parliament, there was little security that the monarch was free to offer to moneyed men, if he wished to borrow.   At the Revolution, the House of Commons obtained a practical control, not only over the taxation levied from the landed men, but also over the advances made by the moneyed classes[5].   The crisis, when Charles I. had been

upon linens, made in that part of Great Britain called Scotland, and in Ireland, which may have been put on foreign linens, in order to vend them as linens of the manufacture of that part of Great Britain called Scotland, or of Ireland." 18 G. II. c. 24.

[1] 5 and 6 W. and M. c. 7, § 10.

[2] The smuggling of wool to the Continent during the period when the export was absolutely prohibited attained enormous proportions; it was estimated in 1788 at 11,000 packs annually (Bischoff, *A Comprehensive History of the Woollen and Worsted Manufactures*, I. 241).   Profitable illicit trade was carried on in many articles of import.   Sir Matthew Decker (*Serious Considerations*, p. 5) alleges the case of one man in Zeeland who exported to England half-a-million pounds of tea.   He had started life as a common sailor, but prospered so that he had come to own four sloops which he employed in running tea.

[3] The assignment of taxes and separate keeping of accounts lasted till Pitt's time, see Chisholm, *Notes on the Heads of Public Income and Expenditure*, in *Reports*, 1868-9, xxxv. Ap. 13, p. 811, printed pag. 327.

[4] The Crown lands were almost valueless at the Revolution, *Parl. Hist.* v. 552.   See also Chisholm, *Reports*, 1868-9, xxxv. Ap. 13, on Crown Lands, p. 915, printed pag. 431.   *Commons Journals*, xLVII. 836, Report of the Board of Land Revenue.

[5] Compare the Resolutions passed in 1681 on this topic.   *Parl. Hist.* IV. 1294.

forced to rely on parliamentary backing in order to obtain
advances, was the turning point in his career[1]. Those
who urged that a bank was inconsistent with monarchical
government were not far wrong[2]; they observed that
such institutions had only flourished in republics, such
as Genoa, Venice, and Amsterdam; a bank created an
imperium in imperio that could not be tolerated under an
absolute monarchy. The Bank trenched in some ways on
the royal prerogative; the maintenance of the purity of the
circulating medium had always been considered as belonging
to the royal honour; but a Bank which had the right to
put its notes in circulation, and was responsible for maintaining their value, came at least to share in this part of

A.D. 1689
—1776.

*to borrow
indepen-
dently.*

[1] 16 Car. I. c. 7. "Whereas great sums of money must of necessity be speedily
advanced and provided for the reliefe of his Majesties Army and People in the
Northern parts of this Realm and for preventing the imminent danger this Kingdome is in and for supply of other his Majesties present and urgent occasions
which cannot be soe timely effected as is requisite without credit for raising the
said moneys which credit cannot be obtained until such obstacles be first removed
as are occasioned by fears jealousies and apprehensions of diverse his Majesties
Loyall Subjects that this present Parliament may be adjourned prorogued or
dissolved before Justice shalbe duly executed upon Delinquents publike grievances
redressed and firme Peace betweene the two Nations of England and Scotland
concluded and before sufficient provision be made for the repayment of the said
moneys so to be raised all which the Commons in this present Parliament assembled having duly considered Do therefore humbly beseech your Most Excellent
Majestie that it may be declared and enacted And be it declared and enacted
by the King our Sovereign Lord with the assent of the Lords and Commons in
this present Parliament assembled and by the Authority of the same That this
present Parliament now assembled shall not be dissolved unlesse it be by Act of
Parliament" etc. *Note.* "This Act was not found amongst the original Public Acts
of this Session at the Parliament Office, but is annexed to the Act for the Attainder
of the Earl of Strafford amongst the Private Acts, and both the said Acts received
the Royal Assent by Commission, being the only Acts which appear to have passed
in that manner during this Session." *Statutes of the Realm*, p. 103.

[2] One of the first advocates of the establishment of a bank, Henry Robinson,
argues against this view, which must have been current in 1641. *England's
Safety*, in Shaw, *Writers on English Monetary History*, p. 56. Balthasar Gerbier
urged on the Council of State that they had an excellent opportunity of founding
a bank, as there was no longer a danger of its money being seized by the king.
Some considerations on the two grand Staple Commodities of England, p. 6 (1651).
The alleged incompatibility was felt, not only by the projectors of banks but by
politicians. The objection is well put by T. Violet, *Appeal to Caesar* (1660),
p. 20; and was borne in mind by the founders of the Bank of England, who say
in anticipating the objections of opponents, "In all their Peregrinations they
never met with Banks nor Stocks anywhere, but only in Republicks. And if we
let them set footing in England we shall certainly be in danger of a Common
wealth." *A brief account of the intended Bank of England* (1694), p. 8. Brit.
Mus. 1139. d. 10.

monarchical responsibility.   It had long been notorious, too,
that the possession of wealth gave the command of power[1];
the concentration of wealth in the hands of the Directors of
the Bank enabled them to exercise an economic influence;
the resources at their command were not exceeded by the
and
changed
the centre
of gravity
in the
State;
sums which the King could control; it was hardly too
much to say that the Bank overbalanced the Crown as a
power in the State.   Hitherto the continuity of the government had depended chiefly on the succession to the throne;
and there were possibilities of violent reaction with each
new accession; but the existence of the Bank gave an
important guarantee for the maintenance of the same
general principles of rule under any monarch; national bankruptcy, rather than the dangers of disputed succession to the
Crown, became an object of dread.   The Bank proved itself
to be compatible with monarchy, only because the monarchy
was now greatly limited by the provisions of the constitution[2].
Hence it came about that the moneyed men, whose prosperity was involved in the maintenance of credit, were
intensely afraid of the return of the Stuarts, and lent
the whole of their influence to the Whig party and the
Hanoverian succession.   They were thus in a position[3] to
expect that attention should be paid to their views on
economic questions, during the period of Whig ascendancy,
and they were not disappointed.

The foundation of the Bank of England was by far the
most striking incident of the period, in the economic history
of the country internally.   We have seen, during the seventeenth century, the importance of new opportunities for the

---

[1] This Aristotelian principle is applied to the internal affairs of modern
countries by Harington in his *Oceana*.   He traced a connection between the
distribution of wealth and the distribution of power within any country.   His
treatise was suggested by considering the changes (Toland's Life, prefixed to
Harington's *Works* (1737), p. xvii] of property and power which had occurred
since the time of Henry VII.   The rise of a moneyed class, in the latter part
of this period, with the rivalry between the landed and moneyed interest which
ensued, is an interesting illustration of his principle.   In accordance with republican doctrines, to which he was strongly attached, it followed that a wide
distribution of wealth was a necessary condition for good popular government
[Harington's *Works* (1737), 73], so that the possessions of the many might over-
balance those of the few.
[2] Addison, *Spectator*, March 3, 1711.
[3] Compare the influence of moneyed citizens under Richard II. Vol. i. p. 381.

formation and intervention of capital, but these were im- A.D. 1689 —1776.
mensely enlarged in the eighteenth century, by the rapid
development of credit in all its forms. The institution *and the Bank*
of the Bank of England not only gave stability to the *also gave*
Government, but provided the means for material progress *facilities for com-*
of every kind. It has been the very heart of the economic *mercial advance.*
life of the country during the last two hundred years, and
we must look closely at the character of the new Bank, and
the circumstances under which it was launched. We shall
then see how these new facilities for the formation and
investment of capital gave scope for extension in commerce
and in industry. The greater activity at the centre, synchronised with an expansion of the sphere in which the
commercial system of England was consciously maintained.

212. The success of the representative assembly, in *The Whigs*
controlling the power of the Crown, led indirectly to an *exercised their new*
enormous expansion of its sphere of influence. At the *power over the planta-*
time of the accession of James I., Parliament had no occasion *tions*
to concern itself with anything outside the limits of England
and Wales. Scotland was a distinct realm, with its own
Parliament; Ireland was also a separate kingdom, in which
the House of Commons took little interest; foreign trade
was in the hands of companies, which held patents from
the Crown ; and as the plantations were founded, they were
similarly controlled. It was only as trade reacted on the well-
being of English taxpayers, that Parliament had ventured to
meddle with it at all. But after the Revolution, this was
entirely changed; the increased power of Parliament gave it
a status for exercising both an economic and political control
over the whole of the territory under English rule. The
dominant party in Parliament was inclined, by its traditional
principles, to take a somewhat narrow view of its duties to *in a jealous*
Englishmen in distant regions, while the colonists were even *spirit,*
more jealous of the interference of Parliament than of the
exercise of authority by the Crown[1].

It was, of course, true that the establishment of the
plantations had involved a considerable drain on English
resources, both in men and money ; there were many people

[1] Fiske, *Civil Government*, 156.

A.D. 1689
—1776.
in England who were indifferent to the existence of the colonies, and who only approved of them in so far as they supplemented the resources of the English realm as a whole. There was a general consensus of opinion that the colonies should not be permitted to do anything that would undermine the power of the mother country; and the Whigs especially insisted that the growing communities should not enter into hostile competition with the industry and trade from which the revenue of the mother country was largely drawn. Hence there was room for much economic jealousy of the American plantations and of Ireland; this worked more or less strongly according as the products of the dependency interfered with those of England, or did not. There was no economic rivalry between England and the West Indies or Virginia, as the sugar and tobacco they produced had not been grown at home. The Northern colonies, on the other hand, were well adapted, by climate and situation, to furnish some of the products which the mother country could and did supply. In the case of Ireland this was still more marked; for Englishmen had actual experience of being undersold, in the victualling trades and the woollen manufacture, by the inhabitants of that island. Scotland, less favoured as it is by climate and soil, excited no similar fears. The degrees of favour or disfavour shown to different members of the English economic system under Parliamentary rule, can be traced to the application of this principle of refusing to tolerate hostile competition with the products and industry of the predominant partner.

as they were afraid of any hostile competition with the mother country,

Not only were the sister kingdom and the colonies injuriously affected by the economic doctrines of the Whigs, but also by their political jealousies. Their bitterness against France, and the success which they achieved in preventing the resumption of trade with that country after the Treaty of Utrecht, were distinctly baneful to many of the members of the English system. Scotland and Ireland had long had a profitable trade with France, and they were forced to relinquish it, or to have recourse to illicit methods of conducting it. The Northern colonies suffered too, for

or of any colonial intercourse with the French,

they were hampered in their efforts to establish commercial relations with the French West Indian islands. By far the larger part of the grievances which were felt under Parliamentary rule, both in Scotland after the Union, and in America before the Declaration of Independence, was created by the anti-French economic policy which found favour in Parliament.

The prosperity of the colonies was sacrificed, in so far as the views of the Whigs on foreign policy prevailed, and their dread of royal authority exercised an even more malign *and specially* influence. The Whig party in Parliament were heirs of a *jealous of* firm determination to limit the power of the Crown; they *the increase of any inde-* looked with jealousy on the prosperity of any part of the *pendent sources* British dominions from which the king could draw in- *of royal revenue.* dependent support. This motive had been consciously at work in the legislation in regard to Irish cattle, and it had not a little to do with forcing on the Parliamentary Union between England and Scotland. The English House of Commons were in serious difficulty about using the power of trade regulation, they had gained at the Revolution, till the time came when they were able to make their authority felt over the whole of Great Britain. The Darien *The Scottish* scheme brought the possibilities of trouble into clear light. *Darien* The ambition of the Scotch to engage in the commerce of *scheme* the great world, might possibly have been advantageous to the head of a Dual Monarchy[1], or it might not; there could be no doubt, however, that it was fraught with dangers of every kind, political and commercial, to the English Parliament. Englishmen recognised that Scotland was in a position to inflict irreparable damage on their commerce, and that the existence of an independent Scottish Parliament was a source of serious danger[2]. The Darien Company had been authorised by the Scotch Parliament, in 1695, to colonise, make fortifications, fit out vessels of war and contract alliances. Their settlement in Darien was to have been a free port, which would have seriously affected the success of the English navigation policy. They hoped to

---

[1] On the possible arming of the Scots, see Swift, *Public Spirit of Whigs, Works* (1824), IV. 250.   [2] Mackinnon, *Union of England and Scotland*, 25.

*awakened
hostility
and sus-
picion*

break through the monopoly of the East India Company;
they had secured the Parliamentary authorisation for which
the English Company were pleading in vain; they opened
an office and received subscriptions in London. They were
preparing to compete in those trades which Englishmen
prized most highly; while the Scottish project also aroused
the Spaniards, and strained their relations with Englishmen,
both with regard to the West Indian and the African trade.
The schemes for trading with Archangel, which the promoters of the Darien Company cherished, and of carrying
on the whale fishery, were opposed to the interests of the
Russian and Greenland Companies. On every side the
leading English trades were threatened; and the embroglios
with the Spaniards which followed rendered it impossible
for King William to support his northern subjects in their
great undertaking. The seeds of failure were thus sown in
the expedition from the first; and the Scottish indignation,
which was roused by the narrative of the survivors who
returned from Darien, was embittered by the sense of a
pecuniary loss which the country could ill afford. The

*which
could only
be set at
rest by a
legislative
Union.*

English merchants were anxious to prevent the recurrence
of similar attempts at competition. They had learned that
a complete legislative Union of the two countries must be
procured at any cost[1].

The Dual Monarchy had not been a satisfactory arrangement from any point of view. There was a trend, both of
men and money, from the northern kingdom to the seat of
government, which was not welcome in England, and which
was bitterly denounced in Scotland. Their brief experience

[1] For an excellent account of the Darien Company see J. H. Burton, *History
of Scotland from the Revolution*, I. c. viii. The Darien Company suffered from
the want of experience of its directors, and from almost every one of the difficulties
which were felt in the more powerful English companies. As a trading concern,
the management was entirely ignorant of the right commodities for export; as
a colony, there was no proper government which could restrain the disorderly and
buccaneering elements; and the capital was quite insufficient for the projects they
had in view. It had been raised with some difficulty in Scotland, and though the
shares were all taken up, it was not a *bona fide* subscription, as some of the shareholders received promises from the Company guaranteeing them against actual
loss (*ib.* I. 297). The general impression which was abroad, that the tropics were
fertile and wealthy, prevented the directors from sending out the supplies which
might have saved the colonists from utter ruin.

of freedom of intercourse, during the Interregnum, led many of the Scotch to desire a commercial union between the countries. The project was the subject of negotiations in 1667[1], but no terms were arranged and the distress in Scotland continued. It was asserted that Scotland had declined *The Dual Monarchy* rapidly both in population and wealth since the union of *had* the Crowns. "Into this Condition hath this Nation been *worked unsatis-* brought by this loose and Irregular tye of the Union of the *factorily in Scotland,* Crowns, a state wherein we are not considered as Subjects nor allies, nor Friends nor Enemies, but all of them, only when, where, how and how long our Task Masters please[2]." It had thus become apparent that some change was requisite in the relations which subsisted between the two countries; and when the Commissioners met to devise a scheme, the English were determined to have a legislative, as distinguished from any form of a federal union, and insisted that this matter should be voted on first, before entering on the discussion of any points of detail[3]. When this principle was once secured, they appear to have treated the *and the details of* Scotch Commissioners generously on all points of detail. *the actual* The quota which Scotland was to pay towards a land tax *scheme of Union* of four shillings in the pound was £48,000 as against £2,000,000 from England[4], while certain duties on malt and coals, which were to expire within a brief period, were not imposed upon Scotland at all. But besides this, Scotland received a considerable payment as an equivalent for incurring a share of responsibility in the debt with which England was burdened. The portion of each class of taxation, whether customs or excise, which was appropriated to the English debt was taken, and the proportion which they bore to the whole customs and excise in England was calculated out[5]. Similar calculations in regard to the different branches of the Scottish revenue brought out the fact that £398,085. 10s. would be a fair equivalent to be paid to Scotland, for accepting obligations in respect of

---

[1] *Hist. MSS. Comm.* I. Ap. 55. Mackinnon, *Union of England and Scotland*, 10.

[2] *Proposals and Reasons for Constituting a Council of Trade*, 1701, Introduction, p. 3. Brit. Mus. 1029. a. 6 (1).

[3] Burton, I. 407.   [4] *Ib.* I. 412.   [5] *Ib.* I. 415.

A.D. 1689
—1776.
the English National Debt by submitting to an incorporating union. This sum was to be applied to winding up the Darien Company and paying other debts[1], and to making the necessary changes in the coinage; while the balance formed a fund for promoting Scotch fisheries and manufactures[2].

disarmed Scotch opposition generally, The treaty, thus arranged, was carried through the Scotch Parliament in spite of the indignant protests of Lord Belhaven. There was indeed one trivial circumstance which caused much friction, after the matter was settled[3]. The collection of the Scotch customs had been farmed out, and naturally this arrangement came to an end when the separate Scotch taxation ceased. The farmers of taxes, knowing that their time was short, found it most profitable to levy small duties and admit large quantities of goods, with which the English markets were eventually flooded. This brought about considerable commercial disturbance for a time, but no special measures were taken, as there seemed to be no likelihood that the occurrence would be repeated.

The figures as to revenue, given above, may perhaps serve better than any others that are available, to indicate *but the economic effects were not obviously beneficial at first,* the relative economic importance of the two kingdoms at the time of their union. It does not appear that much progress was made in Scotland during the first half-century after the Union[4]. It is not improbable that Scottish manufactures suffered by free communication with English towns, and that the steel manufacturers at Falkirk, and the glovers of Perth, were not so prosperous after the Union as they had been before. There can, however, be no doubt that, despite this immediate loss, Scotland gained eventually from being included in the inner circle of the English economic system, and sharing in the fostering care which Parliament bestowed on the commerce and manufactures of Great Britain. The

---

[1] The amount actually allotted to this purpose proved to be insufficient, and the creditors were incorporated as the Royal Bank of Scotland in 1727. The monopoly of the Bank of Scotland was thus broken down. See p. 454 below.

[2] See below, p. 454.

[3] *Parl. Hist.* vi. 579.

[4] Mackinnon, *op. cit.* 469, 482. For an excellent account of the condition of Scotland just before the Union see *Proposals and Reasons for constituting a Council of Trade* (1701).

trading and industrial classes in the Lowlands found that, A.D. 1689
during the period of Whig ascendancy, their political —1776.
principles had the upper hand, and that the economic *though the*
ultimate
maxims, which were influential at Westminster, were most *results have*
been good.
favourable to their own material interests. Since 1707 the
fiscal and economic affairs of the whole island have been
effectively controlled from one centre; and under the Parliament of Great Britain, Scotland has been stimulated into
developing a vigorous economic life, which is moreover remarkably independent of that of the southern kingdom.

XII. Public Finance.

213. Attention has been directed above to the profound *The organi-*
sation of
political significance of the formation of the Bank of England[1], *the Bank*
superseded
and to its bearing on the authority of a constitutional mon- *the practice*
arch. The changes in business practice it brought about and
the stimulus it gave to trade were important, but the main
motive of its founders lay in the fact that they had devised
a new expedient in finance[2]. The Bank rendered public
borrowing much less onerous than it had ever been before[3].

The Kings of England had been in the habit, from time
immemorial, of borrowing in anticipation of the taxes, and
obtaining money for immediate use by guaranteeing repayment when certain forms of revenue were collected.
Charles I. had been deeply indebted to the farmers of the

[1] See p. 411 above.

[2] The Bank of Genoa had been called into existence in 1407 to finance the
State debts, and its foundation was in some way analogous to that of the Bank of
England. The Banks of Venice (1587) and Amsterdam (1609) were called into
being to meet commercial rather than political requirements.

[3] For its influence on the currency and the trading community see below,
p. 442. There was little that was original in the project, as many similar schemes
had been proposed; but none of them had taken practical shape. One of the
earliest was that of Christopher Hagenbuck in 1581 (S. P. D. El. cl. 73). Compare
also Sir Paul Pindar's letter, *A Discourse concerning the erecting a Bank for the
Crown upon occasion of the King's demanding a Loan from the City* (Brit. Mus.
Lans. MSS. cviii. 90); also Sir Robert Heath's project in 1622 (S. P. D. J. I.
cxxx. 29, 31, 32). W. Potter suggested a land bank, under the Commonwealth
(*Humble Proposals*, 1651). Sir John Sinclair mentions *A Description of the Office
of Credit* (1665) and the *Proposals to the King and Parliament of a large Model
of a Bank*, by M. Lewis (1678), *History of the Public Revenue*, iii. 237.

customs[1]. When the Long Parliament declared them delinquents for their action under the personal government
they got into serious trouble[2]; but the same practice was
of borrow- continued by Parliament[3]. Charles II. habitually relied on
ing in anti-
cipation of advances[4] from the Goldsmiths; and even the stop of the
particular
branches of Exchequer in 1672, by which the repayment of moneys
revenue; lent to the Government on the assignment of taxes was
indefinitely deferred[5], did not put an end[6] to a practice
which the Commons viewed with much suspicion. But
the demands of William III. could not be met by such
expedients; the sums required were so large, as to exceed
the proceeds of any possible taxation. As the accustomed
security for the money lent was not forthcoming, borrowing
in anticipation of revenue became more and more difficult.
Attempts were made to procure the necessary supplies by
Tontines and Life Annuities, and subsequently by the issue
of Exchequer Bills[7]. The proceeds thus obtained proved
comparatively small, however; and the immediate success
and the attained, when the Bank of England was actually floated and
granting of
permanent the necessary capital subscribed, came as an immense relief
annuities
gave the to the Government, which was in terrible straits for want
Govern-
ment of money. The State obtained £1,200,000, without giving
command any security for the return of the principal, and by merely
providing for the regular payment of £100,000 as interest.
This scheme, the credit of which appears to be due to
William Paterson[8], was attractive to those persons with

---

[1] He does not appear to have been able to repay these advances. On Charles's alleged breach of faith in regard to the money of English merchants, see Robinson in Shaw, *Select Tracts and Documents illustrative of English Monetary History*, 56.

[2] The Long Parliament fined the farmers £150,000 as delinquents, for collecting the revenue on regal authority (*Commons Journals*, II. 156, 157).

[3] *Commons Journals*, III. 2.

[4] The possibility of dispensing with these advances and thus saving interest was one of the advantages which led Killigrew to advocate the erection of a Bank in 1663. *A Proposal*, p. 5.

[5] Shaw, *The Beginnings of the National Debt*, in *Owens College Historical Essays*, 391.

[6] Compare Mr Chisholm's *Notices of the various forms of Public Debt*, in *Accounts and Papers*, 1857-8, XXXIII. ms. pag. 247, printed pag. 92.

[7] See below, 441. Power to issue these bills, bearing interest at 5*d*. per cent. per diem, was given by 8 and 9 W. III. c. 20, §§ 63, 64.

[8] Andréadès, *Histoire de la Banque d'Angleterre*, I. 82. The failure of Paterson's other great project—the Darien scheme—ruined the reputation of this remarkable

money, who desired to bargain for the payment of interest *A.D. 1689*
in perpetuity, and did not wish to insist on having a right *of large*
to claim the repayment of the principal at a definite date. *sums on*
The terms offered were criticised at the time as unnecessarily *easy terms,*
favourable[1] to the lenders, but it was certainly an advantage
to William to obtain the command of the money so easily.

The new expedient thus devised proved convenient to
the Government and popular with moneyed men, so that both
political parties had recourse to it in turn. This financial
policy was, however, more especially associated with the
Whigs. Its inception was due to them, it harmonised with *but in*
their fundamental principle of keeping the resources of the *the Whig*
realm under Parliamentary control; and as many of their *principle*
supporters had subscribed to the Bank, its prosperity as *of parlia-*
an institution coincided with the interest of their political *control.*
friends. But from the first it roused the jealousy of the
landed interest; they felt that they were placed at a disadvantage, since they were heavily burdened with permanent
taxation, by a system of finance which afforded the moneyed
men a remunerative investment. The Tory scheme of a
Land Bank was an attempt to organise the new finance on
lines in which it should subserve the interests of landed
men; but after its impracticability had been demonstrated[2],
the jealousy felt by the landed proprietors of the power of
goldsmiths and bankers became more pronounced. For
all that, the Tories were forced to acknowledge and rely on
their help. So long as successive administrations had urgent
need of money, and found men who were willing to lend it,
they could hardly be expected to adopt the unpopular course
of largely and immediately increasing the taxes.

The fact that the new system was convenient is suffi- *The*
ciently obvious, but there is some reason to doubt whether *financial expedient*
it was justifiable. The question whether it was really of *proved convenient,*
man, and has inclined subsequent writers to discount his share in starting the
Bank. Doubleday assigns a large part in the inception of the Bank to Bishop
Burnet, who is also said to have followed Dutch precedents in the matter (*Financial History*, p. 64). The Dutch debt at this time involved an annual charge of
£1,000,000 in interest, Davenant, I. 248.

[1] Davenant, *Essay on Ways and Means*, I. 24, thought the attraction of 8 %
diverted capital from trade. Many Dutch capitalists were glad to take advantage
of the offer.   [2] See below, p. 452.

political advantage to the country, in the long run, has provoked an immense amount of discussion[1].   Various writers
have held that each generation should make immediate
*but there
was a real
danger of
imposing
a burden on
posterity*
provision[2] out of taxation for paying off the debt incurred
by any wars in which they had engaged, and that it was
unfair to burden posterity with the cost of their undertakings[3].   But it was often plausible to urge that after-
generations were gainers by the struggles in which their
fathers engaged, and that it was entirely just that the
burden should be distributed over a long period of years.
If the funds are used in connection with some contest
which involves the very existence of the nation, there is
much to be said for this view; but the precise benefit ac-

---

[1] The public mind has become habituated to the existence of national debts, but
the case against them occasionally finds a vigorous exponent, especially in view of
the decline of Holland, which was regarded as due to the pressure of the taxation
which was necessary in order to meet the interest on the debt.   "Up to times of
comparatively modern and recent date, therefore, the idea of any persons, in
a real national exigence, when perhaps national existence was at stake, offering
to lend money to their country 'at interest,' was deemed just as absurd as
would be a child offering to lend its pocket-money to its father 'at interest,'
when both were in danger of wanting a dinner!   It was reserved for what is
strangely termed 'an enlightened era,' to hatch this monstrous absurdity, which,
until it was put into practice, would not have been deemed wicked, but silly.
Strange turn for matters to take at an 'enlightened era'; and stranger still, that
such a notion should first strike root in the skull of a countryman of 'Grotius':
but so it was.   It was in the muddy and huckstering brain of a Dutchman, some-
where about the middle of the seventeenth century, that this pestilent scheme
was engendered; and in the huckstering country of Holland was first presented
to the eyes of the world the spectacle of a 'National Debt.'   The 'Lernaean
Fens' engendered the 'Hydra'; and amidst the swamps of the 'Zuyder Zee' was
generated this far worse than the fabled monster of the poets!   After all, however,
the soil is sufficiently worthy of the tree.   The Dutch, though they have produced
one or two great men, are a nation remarkable for low, peddling, greedy, and
huckstering notions; but they have this excuse, that, being a small and weak
state, they have been continually, by their position, compelled to make efforts
beyond their strength; and this it was, no doubt, which first tempted them to
plunge into that most preposterous and wicked system, of which I am now to
give the detail.   With a country almost naturally defenceless, engaged by position
and religion in conflicts far beyond their real national strength, surrounded by
strong and often hostile powers, the Dutch at length became so exhausted by
the pressure of the taxes they paid, as to sacrifice before the shrine of mammon
those liberties which they had preserved from ambition."   Doubleday, *Financial,
Monetary and Statistical History of England*, 43.   Compare also the writers
quoted by Macculloch, *Dictionary*, s.v. Holland.

[2] An attempt in this direction was made by the Acts 8 and 9 W. III. c. 20 § 41.

[3] Davenant, I. 80.   He thought it specially unfair in England, *ib.* 256.   This
principle is laid down by Jefferson, *Memoirs, Correspondence, etc.*, IV. 200.

cruing to subsequent generations from the military triumphs A.D. 1689
—1776. of the past, can hardly be assessed in terms of money. It is impossible to say what quota of the expense of Marlborough's campaigns could be fairly imposed on Englishmen in the latter part of the nineteenth century. Political gains and military successes are often very transient advantages. If it is fair to postpone the reckoning, it is also necessary to take account of the rapid depreciation which affects this *without compensating benefits,* species of national gain. It is not easy to adduce good reasons for deferring payment for military expense for more than a generation, and there is an undoubted danger that statesmen, who find they can obtain money easily, may be more tempted to engage in reckless undertakings, than if they were compelled at every step to look at ways and means. However this may be, it may still be said that the possession of such a powerful instrument of finance cannot but be beneficial to the country, even if we are forced to admit that it has not always been used with discretion.

The chief point, at which the new system of finance lay open to criticism, was in the rapid increase in the charges *and of increasing* which had to be defrayed by annual taxation, in consequence *the charges* of the necessity of paying interest on the growing national *on revenue,* debt. Charles Davenant, who discussed the new methods from a Tory standpoint, noted that when there is a heavy permanent burden, there tends to be less room for new exactions on occasions of special emergency[1]; and after twenty years' experience, this objection ceased to be closely associated with Tory jealousy. It became obvious to all dispassionate observers that the system had been pursued to a dangerous extent. Archibald Hutcheson wrote most judiciously on the subject, and analysed the losses to the community from the pressure of debt, in the rise of prices, the depression of trade, and payment of interest to foreigners[2]. He urged that immediate steps should be taken to effect the repayment of the debt, as it stood in 1717. He would have appropriated a tenth part of all real and all personal estate to this object, as he believed that there would be such a revival of prosperity, when the pressure of taxation was lightened, that the landed interest, the trading interest, and the moneyed

---

[1] *Essay on Ways and Means,* in *Works,* i. 23.　　[2] *Collection of Treatises,* p. 20.

A.D. 1689
—1776.

interest alike would share in the general gain[1]. As an alternative he proposed that a million should be set aside annually to form a sinking fund, in the expectation that, if no new wars broke out, the nation would be relieved of the burden of debt in the course of thirty years[2]. A somewhat similar scheme was actually set on foot by Sir Robert Walpole[3]; but he was not sufficiently careful to introduce the necessary safeguards, and to ensure that the money set aside should be actually devoted to the repayment of debt, and to no other purpose. In the first few years of the existence of this Fund, there was an inconsiderable reduction of total indebtedness[4], as the new debts incurred did not quite equal the amounts paid off. After 1733, however, all attempts to keep the Sinking Fund inviolate ceased, and it completely changed its character; payments of every sort for current expenses were habitually charged to it, and it was replaced, in 1786, by the establishment of the Consolidated Fund. At that date, out of the £200,607,110 which had been paid to the credit of the Fund during the seventy-two years of its existence, only £23,984,344 had been devoted to its ostensible object[5]. No real success attended the attempts of financiers to reduce the total of the national obligations, though they were occasionally able, by a process of conversion, to diminish the charges for interest[6]. They were, moreover, forced to be constantly on the outlook for additional sources of revenue, from which the expenses of government and the payment of interest might be defrayed, and this necessity was the underlying motive for the scheme of taxing the colonists.

and Walpole endeavoured to pay off the principal by means of a Sinking Fund.

The fiscal system of the country

214. The fiscal system of the country had been entirely reconstructed during the Civil War. The fifteenths and tenths, and the Tudor subsidies, which remained under Charles I., had failed to meet the requirements of Government, and his opponents had to organise a revenue system

---

[1] Hutcheson, *Collection of Treatises*, pp. 20, 22.   [2] *Ib.* p. 78.

[3] 3 Geo. I. cc. 7, 8, 9.

[4] Nathaniel Gould, *Essay on the Publick Debts of this Kingdom* (1727), in Macculloch, *Select Collection of Scarce Tracts on the National Debt*, p. 68.

[5] Chisholm's Report in *Accounts and Papers*, 1868-9, xxxv. 767.

[6] In 1717 the rate of interest on Government securities was reduced from 6 to 5 per cent. and in 1727 from 5 to 4 per cent. Bastable, *Public Finance*, 553.

under the pressure of immediate necessity. The practical A.D. 1689 —1776.
common sense of the Parliamentary party, in meeting the
sudden emergency caused by the War[1], received the highest *had been*
proof of approbation from the Restoration Parliament; since *reconsti-* *tuted*
financial expedients, which had been specially devised in *during the* *Inter-*
order to meet temporary exigencies, were deliberately re- *regnum,*
tained as convenient for raising a permanent revenue. The
scheme, which was adopted at the Restoration, did not
prove sufficient for the ordinary expenses of government[2],
and was totally inadequate as a means of raising money
for the great continental struggle in which William was
engaged; and much interesting discussion took place as to *and pro-*
the best ways and means of supplying the war. Davenant, *posals were* *made to*
and other Tory writers, had argued that a readjustment of *render* *it more*
the taxes levied on commodities would prove very fruitful; *equable and* *fruitful*
they believed that an ample revenue might be provided in
this fashion, and that it would be unnecessary, except in the
direct emergencies, to have recourse to the dangerous system
of borrowing. They maintained the principle that the incidence of taxation should be distributed as equitably as
possible, so that all the various sections of the community
might be called upon to contribute according to their means
to the necessities of State. It appeared to them that the
burden of taxation pressed with undue severity on the
landed men. Davenant points out that in ancient times
personal as well as real property had been taxed, and insists
that the same course should be taken in his own day. " The
usurers, who are the true drones of a commonwealth, living
upon the honey without any labour, should, of all people, be
brought in to bear their proportion of the common burthen.
As yet they could never be effectually reached, but they may
be fetched in by the wisdom of a Parliament, if the House of
Commons would please resolutely to set themselves about
it[3]." Davenant himself would have liked to see the income

---

[1] " The late king having the command of the Inlands and the Parliament of
most of the seaports, they had no better way than to put an excise on goods,
whereby their enemies, making use of the said goods, paid the excise, and so the
Parliamentary Army." *Trades Destruction is England's Ruin, or Excise Decryed,*
by W. C., 1659, p. 5 [Brit. Mus. 518. h. 1 (2)].

[2] Shaw, *Beginnings of National Debt,* in *Owens College Historical Essays,* 400.

[3] *Ways and Means,* in *Works,* I. 57.

A.D. 1689
—1776.
from money subjected to direct taxation, which might correspond to the tax on the rental of land[1]; but the times were not yet ripe for anything of the nature of an income tax[2]. As an alternative expedient for distributing the incidence of *by develop-* taxation more widely, he had to fall back upon an excise[3]. *ing the* This had been the favourite expedient of Charles I.'s advisers, *excise,* though it had not been enforced till Pym took it in hand[4]. Davenant was aware that the scheme might prove impracticable; " unless the nation does unanimously and freely give into excises, upon the full conviction that they are the best ways and means of supplying the government, it will not be the interest of any king to desire such a revenue. For if they are carried but by a small majority, against the sense and grain of a considerable part of the House of Commons, they will come so crampt in the act of Parliament, and loaded with so many difficulties, that they will only occasion great clamours in the kingdom, and not yield much money[5]." There was much ingenuity in his scheme for graduating it, so that it might fall chiefly upon the luxuries of the rich, and to only a small extent upon the necessities of the poor[6]. He hoped that, by a strict enforcement of the assize of bread and beer, it might be possible to prevent such a tax from having a serious effect upon prices[7]; and that the machinery of collection might be organised without the necessity of inquisitorial interference with private life[8]. But, when the advocate of the scheme admitted that so many difficulties had to be faced, there need be little surprise that responsible statesmen made little attempt to follow *though* his advice. There were besides two objections to the ex- *this was* *objected to* tension of the excise. Economic theorists like Locke[9] were *both on* *economic* opposed to it; they held that all such taxation fell ultimately upon the land[10]; they argued that it was wiser to levy it

---

[1] He calculates the money lent in interest at £20,000,000; and takes the rate of interest as 5% and the income as £1,000,000. A four shilling rate on this sum would yield £200,000 (*Works*, I. p. 58). A similar proposal was revived in 1759 by the author of *Thoughts on the pernicious consequences of borrowing money* (Trin. Coll. Lib. T. 2. 133).   [2] See p. 839 below.

[3] Davenant was himself a commissioner of excise.

[4] Dowell, *Taxation*, II. 9.

[5] *Ways and Means*, in *Works*, I. 71.   [6] *Ib.* 63.   [7] *Ib.* 64.   [8] *Ib.* 67.

[9] *Considerations*, in *Works*, v. 57.

[10] Davenant did not deny that "all taxes whatsoever are in their last resort

directly on that fund, rather than to cause disturbance to A.D. 1689
prices by levying it on commodities[1]. But there were also —1776.
objections of a political character; the excise was a branch *and*
of revenue which had been assigned to the Crown; to touch *grounds.*
it in any way was difficult; and to leave it in royal hands, and
make it much more productive, would be to render the Crown
less dependent on Parliament[2]. Under the circumstances,
it is not surprising that little was done to give effect to
Davenant's views; the taxes on malt[3], and leather[4] imposed
under William III., were in accordance with his principles,
and further steps were taken during the reign of Anne, in
charging duties on candle-making, soap, painted calicoes and
starch[5]; the Stamp Act, which was levied on newspapers
and advertisements, may be placed in the same category.

a tax upon land," but held that "excises will affect land in no degree like taxes
that charge it directly." *Ways and Means*, in *Works*, I. 77.

[1] Sir Matthew Decker advocated a graduated tax on houses, as a means of
imposing an equable burden on all classes and raising a million annually which
might be used for the discharge of the debt. *Serious Considerations on the
several High Duties*, London, 1744, p. 17. This is undoubtedly Decker's; the
seventh (1756) edition bears his name, as well as the title-page of Horsley's reply
(*Serious Considerations examined*, 1744). A more ingenious proposal was put into
shape in 1739 in an *Essay on the Causes of the Decline of the Foreign Trade* (1744),
Brit. Mus. 8246. h. 1, which was attributed to Richardson. It is full of excellent
criticism on the then existing arrangements for taxation, and it proposes to replace
all existing exactions, both local and national, by a single tax which should fall on
everyone all round; so far it coincides closely with the plan that was advocated by
Sir Matthew Decker, but this new tax was not to be a tax on consumption but
a tax that should be levied directly, by compelling everyone to take out a license
for all sorts of articles of luxury which they might intend to use. The tract was
reprinted more than once and appears to have attracted a good deal of attention.
It is mentioned here as a curiosity in sumptuary proposals, and as an ingenious
attempt to touch the pockets of the consumers directly with the least possible
interference with trade, p. 44. Temple (*Vindication of Commerce*, p. 37)
and Caldwell (*Debates*, II. 782) attributed it to Decker, but the disregard of
Decker's own scheme, and the condemnation of the Navigation Acts, which
Decker approved, render this most unlikely. Still more interesting is the
proposal (*Thoughts on the pernicious consequences of borrowing money*, 1759)
for substituting direct taxation on land and funded property, for the indirect
taxes which hampered trade, and which, as Locke had argued, ultimately fell
upon land.

[2] The feeling is alluded to in general terms by Davenant, *Ways and Means*,
I. 76. William had the excise for life, but not the customs (*Parl. Hist.* v. 561), an
arrangement which did not satisfy him, but which Bishop Burnet persuaded him
to accept.

[3] Dowell, *Taxation*, II. 56.

[4] 8 and 9 W. III. c. 21.   [5] Dowell, II. 76.

All these were of the nature of excises, or taxes which fell on home manufactures.

The extensive changes in the fiscal system of the country, which were carried through by Walpole, were based on a very different principle. He endeavoured to take consistent account of the effect of the tariffs upon the material prosperity of the country, and to reform all duties so as to give the greatest possible stimulus to the trading and manufacturing interests. By this means he hoped to develop the industrial and commercial resources of the country; there is a close affinity between his fiscal system and the particular form of mercantilism[1] which was current in his time. He acted in complete accord with the best commercial opinions of the day[2], and it has been said in his commendation "that he found the book of rates the worst and left it best in Europe[3]." It is worth while to quote his own statement of the principles which actuated him as it occurs in the Speech from the Throne at the opening of the session of 1721. "In this situation of affairs we should be extremely wanting to ourselves, if we neglected to improve the favourable opportunity which this general tranquillity gives us, of extending our commerce, upon which the riches and grandeur of this nation chiefly depend. It is very obvious, that nothing would more conduce to the obtaining so public a good, than to make the exportation of our own manufactures, and the importation of the commodities used in the manufacturing of them, as practicable and easy as may be; by this means, the balance of trade may be preserved in our favour, our navigation increased, and greater numbers of our poor employed.

"I must therefore recommend it to you, Gentlemen of the House of Commons, to consider how far the duties upon these branches may be taken off, and replaced, without any violation of public faith, or laying any new burthen upon my people. And I promise myself, that by a due consideration of this matter, the produce of those duties, compared with the infinite advantages that will accrue to the Kingdome by

---

[1] See above, p. 396, also below, 457.   [2] Tucker, *Civil Government*, p. 222.
[3] Coxe, *Memoirs of Sir Robert Walpole*, IV. 354.

their being taken off, will be found so inconsiderable, as to leave little room for any difficulties or objections[1]." He practically took off all import duties on naval stores and drugs, and the other materials of our manufactures, and arranged that all the products of our industry should be exported duty free. The creation of the Bank of England had led the moneyed men to rally round the Whigs, but Walpole's reforms cemented the attachment of the manufacturers to the same interest.

Nor were the commercial men forgotten. Walpole was *and commerce,* anxious to leave the carrying trade as free as possible, and to substitute, for duties on the importation of foreign goods, excises on their consumption at home[2]. He hoped by this means to render the whole island " one general free port and a magazine and common storehouse for all nations[3]." He managed to effect this change in regard to tea, coffee, and chocolate, which were deposited in bonded warehouses and charged with duty when taken out for home consumption, and he was able to increase the revenue from these commodities £120,000 a year. When he attempted to extend the principle, however, to all imported goods as well as to articles of home production, like salt, the deep-seated prejudice against an excise was at once aroused. Walpole endeavoured to allay the excitement by a pamphlet entitled *Some general considerations concerning the alteration and improvement of the Revenues*[4]; and a commitee of the House of Commons exposed the frightful amount of fraud and illicit trade which went on under the existing system[5], and which Walpole hoped to check. How far he would have been successful in this last aim must always be doubtful, for he never had the opportunity of carrying his views into effect. The dislike of an excise as inquisitorial was intense, and coupled with this was the curious allegation that the citizens, if once accustomed to it, would feel it so little that they would cease to take an interest in checking the vagaries of the Government. Walpole explained his

---

[1] *Parl. Hist.* VII. 913. [2] Coxe, *op. cit.* III. 66.

[3] Tucker, *Elements of Commerce*, 148 n.

[4] Coxe, *op. cit.* III. 68. [5] *Ib.* 71.

intentions in an admirable speech, in which he expressed his hope that the measure would "tend to make London a free port and by consequence the market of the world[1]." But his opinion was not endorsed by the City men themselves; the Bill was carried in the House of Commons by 249 to 189, but an agitation against the measure was fomented in London, Nottingham, and other towns; and Sir Robert Walpole, sensible that "in the present inflamed temper of the people the Act could not be carried into execution without an armed force[2]," determined to abandon the scheme.

Had the measure been successful, Walpole expected that he would be able to redress some of the admitted inequalities in the incidence of taxation. He had succeeded in reducing the advantage, which the moneyed men enjoyed from the new finance, by lowering the rate of interest on the public funds from 8 or 6 to 4 per cent.; and as he had *so that he might be able to dispense with the land tax,* also reduced the land tax from 4s. to 1s.[3], he had done something to mitigate the sense of injustice from which the country gentlemen suffered. He hoped to be able to go farther, and abolish the land tax altogether; there were extraordinary inequalities in the manner in which it was levied[4], and Walpole asserted that it had "continued so long and laid so heavy that many a landed gentleman in this kingdom had thereby been utterly ruined and undone." But with the failure of his excise scheme, and the impossibility of finding any other source of revenue, it was inevitable that

---

[1] Coxe, *op. cit.* III. 106.   [2] Id., *op. cit.* III. 115.

[3] In 1731 and 1732. Dowell, *op. cit.* II. 96.

[4] Davenant, who examined into the matter with great care, showed that the home counties were assessed much more heavily than those in the north and west. This had been due at first to the manner in which the Commonwealth had laid the heaviest burden upon the counties on which they could rely. An unsuccessful attempt was made to correct this at the Restoration, when the assessment for ship money had been taken as a model, on account of the known care with which it had been made. An excellent account of the method adopted in 1634 will be found in Mr E. Cannan's *History of Local Rates in England*, 50. Davenant endeavours to show, by appealing to the excise, the poll tax, the hearth rate and the poor rate, that the northern and western counties had improved more rapidly than the home counties in the intervening period, and should therefore pay a larger quota than was charged upon them in the property tax (Davenant, *Ways and Means*, in *Works*, I. 32—62). The property tax was thus doubly unfair, since it fell exclusively upon real property, and as land of equal value in different counties bore very dissimilar shares of the burden. See p. 604 n. 3 below.

the land tax[1] should be continued; and the landed interest *A.D. 1689* *—1776.*
were, partly by their own action in raising an opposition to
the excise, left to nurse their grievance about the unfair *but the*
share of the burden of taxation which they were called upon *agitation they roused*
to bear[2]. The subsequent wars rendered it impossible for *rendered his reforms*
any statesman to attempt systematic reforms, and the fiscal *imprac-ticable.*
arrangements of the country continued to give special
support to manufacturers. Capitalists of every class were
relieved of any heavy burden, and special pains were taken
to stimulate industry, both native and exotic.

XIII. CURRENCY AND CREDIT.

215. The condition of the currency was an important
element in all the controversy which preceded and accompanied the founding of the Bank of England. At a time
when the only recognised circulating medium consisted of *The de-ficiency of*
the precious metals, there was a general, if mistaken, anxiety *standard coin,*
that the amassing of money in a bank would tend to denude
the country of the circulating medium. It was contended
that the starting of such an institution would tend to inconvenience traders, to bring about a rise of prices, and to
cause increased trouble in collecting the king's taxes. The
deficiency of currency was a very real and serious difficulty
which pressed on many persons; and it was so far aggravated, during the re-coinage of 1696, that the Bank was
unable to cash its notes with the accustomed punctuality.
The story of the amendment of the silver coins, in 1696, is *which ne-cessitated*
not so well known as that of the Elizabethan re-coinage; *the re-*
but it throws some interesting side lights on the conditions *coinage of 1696,*
of the times, and deserves more than a passing notice. The
causes, which had reduced the currency to such a state that
re-coinage was necessary, were different from those that had
brought about the similar evil in Tudor times. The debased

[1] There is a curious parallelism and a curious contrast between the views of
Davenant and those of Walpole: they start as it were from opposite principles,
but the goal towards which they worked was similar. Davenant advocated an
excise as a substitute for borrowing, Walpole as a substitute for the land tax:
Davenant would have avoided incurring a debt, Walpole attempted to pay it off.

[2] On the effects of this in 1815, see below, p. 729.

*was not
due to de-
basement
of the
issues.*

currency, with which Elizabeth had to deal, had been deliberately issued by her father and her brother; but there had been no decided debasement of English coinage under any of the seventeenth century governments. Charles I. had been tempted to have recourse to this expedient, but his advisers ˉon the Council convinced him that the step was unwise[1]. The coins issued from the Mint continued to be of the fine standard and full weight, all through the century; and such masses were minted that it was surprising that silver coins should be so scarce, and that so many of the examples in circulation should be light, defective and debased. The constant drain[2] of good money caused a very serious loss to the nation[3], and it was not easy to see to what it was due, or how it occurred; it certainly did not appear that any fault attached to the Government.

*The results
of allowing
the un-
restricted
export of
bullion*

Soon after the Restoration, the government of Charles II. adopted, on the advice of the Council, a singularly liberal monetary policy. As some critics thought unadvisedly, and as others would say prematurely[4], they took the bold step of allowing the export of gold and silver bullion without licence[5], and of undertaking the free coinage of bullion[6] brought to the Mint. To break so entirely with the bullionist tradition was a bold stroke, and the report of the Council of Trade, which recommended it, marks an era

---

[1] See the speech attributed to Sir Robert Cotton; Shaw, *Select Tracts, Documents illustrative of English Monetary History*, p. 27.

[2] See S. P. D. James I. 73, 18 May 1611, *A Proclamation against melting or conveying out of the King's Dominions of gold or silver current in the same*. Also Charles I. 25 May 1627. Brit. Mus. 21. h. 1 (38).

[3] Haynes (*Brief Memoirs relating to the Silver and Gold Coins of England with an Account of the Corruption of the Hammer'd Monys and of the Reform by the Late Grand Coynage at the Tower and the five Country Mints*, 1700. Brit. Mus. *Lans. MS.* DCCCI.) puts it at between two and three hundred thousand annually, from 1689, p. 74. He thinks that the worst clipping occurred in 1695 when the recoinage was imminent, p. 100. He estimates the total loss on running silver cash as £2,250,000, p. 75.

[4] Shaw, *The History of Currency*, 163.

[5] 15 Charles II. c. 7, § 9. The preamble of the section is worth quoting: "And forasmuch as severall considerable and advantagious trades cannot be conveniently driven and carryed on without the Species of Money or Bullion, and that it is found by experience, that they are carryed in greatest abundance (as to a Common Market) to such places as give free liberty for exporting the same, and the better to keepe in, and encrease the current Coyens of this Kingdom, be it enacted," etc.

[6] 18 Charles II. c. 5.

in monetary history[1]. The policy of allowing the export of bullion has on the whole been maintained, although it was frequently set aside by proclamation[2] under Charles II.; and the practice of coining money, without making a charge for seigniorage, has been regularly followed, in spite of occasional protests[3]. As a result, the English currency became liable to be depleted, through the very slightest fluctuations in the value of the precious metals. The changing ratio of gold and silver was doubtless a constant cause of trouble; and frequent difficulty arose from the fact that silver was rated so low in England[4] that it was occasionally remunerative to melt down the silver coins, issued from the Mint, in order to sell them as bullion. Besides this, till the mill and press were introduced[5] in 1663, the currency consisted entirely of hammered money, and the pieces varied considerably from one another, in size and weight. As payments were made by tale, there was a frequent temptation to hoard the new pieces which issued from the Mint, or to melt them down for sale to silversmiths and for purposes of export[6]. The coins left in circulation became more worn and defective as time passed, so that the difference, between the nominal value of the coins as money and their real value as silver, became

A.D. 1689 —1776.

and the practice of free coining

of hammered money

---

[1] It has been reprinted by J. R. Macculloch, in *Select Collection of Rare Tracts on Money*, p. 145.

[2] Shaw, *History of Currency*, 163.

[3] E.g. by Dudley North. *Discourse of Trade*, quoted by Shaw, *History of Currency*, 221; also Ruding, *Annals of the Coinage of Great Britain*, II. 12.

[4] See above, p. 137. This difficulty appears to have been felt, though in a less degree, in the reign of James I. (Proclamations 18 May, 1611, S. P. D. J. I. LXIII. 88, and 23 March, 1614, S. P. D., J. I. CLXXXVII. 37. Some confusion was caused at that time by the rate at which Scotch gold coins were rendered current in England (Ruding, I. 362, and Proclamation 8 April, 1603, Brit. Mus. 506. h. 10 (5)). Owing to the scarcity of silver, an attempt was made to put farthing tokens, duly issued from the Mint, into circulation. Proclamation 19 May, 1613, Brit. Mus. 506. h. 12 (75).

[5] H. Haynes, *op. cit.* p. 40.

[6] Haynes describes the conditions in some detail. "But tho' all the pieces together might come neer the pound weight or be within remedy; yet diverse of 'em compar'd one with the other were very disproportionable; as was too well known to many persons, who pick'd out the heavy pieces, and threw 'em into the Melting pott, to fitt 'em for exportation, or to supply the Silver Smiths. And 'twas a thing at last so notorious, that it 'scap'd the observation of a very few; for 'twas pretty commonly known that the following pieces of hammer'd mony

C. 28

A.D. 1689
—1776.

afforded profitable opportunities for clipping and sweating the coin

more noticeable[1]. The attempt to keep heavy and light pieces in circulation together proved a failure, and only resulted in the constant melting down of new coins as issued from the Mint.

In the meantime the old hammered money was being seriously maltreated by dealers in coin. Some of the pieces were thicker than others, and they were filed down to the usual size; others were stamped with the impression at one side, and the margin left bare was trimmed off; at first the men who tampered with the coinage were "pretty modest" in clipping. Defective coins were only occasionally met with in 1672, but after 1685[2] the practice became a very serious evil indeed. Not only did clipping become a regular business, but the old and worn coin lent itself to fraudulent imitation, and a considerable amount of base money was put into circulation by coiners[3]. Altogether, the condition of

tho' never clip'd, did many of 'em in their weight and value want or exceed the legal Standard in the under written disproportion, viz.

Some of		*were in value by their under-weight*				*and other pieces of the same species were in value by their overweight*				
		s.	*d.*	*d.*	*d.*	*s.*	*d.*	*d.*	*d.*	
the crown pieces		4.	9,	10,	11	5.	1,	2,	3	crowns
the ½ crown pieces		2.	4,	5,	0	2.	7,	8,	0	½ crowns
the shillings		0.	10½,	11,	0	1.	1,	2,	0	shillings
the sixpences		0.	5,	5½,	...	0.	0,	0,	0	sixpences were not of an exact assize

Now when pieces so very ill siz'd as these came out of the Mint, and the lighter pass'd under the same Name, and at the same value with the heavyest, this presented the Clippers with too fair an opportunity of rounding the weighty pieces with the Sheers and the file, til they reduc'd 'em to an equall weight, and size with the rest; for they were pretty modest in the practice of clipping, 'til after the year 1685." *Op. cit.* 63.

[1] The fundamental principle in Locke's argument on the subject of coinage was the identity in exchange value between one ounce of silver and another, *Further Considerations concerning raising the Value of Money* (1695), p. 2. But Barbon showed conclusively that within certain limits, silver, which has the stamp of money, may circulate for more than its value as bullion, *Discourse concerning Coining the New Money Lighter*, p. 28. This was indeed a matter of common experience at the time, *Review of the Universal Remedy for all Diseases incident to the Coin* (1696), p. 12 (Brit. Mus. 1139. d. 6 (2)). The writer points out that "every Degree of Currancy given to defective Coin, is a new Lock put upon the Good," p. 39.

[2] Haynes, *op. cit.* 64, 67.

[3] Haynes, *op. cit.* 66, 69. They fabricated base money which looked like old coin that had been clipped; *ib.* 77.

the currency was most deplorable. Very little silver was A.D. 1689
—1776.
to be had, and what was forthcoming was defective and
debased. As Lowndes says, "Great contentions do daily *so as to*
arise amongst the King's Subjects, in Fairs, Markets, Shops, *cause great incon-*
and other Places throughout the Kingdom, about the Passing *venience*
or Refusing of the Same, to the disturbance of the Public
Peace; many Bargains, Doings and Dealings are totally
prevented and laid aside, which lessens Trade in general;
Persons before they conclude in any Bargains, are necessitated first to settle the Price or Value of the very Money
they are to Receive for their Goods; and if it be in Guineas
at a High Rate, or in Clipt or Bad Moneys, they set the
Price of their Goods accordingly, which I think has been
One great cause of Raising the Price not only of Merchandizes, but even of Edibles, and other Necessaries for
the sustenance of the Common People, to their Great
Grievance. The Receipt and Collection of the Publick Taxes,
Revenues and Debts (as well as of Private Mens Incomes)
are extreamly retarded[1]." The larger silver pieces had
suffered most and the smaller coins were comparatively
uninjured; but the malpractices had been carried so far *and to*
that the prices of commodities in silver appear to have risen *bring about a rise of*
considerably. This metal was still the recognised standard *prices as calculated*
of currency, and the fall in the value of silver coins became *in silver.*
apparent, both in the high rates which had to be paid for
guineas[2], and in the unfavourable state of the exchanges[3].

It became obvious that no satisfactory remedy could be
carried out, unless the evil was dealt with in a thorough-
going fashion, and the old coinage was called in. An ingenious scheme for amending the silver coinage, with the
least possible disturbance to prices, was put forward by
Mr Lowndes, the Secretary of the Treasury. He proposed *Lowndes'*
that the new money should be issued at higher denomina- *scheme for amending*
tions; a silver coin of the weight and fineness of the old *the coin with the*
crown should be made current, not as 60, but as 75 pence, *least dis-*
and the half-crown should represent, not 30, but 37½ pence. *turbance to prices*

---

[1] *Essay for Amendment* (1695), in Macculloch, *Tracts*, p. 233.

[2] The silver price of guineas was from 24/- to 30/. Haynes, *op. cit.* 120.

[3] The discount on English drafts in Amsterdam varied between 13·7 per cent. and 23·5 per cent. Thorold Rogers, *First Nine Years of the Bank of England*, 40.

28—2

A.D. 1689
—1776.

*was in-
genious
but incon-
venient*

A proposal for raising the money had been approved by a committee of the House of Commons[1], and would in all probability have been carried into effect, but for the intervention of Locke, who denounced it in vigorous terms. He succeeded in impressing Montague, the future Lord Halifax, who was framing the scheme for re-coinage[2]; and as a result, the new coins were issued at the old denominations. The hopes of the bankers and moneyed men, who had hoarded new silver in the hope that the value would be raised, were balked[3]; and the landed men, who had let their lands on terms calculated in defective coins and subsequently received payments in the amended coin, would be gainers by the fact that the old denomination was retained[4]. It is at

*and the old
denomina-
tions were
retained*

all events obvious that it was much more convenient to keep to the old denominations; the difficulty of counting up any large payment in coins worth 3s. 1½d. each would have been considerable[5].

*in the
re-coinage*

The difficulties which arose from the scarcity of money were distinctly aggravated during the process of re-coinage[6], when a large number of pieces were necessarily withdrawn from circulation. Five country mints were established[7] to facilitate the process of recoinage. Sir Isaac Newton was at

[1] One of the resolutions reported by the committee on 12 March 1695 was in favour of raising the new silver crowns 18% so as to pass for 5/6. Ruding, ii. 36.

[2] Thorold Rogers, *First Nine Years*, 44.

[3] The crucial decision was taken on 20th October 1696, when the House decided not to alter the denomination of the coins (*C. J.* xi. 567). After this, according to Haynes, the new money which had been hoarded began to come into circulation much more rapidly, p. 149.

[4] It is said that Montague only succeeded in carrying through his scheme because the landed men were convinced that it was to their interest to retain the old denominations, and after he had purchased a considerable amount of support from other members of the House of Commons. The arguments *pro* and *con* are clearly stated by Kennett, *Complete History*, iii. 705. Among the most effective writers on Lowndes' side was Sir R. Temple, who argued that to "keep up an old Standard under an old Denomination below the value of Bullion is the greatest Folly imaginable," *Some Short Remarks upon Mr Locke's Book* (1696), p. 8. In a rejoinder E. H. argues that raising the value of the coin would certainly bring about a rise in the price of commodities, *Decus et Tutamen* (1696), 23. Ruding comments severely on the wrongheadedness of the Chancellor in being guided by Locke's view, *Annals*, ii. 58.

[5] Lowndes, *Essay on Amendment*, p. 214; Macculloch, *A Select Collection of Tracts on Money*, and criticism by Haynes, 203—235.

[6] Sir John Dalrymple, *Memoirs*, 1790, Part iii. book iv. p. 86.

[7] At Exeter, Bristol, Chester, York, and Norwich.

pains to get the maximum product out of each of the presses in London[1]; but the manner in which the work dragged on gave some opportunity for political intrigue[2], and offered a considerable field for speculative dealings in coin[3]. The first steps were taken in the Proclamation of 19 Dec. 1695[4], by which clipped crowns were to cease to be current after 1 Jan. 1696; provision was made for the continued use of un-clipped hammered money, which was punched and retained in circulation temporarily[5]; and the whole operation was con-cluded by 1 March, 1698, when all hammered money was

A.D. 1689
—1776.
which was
carried
through by
Sir Isaac
Newton,

---

[1] Haynes, *op. cit.* p. 138. Newton's technical skill was also effective in exposing the mistakes in Challoner's proposed method of coining, *ib.* p. 174. Haynes bears interesting testimony to his general influence on the work which was carried on under his supervision. "For 25 March, 1696, Mr Isaac Newton, publick Professor of the Mathematicks in Cambridge, the greatest Philosopher, and one of the best Men of this age, was by a great and wise Statesman recom-mended to the favour of the late King for Warden of the King's Mints and Exchanges, for which Station he was peculiarly qualified, because of his extra-ordinary skill in numbers and his great integrity; by the first of which he could judge perfectly well of the Mint Accounts and transactions, as soon as he enter'd upon his office; and by the later, I mean his Integrity, he sett a standard to the conduct and behaviour of every Officer and Clerk in the Mint. Well had it been for the Publick, had he acted a few years sooner in that Station; it's more than probable a good part of the silver monys had been preserved by his vigilant and indefatigable prosecution, from the havock that was made upon 'em by clipping and counterfeiting. And the Assize of our gold monys had been brought to that exactness, as to have prevented a very ill, but a very ordinary practice of picking out and remelting the weighty pieces. This was a very beneficial trade to some persons, but fatall to the Standard and increase of the publick Treasure. Since the Assize of the Coin has been more immediately a part of this Gentleman's care, wee have seen it brought to that extraordinary nicety, especially in the gold monys, as was never known in any reign before this, and perhaps cannot be parallel'd in any other Nation. So that in time we may defy the cunning and Artifice of all mankind to make any advantage by the inequality of the pieces coyn'd at the Tower. Of so great consequence to the State is the well executing the office of Warden of the Mint, and of so good consequence has the execution of it been under this admirable Gentleman that in time he will be no less valued at Home on this account than he is admired by all the *Philosophic World* abroad for his wonderful advancement of the *Mathematicall Sciences*; by the last he has benefitted Mankind, and by the first he has done justice to the English Nation, of which he is one of the chiefest Glorys." pp. 131, 132.

[2] Dalrymple, *op. cit.* Part III. book IV. p. 85.

[3] Evelyn, *Diary*, 1850 (June 11, 1696), II. 343. Kennett, *Complete History*, *William III.* Vol. III. p. 725.

[4] [Brit. Mus. 21. h. 3 (175)]. Permission was given to pay them to the re-ceivers of taxes till a later date, and another Proclamation was issued 4 Jan. 1696 (Brit. Mus. 21. h. 3 (178)), insisting that the Collectors should accept this money.

[5] 7 W. III. c. 1 (9). F. Philipps suggested an ingenious scheme for a temporary token currency of inferior metals. *Archæologia*, XIII. 188.

A.D. 1689
—1776.

demonetised[1]. The cost, in the difference between the value of the defective coin that was accepted, and the new money that was issued, amounted to £2,400,000, and this was defrayed by a house and window tax; but the administration at once felt the benefit from the improved rates at which they could remit money for the expenses of the war.

The recoinage of 1696 had done away with the evils which arose from the existence of a corrupt silver currency; but, in so far as the disappearance of silver had been due to the high rate which it bore relatively to gold, the recoinage had made no difference. Parliament had indeed called down the price of guineas from 30s. to 26s.[2] It was further reduced to 22s.[3], but even at this rate merchants found it worth while to import gold, in order to buy English silver for export. Locke had maintained that the low rating of gold—which kept it from becoming the standard for ordinary payments— was in itself advantageous[4], but common opinion regarded the effects of the arrangement as mischievous. It had been part of Lowndes' scheme for raising the value of silver coins, to bring the nominal ratio of gold and silver pieces into closer *who also* accord with the market rate of gold and silver bullion[5]. It *attempted to settle* was left for Sir Isaac Newton to deal with this problem more *the diffi- culty about* thoroughly[6]; as a consequence, the guinea was called down *the rating of gold.* to 21s. in 1717; but events showed that he had not been altogether successful in his calculations[7], for English silver continued to be exported. Important steps were taken towards the solution of the difficulty in 1774, when there was a general recoinage of gold[8], and silver coins ceased to be legal tender by tale for sums over £25[9]. The demonetisation of silver, which was thus begun, was conclusively justified on grounds of principle by Lord Liverpool in his *Treatise on the Coins of the Realm*, and was carried out more thoroughly

---

[1] 9 W. III. c. 2, § 2.

[2] 7 and 8 W. III. c. 10, § 18.   [3] 7 and 8 W. III. c. 19, § 12.

[4] *Further Considerations concerning raising the Value of Money* (1695), 21, 23.

[5] W(illiam) L(owndes), *A further Essay for the Amendment of the Gold and Silver Coins* (1695), p. 11.

[6] Sir Isaac Newton, *Mint Reports*, in Shaw, *Writers on English Monetary History*, p. 154.

[7] Shaw, *History of Currency*, 231.

[8] Lord Liverpool, *Treatise*, 194.   [9] 14 Geo. III. c. 42, § 2.

in 1816[1], when silver sank to the position of a token money, and gold became the sole standard for legal tender.

216. When action had once been taken for the restoration of the metallic currency, much benefit accrued to the community from the success of the Bank of England in popularising the use of paper as a representative of coined money. This form of circulating medium had been introduced in Sweden in 1658, and Killigrew had advocated its introduction into England in the time of Charles II. There was some doubt at first, both as to the form of wealth which might serve as a guarantee for their payment, and as to the possibility of inducing the public to accept them, though there was a general feeling that if they were rendered available for the payment of taxes[2], ordinary citizens would accept them in discharge of public debts. Both problems were solved in an excellent fashion by the Bank of England; the interest due from Government to this corporation gave it an ample fund to guarantee the convertibility of its notes; and the public were glad to accept this new form of money from a great Company, which offered them loans in its own notes on very favourable terms.

The necessary conditions for the introduction of a convertible paper currency were provided by

The Bank of England consisted of a body of subscribers who lent £1,200,000 to Government in 1694, on the understanding that, out of the payments of tonnage[3], they should receive 8 %, or in all £100,000 per annum. They were also permitted to engage in the business of banking in their corporate capacity; that is to say, they were to receive money on deposit and to lend it out at interest. This sort of business had been carried on to a considerable extent by goldsmiths, but the Bank developed it enormously because they were able to offer better terms. The goldsmiths were accustomed to lend coins, or bills which represented bullion actually in their possession. The Bank was able to make loans to an amount which exceeded the total of the deposits it received; for it could issue notes, to meet which it had no

the Bank of England,

which advanced money on more favourable terms than the goldsmiths.

---

[1] 56 Geo. III. c. 68.

[2] Killigrew, *A Proposal showing how this Nation may be vast gainers by all the sums of money given to the Crown*, p. 8. [Camb. Univ. Lib. II. 24, 8 (1).]

[3] A tax levied on ships according to their tonnage, not on tuns of wine, as in the phrase tunnage and poundage.

A.D. 1689 —1776. cash in reserve, on the faith of the interest due to it from the Government. Foreign bills were discounted at 6 %, and home bills at 4½ %, customers' bills were discounted at 3½ %, and the Bank announced its readiness to make advances on plate, or any of the useful metals at 4 %.

The credit of its notes was attained during the re-coinages, From its formation and until 1844, the banking business of making advances to traders, and the issue of notes by the Bank, were inextricably connected. The success of the new institution, as a bank which offered to advance money at low rates, helped to render its notes generally acceptable. The critical moment in regard to the new currency occurred during the re-coinage in 1696; on the 4th of May, when most of the current cash of the country was withdrawn, and few new coins had been issued from the Mint, an organised attack was made upon the Bank by goldsmiths, who had collected large numbers of its notes and presented them for immediate payment. The Bank was unable to meet its engagements[1], though it continued for a time to satisfy the demands which came upon it in the ordinary course of trade. By making a call upon its proprietors, and by the indulgence of certain creditors, the directors were able to tide over the evil day. Coinage was so scarce for many months that traders were forced to fall back upon substitutes for money[2], and became gradually more habituated to the use of paper

but despite some hesitancy on the part of the public currency; but during the re-coinage there was so much hesitancy about it, that the difficulty of the time was increased. Haynes, as a Mint official, spoke with some contempt of all forms of money, other than the precious metals[3], and there were doubtless many others who shared

---

[1] For excellent suggestions as to the course which should have been pursued by the Directors at this time, Aug. 31, 1696, see *Review of the Universal Remedy of all the Diseases incident to Coin*, p. 56.

[2] Kennett, *Complete History*, III. p. 725.

[3] "The great Arrears of the Government like an Inundation and all sorts of Paper creditt in Orders, Bills, Noats, Bonds, Assignments etc., overflowed the Kingdom. All our wealth seem'd to consist in a little Gold and adulterated Silver, a world of wooden Scores and paper Sums. Never was there known before such vast debts owing for Excise and Customs, upon Bills and Bonds unsatisfyed. All sorts of Provisions grew to an extravagant Price, which was an additional hardship to day labourers and Artificers, besides their want of Mony and Credit. Upon the whole, wee had all the symptoms upon us of a Bankrupt sinking State and an undone people." Haynes, *op. cit.* 94.

his views[1]. For a time the various forms of credit were scarcely negotiable[2]. The notes of the Bank of England were subject to 20 % discount, and Government tallies[3] sank 40 %, 50 %, or even 60 %, according to the nature of the funds assigned in security, since some of them did not yield the expected amounts, while some of the tallies had no specific security assigned them. Montague took active steps for the restoration of public credit on the assembling of Parliament in October, 1696. The Commons resolved to grant a supply, which should make up these deficiencies and give ample security for the punctual payment of tallies[4]; the Act of 1697[5], not only enlarged the capital, and improved the status of the Bank of England, but restored the credit of the administration as well. Tallies, bank-notes and Bank- *various forms of paper credit came into general use,* bills all began to circulate freely[6]. Encouraged by his success, Montague proceeded to issue a large amount of paper currency in the form of Exchequer Bills, bearing interest[7]; without some such money, it would have been physically impossible to collect the taxes required for the support of the war; but by these various expedients " Parlia- *and the issue of Exchequer Bills* ment laid a good Foundation for *Paper Money* to supply the Place of our Silver Coin; for so many Payments were at this time to be made into the *Exchequer*, that when the People had assurance given them that the *Exchequer* notes should be received back again in the payment of the King's Taxes, they were very well satisfied to take them, at first indeed at small Discount but not long after at an Equality. A great number of these Notes were only for Five or Ten Pounds

---

[1] "The ill State of the Coin by Diminution on one Hand, and Adulteration on the other, and the Plan which had been laid for the circulating a sort of fictitious Wealth, such as Exchequer-Tallies, Bank Bills and Government Securities, instead of Gold and Silver, were two other Points which took up the Attention and excited the Concern of every thinking Man." Ralph, *History of England*, II. 564.

[2] The great difficulty of procuring coin, for any purpose, made it improbable that either the Government or the Bank would be able to discharge their obligations in cash.

[3] Tallies were the documents issued when Government borrowed in anticipation of taxes. 9 W. III. c. 44, § 50.

[4] This suggestion is put forward by Robert Murray, *A Proposal for the more easy advancing to the Crown of any fixed sum of Money*, p. 1 (1696).

[5] 8 and 9 W. III. c. 20.   [6] Kennett, *op. cit.* III. 726.

[7] See above, p. 420, n. 7.

which answer'd the necessity of Commerce among the Meaner People, for the Common Conveniences of Life * * *. These Bills passed as so many counters, which the People were satisfied to receive * * * * and these State Counters so well supplied the want of Money, till New Coin was issued from the Mint, that Trade and Commerce were maintained, and Mutual Payments well enough made, to answer the Necessities of the Government and the People[1]." In this way the community at large became habituated to the use of a convertible paper currency. Mercantile bills had long been in vogue[2], and were commonly used by the merchants who frequented Blackwell Hall, or had dealings with goldsmiths. These forms of credit suffered[3] like the rest, during the period when metallic currency was so scarce[4], and there was difficulty in meeting them punctually, but the general effect of the episode was to render paper currency of every sort more familiar than it had ever been before, and so to develop a new and more economical circulating medium.

helped to popularise paper currency.

The Bank also facilitated the formation and employment of Capital,

217.   Important as were these incidental services in floating a public loan and in providing currency, it was as an organ for the formation and diffusion of capital that the Bank gave the greatest impulse to the trading life of England. One projector after another had pointed out the advantages which accrued to Holland from the existence of banks, and insisted that Englishmen might attain similar success if they would employ similar means[5]. One of the earliest of these writers is Samuel Lambe, a London merchant who addressed *Seasonable Observations humbly offered to his Highness the Lord Protector*. In it he advocated the establishment of a bank, not as a means of assisting the Government[6], nor as a body

---

[1] Kennett, *op. cit.* III. 726.

[2] Certain London merchants proposed in 1696 to develop the system by insisting that buyers of goods of £10 and upward should pay in assignable bills. *Commons Journals*, XI. 620.

[3] *Review of the Universal Remedy for all Diseases incident to our Coin* (1696), p. 31.

[4] Complaints of the heavy discount on bills were frequent; *Commons Journals*, XI. Newbury, p. 631; Bury, p. 635 (a); Tamworth, p. 640; Chippenham, p. 624.

[5] See above, 419, n. 2. Compare the Report of the Committee on Decay of Trade in 1669 in the *Hist. Manus. Commission*, VIII. 133.

[6] In 1660 Francis Cradocke proposed the erection of a Land bank. He was aware of the necessity of having a fund of cash, as well as credit, in order to

for enlarging the currency by the issue of notes[1], but as a means of assisting traders generally, and thereby rendering

A.D. 1689
—1776.

make the institution a success, and he suggests expedients by which this may be procured, *An Expedient for taking away all Impositions*, p. 4. He urged that the Crown would be wise to anticipate revenue on easier terms and also would be able to carry on a remunerative banking business, p. 6. His scheme is more fully expounded in his *Wealth Discovered* (1661), and was commended by Charles II. to the consideration of the Council of Trade. Compare also R. Murray's *Proposal for the advancement of trade* (1676) by the establishment of magazines where merchants might deposit surplus stock as security for advances made to them.

[1] Lambe recognised that the merchants who kept their accounts at the Bank could make payments to one another by the transfer of their credit with the Bank; this was one important feature in the practice of the Bank of Amsterdam (Adam Smith, *Wealth of Nations*, Bk. IV. iii. p. 194). "A bank is a certain number of sufficient men of estates and credit joined together in a joint stock, being, as it were, the general cash keepers or treasurers of that place where they are settled, letting out imaginary money at interest at 2 and $\frac{1}{2}$ or 3 l. per cent. to tradesmen, or others that agree with them for the same, and making payment thereof by assignation, and passing each man's account from one to another with much facility and ease, and saving much trouble in receiving and paying of money, besides many suits in law and other losses and inconveniences, which do much hinder trade; for oftentimes a merchant hath goods come from some place beyond the sea, which he is not willing to sell at the price current, knowing either that he shall lose by them, or that he hopes they will yield more in England, or some other country where there will be more need of them; therefore is desirous to keep them, and yet drive on his trade, which peradventure he cannot well do wanting stock, so much of it lying dead in the said commodity, therefore procures credit in the bank for so much as he shall have occasion for, at the rates aforesaid, and receives and makes payment thereof where he hath occasion for it, by assignment in bank. As, for example: The said merchant buys cloth of a clothier for 100 l. value, more or less, and goes with him to the bank, where he is debtor so much money as he takes up, and the clothier is made creditor in account for so much as he sold for to the said merchant, then such clothier having occasion to pay money to a stapler or woolmonger, for wool he doth buy of him; so the said clothier is made debtor, and the woolmonger creditor in account; The said woolmonger hath bought his wool of a country farmer, and must pay him for it; so the woolmonger is made debtor, and the farmer creditor: The farmer must pay his rent to the landlord with the proceed of the said wool; so the farmer is made debtor, and such landlord creditor: The landlord for his occasion buys goods of a mercer, grocer, vintner, or the like; then he is made debtor, and such mercer or other tradesman, creditor; then peradventure such mercer, or other tradesman, buys goods of the same merchant that took up the first credit in the bank, and stands yet debtor there; but upon sale of goods to the mercer, or other tradesman, both clear their account in the bank, and such mercer, or other tradesman, is made debtor, and the said merchant creditor: Thus every man's account is cleared, and so in all trades, as occasion presents; which way, if it be thought fit to be settled for a trial at London, I verily believe will be found so convenient, and such an encouragement to trade, by increase of the stock of the land, and be such an ease to the people, that it will be soon desired that others might be also settled at Edinburgh for Scotland, at Dublin for Ireland, and in some other chief cities and shire towns in England, as York, Bristol, and Exeter, &c., for the

A.D. 1689
—1776.
*and proved,
as had
been antici-
pated, to
be of great
advantage* them better able to compete with the Dutch in foreign trades and to hold their own in English undertakings as well[1]. The Bank would "furnish factors in England with credit to pay custom and charges of a great cargo of goods, which may on a sudden be consigned to them; for many times such English factors may be of a good estate and credit, yet have not always a great cash lying by them for such uses (though the Dutch are seldom without it) therefore may often times be forced to strain their credit, to take up money at interest or sell all, or part with such goods at under-rate for want thereof, which may be a great prejudice to themselves, and loss to their principals; and is believed, causeth many such great commissions to be carried from the English and consigners to the Dutch residing in England, to their great benefit and advantage, and loss and prejudice of the English Nation * * * *. They will furnish many young men with Stock, that have, by their industry and well spent time and travels in their apprenticeships gained good experience in foreign traffic, but when they are come to be for themselves, wanting stock, friends or credit to begin to trade with (being commonly younger brothers)[2], are thereby much discouraged, and thinking to drive away such discontent, do often-times fall into bad company and take ill courses, to the utter ruine of their hopes and fortunes, which otherwise might have made good Commonwealths-Men, which is the greatest reason why so few young men, out of so many entertained, do come to good.

"They will preserve many good men from failing and losing their credit; for instead of losing by trade they will

furtherance of trade, by holding correspondence with each other, that which I do not apprehend or know any way better to equal the Dutch in trade, both at home and abroad, in buying and selling all sorts of commodities, and making quick returns, and also so much exceed them, as by far this land lies more convenient for trade than theirs doth, and will also suddenly inrich the people, and increase and maintain the maritime power and strength thereof." S. Lambe, *Seasonable Observations*, in *Somers Tracts*, VI. 457.

[1] Lambe, *Somers Tracts*, VI. p. 456.

[2] Dutch tradesmen were in the habit of dividing their money equally among their children so as to give all a start in life; while an English tradesman was likely to give "mean portions" to his younger sons and make the eldest "possessor of the greatest part of his estate, who addicts himself often-times to the pleasures of Hunting, Hawking and such like pastimes, betaking himself wholly to a Country Life," *Ib.* p. 453.

by the well regulating of it be more certain of profit, and _{A.D. 1689}
the quick and sure satisfaction of a debt by assignment in ^{—1776.}
Bank will preserve many a good man's credit, which many
times is impaired, though he may have a good estate out in
Trade beyond the Seas and cannot command it, or because
he cannot receive his money where it is owing to him, to
make payment where it is due. It being seldom seen that
any of the Dutch Nation fail: and if any of them by losses
do miscarry, being known to be industrious, are soon credited
again with stock out of bank, or otherwise, to recover themselves again by trade.

"And many other (conveniences) which trial and ex- *to many*
perience will daily discover, as quick and easy, paying bills *trades;*
of exchanges, foreign or domestic, and all other payments,
preventing fraudulent payments, in counterfeit and clipt
coin or mistelling money, rectifying errors in accompts,
which occasion Law suits, preventing theft and breaking
open houses, where money is suspected to lie, and robbing
on the high ways graziers, carriers or others that use to
carry money from fairs, or other places, which may be
returned by assignment in bank, whereas now the several
hundreds in many places are forced to guard such as carry
money for fear of their being robbed, and such hundred
paying them the money they lost as it hath often fallen
out of late times."

This enumeration of the felt disadvantages from the
non-existence of banks throws very clear light on the
advantages which accrued to the trading public by the institution of the Bank of England. As a bank of deposit,
it greatly developed the business already undertaken by
goldsmiths, and gave many people the opportunity of
leaving their hoards in the safe keeping of an institution,
which could use money remuneratively by lending it to
traders. In this way the Bank did a great deal to add
to the available capital of the country. Davenant and the *it did not*
other critics of the Bank had maintained, with considerable *divert
money from*
plausibility, that the Bank would divert capital from pro- *productive
employ-*
ductive employments[1] to be lent to the State; but as a *ments,*

[1] *Essay upon Ways and Means*, in *Works*, I. 24.

A.D. 1689
—1776.
matter of fact this fear proved illusory. The security and facilities for investment, offered by the Funds, tended to the more rapid formation of capital, and conferred lasting benefits on the trading community. From this time onwards it became a usual thing for careful men to trade upon borrowed capital, since they found they could habitually obtain the loan of it on easy terms. During the latter part of the seventeenth century England was hampered in every way, both as to internal development, and commerce, and colonisation, by lack of capital; and the banking system which was inaugurated in 1696 had an enormous influence in remedying these evils.

but gave opportunities for trading on borrowed capital.

218. It was probably inevitable that, until a considerable body of experience had been accumulated, there should be many and serious blunders as to the nature of credit, and the conditions under which the forms of credit are available to serve as money. The men of the eighteenth century found that they had a new and very powerful economic instrument in their hands, and they only gradually discovered how to use it wisely. Strictly speaking credit is not wealth[1], though a man who has credit is able to procure the use of other people's wealth. The forms of credit supply a method of anticipating expected wealth, and of obtaining immediate control over certain sums of money, because of expectations in regard to the future. Whenever the expectations are mistaken, and the actual wealth obtained falls short of the anticipated wealth, there is a danger of serious loss. By the judicious restriction of his advances, the banker may check over-sanguine speculation as to possible gain in the future. His readiness to grant loans on easy terms is of course an encouragement to speculation; it increases the quantity of paper money available, and tends to raise the rates of prices, and to render business more remunerative. On the other hand, the action of bankers in suddenly withdrawing accustomed facilities may create a feeling of alarm and distrust, which will make men unwilling to accept paper money at all, and cause a sudden fall in values of every kind.

The nature and conditions of credit were imperfectly recognised,

---

[1] On the difficulties of various trading companies who sunk their wealth in concessions and had no circulating capital see below, p. 466.

Until considerable experience had been gained, there was special danger that the Bank, which exercised a unique influence over English credit, should on the one hand aggravate the evils of a period of inflation, or on the other should induce commercial disaster by the hasty reduction of its issues. The difficulties of the directors were aggravated by the *business assumed a speculative character,* fact that a change was coming over the habits of ordinary traders; legitimate business was becoming more speculative in character. In the days when regulated companies had kept an effective control over the conditions of commerce, and enforced a system of well-ordered trade, there was little room for enterprise in pushing business. After the Revolution, the companies had so far sunk in importance that it was possible for merchants to ship goods in any quantities they preferred, and to speculate on changes in the market rate for goods. The increased possibility of borrowing capital, when opportunity for using it offered, must have enabled shrewd and well-informed men to rise rapidly to considerable affluence. The system of joint-stock trading rendered it easy for the outside public to have a part in commercial gains, without the necessity of devoting themselves to the cares of business. So many companies were formed, that transactions in their shares became increasingly frequent, and this fresh field of business opened up a new range for speculative dealing. Davenant, Hutcheson, Defoe, and all the leading economic writers of the day, complain of the *especially in connection with the Stock exchange,* rapid development of stock-exchange gambling which occurred at this time. The new trades, which were being opened up, and the new industrial facilities, which the credit system seemed to offer, appeared to have turned the heads of many of the men of that day. Large sums had been made, especially by bankers, and it seemed as if there were no end to the fortunes which might be acquired. There was, in consequence, great violence in the changes of prices. If a business was doing well, the gains were exaggerated, and many men were eager to rush into it, so that the price which had to be paid for shares was forced up unduly; on the other hand, if a stock fell, there seems to have been a regular rush to get rid of it, and the price fell with rapidity.

These violent fluctuations must have given great opportunities to stockbrokers; and one of the reasons why the
new finance was condemned was because of the stimulus
it gave to this gambling spirit; it seemed to divert men
from honest enterprise, and encouraged the wildest speculation[1]. In some cases, indeed, Government played for this
gambling spirit; the great financial expedient, in the year
before the Bank of England was floated, was a lottery; a
sum of money was raised, on all of which interest was to
be paid in the usual way, but every fortieth share was
to be entitled in addition to an annuity of a larger or
smaller amount lasting for life[2]. This speculative element
proved a great attraction, and it may have been the cheapest
way of floating the loan, extravagant as the terms appear;
but it was severely condemned at the time, because of the
countenance which Government gave to the gambling spirit.
and bubble companies were formed This spirit showed itself in its most startling fashion, in
1720, when an extraordinary number of wild projects were
floated[3]; and the shares of other undertakings were quoted
at fancy prices. The public were not accurately informed
as to the possible profits in various lines of trade. They
formed the wildest estimates of the gain that might accrue
from certain political concessions or from new industrial
inventions. Of these schemes the most celebrated was the

---

[1] Compare Sir John Barnard's speech during the debate on the Bill to prevent
the "infamous practice" of Stock-jobbing. *Parl. Hist.* IX. 54.

[2] 5 W. and M. c. 7, § 39.

[3] There had been many such schemes before. Defoe, writing in 1697, complains
of them bitterly. "There are and that too many, fair pretences of fine Discoveries,
new Inventions, Engines and I know not what, which being advanc'd in Notion,
and talk'd up to great things to be perform'd when such and such sums of Money
shall be advanc'd, and such and such Engines are made, have rais'd the Fancies of
Credulous People to such height, that meerly on the shadow of Expectation, they
have form'd Companies, chose Committees, appointed Officers, Shares and Books,
rais'd great Stocks, and cri'd up an empty Notion to that degree that People have
been betray'd to part with their Money for Shares in a *New-Nothing* and when
the Inventors have carri'd on the test till they have sold all their own Interest
they leave the Cloud to vanish of itself, and the poor Purchasers to Quarrel with
one another, and go to Law about Settlements, Transferrings, and some Bone or
other thrown among 'em by the Subtlety of the Author to lay the blame of the
Miscarriage upon themselves....If I should name Linnen-Manufactures, Saltpeter-
Works, Copper Mines, Diving Engines, Dipping and the like for instances of this
I should I believe do no wrong to Truth." *Essay on Projects*, pp. 11—13.

South Sea Bubble, which was formed to carry on trade with Spanish America in the hope that large profits would be reaped from the slave-trade and from whale-fishing. There appeared to be an inexhaustible mine of wealth, and the shares rose rapidly from April 1720, when they stood at £120, till July, when they are said to have reached £1020[1]. But, while on the one hand the possible profit had been overrated, the capital of the Company had been sunk in procuring concessions and in lending money to Government, so that there was no sufficient means of carrying on trade. When such mistakes were made in commerce there is no wonder that men entirely miscalculated the possible profits from new inventions. The list of projects which were floated in 1720 shows an extraordinary willingness on the part of the public to take shares in any scheme however wild[2]. As in more recent times, mining offered a great field for such speculation; there were one or two notorious projectors, like Sir Humphry Mackworth[3], who were for ever producing new

---

[1] Postlethwayt, *Dictionary*, s.v. Actions, I. 14. The South Sea Company was partly a trading and partly a financial company; and as the promoters had secured the assiento contract for supplying Spanish America with slaves, and were also engaged in whale-fishery, they appeared to have great opportunities for profitable commerce (*Parl. Hist.* VII. 628). It was, however, as a financial company that they seemed likely to have a fund of wealth which would give them unexampled facilities for using their credit, as the directors were preparing to take over the whole of the National Debt. Under the influence of these large possibilities of gain the public rushed to buy shares, which rose rapidly in market price (*Parl. Hist.* VII. 653). Immense sums were made by those who speculated for the rise, while many *bona-fide* investors who had bought in when the stock was quoted at a high premium were forced to submit to terrible loss. The proprietors who had held on through the rise and the subsequent fall did not, of course, lose so seriously. The attempt to do justice in connection with the affairs of the Company was beset with many difficulties. On the one hand it was requisite to preserve the public engagements unviolated, on the other it was desirable if possible to punish the speculators for the misrepresentations which had gulled the public, and if possible to deprive them of their ill-gotten gains. But it was exceedingly difficult to discriminate between the different classes of shareholders, who had bought at different dates, in any attempt to reimburse them for their losses. The subject is discussed with great care in a series of tracts which were published at the time by Archibald Hutcheson, the Member for Hastings, who criticised the scheme in its earlier stages and kept his head cool during the disaster. A good account will be found in Andréadès, *Hist. de la Banque d'Angleterre*, I. 179. The career of the South Sea Company in its financial aspect was at an end; it did not find whaling profitable, and had competitors in the slave-trade.

[2] See the Order of 12th July, 1720, and list of Bubbles, *Parl. Hist.* VII. 656.

[3] *Parl. Hist.* VI. 892.

C.   29

A.D. 1689
—1776.

schemes. The terrible crisis of 1720[1] was the occasion of efforts to check the operations of projectors[2], and rendered the public more chary of being beguiled by every romance and made them realise the importance of capital as the basis of credit.

The Bank of England acquired experience

The speculative mania at the time of the South Sea Bubble was the most disastrous in the century, and it was only by paying in sixpences, and having recourse to other expedients for delaying its payments in cash, that the Bank saved its own credit, and survived in the general crash. There were other occasions when the Bank of England was fairly successful in intervening, either to check the fever of speculation, or to facilitate recovery after the beginnings of disaster. The directors profited to some extent by financial

while Law's failure in France was a warning,

disasters in other lands; the failure in 1720 of Law's great scheme in France[3] was a useful warning as to the danger of an over-issue of paper-currency, and it seriously interfered with the development of banking and credit in that country. On the other hand, the growth of British commerce in all parts of the world rendered England an increasingly favourable

and London was becoming the chief financial centre of the world.

field for the investment of capital. London was coming to rival Amsterdam as the financial centre of the world, and the wisdom of the management of the Bank, during the critical year 1763, did much to strengthen its position. The difficulty originated on the Continent, as the Bank of Amsterdam had refused support to a firm named Neufville, which had connections in many business centres, and there were numerous failures in Hamburg and Germany. The effect of these disasters extended to England; but the Bank was able to make such advances as to prevent the results from being fatal to many of the mercantile houses here[4].

The reaction after over-trading

The successive crises of this century were all due to similar causes, and followed on periods of commercial over-trading. From 1769 onwards there was a very rapid increase in the exports from the country[5], and early in the summer

---

[1] Compare the petitions in *Parl. Hist.* vii. 760.

[2] On the Bubble Act, see p. 816 below.

[3] For an account of this remarkable man see J. S. Nicholson, *Money and Monetary Problems*, 165.

[4] Macleod, *op. cit.* i. 502; Adam Smith. *Wealth of Nations*, 131.

[5] Playfair's *Commercial and Political Atlas* (1801).

of 1772, the inevitable reaction came. The Bank was able A.D. 1689
—1776. to support commercial credit satisfactorily for a time; but the unexpected failure of the Heales[1], a large London house, through defalcations amounting to £300,000, by one of the partners named Fordyce, involved so many other firms in disaster that a general collapse ensued, which seemed almost as serious as the bursting of the South Sea Bubble. As Fordyce had also carried on banking in Scotland, the effects of his conduct extended to that country, and brought about the fall of various trading houses. Among these was the *brought about the* newly-founded Ayr Bank, which had been much less success- *failure of* fully managed than its older rivals. A run began on it just *the Ayr Bank in* a week after Fordyce had disappeared; after eight days it *1772.* had to stop payment. There was still £800,000 worth of its paper in circulation, and the distress the failure occasioned in Scotland could only be compared with the disaster caused by the Darien scheme[2].

There was another outburst of commercial prosperity on *The Bank* *warded off* the cessation of the American War in 1782. The sudden *disaster in* opening up of markets encouraged reckless speculation, and *1782,* it is said that the Directors of the Bank were incautious in their issues and thus fostered the evil[3]; but they had wisdom to retrace their steps in time. Their gold reserve was re- duced to a very low ebb, but they thought it was possible, by carefully restricting their issues, to tide over the time till specie should arrive, in payment of goods already sent to foreign markets. The point of safety would be marked by a turn in the exchanges, and they refused to make a loan even to Government, in May 1783. It was not till the following October that the favourable signs appeared, and that they felt justified, with regard to their own safety, in extending their issues, by lending to the Government[4].

Ten years later, with continued peace, there had been *but the* *expansion* a great expansion of trading and there were premonitory *of trade in* symptoms of disaster. The period might perhaps have been *1792* tided over but for the outbreak of the Revolutionary War[5]. Almost immediately afterwards a great firm of corn

---

[1] Macleod, *op. cit.* I. 504.   [2] *Ib.* II. 215.   [3] *Ib.* I. 507.
[4] *Ib.* I. 508.   [5] See below, p. 674.

A.D. 1689
—1776.
merchants was gazetted, and the results were felt immediately all over the country. The bankers in Newcastle[1]
made a gallant but ineffective struggle. It is said that of
*was fol-
lowed by a
crisis*
the four hundred country banks in England at that time
no fewer than one hundred failed, while many others only
succeeded in weathering the storm with the greatest difficulty. The banks in Exeter and the West of England
escaped most easily, but the wave of disaster spread over
the North and the panic extended to Glasgow. There was
a total destruction of credit, and substantial houses were in
imminent danger of failure. It is not perhaps possible to
say that this disaster could have been prevented, but it has
been generally maintained that the directors of the Bank of
*which the
Bank
failed to
minimise.*
England acted with undue precipitancy; the suddenness of
their refusal to allow the usual accommodation, gave a shock
to credit, which would have been much less severe if their
action had been more gradual. Besides this, the extraordinary over-issues of paper in France were causing a flow
of gold to this country; the exchanges were favourable, and
under these circumstances the directors, especially after the
experience of 1782, need not have been so uncompromising
in their attitude and so timorous for the safety of the
bank[2]. Government did much to relieve the tension by
issuing Exchequer Bills[3].

*The
conditions
of issuing
convertible
paper*
Other errors arose from a failure to understand how
important it was that paper-money should be really convertible, and to see that a bank could only be carried on when
it had wealth in a form which could be promptly realised
and used for meeting its engagements. This had been the
fundamental error in Chamberlayne's abortive scheme of the
Land Bank. The public knew better than the projectors[4]

[1] Macleod, i. 510.
[2] Sir F. Baring's evidence before the Bullion Committee. Macleod, i. 510.
[3] Ib. ii. 216. See p. 441 above.
[4] The promoters had also made extraordinary blunders in calculating the
value of landed property. They held that land which a man was entitled to for
a hundred years was worth a hundred times the rent, and not something like
twenty years' purchase, or twenty times the rent. They thus calculated the land,
not at its present value to the purchaser, but at the accumulated value which
would accrue by setting aside the rent annually for a century. The prospective
savings from land a century hence are not the same as the worth of the land now,
but the present worth of the land is the only satisfactory security as a basis
for raising credit now. Dr Chamberlayne's project had been approved by the

that it was impossible to circulate bills on the security of A.D. 1689 —1776. wealth which could not be rapidly realised, and they would not subscribe. Experience as to the depreciation of notes *were becoming* which could be circulated, even though not immediately con- *better* vertible, was gradually acquired. It was brought to light *understood.* in Scotland by the issue of notes with an optional clause[1], which permitted the bank to defer payment for a period of six months, and still more forcibly in England by the phenomena which occurred after the suspension of cash payments in 1797[2].

219. The fact that Scottish economic life since the *The bank-* Union has developed in such remarkable independence of *ing system in Scotland* that of England is principally due to the special features *facilitated the forma-* of the Scottish banking system. Poor as Scotland was, and *tion of* large as is the monetary drain to which she has been ex- *capital* posed[3], she has been able to dispense with the aid of wealthy *there.* outsiders for the development of her resources, and has relied almost entirely on her own capital. There are curious links of connection, and curious differences, between the foundation and the development of banking, both of issue and for deposit, in the two countries.

The Bank of Scotland was founded at the same time as *The Bank* the Bank of England, and on very similar lines so far as its *of Scotland* business was concerned; but as there was no public debt to be financed, the Scotch institution never established close relations with the Government, or obtained a permanent monopoly[4]. It was started in the same year as the Darien Company, and perhaps seemed a less promising enterprise than that unfortunate undertaking. Its capital was to consist of £12,000 sterling (£100,000 Scots), and by the beginning of 1696 £10,000 was paid up[5], so that the Bank of Scotland was able to start business, and to make advances of its notes to the public; and from 1704 onwards it circu- *issued £1* lated the £1 notes[6] which have formed such a leading feature *notes to the public;*

Commons in 1693, and was favoured by the Government in 1696 (Macaulay, IV. 691).

[1] See below, p. 454.   [2] See p. 699 below.

[3] R. Somers, *The Scotch Banks*, 116.

[4] Acts of Parliament of Scotland, 17 July, 1695, c. 88. They had a monopoly for 21 years.   [5] A. W. Kerr, *History of Banking in Scotland*, 23.

[6] There appears to have been an unsuccessful issue in 1699. Graham, *The £1 Note*, 14.

A.D. 1689
—1776.
in the paper currency of Scotland[1]. In that year the Bank had to face difficulties, very similar to those which endangered the Bank of England in 1696. The drain of bullion, and rumour that the Privy Council were about to enhance the coin, caused a run on the Bank. It was *it had to* necessary to make calls upon the proprietors, and to retrench *reduce its* *operations* expenses by giving up the branches at Glasgow, Dundee, *in 1704,* Aberdeen, and Montrose; but eventually the credit of the Bank was completely restored, and it entered on a period of steady prosperity.

and, after *a period* In 1727, the original body found itself exposed to the *of fierce* competition of a rival institution, which obtained a charter *competition* *with the* as the Royal Bank of Scotland. It was an offshoot from *Royal* *Bank,* the body of Commissioners, who had been empowered to administer the money paid by England to Scotland[2] as an equivalent for coming under a share of the Parliamentary obligations with regard to the National Debt. The Commissioners had expended most of the money in meeting the claims which arose in connection with the Darien scheme and fostering fisheries and manufactures; the balance in their hands was considerable, however, and they obtained powers to engage, as a corporation, in banking business. The competition of the two institutions gave rise to some unseemly contests; each tried by collecting the notes of the other and presenting them, with a demand for immediate payment, to cripple its rival; and each had recourse to such expedients as paying in sixpences to balk the attack. Eventually they introduced an "optional clause[3]" into the notes, and this rendered these hostile demonstrations futile, though at some slight sacrifice of the value of the paper, as it was no longer convertible at sight.

This rivalry was not wholly mischievous however; the Royal Bank developed a system of giving cash credits[4] for a definite amount, to any respectable and industrious person for whom two substantial men were ready to vouch. In this

[1] *Report of Select Committee of House of Lords on Promissory Notes*, 1826-7, VI. 473, printed pag. 96.

[2] See above, p. 418.

[3] Kerr, *op. cit.* 45.

[4] *Report of Select Committee of Lords on the Circulation of Promissory Notes*, 1826-7, VI. 380, printed pag. 4.

way it became comparatively easy for any well-doing young *A.D. 1689 —1776.* man to obtain a start in business on his own account. This *developed* method of making advances became exceedingly popular *a system* with the public, and the practice was soon adopted by the *of cash credits* Bank of Scotland as well, and became a second special feature in the Scottish banking system. There does not appear to be any certain evidence that the Bank of Scotland was in the habit of receiving deposits from its customers at first[1]. But it afterwards developed the business, especially *and received deposits.* in the way of accepting sums for definite periods, and granting interest upon them[2].

As, however, there was no restriction in regard to banking in Scotland, a considerable number of new institutions came into being, especially in connection with particular trades. The British Linen Company, the third *The rivalry of well-conducted banks* of the Scotch banks[3] in age, was, as its name implies, founded to assist in the development of the linen manufacture. A local bank was started at Dundee; and a similar institution at Ayr caused wide-spread ruin in the West of Scotland by its failure in 1772. On the whole, however, the system was prudently and successfully carried on; and several private firms developed a banking department in connection with mercantile business. It does not appear that these private banks in Scotland had been, generally speaking, connected with the goldsmiths' trade. The best known of them all, that founded by the Coutts'[4] and associated with the name of Sir William Forbes, was largely engaged in the corn trade.

In one way or another, however, the Scotch became *led to a general adoption* rapidly habituated to the use of a convertible paper currency, and a very large proportion of the population were enabled

---

[1] Graham, *The £1 Note*, 13.

[2] In his evidence before the Commissioners Mr Paul distinguishes the running and deposit account. "The second branch of deposits consists of small sums placed in the hands of the Bank at interest which have been in general the savings of their industry, and which are put into the hands of the Bank to accumulate * * * in general these deposits are very seldom removed, excepting when an individual has occasion to build a house or begin a business." *Report*, 1826-7, VI. 450, printed pag. 74.

[3] A. W. Kerr, *op. cit.* 58.

[4] Sir W. Forbes, *Memoirs of a Banking House*, 7.

A.D. 1689
—1776.
of paper
money in
Scotland.
to take advantage of facilities for accumulating and for
obtaining the use of capital; these appear to have been
the chief agency in bringing about the development of the
Scotch fisheries—to the practical exclusion of the Dutch[1].

XIV. PARLIAMENTARY REGULATION OF
COMMERCIAL DEVELOPMENT.

*Burleigh's
scheme of
fostering
all elements
of power
by regu-
lation had
ceased to be
appro-
priate;*
220. A consideration of the aims, which statesmen set
before themselves after the Revolution, in concluding commercial treaties with foreign powers and regulating intercourse
between different parts of the empire, brings out the fact that
England had already entered on a new phase of economic life.
The main lines of Burleigh's scheme for the promotion of power
were being maintained, but marked differences underlay the
apparent continuity of policy. Burleigh had been primarily
concerned in developing national resources of every kind;
the system of well-ordered commerce had been an appropriate
means for securing the steady progress of trade, *pari passu*
with the improvement of lands and manufactures. During
the seventeenth century, however, the country had outgrown
the facilities which could be offered by the machinery of
regulated trade. The statesmen of the Revolution era were
clear that, in so far as any branch of commerce had a
healthful effect upon industry, it should be pushed as rapidly
and energetically as possible.

*the Tories
would have
given dis-
criminating
permission
to com-
merce of
all kinds,*
There was indeed, as Professor Ashley has pointed out[2],
a remarkable body of men who took an even larger view of
the policy which should be pursued towards trade. They
would have been content to impose preferential duties, so
as to favour our own industries especially, but they were
not prepared to stigmatise any branch of trade as injurious
to the realm. They argued that the very existence of a
trade showed that it was directly advantageous to some
classes of consumers, and they were doubtful whether this
benefit was altogether discounted by possible injury to the
productive energy of the country. At all events, it was clear

---

[1] Report, 1826–7, vi. 507 (Dunsmure), printed pag. 131.

[2] *Surveys, Historic and Economic*, 268.

to these writers that to allow the carrying on of commerce with many lands, while the less desirable branches of trade were subjected to high duties, was an easy method of increasing the revenue of the Crown[1].

The more generous economic policy thus commended itself to the Court party, who took the line of favouring a large customs revenue, even when it was to the disadvantage of the landed interest. Their opponents urged that any *but the Whigs discouraged* branches of commerce, which seemed to compete with the *trades which did* industry of the country, should be prohibited, and that those *not react* which affected the manufacturing interests favourably should *favourably* be developed as far and as rapidly as possible. The opposition *on industry,* statesmen had thus reached a point of view from which they were inclined to discard the policy of well-ordered trade altogether, and to adopt modern tactics in the branches of commerce they approved. They did not limit the supply of English goods with the view of keeping up the price obtainable in foreign markets; they tried to increase the volume of business, even though the prices at which particular transactions took place might sometimes be very low. The struggle in regard to commercial policy between the Court and the Country parties was fought out over the French trade, and the Country party won.

The Whigs were undoubtedly right in attaching a very high *and relied* importance to the influence of trade on industrial progress; *on indications* and the Tories were not in a position to establish their point, *furnished* and make it clear that a real benefit accrued to the country, *by the balance of trade* indirectly and ultimately, through the existence of branches of commerce which seemed to be injurious to certain industries. The public had come to see that the prohibition of the export of bullion should not be applied mechanically. Mun had convinced his readers that, by means of a small export of silver, a series of commercial movements might be set on foot, which would result in the return of a greatly increased mass of bullion to the country. The protectionists employed the balance of trade as an index of what was good or bad in commercial affairs, as if it might be relied on absolutely, and they held the field. Not one of the controversialists of

[1] See below, p. 600.

the day was able to show conclusively that the apparent injury wrought to English industry by the French trade was either illusory, or was indirectly compensated. From this distance of time we can see that there were cases, when the sacrifice of colonial trade to the supposed interests of the realm was detrimental to the manufactures which Parliament was most eager to encourage[1]. But the indirect effects of trade are not easily analysed or exhibited; even Adam Smith could do little more than point out that any gain, which arose from the mercantilist protection of industry, was purchased at an absurdly dear rate.

The effort
to render
trade sub-
servient to
industry
led to

The simmering discontent which had been felt since the time of Cromwell[2], in regard to the rapidly increasing importations of manufactured goods from France[3], gave rise to a vigorous agitation after 1667, when Colbert revised the French tariffs, and imposed prohibitory rates on English cloth. A document was prepared by Houblon, Papillon and other leading London merchants, which put forward statistical data for asserting that England was a loser by nearly a million (£965,128. 17s. 4d.) a year, in her trade with France[4]. The opposition party in Parliament took up the matter eagerly in the following session; but it was not till 1678[5] that they were successful in carrying a bill for the prohibition of French trade. The contest was renewed when James II. came to the throne[6], as the prohibition was removed and a heavy tariff was imposed instead; but at the Revolution the Whigs reverted to the policy of prohibiting the French trade[7] as hurtful. In spite of the large amount

---

[1] The Molasses Act, by hampering the New Englanders in their trade, tended to reduce their ability to purchase manufactures. Ashley, *Surveys*, 330. See below, p. 482.

[2] There are some signs of making common cause with France in the colonial policy of Charles I. (see above, p. 356), but the combined economic and political jealousy of France which was so strongly felt by the Whigs seems to have been aroused by the commercial policy which was pursued by Cromwell and maintained by Charles II. The large imports from France were beneficial to the revenue; and both the Protector and King Charles II. preferred a policy which placed money in the hands of the executive. This was an important element in the curious process of the formation of parties at the Restoration; the Court, rather than the Country party, were following on the lines laid down during the Interregnum.

[3] Ashley, *Surveys*, 272.   [4] *Parl. Hist.* App. cxv.

[5] 29 and 30 C. II. c. 1, § 70.   [6] 1 James II. cc. 6, 7. Ashley, *op. cit.* 282.

[7] 1 W. and M. c. 34. *An Act for Prohibiting all Trade and Commerce with*

of smuggling which was developed under this system of
prohibition, the measure was generally regarded as suc-
cessful in its object of securing the home market to British *the prohi-bition of*
manufacturers of textile goods.   The Act of 1678 was spoken *French*
of as marking an era in the history of English commerce[1]; *trade,*
and it undoubtedly denotes the time when the English commercial system began to be consciously shaped in the form
in which it was successfully attacked by Adam Smith.   From
the Revolution till the revolt of the colonies, the regulation
of commerce was considered, not so much with reference to
other elements of national power, or even in its bearing
on revenue, but chiefly with a view to the promotion of
industry.

This is illustrated very clearly in the attitude which was *and the securing*
taken by the British public in regard to two of the com- *of the*
mercial treaties of the time.   There had been days when *Portuguese market for*
wool, or undressed cloth, had been the chief commodities of *cloth*
English export, but eighteenth century statesmen were more
concerned in trying to secure a better market for finished
cloth.   This was the aim of Mr Methuen, in carrying through
the much vaunted treaty with Portugal, which was concluded
in 1703.   All those who were interested in the widely diffused
manufacture of English cloth, regarded the negotiations as
most successful, since they served to reopen a market which
had been partially closed.   During the preceding twenty
years, the Portuguese, in the hope of fostering a native
manufacture, had prohibited all importation of English
cloth[2].   Mr Methuen was sent as a special ambassador to
Portugal and intimated that it would be very acceptable to

France. "Forasmuch as your Majestyes upon just and honourable grounds have
beene pleased to declare actuall Warr with France and to enter into Severall
Confederacies for carrying on the same and that it hath beene found by long
experience that the Importing of French Wines, Vinegar, Brandy, Linnen, Silks,
Salt, Paper and other the Commodities of the Growth, Product or Manufacture of
France or of the Territories or Dominions of the French King hath much
exhausted the Treasure of this Nation lessened the Value of the native Commodities and Manufactures thereof and greatly impoverished the English Artificers
and Handycrafts and caused great detriment to this Kingdome in generall Bee it
therefore enacted" etc.

[1] Smith, *Memoirs of Wool*, I. 325.

[2] *British Merchant*, III. 82.   This Portuguese manufacture appears to have
been due to the energy of an Irishman in 1680 who took a band of artisans over
with him and established the trade.

the Queen of England "if the woollen cloths, and the rest of the woollen manufactures of Britain, might be admitted into Portugal, the prohibition of them being taken off[1]." He was *by admitting Portuguese wines on special terms.* able to carry this point: on the other hand, he conceded to the Portuguese that their wines should always be admitted into England at two-thirds of the duty paid on French wines. This treaty had some curious minor results; through its operation the culture of the vine was somewhat extended in Portugal[2]; and the wines thus introduced into England supplanted Burgundy[3] on the tables of those who adapted their consumption to the supposed advantage of the realm. The man who drank his bottle of port could feel that he was dealing with people who were large customers for English cloth, and indirectly facilitating the employment of the poor at home. The extent to which Portugal took off our manufactures, and thus encouraged industry in this country, appeared to be measured by the vast amount of Brazilian

---

[1] Chalmers, *Collection of Treaties*, II. 304 (27 Dec. 1703). In his adverse criticism of this treaty Adam Smith (*Wealth of Nations*, IV. c. 6, p. 224) does not take sufficient account of the circumstances under which the agreement was made. Englishmen, who were bargaining for liberty to trade at all, could hardly hope to obtain exclusive or preferential privileges at a single stroke. According to the statement in the *British Merchant* (III. 89) the cloth manufacture in Portugal was entirely ruined when the market was opened to British goods. The subsequent revival of the manufacture by the Marquis of Pombal rendered the arrangement nugatory, so far as English manufacturing interests were concerned. Leone Levi, *History of British Commerce*, 29.

[2] The Portuguese appear to have been very anxious to maintain their special advantage over France in the English market. *Parl. Hist.* VI. 792.

[3] Stanhope, *History of England, comprising the Reign of Queen Anne*, 112. The taste of wine drinkers in America was affected by similar considerations. Madeira wine, not being an European commodity, could be imported directly into America and the West Indies; these countries enjoyed a free trade to the island of Madeira, in all the non-enumerated commodities. "These circumstances had probably introduced that general taste for Madeira wine which our officers found established in all our colonies at the commencement of the war which began in 1755, and which they brought back with them to their mother country, where that wine had not been much in fashion before. Upon the conclusion of that war, in 1763 (by the 4th Geo. III. c. 15, § 12), all the duties, except £3. 10s., were allowed to be drawn back upon the exportation to the colonies of all wines except French wines, to the commerce and consumption of which national prejudice would allow no sort of encouragement" (Adam Smith, *Wealth of Nations*, Book IV. c. 4, p. 204). The long-established taste for French wines which had been developed under the natural trading connections of these countries for centuries was not easily suppressed, and there seems to have been a great deal of illicit trade in this article.

bullion which was annually imported from Portugal. This was estimated at £50,000 per week; and though Adam Smith shows good reason for regarding this as an exaggeration[1], there can be no doubt that the amount of bullion which flowed into England through this trade was very large. We cannot wonder that, according to the ideas of the time, Methuen's achievement was rated very highly[2]: *This Methuen treaty* he had opened up a large foreign demand for our goods, and had thus stimulated the employment of labour at home; while much of the returns from Portugal came to us in the form which was most necessary for restoring the currency, and most convenient for carrying on the great European War.

A still more interesting illustration of the eagerness of the English public to form such foreign relationships as might conduce to the prosperity of our manufactures, is furnished by the failure of the Tory Government to carry *presented an obstacle* out their schemes of trade policy, when they were negotiating the Treaty of Utrecht in 1713. The treaty proposed to open trade, on the basis of the arrangements which had existed in 1664, before the war of tariffs and occasional prohibitions[3], which had lasted for nearly half a century, had begun to rage. Bolingbroke endeavoured, without success, to revert to the traditional policy of the Court party in regard to intercourse with France; by the eighth and ninth *to ratifying the treaty of 1713,* clauses of the commercial treaty, which accompanied the Treaty of Peace, it was agreed that French goods should be imported subject to the duties exacted in 1664 and on the same terms[4] as the most favoured nation[5]. A bill was

---

[1] *Wealth of Nations*, IV. 6, p. 223.

[2] Compare Smith's *Memoirs of Wool*, II. 51 note.

[3] The prohibition of French wine was removed in 1710 by 9 Anne, c. 8.

[4] The existing impost was much more onerous (4 and 5 W. and M. c. 5). This proposal seemed to endanger the Methuen Treaty, as England had promised to show more favour to the wines of Portugal than to those of any other country. If we admitted French wines on as favourable terms as Portuguese, we should infringe the Methuen Treaty, and the Portuguese would then be at liberty to retaliate by prohibiting our woollen goods. The loss of this market would affect the manufacturers, who were engaged in producing cloth, and the landlords, whose rents improved when the price of wool kept up and pasture farming was profitable. The authors of the *British Merchant* were anxious to convince our legislators "that the preserving our looms and the Rents of *Great Britain* was of greater Consequence to the Nation than gratifying our Palates with *French* Wine." *British Merchant*, I. p. ix.   [5] Koch and Schoell, I. 214.

.D. 1689
-1776.

hich
ould have
lowed the
owth of
rench
ade,

drafted¹ to give effect to this agreement and make the necessary alterations in the tariffs, which then imposed more than fifty per cent. on French imports² above what was taken on the goods of other countries. There was a general dread that the proposed arrangement would not only open the home market to the competition of French manufactures, but would indirectly lead to a rupture with Portugal, and the closing of the profitable market for English goods which had been secured in 1703. The proposal roused a storm of indignation; the Government endeavoured to be loyal to their agreement, and tried to secure the suspension of the duties on French wines for two months, in the hope that there would be difficulty in re-imposing them; but though they commanded a majority in the House of Commons, the motion was rejected. A very interesting struggle followed, as both the Government and their opponents endeavoured to win the day by con-vincing public opinion. Daniel Defoe³ was employed to carry on the *Mercator*, which was published thrice a week, and was devoted to demonstrating the beneficial character of the French trade. "As he had," to quote his

¹ This and other documents are printed at length in the *British Merchant*, vol. I. 130.

² Adam Smith summarises the matter thus in the third edition, "Higher duties are imposed upon the wines of France than upon those of Portugal or indeed of any other country. By what is called the impost 1692, a duty of five-and-twenty per cent. of the rate or value, was laid upon all French goods; while the goods of other nations were, the greater part of them, subjected to much lighter duties, seldom exceeding five per cent. The wine, brandy, salt and vinegar of France, were indeed excepted; these commodities being subjected to other heavy duties, either by other laws or by particular clauses of the same law. In 1696, a second duty of twenty-five per cent., the first not having been thought a sufficient dis-couragement, was imposed upon all French goods, except brandy; together with a new duty of five-and-twenty pounds upon the ton of French wine, and another of fifteen pounds upon the ton of French vinegar. French goods have never been omitted in any of those general subsidies or duties of five per cent. which have been imposed upon all, or the greater part, of the goods enumerated in the book of rates. If we count the one-third and two-third subsidies as making a complete subsidy between them, there have been five of these general subsidies; so that before the commencement of the present (1783) war, seventy-five per cent. may be considered as the lowest duty to which the greater part of the goods of the growth, produce, or manufacture of France was liable. But upon the greater part of goods, these duties are equivalent to a prohibition. The French in their turn, have, I believe, treated our goods and manufactures just as hardly." *Wealth of Nations*, IV. 3, Pt. 1, p. 192.

³ Smith's *Chronicon*, II. 105.

opponents' complaint, "a Knack of writing very plausibly, A.D. 1689
—1776. and they who employed him and furnished him with Materials, had the Command of all the publick Papers in the Custom House, he had it in his Power to do a great deal of Mischief, among such as were unskilled in Trade, and at the same Time very fond of French Wine, which it was then a great Crime to be against[1]." The antagonists of France, however, started an opposition paper named the *British Merchant*, which came out twice a week[2]; several leading merchants were among its contributors, and they were practically successful, for the Methuen Treaty was maintained, and no effect was given to the commercial clauses of the treaty with France. Trade between the two *and this* countries was carried on, under scarcely altered conditions, *policy was* *not aban-* for more than eighty years after the signing of the Methuen *doned till* *1786.* Treaty, until the dominant policy was at last reversed, with Adam Smith's approval, under the guiding hand of Pitt[3].

221.   The reasoning which brought about the interrup- *The same* tion of the French trade in 1678 gave rise to a new agitation *principle* *underlay* against the East India Company and its operations. In the *the attack* *on the East* early seventeenth century the export trade of this Company *India Co.* had been the chief subject of attack, as they were so much in the habit of sending silver to the East. The fiercest opposition, in the period of Whig ascendancy, was directed against their import trade; since the goods they brought from the East, served as substitutes for textile fabrics woven in England. It was alleged that Indian muslins and silks interfered with the demand for English goods in the home market, and prevented the export of English manufactures to foreign countries. The Act of 1663, which permitted the exportation of bullion without a license, gave a great impulse to the East India trade; but the Company con-

---

[1] King, *British Merchant*, I. p. x.

[2] This controversy incidentally raised the question as to the alleged superiority of English wool (see p. 504 n. 7, below). Defoe argued in the *Mercator* that England had such an advantage from the character of the raw material available, that she could, by restraining the export of wool, secure to her manufacturers a monopoly of the markets of the world. "This extraordinary assertion put the *British Merchant* under the necessity of showing the real circumstance of England in regard to wool"; this "jury of the most eminent English merchants" held that the French manufacturers had access to ample supplies from other quarters. Smith, *Chronicon*, II. 109 n. and 117.   [3] See p. 602 below.

*which
imported
goods that
competed
in the home
market*

*with
English
manu-
factures,*

*such as
fans,*

tinued to import drugs and spices, as their chief returns, till about 1670, when a considerable quantity of textile goods was brought over, and some artisans were sent out to introduce patterns suitable for sale at home. So great was their success, that a few years later it was alleged that "from the greatest Gallants to the meanest Cook Maids nothing was thought so fit to adorn their persons as the Fabricks of India, nor for the ornaments of Chambers like India Skreens, Cabinets, Beds and Hangings, nor for Closets, like China and Lacquered Ware[1]." It thus appeared that the field for the employment of English subjects was becoming restricted, through the importation of commodities manufactured abroad; it was argued that to divert employment from Englishmen to Hindus was distinctly prejudicial to the good of the realm[2], and that, though the East India trade might have been profitable as long as it was confined to the importation of Eastern products like spices, it became distinctly hurtful when it consisted largely of importing textile fabrics and other goods, which took the place in the home market of articles already made in England[3].

There was a great outcry from the fan-makers, who seem to have been a numerous class[4], but the chief complaint arose in connection with the clothing trades. The Company "finding the Advantage they had of having their Goods cheap wrought by the wretched Poverty of that numerous People, have used sinister Practices to betray the Arts used in their Native Country, such as sending over Artificers[5] and Patterns to instruct them in the way of making Goods, and Mercers to direct them in the Humour and Fancy of them, to make them fit our Markets"; this had affected not only the silk

---

[1] Pollexfen, *A Discourse of Trade, Coyn and Paper Credit* (1697), p. 99.

[2] This was another point argued in the attack made by the Turkish Company on the East India Company in 1681. *The Allegations of the Turkey Company and Others against the East India Company* [Brit. Mus. 522. 1. 5 (8), p. 4].

[3] Compare *A Memento to the East India Companies* [Brit. Mus. 1029. c. 21 (9), (1700), p. 19]. This consists of a reprint of a remonstrance presented by the East India Company to the House of Commons in 1628, with animadversions upon it, showing how much the character of their trade had altered since that time, and that it could no longer be defended upon the same grounds.

[4] *The Fann Makers Grievance* [Brit. Mus. 816. m. 12 (97)].

[5] This was denied, except as regards one or two dyers, by the East India Company in their answer to the *Allegations of the Turkey Company* [Brit. Mus. 522. 1. 5 (8), p. 12].

weavers at home, but the Norwich clothiers also[1]. It was A.D. 1689
argued that the employment of 250,000 manufacturers would —1776.
be injuriously affected by allowing this trade to continue, and *woollen*
that this must react on the price of wool and the prosperity *cloth*
of the landed interest[2]. The case of the Company was
powerfully stated by Davenant; he showed that "the Importation of East India and Persia Wrought Silks, Stain'd
Callicoes, etc., though it may somewhat interfere with the
Manufactures of Norwich, Bristol and other particular
Places; yet, that such Importation adds to the Kingdoms
main Stock and Wealth, and is not prejudicial to the
General Woollen Manufacture of England[3]." But he did
not succeed in convincing the general public that the trade
was not hurtful to the employment of our own people. The
reply was put thus: "Suppose a merchant send £10,000 to
India and bring over for it as much wrought Silks and
painted Calicoes as yield him here £70,000, if they be all *and silk.*
worn here in the room of our own Silk and Woollen manufactures, the Nation loses and is the poorer £10,000, notwithstanding the Merchant has made a very profitable Adventure,
and so proportionably the more and oftner he sends, the faster
he grows rich. and the more the Nation is impoverished[4]."
The attempt to discuss the question, without reference to the
export of Indian silks to other countries in Europe, was unfair
to the Company; but the arguments are of interest as they
proved convincing, and the objectors were successful in
carrying their point, for they obtained an Act of Parliament
in 1700 to restrict the trade, so far as the home market was
concerned[5]. It was alleged, after a brief experience, that the

[1] *The Great Necessity and Advantage of Preserving our own Manufacturies,*
by N. C., a weaver of London [Brit. Mus. 1029. c. 21 (7), (1697), pp. 7, 13].
[2] *Reasons Humbly Offered for the Passing a Bill for the Hindering of the
Home Consumption of East India Silks,* by T. S., a weaver of London (1697), p. 3
[Brit. Mus. 1029. c. 21 (8)].
[3] *An Essay on the East India Trade* (1696), p. 33.
[4] N. C., *Great Necessity and Advantage of Preserving our own Manufacturies,* 6.
[5] 11 W. III. c. 10, *An Act for the more effectuall imploying the Poor by
incouraging the Manufactures of this Kingdom:* "Whereas it is most evident
That the Continuance of the Trade to the East Indies in the same Manner and
Proportions as it hath been for Two Yeares last past, must inevitably be to the
great Detriment of this Kingdom by exhausting the Treasure thereof and melting
downe the Coine, and takeing away the Labour of the People whereby very many

C.   30

A.D. 1689
—1776. results were most satisfactory; Canterbury "was become desolate, they are now returned to their Homes, as before they left them, in Shoals and Companies. Their Houses and their Bellies are full; They rather want Hands than Work, and there is at this Day neither Complaint nor Decay among them for lack of Employment," while Norwich and London weavers were flourishing too[1]. The interest of English manufacturers served to reinforce the agitation, which had been growing among merchants, against the commercial and judicial privileges of this joint-stock Company, and imperilled its very existence[2].

There were also good grounds for criticising the conduct of the Company From the time of the conflict between the two Companies[3], the principle of maintaining a joint-stock company for the management of the East Indian trade appears to have been generally accepted; but there was frequent complaint as to the manner in which the Company's affairs were conducted. The troubles of different kinds, which arose, were not altogether the fault of the Company, but were partly its misfortune. The English Government burdened these privileged associations with heavy political and judicial responsibilities, while the French and Dutch traders, with whom they had to compete, were under no similar obligations. It is true, too, that in order to purchase the right to exist, the East India Company had been compelled to sink a large part of their *with regard to the employment of its capital* wealth in purchasing concessions from Government, and that they were often hampered for want of sufficient ready money with which to carry on their trade. It was the error of not a few commercial men, at this era, that they did not sufficiently realise the limits within which credit will serve to take the place of capital.

of the Manufacturers of this Nation are become excessively burdensome and chargeable to their respective Parishes and others are thereby compelled to seek for Employment in Forreigne Parts." East India goods were to be warehoused for re-exportation and not sold within the country.

[1] *Reflections on the Prohibition Act* (1708), p. 8 [Brit. Mus. 1029. c. 21 (10)].

[2] It seems as if the East India Company owed its continuance to the fact that the Government was under heavy pecuniary obligations to these merchants, and was unable to discharge them immediately. See above, p. 268. Successive administrations were unable to consider the matter dispassionately and to view the question either as one of fair-play among merchants, or of British interests in India. See p. 261, note 9.

[3] See p. 209 above.

During this period the possessions of the Company had *A.D. 1689 —1776.* undergone startling vicissitudes; they had been almost de- *and the* stroyed by the French, but the fortunes of the English were *action of* restored by the skill and energy of Clive, and their influence *its officials* had at last triumphed in all the three Presidencies. Clive's greatest achievements had been effected in open disregard of the instructions of the Directors; and his whole career illustrates the extreme difficulty under which the Company laboured, from its relation to servants who were so far distant as to be exempt from all practical control. He believed that the Company would be better served, if the officials enjoyed a different status and had more freedom from routine. The system on which they were paid was very unsatisfactory; their salaries were small, and they were obliged to eke out their resources by taking part in the internal trade of the country. The Company reserved the trade between the Indies and Europe, as a strict monopoly, for itself; but allowed its servants to engage on their own *in carrying* account in trade between different parts of the Indies. This *on private trade.* private trade led to many imbroglios with the natives, as in certain cases, where the goods of the Company were allowed to go free of custom by the authorities in Bengal, the agents endeavoured, and not without success, to pass their private speculations at the same time[1]. Private trade was looked on with disfavour, because many officers were apt to give their best attention to their own ventures, and to neglect the affairs of the Company they served. One of the reforms which Clive endeavoured to carry through, in 1765, was the establishment of a monopoly of salt, betel-nut, and tobacco; this monopoly was intended to be carried on for the benefit of the superior servants of the Company[2]. The Directors were strongly opposed to this private trade society, and it was abolished in 1768[3].

Indeed it may be said that, while the chief troubles of the Company in earlier times were due to the interlopers, those which occurred during a great part of the eighteenth

---

[1] Mill, *History of British India*, III. 25, 230.
[2] *Ib.* III. 289.
[3] *Ib.* III. 310.

century arose from the conduct of the servants. They often acquired large fortunes[1]; and their successes stimulated the imagination of the proprietors, who recklessly insisted on securing large dividends, and embarrassed the Company by dividing sums which had not been earned, and which, as the Directors knew, exceeded what the Company was able to pay.

The Directors and their agents often differed
Not only were there difficulties in regard to the personal conduct of officials, but the management of the Company's own affairs gave rise to differences of opinion between the Directorate and the Company's agents in India. There was one point in regard to which they were in constant conflict. It was necessary for the Presidential governments to have considerable treasure in bullion to meet emergencies, and they were therefore inclined to limit the amount of their *as to the 'investment'* 'investment' in goods for transmission to England. The profit on the trading, and the dividends, depended on the goods sent to England; it was therefore to the interest of the Directors and shareholders that the investment should be large. Here was one cause of trouble; another arose when, as occasionally happened, the Council of a Presidency tried to replenish their local treasury by opening it to *and 're-mittances';* receive 'remittances'; they would encourage the Company's servants to pay cash into the treasury; money might then be remitted by means of bills to England and the value paid to the representatives of the servants there. But there was danger, at all events, that the Council would issue more bills than the Court of Directors at home were able to meet[2], and this gave much occasion for dispute.

and the business was so intricate
These difficulties of management, from the practical independence of the servants and from the difficulty of maintaining two treasuries so as to meet the necessary payments, were all the more serious, since the trading business itself was exceedingly intricate. Fine muslins and silks were among the largest imports. In the process of buying goods, the

---

[1] Clive is reported to have said that the temptations held out to adventurers in that part of the globe were such as flesh and blood could not withstand. *Parl. Hist.* XXI. 446.

[2] Mill, *op. cit.* III. 312.

European agent was five removes distant from the workman. A.D. 1689
—1776.
Each of the intermediaries obtained his commission; the
complicated machinery of trade gave rise on the one hand
to great oppression of the labourer, while on the other it *that super-*
vision was
afforded frequent opportunities for malversation and fraud. *impossible*
The officials of the Company were organised in four different
classes. They entered as writers; after five years' service
they became factors; three years later, junior merchants,
and after three years senior merchants. The high official
positions were given to senior merchants[1], and promotion
was almost entirely by seniority. The patronage which the
Directors were able to exercise was a very valuable power,
and was of more importance to many of them than the
wealth which accrued from their ownership of shares in the
Company. Under these circumstances there can be little *and cor-*
ruption
wonder that Clive, at the beginning of his second adminis- *rampant.*
tration, should have reported that the whole administration was corrupt[2], or that the Directors complained of the
"deplorable state to which our affairs were on the point of
being reduced, from the corruption and rapacity of our
servants, and the universal depravity of manners throughout the settlement. The general relaxation of all discipline *The mal-*
practice of
and obedience, both military and civil, was tending to a *the officials*
dissolution of all government.... We must add that we
think the vast fortunes, acquired in the inland trade, had
been obtained by a series of the most tyrannic and oppressive conduct that ever was known in any age or
country[3]."

These disclosures aroused wide-spread indignation, which
was fomented by retired servants, and by proprietors
who were discontented with their position. As a result
a Parliamentary enquiry was undertaken, and an Act

---

[1] Mill, *op. cit.* III. 16.

[2] Both the Portuguese and the Dutch had to contend with similar difficulties
in regard to their officials. The utter demoralisation of the Portuguese who
settled in India was perhaps the chief reason of the destruction of their power.
Raynal, *History* (1777), I. 141. On the Dutch, see Raynal, I. 266.

[3] Mill, III. 279. It was one of the great achievements of Lord Cornwallis that
he raised the tone of the Indian service in such a remarkable manner. Chesney,
Indian Polity (1868), 23.

A.D. 1689
—1776.
defining the financial obligations of the Company to Government was passed in 1768. It was evidently drafted[1] on the assumption that the Company had control of enormous riches, *and the im-poverished condition of the Company* whereas the large dividends which had been recently paid had brought them to the verge of bankruptcy[2]. But almost immediately after this Act was passed, the public became aware of the real position of the Company, and there was the strongest excitement against the Directors for having, as it was supposed, frittered away the exaggerated resources at their command. There were two opposite suggestions for remedying a condition of affairs which all regarded as discreditable. The Directors made some endeavours to exercise more complete control themselves over their servants by sending out supervisors, who never arrived[3], and by promoting a Bill for increasing their powers, which the House of Commons would not pass[4]. The opposing scheme was that of giving the English Government a firm hold upon the conduct of the Company, both at home and abroad[5]. The Ministry proposed a series of changes which aroused the alarm of Directors, and they protested that "not*rendered public intervention necessary;*withstanding the Company were thus deprived of their franchise in the choice of their servants, by an unparalleled strain of injustice and oppression, they were compelled to pay such salaries as Ministers might think fit to direct, to persons in whose appointment, approbation, or removal, the Company were to have no share[6]." The opposition was taken up by the City of London, but it had no results, and the new order was constituted in 1773[7].

[1] By this Act (9 Geo. III. c. 24) it was determined that for five years the Company should pay annually into the Exchequer a sum of £400,000, that they should export £380,000 worth of British merchandise, and that their outstanding debts should not be allowed to exceed the amount of the sums due to them from the Government. On the one hand provision was made for reducing the payment, if the dividend fell off, and on the other, for increase of their loans to Government if they had a surplus. A somewhat similar arrangement had been concluded for two years by 7 Geo. III. c. 57.

[2] The French Company, organised by Colbert in 1664, was equally unskilful in its trade; in 1684 they lost half their capital, and they were still in an embarrassed condition in 1722. Malleson, *History of the French in India*, pp. 27, 57.

[3] Mill, *op. cit.* III. 340.   [4] *Ib.* 343, 345.

[5] The probable purity and value of direct Government control must not be judged by present standards. See the debate on Contractors in *Parl. Hist.* XXI. 423.

[6] Mill, III. 349.   [7] 13 Geo. III. cc. 63, 64.

The ultimate effect of the new measures, as they in- A.D. 1689
fluenced the administration in India, was most beneficial; —1776.
so far as the internal constitution of the Company was concerned, the principal change was that of raising the voting
qualification of a shareholder from £500 to £1000. A large *the*
number of the smaller proprietors were thus disfranchised, *smaller proprietors*
to their great indignation[1]; but it was apparently supposed *were dis-franchised,*
that the Directors would be less tempted than before to
try and meet their extravagant wishes for large dividends.
Their demands were undoubtedly due to the extraordinary
over-estimate of the riches which the Company handled,
and the efforts of the Directors to keep down the dividend
rendered them very unpopular with the proprietors, who were
besides able, in 1767, to force the management into courses
which were known to be imprudent. The political and com- *but the*
mercial affairs of the Company continued to be in a position *Company continued*
of serious difficulty, and in 1783 Fox and Pitt put forward *to manage its affairs*
rival schemes for strengthening the public control[2]. Through *under a Board of*
all the changes and difficulties, the East India Company still *Control.*
retained its old character and remained as it had been in
fact, though not at the very first in form, a joint-stock
company. The existence of the Company kept alive a feeling
of jealousy against the members of a privileged body. This
sentiment in the mercantile community was taken up by Adam
Smith, and employed against all citizens who were specially
favoured by Parliament in the pursuit of their callings.

222.   The constant attempt to render commerce subservient to the promotion of home industry had far-reaching
results in connection with the colonial trade. Almost as *As the*
soon as the plantations were established, it had been thought *colonies grew*
necessary to take steps to ensure that the benefit, arising from
the trade in their products, should accrue to England, and not
be diverted into other channels. As time passed, and the
population in the American settlements increased, English
traders and manufacturers became anxious to retain their
monopoly in the colonial market for European goods. The

---

[1] Mill, III. 349.

[2] A Board of Control was established by 24 G. III. c. 25. Its powers, as
interpreted by the Declaratory Act (28 G. III. c. 8), embraced all the affairs of
the Company.

A.D. 1689
—1776.
the Navi-
gation Acts
supplied a
suitable
mechanism Navigation Act lay ready to hand, as a convenient instrument for administering commercial affairs on the new and approved lines of fostering industry; and the expedient of regulating this branch of commerce, by delegating it to a Company, was inapplicable. Though several of the trading Companies survived the Revolution, they no longer served as a satisfactory medium for enforcing rules of trade, as they had *for con-*
trolling done in the times of Elizabeth; the plantation trade could *their traffic* be controlled, without being confined to a privileged body of merchants, through the machinery of the Navigation Acts. There was an elaborate system for the registration of ships, and the owners could be compelled to give bonds for carrying their cargoes to a destination approved by Government. In *so as to* this way it was possible to retain to the mother-country[1] the *promote* *British* whole business of supplying the colonists with imports of *industry,* *and to* every sort[2], and at the same time to render England a staple *render* *England a* for the distribution of the more valuable American products *staple* in other parts of the world. Fish, cereals, and timber, which were the principal commodities of the New England States, might be shipped to any market; but the tobacco of Virginia, the rice and cotton of Carolina, and the sugar of the West *for enume-*
rated com- Indian islands, along with naval stores, were enumerated *modities.* specially, and these commodities were reserved for shipping

[1] The official view of the economic importance of the colonies is clearly stated in 15 C. II. c. 7, § 4, "And in reguard His Majesties Plantations beyond the Seas are inhabited and peopled by His Subjects of this His Kingdome of England; for the maintaining a greater correspondence and kindnesse between them, and keepeing them in a firmer dependance upon it, and rendring them yet more beneficiall and advantagious unto it in the farther Imployment and Increase of English Shipping and Seamen, vent of English Woollen and other Manufactures and Commodities, rendring the Navigation to and from the same more safe and cheape, and makeing this Kingdome a Staple, not onely of the Commodities of those Plantations, but alsoe of the Commodities of other Countryes and Places, for the supplying of them; and it being the usage of other Nations to keepe their [Plantations] Trade to themselves."

[2] As a consequence the balance of trade was steadily against the colonists. "The importation of New England exceeds the exportation, which, if not balanced, will bring this double evil,—it will oblige us to set up manufactures of our own, which will entirely destroy the naval stores trade and employ the very hands that might be employed in stores. * * * The best way to keep the colonies firm to the interest of the kingdom is to keep them dependent on it for all their necessaries, and not by any hardships to force them to subsist of themselves. * * * Allow them to keep the balance of their trade, and they will never think of manufactures." Banister, quoted by E. Lord, *Industrial Experiments in the British Colonies of North America*, p. 133.

to England only[1]. It appears that the efforts to enforce this A.D. 1689
—1776. system after 1696 were more stringent than they had been before[2], and so far as colonial exports are concerned, they seem to have been fairly successful.

The West Indian islands were the most favoured of all the colonial possessions of England, and great pains were taken, both on political and economic grounds, not only to restrain their trade to Englishmen but to secure the development of these plantations. An immense amount of English capital was engaged in the commerce which centred round these islands[3]. The traffic with England was important, as well as that with New England[4]; but there was also much money to be made in the lucrative commerce with Central America, which the Spaniards[5] endeavoured to reserve for

Great attention was given to the West India islands

---

[1] 12 C. II. c. 34. Rice and naval stores were not added to the list till 1706, 3 and 4 Anne, c. 3, § 14. On the whole subject compare the excellent monograph by G. L. Beer, *Commercial Policy of England towards the American Colonies*, in *Columbia College Studies*, III. 45.

[2] See above, p. 211. Beer, *op. cit.* 131.

[3] Bryan Edwards is at pains to point out "that the sugar planters generally speaking are but so many agents or stewards for their creditors and annuitants in the mother country; or if in some few instances they are independent proprietors themselves, it is in Great Britain alone that their incomes are expended and their fortunes ultimately vested" [*History, Civil and Commercial of the British West Indies* (1819), II. 533]. He instituted a comparison between the East India Trade and that with the West Indies (about 1790), which brings out the importance of the latter   The capital employed in the East India Trade was £18,000,000, as against £70,000,000 in the West. The exports to India and China were valued at £1,500,000, while the corresponding figures for the West Indies were £3,800,000. The imports by the East India Company were £5,000,000, while importation from the West Indies was given as amounting to £7,200,000. The duties paid to Government were in the one case £790,000, and in the other £1,800,000; and only 80,000 tons of shipping were employed in East India trade, as compared with 150,000 tons in the West.

[4] On the English efforts to foster this trade in competition with the French, see below, p. 482.

[5] On the history of this dispute see Coxe's *Memoirs of Sir R. Walpole*, IV. 3. Mr Keene, the English representative at Madrid, thus summarised the matters in dispute: "Upon the whole, the state of our dispute seems to be, that the commanders of our vessels always think they are unjustly taken, if they are not taken in *actual* illicit commerce, even though the proofs of their having loaded in that manner be found on board: and the Spaniards on the other hand presume, that they have a right of seizing, not only the ships that are continually trading in their ports, but likewise of examining and visiting them on the high seas, in order to search for proofs of fraud, which they may have committed; and till a medium be found out between these two nations, the government will always be embarrassed with complaints, and we shall be continually negotiating in this country for redress without ever being able to procure it." Coxe's *Walpole*, IV. 9.

A.D. 1689
—1776.

as a depot for Mexican trade

themselves. The illicit trade between the West Indian islands and Mexico[1] was valued by the colonists because it enabled them to procure quantities of silver[2] with which they paid for European goods[3]. But the trade declined in the latter part of the eighteenth century; the Spaniards pursued a more liberal policy towards the settlements in Mexico, so that they had less motive for engaging in smuggling[4]. The English on the other hand began to enforce the Navigation Laws[5] more strictly in 1764, and seized the Spanish vessels trading between the English islands and Mexico. Next year the English endeavoured to rectify this mistake by establishing in Jamaica four free ports, into which foreign vessels were allowed to import the produce of foreign colonies[6]. Unfortunately however, the English officials kept a list of the names of those who imported bullion from Mexico; the Spanish Government succeeded in obtaining a copy of this list and severely punished some traders for the illegal exportation[7].

and in connection with the slave trade,

There was another highly profitable trade which connected the West Indian islands, not only with the Spanish mainland and with some of the English plantations on the mainland, but with Africa as well. The African slave trade appears to have been encouraged, if not devised, from motives

---

[1] The English claimed a right to cut logwood at Campeachy, but the Spaniards repudiated it. *Parl. Hist.* VIII. 684.

[2] F. Hall, *Importance of the British Plantations in America to this Kingdom* (1731), p. 41.

[3] The colonies had some difficulty in finding suitable returns for their purchases from England; hence the advantage from cultivating new products. The introduction of rice into Carolina, where it was immediately successful, helped the southern colonists to discharge their indebtedness. F. Hall, *Importance of British Plantations*, p. 18. Beer, *op. cit.* p. 52.

[4] Edwards, *History of the West Indies*, I. 293.

[5] The Navigation Act of 1660 was amended by 15 C. II. c. 7 by the insertion of a clause which had a very important effect on the West Indies. It enacted that in order to make England a staple, both for colonial products and for supplying the plantations with manufactures, all European goods for the use of the plantations were to be fetched from England, Wales or Berwick, and from nowhere else. This appears to have been aimed at the French, and the wine trade, rather than at the Dutch. It practically repealed the clause which allowed foreign countries to ship their own products to English colonies, and it cut off Ireland from direct trade with the colonies.

[6] Foreign manufactures and produce of British colonies which served as the raw material for British manufactures were not included in this permission. 6 Geo. III. c. 49.

[7] Edwards, *op. cit.* I. 295.

of philanthropy. The American natives were physically unfit A.D. 1689 for hard toil on the plantations[1], and Bartholomew de las $-1776.$ Casas urged that Africans were so constituted that they could work hard in this tropical climate without serious injury[2]. In the northern colonies, where white labourers were able to exert themselves fully, there was no advantage in the employment of negro labour. Though some direct voyages were made from the African coast to Newport[3] and other ports on the mainland, the more usual practice appears to have been to ship the slaves to the West Indian islands from Africa, and thence, as they were needed, to Spanish America and the Virginian plantations.

The ordinary Englishman of the eighteenth century *in which* simply regarded the slave trade as a great branch of the *England was* carrying trade which gave employment to English shipping; *largely in-* the Assiento[4] Treaties were a bargain with the Spanish *terested,* Government, by which England secured the sole right of

---

[1] Edwards, II. 45. This did not give them immunity from slavery, however. "The traders on the Musquito shore were accustomed to sell their goods at very high prices and long credit, to the Musquito Indians, and the mode of payment set on foot by the British settlers, was to hunt the other surrounding tribes of Indians, and seize them by stratagem or force, from whence they were delivered to the British traders as slaves, at certain prices, in discharge of their debts, and were by them conveyed as articles of commerce to the English and French settlements in the West Indies. The person among others, concerned in this shameful traffic, had been the superintendent himself, whose employment was ostensibly to protect the Indians, from whence, as the House will easily perceive, all kinds of jealousy, distraction, and distrust had prevailed: several of the Indians and particularly the King, complained to my friend of the distracted state of the natives, from this species of commerce." *Parl. Hist.* XIX. 62.

[2] W. Robertson, *The History of America*, I. 318.

[3] Washburn, *Slavery in Massachusetts*, 218; Bancroft, *op. cit.* III. 405.

[4] English jealousy was roused by the treaty of 1701, which gave the French Company of Guinea the exclusive right for ten years. The Company was allowed to furnish annually 4800 slaves and in time of war 3000, on payment of 100 livres tournois each for the first 4000, the remainder to be free. For this they advanced 600,000 livres to the King to be paid back during the last two years of the Treaty. The Company had the right to export goods or metals to the value of the slaves imported. The Kings of France and Spain each had a share of a fourth in the Treaty, and as the King of France did not find it convenient to pay his share of the capital, 1,000,000 livres, the Company was to advance it to him at 8 per cent.

In Art. 12 of the Treaty between Spain and England in 1713 Spain gave to England and the English Co. the Assiento to the exclusion of Spanish subjects and all others for thirty years dating from 1713, on the same conditions on which the French had formerly held it. In addition the Company holding the Assiento were given a suitable piece of land on the Rio de la Plata to deposit there the negroes till sold. Specifically the rights were:

i. Leave to import 4800 negroes annually at 100 livres duty per head, on

importing slaves into the Spanish colonies; and there appears to have been an entire want of any humanitarian feeling on the subject. The New England colonists were quite as callous[1], and carried on the trade without scruple; there was some uneasiness in the southern plantations, for the enormous number of slaves was regarded as constituting *both in pre-* a grave political danger. But from the point of view of *serving the* *economic* English merchants, this was a lesser evil than the develop-*dependence* *of the* ment of such an industrial population in the plantations as *plantations* would interfere with the sale of English products. "Were it possible for White Men to answer the end of Negroes in Planting, must we not drain our own Country of Husband-men, Mechanicks and Manufacturers too? Might not the latter be the Cause of our Colonies interfering with the Manufactures of these Kingdoms, as the Palatines attempted in Pensilvania? In such Case indeed, we might have just Reason to dread the Prosperity of our Colonies; but while we can be well supplied with Negroes, we need be under no such Apprehensions; their Labour will confine the *and the* Plantations to Planting only[2]." Besides this, the African *African* *market for* trade took off a considerable amount of English manu-*manu-* *factures.* factures, and the slaves for America furnished a large part of the returns. Both as regards manufactures and shipping, the

condition that 600,000 livres were paid to the King of Spain, to be repaid to the Company during the last ten years of the Treaty.

ii. During the first twenty-five years the Company might import as many, more than the specified number, as it thought fit.

iii. They could employ English or Spanish vessels as they thought fit.

iv. They were allowed to use vessels of 400 tons to export goods from America to Europe, and one ship of 500 tons for importing goods for Indian trade.

v. The Kings of Spain and England were each to have one-fourth of the profit.

The English put the liberty accorded to them to great abuse by mooring the one ship permitted to bring imports and constantly refilling her with goods brought by tenders; they got much of the Spanish American trade into their hands. The arrangement expired with the outbreak of war in 1739, but was renewed in 1748 at Aix-la-Chapelle for four years, to make up for the years of which the Company had lost the benefit. There is no mention of the Assiento in the Treaty of Paris (1763). Koch and Shoell, *Histoire Abrégée des Traités de Paix*, I. 215, 361.

[1] A contrary view is expressed by Bancroft, III. 408; but see Weeden, *Economic and Social History of New England*, I. 103, 148; II. 451, 834. Also Wakefield, *England and America*, II. 25.

[2] *The African Trade, the great Pillar and Support of the British Plantation Trade* (1745), pp. 13, 14. Postlethwayt, who is said to have been the writer, assumes that self-sufficiency was a necessary condition without which the plantations could not secure political independence. "Negro labour will keep them in due Subserviency to the Interest of their *Mother Country*; for while our Plantations

slave trade appeared most beneficial to the mother-country[1], A.D. 1689
—1776. and there are numerous official expressions of the high opinion which Englishmen entertained of its value[2].

That the negroes were terribly degraded cannot for a *The traffic* moment be doubted; dragged as they were from different *had disastrous* African tribes, with no common language, or common customs, *results on the negroes,* they had no traditions or interests of their own. The horrors of the middle passage caused a frightful amount of mortality[3] and must have left most serious results, even in the cases of those who survived. The total number of persons, who were thus exported from Africa, has been very variously estimated; but a writer, who was professedly correcting exaggerations and giving what appeared an unusually low estimate, put it at an annual average of twenty thousand from 1680 to 1786. The trade had attained its "highest pitch of prosperity" shortly before the commencement of the American War. Of the hundred and ninety English ships engaged in this trade in 1771, a hundred and seven sailed from Liverpool[4], fifty-eight from London, twenty-three from Bristol, and four from Lancaster; the total export in a year of great activity was about fifty thousand[5]. The dimensions of the

depend only on Planting by *Negroes* * * * our Colonies can never become independent of these Kingdoms."

[1] There was some anxiety as to the drain on the population of Africa for the sources of supplying the slave markets should be exhausted. Hippisley discusses the conditions of Africa and pronounces these fears illusory. *Essays, &c.*, p. 6.

[2] Bancroft, *op. cit.* III. 414. The only symptoms of humanitarian feeling in England were shown, oddly enough, in dicta which tended to confirm the rights of the slave-holder, when popular opinion did not altogether endorse them. There was a general impression in South Carolina that a Christian could not be retained as a slave—that the rite of Baptism at once conferred freedom. This opinion tended to check any efforts for the instruction and conversion of the slaves. Bishop Gibson, of London, was too good a canonist to countenance it for a moment, and the opinions of the Solicitor and Attorney-General, as to the unaltered right of property in Christian slaves, were eagerly welcomed by George Berkeley and those who had the welfare of the blacks at heart (Bancroft, III. 409).

[3] Bancroft calculates the average loss of life in this way at 12½ per cent. of those exported from Africa, *op. cit.* III. 405.

[4] In 1804 Liverpool possessed six-sevenths of the whole trade. Young, *West India Common Place Book*, p. 9.

[5] Edwards, II. 65. A statement of the trade for several years occurs in *Parl. Hist.* XIX. 302; it appears to place the numbers somewhat lower. A very much higher estimate is given by Raynal, who is said by some authorities to have underrated the numbers. Bancroft (II. 555), however, considers him to have erred on the side of excess; this tends to confirm the estimate given by Edwards.

A.D. 1689
—1776.
trade, and the importance attached to it, are a sufficient
illustration of the manner in which English merchants were
ready to push their commerce at the time; but it is worth
and was of
doubtful
economic
advantage.
notice that subsequent events raised a doubt as to whether
the trade had after all proved beneficial even on the lowest
grounds[1]. The labour, which was supplied by English ships to
the plantations, enabled the foreign planters, as it was said,
to develop more rapidly than they could otherwise have
done; it was held that by carrying on this traffic, England
had, after all, only succeeded in raising up competitors with
whom we found it hard to cope.

The
condition
of slaves in
the West
Indies
There is, as might be expected, a great conflict of evidence
as to the manner of treatment which the slaves received. The
most favourable statement, as to the action of the planters,
is that the negro race as a whole distinctly improved under
the care of their masters[2], physically, intellectually, and
was render-
ed less un-
favourable
morally. The most serious evil in the condition of the
West Indian slaves was imposed by a British Act of Parliament, and in the interest of the British creditors of the
planters[3]. In accordance with this Act, the home of the
negro, who had lived for years on an estate, might be
suddenly broken up, he himself sold to the continent, and
his wife and children scattered. This was a matter of
frequent occurrence, and could not be excused as an exceptional outrage, like an occasional case of severe flogging.
Those who held that, on the whole, the position of the slaves
would not be improved by suddenly giving them freedom
and ruining their masters, argued for such an alteration in
by astrict-
ing them to
particular
estates.
their legal condition that they should be astricted to the soil,
and only sold as part of the estate; and this was effected by
a Bill introduced by Mr Edwards in 1797[4].

The West Indian islands had been highly prized on
political grounds in the seventeenth century, as they might

---

[1] Hochstetter, *Die wirthschaftlichen und politischen Motive für die Abschaffung des britischen Sklavenhandels*, 59.

[2] Against this must be set the fact of the insurrection of the slaves in Jamaica
in 1760 (Macpherson, III. 329). The alleged attempts to incite to insurrection in
southern colonies, during the American War of Independence, show that in common
opinion the slaves were not at all contented with their condition. Burke, *Parl.
Hist.* XIX. 698.   [3] 5 Geo. II. c. 7.

[4] 37 Geo. III. c. 119; Edwards, *op. cit.* II. 184 n.; *Parl. Hist.* XXXIII. 831.

serve as a basis for attacking Spanish America; they were also specially favoured during the eighteenth, since they entered into direct competition with the French sugar colonies, and no effort was spared to outdo these rivals. So much English capital was invested in this trade, or in sugar plantations, that a powerful section of London merchants was always eager to obtain new protective measures. But the result does not reflect much credit on the wisdom *The Navigation Acts* of the Navigation Acts. The planters in the West India *were in-* islands were never able to hold their own against their *jurious to the Islands,* French antagonists. The effort to confine the sugar trade to England was often complained of as prejudicial, and the attempts to force the northern colonies to trade with English rather than French islands, were fraught with disaster[1].

By a curious irony the only colony which directly profited from the Navigation Acts was the province of New England, in which English statesmen felt no special interest. The ostensible object of these Acts had been the fostering of English shipping. There is room for doubt whether the legislation did much to secure this result within the realm, but it seems to have had a considerable effect in stimulating *but helped* shipbuilding and seamanship in the New England planta- *to stimu-* tions[2]. There were many ways in which these colonies *building* suffered from the pressure of the English commercial system, but in this respect they were decided gainers. As Englishmen residing in America, the colonists were able all along to have their share of shipping[3] from which both Scotchmen and Irishmen had been excluded; the facilities, along the Atlantic sea-board, for shipbuilding were so great that there was some anxiety lest the business should be transferred from the old country altogether. The state of the trade at the out-ports was most unsatisfactory, in the time of James II.[4]; and in 1724, the Thames shipbuilders

---

[1] On the Molasses Act, see below, p. 482.

[2] Weeden, *op. cit.* II. 574—576. A. B. Hart, *Formation of the Union*, p. 46.

[3] This is explicitly provided by 13 and 14 C. II. c. 11, § 6.

[4] 1 J. II. c. 18 (*Stat. Realm*) "Whereas for some yeares past, and more especially since the laying a Duty upon Coals brought into the river of Thames, there hath been observed a more than ordinary Decay in Building Shipps in England, and particularly in NewCastle, Hull. Yarmouth, Ipswich, Alborough, Dunwich, Walderswick, Woodbridge, and Harwich, where many stout shipps were yearely

complained bitterly of the disadvantages under which they carried on their business[1]. This was exactly a case where it might have been expected that Government would interfere to prevent the hostile competition of the colonies with an established home industry; but no steps were taken in the *in New England.* matter. American shipbuilding was allowed to develop[2] under the stimulus it received from the opportunity of employment in English trade. This is all the more surprising as there would obviously have been special difficulty in obtaining the use of colonial ships for the purposes of naval warfare or transport. In 1707 Parliament abandoned any attempt to press colonial seamen for the navy[3]; the development of shipbuilding in the plantations did but little for the increase of the power of England on the seas, and colonial shipping was sometimes employed in a manner that was detrimental to English commerce[4].

The advantage which accrued to the shipping industries in the northern colonies, doubtless did much to allay the resentment that might otherwise have been felt at the *British* provisions of the Navigation Act. The only serious dif-*attempts to cut off* ficulty appears to have arisen in connection with the *Colonial inter-* attempts to bring the plantations into line with the Whig *course* policy of avoiding all commercial intercourse with France.

built for the Coale and other Trade, which were of great use to his Majestie in time of Warr and a Nursery for able Seamen; but by the Discouragement that Trade hath ever since laid under, occasioned chiefly by the freedome which foreigne Shipps and Vessels, bought and brought into this Kingdome, have enjoyed in the Coale and other Inland Trade, equall to that of English built Shipps, the Merchants, Owners, and others, have not beene able to build as formerly, which hath caused many of our English Shippwrights, Calkers, and Seamen, to seeke their Imployments abroad, whereby the Building trade is not onely wholly lost in severall of the aforementioned places, and in others very much decayed, but alsoe the Importation of Timber, Plank, Hemp, Pitch, Tarr, Iron, Masts, Canvas, and other Commodities used in building and fitting out Shipps, are greatly lessened, to the apparent prejudice of his Majestyes Customs, the losse of a considerable Imployment for Shipping, and consequently of all other Trades depending thereupon, to the too great Advantage of Forreigne Nations."

[1] Ashley, *Surveys*, 313.

[2] Lord, *Industrial Experiments*, 105; Weeden, *Economic and Social History*, II. 643.

[3] 6 Anne, c. 37, § 9.

[4] Compare the privateering in the Indian Ocean. See above, p. 271. King James II., who was particularly interested in maintaining the East Indian trade, issued a proclamation in 1688 against American privateers. [Brit. Mus. 21. h. 3 (24)].

Many restrictions had been imposed to prevent the consump- tion of French goods by the inhabitants of Great Britain[1]; and to English statesmen it would have seemed intolerable that the colonists should be left free to enrich the common *with the* enemy and her dependencies by their trade. Insistence on *French* this policy involved far greater privation on the part of the colonists than was imposed upon Englishmen at home. There were various branches of trade, with the French plantations, which were particularly profitable to the northern colonies, not only as consumers but as producers, and these were also of advantage to the French plantations. Several of the provisions of the English system were devised with the object of interrupting these trading connections, since they were undoubtedly beneficial to the French islands and afforded the American colonists opportunities for procuring commodities which were prohibited in England.

The New England seamen were in a particularly favour- able position for prosecuting the cod-fishery. In the early part of the seventeenth century there had been some fear that they would absorb this industry, and render it unprofit- able for Englishmen to engage in it at all. It appears that in 1624 some question had been raised as to the rights of British seamen to make voyages for this purpose, or to cut fuel and dry their fish upon the American coast[2]. No definite steps *engaged in* were taken at that time to establish such rights for English- *the New-* men on the Atlantic seaboard generally; they were forced to *foundland* be content with their opportunities in Newfoundland[3]. The *fisheries,* colonists had excellent facilities for such fishing, as they found profitable[4], in their own waters, and were chiefly

[1] As drawbacks were granted and large amounts of duty refunded when foreign goods were re-exported, the planters obtained German wines and other foreign manufactures on easier terms than the inhabitants of Great Britain. A. Smith, *Wealth of Nations*, p. 240; Ashley, *Surveys*, 319.

[2] Compare the draft bill, which appears to have passed the Commons, but to have been dropped in the House of Lords. *Hist. MSS. Com.* IV. Ap. 123.

[3] The status of Newfoundland was long left undefined (Reeves, *Law of Shipping and Navigation*, 1792, p. 123), and the rights of the fishing fleets have given rise to constant dispute.

[4] They were practically excluded from taking fish to the English market by 12 C. II., c. 18, § 5, and found their best market in other European countries or the French West Indies. On other restrictions on fishing, see Hart quoted by Ashley, *Surveys*, 333.

C.   31

A.D. 1689
—1776. attracted to Newfoundland by the chance of supplying the
mariners who visited the fishing grounds with provisions.
Many of the vessels which were engaged in the fisheries were
Dutch or French; and the New Englanders had no scruple
in violating the trade laws.   Wine, brandies, and other
European goods were imported directly into the colonies
and with from Newfoundland.   In the instructions to Governor
the French
West India Andros (1686–7) this island is described as a magazine of
Islands   "all sorts of goods brought thither directly from France,
Holland, Scotland, Ireland and other places[1]."   Intercourse
with the French planters in the West Indies was even more
tempting than trading with French mariners in the north.
The northerners found an excellent market for fish and
cereals in these regions.   The French islands were able to
supply them with rum, or the molasses from which rum was
distilled, on easy terms, as the brandy growers of France
were protected against the competition of colonial spirits[2],
while the English planters could ship rum to Europe.
Under these circumstances an active trade sprang up,
which seemed specially objectionable from the fact that
the northern colonists traded by preference with the French,
rather than the English, West Indian islands.   The returns
which they received by this trade enabled the colonies to deal
with the Indians for furs, which they exported to pay for the
manufactures they imported from England.   In 1733 this trade
was discouraged by heavy duties[3]; but it seems to have continued in full vigour in disregard of this Molasses Act.   During
the war of the Austrian Succession[4] the northern traders added
to the irritation, which was felt against them in England, by
supplying the French colonists with victuals.   If any attempt
was to be made to regulate British commerce at all, there was
ample reason for treating the trade between the northern
colonies and the French islands as prejudicial to the realm.

The rules of the English system, which were intended
to render England the staple where all the trade of the dependencies centred and to prevent hostile competition with
home industries, did not press nearly so heavily on any of

---

[1] Beer, p. 136; C. Pedley, *The History of Newfoundland*, p. 101.

[2] Beer, p. 118.   [3] 6 G. II. c. 13.   [4] Ashley, *Surveys*, 339.

the American colonies, as they did on Ireland[1]. Several of A.D. 1689
—1776. the colonial legislatures appear to have given a practical consent to the system in principle, and it did not in all probability cause any serious injury to individuals. England was a convenient market for colonial produce, even though better prices might often have been obtained, if the planters had been free to send their tobacco to any European port; while the large landed resources of America offered attractive openings to those who were debarred from manufacturing[2]. The rules which were imposed, from antagonism to the *gave rise to* French, were much more serious, and it was this side of *consider-able* the restrictions on their commerce, which raised a sense of *grievance.* grievance among the colonists. They showed themselves ready, on the whole, to refrain from doing any economic injury to England herself, but they were not content to let their affairs be ruled in accordance with political antagonisms in which they did not feel themselves directly concerned.

223.   While so much increased attention was given to *While pro-* discriminating between the commodities in which traffic was *viding for the employ-* carried on, the traditional methods of encouraging maritime *ment of shipping,* power were not neglected, though they were modified on the lines which the eighteenth century specially favoured.

The fishing trades had always been regarded as the great *the states-men of the* school of seamanship; the effort to promote them by in- *day main-* sisting on the observance of fish days had been abandoned, *tained their care for* but there were attempts to accomplish the same result, both *fishing* by the formation of companies which were wealthy enough to undertake the business on a large scale, and by the granting of bounties. The Company of the Royal Fishery of England was never very prosperous; it soon expended its original capital, and the subscribers of a second stock, in 1683, were equally unfortunate[3]. A similar attempt was made in 1750, the special object being to gain the white herring fishery from the Dutch; the cod-fishing was also *for herring,* to be attempted. It was regarded as a political step of the *and cod,* first importance, and had been undertaken in response to an appeal made in the King's speech in 1749. Frequent payments

---

[1] See above, p. 376; also below, pp. 525 and 580.
[2] See below, p. 585.   [3] Macpherson, II. 584.

and allowances were made to support the operations of the Company, but it never answered the expectations of the promoters, and it called out the scathing criticism of Adam Smith.

and for whaling.
Another trade in which the Dutch maintained their supremacy and from which they had ousted the English, in the time of James I., was the Greenland whale fishery. To recover it, a joint-stock Company was formed in 1692[1], which was subsequently permitted to import whale-oil duty-free[2]. In the course of a very few years, however, they ran through their capital of £82,000, and the trade was abandoned, till the South Sea Company endeavoured to re-open it; but they prosecuted it without success. From this time onwards, however, the business was left to the enterprise of private individuals, though Parliament paid large sums with the *Bounties were given* view of fostering it. In 1733 a bounty of 20s. per ton on vessels engaged in the business was offered, in 1740 it was raised to 30s., and in 1749 it was raised to 40s. This large bounty was successful in stimulating the trade, but though it was continued for many years it did not serve to make it prosper. In 1755 no less than £55,000 was paid for this purpose, but in 1770 the tonnage employed had so far declined that the bounties had fallen to £34,800. Arthur Young, who wrote in 1768, did not notice any signs of decay, and thought the merchants at Hull deserved "much commendation for entering into a business so extremely expensive, hazardous, and so often disadvantageous[3]." The alleged justification for this continued expenditure, in attracting English capital to a direction in which it did not find profitable employment, was of course political; it was supposed that we could in this way furnish ourselves with whale-oil on easier terms than by buying it from foreign and more successful fishermen, and this had been the underlying motive from the first[4].

on ship-building,
A similar expedient was tried with regard to the construction of large vessels. Bounties had occasionally been given on the building of big ships[5], and this mode of

[1] 4 W. and M. c. 17.
[2] 7 and 8 W. III. c. 33. For an account of the Iceland trade from Broadstairs, see Pennant, *Journey from London to the Isle of Wight*, I. 112.
[3] *Northern Tour*, I. 158.
[4] Macpherson, II. 563: III. 179.   25 C. II. c. 7.   [5] Vol. I. p. 413.

encouraging the art was systematically pursued, with the A.D. 1689 —1776.
view of securing a fleet of "defensible ships" which were
capable of carrying guns[1]. The resources of the plantations
in America seemed to open up a boundless field, from which
masts, and spars, and naval stores might be obtained, both
for the King's ships and the mercantile marine; persistent,
though not very successful, efforts were made to procure such
products from the colonies. Attention had been called to *and the colonists*
this source of supply by various writers, all through the *were*
seventeenth century[2]; and attempts had been made to form *encouraged to supply*
companies both in New Hampshire and Pennsylvania, which *hemp and naval*
might meet the requirements of the mother country. In *stores*
1696, the newly established Board of Trade and Plantations
sent out commissioners to report on the opportunities of the
plantations for the growth of hemp, the manufacture of tar,
and the supply of masts and spars[3]; they also encouraged
Colonel Hunter, the Governor of New York, in his scheme
for getting over the difficulty due to the scarcity of labour
by importing a number of Palatines in 1710[4]. In the meantime, however, the interruption of the Baltic trade, and the
practical monopoly secured by the Tar Company of Sweden[5],
roused the attention of Parliament, and in 1704 an Act was
passed[6], the preamble of which is an admirable statement of
the current opinion on the subject. "Whereas the royal
navy, and the navigation of England, wherein, under God,
the wealth, safety and strength of this kingdom is so much
concerned, depends on the due supply of stores necessary for
the same, which being now brought in mostly from foreign
parts, in foreign shipping, at exorbitant and arbitrary rates,
to the great prejudice and discouragement of the trade and
navigation of this kingdom, may be provided in a more
certain and beneficial manner from her Majesty's own dominions: and whereas her Majesty's colonies and plantations

---

[1] 5 and 6 W. and M. c. 24. On the competition between American and English ship-building, see p. 479 above and p. 832 below.

[2] Lord, *op. cit.* 2.   [3] Lord, *op. cit.* 9.

[4] Lord, *op. cit.* p. 43. On the Palatines, see Cunningham, *Alien Immigrants*, 249.

[5] Supplies were also obtained from Russia (1721), but the conditions of trade were equally unsatisfactory. *Parl. Hist.* vii. 928.

[6] 3 and 4 Anne, c. 10. See also 8 Anne, c. 13, § 30; 9 Anne, c. 17; 12 Anne, Stat. i. c. 9.

in America were at first settled, and are still maintained and protected, at a great expense of the treasure of this kingdom, with a design to render them as useful as may be to England, and the labour and industry of the people there, profitable to themselves: and in regard the said colonies and plantations, by the vast tracts of land therein, lying near the sea, and upon navigable rivers, may commodiously afford great quantities of all sorts of naval stores, if due encouragement be given for carrying on so great and advantageous an undertaking, which will like wise tend, not only to the further imployment and increase of English shipping and sea men, but also to the enlarging, in a great measure, the trade and vent of the woollen and other manufactures and commodities of this kingdom, and of other her Majesty's dominions, in exchange for such naval stores, which are now purchased from foreign countries with money or bullion: and for enabling her Majesty's subjects, in the said colonies and plantations, to continue to make due and sufficient returns in the course of their trade." It enacted that a *by means of* bounty of £4 per ton should be given on pitch and tar, *bounties.* of £6 per ton on hemp, and £1 per ton on masts and spars. The measure seems to have been successful in calling forth the manufacture of a considerable quantity of tar; but the scheme for promoting the cultivation of hemp was an entire failure[1]; and the attempt to reserve areas of forest[2], as a constant source for providing spars for the navy, roused much local opposition, while the large profits to be made by shipping lumber to Portugal[3] interfered with the export of timber to England. On the whole it may be said that Parliament had singularly little success in controlling this source of supply for public advantage, in the way which Sir Josiah Child[4] and other writers desired.

Increased attention was given The strength of England, as a maritime power, depended not only on the possession of well-built and well-found ships, but in ability to man them; and many steps were taken during this period to improve the lot of sailors, and

---

[1] Lord, *op. cit.* 86.   [2] Lord, *op. cit.* 88, 114.   [3] Lord, *op. cit.* 106.
[4] *New Discourse of Trade*, chap. 10. Compare also Davenant on the danger of creating a rival maritime power in the colonies. *Works*, ii. 9.

especially to induce them to serve in the Royal Navy.
A register was opened for the purpose of inscribing the
names of 30,000 sailors of different classes; they were to *to im-*
receive a retaining fee of £2 per annum on the understanding *proving the prospects of*
that they should always be ready for public service when *seamen in the Navy*
called upon[1]. They became entitled to larger shares of prize-
money than unregistered men, and to have better chances
of promotion to the rank of warrant officers. They, as
well as their widows and children, were to have the right
to be provided for in Greenwich Hospital, an institution
which was to be supported by a sort of compulsory insurance;
6*d.* per month was to be deducted from the wages of all
seamen, whether in the mercantile or royal navy, for
its maintenance[2]. Considerable changes were made under
Queen Anne, when the registration of seamen ceased[3]; but
there was a succession of statutes for enforcing their payments to the support of the hospital[4]. The residue of
the money accruing from the confiscation of the Earl of
Derwentwater's estates, was used for completing the building[5]. The distant prospect of a pension, or a home, must
have been a poor compensation for the inconveniences to
which seamen in the navy were forced to submit. An
attempt was made to remedy their grievances, in 1758, by
an Act for "establishing a regular method for the punctual,
frequent and certain payment of their wages; and for
enabling them more easily and readily to remit the same
for the support of their wives and families; and for preventing frauds and abuses attending such payments[6]." But
despite these measures, the Government was frequently in
difficulty about manning the navy, and had recourse to the
high-handed practice of impressing men[7] to serve.

---

[1] On the difficulty of procuring seamen, compare *Parl. Hist.* VI. 518. Also on
the consequent interference with commerce in 1740 and 1750, *Parl. Hist.* XI.
579 note, XIV. 538.

[2] 7 and 8 W. III. c. 21; 8 and 9 W. III. c. 23; cf. 31 Geo. II. c. 10.

[3] 9 Anne, c. 21, § 64.   [4] 10 Anne, c. 17; 2 Geo. II. c. 7; 18 Geo. II. c. 31.

[5] 8 Geo. II. c. 29. On abuses in connection with Derwentwater property see
Pennant, *Journey from London to the Isle of Wight*, I. 18. For Greenwich
Hospital, see *Parl. Hist.* XIX. 991, 992, and the long account in XX. 475.

[6] 31 Geo. II. c. 10.

[7] The impressing of fishermen, &c. to serve as mariners only, was permitted by
5 Eliz. c. 5, § 41. Charles I. obtained parliamentary powers in 1640 to impress
carpenters, surgeons etc., for his fleet against the Algiers pirates (16 Charles I.

Such were the provisions for those who served in the Royal Navy, and men in the Merchant Service were not forgotten. Attempts were made to give definiteness to the contracts of Masters and Seamen[1], and a corporation was erected for the relief of disabled seamen and of the widows and orphans of seamen in the Merchant Service[2]. During the time of Queen Anne special arrangements were made for apprenticing pauper boys to a seafaring life[3], and great facilities were given for the naturalisation of foreign seamen who had served for two years on English ships[4].

and to
the faci-
lities for
protecting
ships on our
coasts, by
erecting
light-
houses
Public attention was also directed to the dangerous nature of our coasts, and the authorities of Trinity House took in hand the erection of a light-house on the Eddystone. A London merchant, named Winstanley, first proved the possibility of the attempt; by unremitting labour he had succeeded in erecting the wooden light-house in which he eventually perished. The expense, however, of replacing this building far exceeded the ordinary resources of the brethren of Trinity House, and they were empowered to levy 1d. per ton on all shipping in order to carry out this work in 1696. Their light-house was destroyed by a storm in 1703, and resort was had to a similar expedient for its re-erection[5]. In some cases the work of erecting light-houses was undertaken by local bodies, or even by private persons, who were empowered to receive tolls to maintain the light. The first light on the Skerries, near Holyhead, was put up by Mr William Trench[6]; that on the Spurn, at the mouth of the Humber, was reconstructed by one of the neighbouring proprietors[7], though subsequently the matter was taken over by Trinity House[8]. Lights were also erected, and landmarks and buoys placed, so as to facilitate navigation to Chester[9]; there were some signs of improvement in the construction of lights, especially in a house erected near Ipswich in 1778[10].

A good deal of care was bestowed on the improvement of harbours. Some had been destroyed by the carelessness

c. 26). On complaints of the system in London in 1777, see *Parl. Hist.* xix. 1159, and xx. 966.

[1] 2 Geo. II. c. 36.   [2] 20 Geo. II. c. 38.   [3] 2 and 3 Anne, c. 6.
[4] 13 Geo. II. c. 3.   [5] Macpherson, ii. 682; 4 Anne, c. 20; 8 Anne, c. 17.
[6] *Ib.* iii. 157; 3 Geo. II. c. 36.   [7] 6 Geo. III. c. 31.
[8] 12 Geo. III. c. 29.   [9] 16 Geo. III. c. 61.   [10] Macpherson, iii. 624.

of sailors, who threw out their ballast on the shore below A.D. 1689
high-water mark, with the result that the harbours got —1776.
and
silted up; this practice was prohibited by a statute passed *improving*
harbours
in 1746[1]. There was an immense number of Acts for
carrying out repairs at Dover[2], Bridlington[3], Ramsgate[4],
Milford Haven[5], Whitehaven[6], S. Ives[7], Wells (Norfolk)[8],
Great Yarmouth[9], Glasgow and Port Glasgow[10], Ayr[11],
Hull[12], Boston[13], Bristol[14], and for improving the Clyde[15].
It was also found that the charts of the west and north- *and charts.*
west coast of Britain and Ireland were very imperfect; and
a statute was passed, in 1741, for surveying them more
completely[16], while attention was also given to navigation on
the high seas. Rewards were frequently offered for finding
a method for discovering longitude at sea[17]; at last £5000
was paid to John Harrison[18] for his discovery.

224. It is perhaps not unnatural to turn from these *The*
practice of
attempts to preserve ships, to give a brief account of the *marine*
facilities which were now devised for reimbursing those who *insurance*
incurred losses by sea. Loans on bottomry[19] had served the
purpose of marine insurance during the Middle Ages; in
the fifteenth century the practice of premium insurance
became common[20], and there appear to have been a considerable number of people engaged in this occupation in

---

[1] 19 Geo. II. c. 22. This had long been a cause of dispute in regard to the coal
trade. The colliers had little return cargo to fetch back from London to Newcastle
and so carried much ballast, which they had difficulty in discharging without
doing mischief. *Conservatorship of the River of Tyne*, in Richardson, *Reprints*,
III. pp. 15—21.

[2] 31 Geo. II. c. 8. [3] 8 and 9 W. III. c. 29.
[4] 22 Geo. II. c. 40; Pennant, *Journey*, I. 114. [5] 31 Geo. II. c. 38.
[6] 2 Geo. III. c. 87. [7] 7 Geo. III. c. 52. [8] 9 Geo. III. c. 8.
[9] 12 Geo. III. c. 14. [10] 12 Geo. III. c. 16. [11] 12 Geo. III. c. 22.
[12] 14 Geo. III. c. 56. [13] 16 Geo. III. c. 23. [14] 16 Geo. III. c. 33.
[15] 10 Geo. III. c. 104. [16] 14 Geo. II. c. 39.
[17] 12 Anne, st. II. c. 15; 26 Geo. II. c. 25; 2 Geo. III. c. 18.
[18] 3 Geo. III. c. 14. [19] See above, p. 146.
[20] Mr Hendriks (*Contributions to the History of Insurance*, 16) shows that
premium insurance was in use at Pisa about 1400 and at Barcelona before 1435.
The rate from London to Pisa was 12% or 15% "according to the risks apprehended either from pirates or other sources." Foreigners could not take
advantage of these facilities for insurance in Pisa; an attempt was made to
impose a similar restriction in England in the 18th century. *Parl. Hist.* XII. 18;
Morris. *Essay towards deciding the question Whether Britain be permitted * * * to
insure the Ships of her enemies?* (1758). See also *War in Disguise*, 84. On the
Spanish practice, see J. de Veitia Linage, *Spanish Rule of Trade* (1702), 319.

A.D. 1689
—1776.

had been organised under Elizabeth

London in 1574, when a patent was issued for giving a certain Richard Candler the sole right to register policies and instruments of insurance[1]. Subsequently a mixed commission of merchants and lawyers was established to deal with cases arising out of this business[2]. But their jurisdiction gave little satisfaction, and the commission was modified soon after the Restoration[3]. Fire insurance was developing[4] and tentative experiments were being made in life insurance[5] in the latter part of the seventeenth century.

[1] Stow, *Survey*, vol. II. bk. v. 242. For a curious dispute in 1572, see Hall, *Society in the Elizabethan Age*, 57. Compare also the patent for an office for the assurance of merchandise granted in 1634. *Hist. MSS. Comm.* I. 34 (b).

[2] 43 Eliz. c. 12.   [3] 14 C. II. c. 23.

[4] The successive steps that were taken are detailed by a contemporary: "I find this design was first set on foot immediately after His Majesty's Restoration by several persons of quality, and eminent citizens of London, and Proposals about it then printed by them. But tho the Project and Authors of it were then recommended to the Common Council of London by his Majesty's letters, yet it was not admitted by them, for the very same reason for which those Gentlemen now are not to be countenanced in it; *viz.* because they thought it impossible for Private Persons to manage, and unreasonable that they and not the City should reap the Profits of such an undertaking. Hereupon this Design, like some Rivers that sink into the Ground, and break not out again, but at a considerable distance, was no more heard of till the year 1670, when it was afresh propounded to the city by Mr De Laun, tho not prosecuted by them. However in the Mayorality of Sir W. Hooker it was briskly revived by Mr Newbold the Merchant, who proposed the carrying it on by a Joint Stock to be raised among the Inhabitants and Proprietors of the Houses to be insured. This he communicated to the Lord Mayor, and divers other eminent Citizens. From some of these like an Eves-dropper, this Observator caught it; it being then generally discussed and approved of and resolved to be put in practice. * * Mr Newbold therefore waiting for a more favourable conjunction found it not till the Majority of Sir Robert Clayton to whom on New Year's Day Anno 7⅘ he presented the Model of it, and sometime after printed it under the title 'London's Improvement and the Builder's Security.' [Brit. Mus. 816. m. 10 (64).] Sir Robert Clayton approved of the matter, only advised that instead of a joint stock it should be managed by the Chamber of London." *A second letter to Mr M. T.* by L. R., Brit. Mus. 816. m. 10 (80). Within a short time three fire insurances were started; one was managed by a committee of the Common Council, and was opened in December 1681; "but this would not take." The Fire Office at the Back side of the Royal Exchange began business a month earlier, and three years later a Friendly Society was started for doing similar business but on a different principle. The respective advantages of these various offices, the rates they charged [Brit. Mus. 816. m. 10 (71 and 73)], and the security they offered, were the object of a good deal of discussion, in which the respective advantages of municipal action and of private enterprise were freely canvassed. See *A letter to a Gentleman in the country by N B.* attributed by Dr Bauer to Barbon. He preferred the Fire Office to the Friendly Society and called forth a defence of the latter from H. S. [Brit. Mus. 816. m. 10 (74, 75)].

[5] During the Mayoralty of Sir William Hooker there were tentative efforts at organising Life Insurance. A certain Mr Wagstaffe laid his scheme before the

We hear very little of such activity in marine insurance till the time of George I.[1], when more than one attempt was made to form a Company to carry on the business with a joint stock. In 1720 two schemes, which were pushed in concert but under the guise of competition, succeeded in procuring sanction from Parliament[2], and the London Assurance Corporation and Royal

A.D. 1689 —1776.

and was developed by the establishment of

City authorities, who thought so highly of the project that they appointed a select committee to carry it into effect. Subscribers of £20 each, or of multiples of £20, were to be associated according to their ages; each subscriber was to have an annuity at the rate of 6 per cent., and as some of the subscribers died off, the survivors would obtain proportionally increased annuities. "This extraordinary gain being not only lawful but very advantageous, there can be no other way proposed whereby, in laying out so small a sum as Twenty pounds there can be produced so great an Encrease, as by Survivourship will most certainly accrue to many persons and especially to the Longest Liver of this Rank." *Proposals for Subscriptions of Money*, 1674, p. 2 [Brit. Mus. 518. h. 1 (15)]. Despite the tempting prospect, however, this scheme seems to have shared the fate of the City Fire Insurance project and came to nothing.

The reasons for preferring public management would probably be clearer if we knew more of the history of the private adventure offices that seem to have sprung up at this time. But the following extract from a petition regarding Dorothy Petty is at least instructive. It was said "that the said Dorothy (who is the Daughter of a Divine of the Church of England now Deceased) did set up an Insurance Office on Births, Marriages and Services, in order thereby to serve the Public and get an honest Livelyhood for herself. The said Dorothy had such Success in her Undertaking that more Claims were paid, and more Stamps used for Certificates and Policies in her Office than in all other the like Offices in London besides; which good Fortune was chiefly owing to the Fairness and Justice of her Proceedings in the said Business. For all the Money paid into the Office was entered in one Book, and all the Money paid out upon Claims, was set down in another Book, and all People had Liberty to peruse both, so that there could not possibly be the least Fraud in the management thereof." *The Case of Dorothy Petty in relation to the Union Society at the White Lion by Temple Bar whereof she is Director.* [Brit. Mus. 816. m. 10 (82).] The profits of such private offices appear to have been very considerable, if we may trust the estimate of Charles Povey, who complained that owing to a 'cross incident' he was obliged to sell his undertaking of the Sun Fire Office on very low terms. Had he remained in possession it would have brought him in £600 or £800 per annum. *English Inquisition* (1718), p. 37. This was in 1709, and early in the following year the business was organised by a company which has continued to flourish ever since. *Proposals set forth by the Company of London Insurers* (from the Sun Fire Office, April 10, 1710). [Brit. Mus. 816. m. 10 (83).]

[1] Insurance business of different sorts was a favourite field for Company promoters at this time. At the Crown Tavern, Smithfield, a subscription book was opened for establishing "an Insurance Office for Horses dying natural deaths, stolen, or disabled"; at the Fountain Tavern there was started "a co-partnership for insuring and increasing Children's fortunes"; at another place in the City subscribers came to put their names and money down for "Plummer and Petty's Insurance from Death by drinking Geneva." * * * Then there were started offices for "Assurance from lying"; for "Insurance from house-breakers"; for "Rum Insurance"; for "Insurance from highwaymen" and numerous others. Martin, *History of Lloyd's*, 89. [2] *Parl. Hist.* vii. 640.

the London Assurance and Royal Exchange Assurance,

Exchange Assurance Corporation were created. These Companies are still large and flourishing institutions; in their earlier days they had considerable difficulties, especially through the loss of a fleet of Jamaica ships; the London Assurance was deeply involved, and its shares fell within a month from 160 to 60 and thence to 12[1]. The two undertakings had agreed to pay £300,000 into the Exchequer[2], but subsequently, in 1721, half of the sum was remitted. The Act which the Companies obtained[3] gave them the exclusive right of carrying on this business on a joint stock, but did not interfere with the business of private individuals who were engaged in underwriting.

In the early part of the eighteenth century the practice had come into fashion of resorting to coffee-houses for all sorts of intercourse, whether social, political or commercial.

as well as by the concentration at Lloyd's Coffee House of underwriters,

Persons engaged in shipping appear to have used a coffee-house kept by Mr Edward Lloyd, who was a very energetic man, and published a newspaper chiefly devoted to foreign and commercial news in 1696[4]. This did not last very long, however; but it was succeeded in 1726 by *Lloyd's List*[5], which contained ship-news, together with the current rates of exchange, the prices of shares, and so forth. The coffee-house, though convenient, was the resort of some doubtful characters; and it was determined by the respectable brokers and underwriters, who frequented Lloyd's, to establish a new resort for themselves. They secured the property in *Lloyd's List*; and after various attempts to get satisfactory premises had failed, they obtained quarters in the Royal Exchange in 1774[6]. The new Lloyd's Coffee-house, which was there established, contained a public room and also a subscribers' room, and the committee enforced various regulations in

---

[1] M. Postlethwayt, *Universal Dictionary of Trade*, article on *Actions*, p. 15 (a).

[2] Martin, *Lloyd's*, 99.

[3] 6 Geo. I. c. 18.

[4] Martin, *Lloyd's*, 74. The following announcement which first appeared in No. 61 shows the nature of the publication and the aims of the proprietor:—"All Gentlemen, Merchants, or others, who are desirous to have this News in a whole Sheet of Paper (two leaves instead of one leaf), for to write their own private Concerns in, or other Intelligence for the Countrey, may be supplied with them, done upon very good Paper, for a Penny a Sheet, at Lloyd's Coffee-House in Lombard Street."

[5] Martin, *Lloyd's*, 107.   [6] *Ib.* 120, 145.

regard to the business which was done by the members. In 1779, they drew up a general form of policy which is still adhered to, and which has been taken as the model for marine insurance business all over the world[1]. It is curious to notice that they regarded the business of life-insurance[2] with much suspicion, as it seemed to be merely speculative[3] and lent itself to all sorts of nefarious practices. At a meeting of the subscribers, in March 1774, a resolution was passed of which the preamble states that "shameful Practices have been introduced of late years into the business *who refused to engage in Life Insurances.* of Underwriting, such as making Speculative Insurances on the Lives of Persons and of Government securities." It continues that "in the first instance it is endangering the Lives of the Persons so Insured, from the idea of being selected by Society for that inhuman purpose, which is being virtually an accessory in a species of slow murder." The subscribers were therefore to refuse to undertake such business and to show "a proper resentment" against any broker who attempted to introduce it[4].

It thus came about that the underwriters, who had been left outside when the two great Companies were formed in 1720, had practically formed themselves into a body resembling a regulated Company. The forms under which business was done were now definitely established; but the immense increase in the risks of loss which British shipping ran, during the great wars[5], rendered it necessary for all

---

[1] Martin, *Lloyd's*, 157.

[2] Martin, 117, quoting *London Chronicle* for 1768, also pamphlet entitled *Every Man His Own Broker*. See also the Act regulating Life Insurance, 14 Geo. III. c. 48.

[3] The valuation of Life Annuities had been already put on a scientific basis by De Witt (whose treatise has been reprinted by Mr Hendriks in his excellent monograph, *Contributions to the History of Insurance*, 40), and also by Halley, *Phil. Trans.* XVII. 596, but they attracted little attention among practical men. Many actuarial questions are also discussed by Weyman Lee, *An Essay to ascertain the value of leases and annuities for years and lives, and to estimate the chances of the duration of lives* (1738). The Society for Equitable Assurances was the first Company founded on a scientific basis; this was established in 1762, but the promoters failed to procure a charter. E. J. Farren, *Historical Essay on the Rise and Early Progress of the doctrine of Life Contingencies* (1844), p. 94. The Amicable Society, which was incorporated in 1706, was originally a sort of Tontine. *Ib.* p. 35.   [4] Martin, *Lloyd's*, 157.

[5] Compare Debates on Miscarriages of the Navy (1708), *Parl. Hist.* VI. 618;

ship-owners to protect themselves by insuring, and caused a very rapid expansion of the underwriters' business.

XV. CHANGES IN THE ORGANISATION AND DISTRIBUTION OF INDUSTRY.

The foster-ing of industry was the prime object of economic policy during the period of Whig As-cendancy,

225. The promotion of industry of every kind had become the primary object which Parliament pursued in its efforts to build up the wealth and power of England. Sir Robert Walpole had aimed at recasting the tariff so that the materials for our manufactures might be cheap; and the rules for commercial intercourse, which were embodied in treaties, or laid down under the Navigation Acts, were intended to secure a large sale for our goods. During the period of Whig Ascendancy attention was concentrated on this aspect of economic life, and no effort was spared to make England the workshop of the extensive spheres where her influence and her friendship availed to keep the markets open to our manufactures.

and this aim is very defensible.

For this line of conduct there was much to be said. Labour is, to a very large extent, the active element in the increase of wealth[1]; and the more it is brought into play, the more the other sides of economic life will prosper. Industrial development furnished commodities with which to carry on trade, and thus gave employment to shipping and seamen; it provided the means of procuring such foreign products as were most required; it gave occupation to a large population, and thus brought about a demand for food, and encouraged agriculture[2]. There seemed therefore to be good grounds for attempting to foster the growth of industrial activity, not merely through the natural influence of expanding commerce, but by the artificial stimulus of bounties as well.

Merchants' Petition (1742), *ib.* XII. 446, 753; Commercial Losses (Feb. 6, 1778), *ib.* XIX. 709, also XX. 1144. Also on the alarm caused by Paul Jones and pirates on our coasts, *ib.* XXI. 486; Difficulties with Holland, *ib.* 963.

[1] Petty, *Treatise*, 49. See above, p. 383.

[2] Compare Sir J. Steuart, *Inquiry into the Principles of Political Economy,* in *Works,* I. 35, 45, 153. See p. 704 n. 1, below.

There were, however, considerable obstacles to the in- definite expansion of industry; the limit, beyond which it was difficult to carry the development of any trade[1], was set by the supply of materials. The English clothiers were largely *As the* *materials* engaged in working up English wool; it was because of the *for estab-* *lished* abundance and excellent quality of this product that weavers *trades were* had migrated to this country in such large numbers. But *limited,* the wool-supply could not be largely increased at will, especially during a period when arable cultivation was coming more generally into vogue. Similarly the ship- builders and the tanners made use of English-grown ma- terials, while the ironworkers were dependent on the amount of wood available for fuel. It seemed as if each of the staple trades of the country had almost reached its natural limit during the early eighteenth century. Efforts were indeed made to supplement the home production by the import of Spanish[2] and Irish[3] wool, and similar expedients were adopted in other trades; but the landed interest was inclined to take exception to such measures. Hence comparatively little progress resulted from all the care that was lavished on the staple trades.

There was, however, considerable scope for planting and *it seemed* *desirable* developing exotic trades, which consisted in working up im- *to plant* *exotic* ported materials; and circumstances favoured the movement *trades* in this direction. The incursion of the Huguenots had, indeed, been most beneficial, by giving the country the advantage of new methods and superior skill in making use of its own materials; the immigrants were still more welcome as adepts *in which the* in trades which had not hitherto been practised in Britain *Huguenots* *were* with much success. Of the manufactures to which they *skilled,*

---

[1] Protection, which maintains a trade after this limit has been reached, is much less defensible than protection which aims at rendering the utilisation of native resources as complete as possible. The differences come out in connection with the protection afforded by the Corn Laws before and after the period 1773—1791; see below, p. 730.

[2] *A treatise of Wool and the Manufacture of it*, Brit. Mus. 712. g. 16 (21), 1685, p. 9; also *England's Interest by Trade asserted* [Brit. Mus. 1102. h. 1 (8)], p. 22. James, *History of the Worsted Manufacture*, p. 206.

[3] *The Grasier's Complaint*, p. 23 (1726), Brit. Mus. 712. g. 16 (37). Defoe, *Plan of the English Commerce* (p. 156), estimates that 100,000 Packs of Wool were imported yearly from Ireland, besides Scotch wool which was said to be worth £60,000 at the time of the Union.

devoted themselves, the linen industry was one for which the materials could be provided in Ireland and Scotland, and it

came to be completely naturalised; but raw silk and cotton wool were, and continued to be, foreign products. The very existence of such textile manufactures is dependent on the maintenance of intercourse with distant lands. The rapid increase of English commerce gave enlarged opportunities of procuring materials, so that there was room for steady, and eventually for rapid development.

The de-
pendence
of industry
on trade,
for sale
and for
material,

The fact that English industry was becoming dependent for its markets, and to some extent for its materials, on distant countries, involved the intervention of capitalists in an increasing degree. The capitalist merchant was called upon to serve as an intermediary between the English weaver and the purchaser in foreign parts, and to procure the materials which were necessary for the prosecution of certain trades. The judgment of the employer was required to maintain the honesty of the materials and workmanship, and to decide on the fashion and quality of goods which it was best worth while to produce. In the old days of gild regulation, or of the activity of aulnagers and searchers, and under the system of well-ordered trade, there had been little room for the personal skill and judgment of an employer. But in

the eighteenth century, there was full scope for the exercise of these business qualities, and industry could not flourish or expand unless they were brought into play.

The opening of distant markets for English manufactures did not always bring about an increased production[1], but it necessarily affected the character of the industrial system. There was greater scope for supervision by masters, and employment in the textile trades was apt to pass from small independent manufacturers to wage-earners. The eighteenth century commercial system led, not so much to the expansion of industry, as to the development of the class of capitalist employers, whom Adam Smith criticised and the Manchester School admired. This sort of modification in the economic relationships of those who are co-operating in the work of producing some article for the market, may proceed very

---

[1] The limitation of the supply of materials rendered this impossible.

gradually and almost imperceptibly. The change from one type of organisation to another does not necessarily involve any revolution that is apparent to the eye. The wage-earner, who is employed by a capitalist, may pursue his occupation in the same sort of cottage and with the same implements as those that are used by independent workmen. The distinguishing feature of the capitalist, as contrasted with the domestic, system lies in the fact, that under the former scheme, employers or undertakers own the materials[1] and pay the wages, whereas in the domestic system[2] the workman is his own master; he owns the materials on which he works and sells the product of his labour. But there need be no external mark that calls attention to an alteration in the economic status of the craftsman; indeed the same weaver might work for some weeks for an employer and at other times on his own account[3]. On this account it is exceedingly difficult to follow out the course of the change. We can occasionally get definite and precise information on the point, but on the whole we are only able to infer the progress of capitalism from incidental occurrences. The nature of the difficulties and disputes, which arise in a trade, may serve to show whether the labourers were wage-earners or not; and the character of the associations[4] which existed among them, may often give us a suggestion as to the condition of the workmen at some date[5]. It is, for the most

A.D. 1689 —1776.

The reconstruction of industry on capitalist lines may be effected gradually and quietly,

but traces of the change are found in the nature of trade associations and trade disputes.

---

[1] The employers sometimes owned the looms, as well, 2 and 3 P. and M. c. 11.

[2] This term is used in the sense in which it was current in Yorkshire at the beginning of the nineteenth century (*Reports*, 1806, iii. 1058, printed pag. 444). Mr Unwin (*Industrial Organisation*, p. 4), defines the terms quite differently, and opposes the gild to the domestic system, as separate and successive phases of development, but this does not seem to me to apply in English history. I prefer to say that the domestic system existed from the earliest times till it was superseded by capitalism; the craft gilds were a form of industrial organisation which was appropriate to the domestic, rather than to the capitalist system; and that these gilds were convenient instruments for enforcing civic, as contrasted with national policy.

[3] The analogy with the agricultural change is noticeable; the yeoman farmer might often be employed as a labourer to work for a neighbour in return for wages.

[4] The true craft gild was appropriate to the domestic system, but some of the mediaeval London companies were capitalist in character and so were the seventeenth century companies, generally speaking. Trade Unions, as associations of wage-earners, testify by their existence to the severance of classes; the inference to be drawn from the formation of yeoman gilds is doubtful. See vol. i. p. 443.

[5] Even in a great trade centre like London, the cloth-workers continued to be an association of domestic workers in the first half of the seventeenth century.

A.D. 1689
—1776.
part, by examining evidence of this kind that we can hope to trace in any way the gradual progress of capitalism in superseding the domestic system throughout the country.

In the clothing trade the capitalist and domestic systems existed side by side
There are some trades which had in all probability been organised on a capitalist basis from the first. It is likely enough that John Kemp and other Flemish immigrants of his time were large employers[1], and there is no reason to suppose that all English trades were originally domestic, and were recast by degrees on the other model. It is apparent that the capitalist and domestic system existed side by side in the staple trade of the country for centuries[2]. It seems not improbable that circumstances, during the seventeenth century, favoured the domestic system, and that it developed at the expense of the other; but as the capitalist was better able than the domestic worker to take advantage of the expanding commerce of the eighteenth century, and of the mechanical appliances of the nineteenth, he has won the day.

and each had advantages of its own,
The contest between these two systems would hardly have continued so long, unless each had had its own advantages. Under the domestic system, the merchant formed the intermediary between the independent weaver and the London market to which the product of his loom was carried. There was much to be said for this arrangement; the weaver could not but prefer to be his own master, rather than to work under supervision, and at the times his employer desired. Public authorities also looked on the domestic system with favour; it had many social advantages, as there was less danger of the weavers being reduced to destitution

---

S. P. D. C. I. cclvii. 6. *Ordinances of Clothworkers*, 1639 (Brit. Mus. 8248. e. 26), p. 127, also *Letter on Lawes and Orders* (Brit. Mus. 1103. f. 33), p. 14. See p. 511 below.

[1] Vol. i. 306. P. Methwin who introduced fine weaving in Bradford (Wilts.) in the seventeenth century was also a wealthy man: W. H. Jones in *Wilts. Arch. Magazine*, v. 48. The weaving trade when introduced into Florence in the thirteenth century had a capitalist character. Doren, *Studien aus der Florentiner Wirtschaftsgeschichte* (1901), pp. 22, 23.

[2] There is a parallel in the contest between farming on a large and on a small scale in the present day. On the whole the small holding has passed away, but there have been circumstances recently, which have favoured the breaking up of large farms in some districts, especially where land is required for a by-occupation, and as subsidiary to some other employment. Small farms may continue to exist side by side with large ones; and a certain amount of re-arrangement is likely to occur according to changing conditions.

and incited to riot, by being dismissed in periods of bad *A.D. 1689
—1776.* trade; while the merchant was better able than the capitalist employer, to reject inferior cloth, and to prevent it from coming into the market at all[1]. On the other hand, the *but the capitalist* capitalist employer not only supervised the industry, but *was in* established his own trading connections. He was better placed *the best position* for completing a large order by a given date, as the work- *for super-vising* men were more entirely under his control, and he was able to *workmen.* organise the industry on the best lines and to introduce a suitable division of labour. The domestic weaver would have to sell his cloth to a fuller, or cloth-worker[2], practically in his own neighbourhood, before it was a marketable article: he did not come in direct contact with the consumer, either at home or abroad. The large clothier had much better oppor- *gauging the market,* tunities of disposing of his goods, either in a half-manufac- tured, or finished state. Not only so—the domestic weaver would be inclined to go on producing the same make of cloth he had always furnished, but the great undertaker could attempt to gauge the probable demand for different classes of goods, and manufacture with a view to a changing demand. The domestic system may have been better adapted for the maintenance of a recognised standard, though this seems doubtful, but the capitalist was certainly in a better position for introducing improvements and making progress[3]. From the point of view of developing trade, capital was at a decided advantage, but the domestic system managed to *and intro-ducing* maintain its ground, till the introduction of expensive *machinery.*

[1] Compare the remedy for abuses in the Somerset trade, 2 and 3 P. and M. c. 12. A bad piece would be left on the hands of the independent workman and used locally; but if a capitalist manufacturer owned the inferior goods, he would be likely to try to pass them off somehow.

[2] The complete independence of each link of the industry as it existed in Devonshire in 1630 is very remarkable. "First the gentleman farmer, or husband-man, sends his wool to the market, which is bought either by the comber or the spinster, and they, the next week, bring it thither again in yarn, which the weaver buys; and the market following brings that thither again in cloth, where it is sold either to the clothier (who sends it to London), or to the merchant who (after it has passed the fuller's mill and sometimes the dyer's vat), transports it." Westcote, *View of Devonshire*, p. 61.

[3] Duchesne, *L'Evolution économique et sociale de l'Industrie de la Laine*, 60. According to Mr Graham's evidence, *Reports* 1806, III. 1058 (printed pagination 441), the neighbourhood of capitalist factories tended to the introduction of improvements on the part of domestic manufacturers.

machinery, which involved the use of water or steam power, when the triumph of capitalism became complete.

226. While this revolution was proceeding gradually and silently, other important changes were occurring in connection with the industrial life of the country, and the signs *The changes which occurred in the local distribution of industry* of them were patent to the most casual observer. A very noticeable alteration was taking place in the local distribution of industry. The Eastern Counties, which had been so important in the later middle ages, lost ground, while the West Riding of Yorkshire was steadily developing. The iron-works of Sussex died out altogether, while Shropshire and Linlithgowshire made startling advances. It must suffice to indicate the general trend of the migration, and to point out that there is a considerable mass of material available, for those who are interested in the question, as to the progress or decay of particular industries in particular areas. Harrison and Leland have described England, as it was in the latter part of Elizabeth's reign; in the charming essays, which Fuller prefaced to his record of the *Worthies* of the various counties of England, we find many details as to the resources and industries of each in turn. Defoe's *Tour*, with the additions by Richardson, goes over much of the same ground at later dates[1]; and the writings of Arthur Young, and of other contemporary tourists, carry the information to another era. Again and again, in perusing these books, we find evidence of obvious decadence in some parts of the country, and of marked progress in others.

can sometimes be explained on physical grounds In many cases these alterations in the distribution of industry can be accounted for by physical reasons. The exhaustion of the fuel in Sussex rendered it impossible to continue the furnaces there; and the trade naturally shifted to districts where coal and iron were found in conjunction, so soon as the means for utilising mineral fuel became available. In other cases, an industry was attracted to a district where advantage could be taken of water power[2], and facilities for

---

[1] Defoe, in 1724, speaks of Bocking and Braintree as flourishing, but Richardson in the 1748 edition of Defoe's *Tour* (I. 118) gives a very different account. The variations in the prosperity of local industries is curious; in 1724 the Guildford trade had revived (*Tour*, 1724, I. 87), but that at Cranbrook in Kent was extinct.

[2] The Eastern Counties were at a disadvantage in this respect; the West of England was much better provided with fulling mills.

procuring certain qualities of wool, or of clay, would determine the special character of the weaving or the pottery in
particular districts.

There were, however, other circumstances, which have *and some-times by conveni- ence for trade.* little to do with mere physical characteristics, that must be
taken into account. The interruption of trading connections,
which might be occasioned by a war, would be a very serious
blow to an old established industry, and the inhabitants
might have difficulty in adapting themselves, and their trade-
institutions, to new conditions. On the other hand, as we have
already seen in the case of London[1], the centres of increasing
commerce[2] tended to become areas of enlarged industry.

These changes had a necessary bearing on the contest
between the large employers and the domestic weavers. It
is not easy to balance the relative advantages of the two
systems. The concentration of many workmen in a small *The con- centration of trade was favourable to capi- talist or- ganisation;* district gave a convenient opportunity for the introduction of
capitalist organisation; while on the other hand, the domestic
system appears to have been an important agent in the
diffusion of industry over wide areas. It is hardly straining
the evidence to regard the migration of craftsmen from the
towns to the suburbs and to country villages, in the fifteenth
and sixteenth centuries, as due to a desire on the part of the *and the migration of inde- pendent workmen tended to diffuse industry.* workmen to remain independent, and escape from the supervision of employers and the regulations passed by oligarchical
associations of capitalists. The development of the cloth
trade in Yorkshire in the early seventeenth century[3], while
complaints were so rife as to the quality of the wares and
the conditions of employment in the capitalist districts[4],
may be interpreted as an indication that the same motives
continued to operate. The migration of weavers from the
West of England to Ireland after the Revolution was not

---

[1] See above, p. 312. On migration by weavers to London, see the *Weavers' Pretences Examined* (1719) [Brit. Mus. 1029. e. 17 (3)].

[2] From its excellent water communication Norwich appears to have continued to flourish as a weaving centre in 1778. Defoe, *Tour*, I. p. 49. He says that "120,000 people were busied in the woollen and silk manufacture of that city."

[3] Compare the petition in 1640 against the weekly cloth market recently erected at Wakefield, and that only the fifteen charter fairs should be continued which had hitherto sufficed for the trade. *Hist. MSS. Comm.* IV. 36.

[4] See above, pp. 204 n., 297.

A.D. 1689
—1776.

Yorkshire proprietors found it profitable to encourage domestic weavers,

improbably undertaken with the same prospect of retaining individual independence[1]. In the eighteenth century there were Yorkshire proprietors who found it was distinctly to their advantage to encourage the development of the weaving trade in its domestic form[2]. Sir Walter Calverly improved his estate immensely by erecting a fulling mill on the Aire[3] and catering for a class of tenants who could combine domestic industry with pasture farming[4].

There were, therefore, good reasons why the cloth industry, as it spread through the West Riding, should be domestic in character, even though capitalism was becoming dominant in other areas. In the latter half of the eighteenth century the domestic system appears to have had advantages of its own, which counterbalanced the economic conditions that were favourable to capitalist employers. The industrial im-

and they adopted labour saving implements,

provements in the weaving trade of the eighteenth century consisted in the introduction of new implements, or of machines that went by hand-power, rather than of expensive machines that involved the use of water or of steam power, and rendered concentration in factories inevitable. The flying shuttle, which was patented by Kay in 1733, enabled a weaver to do his work without assistance and more quickly; it tended to put all the work in the hands of the best men.

to which wage-earners at the old centres

Though the wage-earners of the Eastern Counties[5] objected to it, since it left some men unemployed, the domestic weavers of Yorkshire took it kindly[6]. They were also able

---

[1] The movement affected the domestic weavers of Devonshire, however, as well as others, and was probably connected with the dearness of living of which Westcote complained at the beginning of the seventeenth century. *View of Devonshire*, p. 62.

[2] There is an excellent account of the development of the domestic system in Yorkshire in Mr Graham's evidence before the Committee of 1806 (*Reports*, 1806, III. 1058 p. 444). He had built cottages on an estate near Leeds with 5, 6, 7, 8 or 10 acres of land attached.

[3] E. Laurence, *Duty of a Steward to his Lord* (1727), 36.

[4] On other artificers who cultivated land as a by-occupation, see p. 564 below.

[5] The Eastern County spinners continued to use the distaff, and had not adopted the wheel in 1780. T., *Letters on Utility and Policy* (1780), 14 [Brit. Mus. T. 220 (7)].

[6] The weavers both in Colchester and at Spitalfields were strongly opposed to the introduction of the flying shuttle; and John Kay was forced to give up the business he had established at Colchester, and to migrate to Leeds; his shuttle was readily adopted by the Yorkshire weavers, but not his power-loom. Woodcroft,

to procure the hand-jennies which were used in spinning, A.D. 1689 —1776. and thus to get more yarn spun under their own roofs. These new inventions of the eighteenth century were quite congruent with the domestic system[1], while the attempt to *took exception.* introduce them gave rise to conflicts between the masters and men in capitalist areas. Up till the eve of the introduction of steam-power, domestic weaving seems to have been readily compatible with the introduction of labour-saving appliances, and to have developed in Yorkshire because of the economic advantages it possessed, though capitalism had been established in the West of England district.

227. The cloth manufacture had been conducted in many *Pains were taken to* parts of the country with a view to foreign markets, from *open and* the fifteenth century onwards, and had to some extent dis- *retain foreign* played a capitalist character at that period[2]. Special pains *markets for English* had been taken that the expansion of English commerce, in *cloth,* the seventeenth and eighteenth centuries, should cause an increased demand for the product of English looms. This object has been kept in view in the struggle about well-ordered trade, in the negotiations for the Methuen Treaty, and in the agitation for maintaining it; and a similar feeling comes out in the conditions which were eventually imposed on the East India Company, in regard to the export of English goods[3]. The government were at pains to foster the cloth trade, not merely by opening up better markets abroad, but by fresh industrial regulation. It is in all probability true that the machinery for maintaining the quality of the manufacture had fallen into disuse[4], and there is very little fresh

Brief Biographies of Inventors of Machines, p. 3. On the other hand, the flying shuttle does not appear to have come into use in the West of England till 1796 (*Reports, etc.* 1840, xxiv. 392, printed pag. 372), and the Eastern Counties weavers had apparently been forced to adopt it before that date. Arthur Young notes at Colchester in 1784, "The manufactory is exceedingly improved by means of a mechanical addition to the loom, which enables one weaver to do the business of two. In wide stuffs they formerly had two hands to a loom, now only one." *Annals of Agriculture*, ii. 109.

[1] The machinery for the finishing of the cloth does not appear to have been compatible with the domestic system. The shearmen in Yorkshire, who were wage-earners employed by merchants, resisted the introduction of gig-mills, while the West of England manufacturers were successful in doing so. See below, p. 661.

[2] See Vol. i. p. 437.   [3] In 1768. See above, p. 470.

[4] An attempt was made to reconstruct it in the West Riding by creating a clothiers' corporation. 14 C. II. c. 32.

A.D. 1689
—1776. legislation on this topic; but much attention was given both to the supply of material and the terms of employment. The measures which were passed on these points seem to show that, as we might have expected, the trade was becoming increasingly capitalist in character.

and to give the English manufacturers a preference in purchasing wool. From time immemorial pains had to be taken by the government to see that English weavers had a sufficient supply of the raw material of their manufacture. The assize of wool, under Edward III., had been intended to check the export of this product at low rates, and thus to give a preference to purchasers at home. In the time of Edward IV., limits were laid down as to the time of year when the Staplers might purchase wool for export; from March 18th till August 24th the home producer had no reason to fear their competition[1]. In the latter part of Elizabeth's reign an agitation sprang up in favour of an absolute prohibition of the export of wool[2], and James I. issued proclamations against it[3].

After the Restoration the export was prohibited, Parliament took up the same line, both at the Restoration[4] and the Revolution[5]. The measures which were then passed were intended, not merely to give English weavers a preference[6], but to starve out foreign competition altogether, by preventing industrial rivals from procuring a supply of English wool[7]. This system of prohibition was

---

[1] 4 Ed. IV. c. 4. Lohmann, *Die Staatliche Regelung der englischen Wollindustrie*, p. 66. This seems to have been specially aimed at a system of contracting beforehand for the purchase of wool.

[2] S. P. D. El. ccxliv. No. 104, 1593.

[3] 26 Sept. and 9 Nov. 1614; this was during the disturbance caused by Cockayne's patent, but similar steps were taken in later years (p. 298 n. 9, above), and by Charles I. in 1632.

[4] 13 and 14 C. II. c. 18.　　　　　[5] 1 W. and M. i. c. 32.

[6] Attention was also given to the supply of other articles used in dyeing (8 G. I. c. 15, §§ 10, 11, also 27 G. II. c. 18) and in cloth working, such as fuller's earth. See the commission of 1622 (Rymer, *Fœdera*, xvii. 412), also 12 C II. c. 32 and 14 C. II. c. 18. Direct encouragement was given to the growth of certain products, such as madder (A. Young, *Farmer's Letters*, 227, and Pennant, *Journey*, i. 96), which were useful in connection with the textile trades. Tassels or teasels, which were used in the wool manufacture, were grown in considerable quantities in Yorkshire, where cloth dressing was carried on (Arthur Young, *Northern Tour*, i. 191). The want of tassels in Scotland is spoken of by Lindsay (*The Interest of Scotland*, p. 109) as one reason why the woollen trade was so backward there.

[7] This was believed to be so superior in quality to foreign wools as to be essential, at all events, for certain branches of the manufacture. Defoe, *Plan of*

maintained during the whole period of Whig Ascendancy. A.D. 1689
—1776.
As in other cases, the effort to put down a profitable branch
of commerce led to the development of an illicit trade; the
great stretch of pasture ground on Romney Marsh offered
special facilities for the successful running of wool[1]. This
policy, which tended towards lowering the price of wool, was
much favoured by the manufacturers, but it roused the *despite*
jealousy of the landed interest, and in all probability it did *the protests of the*
to some extent defeat its own ends. Wool-growing became *landed interest,*
less profitable, almost at the very date when the corn-bounty
Act was giving a new security to those who devoted themselves to tillage. The landowners in the pasture counties
were inclined to resent the special favour shown to corn-
growing, but the experience of depopulation in the sixteenth
century had left an indelible impression on the public mind,
and no proposal to develop wool-growing by a system of
bounties would have had a chance of passing. At the same
time it can hardly be a matter of surprise that, when rules
were enforced which tended to keep down the price of wool,
the supply showed little sign of increase. The West of *and the*
England manufacturers had opportunities of obtaining wool *home supply was*
and yarn from Ireland[2], but even with this assistance, and *supple-mented*
the legal right to the whole of the English clip, the trade *from Ireland.*
fails to show an expansion at all commensurate to the pains
which were expended on fostering it.

    The low price of wool would have been advantageous to
all manufacturers, domestic and capitalist alike; but the
difficulty of transporting a bulky commodity, like wool, gave
an advantage to the dealer, who was able to organise the
means of conveying his purchase. The domestic weaver, who *The*
bought in small quantities for immediate use, could hardly *domestic weaver*
hope to compete with the great stapler, who had facilities for *was at a disadvan-*
buying in any part of the country. The mediaeval legisla- *tage in the purchase*
tion against the regrating of wool was probably designed to *of wool.*

English Commerce, pp. 173, 174, and the *Contrast* (1782), quoted by Bischoff,
Woollen and Worsted Manufactures, 95, 231. See also Smith, *Wealth of Nations*,
IV viii. p. 268.

   [1] *An Abstract of the proceedings of W. Carter* (1694) and *Excidium Angliae* (1727).

   [2] 1 W. and M. 1, c. 32, § 6. The statute only allowed wool from Ireland to be
sent to Liverpool, Chester, Bristol, Minehead, Barnstaple, Bideford and Exeter,
and to no other ports.

protect local weavers against middlemen[1] who purchased for the large employers, or with a view to export[2]. In the sixteenth century, however, the wholesale purchasers seem to have obtained an undisputed position in the wool trade, and the domestic manufacturers could not purchase direct from the grower. Henry VIII. endeavoured to force the dealing in this commodity back on to the old lines by his Weavers' Act[3]; but under Edward VI. it seemed preferable to recognise the new order of affairs. The domestic weavers, and the spinners they employed, were forced to have recourse to middlemen in order to obtain wool, either for carding or combing, in the quantities that they could afford to buy. Hence the general prohibition against regrators was relaxed in favour of the poorer workers, in the neighbourhood of Norwich[4], and also round Halifax[5]. The recriminations against the wool merchants, by the weavers, continued through the sixteenth and seventeenth[6] centuries, but no satisfactory method of giving the domestic spinners and weavers a preference could be devised. The domestic weaver, who could not buy a large stock of material, evidently found it difficult to procure wool or yarn as he required it, and this must have hampered him in the pursuit of his calling; the wealthy undertaker was much less likely to suffer from this difficulty. It may be conjectured that one reason why the domestic system survived so long as it did in Yorkshire was because the little grass farmers round Leeds, who worked as weavers, were able to rely to some extent on local supplies.

Attempts were made to prevent the large undertakers from engrossing it,

The Tudor and Stuart regulation of the wool trade appears to have been intended to protect the domestic weaver from capitalist competition; but the government also busied itself to secure satisfactory conditions for the weavers who were working for wages. This class was not explicitly provided for in the statute of 1563; but authority was given for settling the rates of pay per piece in 1597[7], and in a

and to insist that they should pay the regulated wages,

---

[1] Lohmann, *op. cit.* 66. 27 Edw. III. ii. c. 3; 31 Edw. III. c. 2; 14 R. II. c. 4.
[2] 4 Henry VII. c. 11.   [3] 37 Henry VIII. c. 15.
[4] 1 Edw. VI. c. 6.   [5] 2 and 3 P. and M. c. 13.
[6] See above, p. 298.
[7] Regulations on this and kindred matters were drafted in 1593 (S. P. D. El. ccxliv. 126—130), but the measure became law as 39 El. c. 12.

subsequent statute[1] penalties were imposed on the clothiers A.D. 1689
—1776. who did not pay the wages authoritatively settled. Special protection was afforded, in 1662[2], to the weavers in the North of England, against masters who cut down wages. The increasing attention given to the condition of wage-earners not improbably indicates that this class was becoming larger, and that their good government demanded more attention. This impression is confirmed by the occasional interference *and should* which was thought necessary in times of bad trade. In 1528 *continue to employ* there had been capitalists who had dismissed their hands in *their hands in bad* Essex, Kent, Wiltshire and especially in Suffolk[3]. Similar *times.* trouble arose in Berkshire in 1564[4]. In the unexampled stagnation of 1622[5], the Crown insisted that merchants should purchase cloth, and that clothiers should continue to give employment, in the hope of relieving distress both among domestic workers and wage-earners. In Suffolk[6], and later in Essex[7], the crises involved the ruin of employers as well as the distress of the employed.

The Acts against truck are another series of measures *Wage-* which indicate the existence of the capitalist system[8]; and *earners were* similar evidence is furnished by the recurring measures *accused* against the dishonesty of workmen in embezzling materials[9]. *of embezzling* These causes of dispute could only arise under the capitalist *materials,* system, but the repressive measures give us comparatively little information as to the districts where the trouble was most keenly felt. On the other hand the accounts, which have come down to us, of the disputes in the cloth trade[10] in

---

[1] 1 J. I. c. 6.　　　　　[2] 14 C. II. c. 32, § 15.

[3] Hall, *Chronicle*, 746. Brewer, *Cal. S. P.* iv. 4044, 4239.

[4] S. P. D. El. xxxiv. 43. There was also an interruption of trade in 1587 which was severely felt both at Bristol and Southampton, and it seemed desirable to fix on a new depot for the export of cloth. S. P. D. El. cc. 5, 12.

[5] S. P. D. J. I. cxxvii. 76. See also the reports of the goods from Gloucester, Somerset, Reading, Blackwell, Manchester, Wiltshire and Kent, in Blackwell Hall. S. P. D. J. I. cxxviii. 72—76.

[6] S. P. D. J. I. ccxxviii. 67.

[7] In the depression from 1631—1637. S. P. D. C. I. 1637, cccliv. 92, April 26th, and ccclv. 67, May 4.

[8] 1 Anne ii. c. 18, § 3; 12 Geo. I. c. 34; 29 Geo. II. c. 33.

[9] 6 H. VIII. c. 9; 7 J. I. c. 7; 1 Anne ii. c. 18.

[10] For a dispute in London, 1675, see *A true Narrative of the Proceedings against the Weavers* (Brit. Mus. 1132. b. 79). They seem to have rioted and to have broken looms, which shows that the looms could not have belonged to

the eighteenth century, show how deeply-seated and how wide-spread the severance between capital and labour had *and formed* become.　The struggle had assumed considerable proportions *combina-* in Devonshire, in 1718, when a proclamation against unlawful *tions* clubs was published, reciting that, whereas "complaint had been made to the Government that great numbers of Wool-combers and Weavers in several parts of the Kingdom had lately formed themselves into lawless Clubs and Societies which had illegally presumed to use a Common Seal and to act as Bodies Corporate by making and unlawfully conspiring to execute certain By-laws or Orders, whereby they pretend to determine who had a right to the Trade, what and how many Apprentices and Journeymen each man should keep at once, together with the prices of all their Manufactures and the manner and materials of which they should be wrought; and that when many of the said Conspirators wanted work because their Masters would not submit to such pretended Orders and unreasonable Demands, they fed them with Money till they could again get employment, in order to oblige their Masters to employ them for want of other hands; and that the said Clubs by their great numbers and their correspondence in several of the Trading Towns of the Kingdom became dangerous to the publick peace, especially in *in Devon* the Counties of Devon and Somerset; where many Riots had *and* *Somerset,* been committed, private Houses broken open, the Subjects assaulted, wounded and put in peril of their lives, great Quantities of Woollen Goods cut and spoilt, Prisoners set at Liberty by Force, and that the Rioters refused to disperse, notwithstanding the reading of the Proclamation required by the late Riot Act.　For these causes the Proclamation enjoined the putting the said Riot Act and another Act made in the reign of Ed. VI. (intitled The Bill of Conspiracy of the Victuallers and Craftsmen) in Execution against all such as should unlawfully confederate and com-

---

them as domestic workers. "It is sufficiently known to most persons about this Citty, what great mischief and disorders happened by the Insurrection of the *Weavers* in *August* last, not only to the breaking of the public Peace, but to the great damage of several persons whose Looms and Instruments of Trade they forcibly took away from them and burned." They persisted day after day "in continual tumults" and laid "violent hands on looms."

bine for the purposes above mention'd, in particular, or for any other illegal Purposes contrary to the Tenour of the aforesaid Acts[1]." There were troubles in Gloucestershire in 1727, when the method of paying for piece-work was carefully specified[2], and in 1756, when a new statute was passed conferring on the Justices the power of regulating wages[3]. We hear of occasional strikes such as that in 1754 at Norwich, when three hundred wool-weavers, discontented with their wages, quitted their business, retreated to a hill three miles off, built huts and stayed six weeks there, supported by the contributions of their fellow workmen[4]. The organisations of workmen were becoming so powerful that they were prohibited by legislative enactment. "Whereas great numbers of weavers and others concerned in the woollen manufactures in several towns and parishes in this kingdom, have lately formed themselves into unlawful clubs and societies, and have presumed, contrary to law, to enter into combinations, and to make by-laws or orders, by which they pretend to regulate the trade and the prices of their goods and to advance their wages unreasonably, and many other things to the like purpose"......it was enacted that "all contracts, covenants or agreements, and all by-laws, ordinances, rules or orders, in such unlawful clubs and societies, heretofore made or entred into, or hereafter to be made or entred into by or between any persons brought up in or professing, using or exercising the art and mystery of a wool-comber, or weaver, or journeyman wool-comber, or journeyman weaver, in any parish or place within this kingdom, for regulating the said trade or mystery, or for regulating or settling the prices of goods, or for advancing their wages, or for lessening their usual hours

A.D. 1689 —1776.

in Gloucester-shire,

and at Norwich.

---

[1] Quoted from the Historical Register, issued by the Sun Fire Office, in *Notes and Queries*, 3rd Series, XII. 224. On the troubles at this time, see also *The Weavers' Pretences examined, being a Full and Impartiall Enquiry into the Complaints of their Wanting Work and the true Causes assigned.* By a Merchant (1719). Brit. Mus. 1029. e. 17 (3). Additional information about early combinations in Devonshire will be found in Martin Dunsford's *History of Tiverton*, 205.

[2] 13 Geo. I. c. 23.

[3] 29 Geo. II. c. 33. This action on the part of the legislature seems to show that the practice of assessing wages had fallen altogether into neglect, but it appears to have been maintained in Lincolnshire as late as 1754. See p. 897 below.

[4] Sir J. Nickolls' *Remarks on the advantages and disadvantages of France and Great Britain with respect to commerce* (1754), p. 139.

A.D. 1689 —1776.

of work, shall be and are hereby declared to be illegal, null and void to all intents and purposes[1]."

Masters were allowed to combine to prosecute fraudulent workmen,

At the same time attempts were made to strengthen the hands of the employers in exercising and controlling the men, as it was exceedingly difficult for any employer to exercise effective supervision over a number of weavers each of whom worked in his own home. It was alleged that the clothiers suffered severely from the fraud and negligence of the working manufacturers[2], though it was rarely worth their while to prosecute a poor man, even when he was grossly to blame. Thus masters were allowed to combine for the prosecution of fraud in connection with trade, and in this way a right of combination was conceded to the masters[3], which had been and continued to be denied to the men.

There were other forms of fraud which had occasioned trouble in the export trade of the country in earlier times[4], and against which it was necessary to guard. The excessive straining of broad cloth was injurious to the fabric, and in

and in spectors were appointed to maintain the quality of goods.

1727 the Justices were authorised to appoint Inspectors who should have the power to visit all the premises in Wiltshire, Gloucestershire and Somersetshire where the manufacture was carried on, in order to guard against this abuse[5]. Official inspection was still chiefly directed to the quality of goods, and was not yet applied to the conditions of work.

The differentiation of an employing class occurred in the spinning trade

228. There is ample evidence of the rise of an employing class and re-constitution of industry on a capitalistic basis, not only in weaving, but in other processes connected with the manufacture. The records of the investigation, in 1633, into the condition of the clothing trade in the West of England make it clear that there was a class of market spinners[6] who "sett many spinners on work," and gave " better wages than

---

[1] 12 Geo. I. c. 34.

[2] All through the eighteenth century, the term manufacturer is applied, as in Johnson's *Dictionary*, to the working craftsman, not to the capitalist, who is generally spoken of as a clothier. [Temple's] *Considerations on Taxes as they are supposed to affect the Price of Labour in our Manufactures*, p. 2, is an early (1755) instance of the modern sense of the word.

[3] 17 Geo. III. c. 11 ; 24 Geo. III. c. 3.

[4] Vol. I. 193 and p. 221 n. 1 above.

[5] 13 Geo. I. c. 23. A similar enactment was passed to repress the same evil among the domestic manufacturers in Yorkshire in 1765. 5 Geo. III. c. 51.

[6] S. P. D. C. I. ccxliii. 23 ; also cclxxxii. 81. See p. 96 n. above.

the clothiers"; they were accused, but apparently on in- sufficient grounds, of making false yarn. Many of the poor spinners appear to have been wage-earners, and to have been very badly off. "If the poore spinner shall depend only upon the Clothier for worke, the Clothier at this time gives too little wages, as the poor Spinner can hardly live, it may well be feared they will then give less, and will thus make choyce of the prime spinners out of the whole number of spinners, and turn of the reste, which may be of ill consequence[1]." The competition of two classes of capitalists was evidently regarded as beneficial to labour.

The new method of organisation was also being adopted in the trades which were occupied in finishing the cloth. So long as the domestic system held its own among the weavers, *and in* there was at least a possibility that the cloth-worker would *cloth-working.* be an independent man, who had purchased the goods on which he exercised his skill[2], and this appears to have been the form in which the trade was conducted in London in 1634[3]. But the extension of capitalism, through the energy of employers who desired to control the whole process of production, tended to change the economic status of this calling. Clothworking ceased to be a separate trade, and became a mere department of an industrial undertaking organised by an employer. This change in the position of their business necessarily involved an alteration in the character of the organisations among the cloth-workers. The function, *Capitalist* which their companies had formerly discharged, of maintain- *supervision proved* ing the quality of workmanship, was henceforth performed *beneficial* by capitalist employers, so that associations were no longer needed for this purpose. The transitional phase is clearly marked at Ipswich in 1620. The Clothworkers' Company there, obviously retained its character as an association of domestic workers; certain members protested against the manner in which their Company was controlled " by poor and

---

[1] S. P. D. C. I. ccxliii. 23.

[2] As early as 1565, however, there were drapers at Shrewsbury who purchased Welsh cloth, and employed shearmen and clothiers at Shrewsbury to earn wages by dressing and finishing these goods (8 El. c. 7). In Yorkshire, at the beginning of the nineteenth century, the men engaged in this business appear to have been wage-earners employed either by cloth merchants, or the domestic weavers.

[3] S. P. D. C. I. cclxxviii. 101.

unworthy persons " who only made it an excuse for levying money[1]; while the clothiers desired to be free to see to the business of dressing cloth themselves[2]. There was a conflict between the capitalists and the Company, the members of which were sinking to the position of wage-earners[3], and to a lowered social status, and less secure standard of life. It is highly probable that some of the Companies which survived, came to discharge functions which were closely analogous to those of modern Trade Unions.

There are some cases in which the differentiation of an employing class was apparently due to the success of the *among the* capitalist in exercising supervision wisely. The London *felt-* *makers.* felt-makers[4] insisted that all work must be done under the direct observation of the master, and set their faces against the weighing out of stuff by employers, to be made up at the worker's home. This policy appears to have commended itself to the journeymen also, in the face of the competition to which they were exposed by the French immigrants, and the trade continued to prosper on these new lines. The Felt- *In this* makers' Company seems to have changed in character during *calling* the period after the Restoration, and to have become a body of capitalist employers, rather than an association of small masters; while during the same period an active organisation had come into existence among the men, which had pursued a policy very similar to that which has been generally adopted by nineteenth century Trade Unions.

The possession of material, and ability in supervision, *as well as* combined to bring about the rise of an employing class in *among the* *tailors, the* the tailoring trade. In rural districts, the tailor continued to *rise of* *capitalism* visit the houses of his clients and to work upon the materials they furnished; but in London, the customers preferred to deal with a man who had a stock of materials. They had the advantage of a larger choice of goods, and the head of such a business would acquire special skill in cutting and a knowledge of prevailing fashions. The differentiation of the employer from the employed was almost inevitable; it

[1] S. P. D. J. I. cxii. 64.   [2] S. P. D. J. I. cxii. 63.

[3] The clothiers of Ipswich appear to have been employing cloth-workers in 1639. S. P. D. C. I. ccccxxv. 40, also ccccxxviii. 44, 45.

[4] Compare the interesting article by Mr G. Unwin on *A Seventeenth Century Trade Union*, in the *Economic Journal*, x. 398.

was likely to arise so soon as the master-tailor owned and traded in materials on which he worked. There had been a considerable amount of trouble in the trade, as early as the fifteenth century, when the management of the London tailors' gild appears to have passed into the hands of men who were more concerned in the cloth trade than in making clothes[1]. The journeymen tailors, who worked for wages, had *was followed by organisation among the wage-earners.* become a well-defined class; and early in the eighteenth century, they were definitely organised in a Trade Union. Their society appears to have been a new thing; in 1721[2], it was composed of wage-earners, who were primarily concerned in trying to secure better terms for themselves from their masters; it was not a gild, or company, consisting of independent masters who were anxious to maintain due supervision over the manner in which work was done. It had no direct concern with the public, but only with the relations between masters and men.

The most serious grievances on the part of the workmen, *Capitalism appears at its worst* during the eighteenth century, arose in connection with an industry where the capitalist's position was due not so much to his skill as an organiser or supervisor or his possession of the materials, as to the fact that he owned the machinery which was necessary for the prosecution of the trade. The framework knitting trade had been organised on capitalist lines from the first, and the efforts to control the action of the employers in the interest of the hands, proved ineffective. The stocking frame had been invented in the time of Queen Elizabeth; and a considerable industry had sprung up in Nottinghamshire, as well as in London, where a Company was formed which assumed power to regulate the trade of the Framework Knitters[3]. One very important point in the rules they laid down was that they were careful about limiting the number of apprentices. They had been chartered by Cromwell, and again by Charles II.; and the trade appears to

---

[1] See Vol. I. 444.   [2] F. W. Galton, *Select Documents on Tailoring Trade*, XVI.

[3] One man who objected to their regulations tried to migrate with his frame to Amsterdam, but he had no success. Felkin, *A History of the Machine-wrought Hosiery*, 61. Pains were taken to prevent the trade from being planted in foreign parts, as the exportation of the machinery was forbidden, by Proclamation (15 Jan. 1666), [Brit. Mus. 1851. d. 23 (8)], and by Statute (7 and 8 W. III. c. 20, § 8).

A.D. 1689
—1776.

*in con-
nection
with frame-
work
knitting as
carried on
by pro-
vincial
under-
takers*
have steadily increased till 1710, when the pressure of the
wars was severely felt, and the journeymen drew attention to
the fact that the regulation about apprentices had been
persistently neglected. The journeymen, and some of the
masters, endeavoured to enforce this rule in London, but
without success. The machines of one recalcitrant master,
named Nicholson, were broken; and he, as well as two
others, migrated to Nottingham. The London Company
subsequently attempted to enforce the rule against the
Nottingham masters, but they had no success. There was
in consequence a further migration of the trade to Leicester
and Nottingham; and the Company proceeded to frame a
series of by-laws which they hoped to enforce, as they
obtained the approval of the Chancellor. One of these
regulations roused much opposition among the provincial
masters, who appealed to the House of Commons against

*in defiance
of the
London
Company,*
the new by-laws[1]. A Select Committee[2] reported against
the Company; and the evils it had endeavoured to check
became more and more serious. In the decade before the
Parliamentary decision, the work in provincial districts appears to have been largely done by apprentices bound by
their parishes, who were in many cases badly treated. There
was little or no employment for journeymen, and the quality
of the output appears to have seriously declined. The conditions, which arose through the competition of capitalist
employers in this industry, were not satisfactory from the
point of view either of the labourer or of the public.

*but the
new
organisa-
tion was
everywhere
incom-
patible
with old
regula-
tions.*
From one cause or another, organisation by capitalist
employers[3] was superseding the system of independent workmen in one trade after another, during the seventeenth and
eighteenth centuries, and this change was, generally speaking,
inconsistent with the maintenance of the old machinery for
regulating the quality of production and the conditions of

---

[1] The Company considered that outsiders who bought frames and hired them
out, but who did not themselves deal in the product, exercised an injurious
influence on the trade.

[2] Felkin, *op. cit.* 80.

[3] Dr Sprague has called my attention to an interesting case of combination
among shoemakers' servants at Nottingham in 1619. *Records of the Borough of
Nottingham*, IV. 362.

work[1]. Employers were responsible for guaranteeing the excellence of the product, and they were obviously coming to have a great deal of power in determining the circumstances and terms under which labour was carried on.

A.D. 1689 —1776.

229. While these changes were occurring in the old established industries of the country there was also a considerable development of new trades. There had been very little opening for the planting of new manufactures during the greater part of the seventeenth century, but towards its close an opportunity arose of which Charles II. had been ready to take advantage to the fullest extent[2]. Parliament was also prepared to encourage the religious refugees from France, though the government did not adopt the same measures as had commended themselves to Lord Burleigh under similar circumstances[3]. The legislature did not grant the Huguenots exceptional industrial privileges, but preferred to pass measures which should serve to foster the new industries, in whatever part of the realm they might be carried on. The principal expedient adopted was that of promoting consumption by legislative enactment. The policy of insisting that the public should use certain wares, when other goods would suit them as well or better, is a particularly fussy form of protection. It does not obviously encourage the general industry of the country, but only stimulates one trade at the expense of others. A curious sumptuary law was passed, in 1698, which lays down minute regulations in regard to buttons[4]. These had been the subject of legislation under Charles II.[5]; in the time of Queen Anne[6], button-holes were also taken into consideration; and the substitution of serge for silk in covering buttons and working button-holes gave rise to a stirring debate in 1738[7]. There was similar legislation in

The Huguenot incursion gave opportunities for planting new industries

which Parliament encouraged by legislation for promoting consumption at home

---

[1] As Mr Unwin points out, the exceptional condition of the Feltmakers' trade enabled them to maintain an effective system of regulation after the company had become capitalist in character.

[2] See above, p. 328.

[3] See above, pp. 82, 330.

[4] 10 and 11 W. III. c. 10. Cunningham, *Alien Immigrants*, p. 237.

[5] 13 and 14 C. II. c. 13.

[6] 8 Anne, c. 6. *For employing the manufacturers by encouraging the consumption of raw silk and mohair yarn.*　　　[7] *Parl. Hist.* x. 787.

A.D. 1689
—1776. 1745, when a penalty of five pounds was imposed on those who should wear French cambrics or lawn; a similar fine was imposed on those who sold it[1]. Anderson[2] expresses doubt as to whether it was seriously intended to try to enforce such a measure; but it is in full accord with the policy which was habitually pursued, of giving as much encouragement to the native linen manufacture as could be done without interfering with the supremacy of the cloth trade; and the facts, that it was amended after three years' time, and that the Commons refused to repeal it even when its futility was demonstrated[3], seem to show that the legislators were perfectly in earnest. Parliament also had recourse to another expedient, which found favour at the time, for fostering the silk trade, an industry which did not owe its introduction to, but was at all events invigorated by, the Huguenot immigration. The legislature not only tried to promote home consumption, but to stimulate the export *and grant-* trade as well[4]. This whole system of bounties was a most *ing boun-* *ties on* extravagant mode of encouraging the new industries and *export.* gave rise to effective criticism, especially as there was considerable doubt in many minds as to the advisability of introducing these manufactures at all. They were for the most part exotic trades, the materials of which were not of English growth[5].

New- The silk manufacture was the business which was *fashioned* *textiles* specially cared for; and curiously enough, the new trades, *of silk* which eventually attained the greatest importance, were so far from being favoured that they were positively discouraged. The woollen manufacturers were exceedingly

---

[1] 18 Geo. II. c. 36 re-enforced by 21 Geo. II. c. 26.

[2] His work was incorporated by Macpherson, *Annals*, III. 245.

[3] Sir J. Barnard's Speech (1753), *Parl. Hist.* XV. 163.

[4] In 1722 a bounty of three shillings a pound was granted on the exportation of silks, four shillings on silk mixed with gold or silver, and one shilling on silk stockings. 8 Geo. I. c. 15.

[5] Davenant, *Essay on the East India Trade*, in *Works*, I. 99; also Arthur Young, in *Farmer's Letters*, p. 17, condemns the pains taken to develop such manufactures. J. Massie writes with great discrimination on the kinds of manufacture to be encouraged and the importance of native materials, *Representation concerning the Knowledge of Commerce*, 20; *Plan for the establishment of Charity Houses*, p. 10; *Reasons against laying any further British duties on Wrought Silks*, p. 4.

jealous of the introduction of cotton weaving, or of any textile art that might interfere with the market for their goods[1], and Parliament looked askance on the manufacture *and cotton* and printing of cotton fabrics[2]. The Huguenots started calico printing at Richmond in Surrey[3]. The prohibition of Indian fabrics[4], which had been devised in the interest of the woollen manufacture, told for a time in favour of the new trade; but under Anne, an excise was imposed on English-printed goods[5]. The wares produced in England, by printing white goods imported from India, suited the public taste so well, that the jealousy of the woollen manufacturers revived. It seems that there was a violent outbreak, especially at Colchester. Defoe gives us a curious *were* picture of the conflicting interests at stake. The rioters *thought to supplant* appear to have mobbed and insulted the women who wore *woollen goods,* these fabrics, and they even threw aqua fortis over their clothes and into their carriages. If Defoe's[6] statement is to be relied on, we cannot wonder that the taste for these goods developed so rapidly, as they only cost an eighth part of the price of the woollen fabrics they supplanted. He appears, however, to have sympathised with the weavers, as also did Parliament; for, in 1720, an Act was passed[7] which prohibited the use of these calicoes, whether printed at home or abroad. The trade suffered a severe blow; but was continued in the printing of linens, and later of cotton with a linen warp.

The industries, which were thus introduced and fostered, were, for the most part, developed on capitalistic lines. " If *and these* we take a view of those Towns where the *Silk* and *Cotton* *exotic trades* Trades have settled themselves, we shall find there ten

---

[1] A scheme for increasing the home demand for cloth is contained in *A brief deduction of the origin, etc. of the British Woollen Manufacture* (1727), p. 51. It gives an admirable description of the local distribution of the trade, of its history, with the names of Flemish settlers, and of the development of foreign competition.

[2] Baines, *The History of the Cotton Manufacture*, 259.

[3] Baines, *op. cit.* 259.

[4] 11 and 12 W. III. c. 10. *An act for the more effectual employing the poor by encouraging the manufactures of this Kingdom.*

[5] 10 Anne, c. 19; 12 Anne, ii. c. 9.

[6] W. Lee, *Daniel Defoe*, II. 138.

[7] 7 Geo. I. c. 7, amended 9 Geo. II. c. 4.

Master Manufacturers for one in the space of a few years,
and five times the Number of Workmen. These Towns
owe their greatness as well as the Nation the Trades here
mentioned to the public spirit of two or three Men in
each,......This spreading of Trade and multiplying of Masters
has so astonishingly enlarged these Cities of late years,
and increased the numbers of Workmen[1]." Capitalism was
becoming the prevalent type of organisation, and it was
specially appropriate for exotic trades. Any trade, which
had been constituted under the control of large employers
in its older habitat, was likely to be introduced in the same
tended to develop on capitalist lines. form; and as capital was an important factor in the transferring of a trade to a new area, there was a tendency for
the industry, as transplanted, to conform to the capitalist
type. This trend towards capitalism had already been ex-
emplified in the planting of new industries under Elizabeth[2];
it seems to be probable that both the new drapery and
the cotton manufacture[3] were organised, from their first
introduction to this country, by employers. Though some of
the protestant refugees were mere labourers, others were
men of considerable means[4] and of tried capacity, who were
well able to engage in trades where an expensive plant
was necessary. The gun-making which was developed at
Birmingham, the paper manufacture and glass works which
sprang up in so many places, were necessarily organised as
capitalist undertakings. There were, of course, other cases
where the newly introduced or developed trade was organised
Domestic silk manu- facture seems to have been superseded on domestic lines. This was to some extent true of the silk
industry, from its artistic character, though the cost of the
material rendered it particularly suitable for capitalist intervention[5]. We can find indications of the transformation of
this trade on the capitalist model, which are closely analogous
to the steps in the reconstitution of old-established English

---

[1] *Reflexions upon various subjects* [Brit. Mus. 1144 (8)].   [2] See above, p. 78.

[3] The cotton trade appears to have been organised on capitalist lines in
Augsburg, long before its migration to Antwerp, or to England. Nuebling,
Ulm's Handel in Mittelalter, 142, in Schmoller's *Forschungen,* ix. v.

[4] Smiles, *Huguenots,* 263; Macpherson, *Annals,* ii. 617.

[5] A mere labourer would have great difficulty in purchasing it—on the other
hand the capitalist would run special risks of embezzlement.

industries[1]. The migration of the silk industry, from Canter- A.D. 1689
—1776.
bury to London, is not improbably connected with the greater
freedom for capitalist organisation which seems to have *by the*
characterised the trade in Spitalfields. There is evidence *interven-*
tion of
as to a certain amount of capitalist oppression in the fact *capitalists*
that systematic protection was accorded by the Spitalfields
Acts[2]; but on the other hand, the industry in the country
advanced through the enterprise of those who introduced *and intro-*
machinery driven by water-power for silk-throwing[3]; the *duction of*
machinery.
silk-weaving in Cheshire appears to have been benefited by
these facilities for obtaining materials. The infusion of new
trades was a very striking industrial development at this
date, and it certainly gave an increased importance to
capitalist manufacturers as a class.

The importance of capitalist employers in this connection
comes out in the story of the linen manufacture, in its
various branches. The manufacture of sailcloth, in which *Capital*
was sub-
Burleigh had been particularly interested, was at last *scribed for*
naturalised through the energy of M. Bonhomme[4], who had *manufac-*
turing sail-
recently started the trade on French soil. Capital for his *cloth*
undertaking was provided by the elders of the French
Church in Threadneedle Street. A joint-stock Company[5]
was created, with Dupin[6] at its head, to carry on the linen
industry, which had never flourished in England[7]. The new

---

[1] In Holland the old trades maintained their domestic character and gild
organisation all through the seventeenth century, but the trades which were
introduced by immigrants were for the most part established on capitalist lines.
Pringsheim, *Beitrage*, pp. 32, 40.

[2] 13 Geo. III. c. 68. It is possible that the migration of silk-weaving to
Taunton was due to an attempt on the part of employers to evade these Acts.
Cunningham, *Alien Immigrants*, 236. As regards the silk-manufacture in the
Essex district, which fell within the Spitalfields Act, it appears that the employers
would be able to obtain the services of weavers on easy terms in districts where
woollen weaving had decayed.

[3] Sir T. Lombe's machine was copied from an Italian model and attracted
much interest when it was set up at Derby in 1718. Rees, *Encyclopedia*, s.v.
Silk manufacture.   [4] Cunningham, *Alien Immigrants*, 239.

[5] Its failure, like that of the Royal Lustring Company, was attributed to Stock
Exchange speculation (*Angliae Tutamen*, 24). A joint-stock company with a capital
of £100,000 was formed to carry on the manufacture of fine cambrics in England
in 1764. 4 Geo. III. c. 37.

[6] See Molyneux' *Letters* to Locke, in Locke's *Works*, viii. 389, 436, 448.

[7] "The Linen Manufacture has been attempted at different Times and Places
in Great Britain, as well as most of the Counties in England, on the North Side of

A.D. 1689
—1776.
venture enjoyed royal patronage and appeared to prosper for a time, but it failed to fulfil the anticipations that had been formed, and involved the subsidiary Company which *and the linen trade was developed on a co-operative system in Ireland* had been developed in Ireland in its ruin[1]. The desirability of developing this industry, and its suitability for the Irish climate and soil, had been recognised since the time of Strafford[2]; but it was not till Louis Crommelin[3] took the matter up, and organised an ingenious co-operative system[4] by which the necessary stock-in-trade was contributed, that the Irish industry really took root and began to develop. Great pains had been taken by the Scotch Parliament to foster a linen trade, both by promoting consumption, and by insisting on a uniformity in the cloth exposed for sale[5] *and in Scotland by means of* A large portion of the money which the Act of Union assigned for encouraging the industrial arts in Scotland was devoted to the linen-trade; there were premiums on the growth of lint, support was given to schools where spinning was taught, prizes were awarded to housewives for the best specimens of linen, and considerable pains were taken to procure models of improved looms[6]. But the most important developments occurred after 1727, when the Scottish Board

Trent where they make Linen for their own Consumption, besides a species to Export in Imitation of Osenburgh, but with small success, as it never was pushed with Vigour, or cherished with proper Care and Encouragement from the Publick, or those in Power, by giving premiums as is done in Scotland and Ireland." *An Appeal to Facts regarding the Home Trade and Inland Manufactures* (1751), 55; Brit. Mus. 1144. 7.   See also above, p. 369 n. 2.

[1] See the excellent account of this episode by Dr W. R. Scott. *Proceedings of Royal Soc. Ant. Ireland*, XXXI. 374.

[2] See above, p. 369; also *Reports*, 1840, XXIII. 458, 521. The English Parliament which was determined to check the migration of Devonshire weavers to Ireland was ready to encourage alien linen weavers to settle there. They hoped that the foreign Protestants who were leaving France might be attracted to settle in Ireland and carry on their calling there. "Whereas there are great Sums of Money and Bullion yearely exported out of this Kingdome for the purchasing of Hemp Flax and Linen and the Productions thereof which might in great measure be prevented by being supplied from Ireland if such proper Encouragement were given as might invite Forreigne Protestants into that Kingdome to settle" (7 and 8 W. III. c. 39). In 1709, 500 families of poor Palatines were sent to Ireland to carry on husbandry and the linen manufacture. *State Papers, Treasury*, 1708–14, CXIX. 1; also 1714–19, CLXXXVII. 25.

[3] *Ulster Journal of Archaeology*, I. 212, IV. 206.

[4] See p. 329 n. 2, above.   [5] Bremner, *Industries of Scotland*, 215.

[6] Bremner, 217. On the progress of the art, compare Lindsay, *Interest of Scotland* (1733), pp. 81, 160, 178.

of Trustees for Manufactures invited Nicholas D'Assaville A.D. 1689
—1776. along with experienced weavers of cambric and their families to come and settle[1]. They established themselves in a suburb of Edinburgh, on the road to Leith, and the site of the little colony is commemorated by the name Picardy Place. In *public funds,* 1753, Parliament voted £3,000 a year for nine years to propagate this trade in the Highlands; and such success attended these efforts that, in 1800, the Board thought it unnecessary to open a spinning school in Caithness, as the art was generally understood and there were so many opportunities for learning it[2]. In 1746 an Edinburgh *and the development of* Company had been chartered under the name of the British *credit.* Linen Company. The Company's principal mode of operation was by advancing ready money to the manufacturers, and they thus came to devote themselves to ordinary banking business, outside the limits of the special trade they had intended to subserve at first. The development of the credit system in Scotland and the growth of the linen industry went on hand in hand. Under these various encouragements the Scotch linen trade increased rapidly; and, whereas the average annual production from 1728 to 1732 was only three and a half millions of yards, it had reached just double the amount in 1750[3]. It must be remembered *Scottish linen had* that, in this matter, Scotland was at a very great advantage *better* as compared with Ireland, as from 1707 onwards the Northern *access to foreign* Kingdom shared in all the advantages of English commerce[4], *markets* and the Glasgow merchants were anxious that no step should *than Irish.* be taken which would have curtailed their privileges[5]. Under

---

[1] See above, p. 330 n. 5.   [2] Bremner, 219.   [3] Macpherson, III. 289.

[4] Ireland was only permitted to export her linen direct to the American Plantations. 3 and 4 Anne, c. 8.

[5] Compare the debate in 1778. *Parl. Hist.* XIX. 1117. Also Burke's letters to Bristol Merchants, *ib.* 1100. "Trade is not a limited thing; as if the objects of mutual demand and consumption could not stretch beyond the bounds of our jealousies. God has given the earth to the children of men, and he has undoubtedly, in giving it to them, given them what is abundantly sufficient for all their exigencies; not a scanty, but a most liberal provision for them all. The author of our nature has written it strongly in that nature, and has promulgated the same law in his written word, that man shall eat his bread by his labour; and I am persuaded, that no man, and no combination of men, for their own ideas of their particular profit, can, without great impiety, undertake to say, that he shall not do so; that they have no sort of right, either to prevent the labour, or to

the circumstances, the Irish linen trade did not prosper rapidly, though the Irish Parliament did their best to encourage it[1], and it had attained considerable proportions when the Dublin Linen Hall was founded in 1728[2]. It did not spread over the whole island[3], but it seems to have made steady progress through the eighteenth century[4]. The trade was protected against foreign linens[5] and enjoyed certain bounties[6], but it *and re-* did not have a fair share of the encouragement[7] that was *ceived more* *encourage-* given to British linens[8] There can be no doubt that certain *ment.* English statesmen viewed this trade with some jealousy. They feared that if we did not take our returns from the Low Countries in linen, they would close their ports against English woollen cloth; and thus, while the Irish clothing trade was extinguished, the Irish linen trade was also offered as a sacrifice to the staple industry of this country.

The hard- **230.** The story of the hardware trade during this period *ware trade* *underwent* has somewhat special interest, since it does not present a *little* *change in* close parallel to that of the other trades. There is no reason *organisa-* to believe that the organisation of the industry underwent *tion,* much change. Some departments seem to have been capitalist in character from mediaeval times[9]; though such branches of business as nail-making continued to be in the

withhold the head. Ireland having received no compensation, directly or in-directly, for any restraints on their trade, ought not, in justice or common honesty, to be made subject to such restraints. I do not mean to impeach the right of the parliament of Great Britain to make laws for the trade of Ireland. I only speak of what laws it is right for parliament to make."

[1] *Irish Commons Journals*, II. i. 287 ; 10 and 11 W. III. c. 10, § 2.

[2] Lecky, *History of England in the Eighteenth Century*, II. 321.

[3] *Essay on the Antient and Modern State of Ireland* (Dublin, 1760), 63. Brit. Mus. 116. g. 12.

[4] Newenham, *View of the Natural, Political and Commercial Circumstances of Ireland*, App. No. 7, p. 10. There was a temporary decline for some years after 1771, *Reports from Committees of the House of Commons*, III. 107.

[5] 7 Geo. III. c. 58.   [6] 10 Geo. III. c. 38.

[7] Compare the Report of 1744, *Reports from the Committees of the House of Commons*, II. 69.

[8] 10 Geo. III. c. 40. See also the speech of the Marquis of Rockingham, *Parl. Hist.* xx. 640.

[9] Compare the survey of the possessions of Gilbert d'Umfraville (1245). I. Lowthian Bell in *Brit. Assoc. Report*, 1863, 737. Dr G. T. Lapsley has printed [*Eng. Hist. Review*, XIV. (1899), p. 509] an interesting account of the Bishop of Durham's forge at Bedburn in Weardale in 1408. The hands, of various grades of skill, were all wage-earners, and in years when the works were let at ferm, they were probably rented by a capitalist undertaker.

hands of small independent masters. The history of the A.D. 1689 —1776. trade is almost entirely concerned with the struggle that was *but was* made to overcome the difficulty that arose from the in- *exposed to difficulty* creasing scarcity of fuel; but incidentally, it throws much *from the* light on the policy that was pursued in regard to the indus- *scarcity of fuel,* trial development of the plantations.

The paucity of fuel had caused anxiety even in Tudor times, and there had been legislation with the view of maintaining woods and coppices in the reign of Henry VIII.[1]. The Sussex Ironworks were regarded with special suspicion, *which* as they drew on supplies of timber that might have been *caused a migration* available for shipbuilding and competed with London for *of industry* supplies of fuel. Eventually they were starved out; and the *from Sussex,* iron-trade migrated to Shropshire and the Forest of Dean, where both iron-ore, and fuel for smelting, were more easily obtained. It was obvious, however, that, though this was a temporary relief, it could not prove a permanent remedy. From the sixteenth century onwards, attention had been *and stimu-* directed to the possibility of substituting coal and coke, for *lated the experi-* wood and charcoal, in the various processes of the iron manu- *ments of the Darbys* facture. Neither Dudley, nor any of the other men who *for sub-* devoted themselves to this object, were able to get beyond *stituting the use of* the experimental stage; but the difficulties were gradually *coal for charcoal* solved, and the Darbys made the new processes a practical success. The cast-iron bridge over the Severn, which was erected in 1779, marks the beginning of an iron age, when the metal[2] has been applied to new purposes of many kinds and serves as a monument to the enterprise of this family,

---

[1] 35 Hen. VIII. c. 17. Frequent cases of prosecutions under this Act occur in the Bedfordshire Quarter Sessions Records in the seventeenth century. Compare also for Durham in 1629, I. Lowthian Bell, *Brit. Assoc. Report*, 1863, p. 737. "There is one man, whose dwellinge place is within twenty miles of the cittye of Durhame, which hath brought to the grounde, above 30,000 oakes in his life tyme; and (if hee live longe) it is to be doubted, that hee will not leave so much tymber or other woode in this whole County as will repaire one of our churches, if it should fall, his iron and leade workes do so fast consume the same." A. L., *Relation of some abuses which are committed against the Commonwealth composed especiallie for the Benefit of this Countie of Durhame*, p. 9.

[2] The most important steps in progress may be briefly indicated. Abraham Darby succeeded in 1735 in making coke from coal; this served as a substitute for wood charcoal in the furnaces for smelting the iron, when a more powerful blast was used (Smiles, *Industrial Biography*, p. 338). In 1766 the Cranages introduced a reverberatory furnace in which coal could be used, and superseded the forges in

A.D. 1689
—1776.
who devoted themselves for three generations to the improvement of the trade. The turning-point in the history of the industry may be dated however at 1760. In that year the Carron Works were founded; and the blast furnaces, which Roebuck erected, were built with a view to the use of coal. Still, the progress was not very rapid till about 1790 [1], *for smelting in blast furnaces,* when steam-engines were introduced to work the blast-furnaces. With this more powerful blast they were able to save one-third of the coal hitherto used in smelting. The old blast-furnaces had been worked by water, and considerable ingenuity had to be exercised in order to get a powerful and uninterrupted blast [2] The effect of these improvements was unprecedented, and in 1796 the production of pig-iron was nearly double what it had been eight years before. Mr Pitt had proposed to tax coal in 1796, and pig-iron in 1797, but he was forced to abandon both projects. When the latter plan was revived by Lord Henry Petty in 1806, the Bill passed the second reading by a narrow majority, but was dropped in Committee. The returns which were made, and discussions which took place in connection with these proposals, have put on record an immense amount of information in regard to the manufacture of pig-iron, at the time when these new inventions caused it to advance with the greatest rapidity.

and for puddling. Shortly before these improvements in blast furnaces had been introduced, two very important inventions had been made by Mr Cort, of Gosport; in 1783 he obtained a patent for converting pig-iron into malleable iron with the aid of coal, in a common air-furnace, by puddling [3]; in the following year he obtained a patent for manufacturing the malleable iron into bars, by means of rollers instead of the forge hammers which had been hitherto in vogue. Like so many of the other inventors, Mr Cort derived little personal benefit from inventions which have been of world-wide importance,

which pig-iron had been converted into bar-iron with the help of charcoal (*ib.* 87). Statistics as to the amount of coal and wood consumed in these works just before this invention will be found in Whitworth, *Advantages of Inland Navigation,* p. x. 39 (table).

[1] Scrivenor, *History of the Iron Trade,* 87.

[2] See the account of the Devon Iron-works (Clackmannan), in Sir J. Sinclair's *Statistical Account of Scotland* (1795), XIV. 626.

[3] Roebuck also had claims to this invention.

and the history of this invention is recounted in the petition A.D. 1689 —1776. in which his son pleaded for a grant from the House of Commons in 1812[1]. These last inventions were a great saving of time and labour; but it was the new form of the *The trade flourished in districts where coal was avail- able,* blast-furnace which had the most remarkable effects on the distribution of the iron trade. While it had been dependent on wood, it had flourished in Sussex and the Forest of Dean; when it became possible to use coal with the help of water-power to create a blast, the industry tended to be located in regions where water-power was available; hence the revival of the South Wales iron-works which had been discontinued long before from want of fuel; the use of coal and water-power gave a new impetus to the works at Cyfartha and Dowlais[2]. The application of steam, however, rendered the iron-masters independent of water-power, and blast-furnaces could be erected wherever the presence of coal and iron rendered it convenient. In Gloucestershire, the supply of fuel from the Forest was readily replaced with coal; but in other cases, and notably in Sussex, the ancient iron-works ceased to be of importance; while enormous new centres of activity and industry were created in parts of Scotland, Wales and the North of England, which had been practically barren before.

During the earlier half of the eighteenth century, how- *and manu- facturers were no longer de- pendent on pig-iron from Sweden,* ever, the manufacturers had to be content with wood-charcoal as fuel, and the expense of smelting iron ore was very great. Considerable quantities of pig and bar iron were imported from Sweden, and it appeared that, if smelting could be developed in our own plantations, there would be a distinct saving to the mother country. Soon after the Revolution, an attempt was made to draw on the resources of Ireland. In 1696 and 1697 the duties were removed from bar-iron imported into England from Ireland[3]; this led to a develop- ment of iron smelting in Ireland and a consequent de- struction of the Irish forests; though various measures *from Ireland,* were taken to prevent it, and to promote the planting of trees, they proved utterly ineffective. Not only so, but the exportation of timber to England was permitted on very easy

[1] Scrivenor, 119.   [2] Scrivenor, 122.
[3] 7 and 8 W. III. c. 10, and 8 and 9 W. III. c. 20.

A.D. 1689
—1776.

or the
American
colonies.

terms[1]; and as a result the forests of Ireland were absolutely ruined. There was a better prospect of obtaining an ample supply of material from the American plantations, where both iron ore and fuel were found in abundance, and in 1717 the ironmongers and smiths of London and Bristol, who were dependent on imported material from Sweden, petitioned in favour of encouraging the smelting of iron in the American colonies[2]. The condition of the trade was fully discussed in an interesting report in 1737[3], when a Committee of the House of Commons reported in favour of discouraging this trade as prejudicial to iron smelting at home[4]. It was maintained, however, that there would be no injurious competition if the colonies were only permitted to prepare pig and bar iron for manufacture in England and this line was taken by the Act of 1750[5], which allowed the importation of bar-iron from the colonies, duty free, into London[6], and of pig-iron into any port. At the same time, the use of slitting mills and tilt hammers in the plantations was prohibited; existing works in New England were shut down[7], and Edmund Quincy failed to obtain permission to erect plant for the manufacture of steel in 1773[8].

The change
in the pro-
cesses of

231. The attempt to assist the English hardware trade, by drawing on extraneous sources for the fuel required in

---

[1] 2 Anne, c. 2 (Irish); Newenham, *op. cit.* 154–5.

[2] *Commons Journals*, xviii. 691. The Birmingham nailmakers, who had convenient access to the Midland smelting district, petitioned against encouraging the colonists to engage in this business, *ib.* 733, though opinion seems to have been divided, *ib.* 747.

[3] *Commons Journals*, xxiii. 109.   [4] *Ib.* 157.   [5] 23 G. II. c. 2.

[6] The discussion broke out again in 1757, when the Bristol manufacturers desired to have access to the same supplies of bar-iron as were available for Londoners. *Commons Journals*, xxvii. 830. The whole discussion is instructive; the iron manufacturers desired to get bar-iron cheap from the colonies, but to secure the subsequent processes of the trade for the support of English hands. They were "men of middling fortunes," but were numerous; the iron-masters, who owned the forges, were large capitalists, and they were opposed to the colonies competing in their trade; and the proprietors of woods objected to the intended development of mining and smelting in the plantations as likely to affect the value of woods in England; they were joined by the tanners, who were interested in procuring the bark of the wood used for smelting. See *The case of the Importation of Bar Iron from our own Colonies* (1756), [Brit. Mus. 1029, c. 15]. Also the answer, entitled *Reflections on the Importation of Bar Iron* (1757), [Brit. Mus. 8229, i. 1].

[7] Weeden, *Economic and Social History of New England*, 683.

[8] *Commons Journals*, xxxiv. 93, 117.

preparing the materials, had been resented by the landed A.D. 1689
—1776.
interest; but the proprietors in certain districts gained *iron manu-*
enormously through the development which occurred in the *facture*
stimulated
later part of the eighteenth century. The success of the *the coal*
Darbys, in utilising coal instead of wood for the smelting and *trade,*
manufacture of iron, not only gave a new impulse to that
trade, but caused an immense increase of coal-mining, and
occasioned the introduction of better facilities for internal
intercourse. The coal trade had been growing, but was still
of a limited character; the only fields, which had been
hitherto worked on a large scale[1], were those of Newcastle,
as the product of these mines could be easily shipped.
Throughout the seventeenth century there had been a con- *which had*
been
siderable and growing export trade. Much of the traffic was to *growing*
foreign parts[2], but a very large trade with London[3] was also *through the*
demand for
springing up. The city had come to rely so much on this *fuel in*
London.
supply of fuel, as to feel considerable inconvenience from the
interruption of the coaling trade which occurred during the
Civil War[4]. There was some uncertainty, even under ordinary
circumstances, since the heavily laden colliers[5] were greatly
exposed to storm. Defoe tells a story of more than two
hundred sail of vessels, mostly colliers, with a thousand lives,
which were lost in one storm off the Norfolk coast[6]. The
vessels were also in danger of attack from pirates[7]. We hear
of other difficulties, many of which were due to the action of
the Hostmen of Newcastle[8]; this fraternity had been incorporated by Queen Elizabeth, for the loading and disposing of
pit coals upon the Tyne[9]. The exclusive privileges of these

---

[1] Mining on a small scale had been carried on in Yorkshire from time immemorial. The Halifax coal-field is mentioned in the Wakefield Court Rolls in
1308. For many references to Yorkshire mining, see Mr Lister's article in *Old
Yorkshire*, II. series, edited by Wheater (1885), p. 269. On the arrangements
made for the purchase and supply of coal in Dublin, see Gross, *Gild Merchant*,
I. 137, II. 66 f. [2] *Reports*, 1871, XVIII. 826.

[8] Petty writes of the consumption of coal in houses as a new thing. *Political
Arithmetic* (1699), p. 259; Macpherson, II. 580.

[4] *See coale, Charcoale and Small coale* (1643), quoted in *Reports*, 1871, XVIII. 826.

[5] These belonged partly to Newcastle Merchants and partly to those of Lynn
(Defoe, *Tour* (1748), I. 76), and of Yarmouth (*ib.* I. 66).

[6] Defoe, *Tour*, I. 71.

[7] *Commons Journals*, x. p. 491, 2 Dec. 1690; Brand, *Newcastle*, II. 300.

[8] For complaints in 1604, see *Rep. Hist. MSS. Comm.* VI. Ap. 311.

[9] Brand, II. 271.

A.D. 1689
—1776.

*New enter-
prise was
shown in
mining*

Hostmen were a matter of frequent complaint; while, on the other hand, the Hostmen urged that the action of the Government in pressing keel-men for the fleet caused a serious interruption to the trade[1]. Like other lines of commerce at this period, this trade became more and more open[2]; the charter of the Hostmen was not renewed after 1679, though they were an influential body of traders.

With the growing demand for coals[3] we see signs of increased enterprise in carrying on mining operations. Gray asserts that as early as 1649[4] some " South Gentlemen hath,

---

[1] Brand, *op. cit.* II. 300. All these obstacles must have tended to keep up the price of coal in London; the complaints on this head are of frequent recurrence; C. Povey attributed the evil to the desperate competition among dealers and consequent fraud and oppression (*The Unhappiness of England as to its Trade by Sea and Land*, 28); see also *State Papers, Treasury*, 1708—1714, cxli. 2. A considerable number of petitions were presented in 1731 (Brand, II. 306); and during the frost of 1740, the House of Commons addressed the Crown in favour of enforcing the law about regulating the price of coals (*Parl. Hist.* XI. 435).

[2] The chief struggle over the privileges of the Newcastle men took place in the time of Cromwell. This town possessed very special privileges under a charter granted by Queen Elizabeth in 1601, and these had been specially preserved in the Act of 1624. With these powers the old companies had all come to the front again, and they were brought into bitter hostility with the neighbouring town of Shields. The chief assertor of the common law rights, in opposition to special privileges, was a brewer named Ralph Gardner, who certainly underwent great personal sacrifices in the cause, and brought startling allegations against the Newcastle men for the way they exercised their powers. He asserts that the action of the burgesses from 1642 to 1644 "caused coals to be four pound a chaldron, and salt four pound the weigh, the poor inhabitants forced to flie the country, others to quarter all armies upon free quarter; heavy taxes to them all, both English, Scots and Garrisons; plundered of all they had; land lying waste; coalpits drowned; salt-works broken down; hay and corn burnt; town pulled down; mens wives carried away by the unsatiable Scots and abused; all being occasioned by that corporations disaffection; and yet to tyrannize as is hereafter mentioned." *England's Grievance Discovered*. Address to the Reader. The reply of the Corporation, who were represented in London by Mr S. Hartlib, has been printed from a MS. of Alderman Hornby's on *Conservatorship of Tyne* in Richardson, *Reprints of Rare Tracts*, III. p. 35. Many of Gardner's accusations are met by a simple denial of the alleged facts; in regard to the conservancy of the river, the most serious question, the Corporations said that they had acted on the advice of the authorities of the Trinity House, p. 62. They claimed to retain special privileges on political grounds, however, as their town was a defence against the Scots. One of their trade corporations, the Hostmen, paid £8000 a year to the public treasury and might well expect their privileges to be protected, pp. 43, 44.

[3] As in other trades which looked to a distant market, there were occasional fluctuations, with consequent difficulties between employers and employed, especially in 1740 (Brand, *op. cit.* II. 307, 309), and 1765. (Macpherson, III. 420.)

[4] Gray, *Chorographia*, 25.

upon great hope of benefit, come into this Country to hazard their monies in Coale-Pits. Master Beaumont, a Gentleman of great ingenuity, and rare parts, adventured into our Mines with his thirty thousand pounds; who brought with him many rare Engines, not known then in these parts, as the Art to Boore with, Iron Rodds, to try the deepnesse and thicknesse of the Coale, rare Engines to draw Water out of the Pits; Waggons with one Horse to carry down Coales from the Pits, to the Stathes, to the River etc. Within few years, he consumed all his money and Rode home upon his Light Horse." Early in the seventeenth century, Lindsay, the father of the first Earl of Balcarres, obtained a patent for an engine for pumping water out of mines[1]. Fire engines were apparently in use for this purpose in the middle of the eighteenth century[2], and an improved pump is mentioned in 1778[3]. Brand notes an important invention in 1753, when Michael Menzies devised a machine for raising the coal by balancing it against a bucket of water, and effected a considerable saving in labour[4].

A fresh impetus was given to this growing trade, when the smelting and working iron, with this form of fuel, became

A.D. 1689 —1776.
and in the introduction of pumping and other appliances.

---

[1] Arnot, *Hist. of Edinburgh*, 67, note.

[2] They were used for pumping water from tin and copper mines in 1741 (14 Geo. II. c. 41).

[3] It is not a little curious to find that the prospective expansion of coal-mining, to meet the requirements of the iron-trade, was the cause of some little anxiety in Scotland. It was said that the demand due to blast furnaces would be so great as to raise miners' wages enormously, and thus enhance the price of coal used for domestic purposes. The argument seems to assume that colliers were a special class and could not be readily recruited from outside, which was of course, to a great extent, true. (See p. 531 below.) "Five blast furnaces will require 262 colliers and miners; formerly employed in preparing collieries for work, or in working coals for the domestic consumption of the inhabitants of Scotland. This evil is only beginning to be felt, it being certain, from the present high price and great demand for cast iron, * * that twenty additional blast furnaces will be erected in Scotland within the space of ten years from the present date, requiring a supply of 2,018 colliers and miners. This supply of hands must either be drawn from the collieries now working coal for the consumption of the inhabitants of Scotland,—in which case coal will increase in price above any calculation now possible to be made;—or, erectors of ironworks must be compelled to breed hands for their works, by being prohibited * * from employing any colliers now employed at the collieries." *Reports*, etc. 1871, xviii. 847.

[4] One man and the machine could do the work of three shifts of two horses each driven by two boys. Brand, *op. cit.* ii. 308. See also a *Treatise upon Coal Mines*, 1769 [Brit. Mus. 117. n. 28], p. 100.

A.D. 1689
—1776.

In the
Newcastle
district the
employers
organised
a system
for con-
trolling the
output
a practical success; not only were new fields opened up but the old mines were worked more vigorously than before[1]. The development of the trade and its fluctuations gave rise to a curious system of combination among the great capitalists for the regulation of the out-put; the trade was deliberately organised in the Newcastle district with the view of giving a regular and steady return to all the capital invested in this employment throughout the district.

The 'vend' was an agreement among the Newcastle coal-owners which has curious analogies with the stint[2] of the Merchant Adventurers; it appears to have taken very definite shape about the year 1786. The object apparently was to give the owners of mines, which yielded inferior sorts of coal, a chance. The shipowners preferred to load the best sorts of coal; and if there had been no regulation, the whole trade would have been monopolised by a few collieries which yielded the best qualities, and other owners would be ruined. This result, as was argued in 1800, would not really benefit the public[3], since the few high-class mines that were left would be able to charge what they liked for coals. It thus came about that the 'vend' was organised; it was an agreement which was officially described in 1830. A committee was formed to represent the different collieries, and " the Proprietors of the best Coals are called upon to name the price at which they intend to sell their Coals for the succeeding twelve months; according to this price, the remaining Proprietors fix their prices; this being accomplished, each Colliery is requested to send in a Statement of the different sorts of Coals they raise, and the powers of the Colliery; that is, the quantity that each particular Colliery could raise at full work;

---

[1] The Commissioners of 1871 estimated it as follows (*Reports, etc.*, 1871, xviii. 852):

1660	. . . . .	2,148,000 tons.
1700	. . . . .	2,612,000 ,,
1750	. . . . .	4,773,828 ,,
1770	. . . . .	6,205,400 ,,
1790	. . . . .	7,618,728 ,,
1795	. . . . .	10,080,300 ,,

[2] See above, p. 220. A similar arrangement existed among the Hostmen with regard to the shipment of coals in 1602. Brand, ii. 273 n.

[3] See the evidence of the Town Clerk of Newcastle, *Reports from Committees of House of Commons, Misc. Subjects*, 1785—1800, x. 544.

and upon these Statements the Committee, assuming an imaginary basis, fix the relative proportions, as to quantity, between all the Collieries, which proportions are observed, whatever quantity the Markets may demand. The Committees then meet once a month, and according to the probable demand of the ensuing month, they issue so much per 1,000 to the different collieries; that is, if they give me an imaginary basis of 30,000 and my neighbour 20,000, according to the quality of our Coal and our power of raising them in the monthly quantity; if they issue 100 to the 1000, I raise and sell 3000 during the month, and my neighbour 2000; but in fixing the relative quantities, if we take 800,000 chaldrons as the probable demand of the different markets for the year; if the markets should require more, an increased quantity would be given out monthly, so as to raise the annual quantity to meet that demand, were it double the original quantity assumed[1]."

It was possible to argue that the vend was an arrangement which merely secured a reasonable price, and that, while it benefited the producers as a body, it did not entail ultimate loss on the consumers[2]. But the relations which existed, in some parts of the country, between the coal-owners and the labourers were much less defensible. It was important to the employer to be able to command the regular and constant service of a number of labourers, and customs grew up[3] by which the miners were just as definitely astricted to particular mines as villeins had been to particular estates in the middle ages. This custom was specially noticeable in Scotland; an Act was passed with the view of breaking it down in 1775[4], but apparently with little success, for farther legislation was necessary in 1799[5]. The bondsmen were born in a state of subjection, and an attempt was first made to free them gradually; but many of them failed to take advantage of the opportunity, while others became

A.D. 1689 —1776.

from each colliery,

and the miners in Scotland

were bondsmen,

---

[1] *Reports*, etc., 1830, VIII. 6.

[2] Especially as the arrangement only held good in the Newcastle district which was exposed to competition from other fields. *Ib.* 1830, VIII. 17.

[3] Cosmo Innes considers it was not a vestige of mediaeval serfdom. *Sketches of Early Scotch History*, 199; May, *Constitutional History*, III. 38.

[4] 15 Geo. III. c. 28.   [5] 39 Geo. III. c. 56.

A.D. 1689
—1776.
deeply indebted to their masters, and thus sank to a position
in personal of absolute dependence[1]. In other cases the system of
subjection apprenticeship operated so as to produce similar results.
to their
masters. "Here," said the commissioners in Staffordshire, in 1842,
"is a slavery in the middle of England as reprehensible as
ever was the slavery in the West Indies, which justice and
humanity alike demand should no longer be endured[2]." The
publicity thus given appears to have been of advantage[3], and
a considerable improvement took place within the next few
years.

The im- **232.** The increased demand for coal as fuel and the
provement
of internal prospect of opening up new beds so as to obtain a profit-
water com- able return was the direct motive for the first serious
munication
attempt to improve internal communication by water. The
Duke of Bridgewater, with the help of James Brindley,
embarked on a great scheme for connecting Worsley with
Manchester by a canal, so as to effect a saving in the cost
of carting coal from his pits to the growing city. The
success which attended his achievement led to its being
imitated in many other places, with the result that in the
course of a few years England was covered with a net-work
of canals.

The fact that it was possible to sink money in such large
and expensive undertakings is in itself an indication that
had often capital was more readily available. Many of the schemes
been
projected, which were now carried out had been mooted more than a
hundred years before[4]. In Holland the facilities for water
communication were obvious to every passing traveller, and
an immense amount had been done under Henri IV. to
improve the rivers and construct canals in France[5]. There
were plenty of models for Englishmen to copy; but they
had not the means of effecting such costly improvements.
Yarranton was a writer who argued that the problem of
providing an adequate food supply for London and other

[1] 39 Geo. III. c. 56, § 5. This measure seems to have proved effective.
Reports, etc., 1844, XVI. 9.
[2] *Reports, etc.*, 1842, XV. 54, printed pag. 42.   [3] *Reports*, 1844, XVI. 56.
[4] See the third instruction to the Commission of 1650. *Parl. or Const. Hist.*
XIX. 315. Also 16 and 17 Charles II. cc. 6, 11, 12 (private).
[5] Fagniez, *Economie sociale de la France sous Henri IV.*, p. 188.

large towns could be most easily solved by giving new *A.D. 1689 —1776.*
facilities for internal traffic; he urged that the rivers might
be utilised for the conveyance of corn. He suggested that *for conveying corn,*
great granaries should be built by the London Companies
near Oxford, and that the navigation of the Cherwell and
Thames might be improved so as to render the conveyance
of corn from them very easy[1]. He would have erected
similar granaries at Stratford-on-Avon[2], from which the
towns in the Severn valley might be supplied. There were
also attempts to utilise the Wye in a similar fashion[3], as
well as to connect the Severn and the Thames by a canal at
Lechlade[4]. Charles II., who had seen many things on his
travels, was much interested in these schemes, as well as in
the proposal to render the Medway navigable, with the view
of conveying the timber of the Wealds of Kent and Sussex
for the use of the Royal Navy[5]. During the seventeenth *and the new demand for coal gave better prospects of profit.*
century, when the products of the surface of the land were
the only goods for which internal transport was required,
these schemes seemed impracticable; but in the eighteenth
the increasing traffic in coal promised to be remunerative,
and capital was available in large quantities for attempting
to carry out these costly undertakings. It was the Duke
of Bridgewater who, by his enterprise, demonstrated to the
English public the possibility of success.

His first canal, from Worsley to Manchester, was only *The Duke of Bridge-water constructed a canal from Worsley to Manchester with his own resources,*
eleven miles long, but it presented formidable engineering
difficulties. Tunnelling was necessary to get access to the
pits at a convenient level[6]; and the promoters determined
to attempt to construct an aqueduct over the River Irwell.
This was very desirable for the sake of convenience in
working the canal; though it was generally regarded as an
impossible feat; but Brindley's skill in the choice and use
of materials enabled him to solve the difficulty[7]. In 1761,

---

[1] Yarranton, *England's Improvement*, 180.   [2] *Ib.* 163.

[3] Act for making navigable the Wye, passed June 26, 1651, not printed by
Scobell though mentioned by him.

[4] Phillips, *Inland Navigation*, 210.

[5] On the difficulties of conveying timber, see Defoe, *Tour* (1724), Vol. I.
Letter II. p. 59. The project of 16 and 17 C. II. c. 11 (private) as revived by
13 Geo. II. c. 26 is described in the edition of 1748, I. 204.

[6] Smiles, *Lives of Engineers*, I. 357.   [7] *Ib.* I. 353.

A.D. 1689
—1776.
so soon as the success of this first expedient was ensured,
the Duke employed Brindley to construct a long branch to
connect the original canal with the Mersey at Runcorn, and
and from Manchester to Runcorn through the help of London Bankers, thus to open up improved water communication between
Liverpool and Manchester. This was a more ambitious
scheme; it roused more open hostility[1], and the attempt to
carry it through, entirely exhausted the Duke's resources and
his credit in Manchester[2]. London Bankers, however, took

[1] The nature of the opposition may be understood from the following suggestion
by Richard Whitworth, who was a great enthusiast for canals, and tried to
promote an alternative to Brindley's Grand Canal (*The Advantages of Inland
Navigation*, by R. Whitworth, 1766, 29). " It has been a common objection against
navigable canals in this kingdom, that numbers of people are supported by land
carriage, and that navigable canals will be their ruin; and it has as often been
said, to remedy that inconvenience, that those people may take to other trades,
and turn either farmers or navigators; and instead of driving the waggon they
may learn to steer and navigate a boat, which, in time of war, may turn to the
advantage of the navy, or merchants service (upon both which most of our learned
authors agree that our safety depends); but I, more supple to the inclinations of
my fellow countrymen, am unwilling to unbend the crooked finger, or streighten
the almost distorted joint, inured to tally with the stroke of its accustomed trade,
and at his old age deprive him of the art of his employment, and leave him in his
second childhood to begin the world again: and as the land carriage is chiefly
carried on from trading towns and their neighbourhood, I must advance a very
uncommon alternative, which would free the carrier from any fear of losing his
employment or selling off his stock of horses, viz.—That no main trunk of
a navigable canal ought reasonably to be carried nearer than within four miles of
any great manufacturing and trading town, considering the present state and
situation of affairs, and the proprietors of blending the landed with the commercial
interest; which distance from the canal is sufficient to maintain the same number
of carriers, and employ almost the same number of horses, as usual, to convey the
goods down the canal, in order to go to the seaports for exportation. When any
person considers the advantage of this nation, they must consider that of every
individual, and see that one is not burdened in order to unburthen another;
I therefore have produced this uncommon argument and favour the landed, as
well as the commercial interest, which I think proves, considering both interests
together, that it is not for the benefit of every individual in a trading city, to have
the navigable canal come close to their town, but that the same should be at
a proper distance about four miles, so that each trade may still have some employ,
those that carry the goods and merchandize, as well as those that manufacture
them: there is no doubt but the person who manufactures the goods might afford
to export them to foreign markets much cheaper by having the navigable canal
come close to him, but then we must consider all parties when we talk of trade,
and not let the carriers starve while the traders and manufacturers ride in their
coach and six, exulting over their dejected distressed brethren and fellow
creatures. If a manufacturer can have a certain conveniency of sending his
goods by water carriage within four miles of his own home, surely that is
sufficient, and profit enough; considering that other people must thrive as well as
himself; and a proportion of profit to each trade should be the biassing and
leading policy of this nation." [2] Smiles, *op. cit.* I. 396.

a more favourable view of the situation, and Messrs Child, A.D. 1689
—1776. by successive advances which amounted in all to £25,000[1], enabled him to complete this second undertaking.

Brindley was next employed upon the Grand Junction *and the* canal, which was eagerly promoted by the Wedgwoods. For *scheme of* certain branches of the pottery manufacture, materials were *Junction* required which had to be brought considerable distances— *Canal was* flints from the Eastern Counties and clay from Devonshire *eagerly* and Cornwall[2]. Several of the leading proprietors in Cheshire *taken up.* and Staffordshire were eager to carry out a scheme for opening up their estates by making a water-way, which should start from the Duke's canal near Runcorn on the Mersey, and connect with the Trent at Wilne, near Derby, and also with the Severn at Stourport. It more than realised the most sanguine expectations, as it reduced the cost of carriage to about one-fourth of what it had been[3]. Cheshire salt could be manufactured on a much larger scale, and the Potteries benefited enormously, not only by the improved means of obtaining materials, but by the increased facilities for the safe transport of brittle wares.

The development of internal navigation was of immense *The roads* importance to manufactures of every kind[4], but it also gave *of the* an incentive to agricultural improvement; it was possible to *kingdom* convey produce to more distant and better markets[5]. This *had been* kind of advantage accrued, in an even greater degree, *fall into* through successful efforts to rescue the roads of the country *disrepair* from the frightful state of disrepair into which they had been allowed to fall in the later middle ages. Till the time of Philip and Mary, the maintenance of the roads had been for the most part a matter of private benevolence, and during the fifteenth and sixteenth centuries, they appear to have decayed. In the time of Philip and Mary, parish *despite the* surveyors[6] were instituted, whose business it was to enforce *efforts of* the necessary labour from each parish. The justices had *surveyors* power to punish the neglect of surveyors and to assess the

---

[1] Smiles, *op. cit.* I. 398.   [2] Id., *op. cit.* I. 425.   [3] Id., *op. cit.* I. 447.

[4] Whitworth (*op. cit.* p. 36) gives an interesting account of the local manufactures which would benefit by his proposed canal.   [5] Id., *op. cit.* p. 31.

[6] 2 and 3 Philip and Mary, c. 8. The Bedfordshire Quarter Sessions Records, 1650—1660 have frequent complaints of parishes not appointing surveyors. See also Atkinson, *Yorkshire Quarter Sessions Records.*

A.D. 1689
—1776.

to enforce
statute
duty,
parishes, but the machinery was too cumbersome to be very effective. The 'statute duty,' which could be required from the parishioners, was perfunctorily performed, since there was not sufficient difference between the calls on large and small farmers and on large and small householders. It seemed that the most equitable system would be that "every Person ought to contribute to the Repair of Roads in Proportion to the Use they make of, or the Convenience which they receive from them[1]." With the view of carrying out this

but turn-
pike roads
were better
main-
tained.
principle on the main lines of through traffic, turnpikes were erected and tolls[2] levied on certain highways, under the authority of special Acts. Precautions were also taken against injury to the roads from very heavy weights, or badly constructed waggons[3]; when the wheels were so arranged as to follow one another in the same track, vehicles were freed from half the usual tolls[4]. Though improvement occurred on the highways for which special Acts had been procured, the parish roads were not equally well cared for. Under these circumstances we can well understand that there should have been a great variety in the condition of the different roads; and that some should have been left in a very dangerous condition, while others were fairly good. It was in 1773 that a general measure was passed, which rendered it possible to bring all the highways of the kingdom[5] into the same sort of repair as had been obtained by the various bodies of commissioners for turnpike roads.

That the evil was not cured immediately and that many roads were allowed to remain in a desperate condition is clear enough from the complaints made by Arthur Young[6]:

---

1 Homer, *Enquiry into the Publick Roads*, p. 18.

2 Arthur Young, *Southern Tour*, 137, 161.

3 5 Geo. I. c. 12; 1 Geo. II. c. 11; 14 Geo. II. c. 42.

4 5 Geo. III. c. 38.

5 13 Geo. III. c. 78.

6 "Of all the roads that ever disgraced this kingdom, in the very ages of barbarism none ever equalled that from Bellericay to the King's Head at Tilbury. It is for near 12 miles so narrow, that a mouse cannot pass by any carriage, I saw a fellow creep under his waggon to assist me to lift if possible my chaise over a hedge. The rutts are of an incredible depth....The trees everywhere overgrow the road, so that it is totally impervious to the sun, except at a few places: And to add to all the infamous circumstances, which concur to plague a traveller, I must not forget eternally meeting with chalk-waggons; themselves frequently stuck fast, till a collection of them are in the same situation, that twenty or thirty horses may

but at the very date of his travels another observer was able *A.D. 1689 —1776.*
to congratulate his countrymen on the immense improve-
ment that had taken place in the preceding half century.
Henry Homer regarded the state of the roads and difficulties *In the time*
of internal communication as one of the chief reasons for the *of Queen Anne*
backward state of the country in the time of Queen Anne.
"The Trade of the Kingdom languished under these Impediments. Few People cared to encounter the Difficulties,
which attended the Conveyance of Goods from the Places
where they were manufactured, to the Markets, where they
were to be disposed of. And those, who undertook this
Business, were only enabled to carry it on in the Wintry-
Season on Horseback, or, if in Carriages, by winding
Deviations from the regular Tracks, which the open country
afforded them an Opportunity of making. Thus the very *the state of*
same Cause, which was injurious to Trade, laid waste also *the roads hampered*
a considerable Part of our Lands. The natural Produce of *trade*
the Country was with Difficulty circulated to supply the
Necessities of those Counties and trading Towns, which
wanted, and to dispose of the superfluity of others which
abounded. Except in a few Summer-Months, it was an
almost impracticable Attempt to carry very considerable
Quantities of it to remote Places. Hence the Consumption
of the Growth of Grain as well as of the inexhaustible
Stores of Fuel, which Nature has lavished upon particular
Parts of our Island, was limited to the Neighbourhood of
those Places which produced them; and made them, comparatively speaking, of little value to what they would have
been, had the Participation of them been more enlarged.

"To the Operation of the same Cause must also be *and agri- culture,*
attributed, in great Measure, the slow Progress which was
formerly made in the Improvement of Agriculture. Discouraged by the Expence of procuring Manure, and the
uncertain Returns, which arose from such confined Markets,
the Farmer wanted both Spirit and Ability to exert himself
in the Cultivation of his Lands. On this Account Undertakings in Husbandry were then generally small, calculated

be tacked to each to draw them out one by one." *Southern Tour,* p. 88. A mass
of evidence as to the state of the roads in the eighteenth century will be found in
W. C. Sydney, *England in the Eighteenth Century,* II. 1—43.

A.D. 1689
—1776. rather to be a Means of Subsistence to particular Families, than a Source of Wealth to the Publick. Almost every Estate was incumbered with a great Quantity of Buildings, to adapt them to the convenience of the Occupiers. The clear Emolument resulting from them both to the Proprietors and Tenants was far more inconsiderable than what has accrued from the more extended Plan, upon which that Branch of Business is now conducted.

"The great Obstruction to the Reformation, which has been accomplished, was founded upon a Principle adopted by Gentlemen of Property in the Country, which Experience has since proved to be as erroneous as it was selfish; viz., that it would be injurious to their Tenants to render the Markets in their Neighbourhood more accessible to distant Farmers, and consequently a Diminution of their own *but the* Estates. It ought for ever to be recorded to the Honour *eighteenth century* of the present Century, that it was the first which pro- *proprietors were* duced publick Spirit enough to renounce that Prejudice, *sufficiently public* and by this Circumstance only to have given as it were a *spirited* new Birth to the Genius of this Island. It is owing to the Alteration, which has taken Place in consequence thereof, that we are now released from treading the cautious Steps of our Forefathers, and that our very Carriages travel with almost winged Expedition between every Town of Consequence in the Kingdom and the Metropolis. By this, as well as the yet more valuable Project of increasing inland Navigation, a Facility of Communication is soon likely to be established from every Part of the Island to the sea, and from the several Places in it to each other. Trade is no longer fettered by the Embarrasments, which unavoidably attended our former Situation. Dispatch, which is the very Life and Soul of Business, becomes daily more attainable by the free Circulation opening in every Channel, which is adapted to it. Merchandise and Manufactures find a ready Conveyance to the Markets. The natural Blessings of the Island are shared by the Inhabitants with a more equal Hand. The Constitution itself acquires Firmness by the Stability and Increase both of Trade and Wealth, which are the Nerves and Sinews of it.

"In Consequence of all this, the Demand for the Produce A.D. 1689
—1776. of the Lands is increased; the Lands themselves advance proportionably both in their annual Value, and in the Number of Years-purchase for which they are sold, according to such Value. Nor does there appear to have arisen even any local Injury to particular Estates by this Change of Circumstances; though if there did, they ought to submit to it from the greater Advantage resulting to the Publick; but they are yet more valuable as their Situation is nearer to the trading Towns, and as the Number of Inhabitants in such Towns is enlarged by the Increase of Trade.

"There never was a more astonishing Revolution ac- *to carry out vast improvements* complished in the internal System of any Country than has been within the Compass of a few years in that of England. The Carriage of Grain, Coals, Merchandize, etc., is in general conducted with little more than half the Number of Horses with which it formerly was. Journies of Business are performed with more than double Expedition. Improvements in Agriculture keep pace with those of Trade. Everything wears the Face of Dispatch; every Article of our Produce becomes more valuable; and the Hinge, upon which all these Movements turn, is the Reformation which has been made in our Publick Roads[1]."

There is ample evidence to confirm this account of *in the country generally.* the improvements. It may be inferred from the increasing practice of keeping carriages; hackney carriages were brought down from London to ply between Cambridge and Stourbridge Fair[2]; and it could hardly have been worth while to bring these vehicles for a few days, if the roads had been everywhere of a very defective character. It is not always easy to judge how far the existence of internal trade implied that good roads were available. Corn was usually taken in bags on horses, though waggons were also used[3], and bulky goods were conveyed as far as possible by water[4]; but

---

[1] Homer, *An Enquiry into the Means of Preserving the Publick Roads* (1767), 4.

[2] Defoe (1748), I. 97.   [3] *Ib.* 229; Arthur Young, *Farmer's Letters*, 190.

[4] Manchester goods were brought to Stourbridge Fair in horse packs; similar goods were taken from Essex to London in waggons. Defoe's *Tour*, I. 94, 118.

A.D. 1689
—1776.

it appears that live geese were brought from the Fens to the London market in large two-horse carts, arranged with four stages, which took them a hundred miles to market in two days and a night[1]; and it is difficult to understand how such quantities of Scotch cattle could be driven to the Norfolk and Suffolk marshes[2] unless there was fairly good going.

XVI. Spirited Proprietors and Substantial Tenants.

The Whigs endeavoured to promote tillage

233. The fostering of industry was the fundamental principle in the economic policy of the Whigs; they were chiefly concerned in trying to develop existing and to plant new manufactures. But they did not forget that agriculture was by far the most important of all English employments, and that a very large proportion of the population was engaged in tillage. The party which came into power after the Revolution was eager to promote the interests of the farmers[3], and formulated a scheme, which was entirely consonant with accepted maxims, for achieving this result.

not merely by protecting the English farmer in the home market,

The Court Party at the Restoration had given a large measure of protection to English producers of food stuffs[4]. English agriculturists, as well as English fishermen[5], were secured by prohibitive tariffs against colonial competition in the home market. But this did not satisfy those who were looking further afield, with the view of not only meeting the requirements of their countrymen, but of catering for foreign consumers as well[6]. In 1663 the conditions as to time and price, on which the export of corn was permitted, were relaxed[7]; and an attempt was made by the Whigs to remove the export duty in 1677. This would have meant a reduction of royal revenue, and it was resisted by the

[1] Defoe's *Tour*, I. 54.   [2] *Ib.* I. 63.

[3] Colbert recognised the desirability of taking this course, but he did not pursue it systematically, Clément, *Histoire de Colbert*, I. 365, II. 49.

[4] High rates were levied on the importation of corn by 12 C. II. c. 4 and 22 C. II. c. 13, *An Act for the Improvement of Tillage and the Breed of Cattle*.

[5] 12 C. II. c. 18, § 5.   [6] Davenant, *Works*, v. 424.

[7] 15 C. II. c. 7. Steps had been taken to give more scope for the export of cereals and other agricultural produce under Cromwell. *Calendar S. P. D.* 1656-7, p. 174; Whitelock, *Memorials*, IV. 282.

Tories[1]; but the opinion gained ground in favour of not only protecting but of stimulating agriculture, and the desirability of granting a premium on export was suggested in 1683[2]. This expedient was adopted in 1689, and a bounty was given on the export when the price ranged below 48s.[3]; this was continued, with suspensions in the four famine years of 1698, 1709, 1740, 1757[4]. The result of this measure was very remarkable; from this time onwards corn was treated as a commodity to be grown for export. This policy was almost exclusively English[5], but it had been pursued, at least occasionally, in this country since the agricultural depression of the fifteenth century[6]. The result which followed was twofold; first, the landed interest was so far relieved from loss by low prices, in the case of a plentiful harvest, that there was a distinct inducement to invest capital in the land; and secondly, by encouraging such extensive production of corn there was some security that the food supply of the people would not be deficient. By promoting the growth of corn, to serve as a commodity for export in favourable seasons, a motive was brought into play for growing as much as would meet the home consumption in unfavourable years. The ulterior political aim[7] of this measure was clear; it was intended to render agriculture more profitable, and so to bring about a rise of rents. By far the larger share of the taxation of the country fell on the landed gentry[8]. The Tories aimed at diverting this burden to other shoulders; but the Whigs schemed to foster the agricultural interest, so that the

A.D. 1689 —1776.

but by giving a bounty on the export of corn,

and thus enabling the landed gentry to bear taxation.

---

[1] R. Faber, *Die Entstehung des Agrarschutzes in England*, 111.   [2] *Ib.* 113.

[3] William and Mary, i. c. 12, *An Act for the Encouraging the Exportation of Corn*. As Faber points out, Dalrymple's assertion (*Memoirs*, pt. ii. 74) that the measure was passed in order to disarm Tory opposition to an increased Land Tax is not well founded. R. Faber, *Die Entstehung des Agrarschutzes*, 112.

[4] C. Smith, *Three Tracts*, 73.

[5] Faber, *op. cit.* 2.   [6] Vol. i. p. 447.

[7] The improvement of agriculture also afforded a commodity for export and increased the employment of shipping. N. Forster, *Enquiry into the Causes of the present high price of Provisions* (1767), p. 70. Dr Johnson, *Considerations of the Corn Laws*, in *Works*, v. 321.

[8] According to Locke this was inevitable in any scheme of taxation. *Considerations of the Lowering of Interest*, in *Works*, iv. 57. See p. 426 above, also 839 below.

A.D. 1689
—1776.
landed men might be able to make these large contributions to the expenses of government, both local and national.

The Whig scheme for the economic development of the country did not merely appeal to the moneyed men, whether merchants or manufacturers, but to the landed proprietors[1], in so far as they were ready and willing to devote themselves to the improvement of their estates. The sinking of money in land, with the view of obtaining a regular return by an increased rental, had been recognised as a sound form of business enterprise in Elizabethan and Jacobean times. The spirited proprietors of the eighteenth century were not content, however, with occasional and permanent works, but busied themselves about changing the practice of ordinary farming operations for the better. Whether from lack of energy or lack of security, the tenants do not seem to have done much in this direction at first. The great advance in the management and working of land, which occurred during the eighteenth century, was due to the landlords and was initiated under the influence of men of wealth. In carrying out these improvements they had to contend, not only with the difficulties which were due to deficiency of knowledge, since scientific agriculture did not exist, but with the time-honoured prejudices of those who had practised traditional methods and who were constitutionally averse to any change[2].

The wealthy land-owners of the eighteenth century

were keenly interested in new methods of cultivation

[1] The plan adopted under Locke's influence for recoinage in 1696 favoured the landed rather than the moneyed interest at the time. See p. 436 above.

[2] From the point of view of Norden, a seventeenth century surveyor, the small freeholder was merely obstructive. He writes as follows. *Lord.* "As farre as I can perceive, an observing and painful husband liveth, fareth, and thriveth, as well upon his Farme of ract rent, as many do that are called Freeholders, or that have Leases of great value for small rent. *Surveyor.* There is some reason for it, which every man either seeth not, or seeing it, doth not consider it, or considering it, hath no will or power to reforme it. Some Freeholders, and the Lessees of great things of small rent, bring up their children too nicely, and must needs, forsooth, Gentleize them; and the eldest sonne of a meane man must be a young master, he must not labour, nor lay hand on the plough (take heed of his dis-grace), hee shall have ynough to maintaine him like, and in the societie of gentlemen, not like a drudge. And when this young gentleman comes to his land (long he thinkes) he hath no leasure to labor, for Hawking or Hunting or Bowling or Ordinaries or some vaine or lascivious or wanton course or other, leaving ploughe and seede and harvest, and sale to some ordinary hireling, who may doe what he list, if the poore wife be as carelesse at home, as the husband is abroad; And at his elbowe he hath perchaunce some vaine persons, that disswade from covetousnesse and from too much frugalite, and that he needes not to care

The progress of their endeavours has been recorded in many A.D. 1689
—1776. cases by Arthur Young, who watched their proceedings with interest and admiration. To him they were the greatest of patriots, for whom no praise could be too high. They were "spirited cultivators" who managed their land in such a fashion as to deserve "every acknowledgment which a lover of his country can give." He is full of enthusiasm for their *and in improved implements* experimental farms, new patterns of agricultural implements, *and buildings,* and new plans for laying out farm buildings; as well as for the care which they bestowed on the smallest points of land management. Perhaps we may feel that the judgment of a contemporary, who mixed with these men and discussed their successes and failures, was formed on better grounds than that of writers who, at a distance of more than a century, decry the landlords, and gratuitously attribute to them the meanest motives.

The progress was initiated by wealthy landlords; but in *and the plans were carried out* order to carry out their schemes effectively it was necessary *by a new class of* that there should, if possible, be enterprising farmers too. The owners, who were improving their estates, preferred to throw the holdings together, so as to substitute farms of three hundred acres and upwards, for farms of one hundred acres and under. With the possible exception of poultry farming, there was no department of agriculture in which small farms proved more advantageous to the public[1]. As the usual calculation appears to have been that the capital requisite, in order to work the land, was at least five pounds an acre,

for getting more, he hath no rent to pay, but some to receive, which will maintaine him; and when he is gone, all is gone; spending is easier then getting. And thus by little and little roweth himself and the hope of his posteritie under water, in the calme weather. Whereas, he, that hath a rent to pay is not idle, neither in hart nor hand; he considers the rent day will come, and in true labour and diligence provides for it, and by his honest endeavours and dutiful regard, gets to pay rent to his Lord * * I inferre not yet by this, Sir, that because they sometimes thrive well, that live upon rackt rents, therefore you Landlords should impose the greater rent or fine; that were to do evill that good might come of it, nay rather to doe evill that evill may followe; for if there be not a meane in burdens, the backe of the strongest Elephant may bee broken. And the best and most carefull and most laborious and most industrious husband may be overcharged with the rent of his Land." *Surveyor's Dialogue*, 80–81, also p. 16. Compare above. p. 107, n. 1.

[1] Arbuthnot, *An Inquiry into the connection between the present price of Provisions and the size of Farms* (1773), p. 21.

A.D. 1689
—1776.
the large farmers were men who could start in life with
fifteen hundred or two thousand pounds; and thus we find
signs of a middle class in the country, who were capitalists
substantial
tenants, and employers of labour, but who did not themselves own
land, and did not engage in the actual work of the farm with
their own hands. These men had an advantage over the
small farmers, inasmuch as they were able to hold their stocks
of corn for a longer period, and get the benefit of a rise of
price, whereas the poorest of the small farmers were forced to
realise at once, and were compelled to dispose of their whole
who could harvest by Christmas at latest[1]. The substantial men were
make the
new system also able to afford better seed, better implements, and to
profitable, work the land on better principles, and hence they were able
to pay a larger rent than the small farmers who stuck to
the old-fashioned methods. The rise of an employing class
occurred not only in manufacturing occupations, but in
agriculture also, and the causes at work were precisely
similar. The new facilities for commerce[2] brought about
a development, and led to changes in the character of
the system. There was scope in farming for the talents
of men with business capacity, such as there had never been
before. In the period before the Civil War, when the

---

[1] Smith, *Three Tracts*, p. 12.

[2] Defoe's account of the changes at Chichester was published in 1724. "They
are lately fallen into a very particular way of managing the Corn Trade here,
which it is said turns very well to account; the country round it is very
fruitful and particularly in good Wheat, and the Farmers generally speaking
carry'd all their Wheat to Farnham to market, which is very near Forty Miles, by
Land Carriages, and from some Parts of the Country more than Forty Miles.
But some Money'd Men of Chichester, Emsworth and other places adjacent, have
join'd their Stocks together, built large Granaries near the Crook, where the
Vessells come up, and here they buy and lay up all the Corn which the Country
on that side can spare; and having good Mills in the Neighbourhood, they grind
and dress the Corn and send it to London in the Meal about by Long Sea, as they
call it: nor now the War is over do they make the Voyage so tedious as to do the
Meal any hurt, as at first in the time of War was sometimes the Case for want of
Convoys. It is true this is a great lessening to Farnham Market, but that is of
no consideration in the Case; for if the Market at London is supply'd the coming
by Sea from Chichester is every jot as much a publick good as the encouraging of
Farnham Market, which is of itself the greatest Corn-Market in England, London
excepted. Notwithstanding all the decrease from this side of the Country this
carrying of Meal by Sea met with so just an Encouragement from hence, that
it is now practised from several other Places on this Coast, even as far as
Shampton." *Tour*, I. Letter II. p. 70.

Justices of the Peace insisted that those who had stocks of corn should give a preference to local markets, the well-informed producer could not always hope to reap the reward of his enterprise; but the conditions of the corn trade had *under the stimulus of* completely changed before the eighteenth century opened[1]. *expanding commerce.* Under the influence of increasing commerce, large amounts of capital were applied to the management of land and the cultivation of the soil, and there was room for the energies of an employing class of tenant farmers.

234. During the seventeenth century[2] there had been a *In the seventeenth* very decided increase of knowledge as to the best methods of *century* turning the land to good account; and the suggestions which *there was much* are found in the agricultural treatises of the time appear to *imitation of Dutch* have been put in practice to some extent. As in regard *methods* to so many other sides of Economic life, Dutch methods were held up as an example[3]. The people of Holland were not

---

[1] In the period after the Restoration the character of the seasons tended to render farming a very uncertain business. There were one or two years of excessive dearth, notably 1661-62, when those who had managed to save their crops would realise unusual prices, but the century was curiously remarkable for the way in which the seasons ran in successive periods, of longer and shorter duration, of good years and of bad years. Good years meant but little remuneration for the farmer, as prices were low; bad years might bring in a profit, or might ruin him altogether. No similar run of seasons has been traced by Professor Thorold Rogers in the three centuries and a half which preceded it; and the eighteenth century presented a remarkable succession of fairly good harvests, followed by a long period of great irregularity. In the seventeenth century only, "the good and bad seasons lie in groups of more or less extent. The fact was recognised in a rough way by the agriculturists of the time" (*Agriculture and Prices*, v. 173). The business of the farmers was accordingly a highly speculative one; it might be profitable, or it might be the reverse.

[2] This is especially noticeable in the recommendations of the use of various substances for improving the land. Markham refers to the use of marl as it had been understood from very early ages; and Dymock gives a long list of suitable manures which were available in many parts of England, but which were unknown in Flanders (Hartlib's *Legacy*, p. 43); such as chalk, lime, snagg-root, Cornish sea-sand (7 Jas. I. c. 18), ashes, salt, fish, and even woollen rags. The judicious application of these various fertilisers was an art that seemed to be but little understood, and there are a whole series of writers who dwell upon the advantages which may accrue from the proper use of marl and lime (Blith, *The English Improver or a new Survey of Husbandry*, 60; Platt, *Jewell House*, Part II. *Diverse new sorts of Soyle*, 21; Markham, *Farewell to Husbandry*, 32).

[3] The Dutch were noted for their horticulture, and there is every reason to believe that, under the guidance of the seventeenth century writers on rural affairs, a great improvement took place in English gardening. See Worlidge, *Systema Agriculturae*, 164. Compare also *Adam armed*; an essay presented by the Gardeners' Company which was chartered in 1606. Serious efforts were made under

C. 35

A.D. 1689 —1776.

of raising stock and dairy farming.

much given to the growing of cereals, but they were adepts in cattle-breeding and dairy farming. Englishmen were much impressed with the desirability of imitating them, by growing root crops and artificial grasses, so as to have better means for feeding stock during winter[1]. During the preceding century, grazing had been restricted; in the seventeenth, efforts were made to promote it with regard to cattle; the very statute, which gives fresh opportunity for the export of corn, is strictly protective against the importation of fat cattle, as it had been found by experience that the English cattle-breeders were suffering from foreign competition[2]; and a few years later the cattle-farmers of Ireland[3] were prohibited from continuing an export trade which was proving very profitable. We may gather from Defoe's *Tour* that English farmers who had devoted themselves to this occupation[4] were prospering greatly in the earlier half of the eighteenth century[5], even before the time when Bakewell did so much to improve the breeds of stock of every kind[6].

Improvements in tillage in the eighteenth century

It is obvious, however, that improved methods were also being introduced with regard to the cultivation of cereals. Very full information, on the changes which were taking

---

James I. to introduce the cultivation of mulberry trees, so that the English might be able to provide the raw material for the silk manufacture (Hartlib's *Legacy*, p. 72), a project which was eagerly taken up in France. Fagniez, *op. cit.*

[1] Root crops appear to have been introduced to some extent as a course of husbandry. Weston refers to them (*Discourse of Husbandrie used in Brabant* (1652), p. 25); also Worlidge (*op. cit.* p. 46). Arthur Young had occasion to criticise the manner of growing turnips which had become traditional at the date of his tours; but on the other hand it does not appear that much practical result followed from the recommendation of clover (Weston, *Discourse of Husbandrie*, 11; Hartlib's *Legacy*, 1), sainfoin and lucerne as means of cleaning the fields; the cultivation of these grasses seems to have been one of the distinctive improvements of the eighteenth century.

[2] 15 Charles II. c. 7, § 13.

[3] 18 and 19 Charles II. c. 2, *An Act against importing cattle from Ireland, and other parts beyond the seas.*

[4] Defoe, *Tour* (1724) (I. Letter i. p. 90), notes the existence of wealthy tenants on the dairy farms of High Suffolk. Some had stock worth £1000 " in Cows only."

[5] Compare the insertion in Defoe's *Tour* on the improved pasture at Painshill in Surrey (1748), I. 239. This is not in the edition of 1724. The remark on the increase in the value of pasture near Yarmouth (from 5s. to 20s. an acre), is also an insertion. *Ib.* I. 63.

[6] See below, p. 556 n. 2.

place, has been recorded by Arthur Young, who has left us A.D. 1689
—1776.
an inimitable picture of rural England, as he knew it during *were*
this period of transition. He was a man of very varied tastes *recorded*
by Arthur
and interests, who had engaged in farming on a small scale. *Young,*
His observations, when making a business journey into
Wales through the south of England, excited so much
interest among agriculturists that he planned a northern
tour, with the express object of gathering information on
the state of rural England; he took considerable pains to
render his enquiry as complete as possible. He advertised
in the newspapers which circulated within the area of his
projected tour, and some of his correspondents were able to
supply him with accurate statistical information; in other
cases, he had to rely on what he could gather in conversation
with illiterate farmers, who were suspicious of his motives
for prying into their affairs. " My business was so very unusual that some art was requisite to gain intelligence from
many farmers, etc., who were startled at the first attack.
I found that even a profusion of expense was often necessary
to gain the ends I had in view: I was forced to make more
than one honest farmer half-drunk, before I could get sober,
unprejudiced intelligence[1]." The contrast between his own
habits of accurate observation and the slovenliness of many
of the farmers, is very striking. He asserts that he had *who was*
an accurate
the qualifications for his work which came from practical *observer*
acquaintance with agriculture; but he adds, "what is of
much more consequence towards gaining real experience,
I have always kept, from the first day I began, a minute
register of my business; insomuch that upon my Suffolk
farm, I minuted above three thousand experiments; in every
article of culture, expenses, and produce, including, among a
great variety of other articles, an accurate comparison of the
old and new husbandry, in the production of most vegetables.
But in this, I would by no means be thought to arrogate any
other than that plodding merit of being industrious and
accurate to which any one of the most common genius can
attain, if he thinks proper to take the trouble[2]." His book
abounds with figures in which he was at pains to reduce

---

[1] *Northern Tour*, I. xiii. [2] *Ib.* I. ix.

A.D. 1689
—1776.
the curious and complicated local measures to a common standard, for the convenience of his readers it is true, but to the loss of those who are curious in metric systems.

and notes some interesting survivals
There are, however, many passages in his writings which describe the survival of primitive practices[1]. Thus at Boynton, in Yorkshire[2], he found remains of extensive culture[3]. He was informed by Sir Digby Legard that the farmer on the wolds of the East Riding "every year has been accustomed to plough up a fresh part of his sheep walk, to take a crop or two, and then let it lie fifteen or twenty years till the natural grass has again formed a kind of turf, but it will sometimes be forty years before the land is completely sodded over. This ruinous practice is but too common ; and where it has long prevailed, the farmer seldom has a three-fold increase[4]."

of mediaeval practice.
There were other cases where the two-field or three-field system was still in vogue ; thus in the neighbourhood of Ecclesfield, in Hallamshire, the usual course was as follows : first fallow, second wheat, third clover, and fourth wheat[5]. This is obviously the two-field system, with the introduction of clover in place of every second fallowing. His comment is a sweeping condemnation of the early middle ages, "This is very bad husbandry." At Beverley[6] there was a similar modification of the two-field system, with the use of peas in place of clover. He notes the three-field system at Ecclesfield, first fallow, second wheat, third oats, but does not criticise it[7].

He severely criticised thriftless ploughing,
What, however, roused his strongest condemnation was the extravagance of the ploughing[8]. Near Woburn "they use four or five horses at length in their ploughs, and yet do no more than an acre a day. The reader will not forget

---

[1] These were genuine survivals. The primitive character of English Agriculture in the seventeenth century, is shown from the nature of the arrangements which were transplanted to New England ; see the accounts of common field cultivation, common fencing, herding, etc., in Weeden, *Economic and Social History of New England*, 58. But these practices in the plantations might be to some extent revivals, rather than survivals, since the special conditions of the new country would make reversion to primitive practice advisable.

[2] *Northern Tour*, II. 7.   [3] Vol. I. p. 33.   [4] *Ib.* II. 14.
[5] *Ib.* I. 126.   [6] *Ib.* II. 1.   [7] *Ib.* I. 126.
[8] *A six weeks Tour through the Southern Counties*, 298, 300.

the soil being sandy, the requsite team is certainly nearer a single jackass than five horses. This miserable management cannot be too much condemned[1]." At Offley, near Hitchin, "they never plough without four horses and two men, and do but an acre a day; this terrible custom, which is such a bane to the profits of husbandry, cannot be too much condemned; for the whole expense (on comparison with the common custom) of tillage might be saved by the farmer if he would adopt the rational method of tillage with a pair of horses, and one man to hold the plough and drive at the same time[2]." He was, however, by no means a reckless innovator; he was much interested in weighing the relative merits of oxen and horses for ploughing and draught[3], and was inclined to question the wisdom of dispensing with oxen[4].

The raising of peas and beans formed part of the *and careless cultivation of beans,* traditional agriculture; near Woburn "they give but one tilth for beans alone, sow them broadcast, never hoe them, but turn in sheep[5] to feed off the weeds, and reckon three quarters a middling crop" from four bushels sown. "This is an execrable custom, and ought to be exploded by all landlords of the country." In fact, the prevailing evil of the old husbandry was the mass of weeds, which sometimes appear to have got the better of the crop altogether. Thorough ploughing and fallowing did much to clear the land; but it appears that some of the earlier attempts at improvement were most unsatisfactory. Thus the introduction of turnips in the East Riding of Yorkshire seems to have been positively mischievous though "the soil is good turnip land, but," as he continues, "their culture is so wretchedly defective, that I may, without the imputation of a paradox, assert, they had better have let it alone. Very few of them hoe at all, and those who do, execute it in so slovenly a way, that neither the crop nor the land are the least the better for it. With such management, turnips are

---

[1] *Northern Tour*, I. 41.   [2] *Ib*. I. 22.

[3] *Ib*. I. 169, II. 70, and *Southern Counties*, 151, 203, 212.

[4] *Northern Tour*, I. 146. He argues for oxen in the *Farmer's Letters*, 166.

[5] *Northern Tour*, I. 40, 41. Compare the Scotch practice (1735), as described in Alexander's *Notes and Sketches of Northern Rural Life* (1877), 25.

by no means beneficial in a course of crops, as they leave the soil so foul that a fallow rather than another crop ought to succeed. The great benefit of turnips is not the mere value of the crop, but the cleaning the land so well as to enable the farmer to cultivate the artificial grasses with profit...... The farmers of this country ought therefore to neglect turnips totally, or cultivate them in the clean-husband-like manner that is practised in many parts of England, of thoroughly pulverizing the land and hoeing them twice or thrice, or as often as necessary, to keep them distinct from each other, and perfectly free from weeds. Turnips would then be found an excellent preparation for barley or oats, and for the artificial grasses sown with them[1]." Root crops had been introduced during the seventeenth century, but they were often badly managed; and in some districts the farmers and butchers preferred to raise small and inferior rather than large and good turnips[2]. In such cases the slovenly habits, which characterised the growth of cereals, also affected the green crops that had been much more recently introduced. There were, however, some districts where they were little known and might have been tried with advantage; on the whole, what was needed was the better working of the ground, so as to keep it clear from weeds. In regard to these matters, agricultural science was fairly advanced, but agricultural practice lagged behind.

He advocated the introduction of clover and rye grass

On the other hand, little progress had been made anywhere with the cultivation of seeds and the extension of clover and rye grass. Arthur Young is particularly careful to note what success attended attempts to cultivate these grasses and improve pastures[3], and he gets quite enthusiastic over the accurate results which were recorded at various experimental farms. He was interested in the increased cultivation of potatoes, carrots, cabbages or anything else; but the growing of artificial grasses was the department in which agricultural science, as distinguished from agricultural practice, made most progress during this century[4]. The

---

[1] *Northern Tour*, I. 217, 218.   [2] *Ib.* I. 107.

[3] *Northern Tour*, I. 277; II. 237, 243; IV. 149.

[4] Thorold Rogers, *Six Centuries*, 468.

great principle of the so-called new husbandry was to in- A.D. 1689 —1776. troduce the cultivation of roots and seeds in such a fashion as to supplement corn-growing. There was no desire to substitute anything else for corn-growing, as pasture-farming had been substituted for arable cultivation in the fifteenth and sixteenth centuries. The point maintained throughout *so as to* was, that, if careful attention were given to the qualities of *give a five- course* the soil, and energy were expended on the working of the *husbandry.* land, these root and grass crops might be introduced so as to render unnecessary the fallow shift, every second or third year. Thus, what he commonly recommends, is a course of turnips, barley, clover and wheat, an arrangement which may be said to be a development of alternate cropping and fallowing. He preferred, however, that the land should be two years under clover, which thus gave a five-course husbandry[1]. He was, of course, well aware that this rotation of crops would only prove satisfactory where the land was carefully cultivated: in particular if the turnips were not properly tilled, there was reason to fear that the land would never be free from weeds. A great impulse had been given to the introduction of the new husbandry by the example of Jethro Tull, who invented a drill for sowing, and devised a method of cultivating turnips, which was sound in principle[2], and which he found successful in practice.

In this way, cattle-breeding, which along with dairy *while Bakewell* farming and poultry farming had been the department in *improved* which the small farmers had a special advantage[3], came to *the breeds of sheep* be an important element in capitalistic land management, *and cattle.* and attracted the attention of improvers. Through the Middle Ages, sheep had been chiefly bred for the sake of their wool, and cattle for the sake of their powers of draught as oxen; but in the latter half of the eighteenth century these points were treated as subsidiary, and the breeding of sheep and cattle was pursued with reference to the food supply[4]. Mr Bakewell of Leicester appears to have been the pioneer in both sheep-breeding and cattle-rearing; and he was

---

[1] *Northern Tour*, I. 165. Turnips, barley, clover (2), and wheat.

[2] *Horseshoeing Husbandry* (1773).

[3] H. Levy. *Entstehung und Rückgang des landwirthschaftlichen Grossbetriebes in England*, 6–10. [4] Prothero, *op. cit.* 51.

A.D. 1689
—1776.

specially successful in improving the breed of sheep. During this period, the high price of corn and facilities for feeding stock rendered agricultural improvement profitable, and it also became fashionable. King George III. devoted himself enthusiastically to the concerns of his Windsor farm; he wrote articles which he signed Ralph Robinson, and many of the nobility in different parts of the country followed him in these pursuits[1], and set an example which found many imitators and which proved exceedingly profitable at all events to those who had sufficient capital.

The pro-
gress of im-
provement
and en-
closure

235. Throughout the seventeenth and eighteenth centuries, the enclosure of common waste and common fields was an outward and visible sign of the progress of improvement in the management of land. The primitive method of laying out the land of the freeholders and tenants as scattered strips in common fields, with pasture rights on the common waste[2], presented an obstacle to any changes for the better. The existence of common fields, cultivated by common custom was a hindrance to improved husbandry[3]; and the pasturage on common wastes was often spoiled from lack of better management[4]. When the land was devoted to its most profitable uses, there was an increased food supply, and a much larger fund from which taxation could be drawn, so that the increase in national wealth was undoubted[5]: but the effects on the rural population are much more difficult to

---

[1] The Duke of Bedford was one of the leaders in this movement; and the sheep-shearings of Woburn were remarkable gatherings of gentry who were interested in encouraging the breeding of sheep. Prizes were given for this object as well as for the improvement of agricultural implements. There was an even more celebrated meeting, instituted by Mr Coke of Holkham in Norfolk, where the prizes offered included rewards for labourers who showed special skill in particular departments of farm work (*Annals of Agriculture*, xxxix. 42, 61).

[2] For an excellent map of this arrangement as it survived in 1905 at Upton S. Leonards, see *Victoria County History, Gloucester,* ii. 167; also for maps of Walthamstow, Bestmoor, Barton-le-Street, Donisthorpe, and Shilton in 1844, see *Report from the Select Committee on Common Enclosure* 1844, v. 489—497.

[3] S. Taylor, *Common Good,* p. 13.

[4] Worlidge, *Systema Agriculturae* (1687), 10.

[5] John Lawrence, rector of Bishop's Wearmouth, wrote decidedly in favour of the change in his *New System of Agriculture* (1726), p. 45; so too Edward Laurence, *Duty of a Steward to his Lord* (1727), p. 37; and John Mortimer, *Art of Husbandry,* p. 1 (1707); and the anonymous authors of the *Great Improvement of Commons that are enclosed* (1732), Brit. Mus. T. 1856 (7), and an *Old Almanack* (1735). Brit. Mus. T. 1856 (9). See p. 558, n. 2 below.

trace, and it is not easy at this distance of time to strike a A.D. 1689
—1776. balance between the evil and the good. That natural economy and subsistence farming appear to have practically *put an end to subsist-* died out altogether, and that there was much more of a *ence farm-ing* national market for farm produce[1], and therefore of effective competition between different districts in the country, are the two points to be chiefly noticed.

There were three classes, at the beginning of the seven- *on the part* teenth century who practised subsistence farming, either as *of artisans,* their sole avocation, or as an adjunct to some other means of earning a living. Among the last were comprised all village artisans; not only those who, as smiths, wheelwrights or shoemakers, supplied the needs of their neighbours, but also the domestic weavers who were found in large numbers[2], especially in the West of England. They had the opportunity of leading an independent and comfortable life, in healthy surroundings[3], such as would be greatly prized by the manufacturing population of the present day[4], but they did not have a very good reputation for industry[5]. They were not a welcome element in the rural districts, and it seemed that they would do better if they devoted themselves exclusively to manufacturing. With the progress of enclosure, they seem to have been more cut off from opportunities of eking out their subsistence with the help of small holdings or pasture rights. Thus these manufacturers became mere wage earners who were wholly dependent on the state of trade for their daily bread. When trade was slack they had no resource but to come upon the rates, and in periods of depression they were not unlikely to break out in riots[6].

Besides these manufacturers, there was a large class of *cottiers,* cottiers and squatters on the waste who, had no obvious means of subsistence, besides the supplies they got from the land[7]. In the fens, they must have been a sturdy people, leading an

---

[1] H. Levy, *op. cit.* 9.
[2] On the growth of this class in the seventeenth century see R. F. Butler in *Victoria County History, Gloucester*, II. 165.   [3] See below p. 564.
[4] On the desirability and practicability of reintroducing "subsistence-farming" by wage-earners see my article on *Back to the Land,* in the *Economic Review,* October 1907.
[5] *Rowland Vaughan,* p. 31.   [6] See below p. 562 n. 1.   [7] II. Levy, *op. cit.* 5.

independent life. But throughout the country generally they seem to have been regarded as lazy and undisciplined[1], and public opinion was in favour of forcing them to take to more regular habits[2].

and small farmers.

The remaining class, whose fate elicited most sympathy was that of the small holders—whether tenants or freeholders —who worked the land on traditional methods, and lived on the produce. They were regarded as the backbone of the country; but their cultivation was apt to be slovenly[3], and there were difficulties in allowing it to continue side by side with the improvements which more adventurous men were making on their estates. There are many complaints from the earlier part of the seventeenth century of the encroachment on pasture rights, so that the small farmers could no longer feed their stock[4]; or encroachment on the common fields might interfere with the customary husbandry of a village[5]. Sir W. Dolben's Act in 1773, which facilitated the improvement of the common custom of tillage so as to render it less necessary to break up the common fields into severalty, was an attempt to enable the old race to move with the times[6], but the trend of circumstances was too strong[7]; and

---

[1] "Destroying of Manors began *Temp.* Hen. VIII., but now common, whereby the mean people live lawless, nobody to govern them, they care for nobody, having no dependence on any body." Aubrey, *Introduction to Survey of North Wiltshire, Miscellanies* 1714, p. 30.

[2] S. Taylor, *Common Good*, 37, Pseudonismus, *Considerations*, 9. See below p. 567 n. 1. The advocates of enclosure continued to insist that the commons were a source of moral evil as well as of economic loss, *Reports* 1844, v. Questions 71, 774, 1811, 3091, 4203.

[3] The chief excuse for pushing on the enclosure of common fields lay in the prevalence of weeds; a single lazy farmer who allowed his strips to be covered with thistles and allowed these thistles to seed, would do an infinity of mischief to all his neighbours. The case of Farmer Riccart near Audley End brought this home forcibly to Arthur Young. *Southern Counties*, 386.

[4] Compare the very interesting petition from Wooton Bassett printed by J. Britton, *Beauties of Wiltshire*, III. 39.

[5] Aubrey, *Topographical Collections*, 131.

[6] T. Stone a Bedfordshire surveyor, writes as if a common custom of tillage was prevalent in his experience; he approves of Sir W. Dolben's Act (13 Geo. III. c. 81), but regards it as inoperative. *Suggestions for rendering the Inclosure of common fields and waste lands a source of population and riches* (1787), p. 13. In 1801 the Act was revived with the view of enabling occupiers to take a crop of potatoes (41 Geo. III. c. 20). Slater, *The English Peasantry*, 87.

[7] The exceptional case of Weston Subedge, where the communal system was maintained till 1852, is fully described by C. R. Ashbee, *Last Records of a Cotswold Community*.

as enclosure went on, there was less and less room for the small farmer who carried on a traditional husbandry with a view to subsistence.

As these men were replaced by tenants who farmed for the market, another change became more noticeable; there was a tendency to unite small holdings in the hands of one man[1]; a successful yeoman[2], who had saved some capital and could do his marketing to advantage, would be glad to take *Enclosure* additional lands. The consolidation of holdings was favoured *led to the consoli-* by manorial lords[3] who found that they were put to less *dation of holdings* expense in connection with farm buildings. There were in consequence, as enclosure proceeded, fewer farm houses; and during the seventeenth century, when so much attention was given to grazing, there was probably a diminished demand for labour; in the eighteenth century, it was alleged that enclosed land gave employment to a larger number of hands than unenclosed[4], but there would not necessarily be a larger population. The number of cottages had diminished, so that the rural labourers opportunities of marrying and settling would be curtailed[5], as well as his chance of bettering his position[6]. Hence it came about that the anticipations of Fitzherbert and others, who had argued in favour of enclosure for improved husbandry, as an all round benefit[7] were falsified. The progress of enclosure brought about a decrease in the *and the* number of farm households and of cottages in one village *displace-ment of* after another, so that the depopulation of the rural districts[8], *rural popu-lation.*

[1] On this and other points I am much indebted to the excellent paper by E. M. Leonard on *The Inclosure of Common Fields*. Royal Hist. Soc. Trans. N. S. XIX. 118.

[2] For early instances of yeomen who prospered and rose in the world, see E. C. Lodge, *Victoria County History, Berkshire*, II. 208; also S. J. Elyard, *Annals of Purton* in *Wiltshire Notes and Queries* (1895), I. 532.

[3] Pennington, who was an advocate of enclosure, deprecates this practice, which he regards as injurious; he held that it was commonly but not necessarily asso-ciated with enclosure. *Reflections on the various advantages*, p. 56.

[4] Hale, *Compleat Book of Husbandry* (1758), I. 208.

[5] *Enquiry into the advantages and disadvantages resulting from Bills of Inclosure*, Brit. Mus. T. 1950 (1), (1780). This is an admirable statement of the case against enclosures, and deals specially with the unfair methods by which they were carried through. See below, p. 558.

[6] See below p. 714.

[7] Compare the argument in John Houghton's *Collection of Letters for the Improvement of Husbandry and Trade*, I. (8 Sept. 1681), p. 10.

[8] This is implied in Moore's argument (see below, p. 557 n. 3) in the time of Cromwell: also in Cowper's vigorous tract *An Essay proving that enclosing commons*

A.D. 1689
—1776. of which so much complaint had been made in Tudor times, did not by any means cease when the profit on sheep-farming declined[1]. Some of the displaced population migrated to other commons, some to towns[2], and some appear to have emigrated[3].

Different localities competed in a national market   The difficulty of following the effects of the change is greatly increased by the fact that substantial loss in certain districts must be set against the gain in others. By new methods of manuring it was possible to bring land into cultivation which had never been tilled before[4]. The exhausted common fields could not compete against the produce

---

is contrary to the interest of the nation (1732), Brit. Mus. T. 1856 (8). He argues that if inclosure became more general there would be less agricultural employment, and that the by-employments of spinning and manufacturing wool would also decline as well as all the subsidiary village trades,—such as wheelwrights, smiths, etc. (pp. 3, 7, 8). See also the *Enquiry into the reasons for and against Inclosing the open Fields* (1767), Brit. Mus. 1959 (3), p. 29, where special reference is made to Leicestershire. In a reply to this pamphlet Pennington argues that if the processes of manufacture are included, the raising of wool affords far more opportunities of employment, before it is ready for the use of the consumer, than the raising of corn. *Reflections on the various advantages resulting from the draining, inclosing and allotting of large commons* (1769), p. 19. The same line of argument had been taken by Homer (*Essay on the Nature and Method of ascertaining the Specific shares of proprietors upon the Inclosure of Common Fields* (1766), p. 35; he looked with complacency on the movement of the population from the villages. "There is a natural Transition of the Inhabitants of Villages, where the Labour of Agriculture is lessened, into Places of Trade, where our Naval Superiority, as long as it lasts, will furnish Sources of perpetual Employment. Whether the hands, thus directed from Agriculture to Manufacture, are not in that Station more useful to the Publick, than in their former, is an Enquiry which might perhaps be prosecuted with some Entertainment to the Reader."

[1] See above p. 101. Dyer writing in 1757 insists that enclosure is desirable in the interests of the quality of wool; but he is thinking of a flock in conjunction with tillage. *The Fleece:*—Anderson—*Poets of Great Britain*, IX. 564.

[2] Leonard, *op. cit.* 123.

[3] "Inclosure with depopulation is a Canker to the Commonwealth. It needs no proof; woful experience shows how it unhouses thousands of people, till desperate need thrusts them on the gallows. Long since had this land been sick of a plurisie of people, if not let blood in their Western Plantations." Fuller. *Holy State* (1642), Bk. II. c. 13. Also in the following century. *Cursory Remarks on Enclosure by a Country Farmer*, 1786, p. 6.

[4] "The Downs or Plains which are generally called Salisbury plain...were formerly left open to be fed by the large flocks of sheep so often mentioned; but now so much of the Downs are ploughed up as has increased the Quantity of Corn produced in this country in a prodigious Manner and lessened their Quantity of Wool, as above; all which had been done by folding the sheep upon the plow'd lands, removing the fold every night to a fresh Place, till the whole Piece of Ground has been folded upon; this and this alone, has made these lands, which in themselves are poor, able to bear as good wheat as any of the richer lands in the

of this fresh soil, and Aubrey describes how in Wiltshire, A.D. 1689 —1776. "as ten thousand pounds is gained in the Hill Country, so the Vale does lose as much, which brings it to an equation[1]." The same sort of change was taking place over larger areas; Leicestershire and Northamptonshire had been great corn-growing areas, but in the seventeenth century, tillage gave place to pasture farming; the inland shires were[2] apparently at a disadvantage in disposing of their grain; cattle-breeding and sheep-farming were the most profitable uses of the soil. The Council of James I. and Charles I.[3] had taken active measures to check the movement of turning arable land to pasture in these districts, both by writing to the justices and by instituting proceedings in the Star Chamber[4]. With the *and no effort was made to maintain separate markets.* fall of the monarchy, there was no longer any effective means of attempting to maintain the special conditions of either agriculture or industry in particular localities, and pasture farming spread more rapidly[5].

The movement for enclosure does not appear to have

Vales, though not quite so much....In Wiltshire it appears to be so very significant that if a Farmer has a Thousand of Sheep, and no Fallows to fold them on, his Neighbour will give him Ten Shillings a Night for every Thousand." Defoe, *Tour* (1724), Vol. ii. Letter i. 49.

[1] *Natural History of Wiltshire*, 111. His own rents at Chalke had fallen £60 since the Civil War.

[2] See above p. 544 n. 2.

[3] Leonard, *op. cit.* 126.   [4] *Ib.* 129.

[5] Some discussion arose on the subject during the Interregnum, in consequence of the allegations of the Rev. John Moore of Knaptoft, who seems to have thought that a great deal of enclosure with depopulation had recently occurred in Leicestershire (*Crying sin of England of not caring for the poor wherein Inclosure viz. such as doth unpeople Townes and uncorn fields is arraigned*), and that as a consequence tenants were unable to get farms, and cottiers were deprived of employment in various agricultural operations which he enumerates (p. 11). 'Pseudonismus' replied that the law provided sufficiently against any danger of depopulating, and that this could only arise from carelessness in enforcing it. *Considerations concerning Common Fields* (1654), p. 8. This answer to Moore's pamphlet has been attributed, by Nichols (*History and Antiquities of the County of Leicester* (1807), iv. i. 85), to the Rev. Joseph Lee, Rector of Cottesbach in Leicestershire. See also *A Scripture word against Inclosure* (1656), from which it appears that petitions on the subject from Leicestershire were presented to the Lord Protector and his Council. The further reply of Pseudonismus, *Vindication of the Considerations*, includes a vigorous statement from a Leicestershire gentleman of the waste and mischief which arose from the common fields (p. 41); this is quoted by Nichols, *op. cit.* iv. i. 93. Lee distinguished the enclosing he approved from that of Tudor Times. Εὐταξία τοῦ ἀγροῦ, or *A Vindication of a regulated Enclosure*, (1656). Considerable extracts are printed by Nichols, *History and Antiquities of the County of Leicester*, iv. i. 94.

A.D. 1689
—1776.

been pressed on with such rapidity in the seventeenth[1] and early part of the eighteenth century as was the case toward its close. Even though the advantage to agriculture was considerable[2], the small farmers could not afford to have any part in this boon. It undoubtedly was not easy to

The expenses of enclosure were great

re-allot the lands fairly, so that each of the landholders should have such a piece as was really the equivalent of the scattered strips and patch of meadow and pasture rights which he had previously possessed. This was a difficult duty, and one which was generally assigned to strangers, who might be supposed to make an award unbiassed by personal friendship. Apart from parliamentary and law expenses, the change was costly. The new farms were permanently separated from one another, and it was necessary to fence them; a very heavy burden was imposed on the village, and the shares of the poorer inhabitants for these expenses, involved many of them in debt and led to their ruin[3].

It appears to have been the usual procedure, in the seventeenth century, to procure an agreement among those concerned, and to have this agreement authorised by a decision in Chancery or the Exchequer[4]. In the eighteenth

and the procedure inflicted much hardship

century the method of proceeding by private bills came into vogue[5]; these were often passed through Parliament without sufficient enquiry, and when many of the inhabitants were quite unaware of the impending change or were at all events

---

[1] Houghton estimated in 1692 that a third of all the kingdom was in common fields. Dr Plot had made this calculation for Staffordshire, and Houghton apparently generalised it for the kingdom as a whole: how rough his calculation is, may be gathered from the fact that he corrected his estimate of the acreage of England from 29,000,000 to 40,000,000 acres. Houghton, *Collection of Letters for Improvement of Husbandry and Trade*, 1 June, 1692.

[2] Burke, *Works*, II. 347. The enquiries of the Board of Agriculture, embodied in their *General Report on Enclosures* published in 1808, appear to be decisive on this point. See also the *Report from the Select Committee on Enclosing Commons*, 1814, v. 3.

[3] A. Young, *Northern Tour*, I. 223.

[4] Leonard, *op. cit.* 108.

[5] In the reign of Anne there were 3 private bills for enclosure; in that of George I., 16; under George II., 226; and in the reign of George III., from 1760–1775, there were 734; from 1776–97, 805; from 1797–1810, 956; and from 1810–20, 771; besides this, there was a general enclosure Act in 1801 (Tooke, I. 72; Prothero, *Pioneers and Progress of English Farming*, 257). See also Clifford, *Private Bill Legislation*, I. p. 21. The period of parliamentary enclosing has been investigated in great detail by Dr Slater, *English Peasantry*.

powerless to resist it[1]. Very clear light on this subject is A.D. 1689
—1776. given by a debate in the House of Lords in 1781; the Bishop of S. David's[2] objected to the manner in which the claims of the tithe-owner were adjusted when land was enclosed; Lord Thurlow, who was then Chancellor, expressed himself in very strong terms as to the injustice to small proprietors which frequently occurred in connection with such measures[3], and the pamphlet literature of the day corroborates this statement[4].

To those who were unable to conform to the new conditions of profitable agriculture it was an additional hardship that the change was hurried on by inconsiderate legislation; but it may be doubted whether any parliament could have seriously attempted to restrain the economic forces, which were rendering the continued existence of the small farmer increasingly difficult. Corn prices ranged high, *on the small farmers*

---

[1] The bill for enclosing Bisley was thrown out in 1733, because of the opposition of the weavers, who were also small farmers. R. F. Butler in *Victoria County History, Gloucestershire*, II. 167.

[2] *Parl. Hist.* XXII. 47. In enclosing common fields there was great difficulty about making a satisfactory allotment of tithes. The Bishop of S. David's was the spokesman of a large number of clergy who disliked a change by which they were forced to undertake the management of a glebe, instead of obtaining tithes from the occupiers (*Parliamentary History*, XXII. 49). On the other hand, the agricultural improvers could not but feel that tithe was a form of tax which had a baneful influence upon agriculture. Mr Howlett, the vicar of Great Dunmow, calculated that the tithes in his neighbourhood had increased in value twelve times as much as the rent (*Annals of Agriculture*, XXXVIII. 132). While a charge of this sort was a real obstacle to improvement, the recent changes made it more difficult for the clergy to consent to accept an arrangement, by which they agreed for themselves and for their successors, to forego the advantage which might arise from any further increase of cultivation. The benefits which had come to the Universities from the law which assigned to them corn-rents were well known, and it was not obviously politic to accept a change in system. In this way it came about that the tithe-owners were inclined to regard the Board of Agriculture and their supporters with much suspicion, and this was in all probability one of the influences which caused the discontinuance of this department in 1819.

The existence of tithe had also a curious effect upon the farmers in making them prefer the policy by which labourers were maintained out of the rates to that of raising their wages. Tithes are levied on the produce after the rates have been allowed for, but without taking account of the expenses of cultivation, so that the farmer who employed labour would pay a smaller tithe if the rates were high and wages low than he would have to do on the same crop if rates were low and wages high. This is another of the minor causes which contributed to render the pauperising policy of allowances popular with the large farmers. (*Annals of Agriculture*, XXXVIII. 134.)

[3] *Parl. Hist.* XXII. 59.

[4] *Enquiry into the advantages and disadvantages resulting from Bills of Enclosure* (1780).

A.D. 1689 —1776.

who did not benefit by the high price of corn

but the small farmer did not, generally speaking, devote himself to the production of corn for the market; and if he did, the times were too uncertain for him to steer his course with success. If he were a freeholder, he might of course be able to maintain his position, though bad seasons might make it necessary for him to borrow[1], and he might sooner or later be forced to sell[2], as the only means of escaping the burden of debt. The copyholder, with the obligation to pay occasional fines, and the yearly tenant had a less firm grip on the land, and were less able to compete successfully with the large capitalists. In the last quarter of the eighteenth century England ceased to be a corn-exporting country; there was no margin of production in ordinary years above the requirements of the country, and as a consequence there were unprecedented fluctuations of price according as the seasons were good or bad[3]. Farming had become a highly speculative business in which poor men could hardly hope to hold their own. The violent changes of price would often give the capitalists, who could hold large stocks of corn, opportunities of making enormous profits. On the other hand, the small farmers, whether they worked in common fields or in separate holdings, were forced to realise their corn immediately after harvest, and suffered immensely. In 1779 in particular, prices were so low that many farmers were ruined[4]. Somewhat later prices fell again, and there was another great period of

---

[1] A full discussion of these influences and of the destruction of this class will be found in the Report of the Committee of 1833. *Reports from Select Committee on Agriculture*, 1833, v., Questions 1262 (Wiltshire), 1691 (Worcestershire), 3103 (Yorkshire), 4862, 9269 (Somerset), 6056 (Cheshire), 6156 (Shropshire), 6957 (Cumberland), 12216 (Nottingham).

[2] When they did so there were no men of their own class to buy their properties, and these went to large owners. Prothero, *Pioneers and Progress*, 83.

[3] On legislative action in this period see below, p. 723. The season from 1765 to 1774 were specially inclement, and from 1775 onwards they were very irregular; thus in 1779 there was an unusually plentiful crop, while 1782 was a very bad year, which was followed by two others that were distinctly below the average. It thus appears that the inclemency of the seasons does not serve to account for the high range of the average prices; but the irregularity of the seasons had a great effect in producing sudden fluctuations of price. At Lady-Day 1780, the price of wheat was thirty-eight and threepence; at Michaelmas forty-eight shillings; and at Lady-Day 1781, fifty-six and eleven-pence (Tooke, I. 76).

[4] Arthur Young, *Annals of Agr.* xxv. 460.

agricultural distress, which caused very widespread disaster; A.D. 1689 —1776. the capitalists may have held out longer than the small farmers, but many of them were forced to succumb[1].

The small farmers who continued to devote themselves *while they lost on other produce* to cattle-breeding and dairy farming, also found themselves in serious difficulties. The price of these products did not rise correspondingly with the price of corn; indeed there was a relative fall of price, as the labouring population which was forced to pay more for bread, found it necessary to economise in other articles of diet[2]. The business of the small farmer became less and less remunerative during the last decade of the eighteenth century and the beginning of the nineteenth, while there was an eager demand for every rood of land that could be utilised for the growth of corn. Some of the yeomen were doubtless bought out, and some were crowded out, but in the changed conditions they could not maintain themselves by their traditional husbandry.

Some of the other changes of the times were specially *and were crushed by the burden of rates.* burdensome to the small farmers, as compared with their wealthier neighbours. They were heavily charged for the maintenance of the poor, especially at the close of the eighteenth century after the adoption of the Speenhamland policy[3] of granting allowances out of rates in addition to wages. The small holder was a rate-payer and had to make increased contributions; since the labourers were not maintained by the wages paid by their employers, but partly subsisted on poor-relief, it followed that the small holders were taxed for the benefit of the large farmers[4]. All the circumstances of the day combined to render the position of the small farmer untenable. "Perhaps it may not be an extravagant conjecture to venture[5], if one were to affirm that if the small farmers should remain under a pressure of poor's

---

[1] About the year 1782 a number of country banks had been formed; this was a sign of the increased facilities for saving money and for applying capital to land (Tooke, I. 193); but in 1792, when prices were low, a considerable proportion of these country banks appear to have got into difficulties: there were a large number of failures in that and the following year, so that the whole credit system of the country (*Ib.* 195) was seriously affected.

[2] Levy, *op. cit.* 17, 58.

[3] That this policy was practically in operation for some years before is shown by David Davies, *Case of Labourers in Husbandry* (1795), p. 25.

[4] *Annals of Agr.* XXXVII. 106, 109.   [5] *Ib.* 109.

C.   36

rates for ten years to come equal to the pressure which they
have experienced during the last ten years, that so useful and
respectable a set of men must necessarily be exterminated
entirely in many districts of the kingdom, and many respectable fathers and mothers of families would themselves
become objects of that charity which they had been ruined
to support; their farms would, on the first vacancy, be
purchased by neighbouring gentlemen or by opulent farmers;
and eventually, by the entire suppression of small occupations, every hope would be taken away from the labouring
poor of ever bettering their condition by renting and cultivating a few acres for their own comfort and advantage."
The progress of agricultural improvements left its mark by
drawing hard and fast lines of cleavage between the classes
in rural society[1]; the smaller farmer who had succumbed in
the struggle was all the more to be pitied, because the
labouring class in which he had been merged was entering on
a terrible period of privation and degradation[2].

236. The development of manufacturing had done much
to stimulate agricultural production, but it also had serious
*The
pressure of* results in imposing fresh burdens on the proprietors of the
*pauperism
called forth* soil[3]. In many places the wage-earning population had no
discussions means of support to fall back upon, in times of bad trade;
the pressure of the poor rates was occasionally a very heavy
burden, and prudent men were desirous of avoiding the risk
of being exposed to it. Changed circumstances gave rise to
new social problems, and there were some alterations in the
administration of the Elizabethan system of poor relief; it
was also supplemented by Private Bill legislation[4]. Still

---

[1] Compare H. Levy, *op. cit.* p. 48 on the bitterness this change engendered.

[2] See below pp. 713—715.

[3] "This clothworking I have named a commodity of this country, and so is it
generally taken to be and I suppose you conceive it is so; and so it is a great use
to the kingdom. But I may tell you secretly in council not so much for this
country (some few excepted), to whom it is more burdensome than profitable; for
having engrossed so great a trade it hath made the towns and country so populous
that notwithstanding all their best endeavours in husbandry, yet yields hardly
sufficient of bread, beer and victual to feed itself....And in every rumour of war or
contagious sickness (hindering the sale of those commodities), makes a multitude
of the poorer sort chargeable to their neighbours, who are bound to maintain
them." Westcote, *A view of Devonshire in MDCXXX.* On the inability of
Devonshire to feed its large manufacturing population in 1620, see Giles, *Parl.
Hist.* I. 1196.

[4] Clifford, *Private Bill Legislation,* I. 266*. There were more than 150 local

the fundamental principles of the system held their ground A.D. 1689
—1776.
for two hundred years till it broke down at last under the
pressure caused by the Industrial Revolution. The discussions which centred round this topic have an abiding
interest, however, even when they seem to have been barren
of any direct result. The criticisms to which the Elizabethan *which*
scheme was subjected, and the modifications which were *throw light on*
proposed from time to time, afford evidence, which is none *contempo-rary social*
the less interesting because it is indirect, as to the changes *conditions.*
which were occurring in social and economic conditions.

The amendments were avowedly in regard to the practical
administration of the system. In attempting to trace them
we shall do well to remember how large was the sense in
which the State had interpreted its duty to the poor. There
was, in the sixteenth century, a clear opinion that the Government ought to have a care for all those who were dependent,
and not merely for the impotent, or for children. The substantial man, who had the means of employing himself on
his own land, or in his own calling, might be left to himself;
but it was felt by Elizabeth and her advisers that supervision
was needed to secure the welfare of the labourer, both as
regards the conditions of his work and the periods when
he was unemployed. It is clear that assiduous efforts were *The decline in the power of the Council after the Civil War*
made to enforce this system until the time of the Civil
War[1]; but it is probable that after that event the pressure
was relaxed. The frequent supervision which had been
exercised by the Privy Council appears to have fallen into
abeyance; and as separate counties and parishes were no longer
subjected to constant centralised control, they could pursue
the course of greatest advantage to their own neighbourhood.
Under these circumstances there need be little surprise that
the authoritative assessment of wages should have become a
mere formality[2], or should have fallen into entire desuetude[3],

Acts chiefly passed in the reigns of Geo. III. and Geo. IV. giving power to the
local authorities for the relief of their poor.

[1] Morant (*Essex*, I. 180) gives an excellent history of the provision for the poor
in Colchester and testifies to the good working of the Elizabethan Act for about
40 years.   [2] See above, p. 43.

[3] In addition to evidence adduced above compare H. Fielding, *An Inquiry into
the causes of the late Increase of Robbers* (1751), p. 55.

A.D. 1689
—1776.

*gave scope
for the con-
sideration
of local to
the neglect
of national
interest.*
and that the administration of the poor should have become intensely parochial. It was inevitable that this should be conducted with a primary regard to local convenience[1], so that there was danger of insufficient care for the needs of the poor, and of scant attention to the national interest.

So far as I am able to judge, however, the breakdown of the system of State supervision over the terms of employment had no injurious effect on labourers' standard of comfort, during the seventeenth century and the first half of the eighteenth. There was a rapid growth of trade and an increased demand for labour of many sorts; the progress of enclosure, though it told against the small farmers, increased the demand for the services of hired labourers; while the general diffusion of the art of spinning would give a considerable increase to *Labourers had a double source of income,* the family income. The rural labourer could eke out his wages, not merely by the exercise of privileges on the commons, but from the connection of his family with the manufacturing interest. On the other hand, a very considerable part of the artificers had direct connections with the soil. The Survey of 1615 shows that Sheffield cutlers, who had a considerable struggle to pay their way, combined the management of some land with the production of whittles[2]. At Pudsey, in the neighbourhood of Leeds, the woollen weavers practised agriculture as a by-employment at the beginning of the nineteenth century. They were able to add considerably to their personal comfort

---

[1] The introduction of a central authority to give unity to the whole system was the most important change effected by the Poor Law Reform of 1834 (see below, p. 772). The inconvenience of allowing each parish to be an independent administrative unit had long been felt. See a proposal in 1652, *State Papers addressed to Oliver Cromwell*, edited by Nickolls, p. 89. Also compare the proposal of Nickolls, *Advantages, etc.* (1754), p. 207, and the argument, in 1758, by Massie, who held that the poor law of Elizabeth was one of the chief causes for the growth of pauperism. "As Multitudes of working People," he continues, "are obliged to travel from Parish to Parish, and from County to County, in order to find Employment, proper Maintenance or other Relief ought to be provided for them, when and where they want it; because there cannot be a better Motive for their travelling, than a Desire to get an honest Livelihood; and therefore they should have all possible Encouragement to persevere in doing what is Best for the Nation, and for Them. Giving every poor Person a Right to Relief, when and where he or she shall want it, would put an End to all Law Suits, about the Settlement of the Poor" (*A Plan for the Establishment, etc.*, 112).

[2] Hunter, *Hallamshire*, 148. The pressure of pauperism at this place was very severe. See above, p. 347, n. 3.

and to pay high rents for pasture land[1], though their agri- culture was backward in the extreme[2]. The woollen weavers, in all parts of the country, appear to have enjoyed allotments or large gardens; but some of those who were engaged in the more recently introduced cotton industry were aggregated in towns, and suffered from the want of healthful relaxation which could be combined with work at their looms[3]. In many small towns like Kettering[4] the artisans had allotments or pasture rights; and hence it may be said that, at the beginning of the nineteenth century, there was a large part of the industrial population[5] which was not yet divorced from rural employments.

This double source of income gave an immense stability *and their* to the labourers' position; but it did not necessarily con- *was so* duce to energy. Labourers and artisans could afford to be *secure* idle at times, and they had comparatively little incentive to work; the possibilities of enjoyment within their reach were very limited. The yeoman farmers, who formed the class immediately above the labourers, led a sordid life[6];

---

[1] *Annals of Agriculture*, XXVII. 309.

[2] *Ann. of Agricul.* XL. 135. "The land in this part is almost wholly occupied in small plots or farms, by manufacturers, merely for the convenience of keeping a few cows, for milk for their children, apprentices, and inmates, and a horse to job to and from the mills, market, etc., hence it is, that the business of a farmer has, for a long time, been a subordinate consideration with almost every manufacturer, his views and ideas are narrow and contracted, and are confined to the cloth trade; in this method he jogs on; and such is the force of prejudice, that if anyone does not follow the old course of husbandry, he is frequently laughed at by his neighbours, and very invidiously considered as a visionary and an innovator; and the chief reason which they advance in defence of this old antiquated procedure, is that their forefathers have practised it."

[3] *Ib.* XXXVIII. 546.

[4] *Ib.* XXXIX. 259, 211 note.

[5] At West Bromwich, the seat of the nail trade, agriculture "is carried on so connectedly with manufactures that it is subservient to them." *Ib.* IV. 157.

[6] Arthur Young's testimony is clear: "From all the observations I have made, I am convinced that the latter, when on an equality with the former (little farmer) in respect of children, is as well fed, as well clothed, and sometimes as well lodged as he would be, was he fixed in one of these little farms; with this difference—that he does not work near so hard. They fare extremely hard— work without intermission like a horse—and practise every lesson of diligence and frugality, without being able to soften their present lot" (*Farmer's Letters*, 114); and their hopes of saving enough to take a larger holding were seldom realised. Harte also expresses himself decidedly; he holds that the little farmer at a rent of thirty or forty pounds a year "works and fares harder and is, in effect, poorer than the day labourer he employs. An husbandman thus circumstanced, is, beyond

the standard of comfort was low, and the labourer was generally speaking in a position to satisfy his requirements *that they could afford to be idle;* without strenuous exertion[1]. Under these circumstances we can hardly be surprised at the repeated charges of idleness which are brought against the poor; this was a constant complaint on the part of the employers[2], and was put forward by many writers as the real cause of lack of employment and poverty[3].

On this assumption, that idleness was the only cause of pauperism (apart from sickness and old age), it was obvious *additional opportunities of employment* that additional opportunities of employment would have little effect on those who were unwilling to work at all. It may perhaps be said that the hard tone, which popular opinion associates with the dismal science, first shows itself at a period, when philanthropic measures were denounced on economic grounds, as either useless[4] or baneful, and when

dispute, a worthy object of our commiseration and assistance" (*Essays on Husbandry*, 205).

[1] The rural labourer could count on regular employment, since agricultural industry was not liable to such violent fluctuations as manufacturing (A. Young, *Farmer's Letters*, 21), especially in trades for which the materials came from abroad. The employees of the capitalist farmer were, however "free hands," to quote Sir James Steuart's phrase, as distinguished from peasants whose interest bound them to the soil.

[2] Compare Temple, *Vindication of Commerce* (1758), p. 13. Also *Essay on Trade and Commerce*, Brit. Mus. 1139. i. 4 (1770), p. 15: "The manufacturing population do not labour above four days a week unless provisions happen to be very dear." "When provisions are cheap they wont work above half the week but sot or idle away half their time." Richardson, *Causes of Decline* (1750), p. 6. Even when the men were industrious, the conditions of domestic industry in the West Riding were such that the men lost about a third of their time. *Annals of Agriculture*, xxvii. 511.

[3] Locke (*Report of Board of Trade* [1697] in *Account of Society for the Promotion of Industry in Lindsey*, p. 108 [Brit. Mus. 103. 1. 56]). Defoe is perhaps the writer who lays most stress on the faults of the poor: "I make no Difficulty," he says, "to promise on a short Summons to produce above a Thousand Families in England, within my particular knowledge, who go in Rags and their Children wanting Bread, whose Fathers can earn their fifteen to twenty-five shillings per week but will not work, who may have Work enough but are too idle to seek after it, and hardly vouchsafe to earn anything but bare Subsistence and Spending Money for themselves." *Giving Alms no Charity*, in *Genuine Works*, II. 448. Eden (I. 244) stated the opinion, that a large proportion of paupers, besides the regular tramps, were merely lazy, and that the complaint of want of work was a mere pretence. The high prices of the dear years had not inoculated the English with the frugality which the Dutch displayed.

[4] "Suppose now a workhouse for the employment of poor children sets them to spinning of worsted. For every skein of worsted these poor children spin there

the frugality of Dutch craftsmen and French peasants was held up as an example to Englishmen. Hard-headed men at the close of the seventeenth and beginning of the eighteenth century protested against the observed effects of indiscriminate State charity. We have, moreover, abundant *did not absorb the* evidence that despite the facilities for employment which *vagrant* were open, there was a very large half-pauper and half-criminal *population,* class, who were never absorbed in industrial pursuits of any kind. One writer after another inveighs[1] against them, and makes suggestion as to the best means of dealing with this social danger.

The obvious expedient, to which the authorities had *who were permitted* recourse, was that of permitting and even encouraging these *in the* vagrants to settle on unoccupied ground. An Elizabethan *seventeenth century* Act had provided for the building of cottages on the waste, and many landlords appear to have been willing that additional accommodation should be erected, though they were not always ready to assign allotments of land to be held along with these houses[2]. Silvanus Taylor complains

must be a skein the less spun by some poor person or family that spun it before; suppose the manufacture of making bays to be erected in Bishopsgate Street, unless the makers of these bays can find out at the same time a trade or consumption for more bays than were made before, for every piece of bays so made in London, there must be a piece the less made at Colchester."

"If these worthy gentlemen, who show themselves so forward to relieve and employ the poor, will find out some new trade, some new market, where the goods they make shall be sold, where none of the same sort were sold before, if they will send them to any place where they shall not interfere with the rest of that manufacture, or with some other made in England; then indeed they will do something worthy of themselves, and they may employ the poor to the same glorious advantage as Queen Elizabeth did." Defoe, *Giving Alms no Charity*, in *Works*, II. 434.

1 "The two great Nurseries of Idlenesse and Beggery etc., are Alehouses and Commons," Taylor, *Common Good* (1652), 51. In 1683 Sir M. Hale wrote, "Whereas in that State that things are, our Populousness, which is the greatest blessing a Kingdom can have, becomes the burden of the Kingdom, by breeding up whole Races and Families, and successive Generations, in a mere Trade of Idleness, Thieving, Begging and a barbarous kind of life which must in time prodigiously increase and overgrow the whole face of the kingdom and eat out the heart of it." *Discourse touching provision for the Poor* (1683), p. 11. See also *Observations on a pamphlet entitled An Enquiry*, Brit. Mus. T. 1950 (2) (1781), p. 5. Even when the cottagers did not deserve the bad character which they often bore they were apt to be at cross purposes with the farmers. *Political Enquiry into the consequences of enclosing waste lands* (1785), p. 48. Brit. Mus. T. 1950 (3).

2 This was ordered to be a matter of official enquiry by the Commissioners in 1631. A case came before the Bedfordshire magistrates at the January Sessions

that people were too ready to give way to the building of
cottages, " for the ease of your parish, or out of a base fear
of your Lord. The Parish sometimes wants habitation for
to squat on
the common
wastes
their poor, and then with consent of the Lord there is a
new erection, and for which there are very few Lords, but
contrary to Law do receive rent, so that he careth not how
many are erected. Again, many times the Lord gives way
to erect without consent, either of Free or Copyholder, and if
such are presented yet very seldome redressed[1]." There was
soon reason to suspect, however, that this mode of dealing
with the difficulty was a mere palliative, and that the practice
in the long run fostered the evils of pauperism. Dymock
propounds some searching questions on this subject; "whether
Commons do not rather make poore by causing idlenesse,
than maintaine them; and such poore who are trained up
rather for the Gallowes or beggary, than for the Commonwealth's service ? How it cometh to passe that there are
fewest poore where there are fewest Commons, as in Kent,
where there is scarce six commons in a county of a considerable greatnesse[2] ? " The remedy he suggests is that of
enclosing the commons and allotting a couple of acres, or so,
to each of these families. Taylor is still more explicit; he
would have tried to train these people to engage in spinning
and manufacturing rather than that they (as usually now
they do) "should be lazying upon a Common to attend
one Cow and a few sheep for we seldom see any living on
Commons set themselves to a better employment. And if
the father do work sometimes, and so get bread, yet the

---

in 1654. Where the man could obtain four acres of ground there was no legal
objection to the erection of a cottage, as he was supposed to have the means of
supporting himself. A. Moore, *Bread for the Poore* (1653), p. 15.

[1] *Common Good*, 38.

[2] *Hartlib's Legacie*, 54. Samuel Hartlib is sometimes credited with being
the author of this work, as for example by Thorold Rogers, *Agriculture and
Prices*. But his own Prefaces, as well as the Memoir by Dircks, make it clear that
this is a mistake. Hartlib constituted himself into a sort of Society of Arts, and
had a large correspondence with specialists in different departments. Of his own
acquaintance with the subject of husbandry he observes:—"I cannot say much of
mine own experience in this matter, yet Providence having directed me by the
improvement of several relations with the experience and observations of others,
I find myself obliged to become a conduit pipe thereof towards the Publick."
(Dircks, *Biographical Memoirs of Hartlib*, p. 63.) Dircks attributes this tract to
Cressy Dymock, p. 69.

children are seldom brought up to anything; but being nursed up in idleness in their youth, they become indisposed for labour, and then begging is their portion, or Theevery their Trade, so that though Commons be a help to one, yet its a ruine to many[1]." Worlidge also argues that the common rights of the "Poor do very much injure them and the Commonweal in general. For here, by reason and under colour of a small advantage on a Common, and *instead of working,* by spending a great part of their time in seeking and attendance after their cattel; they neglect those parts of Husbandry and Labour, that otherwise would maintain them well, and educate their Children in these poor Cottages, as attenders on their small Stocks, and their Neighbours' greater, for a small allowance; which is the occasion that so many poor Cottagers are near so great Wasts and Commons. These open and Champion Counties, by reason of the multitude of these Cottagers, are the Producers, Shelterers and Maintainers of the vast number of Vagrants and Idle Persons, that are spread throughout the greatest part of England; and are encouragements to Theft, Pillage, Lechery, Idleness and many other Lewd Actions, not so usual in places where every man hath his proper Lands Inclosed, where every Tenant knows where to find his Cattel, and every Labourer knows where to have his day's Work[2]."

In so far as the Civil War caused the dislocation of agriculture[3], or of trade, the means of charitable relief[4]

---

[1] Taylor, *Common Good*, 8.   [2] Worlidge, *Systema Agriculturae*, 13.

[3] Sir John Cooke writes in 1648 (*Unum necessarium*, p. 5) : "There was never more need to make some provision for the poore then this yeare;...a Labourer will thrash as much corn in a day, as the last yeare in two; and corn being deere, those that kept three servants the last yeare, will keep but two the next; those that had two but one, and those that had one will do their work themselves; and every one projects for himselfe, to spend as little as may be, but who takes care for the poore, how shall they be provided for? If a poor man have work all this winter, and get six pence a day; what will three shillings a week do to maintain himselfe, his wife, and three or foure children? For English families commonly consist of six or seven." The remedy he suggests is that of preventing or limiting brewing so that barley may be available for food (p. 29). He discusses the practice in other countries of authoritatively fixing the price of corn (p. 7), but is curiously silent about the powers of the Justices to raise wages.

[4] "In respect of the troubles of the times, the meanes of the said Hospitall hath very much failed for want of charitable benevolences which formerly have

would be curtailed, while there would be a tendency for the numbers of this pauperised class to increase. The existence of this social element, and the shifting of population consequent on enclosure, gave occasion to the measure of 1662, by which the claims of the poor, and the responsibilities of each parish were more clearly defined. There had been some

till they were checked by the Act of 1662,

scandalous instances of towns and villages, which had tried to shirk their obligations[1]; and it was necessary to restrain the vagrants from taking unfair advantage of the ratepayers in places where the children of the poor were cared for[2]. " The necessity, number and continual increase of the poor," says the Act[3], "not only within the cities of London and Westminster, with the Liberties of each of them, but also through the whole kingdom of England and Dominion of Wales, is very great and exceeding burdensome, being occasioned by reason of some defects in the law concerning the settling of the Poor[4], and for want of a due provision of the Regulations of Relief and Employment in such parishes or places where they are legally settled, which doth enforce many to turn incorrigible rogues, and other to perish for want": it adds, "that by reason of some defects in the law, poor people are not restrained from going from one parish to another, and therefore do endeavour to settle themselves in those parishes where there is the best stock, the largest commons or wastes to build cottages, and the

beene given and are now ceased, and very few legacies are now given to Hospitals, the Rents and Revenues thereunto belonging being also very ill paid; besides the want of bringing cloth and manufactures to London, which have formerly bin brought to *Blackwell Hall*; the hallage whereof was a great part of the poore children's maintenance, which being decayed by these and other meanes, the said Hospitall hath not been able to take in any children for two yeares past." *True Report of the Great Costs and Charges of the Foure Hospitals* (1644), Brit. Mus. 669. f. 10 (2). *World's Mistake in Oliver Cromwell*, in *Harl. Miscel.* I. 289.

[1] Eden (I. 144) quotes from a pamphlet published in 1698 that no rates were levied in some parishes for 20, 30, or 40 years after 1601. "Though the number of the Poore do dailie encrease, there hath beene no collection for them, no not these seven years, in many parishes of this land, especiallie in countrie townes, but many of those parishes turneth forth their Poore, yea, and their lustie labourers that will not worke, or for any misdemeanor want worke, * * so that the country is pittifully pestered with them" (*Grevous Grones*, by M. S., 1622; Eden, I. 155).

[2] 7 James I. c. 4, § 8. The evil of vagrancy took many forms; it was necessary to protect well-provided commons from the depredations of Squatters by 28 Geo. II. c. 19, § 3.   [3] 13 and 14 Charles II. c. 12.

[4] On the law of settlement under the Commonwealth see Inderwick, *Interregnum*, 91.

most woods for them to burn and destroy[1], and when they have consumed it, then to another parish, and at last become rogues and vagabonds, to the great discouragement of parishes to provide stocks, where it is liable to be devoured by strangers." According to the preamble the statute was aimed at this vagrant class, and gave powers to remove a new-comer within forty days, if there was a danger of his becoming chargeable to a parish, to the place where he had last been legally settled. But like so many *which imposed serious restrictions on the labouring poor.* pieces of social regulation it had most unforeseen effects, and a measure, which had been intended to fix local responsibility and check vagrancy, came in the succeeding century to have a most disastrous effect on the English artisan[2]. It interfered with the employment of the industrious, and it chained the unemployed to districts where no work could be obtained. In the course of the eighteenth century, when industry was migrating to new centres, it must have tended to the creation of a class of pauperised artisans[3] in addition to the half-vagrant cottagers on the commons.

Though there seems to have been a considerable development of commerce, with a healthful reaction on industry, during the years which intervened between the Restoration and the Revolution, it is perfectly clear that the unemployed class was not absorbed by the increased opportunities of

---

[1] The importance of woods as the chief source of fuel comes out in these discussions. One of the severest attacks of a socialistic kind, on the privileges of manorial lords, was a claim on the part of commoners to have their share in all wood grown on the commons. *Declaration from the poor oppressed people of England* (1649) [Brit. Mus. 1027. i. 16 (3)]. There were also complaints that rich men who put large flocks on the commons for a time, and ate them bare, gained at the expense of other commoners, *Hartlib's Legacie*, 54. The destruction of commons and need of enclosing in the interest of commoners comes out in regard to Herefordshire. 4 James I. c. 11.

[2] Adam Smith, *Wealth of Nations*, pp. 57–59, 191.

[3] Massie noticed a general course of migration, "from Rural Parishes to Market Towns, and from both of them to the Capital City; so that great Multitudes of People, who were born in Rural Parishes are continually acquiring Settlements in Cities or Towns, more especially in those towns where considerable manufactures are carried on; and as Trade is not only of a fluctuating Nature, but many Towns in England carry on Manufacturies of the same Kind, and are always gaining or losing with respect to each other, although there be an encrease of Manufacturies upon the Whole; it must necessarily follow, that there will be frequent Ebbings in the Manufacturies of one or other of our Trading Towns." Massie, *A Plan for the Establishment of Charity Houses*, p. 99.

*Fluctua-
tions of
trade in-
creased the
numbers
of un-
employed;*

*and
methods of
relieving
the rates*

employment. It is indeed conceivable that the changes which were going on in the character of industry aggravated the evil; and that the occasional interruptions of trade inflicted periods of enforced idleness on weavers and others, and thus reduced them to the level of paupers[1]. However this may be there can be little doubt that the charge which arose in connection with the maintenance of the poor was becoming intolerably severe. Gregory King calculated that the total population was five million, five hundred thousand; and apparently about a fourth of the total population was more or less dependent on parochial relief[2]. In 1685 the total poor rates for England were estimated at over £665,000[3]; and in the succeeding years, with bad seasons, heavy war expenses and interrupted commerce, pauperism appears to have gone on increasing with rapidity[4]. It had become obvious that little could be done by planting the poor on the land, and many schemes were now devised for drafting them into industrial employments. This seems to have been specially noticeable in the years succeeding the Civil War, when a good many pamphlets were issued, with proposals for building hospitals and setting the poor at work. *Stanley's Remedy,* the work of a repentant Elizabethan highwayman, who desired to confer a benefit on the public he had injured, was printed in 1646; Sir John Cooke,—the lawyer who suffered, in spite of his able defence, for his part in the execution of King Charles,—published his *Unum necessarium*

---

[1] The author of a tract speaks of the poor rate in Elizabeth's time being 6*d.* "Whereas in our unhappy Days, 3*s.* in the Pound throughout the Kingdom is not sufficient to sustain them in a poor and miserable Condition more especially in the great Cities, and cloathing Countries; for in many places, where there is most of our Woollen Manufactory made, the Poor Rate is from half a Crown to six or seven Shillings in the Pound, for the trading Poor have no way nor shelter but their Trade which if that fail once they are downright Beggars presently, whereas the contrary is to be understood of poor Husband-men who have many ways to shelter themselves, as, a Common, a Cow, a Wood, gleaning of Corn in Harvest, Day Work, Children to look after Cows, Hogs, going to Plow, etc. Besides all provisions 40 per cent. cheaper." *A Brief History of Trade in England,* 1702 (Brit. Mus. 1138. b. 3), p. 63.

[2] Davenant, *Balance of Trade,* in *Works,* II. 184 and 203.   [3] *Ib.* I. 41.

[4] The figures commonly accepted for 1698 put the outlay at £819,000, but Sir George Coode saw reason to believe that this estimate was based on insufficient data. *Report to the Poor Law Board on the Law of Settlement and Removal,* in *Reports,* 1851. XXVI. 219, printed pag. 23.

in 1648, in which similar measures are advocated; and
Parliament intervened in 1647 by erecting a corporation
for employing the poor in London[1]. In 1649 a pamphlet
appeared, entitled the *Poor Man's Advocate*[2], which suggests
that the remains of the crown lands, as well as of the
episcopal and cathedral revenues, should be utilised in this
way. Sir Matthew Hale[3] wrote in the same vein in 1683;
and many schemes were put forward for providing employment[4]. After the Revolution[5] expedients of this kind were
urged more frequently. One of them was brought before
Parliament in 1698, and is highly commended by Davenant[6];
another was drafted by Locke[7], who was one of the commissioners of the Board of Trade, another by one of the
Worcester justices, Mr Appletre[8], and another by Mr Dunning
of Devonshire[9]. Locke brought a Bill into Parliament in

[1] 16 Dec. 1647. This is not printed by Scobell but merely mentioned. There
is a copy in the British Museum [1027. i. 16 (2)]. "An ordinance of the Lords and
Commons for the constant Reliefe and Imployment of the Poore * * * also
inabling the severall Counties and Corporations in the Kingdome of England and
Dominion of Wales for the like Relieving and Regulating of the Poore in their
respective Places."

[2] By Peter Chamberlen. [3] *Provision for Poor.*

[4] Several tracts were written by men who were eager to promote some branch
of industry and who refer to the employment of the poor as one of the incidental
advantages it would subserve. It is in this spirit that Haines advises that the
poor should be employed in the linen manufacture (*Proposals for building * *
a Working Almshouse* (1677), in *Harl. Misc.* IV. 489). This was the favourite experiment when workhouses were necessary and were established, as for example by
Firmin in London, in 1678 (Eden, I. 202 and note). The account of Haines' scheme
shows that the class of poor, for whom employment was sought, was not the same
as the able-bodied vagrants whom Stanley had in mind, and for whom Harman
provided. Eden, I. 168. Goffe (*How to advance the trade of the nation and employ
the poor*, in *Harl. Misc.* IV. 385, a tract which is undated but apparently of the
time of Charles II.) and others [*Grand Concern*, in *Harl. Misc.* VIII. 581; I. D. in
A Clear and Evident Way (1650), [Brit. Mus. 1027. i. 16 (5), p. 15], urge that
the poor might be employed in connection with fishing; and Yarranton
(*England's Improvement* (1677), pp. 47, 56) enunciates different possibilities for
different parts of the country, such as bone lace for the girls, toy-making for the
boys, and iron working. In Guilding, *Records of Reading*, much information will
be found about the workhouse and stock for employing the poor, but apparently
the utensils were sold and the scheme abandoned in 1639. *Ib.* III. 455.

[5] The subject was mentioned in the King's Speech, 16 Nov. 1699, and a committee of the House of Commons was appointed to deal with it (C. J. XIII. 4).
Cary, *A Proposal offered to the Committee of the Honourable House of Commons
appointed to consider of Ways for the better providing for the Poor and setting
them on Work* [Brit. Mus. 1027. i. 18 (6)]. [6] Davenant, II. 207.

[7] Eden, I. 244, 245. [8] *Ib.* 239. [9] *Ib.* 248.

A.D. 1689
—1776.

*were tried
in many
towns.*

1705, but no general Act was passed: though an important experiment was tried in Bristol[1], and the different parishes in the city were incorporated and proceeded to erect a workhouse for employing their poor. The Bristol scheme appears to have been carried through by Mr Cary, who was then a well-known writer on commercial subjects; within a very few years the example, which had been set at Bristol, was followed at Exeter, Hereford, Colchester, Hull, Shaftesbury, Lynn, Sudbury, Gloucester, Plymouth, and Norwich[2]. The Bristol experiment was not, however, a pecuniary success; and in 1714 the Corporation found themselves in great difficulties, as they had entirely lost the fund with which they had started.

As a matter of fact, it was extremely difficult to organise an undertaking of this kind in such a manner that it should be a commercial success. This had not been easy, even in the Elizabethan period; but the more industrial organisation and industrial skill developed, the more difficult must it have been to set the casual and untrained poor on remunerative work. According to Defoe[3] the whole attempt was illusory, and could only result in diverting occupation from the frugal and industrious who were employed in the ordinary course of trade, and subsidising the lazy and inefficient. His criticism sufficed to kill the magnificent scheme of that ingenious projector Sir Humphry Mackworth, whose Bill for establishing a factory in every parish, after being passed by the House of Commons, was dropped in the House of Lords. But the advocates of providing employment were not daunted[4]; a much humbler plan of a similar kind[5] was

*The estab
lishment*

---

[1] John Cary, *An Account of the Proceedings of the Corporation of Bristol* (1700). The children could not spin woollen yarn so as to pay for their own keep until they learned to spin it specially fine, p. 13. [2] Eden, I. 257.

[3] *Giving Alms no Charity*, in *Genuine Works*, II. 435.

[4] L. Braddon, *Particular Answers to the most Material Objections made to the proposal...for Relieving, Reforming and Employing the Poor of Great Britain* (1722). Brit. Mus. 1027. i. 18 (7).

[5] A mass of very interesting information on the workhouses in England, their history and management, will be found in *An account of several workhouses for employing and maintaining the poor* (1725), Brit. Mus. 1027. i. 18 (9). It appears that there were about 124 workhouses known to the writer in different parishes in England at this date. The distribution is very curious. They were mostly concentrated in Essex, Hertfordshire, Northamptonshire, Bucks. and Bedfordshire—

brought into operation in 1723[1]; it empowered a parish, or A.D. 1689 —1776. a union of parishes, to erect houses for the lodging and employing the poor. The plan was often adopted of letting *of work-houses and the system* the house to contractors, who either undertook the care of *the system* the poor, as a whole, for a definite sum[2], or provided for them *of farming the poor* in the workhouse, at so much a head[3]; they sometimes gave out-door relief, but those who farmed the poor per head appear to have put great pressure on the poor to go into the houses[4]. The immediate effect of the introduction of this

as well as in Middlesex. There was only one each in Lancashire, Lincolnshire, Norfolk, Suffolk, Warwickshire, Wiltshire and Worcestershire.

[1] 9 Geo. I. c. 7.

[2] Sir Frederick Eden reports of Stanhope in Durham in 1796: "The poor have been farmed for many years: about 25 years ago they were farmed for £250, but the expense has gradually increased since that period; the year before last the expense was £495 and last year £494; and the Contractor says that he shall lose £100 by his last bargain, and will not take the poor this year under £700. Twenty-two poor people are at present in the house, and 100 families receive weekly relief out of it; these out-poor the Contractor says will cost him £450 for the year ending at May Day last. The Poor-house was built about fifteen years ago; it is, like most others in the hands of Contractors, in a very dirty state."

[3] At Newcastle, according to Eden, writing in 1796, "the Gateshead contractor is allowed 2s. a head for each pauper in the poor-house, and his earnings. The parish house in addition gives him this year a gratuity of £10, but it is supposed he will be a considerable loser by his bargain." *Ib.* 554.

At Downham in Norfolk there was a combination of those systems. "The poor are partly farmed. The contractor has the use of 4 acres of land, and a work-house in which he maintains such poor as the parish please to send him. They find beds, &c. and clothe the poor, when they go into the house; but the farmer provides clothing during their residence with him. He is paid £95 a year provided their number does not exceed 20, and for all above that number 2s. a week each, he is likewise entitled to their earnings. * * * The officers give weekly allowances to such poor as can support themselves upon a less sum than what is charged by the master of the poor-house." *Ib.* 450.

[4] The effects of the two systems of farming as practised in different counties on the Welsh border is discussed by Mr A. J. Lewis. "It is to be observed, that the mode of farming the poor as practised in Monmouthshire is materially different from what obtains in Shropshire and Herefordshire. In the former the practice is to contract for the farming of the poor, impotent and able-bodied, at a gross annual sum; in the latter, the parish enters into an agreement with the governor or manager of the workhouse to allow him a certain sum per week for each pauper relieved in the workhouse, and in general the agreement specifies the quantity and quality of the food with which each pauper is to be daily supplied. The effects of the two systems are also different; in the latter it is the interest of the contractor to get as many paupers into the workhouse as he possibly can; in the former, he admits as few as possible. The person who is allowed a given sum per week for each pauper relieved in the workhouse finds, that the more he has to maintain the greater is his profit. He who contracts to maintain them at a gross annual sum, saves more out of that allowance by keeping the poor out of the workhouse, for the poor invariably prefer the smallest pittance as out pensioners rather than

system was a great decrease of the rates; but there were difficulties in carrying on such establishments satisfactorily[1], and the condition of some of the houses which survived in 1833, where the poor were huddled together without distinction of age or sex, was disgraceful in the extreme[2].

Though the establishment of these institutions did not realise the expectations of their promoters, they served indirectly to check the increase of pauperism. Overseers were empowered in 1723 to refuse relief to persons who *checked the* would not enter the houses, and there was in consequence *increase of* a great check upon the growing expenditure on the poor. *rates,* The decline in the rates during this period is sometimes spoken of as a proof of the flourishing condition of the labourer in the eighteenth century; more probably it merely indicates the increased stringency on the part of the officials. *as did* This was shown, not merely in the diminution of the charge *the war* *on cottages.* for maintenance, but in the war which was carried on, in many parishes, against cottages. There was a regular crusade against the half-vagrant, half-pauper class that subsisted on the commons; and the tendency of the authorities

---

enter the workhouse, and the fact is, that what the contractor gives a pauper in the shape of allowance out of the workhouse, is not by a half or a third so much as it would cost him, were he to maintain such pauper in it. Hence it is that in the parishes in Monmouthshire yon will find the workhouses almost deserted. Their workhouses or poorhouses seem scarcely to answer any other ends, but that of terrifying paupers into a willingness to accept the quantum of allowance the contractor may think fit to offer them." *Reports*, 1834, xxviii. 664.

[1] Henry Fielding wrote on the subject in 1753 in a *Proposal for making an effectual Provision for the Poor*. The experience of half a century as to the management of workhouses and the trades which could be carried on in them was summed up by Mr W. Bailey of the Society of Arts in his *Treatise on the Better Employment of the Poor* (1758). Pennant writing in 1787 speaks with much enthusiasm of the large house of industry in the Isle of Wight, and enumerates the employments. *Journey*, ii. 156.

[2] The Chatham case was particularly bad (*Reports*, 1834, xxviii. 224), also the management of Preston in Sussex (*Ib*. 539), and in some of the large London parishes the authorities had not sufficient powers to cope with the hardened offenders, *Ib*. 78. The commissioners reported that in by far the greater number of cases the workhouse "is a large almshouse in which the young are trained in idleness, ignorance and vice; the able-bodied maintained in sluggish sensual indolence; the aged and more respectable exposed to all the misery that is incident to dwelling in such a society, without government or classification, and the whole body of inmates subsisting on food far exceeding both in kind and in amount, not merely the diet of the independent labourer, but that of the majority of persons who contribute to their support." *Reports*, 1834, xxvii. 31.

was to treat their poverty as a crime. The local adminis- A.D. 1689 —1776.
tration was carried on in the same spirit, for every overseer
seemed to regard it as his primary duty to keep down the
rates at all hazards[1]. The policy proved successful in its *but at the*
main object, though at what expense of suffering we shall *cost of much*
never know. Under the influence of the workhouse test and *suffering.*
the harshness of overseers the sums expended in poor relief
diminished from £819,000 in 1698[2] to about £689,000 in 1750.

The last half of the eighteenth century saw the beginning of a reaction against this stringent administration of
poor relief; the change was not merely due to the ebb
and flow of sentiment, but was to some extent justified by
intelligent consideration of the causes of pauperism. If it *Since some*
had been true to say that all poverty was due to the fault of *persons fell into*
the distressed and his idleness, there would have been some *poverty through no*
excuse for insisting that the poor should be treated harshly. *fault of*
But as Joseph Massie showed most clearly, distress did not *their own,*
always arise from the fault of the sufferers, but sometimes
from their misfortune. He pointed out that the tendency
of the new development of manufactures[3], as well as the effect
of enclosure on the tenantry, was to divorce the poor man
from the soil, and to expose him to risks from all the uncertainties of business. "Many People are reduced to that
pitiable Way of Life, by Want of Employment, Sickness or
some other Accident; and the Reluctance, or ill Success,
with which such unfortunate People do practise begging,
is frequently manifested by a poor and emaciated Man or
Woman being found drowned or starved to Death, so that
though Choice, Idleness, or Drunkenness may be reasons
why a number of people are Beggars, yet this Drowning,
and perishing for Want, are sad Proofs that the general
cause is Necessity. And if any person thinks those Proofs
are insufficient, the great Numbers of Thieves, and Pick-
pockets which daily infest this metropolis, will put the
Matter beyond all Doubt; for their not being Beggars

---

[1] See below, p. 768.

[2] See above, p. 562 n. 4, and 571, also 608 and 638 below.

[3] Samuel Richardson in his additions to Defoe's *Tour* notes the heavy poor
rates at Bocking in Essex in consequence of the decay of manufactures (1742),
I. 118. See above, 562 n. 4.

C. 37

instead of Thieves, etc., is owing to the different Effects which Necessity produces in different People, according to their Turn of Mind, Time of Life, etc., and not to another Cause[1]." The peasant with his own holding was rooted to *owing to the fluctuations of trade,* the soil, the labourer who worked for wages was dependent upon trade. "The Real Strength" of a country, he says, "doth not consist in the Number of Men who live there, but in those who Defend it; and the Source of that astonishing Disparity between the One and the Other in England, is Removing multitudes of people from our natural and fixed Basis, Land, to the Artificial and Fluctuating Basis, Trade[2]." His insight was abundantly justified, in the evil days of the Industrial Revolution, and he gave expression to a feeling which many people shared, and which eventually found expression in parliamentary enactments.

The turn of the tide was marked by the passing of *there was a reaction against stringent administration in 1782,* Gilbert's Act in 1782[3]. At the Restoration the parishes of England had been armed with powers for defending themselves against the poor[4]; on the eve of the Industrial Revolution, facilities were given for granting relief lavishly. The new Act was an experimental measure, and did not apply to the whole country, but only to those parishes which decided to adopt it, and to unite with others. In these new Incorporations the practice of contracting for the labour of the poor was brought under strict supervision; able-bodied men were not set to tasks in the house, but were encouraged to take such employment as they could get in the district, and might have their wages supplemented by parochial allowances. The workhouse test practically ceased to operate, since the houses in the Gilbert Unions were employed for the reception of the impotent[5] rather than as Houses of Industry. At the same time, the responsibility for carrying out the provisions of the measure was transferred from the parochial officials to men of better social status[6], who, as guardians and justices of the peace, acted for the several parishes combined in a Union; in the districts where Gilbert's Act was adopted, the churchwardens and

---

[1] *A Plan, etc.*, 50.　　　[2] *Ib.* p. 69.　　　[3] 22 Geo. III. c. 83.
[4] Sir G. Coode, *Report on the Law of Settlement*, in *Reports*, 1851. xxvi. 251, printed pag. 57.　　　[5] *Parl. Hist.* xxii. 301.
[6] T. Gilbert, *Considerations on the bills for the better relief of the poor* (1787), 18.

overseers ceased to be concerned in the relief of the poor A.D. 1689 —1776. farther than by the collection of rates. It may almost be said to have established a new system which was based on new principles, and which existed side by side with the old, according as different parishes exercised their local option[1]. The confusion in the whole of the arrangements was farther confounded by the special provisions which were adopted in various towns and districts under the authority of private Acts of Parliament.

A farther relaxation of the severity of the system, as it *and against the settlement* had been administered in the greater part of the eighteenth *restrictions* century, was effected by modifying the unfair restrictions *in 1795,* which the law of settlement placed on the artisan. The tyranny of the overseers had been specially felt by such new-comers in a parish, as might become chargeable at some future time; but in 1795, an Act was passed which protected them from interference, until they actually became chargeable. This measure did not render it easier to obtain a new settlement; but it enabled labourers to live and work in any parish, so long as they could pay their way and did not come upon the rates; and it protected them from the cruelty of sudden and injudicious removal, if, through sickness, they did become dependent on parochial relief[2]. These re- *so as to render the* laxations were in themselves harmless, but they prepared *granting of lavish* the way for that granting of lavish relief, in the early part *relief more* of the nineteenth century, which led to the growth of a *common.* pauperised class of a new type, and one which proved more difficult to deal with than the half-criminal, half-pauper cottagers on the commons had been. The provision of maintenance on the land for persons, who were under no obligation to work, could not be extended indefinitely; but the lavish distribution of outdoor relief seemed to have unlimited possibilities of mischief. It pauperised a large proportion of the rural poor and contaminated many other persons as well, before it was effectively checked.

---

[1] At first very little use was made of it (Young, *Considerations on the subject of Poor houses*, 1796, p. 29); before 1834, 924 parishes had adopted it.

[2] 35 Geo. III. c. 101. *An Act to prevent the removal of poor persons until they shall become actually chargeable.* The attempt to remedy hardships, by 8 and 9 W. III. c. 30, had proved ineffectual.

A.D. 1689
—1776.

*The en-
courage-
ment of the
English
landed
interest*

237. Such were the changes at work within the realm, but the encouragement given to particular interests at home affected other parts of the British System. The systematic efforts of the legislature to increase the shipping and foster the industries of Great Britain had a marked, and, to some extent, an injurious effect upon the development of the American and West Indian plantations. These colonists were scarcely touched by legislation in regard to the English landed interest, except in so far as the protective tariffs, imposed by the Restoration Parliament, prevented them from establishing a trade in cereals. The case of Ireland was entirely different: the sister island had suffered severely from the Navigation Acts, and from the repression of her industries; but the chief grievances of which she had cause to complain arose from the agricultural, rather than from the industrial, or commercial, policy of the British Parliament. In climate and position Ireland is so far similar to Great Britain that her products entered into direct competition with those of the English soil. Probably nothing did greater harm to Ireland than the system of bounties by which English corn-growing was encouraged. The English farmer found it profitable to grow corn, and with the help of the bounty he was able to export it to Dublin, at rates which defied competition in a country where wheat-growing had

*reacted un-
favourably
on Irish
land-
manage-
ment,*

made but little progress. The very same measure which encouraged the application of capital to the English soil, rendered it utterly unprofitable to invest money in improving the cultivation of Ireland[1]. The graziers had suffered under Charles II.; wool-growing was less profitable than it would have been, if the drapery trade had had a fair chance; while tillage was depressed by the English bounties. The backward condition of agriculture, despite the excellence of the soil, made a very deep impression on Arthur Young, and the causes are fully described by Mr Newenham. "The different disadvantages which the agriculture of Ireland laboured under * * * had, almost necessarily, the effect of preventing an accumulation of

[1] For an exceptional case of cultivation for export, see Pococke, *Tour in Ireland* in 1752, p. 54.

capital among those who, with a view to a livelihood, A.D. 1689
were principally concerned in that pursuit. The wealthier —1776.
occupiers of the land were generally engaged in the business
of pasture; and the profits thence accruing to them were,
for the most part, expended in the purchase of those articles,
which the prevailing practice of excessive hospitality required; seldom or never in agricultural projects. Several
of the country gentlemen pursued tillage in their respective
demesnes with some spirit and some skill, chiefly with the
view of supplying the demands of their families; but few *and few of*
of them extended their views to the augmentation of their *the land-*
rentals, by the improvement of the waste and unproductive *devoted*
land which they possessed. * * The generality of them in *improving*
Ireland could not, or at least thought they could not, con- *tillage,*
veniently abridge their annual expenses, in such a manner
as to enable them to collect a sufficient capital for carrying
into effect extensive plans of improvement; and many of
them were probably deterred from adding to the burdens
of their encumbered estates by borrowing money for such a
purpose. The tillage of Ireland for home supply, for there
was not sufficient encouragement held forth to cultivate corn
for exportation, was chiefly carried on by those who engaged
in it with no other capital than the aid of three or four lusty
sons as partners, whose united endeavours were directed,
during their short leases, to extract from the land as much
as the condition in which they found it would admit of;
and whose annual profits, hardly earned, after defraying the
trivial expenses of their food and clothing, were very rarely
sufficient to qualify them for any agricultural undertaking
which seemed likely to be attended with even moderate
expense. Hence it happened, that the waste land of Ireland,
presenting such an immense source of wealth, was left almost
neglected until near the close of the last century[1]." We may
here see the greatest of the evils which was brought upon
Ireland by absenteeism. In England during the eighteenth
century the "art of agriculture progressed by leaps and
bounds, and this was due to the fact that during the
eighteenth century the great landowners were the most
zealous students of agriculture, and the boldest experi-

[1] Newenham, *View of the resources of Ireland*, 76.

mentalists in new methods of culture[1]." Absentees could take no such interest in their estates; and the existing laws did not ensure such profit to the agriculturist as to render tillage a tempting investment in Ireland. The trivial bounties[2] which were eventually given on export (unaccompanied as they were by any protection against the constant importation of bounty-favoured corn from England) did not render tillage profitable. Landlords were on the whole opposed to it[3], and the measures, which tried to force them to adopt it, remained a dead letter[4]. It was not till England had begun to lose her position as a European granary, and the necessity for import was coming to be regularly felt, that Ireland was put on anything like an equality with her in regard to the encouragement of corn-growing[5].

while their pasture farming was discouraged,

The landed men, in the pasture counties of England, were inclined to be jealous of the favour extended to their corn-growing compatriots; and this made them all the more eager to obtain protection against the competition of Irish graziers. Their success in prohibiting the legitimate trade in Irish wool, and Irish provisions, was most detrimental to the economic interests of the realm as a whole; Irish wool was smuggled to the continent in considerable quantities, and supplied the staple material for manufactures which threatened to rival our own[6], while the Dutch and the French had the advantage of providing their ships on easy terms with Irish victuals, since there were so many hindrances to the purchase of them for English vessels[7]; but the landowners in the grass counties were inclined to demand farther protective measures[8].

---

[1] Thorold Rogers, *Agriculture and Prices*, v. p. vii.

[2] Newenham, 124, 130.   [3] *Ib.* 126.

[4] 1 Geo. II. c. 10 (Irish); Newenham, 128.

[5] 19 and 20 Geo. III. c. 17 (Irish); Newenham, 142.

[6] See above, pp. 374, 378.

[7] Ireland had been allowed a direct trade with the colonies in 1660, but this permission was withdrawn by the terms of 22 and 23 C. II. c. 26, and 7 and 8 W. III. c. 22. The first relaxation of this restriction, 4 Geo. II. c. 15, only enabled her to procure rum on easy terms from the West Indies, and this again may be represented as sacrificing native distilling to a trade in which much English capital was invested (Newenham, 100). It also encouraged the Irish to purchase West Indian products from the French Islands; and to pay for them by victualling French ships. Caldwell, *Enquiry*, in *Debates*, 771.

[8] W. Allen, *The Landlord's Companion* (1742), p. 21.

It is also true that the forests in Ireland were ruthlessly
wasted, at a time when anxiety was keenly felt in regard
to the preservation of English woods. The English iron
manufacturers, suffering as they did from dearness of fuel[1],
were glad to have smelting carried on elsewhere, so long as
they had advantages in working up the material provided
for them. In 1696 and 1697 the duties were removed
from bar iron imported into England from Ireland[2]; this
led to a rapid destruction of the Irish forests[3]; though
various measures were taken to prevent it, and to promote
the planting of trees, they proved utterly ineffective. Not
only so, but the exportation of timber to England was
permitted on very easy terms[4], and as a result the forests of
Ireland were absolutely ruined. As Ireland had at one time
been specially well provided with the materials for building,
fitting and provisioning ships[5], this wanton waste prevented
her from taking the part she might have otherwise done in
the work of ship-building or in the shipping trades. In brief
it may be said that all the encouragements, which were given
in England, acted as positive discouragements to the development of Irish estates, and that she derived no countervailing
advantage for the disabilities which were imposed upon her
by the British system.

XVII. THE BEGINNING OF THE END.

238. The Declaration of Independence has had many
results; for our purposes it is important to note that it
occasioned a revulsion in the economic policy of this country.
Parliamentary Colbertism had aimed at controlling the development of all the territories under British rule in such a
way as to react on the prosperity of British industry. When
the thirteen colonies threw off the authority of the Mother

---

[1] On the other hand, the glass manufacture in England had an exclusive right
to the exportation of glass; the prohibition of export hindered the development of
an Irish trade, though the country was especially suited for it, until 1779.
Newenham, *op. cit.* 104, 192.

[2] 7 and 8 Wm. III. c. 10, § xvii., and 8 and 9 Wm. III. c. 20, x.

[3] The manufacturers subsequently agitated for the admission of bar iron from
America. See above, p. 526.

[4] 2 Anne, c. 2 (Irish); Newenham, 153–4.   [5] *Ib.* 156.

A.D. 1689
—1776.
Country, a most important member of the body economic
was lopped away.   It was no longer possible to control this
great branch of commerce so as to render it subservient to
and dis-
credited its
principles.
the promotion of English manufactures.   The system had
fallen to pieces and was at once discredited, since it seemed
to have brought about a blow to British prestige.

Economic
grievances
gave
occasion to
the breach,
The economic effects of the severance were far reaching;
but the extent to which economic causes contributed to bring
about the revolt of the Americans has been exaggerated.
Contemporary observers, and later historians, have been
accustomed to insist on the commercial and industrial
grievances of the colonists, as not only the occasion, but the
principal reason of their determination to break with the
Mother Country.   There was no other obvious ground for
their decision ; they had no religious disabilities, and they
had a large measure of political self-government; it seemed
as if the secret of their dissatisfaction must have lain in the
galling nature of the control exercised over their commerce
but they
would
not have
pressed
seriously,
and industry.   That they had grievances is true, and for
these the Parliamentary Colbertism of the Whigs is undoubtedly to be blamed[1]; but Professor Ashley has shown
that the pressure of these annoyances has been over-rated to
some extent[2].   The colonists seem to have been not indisposed
to accept the restrictions imposed on their trading out of
regard to the economic welfare of the Mother Country; it
is rather true that the increasing political cleavage rendered
the economic situation strained.   The colonists felt no duty
to contribute from their meagre resources towards the maintenance of any particular interest on the continent of Europe.

if it had not
been for
the colonial
lack of
interest in
Hano-
verian
politics,
The colonial sentiment of attachment to the Crown might
possibly have been stronger, if the English Revolution had
failed ; for it certainly was not transferred to the Hanoverians
and their belongings.   There were many Englishmen who
regretted the fact that their country was so frequently em-
broiled in continental struggles from which she had little to
gain ; the colonists were reluctant to sacrifice anything in

[1] See above, p. 481, and 586 below.
[2] *The Commercial Legislation of England and the American Colonies*, 1660—
1760, in *Surveys*, 309—335.

such a cause, and they were careful to guard themselves against being called on to bear a direct share in the cost.

Comparatively slight economic grievances sufficed to rouse the colonists to throw off their allegiance, not only because the ties with English authority were being weakened, *and from* but because they were learning to cherish positive political *the fact that the* ambitions of their own. The plantations had grown up into *colonists felt strong* vigorous communities with an active life, and they desired *enough* to stand alone. The northern colonies had been forced in self defence to rely to some extent on local industries, and they could see their way to a position of economic independence. It was because of the healthy activity, which they had developed under British tutelage, that they cherished aspirations after a freedom from control which should give them the opportunity of realising their own ideals. The Pilgrim Fathers had gone to the New World in the hope of carrying out their own views of what religious life ought to be[1]; by joining in the Declaration of Independence, their descendants in New England seized an opportunity of claiming the right to work out their own ideals of political life, apart from the conflicts and entanglements of the Old World. This was the positive aim in the minds of the leading men of the time, and any economic grievance sinks into insignificance by its side. In so far as economic causes affected them at all, it was chiefly because the extent and resources of their country rendered the colonists self-reliant. The men *to work out* of Massachusetts had a consciousness of their own economic *their own political* independence as a community, which gave them confidence *destiny* in asserting a claim to follow their own political destiny for themselves. The New Englanders had little sense of obligation[2] to the Mother Country. In the early days the pioneers had cleared the ground, and fought against the Indians; bit by bit their descendants had pushed farther into the continent; they had taken an active part in the struggle with France, and had proved their capacity in

[1] Religious ideas did not enter very largely into the struggle, though the fear that they would lose their uncontrolled position by the introduction of an episcopate was a motive which influenced the ministers to take the side of independence. in a way that the educated classes generally were loth to do.

[2] On the other hand the people of England were very much impressed by the sacrifices they had made for the plantations.

the field. When at length the French power was broken at Quebec, the colonists felt that they could hold their own on an enormous continent; it was inconceivable that they should look again to anyone but themselves for protection *without British protection.* against a foe. Hence the authority of the Mother Country was entirely sapped; it could only have been permanently maintained by a constant exercise of wisdom on the part of the Government at home, and by the highest tact on the part of its representatives in America. It was not from grievances caused by economic dependence, but from the economic strength of the colonies, that the desire to sever their connection arose[1], and it may be doubted whether any concessions in the way of Parliamentary representation would have rendered them content to remain in a condition of political dependence, for all time.

The principles of the British system
The economic treatment of the colonists by the Mother Country doubtless gave rise to some inconvenience; we cannot gauge its full extent. The principles on which it rested however, were not in themselves unreasonable; no serious statesman would have expected a country to tolerate hostile competition on the part of its dependencies; but the principles were applied to the colonies in a manner which rendered the action of the Mother Country irritating to all sections of the community.

were applied in America, so as to affect consumers
The enactments for Ireland had been a blow to certain producers, and stamped out trades that were beginning to flourish; but in America, the grievance was chiefly felt by the consumers, who had to pay very heavily for all their clothes and implements. The duties which were levied on their raw produce and fish, after the Restoration[2], put them to considerable straits to find goods with which to purchase stores; and they had begun to manufacture as well as they *of manufactured goods* could, because of their inability to buy. Had they been permitted to manufacture for the local demand, they might possibly have acquiesced in any legislation which prevented

---

[1] This danger had been indicated by various writers. Compare Child's argument in support of the thesis "that New England is the most prejudicial plantation to this kingdom." *New Discourse of trade* (1694), p. 212. Gee, *Trade and Navigation of Great Britain* (1767), p. 173.

[2] Beer, *Commercial Policy of England*, 74.

them from competing with the Mother Country in other A.D. 1680
markets.   But the statesmen of the period appear to have $^{—1776.}$
thought that it was easier to prevent these industries from
coming into existence at all, than to control them when *and to*
once they were planted, as they had tried to do, not very *repress*
successfully, with the manufacture of hats[1].   With this *industries,*
view they endeavoured to prevent the migration of skilled
artisans[2] to the colonies, and to reserve the colonial market
as a monopoly for English producers.   During the period of
Whig ascendancy these principles were applied in turn to
the woollen trade[3], and to iron-manufactures, for which
one or other of the colonies were admirably adapted.   The
policy of stimulating English industry was pursued with
ruthless consistency, and constituted an economic grievance
from which all the colonists suffered somewhat, and which
many of them resented.

Whether the economic grievances were great or small, we *but*
can hardly regard them as the determining cause, when we *American economic*
look either at the incident which brought about the breach, or *grievances did not*
at the line along which the cleavage took place.   Economic *determine*
considerations had very little to do with the Boston tea
party[4]; the colonists resented the exclusive privileges of
the East India Company, but the disabilities of which they
complained extended to all private shippers in Great Britain
as well.   Nor was the new duty in any way oppressive.

---

[1] This industry was carried on in London by a very limited body, who probably
kept prices up; the London hatters managed to get an Act in their favour (5 Geo.
II. c. 22), but this American industry appears to have been the only colonial
manufacture that developed enough to compete with the mother country.   Beer,
op. cit. 82.

[2] A stringent measure was passed in 1718 which prohibited artisans from going
across the sea at all, and insisted that those who had done so should return
(5 Geo. I. c. 27, *An Act to prevent the inconvenience arising from seducing
Artificers in the Manufactures of Great Britain into foreign parts*).   Compare the
South Sea Kidnapper, by J. B. (1730), for Spanish attempts to entice away our
artisans.   See also below, p. 755.   [3] Beer, *op. cit.* 78.

[4] "One fact is clear and indisputable.   The publick and avowed origin of this
quarrel was on taxation.   This quarrel has indeed brought on new disputes on
new questions; but certainly the least bitter, and the fewest of all, on the trade
laws.   To judge which of the two be the real, radical cause of quarrel, we have to
see whether the commercial dispute did, in order of time, precede the dispute on
taxation?   There is not a shadow of evidence for it."   Burke, *Speech on Con-
ciliation with America*, in *Works*, I. 193.

A.D. 1689
—1776.
Pains had been taken to render the tax on tea a charge that was little more than nominal, and that would hardly affect the consumers[1]. The destruction of the chests was the act of a community, conscious of its own vitality, and determined to protest against the control of any outside

the line of cleavage on which severance occurred.
authority, whether king or parliament. The first blow was not instigated by economic motives, and the lines of cleavage in the colonial possessions had no perceptible connection with the areas which were exposed to the pressure of grievances under the British System. The sugar and the tobacco plantations, which had received very similar care, took opposite sides; so, too, did Canada and New England, which had developed under very similar economic conditions. It was unintelligible to the English colonists that the French settlers should not be ready to take the opportunity of throwing off a yoke that had been so recently imposed; but the Canadians were deeply embittered against their neighbours in America, and had no special grudge against King George III. Little cause as the Canadians had to love the British Crown, they had far more grounds for resentment against the patrons of the Five Nations, and would not make common cause with their English-speaking neighbours. The responsibility for the desolation of Acadia[2] was held to lie, not so much with the English Government, as with the contractors and sailors who had carried off the *habitans*, and scattered them in the English plantations. Physical contiguity and social antipathy defined the lines along which the colonial system split up, and economic grievances were hardly perceptible in connection with the actual breach.

British statesmen were led
239. Economic and fiscal objects had determined the course taken by British statesmen themselves[3], but their belief

---

[1] Fiske, *War of Independence*, p. 80.

[2] The judgment of Burke and the picture drawn by Longfellow seem to me to be substantially correct. Parkman has attempted to justify the deportation of the Acadians (*Montcalm and Wolf*, 1901, I. 284), but he was not acquainted with some of the most important documentary evidence which has been more recently printed by Casgrain. The British Governors prevented the Acadians from exercising the right of emigration to French territory which had been secured to them by the treaty of Utrecht; the Acadians were forced to remain unwillingly on British soil, and then punished because of their divided loyalty. Casgrain, *Un pèlerinage au Pays d'Evangéline*, p. 112.   [3] See above, p. 421.

that economic grievances were the fundamental reason for the A.D. 1689
revolt, on the American side, appears to have been mistaken. —1776.
Still, this opinion had immediate and important results on *by the*
the remaining members of the colonial system, especially in *American revolt*
the country which had suffered most severely from British
economic policy[1]. In 1779 Lord North endeavoured to remove the main commercial disabilities of Ireland[2]; and
after 1782, when the Nationalist movement had been so far
successful as to obtain a fuller Parliamentary freedom[3], a *to treat Ireland*
serious effort was made by the Irish to imitate the policy *more favourably.*
that had been adopted in England, and thus to foster their
agriculture and industry.

A large number of measures, with these objects in view, *The Irish in 1783*
was passed in the Parliamentary session 1783—4; but it is
not clear that sufficient pains were taken to consider the real
requirements of the country. This objection may certainly be
made in regard to the Act which followed the English policy
of giving bounties on corn. The circumstances of the two *imitated Parlia-*
countries were somewhat different; for corn did not constitute *mentary*
the food of the Irish peasant, who subsisted chiefly on potatoes; *Colbertism,*
premiums on the growing of corn were a boon to farming as
a trade, but did not directly maintain the food supply of the
country. Hence the political bearing of the Irish corn bounties
was different from that of the English, even though many of
the economic results may have been similar. The bounties
gave no encouragement to provide a surplus of food, and no
security that a slight failure of the food supply would not result
in famine. According to the new law the Irish farmer could
count on getting nearly 30s. a barrel for his wheat; a bounty
of 3s. 4d. was given on export, when the price was not
above 27s.; exportation was prohibited when the price was

[1] Burke in 1778 put forward the doctrine that Ireland should be free to use its
natural facilities. *Works*, I. 224; Salomon, 100.

[2] 18 Geo. III. cc. 55 had opened up the colonial trade, and free trade was
granted by 20 Geo. III. cc. 6, 10, 18, *An Act to permit the exportation of certain
goods directly from Ireland into any British plantation in America, or any British
settlement on the coast of Africa, and for further encouraging the fisheries and
navigation of Ireland.*

[3] By the repeal of Poynings' Law which gave the English Privy Council
control over Irish legislation, and of the Declaratory Act (6 Geo. I. c. 5), which
asserted the right of the English Parliament to legislate for Ireland. Lecky,
England, IV. 551.

at or above 30s.; and a duty of 10s. was imposed on every
barrel of wheat imported when the price was below 30s.[1]
Irishmen believed that the effect of this measure was im-
with regard to tillage mediately perceived in the stimulus given to agriculture.
The exports of wheat and barley rose very rapidly from 1785,
and though they fell back for a time in the last years of the
century, this may be partly accounted for by political disturbances, partly by the character of the seasons which were
most unfavourable, and partly by the rapid development
of the Dublin breweries, which offered an excellent home
market for cereals. The manufacture of porter in Dublin
may be said to date from 1792[2], and its influence should
certainly be taken into account; but even when this is done,
it is difficult to see that the bounties of 1784 did more than
give a temporary stimulus, or that they really induced
any considerable improvement in Irish agriculture by the
application of additional capital to the land[3].

and internal communication,
Much greater success attended attempts to utilise
the natural facilities of Ireland for internal communication[4]
by water. These had been taken into account many years
before, and early in the reign of George I. some undertakers
were empowered to improve the navigation of the Shannon[5].
In the reign of George II. commissioners were appointed
to devote the produce of certain taxes to this object; and
somewhat later, they were formed into a Corporation for
promoting and carrying on Inland Navigation in Ireland[6].
They accomplished but little, however, and it was only in
1784 that the matter was heartily taken up, and the work
pushed forward energetically, and perhaps extravagantly.
The Grand Canal, which connects Dublin with the Shannon,
was completed[7] at an expenditure of more than a million of
money; and the navigation of the rivers Boyne and Barrow
was improved.

---

[1] 23 and 24 Geo. III. c. 19, 1783-84 (Irish).   [2] Newenham, *op. cit.* 227.

[3] See the figures in Newenham, *op. cit.* p. 216, and Martin, *Ireland before and after the Union*, 63.

[4] The roads in Ireland seem to have impressed travellers very favourably. Tyerman, *Life of Whitfield*, I. 147; A. Young, *Tour in Ireland* (1780), II. 150. On road-making at Letterkenny, compare Pococke's *Tour*, 53.

[5] Newenham, 143.   [6] 25 Geo. II. c. 10 (Irish). Newenham, 147-8.

[7] Newenham, 202.

So far for internal traffic; but attempts were also made to A.D. 1689 —1776. develop the industries of the country as well. Fishing busses *and in* were subsidised, so was the cotton manufacture, and Irish *promoting fisheries* trade increased enormously for a time. Still it may be *and manu- factures.* doubted whether the bounties really brought about this change, and it is certain that they were not the only reason for the new development. At all events they were a costly expedient[1], and the fraud and peculation to which they gave rise[2] were a serious drawback to the system. It seems probable that the sudden, though brief, expansion of Irish trade was due to other causes which affected her commerce, and especially to the improved facilities which were given for trade with France by Pitt's treaty. Though the custom-house books do not seem to show it, there can be little doubt that the French trade had always been considerable; the "running" of wool had been a matter of constant complaint[3], and the claret, which was so lavishly consumed in Ireland, must have been paid for in goods, even if much of it evaded the duty. The decline of the new era of prosperity appears to synchronise with the fresh rupture with France; and the rebellion of 1798, with the subsequent reconquest of Ireland, sufficiently account for the decline.

The changes which had placed the economic life of *The English* Ireland outside the control of the British Parliament had *House of* created a somewhat anomalous situation. By the new *Commons was deter-* position which Ireland had acquired, in 1782, it became *mined to* necessary to arrange for the commercial relationships on *control* the basis of a treaty between the two kingdoms, and not, *economic life* as hitherto, by the regulations which England chose to *throughout the British* impose on a dependency. In 1784 a committee of the *Isles,* British Privy Council examined the trade between the two countries, and framed a report which was regarded in Ireland as admirably impartial[4]. Early in the following year a scheme, based upon it, was submitted to the Irish House of Commons and readily accepted by them; but it was not

---

[1] Martin, 43. Compare Mr Cavendish's motion for retrenchment in 1784, Newenham, 206. This was an old complaint in regard to other bounties. Caldwell, *Debates on affairs of Ireland*, 133, 303, 521.

[2] Martin, *op. cit.* 43; Newenham, *op. cit.* 206.

[3] See above, p. 550.   [4] Newenham, 253.

A.D. 1689
—1776.
so satisfactory to the English House of Commons; and the draft which contained their amendments roused a strong feeling of resentment throughout Ireland. But the existence of these conflicting views brought out the necessity of creating some ultimate authority which might settle differences as they arose. The English House of Commons had attempted to reserve the power of final decision for England, and this had been the main ground of dissatisfaction with the revised scheme of commercial intercourse. Two other possible arrangements remained; either a legislative union, or the " establishment of a board, constituted of independent commissioners, equally and impartially drawn from both kingdoms[1]." This last suggestion was never carried into effect, and a legislative union seemed to offer the only possible solution of the commercial difficulties[2]. The policy of fostering national industry, on which the Irish Parliament had entered, was already discredited in England; and the demands, which were commonly heard in Ireland, for the prohibition of British manufactures[3], could not be favourably received in England.

and a legislative union was the only course available,

In the first decade of the eighteenth century, the organisation of the Darien expedition had opened the eyes of Englishmen to the necessity of treating Great Britain as one economic community, for the purposes of commerce and colonisation; they had been glad to arrange for Scottish representation as a means of securing this result. In the last year of the eighteenth century Englishmen were becoming convinced that Great Britain and Ireland must also be treated as one community for industrial and commercial purposes, and once more a legislative Union was carried into effect. The representation for which the American colonies had appeared to pine was granted to the Irish[4], and it might have proved a sufficient remedy in a country that was less distracted by internal differences. In the case of Ireland the grievances had been very serious, but they were merely

as had been already found in regard to Scotland.

[1] Newenham, 255.

[2] Compare Lord Sackville, *Parl. Hist.* xxv. 877.

[3] *Ib.*, 870; Martin, 19.

[4] On the effects of the Union, see below, p. 845.

economic. There was no positive political ideal which ap- A.D. 1689 —1776. pealed to the various elements of the population alike and which they were anxious to realise. The simplest scheme for preventing the recurrence of economic mischiefs in Ireland, and in regard to its relations to England, seemed to be the absorption of both countries under the control of a single Parliament, in which both were represented and which should treat both alike.

240. The break-down of Parliamentary Colbertism, *Adam Smith sup-* through the Declaration of Independence in 1776 and the *plied a* changed policy adopted towards Ireland in 1779, syn- *justifica-tion for* chronised with the diffusion of certain new ideas of economic *this change;* policy which were inconsistent with the reconstruction of the Mercantile System in any form. In 1776 Adam Smith published the *Wealth of Nations,* and the argument of that epoch-making book went to show that the principles, on which all systems of national economy had rested, were in themselves untenable. It is not necessary to follow out the interesting investigations which have recently taken place as to the obligations of Adam Smith to other writers, or as to the manner in which his opinions took shape in his own mind[1]; we are merely concerned to note their extra-ordinary practical importance in sapping the foundations of the economic policy which had been in vogue, in our own and other lands, for some centuries.

Till his time the main object, which publicists who dealt *by treating* with economic topics had had before their minds, was the *National Wealth* power of the country; they set themselves to discuss the particular aspects of industry and commerce which would conduce to this end, according to the circumstances of different countries. The requirements of the State had been the first consideration of seventeenth century writers, and they had worked back to the funds in the possession of the people from which these requirements could be supplied. Adam Smith approached the subject from the other end. The first object of political economy, as he understood it, was "to provide a plentiful revenue or subsistence for the

---

[1] See the introduction to his edition of Adam Smith's *Lectures on Justice, Revenue and Arms,* by E. Cannan.

people," the second was "to supply the State or common-wealth, with a revenue sufficient for the public services[1]." He simply discussed the subject of wealth; its bearing on the condition of the State appeared an after-thought. He isolated the connection of National Wealth and put it forward as the subject matter of his treatise; and in this way he may be said to have brought into clear light the principles which underlay Parliamentary Colbertism. Those who developed this system had concerned themselves about increasing the mass of national wealth of any and every kind, as the indirect means of securing national power.

without direct reference to power, he created Economic Science.

Adam Smith gave clearness to the notions which were implied in their practice. It was his main achievement to treat national wealth as separable from other elements in political life, and in this way he defined the scope of the scientific study of Economics[2].

It thus came about that he cut away the political grounds which had been commonly urged for interfering with the ordinary course of business. In former times it had been possible to insist that some kinds of wealth were more important for the promotion of national power than others, and that it was the work of the statesman to play

---

[1] *Wealth of Nations*, IV., introduction, p. 173.

[2] By isolating wealth as a subject for study he introduced an immense simplification. The examination of economic phenomena became more definite; and just because Adam Smith achieved this result his work rendered it possible to ask new questions, and so to make a real advance in every direction of social study. Not till we isolate wealth and examine how it is procured and how it may be used, can we really set about enquiring how material goods may be made to subserve the highest ends of human life. National rivalries and national power are but mean things after all; but till the study of wealth was dissociated from these lower aims, it was hardly possible to investigate empirically how we could make the most of the resources of the world as a whole, and how material goods might be best applied for the service of man. It is owing to Adam Smith, and the manner in which he severed Economics from Politics, that we can raise and discuss, even if we cannot solve, such problems to-day.

Similarly, we find the clearest testimony to his greatness in the new form which the old enquiries assumed. He severed economic science from politics; he dealt with it as concerned with physical objects and natural laws. To his English predecessors it had been a department of politics or morals; while many of his English successors recognised that in his hands it had become more analogous to physics, and delighted to treat it by the methods of mechanical science. Whether consciously or unconsciously, he gave the turn to economic problems which has brought about the development of modern economic theory.

on private interests so as to guide them into the directions A.D. 1689
—1776. in which they would cooperate for the maintenance of national power. Sir James Steuart[1] and other writers had attenuated the reasons and occasions for such interference more and more, but Adam Smith swept them away. The military and naval power of a country is clearly distinct from the powers of the individual citizens as separate and distinct persons; but there is no such obvious distinction as regards their possessions. It is at least plausible to say that *He held that if each were free to seek his own wealth the national wealth would increase,* the aggregate of the wealth of individual citizens makes up the wealth of the nation, and that if each is as free as possible to pursue his own gain the wealth of the nation will be sufficiently attended to, and its power will follow as a matter of course. The concentration of attention on the wealth of the nation renders a thorough-going doctrine of economic individualism possible[2]. When the new conception was once clearly grasped it became obvious that interference with any individual, in the way he conducts his business, can scarcely ever be justified on strictly economic grounds, and that costly attempts to foster exotic trades or to stimulate native industries are on the face of it absurd.

The standpoint, which Adam Smith thus took, enabled *and that special encouragements were needless* him to render his attack on these special encouragements much more forcible than would otherwise have been the case. In the seventeenth century the agitations for economic and for political liberty had been blended; exception was taken to the special privileges accorded to the Merchant Adventurers and the patentees, because other Englishmen were excluded from certain opportunities of trade. This criticism no longer held good[3] during the period of Whig Ascendancy;

---

[1] Sir James is still definitely within the circle of the Mercantilist's ideas, since he holds so strongly that it is wise for the statesman to direct industry and commerce into the right channels; though he realises, as few of his predecessors had done, that this is a most difficult and delicate operation.

[2] Oncken has pointed out that Adam Smith recognises functions and interests of government which do not belong to any individual, and is thus separated from the standpoint of the Manchester School. *Z. f. Socialwissenschaft*, 1898, I. 1-3; see also Salomon, *William Pitt*, 196.

[3] It reappears in the controversies over the East India Company; Fox's Bill would have shorn it of its powers; Pitt's policy was to continue the power and efficiency of the Company, but to bring it under proper control.

all Englishmen were treated alike; Adam Smith's objection
was a purely economic one, as to the expense of attempts
to encourage industry, and the loss incurred through the
misdirection of capital. He attacks all systems for the
development of a nation's resources, not on the ground of
political unfairness, but simply as a matter of economic
expediency. His reasoning went to show, not only that
Parliamentary Colbertism had been bad, but that no attempt
to reconstruct some better scheme in its place could be
advisable.

His new view of the subject matter of the study was all
important in its bearing on the internal economy of the
country; but still more striking results followed, in regard
to international affairs, from his analysis of the nature of the
gain which accrues from exchange. From time immemorial
men had believed that when a fair exchange took place and
each party really gave an equivalent for what he received,
there could be no gain to either; each was as well off as he
had been, and if either gained it must be because he had
not really given an equivalent, but had won something at
the expense of his neighbour. By bringing out the sub-
jective aspect of value, Adam Smith showed that in every
exchange that occurs, both parties gain, more or less; each
obtains something that is more useful to him than the commodity he has disposed of. When this principle is applied
to international relations, it appears that there is no need
to watch the course of trade with a possible enemy very
jealously, in order to ensure that foreigners do not gain
at our expense; if each nation benefits by trade, there is
comparatively little reason to scrutinise the balance with
particular nations closely, and no reason to fear that intercourse with them is strengthening the sinews of their power
at the expense of our own. "The wealth" he says "of
neighbouring nations, however, though dangerous in wealth
and politics, is certainly advantageous in trade. In a state
of hostility it may enable our enemies to maintain fleets and
armies superior to our own, but in a state of peace and
commerce it must likewise enable them to exchange with
us to a greater value and to afford a better market either

for the immediate product of our own industry, or for A.D. 1689 —1776. whatever is purchased with that produce[1]." From his standpoint it was possible to regard international trade, not merely as the fruitful cause of disputes, but as creating economic ties which may tend to political peace.

Many years were to elapse before these new principles *he revolutionized* could exert their full influence on our commercial policy, *current* but their immediate effect was most remarkable. This was *maxims of trade in a* partly due to the extraordinary simplicity and clearness of *way* his treatment as well as to the excellence of the style. But this simplicity was secured by the definiteness of his new conception as to the object of political economy. It had to do with the necessaries and conveniences of life, material commodities, definite concrete things. There was much clever compilation in the book, but it made no demand for additional statistics, nor was much stress laid on that impalpable abstraction, the spirit of the nation; and the "disagreeable discussion of metaphysical arguments" was avowedly abjured[2]. It was all to be plain sailing for the man of ordinary intelligence; and within a few months of its publication, the book had become a considerable power. National prosperity and relative superiority were vague and difficult notions, but when the whole discussion was made to turn on wealth, the treatment seemed to be more concrete and definite, and it took hold upon the public mind. Perhaps, however, the most important element in its success lay, not in any of the qualities of the book, but from the manner in which it appealed to each of the great political parties, at a juncture when Mercantilism was discredited and statesmen were at a loss as to the course which should be pursued on pressing economic questions. Adam Smith not *that commended* only brought into light the underlying principles of Whig *itself both* Policy, by his new treatment of wealth, but by his analysis *to Whigs and Tories.* of exchange supplied a satisfactory basis for the maxims of trade which had long before commended themselves to the Tories.

241. There has been occasion to enter at some length *Tory politicians* into the views of Whig statesmen during the long period *treated*

---

[1] *Wealth of Nations* (ed. Nicholson), 201. [2] *Ib.* 349.

A.D. 1689
—1776. when that party was in power. It is worth while, by way of retrospect, to indicate the line which had been taken by the Tories. Though the various points in the policy of the party have been indicated in contradistinction to the Whigs, no attempt has been made to show the strength of their position, and the coherence of Tory policy as a whole. Their dissent from Whig measures was not the mere negative criticism of an irresponsible opposition. The Tory policy had a definite character of its own, and may be easily contrasted with that of the party who held the reins of *land as the main factor in economic prosperity,* power for so long. While the Whigs relied on industry as the main factor in material prosperity, the Tories looked to the land as the element on which the sound political life *and desired to relieve* of the community depended. They were prepared to protect *its burdens,* agriculturists from hostile competition[1], but they did not go further. Their main object, so far as the agricultural interest was concerned, was to lighten the pressure of the taxation which fell upon the landed proprietors; they were not convinced that the expenses of government must necessarily be defrayed, directly or indirectly, by the owners of the soil, and they had little sympathy with the policy of stimulating agriculture so that it might sustain this heavy weight. They had no desire to keep the burden and the control of *but were not jealous of the Crown,* national policy in their own hands. In old days the King had been accustomed to live of his own, with occasional assistance from the subjects, for many centuries; and the Tories saw no valid objection to the continuance of that system. If he could develop a crown domain in Ireland, or in the lands beyond the sea, so much the better, so long as the bonds of political attachment were really strong. The Tories did not share the jealousy of monarchical influence which actuated the country party in their measures towards Ireland.

Nor is it difficult to discern a difference in the position taken by leading men of the two parties, in regard to the American colonies. The Whigs were chiefly concerned with building up the wealth of the mother country, and cared for the colonies in so far as they served this object, but no further.

---

[1] Compare C. Smith's *Tracts on the Corn Laws,* p. 11.

The Tories on the other hand recognised the political importance of these communities[1], and regarded the measures
which secured their economic dependence[2] with satisfaction,
because they believed that this restriction would strengthen
the political ties. Events proved that they were mistaken
in this forecast; but it is not a little noticeable that Chatham,
after his definite breach with the official Whigs in regard to
the question of raising revenue from the colonies, gave
vigorous expression to views which are in close accord with
the traditional aim of the Tories[3]. He attached the highest

[1] According to Davenant, "Colonies are a strength to their mother kingdom, while they are under good discipline, while they are strictly made to observe the fundamental laws of their original country, and while they are kept dependent on it. * * * Our colonies, while they have English blood in their veins, and have relations in England, and while they can get by trading with us, the stronger and greater they grow, the more this crown and kingdom will get by them; and nothing but such an arbitrary power as shall make them desperate, can bring them to rebel." *Works*, II. 10.

[2] "The principal care will always be to keep them dependent upon their mother country and not to suffer those laws, upon any account, to be loosened, whereby they are tied to it, for otherwise they will become more profitable to our neighbours than to us." *Ib.* II. 24. See also p. 476 n. 2, above.

[3] See the preamble of his Bill. "Whereas by an Act 6 Geo. III. it is declared, that parliament has full power and authority to make laws and statutes to bind the people of the colonies in all cases whatsoever; and whereas reiterated complaints and most dangerous disorders have grown, touching the right of taxation claimed and exercised over America, to the disturbance of peace and good order there, and to the actual interruption of the due intercourse from Great Britain and Ireland to the colonies, deeply affecting the navigation, trade, and manufactures of this kingdom and of Ireland, and the British islands in America: now, for prevention of these ruinous mischiefs, and in order to an equitable, honourable, and lasting settlement of claims not sufficiently ascertained and circumscribed, may it please your most excellent Majesty that it may be declared, and be it declared by the King's most excellent Majesty, by and with the advice and consent of the Lords spiritual and temporal, and Commons, in this present parliament assembled, and by the authority of the same, that the colonies of America have been, are, and of right ought to be, dependent upon the imperial crown of Great Britain, and subordinate unto the British parliament, and that the King's most excellent Majesty, by and with the advice and consent of the Lords spiritual and temporal, and Commons, in parliament assembled, had, hath, and of right ought to have, full power and authority to make laws and statutes of sufficient force and validity to bind the people of the British colonies in America, in all matters touching the general weal of the whole dominion of the imperial crown of Great Britain, and beyond the competency of the local representative of a distant colony; and most especially an indubitable and indispensable right to make and ordain laws for regulating navigation and trade throughout the complicated system of British commerce, the deep policy of such prudent acts upholding the guardian navy of the whole British empire; and that all subjects in the colonies are bound in duty and allegiance duly to recognise and obey (and are hereby required so to do) the

A.D. 1689
—1776.
so long as
political
control was
main-
tained.importance to the maintenance of the political connection with the Americans, as establishing a barrier against Bourbon pretensions. The dream which he indulged of an empire of federated constitutional monarchies[1] was premature; even with the greater facilities for communication, the development of democratic institutions at home, and of responsible government in the colonies, the problem of imperial rule is difficult enough. It may be doubted whether any statesman could have controlled the forces that made for disruption; but it was undoubtedly the policy of the Whigs, and the stress they laid on fiscal and economic objects, that occasioned the breach.

The Tories desired to distribute the burden of taxation,   The differences between the Whigs and Tories are also noticeable when we turn to a consideration of fiscal policy. The Tories were in favour of placing the finances of the country on a broad basis, so that all classes of the community should contribute towards the expenses of the state[2]. They were anxious that the moneyed men should pay their quota; though the difficulties of organising a system of assessment, which should include them, proved insuperable in the seventeenth and eighteenth centuries. They were also inclined not to prohibit the French trade[3], or any branch of commerce, but to make it a source of supply, and they desired to adjust the tariff for revenue purposes, rather than with regard to its ulterior effects on industrial development. So far as their fiscal policy was concerned, they were inclined to look at the immediate results; the Whigs carried economic analysis farther, and laid stress on the ulterior and indirect effects of the course which they advocated.

and were not con- cerned   With the fostering of manufactures the Tories had not much sympathy; with the planting and nourishing of

---

supreme legislative authority and superintending power of the parliament of Great Britain as aforesaid." Chatham, *Correspondence*, IV. 533, 534.

[1] Hubert Hall, *Chatham's Colonial Policy*, in *American Historical Review*, V. 673. An interesting plea for an Imperial Parliament will be found in an anonymous *Letter to Dr Tucker on his proposal for a separation*, 1771. Brit. Mus. T. 691 (3).

[2] See above, p. 425. The opposition of the Tories to the abandonment of the Hearth Tax in 1689 may have been merely factious as Dalrymple asserts (*Memoirs*, part II. p. 10), but it certainly accorded with their fiscal principles.

[3] See above, pp. 456, 458.

exotic trades they had none. Manufactures, which worked A.D. 1689 —1776. up native products, were advantageous in many aspects, but *to promote* even these the Tories did not view with much enthusiasm. *manufactures.* Where industry was organised on the domestic system, and the artisan had by-occupations available, there was little risk. But the existence of a large wage-earning body of artisans was a cause of considerable anxiety, especially in times of bad trade, and added largely to the numbers of those who might be chargeable to the rates[1].

On the whole it may be said that the Tories regarded trade from its immediate effects on the consumer, while the Whigs endeavoured to look farther, at its ulterior effects on the development of the country. Since they were indifferent to the fostering of industry, the policy of the Tories appears to have some affinity with the *laissez faire* views which eventually triumphed; and to a certain extent this was the case. The Tories were content to let things develop slowly, and took no keen interest in active measures to stimulate either agriculture or industry. That the Whigs *The results of* made grievous mistakes is true, but it is also true that the *applying* main object they had at heart was achieved to an extra- *Whig principles had* ordinary extent, during the period when they were in power[2]. *been immense,* At the time of the Civil War, English industry was but little developed, and English agriculture was very backward. When the *Wealth of Nations* was published, both had advanced enormously. We may condemn the artificial stimulus Whig measures induced, while yet we recognise the advantage of a forward policy. The principles of the Mercantilists had been more compatible with pushing trade, and with progress, than those of the Bullionists, and survived. The principle of Joint Stock enterprise had been more favourable to the energetic development of commerce than the rules of regulated Companies, and these had practically disappeared. In so far as economic interests helped to determine political issues, the Whigs came into power and maintained their position, because they were eager to stimulate material progress both in rural and urban employments.

[1] See above, p. 562 n. 4, and 571, 577; also 638 below.
[2] Salomon, *William Pitt*, 64.

A.D. 1689
-1776.

*ut the
country
had out-
grown
them,
Even those students who sympathise most strongly with the policy pursued by the Whigs, as expedient at the stage of national development which England had reached at the Revolution, may yet be willing to admit that the country had outgrown this phase before 1776, and that the rules of the mercantile system were proving unnecessary and noxious. The swing of the pendulum brought Chatham and Pitt, who inherited much of the tradition of Toryism, into power; and

*and Pitt
*as well
*dvised in
*iscarding
*hem
under the influence of the younger Pitt, the system the Whigs had built up was discarded, and the economic policy of the country was completely recast on lines which were in accordance with the commercial and fiscal policy that had been advocated by the Tories.

It had been the fundamental principle of Parliamentary Colbertism that commerce should be regulated so as to react favourably upon native industry. But there is another view of the benefit conferred on a nation by commerce; we may desire to extend trade because of the increased supply of the comforts of life which it brings from abroad to the con-sumer. This had been a recognised object of policy since the time of Edward III.[1], and it had been consciously adopted

*and re-
*erting to
*he Tory
*radition,
*s to the
*enefit of
*rade
by the Tory party in their advocacy of facilities for trade with France, especially in 1713[2]. They had been out-voted then, but under changed circumstances their policy was carried into effect in 1786[3]. The Physiocrats had over-thrown the power of Colbertism in France, so that our old rival was more ready to offer favourable terms; while the revival of Portuguese industries under the Marquis of Pombal had rendered the alleged benefits of the Methuen treaty worthless. Under this conjunction of circumstances

---

[1] See Vol. I. p. 470.   [2] See above, p. 461.

[3] Dowell, II. 191. This treaty favoured French agriculture—particularly the production of wines, brandy and oil—and also the manufacture of glass, jewelry, French muslins and millinery. Competition forced the French cotton, hardware, saddlery and crockery manufacturers to improve their goods, but until they reached the English standard of excellence there was a temporary loss to France.

The importation into England of silks, and of cotton and woollen materials mixed with silk, being still prohibited, the French manufacturers neither gained nor lost. It was urged in England that the treaty was in favour of France, since it ensured a sale for her natural products, and rendered industrial equality possible. Koch and Schoell, I. 461.

Pitt was able to carry his commercial treaty with France; there was a very considerable reduction of tariffs on each side, though the increased facilities for intercourse were not favourably received by some of the manufacturers in either country. Despite the temporary irritation which was caused, however, the trade with France expanded greatly[1]; and consumers in each country felt the advantage of the increased intercourse.

The attitude taken by various critics, towards the policy of the Navigation Acts, was closely associated with this view as to the nature of the chief advantage derived from trade. These measures were ostensibly intended to increase the shipping and develop the maritime power of the country, but they tended to limit the quantities of goods imported, and thus to diminish the receipts from customs and to raise prices to the consumers of foreign goods[2]. The benefit which accrued to the shipping of the country was problematical. Cecil had pronounced against the policy; and during the Restoration period, the Navigation Act seriously interfered with the provision of stores for the navy; it was a doubtful boon, and constant efforts had been made by the advisers of Charles II. to set it aside, or to obtain the Parliamentary relaxation of some of its prohibitions. There had never been much success in enforcing it, so far as the American colonies were concerned, but in 1796 the attempt to do so was *in relaxing the Navigation Acts,* definitely abandoned; and the rule that all goods from America should be imported in British ships was relaxed in favour of the United States[3]. The great expansion of American trade which took place at this time amply justified the views of Dean Tucker[4], who had argued that no commercial advantage was to be gained from maintaining a political control over the plantations in America. The interest of the consumer of American produce[5] asserted

---

[1] It is an incidental proof of the industrial progress of England that, whereas in the seventeenth century French commodities had been so fashionable here, at the end of the eighteenth English manufactures were much sought after in France.

[2] See Vol. i. p. 490.   [3] 37 Geo. III. c. 97. Leone Levi, 160.

[4] *The True Interest of Britain set forth in regard to the Colonies*, 1776, pp. 50—53.

[5] The fact that raw cotton was now coming from the States would render the manufacturers of cotton goods glad of the relaxation.

A.D. 1689 —1776.

itself against the maintenance of a restriction which had always been a matter of controversy[1].

Another fundamental principle of Parliamentary Colbertism had been that taxation should be levied, so far as possible, in forms that were not unfavourable to the industry of the country. This had been the basis of Walpole's scheme, whereas Davenant and the Tories attached the first importance to questions connected with the incidence of taxation. They desired that contributions should be drawn from all classes of the community, though the burden should be made to rest as lightly as possible on those who were least able to bear it; and these principles were clearly borne in mind in Pitt's fiscal reforms[2]. Many of these were of an administrative character[3], but his view as

and as to the desirability of distributing

---

[1] The party cleavage on the policy of the Navigation Acts is not so marked as on other questions. Child, and more doubtfully Davenant, pronounced in their favour. Their alleged advantage in promoting shipping was probably more apparent in some trades, *e.g.*, the East India Trade, than in others.

[2] The Tory tradition was maintained by Lord Liverpool; see *Dict. Pol. Ec.*, s.v.

[3] Owing to the gradual additions which had been made to the sums levied, the customs rates were extraordinarily confused; each article imported paid a number of separate taxes which were answered under different headings. The collection and administration of such a complicated system was most wasteful; while the taxes, when taken together, were so high as to interfere seriously with the consumption of the article and to offer a great temptation to the smuggler. Adam Smith had laid stress on these matters, and had advocated the policy of simplifying the departments and diminishing the taxes in the hope of lessening the frauds and of putting down smuggling. The duty on tea was reduced from 119 to 12½ per cent. But such a considerable change appeared to be a very rash step. As Adam Smith had pointed out, what was required was an entire change of system (*Wealth of Nations*, 374). On the pressure of existing taxes, see *Parl. Hist.*, xxi. 398 (Bunbury); but while Pitt set himself to face the difficulties of carrying this through, he was also determined to have a sufficient margin in case the project did not answer his expectations. He therefore levied additional duties on windows and on houses, by the Commutation Act (1784); and was thus able to make his reduction and to wait for the expected expansion of the revenue without hampering any of the departments of Government. The reform thus initiated established Pitt's reputation as a financier; he also set to work to improve the fiscal administration by grouping a certain number of exactions on carriages, men-servants, horses, etc., and treating them as *Assessed Taxes* (Dowell, II. 188, 1785), which fell almost entirely upon the richer classes. In a somewhat similar fashion the complicated customs duties were replaced by a single tax on each article; the methods of collection were improved, and the proceeds of the whole were lumped together as a *Consolidated Fund* (1787), instead of being kept under separate accounts. Pitt's success, in carrying through these simplifications and changes, was partly due to the care he took to provide some new form of revenue which might tide him over the period of transition (*Ib.* 192).

to the directions in which changes should be effected is very A.D. 1689 —1776.
obvious. The glaring inequalities[1] of the land tax had been *the burden*
somewhat reduced, and the moneyed men had been forced to *of taxa- tion*
contribute through the inhabited house duty and the assessed
taxes. But Pitt was desirous that the poorer classes should be,
so far as possible, relieved from the burden. This view comes
out in the measures which he took, when the prosperity of
the country enabled him to reduce the Government demands.
In 1792 he was able to repeal the tax on women servants[2]
in poorer families, the taxes on carts and waggons, the
window tax on small houses[3], a portion of the tax on candles,
and a recently imposed duty on malt[4].

Following the same principles, Pitt showed himself most
reluctant to impose any taxes upon necessaries, when the
Revolutionary War unexpectedly burst upon him; and he
devoted himself, so far as possible, to raising the necessary
supplies by taxes which should fall upon property[5]. The *so as to*
first of these was an expedient which Adam Smith had *reach the owners of*
recommended, and which North had attempted, of taxing *personal property,*
successions[6]. North's tax had been easily evaded as it was
levied on the receipts given by legatees, but executors
connived at a fraud on the revenue, and did not insist on
having receipts. Pitt taxed the property while still in the
hands of the executors. He originally intended to include

---

[1] The tax since 1697 had been regarded as a fixed sum of about £500,000, when
the tax was 1s. in the pound, and thus it got into the same groove as the tenths
and fifteenths had done in 1334, and the Tudor subsidies at a later date (Vol. I.
547, 548). Further "it happened that as the tradesmen and others assessed in
respect of their personalty died off or departed from the particular district, the
assessors charged their quota upon the land, adding it to the previous charge upon
the landowners; so that the tax, which was intended to rest in the first instance
upon goods and offices, the residue only being charged on the land—intended for
a general tax upon property, gradually became in effect a tax on land, and a most
unfair one, because originally the division of the whole sum representing the rate
was extremely unequal, and the relative riches of the different counties specifically charged altered, the unfairness increased." (Dowell, *op. cit.* II. 53.) On
Davenant's criticism of the assessment, see above, p. 430 n. 4.

[2] This tax had been proposed in 1785 when the group of assessed taxes was
formed; this and a shortlived tax on shops, according to the rent of the shop,
were intended to draw from the shopkeeper class. Dowell, II. 90. 25 Geo. III.
c. 43 and c. 30.

[3] With less than seven windows. Dowell, II. 197.

[4] Compare Pitt's oration, Feb. 17, 1792. *Parl. Hist.* XXIX. 816.

[5] Dowell, II. 213.   [6] *Wealth of Nations*, 363.

A.D. 1689
—1776.
all collateral successions to property of every kind, but while
he succeeded in the measure which dealt with personal
property (1796), that which concerned real property had to
be dropped[1]. Another expedient was adopted in 1797 which
told in the same way, and brought pressure to bear directly
on the propertied classes[2]. This was the so-called *Triple
Assessment*; it was intended to be a tax which should fall
widely, and which should yet be so graduated as to press
less heavily on the poorer classes than on others[3]. The
principle of the assessed taxes was that a man's return as
to his establishment for the previous year was the basis of
payment in the current year according to a graduated scale,
"which had the effect of increasing the tax for every subject
of duty in the larger establishments[4]." In 1797 Pitt proposed that in the following year the payments should be
greatly increased, those whose assessment had been under
£25 were to pay a triple amount, those who had paid
between £30—£40 were to make quadruple payments, while
assessments of £50 and upwards were to increase fivefold.
The following year it appeared that a better result could
be obtained with less elaborate machinery, by imposing a
ten per cent. income tax on incomes of £200 and upwards.
It was graduated for incomes between £60 and £200, and
incomes of less than £60 were free[5]. The income tax was
repealed by Addington on the close of the war, but had of
course to be re-imposed in the following year. A more
convenient form of return was adopted, under five distinct
schedules.

*though he
was also
forced to
borrow
largely, and
in a costly
fashion.*
This was the principal new departure made under the
strain of the great French wars. Pitt and his successors
were anxious so far as possible to pay the current expenses
out of the year's receipts. It was only under the pressure
of necessity that he had recourse to the expedient, which had
come into fashion in the time of William III., and permitted
himself to throw a burden of debt on posterity. When he
was forced to fall back on these financial methods, he gave
the last great example of the disastrous results of misunder-

[1] Dowell, II. 214.   [2] Dowell, 220.   [3] *Parl. Hist.* XXXIII. 1047.
[4] Dowell, II. 221.   [5] *Ib.* II. 222.

standings about credit, both in the principles of the Sinking Fund[1], and in forcing on the Suspension of Cash payments[2]. He seemed to inherit not only the principles but the weaknesses of Tory finance.

Under Pitt's peace administration, the application of these Tory principles was not unfavourable to English industry, but the old jealousy between the landed and the *The Tory* moneyed interest was by no means extinct. Industry was *jealousy of the* assuming capitalist forms, and there was much in the new *moneyed interest* development of manufacturing that jarred upon Tory sentiment. The country gentleman cherished a suspicion that his interests had always been subordinated to those of some trade; in the pasture countries, he had grumbled at the measures which were intended to keep down the price of wool; in woodland districts, he had felt aggrieved because the iron-masters were permitted to dispense with his fuel in smelting and to import bar-iron from the colonies. The capitalist, who succeeded in getting these necessary materials cheap, was his natural enemy; and the landed men were all the more ready to give credence to complaints in regard *was asso-* to the moneyed men's attitude towards labourers. That *ciated with humani-* personal property contributed little towards the relief of *tarian agitation* the poor was clear; while there was some reason to suppose that the development and migration of manufactures were largely responsible for the continued difficulties in regard to pauperism. The callousness of the trading interest beyond the sea to the distresses of kidnapped servitors and the miseries of the slave trade, gradually roused a philanthropic *in regard* sentiment, which was eventually to exercise a powerful in- *to the slave trade* fluence on the condition of labour at home. This was perhaps the most wholesome form which the immemorial jealousy of the landed for the moneyed interest had taken, but it is not a mere accident that so much of the humanitarian activity of the eighteenth and early nineteenth centuries should have emanated from the Tory camp. Samuel Johnson was one of the earliest and most vehement opponents of the slave trade, and it was at the table of his

---

[1] See below, p. 696.

[2] See p. 692 below.

friend Bennet Langton[1], that Wilberforce and Clarkson met some influential men, and that the agitation against the slave trade first took practical shape[2]. The struggle on behalf of labour against capitalism at home[3] had similar political affinities, for it was commenced by Michael Thomas Sadler, a Tory member of Parliament, and supported by the landed interest at a time when the labourers themselves were apathetic. At the close of the eighteenth century the lines were being already formed for the struggles of the nineteenth. The capitalists were preparing to demand greater freedom from restriction of every kind, and to abolish the survival of by-gone institutions in the name of economic science; but the principles and sentiments to which the Tories were attached were to have no little share in the positive work of re-constructing a new order, in which human welfare would be the primary consideration.

---

[1] *Dict. Nat. Biog.*, s.v. Wilberforce.

[2] Comparatively little progress was made till the philanthropic agitation was re-enforced by political and economic reasons for abandoning the trade as detrimental. Hochstetter, *Die wirthschaftlichen Motive für die Abschaffung des britischen Sklavenhandels*, 33.

[3] An interesting illustration of the common interest of these classes occurs in the Report of the Select Committee on the Calico-Printers: "Without entering into the delicate and difficult question, as to the distribution of profits between Masters and Journeymen, in this as well as the other mechanical professions, Your Committee may venture to throw out, for the consideration of the House, whether it be quite equitable towards the parties or conducive to the public interest that on the one part there should arise a great accumulation of wealth, while on the other there should prevail a degree of poverty from which the parties cannot emerge by the utmost exertion of industry, skill and assiduous application, and may at an advanced period of life, notwithstanding perpetual labour, be obliged to resort to parish aid for the support of their families. Is it just that such a state of things should be permitted to exist? Is it fair towards the Landed Interest in those districts in which Manufactories are established that they should be called upon to contribute from the Poor Rates to the support of those who ought to be enabled to derive a support from their labour, and who are at the same time contributing to establish a fortune for the Principals of such Manufactories?" *Reports*, 1806, III. 1160.

For EU product safety concerns, contact us at Calle de José Abascal, 56–1°,
28003 Madrid, Spain or eugpsr@cambridge.org.

 www.ingramcontent.com/pod-product-compliance
Ingram Content Group UK Ltd.
Pitfield, Milton Keynes, MK11 3LW, UK
UKHW042210180425
457623UK00011B/133